COST ACCOUNTING

To my parents, who wanted me to write like Hemingway.
Sorry, folks.

COST ACCOUNTING

A Comprehensive Guide

Steven Bragg

JOHN WILEY & SONS, INC.
New York • Chichester • Weinheim • Brisbane • Singapore • Toronto

Copyright © 2001 by John Wiley and Sons, Inc. All rights reserved.

Published simultaneously in Canada.

Library of Congress Cataloging-in-Publication Data:
Bragg, Steven M.
    Cost accounting : a comprehensive guide / Steven Bragg.
        p. cm.
    Includes bibliographical references and index.
    ISBN 0-471-38655-3 (cloth : alk. paper)
        1. Cost accounting. I. Title.

HF5686.C8 B673 2001
657'.42—dc21   00-047992

Contents

CONTENTS

CONTENTS

Preface

This book is written for the practicing cost accountant or accounting manager. It addresses an enormous array of cost accounting topics, most of which the professional cost accountant deals with during his or her daily or weekly activities. The chapters are specifically designed to cover the key operational problems encountered while designing costing systems, collecting cost data, converting it into usable information, and incorporating the information into valuable suggestions for the management team that can enhance a company's overall level of effectiveness and efficiency.

We start with a discussion of how cost accounting can be used to assist the modern-day management team in running a company, as well as how the cost accountant's job should be structured in order to provide the maximum degree of assistance to management. In the next set of chapters we deal with the collection of cost accounting data—how to select the best computer system, set up a chart of accounts to store incoming information, and collect cost information in the most efficient manner. These are crucial topics that the cost accountant must deal with every day to ensure that the data used for a variety of cost analyses is accurate, timely, and relevant.

Next, we consider a number of different costing methodologies that can be used to convert all this newly collected cost data to information that can be used for management decisions. Examples of these procedures are the commonly used job and process costing, as well as direct costing, standard costing, activity-based costing, and throughput costing. These methodologies are compared and contrasted in a summarization chapter, where we note the problems and advantages of each one, as well as how to implement controls that can mitigate any deficiencies.

We then take the accumulated costing information and cover a number of methods for analyzing it, using such tools as variance analysis, spoilage and scrap tracking, and cost-volume-profit analysis.

We then proceed to a series of chapters that address the management issues that the cost accountant can provide valuable information about. These include the use of feedback loops, capital budgeting, capacity management, material requirements planning, manufacturing resources planning, just-in-time production techniques, the cost of quality, and issues related to the variability of costs.

Next, we touch on several pricing issues in which the cost accountant can become involved, such as transfer pricing and the impact of federal regulations on dumping and price fixing.

Finally, we conclude with a series of chapters that address more specialized topics, such as the role of cost accounting in the creation of corporate strategy, inventory valuation, costing best practices, the use of electronic spreadsheets, taxation, and fraud in the cost accounting arena. A glossary provides a comprehensive set of costing terms and definitions.

Given its ability to address a broad array of problems on nearly any topic that the cost accountant is likely to encounter, this book should become a permanent part of the essential tool kit for any cost accountant.

A special note of thanks to my managing editor, Sheck Cho, who has assisted in the completion of so many manuscripts.

August, 2000
Englewood, Colorado

Introduction

This book is intended to give the cost accountant enough information to complete 95% of the tasks that he or she will confront. To achieve that goal, the book is divided into 40 chapters, a bibliography, and a glossary that cover a broad range of topics. With the book segmented into so many chapters, the reader can find most topics simply by scanning the table of contents, rather than digging through the index.

The book consists of seven parts, each of which addresses a different segment of the cost accountant's job:

1. *Purpose of Cost Accounting.* This part describes the basis of the cost accountant's job—why the function is necessary, the exact tasks involved, and how ethics must be considered in completing one's work.

   • *Role of cost accounting.* Chapter 1 presents an overview of the various tasks assigned to the cost accountant and shows how the resulting information is used by the organization. There is also a short discussion of how the cost accountant's role may evolve in the future.

   • *Cost accountant's job.* Chapter 2 includes a complete description of the cost accountant's job that is useful for those who have little direction on the job, or who are new to a position, and have the opportunity to design the job themselves. This information can also be used by an accounting manager who needs ready access to a standard job description.

- *Ethics.* The cost accountant operates at the core of many of a company's most important transactions. In that position he or she is sometimes exposed to ethical quandaries, perhaps involving other employees, weak systems, or pressure for rapid growth, that bring out the worst in employees or systems. Chapter 3 explains why ethical problems arise, the various types of problems, and how to deal with them.

2. *Costing Systems and Data Collection.* The cost accountant cannot operate without a pool of data from which to compile analyses. Obtaining this information requires some knowledge of what system requirements should be in place, how data is collected and summarized, and how this can be done in the most efficient and effective manner. The five chapters in this part cover the complete range of necessary topics—data collection, categorization, and storage.

- *Data collection systems.* There is no longer any need to laboriously record information on a piece of paper, forward it to the accounting department, and have the clerks there summarize it into a format suitable for further analysis by the cost accountant. Chapter 4 covers the latest technologies now being used to collect data in the most automated, error-free way.

- *Timekeeping.* The most laborious type of data collection has always involved the gathering of information related to direct labor. In Chapter 5 the applicability of this data to modern decision making, how to adjust the level of data collection effort to this applicability, and how new data collection methods can still result in a considerable volume of detailed data being collected are discussed.

- *Chart of accounts.* Once data is collected, it must be summarized somewhere. This is done through the chart of accounts (COA), which must be carefully structured to ensure that data is segregated into areas that can be used by the cost accountant for further analysis. Chapter 6 covers the process for creating this structure, and describes several possible account structures.

- *Cost accounting software.* The accounting software used to process costing data requires different functions, depending on the type of costing system used. To a large extent the cost accountant is stuck with whatever costing-related features are incorporated into the packaged accounting software purchased by the company's controller. Nonetheless, Chapter 7 describes the functions that are most useful for costing work in case the cost accountant has some input into the purchase of packaged software or in case the accounting system is custom-designed and additional features can be added.

- *Paper-based documents.* Despite advanced levels of computerization at many companies, there is typically some residual use of paper-based documents that are separate from the accounting database but are still needed by the cost accountant to conduct his or her work. Chapter 8 covers the types of paper documents still most commonly used, how they can be integrated into the overall accounting system, and how they can be replaced with computerized solutions.

3. *Costing Methodologies.* Once the cost accountant has compiled a large volume of data, what is to be done with it? There are a number of different views on how to treat costing information, most of which result in different outcomes or recommendations for action to be taken by the management team. The 10 chapters in this part cover the most common methodologies (each one is actually a separate paradigm for how to look at costing data) used to interpret costing information. Though the procedures presented here may not appear related, or even be intended for use in the same manner, they all represent different ways of viewing the use of costing data.

   - *Job costing.* The most common method for summarizing costing data is through job costing, which is presented in Chapter 9. In essence, it assumes that the bulk of all costs incurred can be assigned to specific jobs that run through the production process.

   - *Process costing.* This methodology is used when the manufacturing process results in a continuous flow of finished goods to which costs cannot be specifically charged on a unit-by-unit basis (such as gasoline flowing from a petroleum refinery). Its mechanics are discussed in Chapter 10.

   - *Direct costing.* The fallacy behind the two preceding systems is that they both assume that overhead costs can be allocated in a meaningful way to individual products, which is not a useful allocation in some circumstances. Chapter 11 addresses the uses to which direct costing can be put so that the impact of overhead costs on various decisions can be ignored.

   - *Standard costing.* A common approach in developing product costs is to assign standard costs to each component of each product, usually updating these costs once a year, and then measure actual performance against those standards. The cost accountant's main role is to calculate these variances and investigate why they occur. Chapter 12 describes this process.

   - *Last-in first-out (LIFO), first-in first-out (FIFO), and average costing.* A single cost cannot be applied to a component or product because there is actually a layered series of costs that are applicable to any given situation, depending on changes in costs incurred while a product is being manu-factured. Chapter 13 describes the cost layering concept, as well as the ways in which it is most commonly used.

- *Throughput costing.* A school of thought holds that the bulk of all cost-related decisions should focus on just one area—the bottleneck operation. There are many convincing arguments in favor of this approach, which are presented in Chapter 14. This discussion is highly recommended to the reader.

- *Joint and by-product costing.* The application of costs to products is not as simple when a single production process results in the creation of more than one product. The methods most commonly used to allocate these joint costs are described in Chapter 15.

- *Activity-based costing.* This procedure allocates overhead costs to prod-ucts and activities more accurately than was previously possible with al-locations based on just one activity measure such as direct labor dollars. By using this approach, as described in Chapter 16, one can determine costs much more precisely, which leads to better management decisions.

- *Target costing.* This method operates on the assumption that cost infor-mation is of no use unless it is immediately fed back into the product de-sign process so that the new-product engineering staff can determine the cost of new designs more precisely, which in turn leads to the develop-ment of more cost-effective models that will unfailingly hit their prof-itability targets. This concept is covered in Chapter 17.

- *Costing systems summary.* Chapter 18 summarizes all the costing methodologies presented in this part, noting the situations in which each one is the most (and the least) useful.

4. *Using Costs in Pricing, Variance, and Operational Analysis.* Thus far we have listed a number of ways to collect and organize information but not how to analyze it. The four chapters in this part cover several types of vari-ance analyses that are useful for determining price points, controlling costs, and determining profit levels at various amounts of unit sales volume.

   - *Variances.* If a company uses standard costing, as described in Chapter 12, there will be variances from these standards when actual costs are added up and compared to them. Chapter 19 describes how to calculate and use these variances.

   - *Spoilage, waste, and scrap.* A type of variance that does not require a baseline standard cost is any variance related to labor or materials that are lost in the production process, such as spoilage, waste, and scrap. Chapter 20 considers each of these variances, how to calculate them, and what to do with the resulting information.

- *Cost-volume-profit.* A different type of analysis is determination of the point at which a company's sales volume allows it to earn exactly no money—its break-even point. This is also known as the cost-volume-profit relationship, permutations of which are noted in Chapter 21.

- *Analysis reporting.* Once the cost accountant has collected good variance information, what should be done with it? Chapter 22 explains how this information can be compiled into a presentation, as well as *how* to present it and follow up on any resulting decisions.

5. *Managing Costs.* At this point the cost accountant has compiled a large amount of data, sorted through it, and prepared a variety of reports related to variances. However, these actions do not reflect the full range of actions that can be taken. The chapters in this part cover a number of ways to use costing information to manage costs through the use of cost control systems, fixed-asset analyses, various production control systems, and quality reviews.

- *Control systems.* One of the key methods for controlling costs is to set up systems that spot excessive costs, determine why they are occurring, and feed the resulting information back to the responsible parties for corrective action. Chapter 23 considers the nature and uses of cost controls and feedback loops.

- *Capital budgeting.* Companies have a limited amount of capital available to spend on new projects, and usually far more projects being pushed by eager managers than money. We use capital budgeting to determine which of these projects are most likely to yield the best return on invested funds. Chapter 24 covers the details of the capital budgeting process.

- *Capacity management.* It is not the direct responsibility of the cost accountant to manage a company's asset base, but it is certainly acceptable to track the level of use of all machinery and to report this information to management along with recommendations for adding or deleting fixed assets. These issues are dealt with in Chapter 25.

- *Material requirements planning.* This is a commonly used system that breaks down the components required to create a finished product and schedules the purchasing and production of all necessary components in a time-sequenced manner. The information generated by this system is of great value to the cost accountant, as discussed in Chapter 26.

- *Just-in-time.* The single most influential production management concept developed over the last two decades has been just-in-time (JIT), which is an amalgamation of several advances that focus on the ability of a company to use the minimal amount of resources to create products only when they are needed. Chapter 27 describes how the cost accountant fits into this methodology.

- *Quality.* An increasing degree of management attention is being focused on the cost and origins of quality problems since it has been discovered that an inordinate amount of a company's collective time (and related costs) is devoted to solving quality-related problems. Chapter 28 describes the various components of the cost of quality, how they can be measured, and what to do with this information.

- *Cost variability.* Costs are usually divided into such categories as fixed, variable, and semivariable. Chapter 29 has been included to disabuse the reader of any notion that these classifications are set in stone. As it points out, the relative level of variability changes over time and volume.

6. *Pricing Issues.* The cost accountant usually feels that his or her position is related to an item in the job title—cost. However, costs are used in the derivation of prices in some instances or can be used as a defense in avoiding federal prosecution for price fixing or dumping violations. Accordingly, the two chapters in this part address the problems of transfer pricing and government price regulation.

- *Transfer pricing.* For companies with multiple international locations, it is important to recognize the largest amount of income in countries with the lowest tax rates, and the least income in countries where tax rates are the highest. The cost accountant can be of great value in setting up transfer prices between locations that will result in a lower overall level of taxation. Chapter 30 covers the various methods for establishing transfer prices, as well as cautions about the need for consistent, defensible transfer prices acceptable to tax authorities.

- *Pricing laws.* The cost accountant is frequently consulted in the matter of setting prices, as well as in determining the cost structure of competitors and the types of margins they are probably experiencing. In this role one can determine if possible dumping or price fixing violations are occurring. Chapter 31 considers the main federal regulations related to pricing, as well as how violations are determined under these laws.

7. *Other Topics.* Despite the large number of parts in this book, there are still several topics that defy clustering. These are:

- *Corporate strategy.* Chapter 32 discusses how one can integrate information from the cost accounting area into a company's overall strategy in order to arrive at the most effective plan for achieving a high level of profitability in the future.

- *Benchmarking.* Chapter 33 addresses benchmarking—what it is, how to conduct a survey, and how to integrate the results into in-house operations.

- *Valuing inventory.* Valuation of inventory occupies an inordinate amount of the cost accountant's time. Chapter 34 covers the various valuation methods used, as well as the pitfalls and advantages of each.

- *Best practices.* As in all functional areas, there is a normal way of doing things and a more advanced method that can result in greater efficiency and effectiveness. Several of these advanced methods, known as "best practices," are covered in Chapter 35.

- *Budgeting.* The cost accountant can become deeply involved in the budgeting process since much of the information needed to complete a comprehensive budget requires information about product and functional costs, cost variability, and the impact on profits of prospective changes in inventory levels. Chapter 36 gives the reader the tools needed to provide valuable input to the budgeting process.

- *Services.* Companies deeply ensconced in providing services present unique problems from the cost accountant's perspective because there is no "hard" product whose cost can be analyzed, nor can most of the traditional variances be calculated. Chapter 37 discusses how cost accounting can be modified to provide value in this environment.

- *Electronic spreadsheets.* Though much of the information used by the cost accountant is stored in central databases, there is still a need to transfer some of this information to electronic spreadsheets for further review. Chapter 38 covers a number of useful formulas available in the Excel spreadsheet that can be used for analysis tasks.

- *Taxation.* Valuation of inventory and other means for recognizing or deferring income have a direct impact on the amount of income taxes a company pays. Though this book does not claim to present an in-depth discussion of the vast area of income tax rules and regulations, Chapter 39 provides enough background information for the cost accountant to understand why the selection of certain costing methodologies and other actions has a direct bearing on the amount of taxes paid.

- *Fraud.* There are a surprisingly large number of ways to commit fraud in the functional areas in which the cost accountant conducts analyses. Chapter 40 describes each type of fraud, how it is achieved, and how to prevent it. This chapter provides a good review for companies that want to improve their control systems and need to know what types of problems must be prevented.

8. *Bibliography and Glossary.* The bibliography includes the most essential cost accounting articles, pamphlets, and books. It is not a comprehensive list

of cost accounting references since such a list would require a 1000-page book just for the most recent publications. Instead, a limited set of references that are top-notch representations of the particular class of knowledge they address have been chosen. The Glossary contains relevant cost accounting terms. Though the reader is assumed to be a practicing cost accountant with a reasonable grasp of the associated terminology, many terms related to the wide range of topics touched on in this book may still be unfamiliar. Also, there may be terms whose definitions are similar and so are hard to distinguish. The Glossary is provided as a reference for these situations.

PART I

Purpose of Cost Accounting

CHAPTER 1

Role of Cost Accounting

When properly implemented, the cost accounting function can have a pervasive influence in the modern corporation. Unfortunately, it is not always properly implemented because management often is not completely aware of all the uses to which the cost accounting function can be put. This chapter describes the main categories of activities in which this function can become involved, and can be used as a guide by the controller in creating a well-rounded niche for the cost accountant.

EXTERNAL REPORTING

The key task for the cost accountant is contributing information to a company's external financial reports. In many cases where the main accounting function is perceived to be financial reporting (such as in a publicly held company), the other tasks of the cost accountant may very well be subordinated to providing various types of information for these external reports.

A key piece of information provided by the cost accountant is inventory valuation, which in turn impacts the cost of goods sold. Several tasks are involved here, such as deciding on the type of cost layering technique (Chapter 13), ensuring that inventory quantities and costs are accurate, and compiling the resulting data into the formats required for external reporting.

Other related work may also be needed, such as compiling profitability levels for various product lines, or profit levels by division. The cost accountant may also become involved in the compilation or updating of a few footnotes to the financial statements, though most of these are handled by the financial accounting staff.

INTERNAL REPORTING

The advantage of having cost accountants create reports strictly for internal consumption is that they are not restricted to generally accepted accounting principles (GAAP) when preparing these reports. GAAP requires the use of full-absorption costing in the creation of external reports, which may not be necessary or may even be counterproductive for internal reporting purposes. Accordingly, the cost accountant is free to use any costing paradigm that will result in the most informative reports for the management team—job costing, process costing, direct cost costing, activity-based costing, direct costing, throughput costing, and so on (chapters 9 through 18). For example, direct costing can be used for an internal report that focuses specifically on activities in the extreme short term, where there is no impact associated with overhead costs. Alternatively, a report can be based on throughput costs if the issue is how to push the correct product mix through a bottleneck operation in order to derive the highest possible profit. Further, full-absorption costing can be used for reports that focus on long-term decisions. The accounting method can therefore be precisely tailored to the use to which the report will be put.

The format and content of internal reports can also vary substantially from the format used for external reporting. External report formats are precisely defined by GAAP: Revenues and costs are categorized in a specific manner and only a certain number of reports are allowed. None of these rules apply to internal reporting. Some examples of different reporting structures include:

- **Corporate-level reports.** These reports may include only trend lines of information about a few critical success factors that senior managers are most interested in influencing, bottom-line profits and return on assets for each production facility or store, and perhaps forecasts at the product line level. The exact format used varies not only by company but also over time within each company, as different reporting items become less or more important to the senior management team. There is certainly no reason to include deeply detailed reports in the reporting package that goes to senior managers—they do not have the time to wade through such a morass of information.

- **Business unit-level reports.** These reports must include a much larger quantity of information, for the recipient (the plant manager) needs to know about the operation of each department, as well as a host of operational issues such as the cost of quality, inventory turnover, machine utilization, profitability, and cash flow projections. This tends to be the most voluminous of all reporting packages, as well as the one that includes the greatest mix of financial and operational information.

- **Function-level reports.** These reports can be issued to individual departments or at lower levels, for example, to the supervisors of individual machines. Such reports are custom-designed for each recipient, with some requiring more financial data (e.g., for the sales manager who wants to know about customer bad debts or orders booked) and others including almost entirely operational information (e.g., for the warehouse manager who is interested in inventory turnover, kiting percentages, and receiving accuracy).

- **Project-specific reports.** A project report is slanted more toward just those costs being incurred for a specific purpose and so tends to be heavy on direct costs and light on most other allocations. This report usually compares incurred costs against budgeted costs expected to have been incurred at various stages of the project. If a project is already bringing in revenues, the reporting structure can be converted to a profit center format. This format tends to have few operational statistics besides percentages of completion and lists of to-do items that must be finished in order to ensure conclusion of the project.

- **Decision-specific reports.** Many times the cost accountant is called on to report on a specific issue that occurs only once, after which the report is discarded. For example, a report may be needed that describes the particular quality costs associated with the selection of three prospective production processes the management team is considering installing. Once the decision is made and the installation completed, there is no longer a need for the report. Another example is a review of waste in a production process—the report may cover such information as times elapsed when moving products between manufacturing stations, setup times, cycle times, and the amount of space occupied by idle work in process; this report is concerned less with financial issues than with process efficiency, but it is still the cost accountant's job to complete it. Clearly, these reports can cover virtually any topic and can include any type of information—financial, operational, or a mix.

An enormous range of topics can be covered by internal reports. Because they lack the amount of structure imposed on external reports, they are much more interesting to prepare, giving the cost accountant free rein to express creativity in designing the perfect format that will result in easy readability and effective management decision making.

SCOREKEEPING

The last two sections have focused on the role of cost accounting in the preparation of formal reports. However, in terms of volume, the cost accountant probably issues more scorekeeping report cards than reports. These are simple reports, usually presenting a trend line of performance for a single key measurement that is posted frequently—perhaps daily. For example, the accounting staff may be called on to create a graph of machine utilization for each machine and post it on the appropriate machine every day. This is a highly standardized repetitive format that is easy to prepare and is targeted at a specific performance criterion. One can count on creating and distributing hundreds of these reports over the course of a full career in accounting.

BUDGETING

Several of the subsidiary-level budgets that roll up into the main corporate budget involve information to which the cost accountant can contribute a great deal (Chapter 36). For example, the production budget includes estimated direct costs for each product the company expects to manufacture in the upcoming year, as well as estimated overhead allocations per unit based on expected production volumes. Cost accountants are in the best position to supply this information since they have access to all the needed information—bills of material, routings, throughput capacity constraints, and sales estimates by unit. Similarly, the direct labor budget requires input about expected labor costs, which requires information from the cost accountant regarding expected labor utilization rates and overtime estimates. If there is no human resources department to provide information about labor and benefit costs, the cost accountant is expected to supply this information too. It may also be necessary to assist in compiling estimated costs for various departments that do not have an internal staff skilled in such work and help them determine cost estimates for the upcoming budget period. Finally, the cost accountant is frequently called on to estimate facilitywide budgeted costs, including those in such categories as repairs and maintenance, insurance, and utilities. Given the wide-ranging nature of these costs, it is evident that the cost accountant can expect to allocate a great deal of time to the budgeting activity at the times of the year that it is performed.

COST REDUCTION ANALYSIS

Cost accountants should be true to their job title and create in-depth examinations of the costs of many functions throughout a company. This is a wide-ranging activity, for it can involve cost studies virtually anywhere—in engineering, production, sales, and so on. No matter what the topic may be, the process followed is quite standardized—obtain a detailed list of all costs incurred, track down the origins of each one, insert this information into a process flow for the functional area where the costs are incurred, and see which costs can be reduced or entirely eliminated by omitting the associated process steps. This task is essentially a determination of what process steps create value for a company, and which ones can be eliminated.

PRICING

The responsibility for setting product prices should be part of the sales and marketing function, which has the best knowledge of current pricing in the marketplace. This group needs to know the cost of each product sold so that it does not set prices that are below a product's cost, thereby creating loss on every unit sold. The cost accountant is in charge of compiling these costs and presenting them to the sales and marketing staff. This task is of particular importance when customers come to the company with offers to accept large volumes of product only if the sales price is substantially lowered. In these instances the cost accountant must determine the direct cost of the product in question, as well as the added cost of overhead directly associated with the production run that creates the customer's product. It may also be useful to determine the overall impact on company profits via a throughput accounting analysis (Chapter 14). A separate analysis must usually be made for each customer pricing request; since larger companies may face these issues on a regular basis, they may employ teams of cost accountants who deal with only this type of work.

Another important pricing-related task is determining the profitability of individual customers, products, product lines, and facilities. Each of these calculations must incorporate only the costs relevant to the particular analysis. For example, a review of profits by customer may include only direct costs (Chapter 11) if the analysis is meant to cover a short period of time, but should use activity-based costing (Chapter 16) if the company's long-term impact on profits is the objective of the analysis. For short-term analysis profit impact using throughput accounting (Chapter 14) should be included. Given the wide range of costing methods available, these analyses can take a great deal of time and require extensive explanations for the management team so that they fully understand the consequences of any actions taken based on this information. Typical actions are the dropping of low-profit customers, products, and facilities in favor of focusing attention on those that are the most profitable.

SYSTEMS DEVELOPMENT AND MAINTENANCE

The cost accountant has a great deal of influence over the types of data collection and summarization systems used by a company, as well as over systems that one would not normally associate with the cost accounting function, as will be described in this section.

A main concern of the cost accountant is collecting a large enough quantity of data to create a sufficiently large pool of information that can be used for various types of costing analysis. However, there is a cost associated with the collection of data, so higher costs are incurred in collecting more data. Consequently, the cost accountant must spend some time exploring new types of data collection automation (Chapter 4) to keep these costs low, while still providing sufficient quantities of data. For example, replacing manual time cards for direct labor personnel with automated bar code scanning equipment eliminates a significant amount of the labor costs associated with collecting and processing direct labor-related data.

When an activity-based costing system is used, the cost accountant is probably its primary maintainer. He or she carefully investigates the nature of all costs feeding into the system, determines which costs will be collected into which cost pools, selects cost drivers for each pool, and verifies that there is indeed a causal relationship between the drivers and the pools (Chapter 16). These relationships change over time, so the cost accountant is required to investigate and make changes as necessary.

It is also common to become involved in the assignment of costs to various entities, such as departments or product lines, and to constantly re-review this information and reassign the costs as needed. This is a particularly common activity in organizations where managerial compensation is based on localized profits, since managers are constantly attempting to shift cost allocations away from their areas of responsibility, thereby producing instant improvements in the profits attributed to them.

Rather than allocating costs, as just noted, the cost accountant may be asked to take the reverse approach, that is, to determine why costs have been incurred and allocated in a certain manner by tracing them back through the accounting system, perhaps all the way back to their originating source documents. This information can then be used for a simple report to management regarding the causes of costs, or it can be used as the foundation for a project to alter the system to allocate costs in a different manner.

COST-BENEFIT ANALYSIS

A cost-benefit analysis is used when management wants to know if it makes sense to acquire or dispose of a piece of equipment, as well as to determine all of its associated costs. This is not a simple analysis, requiring the accumulation of all related cash flows and their reduction to a net present value with the use of a discount factor (Chapter 24). It may be necessary not only to delve into the inner workings of such prospective projects but even to be attached to them until they are completed, in order to ensure that all cost additions are within the original approved funding levels. This activity represents an entire subcategory of cost accounting called project accounting.

INTERNAL CONSULTING

It is also common to be assigned to any number of cost-related projects as an internal consultant. For example, a department manager may want to know what will happen to costs if certain functions are outsourced to a supplier. Alternatively, the warehouse staff may want assistance in determining the amount by which working capital requirements will be reduced if a new project to shrink inventory levels is implemented. In addition, it may be necessary to conduct a benchmarking study (Chapter 33) to find better ways to complete a task, either by searching within other divisions of the company or (more commonly) looking outside the company for better "best practices" (Chapter 35). These activities may stop with a presentation of the suggested improvements to management but can continue through monitoring of the implementation of these best practices—a common activity for the cost accountant. Thus, the cost accountant may be asked to review a wide variety of function-specific activities on a project basis.

GOVERNMENT BILLINGS

An extremely specialized area is government billings. Though many government purchases are now made through standardized pricing schedules, such as those issued by the General Services Administration or through a government-wide agency contract (GWAC), a significant volume of purchases still involve the use of cost-plus contracts. Cost-plus purchases are made in situations where the government wants to acquire something so unique (such as innovative new defense equipment) that it has never before been produced. Companies do not want to quote a fixed price for such items since they have no idea if they can actually manufacture them and still turn a profit. Accordingly, the government is compelled to offer a cost-plus contract under which a company is reimbursed for all costs related to the work being done for the government, plus a percentage allowance for profit.

This is a key role for the cost accountant, whose job it is to learn the byzantine costing rules of the government and then create a cost accumulation system that records the costs for which the government requires records. In addition, one must determine the allowable allocation of overhead costs that can be applied to project costs and billed to the government. The rules for these procedures are mind-numbing.

The allowable costs that can be billed to the government are drawn from different functional areas of a company, which requires the cost accountant to have considerable knowledge of the research, product design, production, and administrative functions and how each of these areas tracks its costs.

Government contracting officers are assigned to review the billings issued by a company and may protest and refuse to pay for certain line items if they feel that the billing is not supported by government cost reimbursement rules. In these instances it is the cost accountant's job to research the rules and present a case to the contracting officer that argues in favor of reimbursement. These cases can go to court for final resolution, and the cost accountant is then required to assist in preparing legal justification for the company's case and may even be called on to testify.

Government billings require cost accounting skills of the highest caliber. A top-notch costing professional in this area has a direct impact on company profits and is considered an important part of the management team in companies that engage in this sort of work.

FUTURE ROLE OF COST ACCOUNTING

The future role of cost accounting will certainly include a greater emphasis on corporate strategy. The cost accountant can contribute several types of costing information to the planning process (Chapter 32) that are of assistance in making strategy alterations that will result in enhanced levels of profitability or at least in the avoidance of low-profit strategy alternatives. A large part of this information comes from a database of costs that encompass a much wider range of potential production volumes than those currently used by the company. This information is derived from interaction with the purchasing department, vendors, and industrial engineers, all of whom can contribute information about changes in costs at various volume levels. With this information, strategy planners can determine what will happen to internal costs if the company pursues various strategies that either increase or decrease sales (and therefore production) volumes for various product lines.

Another contribution to corporate strategy is the use of throughput accounting (Chapter 14). This method allows the corporate planning staff to determine which equipment is currently causing the primary production bottleneck. It can use this information to shift the bottleneck to a different point in the production process if it will result in changes in the mix or in the volume of products manufactured that will cause a significant alteration in profits. One can also use this information to create a plan for producing a specific set of products that will make the most effective use of the existing bottleneck right through the planning period; this allows a company to redirect all its sales and marketing, production, and materials management activities around the sale and manufacture of only these products, thereby maximizing profit levels.

SUMMARY

Despite the large number of categories of work discussed in this chapter, it does not begin to reflect the full range of tasks that the cost accountant may be involved in during her career. The cost accountant can reliably expect to be assigned tasks in every nook and cranny of a corporation, which is what makes the job such an interesting one, far more so than that of a financial accountant, whose job is much more closely defined by external accounting reporting rules.

The only common denominator among the various cost accounting tasks is that they focus on providing information for management decision making. Typically, the task is to conduct a short analysis of a specialized topic, draw conclusions, and make recommendations that will be acted on by management to make improvements. The responsibility here is great, for the cost accountant's recommendations ultimately have a direct impact on company operations and overall profitability.

CHAPTER 2

Cost Accountant's Job

In far too many organizations the cost accountant is considered a glorified clerk who pores over reports and issues profitability statements for a few products or jobs each month. In this chapter we discover that the modern cost accountant should actually be a highly educated, sociable person who roams through an organization examining key systems, assisting design teams, and creating many of the most fundamental reports required by management to run a business. To that end, the following sections consider the cost accountant position within the corporate hierarchy, including the responsibilities, education required, and a job description. We end with a short discussion of the organizations and reference materials that are of most use to both the aspiring and the experienced cost accountant.

COST ACCOUNTANT'S POSITION
IN THE CORPORATE HIERARCHY

The cost accountant is generally a member of the accounting department. As noted in Exhibit 2.1, however, the position can have a number of different reporting relationships. When a company is small and has only a small accounting staff, the most likely situation is for the cost accountant to report directly to the controller (option 1 in the exhibit). The next most likely case is one in which a company grows to a sufficiently large size that the controller acquires one or more assistant controllers who take on much of the controller's supervisory work. In this instance, the cost accountant

EXHIBIT 2.1. Cost Accountant's Place in the Corporate Hierarchy

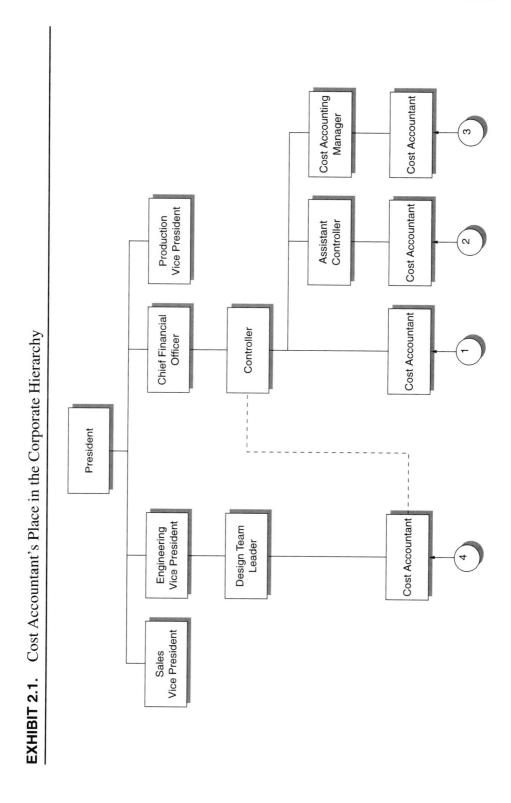

reports to an assistant controller (option 2). Then, if a company grows to an even larger size, there may be so many cost accountants that they are all grouped together under a cost accounting manager who in turn reports to an assistant controller or to the controller (option 3). Finally, when a company uses target costing (Chapter 17), a cost accountant can be permanently or temporarily assigned to a design team leader in the engineering department, though he or she still has some "dotted line" reporting responsibility back to the controller in the accounting department (option 4). This arrangement is most likely in product-driven companies that base their strategies on product designs. Also, when there are many corporate divisions, it is most likely that the cost accountant reports to the most local controller, such as one at the level of plant controller (though there may be a few cost accountants who report to the corporate controller and whose responsibilities involve a detailed review of corporatewide issues such as the acquisition of new facilities or subsidiaries). Consequently, the precise positioning of a cost accountant within the corporate hierarchy is largely driven by the size of the organization and its use of target costing.

Most of the cost accountant reporting relationships noted in Exhibit 2.1 are appropriate ones for a junior cost accountant—he or she receives a sufficient amount of management attention in three of the four reporting relationships. The problem is the fourth one, where the cost accountant is assigned to a product design team. In this case, only the most senior cost accountants should be assigned to a product design team because there is some risk that they will not be adequately supervised by the design team leader, who is not only very busy but is also not used to dealing with accountants. Accordingly, this reporting relationship is best avoided if there is not a sufficiently well-trained, experienced cost accountant available for the position.

COST ACCOUNTANT'S RESPONSIBILITIES

What does the cost accountant do during a typical workday? In this section we explore a multitude of tasks that cost accountants perform. The range of activities covered here are carried out by an entire cost accounting department since it would be difficult for one person to complete them all. They are:

- **Review the adequacy of activity-based costing systems.** If there is no activity-based costing system, the cost accountant should play the driving role in creating and maintaining one (see Chapter 16 for more information about activity-based costing). This is an exceedingly important system for determining the applicability of overhead costs to activities and should be present in virtually every kind of business.

- **Review the adequacy of data collection systems.** The cost accountant uses reams of data from all parts of a company, and if the data collection system does not work properly, the resulting analyses will be incorrect or misleading. Consequently, the cost accountant must periodically review all data collection systems to ensure not only that the correct information is being obtained but also that it is complete and relevant for the analyses in which it is used.

- **Review system costs and benefits.** Every company operates dozens, if not hundreds, of different systems. Many of these systems entail significant costs and so require a periodic costing review to see if they are operating in an efficient manner and providing improved service to downstream customers. Cost accountants are increasingly being called on to review these systems from a cost-benefit perspective to see if changes should be made.

- **Audit all costing systems.** In organizations where there is no internal auditing staff, the cost accountant can expect to review the adequacy of all costing systems through periodic system audits. Even if there is an internal auditing staff, the cost accountant may be asked to lend special expertise to the completion of such audits.

- **Report on product target costing variances.** One of the most rewarding activities for any cost accountant is to serve on a product design team that uses target costing principles (Chapter 17) since this practice results in higher product margins. In this role the cost accountant gives constant feedback to the design team regarding the cost of current design concepts, as well as the amount of costs still to be eliminated from a product design in order to achieve targeted profitability levels.

- **Report on activity-based costing overhead allocations.** The cost accountant must be able to interpret the allocation results of an activity-based costing system, determine the reasons for changes in the costs of various activities, investigate anomalies in costing information, and communicate the results to company management.

- **Report on break-even points by product and division.** There should be a current analysis on hand for the sales break-even point for every product, product line, and operating division of a company. This information is useful for determining the sales volume levels at which the company makes money, as well as for identifying the areas in which fixed costs are so high (or variable margins so low) that earning a profit is extremely difficult. The cost accountant should continually calculate, review, and communicate this information to the management team.

- **Report on margins by product and division.** The cost accountant should regularly review the margins being earned on all products, product lines, and operating divisions, as well as trends in these numbers and the reasons for changes. The resulting information is of major importance to managers, who use it to identify and resolve profitability-related issues.

- **Report on periodic variance analyses.** The cost accountant must determine which variances to calculate, which variance levels require further investigation, which investigative results are important enough to pass along to management, and how this information should be communicated to management.

- **Report on special topics as assigned.** This is one position in which there is a reliably steady flow of requests for additional reports on a wide array of topics, frequently stemming from anomalies that appear in standard reports issued by the costing staff. The cost accountant should block out a significant part of her work schedule to deal with these requests.

- **Report on capital budgeting requests.** In some organizations capital budgeting requests are handled by the cost accounting staff, though larger organizations route them to a separate financial analysis staff. In the former case the cost accountant must review capital request assumptions, cash flow projections, and risk levels and express a considered opinion on whether or not to proceed with an investment.

- **Assist in development of the budget.** There are several parts of the annual budgeting process in which the cost accountant should be deeply involved, such as the production budget, labor budget, manufacturing expense budget, inventory budget, and cost-of-goods-sold budget. The cost accountant is not directly responsible for any of these budgets but can give a great deal of advice to the responsible managers in regard to them.

- **Work with the marketing staff to update product pricing.** A company should not set product prices without a detailed analysis of the underlying unit costs, as well as the overhead costs that can be recovered only by selling beyond a certain minimum level. Cost accountants are of great use in this price-setting process because of their in-depth knowledge of both direct and overhead costs.

Though there may be a few other incidental activities in which cost accountants become involved, the activities described here are their chief responsibilities. We now translate these responsibilities into a formal job description.

COST ACCOUNTANT'S JOB DESCRIPTION

Based on the list of responsibilities outlined in the last section, we can now create a formal job description for a cost accountant. However, the job description that follows is based on *all* the possible tasks a cost accountant performs, which would require a superhuman effort for a single person to complete. Rather, this job description should be used as the foundation for a number of lesser job descriptions that are each a subset of the description provided here.

Job Title: Cost Accountant

Reports to: Cost Accounting Manager/Assistant Controller/Controller

Responsibilities	*Timing*
Systems Tasks	
Review adequacy of activity-based costing system	Quarterly
Review adequacy of data collection systems	Quarterly
Review system costs and benefits	Quarterly
Audit costing systems	Monthly
Analysis and Reporting Tasks	
Report on product target costing variances	Monthly
Report on activity-based costing overhead allocations	Monthly
Report on break-even points by product and division	Monthly
Report on margins by product and division	Monthly
Report on periodic variance analyses	Monthly
Report on special topics as assigned	Ongoing
Report on capital budgeting requests	Ongoing
Assist in development of the budget	Annual
Pricing tasks	
Work with marketing staff to update product pricing	Ongoing

COST ACCOUNTANT'S EDUCATION AND ONGOING TRAINING

The foundation of the cost accountant's education is a bachelor's degree in accounting. However, this degree focuses on many other areas besides cost accounting, perhaps limiting costing training to as little as one or two courses. Consequently, the newly graduated cost accountant does not really have a good understanding of how costing systems operate or how to interpret information extracted from them. This knowledge can be acquired from a variety of additional sources.

One is through certification work. The best is a certificate in production and inventory management offered by the American Production and Inventory Control Society (see Reference Materials and Organizations for the Cost Accountant for contact information). The certification requires one to pass seven tests covering these areas:

- Basics of supply chain management

- Inventory management

- Just-in-time

- Master planning

- Material and capacity requirements planning

- Production activity control

- Systems and technologies

Though this certification is designed primarily for people involved in the management and operation of production and inventory systems, these are also areas in which a cost accountant spends an inordinate amount of time. Consequently, this is one of the best possible ways to further education oneself in the systems that are so central to the operation of a quality cost accounting function.

Another objective worth pursuing is a Certified Management Accountant, which is a certification issued by the Institute of Management Accountants (see Reference Materials and Organizations for the Cost Accountant for contact information). The required 3-day test covers far more than just cost accounting topics but still includes a significant number of costing topics.

Besides certification, an aspiring cost accountant should strongly consider acquiring an additional college degree at the master's level. This can be a master's degree in business administration, which provides a good foundation in management and financial analysis principles, or a master's degree in finance; the latter degree is of particular interest to those who want to ascend in the accounting hierarchy to manage both cost accounting and financial analysis staffs (a common combination because of the heavy reliance of both functions on analytical skills).

A final warning to any cost accountant is that no level of training is sufficient. One must constantly root out the newest information, not only on accounting systems but also on the latest advances in technology, because both these areas have a considerable impact on the types and quality of information that can be extracted from a company's operations. This information can be acquired from magazines, the Internet, consultants, or attendance at conferences. The best approach is to continually pursue all avenues of information dissemination.

The recommendations listed here may seem extreme, for they require literally years of study beyond the bachelor's degree. However, cost accounting is a technical position that requires a great deal of knowledge, so the continuing pursuit of more knowledge is the only way to stay at the top of the profession.

COST ACCOUNTANT'S CAREER PATH

Cost accounting is one of the skills most sought after by many larger corporations because it calls for specific technical abilities that many accountants do not have. The downside of this level of demand is that a good cost accountant has no career path—companies want them to stay right where they are, especially if the organizations are so small that there is no easy way to train someone to take their place on promotion. To keep from being locked into a cost accounting position for life, it is best for an accountant to take a position in a company with a sufficiently large accounting staff that promotions occur with a reasonable degree of rapidity. In this type of environment it is not unreasonable to expect a promotion to either cost accounting manager or assistant controller. At this level the breadth of supervision probably encompasses not only the cost accounting staff but also all financial analysts—these are both analysis positions, and so it makes sense to cluster them together under the same supervisor.

However, because of the high degree of specialization of the cost accounting position, one can still reach a career dead end at this next-higher level unless one has spent a sufficient amount of time in other areas of the department, especially in the key transaction processing areas of accounts payable and accounts receivable. Only after obtaining this broader level of experience does one have a serious chance of moving up another notch to the controller position.

Another career path problem is being assigned to a target costing team. Since this type of work can lead to a permanent position within the engineering department, there is some risk that a cost accountant who accepts such a position will never return to the accounting department or will come back after so many years that his career will be effectively sidetracked into that of a target costing specialist. To avoid this, one should reach an agreement (in writing) with the cost accounting manager that specifies how long a target costing assignment will last, so that there is some basis for demanding a return to the accounting department after a reasonable period of time. The alternative for employees not interested in a promotion is to permanently stay in a target costing role; it is one of the most valuable and rewarding accounting positions and may be a satisfactory position in which to remain.

Thus, the cost accountant must be mindful of obtaining experience outside the cost accounting field and avoiding long-term assignments outside the accounting department, while also looking for larger organizations that are big enough to ensure some type of promotion within the accounting department.

REFERENCE MATERIALS AND ORGANIZATIONS FOR THE COST ACCOUNTANT

There are a number of valuable cost accounting texts that should be on every cost accountant's desk. The bibliography at the end of this book contains a list of the most commonly used texts. For the most up-to-date research materials on cost accounting topics, it is also useful to purchase the complete catalog of publications from the Institute of Management Accountants (IMA) Foundation for Applied Research, Inc. This group is a nonprofit branch of the IMA and publishes research reports on a wide array of topics, such as direct costing, transfer pricing, and the cost of quality. The easiest way to review this catalog is to examine it on the Internet at http://www.imanet.org/, while books can be ordered by calling 800-638-4427, extension 235.

The most relevant organizations for a cost accountant to join are the IMA and the American Production and Inventory Control Society (APICS). The IMA is an extremely active group that produces several quality magazines covering a number of management accounting topics. Cost accounting issues of various types are discussed in nearly every issue, including case studies. The IMA can be contacted at 10 Paragon Drive, Montvale, New Jersey 07645-1760, or by calling 800-638-4427. APICS is a large organization concerned with the dissemination of information about production and inventory control issues; since these topics are central to the work of a cost accountant, it is well worth reviewing the APICS magazine as well as its enormous catalog of books. APICS can be contacted at 5301 Shawnee Road, Alexandria, Virginia 22312-2317, or by calling 703-354-8851; its Web site is at http://www.apics.org/. A cost accountant should consider membership in both these organizations mandatory.

If accounting system control issues are of interest, it may be useful to join the Institute of Internal Auditors (IIA), though the topics this organization deals with are more peripheral to cost accounting issues. The IIA can be reached at 249 Maitland Avenue, Altamonte Springs, Florida 32701, or by calling 407-830-7600. The IIA also publishes a book catalog.

SUMMARY

This chapter has focused on the cost accountant's role and position within the modern corporation. As can be seen by perusing the cost accountant's job description, this is a highly technical, demanding position that requires an in-depth knowledge of production and inventory control systems, as well as accounting principles, and that can lead to a rewarding career within the accounting function. In the remainder of this book, we cover the key topics that will assist an aspiring cost accountant in her career, including costing systems and methodologies, variance analysis, cost management, and pricing issues.

CHAPTER 3

Impact of Ethics on the Cost Accountant

Before we review the detailed types of data collection and costing systems to be discussed in the next few dozen chapters, it is important to understand that the results produced by these systems can be seriously skewed if the ethical basis of a company's operations is downgraded. For example, constantly shifting forward the month-end closing date used to create monthly financial statements alters the reported financial results so that no one knows the actual monthly results. Further, any alteration of costing records, such as bills of material, can seriously distort the reported cost of goods sold, not to mention the period-end inventory balance. If a company has problems in these areas, the cost accountant will have a difficult time extracting accurate information from the existing systems—not because the systems are faulty but because their operators are.

In this chapter we explore the main types of ethical issues faced by the cost accountant, discuss the resolution of ethical problems, and consider the special ethical problems faced by managers. Though these issues may seem to be "high level" and divorced from the reality of daily operations, they are not. In the author's experience ethics problems arise continually, at least once a month, and must be dealt with in a careful, well-reasoned manner in order to ensure that the cost accountant's actions improve company operations, result in consistently accurate costing information, and give the accountant a sense of upholding a high standard of ethical conduct.

CAUSES OF ETHICS PROBLEMS

There are three main causes of low standards of ethical behavior. The first is inadequate personnel screening. Companies who are in a rush to fill positions may do so without conducting adequate reference checks, background investigations, or thorough interviews. Though hiring departments may think that they are achieving cost savings and accelerating the hiring process by avoiding these tasks, they are really lowering the company's hiring criteria, which allows more people with a history of questionable ethics to be hired. The best ways to avoid this difficulty are the opposite of the practices just stated—intensive discussions with references, use of a preplanned list of questions covering all aspects of a recruit's behavior patterns, and thorough background investigations by outside review firms that specialize in accessing historical records of recruits that may provide evidence of improper behavior in the past. Finally, interviews should involve several employees, each of whom is trained in interviewing techniques that force job applicants to describe their reasons for past failures as well as successes. These investigations should be conducted with particular thoroughness for potential management hires, since these individuals can have an inordinately large impact on the ethical behavior of their subordinates. All these techniques are needed in order to acquire high-quality employees.

The second reason for low standards of ethical behavior is poor company procedures. If there is not a regimented way of doing business, over and over again, employees will find their own way of doing business. These methods vary over time, so much that employees begin to alter procedures just to fit the circumstances, whether it be for ease of use, in order to alter financial results, or for some other reason—they simply pull out the homemade procedure that fits and use it until it is no longer necessary. Of course, this problem is best dealt with through the strict implementation and use of a single set of rigidly enforced procedures, requiring internal auditors to discover any possible loopholes, systems analysts who can design the best systems, and committed managers who are willing to implement and enforce policies.

The third reason for substandard ethical behavior is the one that also seems to attract the most attention in the business press—high performance expectations. When top-level managers set unrealistically high performance goals and tie compensation to their achievement, it is amazing what employees will do to ensure that these goals are reached. One may see the creation of false customer orders, early shipments of products not yet wanted by customers, falsification of inventory records to show a higher profit, and all kinds of skullduggery related to the modification of financial reports. And this is seen in people who normally would not be tempted to stretch their ethical boundaries at all. In this instance, the best preventive measure is to scale back on performance goals and related compensation measures. If this is not possible [i.e., the chief executive officer (CEO) does not listen to the cost accountant's advice], the costing staff should be on the lookout for any type of record falsification in the areas they investigate and bring any problems to the immediate attention of senior management. The problem in this case, which makes it one of the worst causes of ethical failure, is that the management team itself may be deeply involved in financial misstatements, so that all warnings from the costing staff go unheeded.

Of the three reasons for ethical misconduct noted here, the worst is the last. The motive for ignoring one's sense of ethics is simply too strong—personal gain through the achievement of performance goals, which is made easier when everyone in the company is straining to attain the same goals, thereby allowing for the possibility of widespread collusion. The other reasons tend to result in spotty ethics problems related to specific individuals or procedural weaknesses and so are more easily identified and controlled. Next we address the types of ethical problems with which the cost accountant may be confronted.

CONFIDENTIALITY ISSUES

One of the major ethics areas about which a cost accountant should be concerned is confidentiality. This issue is particularly important because cost accountants have detailed access to all kinds of "secret" information, such as payroll records, product costs, and profits by product line. This information can be used by other entities, such as labor unions and competitors, to damage the company, either by demanding wage concessions (labor unions) or by hiring away key staff or pricing their products to attack weak company products (competitors). Furthermore, acquiring a reputation for not keeping quiet about confidential information eventually results in a cost accountant being locked out of access to much of the information needed to do his job.

Given the number of problems associated with confidentiality, there are several steps one should take to avoid ethics issues in this area. First, the cost accountant should personally assist in locking up sensitive information. This may involve recommendations to encrypt data, physically lock paper-based files in safes, or control access to certain offices. Furthermore, one can adopt a rigid attitude toward the control of information that is in the cost accountant's possession, which may include locking up one's office when sensitive data is kept there, locking one's briefcase when transporting such data, and using password protection on one's computer. Additionally, the cost accountant should be aware that "loose lips sink ships"—in other words, many cost accounting topics should not be the subject of casual conversation. If others attempt to bring the subject of conversation around to a confidential topic, one must find a way to redirect the discussion or to politely point out that one cannot discuss the issue at all. Though this can make one feel like a social pariah, others will respect the need for confidentiality once they realize that certain topics are off limits.

It is also important that the cost accountant watch for confidentiality problems in others and point them out, either directly to the employees in question or to their supervisors. This attentiveness ensures that other employees are constantly made aware that certain kinds of information must be kept confidential.

The discussion here is not intended to suggest that a company should be on a war footing or that there is constant traffic in stolen information. There are usually only a small number of situations in which confidentiality of information must be maintained. Most of the time, the bulk of the information that passes through a cost accountant's hands can be discussed freely with anyone. Care is needed only in a minority of cases.

INTEGRITY ISSUES

The general topic of integrity involves the largest number of ethical pitfalls for the cost accountant simply because there are so many topics within this category of which the accountant must be aware.

One of the key integrity issues is recognizing when one's training and experience are not sufficient to complete an assigned task. This happens frequently when a cost accountant is assigned to analyze a special project area that falls outside his or her area of expertise. For example, there may be a need to review the process flow within the engineering department or perhaps to determine the fully absorbed cost of fuel oil after it has been processed at a refinery. To accomplish these tasks one must determine what additional skills are necessary and acquire them before proceeding with the project. This may not seem like an ethical issue at all, but consider the alternative—completing the work knowing that one is operating from a foundation of insufficient knowledge. The results of the analysis may draw conclusions and recommend actions that are completely erroneous, simply because the cost accountant was aware of his own knowledge limitations but did nothing to improve the situation. This is a common cause of poor performance reviews, if not dismissal from a company.

Another integrity issue is conflict of interest. This situation can arise when a cost accountant develops a close relationship with the person whose area of responsibility is currently under review, perhaps because of something as seemingly innocent as a few free meals or tickets to a sports event. Though these favors seem minor, they can build up a sense of obligation in the cost accountant's mind that the current analysis should be modified ever so slightly to cast the reviewee in a more favorable light. This problem can be greatly reduced if a company has a standard policy outlining the extent to which favors of any kind can be accepted by employees—such as a hard dollar limit of $10 for any gift.

Another integrity issue involves the use of company assets. There is a temptation for employees to borrow company equipment or even access it for personal use while in the office. When a cost accountant does this, it creates a "gray area" in that person's mind regarding the extent to which assets can be used for other than company-specific purposes. This may lead to the cost accountant's overlooking any similar practices found during various cost accounting reviews if he or she finds that other employees are also borrowing company assets. As a result, accounting reports concerning the levels of control over company assets may not reveal that there is a usage problem.

A more general integrity issue is a cost accountant's propensity to actively or passively undermine a company's ethics policies. The most common instance is *passive* subversion, in which the accountant sees behavior that is clearly unethical but fails to report it on the grounds of not wanting to "rock the boat" or be a whistle blower and tries to curry favor with the person engaged in the illicit activity. This passive behavior is extremely destructive in the long run for the entire company, for it results in unchecked adverse behavior, not to mention a general sense among other employees that the company is ignoring clearly identifiable ethics problems.

It hardly needs to be mentioned that the *active* subversion of ethics policies by a cost accountant reflects poorly on the profession as a whole and on the accounting department in particular. There are no excuses for such activities, and an accounting supervisor is well advised to deal with such behavior by immediately dismissing the perpetrator.

OBJECTIVITY ISSUES

An important issue with which the cost accountant is constantly confronted is objectivity. This involves presenting cost analyses in a fair, well-balanced format that discloses all relevant information pertaining to a decision. Though it may seem obvious, the cost accountant can be under considerable pressure by department managers whose operations are being reviewed to skew reported information in such a way as to make the managers appear to be better performers than they really are.

The best approach to this problem is to communicate regularly with employees who are being subjected to reviews by the cost accountant. This allows them to have a fair amount of access to the analysis, which they can then use, if they so desire, to present their own views of the costing reviews to senior management. By taking this approach employees who would normally be encouraged to pressure the cost accountant to modify the final reports are instead channeled into presenting their own opinions as a separate document. It is important to give these people advance reviews of the analyses so that they feel they have sufficient time to prepare their own defenses of the cost accountant's work.

ETHICS PROBLEM RESOLUTION

Despite a cost accountant's best efforts to avoid ethical problems, they appear regularly. In the author's experience rapidly growing organizations in particular encounter a variety of ethical problems caused by inadequate personnel screening, minimal procedures, and intense pressure to meet financial projections. In these instances ethical issues pop up with disturbing regularity—as often as once a week and certainly not less than once a month. This frequency is much lower in large, well-established companies where systems have been firmly implanted for a long time, personnel have been thoroughly screened during the hiring process, and there is a substantial core of experienced financial analysts who can readily and accurately predict financial results. Nonetheless, ethical problems come up in all situations at one time or another. What steps should the cost accountant follow when they arise?

The first step is to determine if the issue at hand is one that involves ethics. A problem may crop up that is outside the cost accountant's experience and may or may not be an ethical problem—one simply is not sure. To clarify the situation one can consult a book on the subject or talk to an advisor. The advisor may be one's supervisor or mentor—someone with long experience in the field who is well grounded in the proper types of behavior. If this sort of person is not available, one can contact the ethics advisor at one of the professional accounting organizations, such as the American Institute of Certified Public Accountants or the Institute of Management Accountants, for an opinion.

Once the issue has been clarified through discussion with an advisor, the cost accountant must determine some course of action. Is the ethical issue one that is so minor that it can be ignored or does it lie somewhere further along a continuum of ethical problems and represent a more severe issue? One person may decide that some action must be taken, no matter how insignificant, whereas others may conclude that there is a minimal level of ethics below which they are comfortable ignoring any problems. For ethical problems that appear to be the most severe, or for which there may be some retribution against the cost accountant, it may be necessary to consult an attorney regarding any legal ramifications.

At this point the cost accountant must take some sort of action. Whatever this action is, it is important to carefully consider the exact wording to be used in dealing with the issue (so that the reason for taking corrective action is conveyed in a convincing manner) and the steps to be taken to correct the ethical problem. It is not necessary to make an "I'm doing this, or else there will be consequences" statement at this point since the cost accountant's initial position may be accepted at once, with no further issues arising. There is no reason to create a contentious environment by making such statements before there is any evidence of resistance. However, additional steps taken by the cost accountant to resolve the problem should be thought out in advance in case a problem situation rapidly escalates.

If the ethical problem continues in spite of the cost accountant's stated position, then it is time to communicate to the offending party the further action that will be taken if the situation occurs again. This can become a confrontational situation that is extremely uncomfortable for all involved parties, so it is important to state one's position clearly but politely, thereby avoiding an emotional display.

The situation may still be in evidence after all the preceding steps have been taken. Then what? First, make sure that the problem is still occurring. There may have been some improvement, though not to the extent that the difficulty is completely resolved. If so, it may be worth iterating one's position to see if the problem gradually declines over time. If not, and if the problem is sufficiently severe, the cost accountant must seriously consider leaving the company. Though this seems like a drastic step, one cannot let one's ethical principles be compromised by ongoing misguided behavior, nor is it wise to let one's reputation be potentially damaged by association with an organization whose lack of ethics may eventually become public knowledge. There are many highly ethical organizations that would welcome a cost accountant's services. Seek them out.

ETHICS FOR THE SUPERVISOR

The supervisor is in the unique position of either improving or weakening a company's sense of ethics because she can influence the behavior of those reporting to her. If the supervisor is willing to adopt low ethical standards, it is likely that a large portion of her staff will copy her actions and that the remainder who disapprove will find work elsewhere.

Several steps can be taken to ensure that supervisors' standards, as well as their actions in dealing with their staffs about this issue, be kept as high as possible. Here are some possibilities:

- **Proper job screening.** Job screening is especially important for anyone who is either hired or promoted to a supervisory position. Even if a company conducts minimal background checking and interviewing for nonsupervisory positions, in the case of managers it must do so with great thoroughness. This keeps people who have a record of problem behavior from reaching influential positions.

- **Ethics training.** Supervisors should be required to attend formal ethics training classes at least once a year, as well as to administer such training to all their subordinates.

- **Match ethics training materials to company policy.** It does not do much good to conduct ethics training classes if their content varies from the official ethics policy of the company. When this happens, employees are caught between differing standards and must choose their own solutions to problems, which may not result in behavior condoned by the senior management team.

- **Performance reviews.** The annual reviews of both supervisors and their staffs should include a discussion of any ethical issues that have arisen during the past year, the thought processes that occurred in dealing with them, and their outcomes. These discussions should be documented in the annual review paperwork and forwarded to the human resources staff, which should keep track of this information and notify senior management if such discussions are not taking place.

- **Follow up on problems at once.** A major issue is that supervisors be required to follow up on any reported ethics issues *immediately*. Otherwise, employees feel that company management likes to talk about ethics but does not take any action to underscore that talk. This eventually results in the staff completely ignoring management's statements about ethics.

The points made here relate to a mix of issues—job screening, training, performance reviews, and immediate attention to ethics issues. All involve managers to some degree because they are responsible for training employees, reviewing their ethics performance, and correcting ethics-related problems. Given the number of situations in which managers must become involved, it is apparent that senior management must be assured of having complete agreement regarding the need for high ethical standards within its supervisory ranks in order to be assured of proper ethical behavior throughout the organization.

SUMMARY

This discussion of ethics is not meant to imply that today's corporation is rife with ethical problems that the typical employee must deal with on a daily basis. Nonetheless, ethical issues arise regularly, if only because the cost accountant works in an area of the company where ethical irregularities are most likely to occur. Several sections in this chapter were designed to provide some guidance for the cost accountant in terms of what issues present ethical problems, as well as how to deal with them. For the opposite view—that of the perpetrator—the reader should refer to Chapter 40, which deals with fraud and provides a better view of the specific areas in which problems can arise.

PART II

Costing Systems and Data Collection

CHAPTER 4

Using Data Systems to Collect Costing Information

The classical view of data collection for the accounting function is that of employees filling out forms of various kinds throughout the company, which are then forwarded to a central data entry location where hordes of clerks keypunch the data into a central computer database. Though this was a reasonably accurate view of the situation in the past, there has been a major improvement in the types of systems available for collecting information in a more efficient, effective manner. These systems were developed because of a growing recognition that traditional data collection methods require a great deal of employee time that could be better spent on value-added tasks. Also, having a secondary data entry step increases the likelihood of keypunching errors, which can be completely avoided by some of the new data collection methods discussed in this chapter.

Some of the data systems that can be used to collect costing information are shown in Exhibit 4.1. They lie along a continuum that begins with loosely formatted data, such as that found on a faxed document, and ends with perfectly formatted data that can be directly entered into a computer system without alteration, such as electronic data interchange (EDI) transactions or transactions entered through an electronic form. A special case is document imaging, which can be tightly coupled to a company's computer systems or maintained as a free-standing system with no linkages at all. Accordingly, it is surrounded by a larger box in the exhibit, indicating the range within the exhibit that it can occupy. Based on the information in the

EXHIBIT 4.1. Characteristics of Data Collection Systems

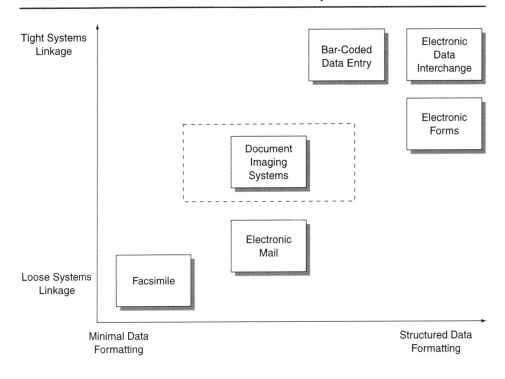

exhibit, it is evident that a cost accountant should recommend installation of the systems noted in the upper right-hand corner because they provide the best means for collecting the highest-quality costing information that can be injected directly into a company's central database of costing information.

BAR CODING

Let us say that Company Alpha wants to track the progress of a product through every step of its production process. Being a technologically advanced organization, it has installed data entry keypads at each of its workstations. One of these products is coded AD-546-798. The operator of each workstation is required to enter the part number into a keypad, followed by the number of units completed. The cost accountant uses this information to determine the progress of work-in-process batches as they move through the plant. The trouble is that the part number is so meaningless that 3 of the 10 workstation operators enter the information incorrectly by transposing numbers. The 546 part of the number is in the same row on the keypad as the 798 portion of the number, so that transpositions are difficult to avoid.

This error results in unreadable reports that the cost accountant must manually correct by going to the shop floor and tracking each job by hand. Obviously, data entry inaccuracy is a big problem in this instance. In the real world it is an enormous issue because employees are asked to enter data into computer systems even if they are not properly trained in data entry. The author recently observed a situation where a workforce whose primary language was not English, and which also experienced an annual turnover rate of greater than 200%, was asked to enter production data into a warehouse database; the results were continuing inventory record inaccuracy levels of 50% or greater despite weekly cycle counts. In short, the human element of data entry can cause considerable difficulty in ensuring that accurate data is entered into a computer database. This problem can be resolved through the use of bar codes.

A bar code is a set of alternating parallel bars and spaces of different widths that signify letters, numbers, and other characters. When scanned by a laser beam attached to a computer chip containing a decoding algorithm, this cluster of bars and spaces is converted to an alphanumeric character. There are several algorithms that result in different types of bar codes. One of the most popular is Code 39, which contains both letters and numbers (i.e., is alphanumeric) and is heavily used in manufacturing. Another is Interleaved 2 of 5, which contains only numeric characters; this bar code is most commonly found in the automotive, warehousing, and baggage handling industries. Yet another variation is the universal product code (UPC), which is primarily found in supermarkets and in the retailing industry. Whatever the method used, all these bar codes can be generated within a company by entering the required characters into a computer, which converts them to the needed bar code format and sends them to a printer. A laser printer is recommended because it yields a higher-resolution bar code, though ink-jet printers are close in comparative levels of resolution. Dot-matrix printers are not recommended for bar code printing because of their much lower resolution levels.

Whatever the type of bar code used, the subsequent processing steps are the same. A bar code is manufactured at the point of use, typically by a special application printer that produces only bar codes. The bar code is typically a self-adhesive one that is affixed to the item to be tracked; this procedure can be automated if the volume of activity warrants investment in such machinery. Then the item being tracked moves through whatever process is occurring and is scanned at fixed points in the process. This scanning can be conducted by a person with a hand-held scanner or by an automated scanning station. The scanner extracts information from the bar code and feeds it directly into the computer database.

There are several types of scanners, and the choice of model depends on the application. The main categories of scanners are:

- **Light pen.** This is the least-expensive type, requiring a user to manually drag the scanning device across the bar code. It has a low success rate and may require a number of scans before an accurate scan is completed. It is most commonly used for low-volume applications, where speed of scanning is not important and where low cost is the main determinant of use.

- **Hand-held scanner.** This device contains a motor that rapidly sends a series of laser scans across a bar code, resulting in a much faster scan. It can also be used with bar codes printed with relatively poor resolution. This scanner can be used with a direct wire linkage to a computer or through radio transmission to a local radio receiver, thereby allowing roving use of the device. A hand-held scanner is several times more expensive than a light pen, while radio-frequency scanners usually cost several thousand dollars each.

- **Stationary fixed-beam scanner.** This device is not intended for manual use. Instead, it is fixed in place at a point past which items are moved, such as on a conveyor belt. The scanner must achieve success on a single scan of any passing bar code or no read will result. To handle this situation, the conveyor belt must be equipped with a shunting gate so that unscanned items are pushed to one side, allowing machine operators to move them back through the scanning station for a second attempt.

- **Stationary moving-beam scanner.** This device is the same as a stationary fixed-beam scanner except that it is equipped with a motor that sends a series of scans over each bar code, ensuring a high percentage of successful scans. This type of scanner is more expensive than the fixed-beam variety, but its added cost can be offset against the reduced (or eliminated) need for a shunting gate and the manual labor associated with it.

There are a number of applications for which bar coding is useful. For example:

- **Inventory transactions.** An inventory identification number is frequently one that is randomly assigned to a component or product and so has no meaning to the person entering it into the computer system for a transaction. This situation leads to inaccurate data entry. To avoid this problem, bar codes can be attached to all inventory items, which are then scanned as part of any inventory move transaction.

- **Labor tracking.** When employees manually fill out a time card for submission to the accounting department, their writing may be so unclear that the accounting staff makes errors when transcribing this information into the payroll system. To avoid this problem, employees can be issued bar-coded time cards which they slide through a time clock equipped with a scanning device. In this way, all data entry is eliminated.

- **Fixed-asset tracking.** It is customary for the accounting staff to make an annual comparison between the fixed-asset database and assets that can actually be located in the facility. This is a difficult task when the assets are poorly labeled or if the labels used are easily damaged. Bar codes help to resolve this problem because they are easily attached to assets, can be damaged to some extent and still be successfully scanned, and cost little to produce.

- **Accounting transactions.** The accounting department itself can profit from the use of bar coding. For example, this department is frequently called on to enter data for transactions recorded by other departments, particularly the production and warehousing departments. One such document is the labor ticket for a specific job, which can be posted next to a machine and filled out by anyone working at that work center. Often it is difficult to read the standard information on the sheet, such as the identification number of the machine. A bar code can be added to the document when a fresh one is distributed to the machine locations each week. Then, when the document is completed and returned to the accounting department, the data entry clerk can scan the bar code into the computer, achieving a perfectly accurate entry of the bar code identification information.

- **Shop floor control.** As a job works its way through the production area, some companies require the production staff to extract information from a routing sheet attached to the job and enter it into a local data entry terminal. This information tells the production control staff where the job is located in the production process and can also be used by the accounting staff to determine the costs each job has thus far compiled. It is possible for the data entry person to enter this identification information incorrectly, so bar codes can be added to the routing sheet in place of written identification information. The data entry person then scans the bar codes into the local data entry terminal instead of making a typed entry.

Clearly, there are many uses to which bar coding can be put. It is ideal for situations where the risk of data entry error is high and is also useful when a company wants to use automation to avoid manual data entry. However, there is a cost associated with the purchase and implementation of bar code printing and scanning equipment, so the cost accountant should first calculate the costs and benefits associated with the use of this equipment before proceeding to an actual installation.

WIRELESS TRANSMISSION

When a transaction is entered into a computer terminal, it travels through a wire or fiber optic cable to a database for storage. Unfortunately, this data entry method requires one to walk to a fixed terminal location in order to enter data, which is not always possible for employees who collect data as they travel through a facility or are on the road.

The answer to this problem is to create a terminal that sends wireless transmissions to a receiver that in turn is directly linked to a database. This allows data entry to take place virtually anywhere. This mode of data entry has improved at a rapid rate, and several types of portable terminals have been developed. One is the radio-frequency bar code scanner, which is an integrated liquid crystal display, keyboard, and scanner. It is frequently used in warehouses, where cycle counters can enter quantity changes on the spot rather than write them down, walk to a terminal, enter the data, and then walk back to the counting area. Another terminal is the wireless Palm computer (and several knockoff versions thereof) into which one can enter information with a stylus and then send it to a Web site from which it is sent as an electronic message to a company's database. Yet another variation is a portable computer linked to a cellular phone; a modem connection is made through the phone, which transmits the data to a modem at the company, where it is converted to a digital signal and sent to the company database. Other devices are appearing all the time, though they are still looking for applications—such as wrist-mounted computers and voice-activated computers that convert spoken words to data and transmit the results to a database. This is an exciting new area that will allow companies to perform data entry from virtually any location. These are some examples of the applications to which wireless transmission can be put:

- **Inventory transactions.** A major problem with any inventory system is that the warehouse staff conducts a transaction and then must find a computer terminal into which to enter the information. This may involve a long walk, so there is some risk that the worker will forget some of the information to be entered or entirely miss making the entry. Radio-frequency bar code scanners avoid this problem because they are readily available for use no matter where the worker travels within a facility. The information is scanned or punched into the portable unit, and the transaction is immediately sent to the central computer database for updating.

- **Cycle counting.** Any warehouse manager who wants to ensure a high level of inventory accuracy must send an employee into the warehouse to confirm that the inventory quantities listed in the computer are the same as those on the shelves. The trouble is that the cycle counter must plod through the warehouse with a thick sheaf of inventory reports, locate the item to be counted in the report, find it on the shelf, write down any corrections, go back to a terminal, and enter any changes. Clearly, this is a time-consuming process. A better approach is to use a radio-frequency bar code scanner to scan the part number of the item on the shelf, scan the bar code for the item's warehouse location, have the scanner immediately reveal whether there is a counting discrepancy by accessing the central database, and then making a correction on the spot.

- **Fixed-asset tracking.** Larger companies want to keep track of where all their fixed assets are located. To do so, they affix a bar code label to each asset when it is purchased. Periodically, someone walks through the facility and scans each bar code, which is transmitted to a central database for comparison to a central asset listing.

The scanner may even be able to receive transmissions back from the central database, indicating which assets have not yet been scanned at a given location.

- **Customer order entry.** Salespeople can enter orders at customer sites, either on a laptop computer with a cellular phone connection or into a wireless Palm computer. The entry can then be sent straight to the company's order processing system without the hassle of mailing or faxing (which would also require rekeying of the data). This method also reduces the time required to put the order into a company's system, resulting in faster order turnaround time and therefore a higher level of customer satisfaction.

DOCUMENT IMAGING

The assumption in most organizations is that a paper document must be manually transcribed into a computer database. However, an alternative to this labor-intensive approach is to simply insert the document into a scanner and punch an indexing number into an attached computer terminal, thereby converting the document directly to a digitized format and making it easily accessible from any linked computer terminal throughout the company.

The basic structure of this document imaging system is shown in Exhibit 4.2, which illustrates several ways to input documents into a computer, the most common being the use of a scanner. When a document has been converted to a digital format by this means, it still cannot be stored in the computer database since there would be no way to retrieve it. Consequently, one or more indexing numbers must be punched in. For example, these could be the unique number assigned to the scanned document, the name of the customer, the date, or any other information that allows a user to readily access the document again. The key issue is to ensure that the document is not lost in the database.

The digitized document is then stored in a high-capacity storage device, usually a compact disc (CD) jukebox. This is a device that contains a large number of CDs and allows rapid access to the data on each one (as opposed to tape storage systems). The jukebox format can store many gigabytes of data, and it needs to—a single document stored at a high-image-quality level can require up to $\frac{1}{2}$ megabyte of storage capacity. However, it is more common to choose a lower level of document resolution when scanning into a database, which results in much lower storage requirements, usually in the range of $\frac{1}{10}$ megabyte. The indexing file is stored separately in a high-speed storage device that can rapidly sort through a large indexing file to find the correct document. This index is then used to extract a file from the CD jukebox and send it to a user on demand.

There are a number of ways to output the data from a document imaging system. The most common one is direct output to a user terminal, which has the dual advantages of saving paper and of allowing users to see a document on their screens side-by-side with other pertinent information. Other types of output include

EXHIBIT 4.2. Overview of the Document Imaging Process Flow

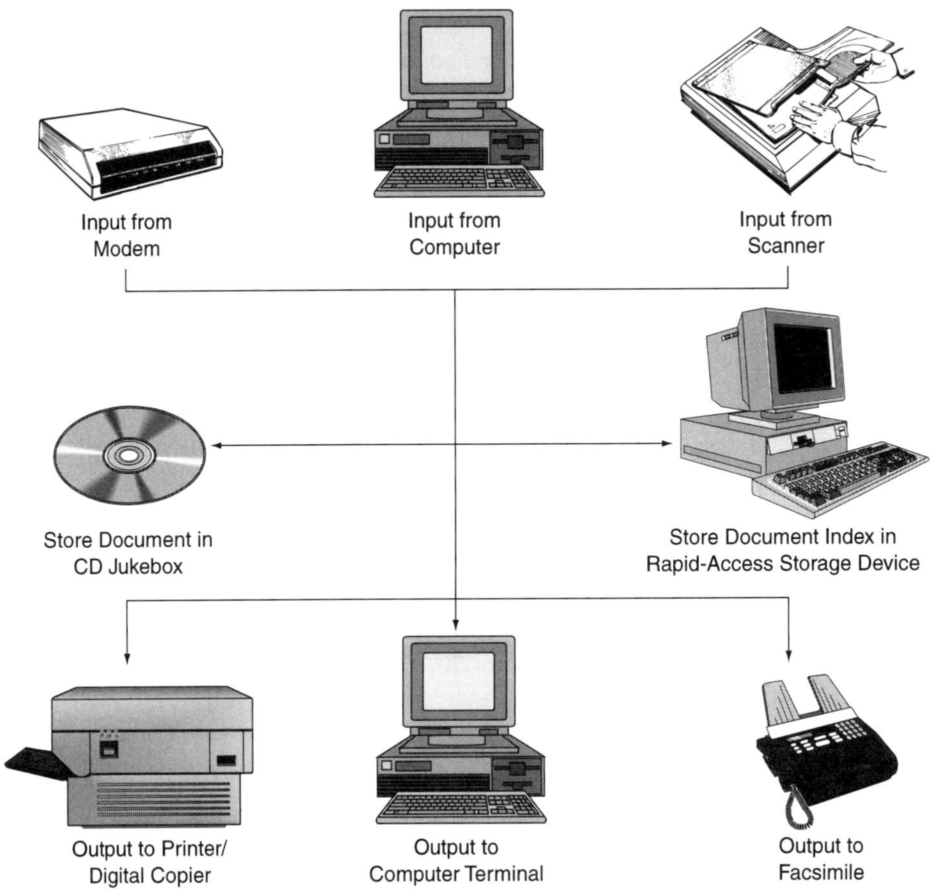

Input from
Modem

Input from
Computer

Input from
Scanner

Store Document in
CD Jukebox

Store Document Index in
Rapid-Access Storage Device

Output to Printer/
Digital Copier

Output to
Computer Terminal

Output to
Facsimile

printing, facsimile transmission, and modem transmission. The most common output is straight to a terminal.

The use of document imaging by a cost accountant is primarily for drill-down analysis. It makes research efforts much easier by allowing the cost accountant to find all the materials relevant to an information search without ever having to leave his terminal. For example, if he is looking into the reason for a specific purchase, he can drill down into the accounting system from the general ledger account to the purchasing journal, which shows the date and amount of the purchase as well as the purchase order number. If the system is linked to a materials management system, he may even be able to drill down to a copy of the purchase order but cannot reference the purchase requisition used to derive the purchase order. Now, with a document imaging system, he can use the requisition number noted on the purchase order to index the scanned requisition which shows precisely what was ordered and who ordered it. There is no need to conduct research in paper file which makes this a much faster way to conduct cost accounting research.

An added benefit of document imaging is that more than one accountant can review the same document at the same time. With a paper-based system there is always the problem of files being missing because they are being used by someone else (and the added problem of their not being returned to the appropriate location), resulting in a delay in research efforts until they are returned. With a document imaging system the file remains in the same storage location in the CD jukebox, no matter how many users are reviewing it at the same time. Thus, research is never delayed by missing documents.

The document imaging solution is a good one, but its cost must be considered. For a small organization, the cost of the computer hardware and software may be too high in relation to the cost savings anticipated from converting a small volume of documents to a digitized format. However, large-volume organizations dealing with tens or hundreds of thousands of documents, such as insurance companies, find that the cost of such a system is negligible in comparison to the benefits to be gained. Prices are constantly dropping in this area, as is the case for all computer equipment, so it is difficult to itemize imaging system prices that will be valid for any length of time. In general, a low-end imaging system can be obtained for a price in the low five-figure range, while a high-volume transaction solution can easily cost up to more than $1 million. When preparing a cost-benefit analysis for a document imaging system, one should consider the benefits not only of reduced research time but also of eliminated rent for document storage space, eliminated staff positions for filing work, and (a surprising large item) the eliminated cost of lost documents.

ELECTRONIC DATA INTERCHANGE

Data collection is particularly painful when data is received from a company's trading partner and must then be reentered into the company's database. The problem is that the information sent to the company may not be the same as that required by the internal system, so that someone must contact the trading partner for the missing information. In addition, there is always the risk of data entry errors, which can be caused by simple retyping mistakes, or a misreading of the received document (such as a blurry fax). All these costs are non-value-added since they contribute nothing to the underlying value of the product or service the company provides. All these issues can be eliminated through the use of electronic data interchange.

For a few hundred dollars one can purchase an elementary EDI software package that reveals an electronic form on the computer screen. One enters all the data needed into a set of required fields for whatever standard transaction is required—more than 100 of which have been carefully defined by an international standards organization. Once all the transactions have been entered, the computer sends the information to the business partner by modem. The recipient then accesses the data through its modem, prints it, and manually transfers the information to its computer system. Though very simple, this approach is not much better than sending the same information by a fax machine, since it still requires manual entry of data at both ends of the transaction. The only improvement over the fax machine is that the information can be accessed only by a specific computer at the receiving company, so that the risk of losing the document (as would be the case at a publicly available fax machine) is eliminated.

A much better approach is to have the computer system at the sending organization automatically reformat a transaction into EDI format and also send it automatically—no operator intervention required! The same process can be achieved at the receiving end, where incoming transactions are automatically received, reformatted, and inserted into the in-house computer system. With this approach all risk of data entry error is completely eliminated. This is a particularly valuable capability at companies with large volumes of data flowing between them and their trading partners.

A final issue for EDI application is how to send a transaction between companies. It is possible to send a transmission directly to each business partner, which can have a computer permanently available to receive the transaction. However, this computer may be tied up receiving a transaction from some other company and the transaction cannot go through. Also, the sending company may be sending at a transmission rate too high to be received at the other end. The best way to avoid these problems is to sign up with a value-added network (VAN), which is a central computing facility that receives EDI transmissions from trading partners and stores them in electronic mailboxes for recipients. The recipients automatically poll their mailboxes every few hours and extract the messages that have arrived. Though the VAN operator charges a fee for each transaction flowing through its computer system, this arrangement provides a much more error-free environment in which to transact business. The complete EDI process flow is shown in Exhibit 4.3.

Despite its advantages, EDI is not used by many companies. There are several reasons for this. One is that it takes a great deal of time to set up, involving travel to the locations of business partners to convince them to participate. Given this difficulty, many companies use it only with their highest-volume trading partners. Another issue is that the automated interfaces between the EDI system and internal computing systems must frequently be custom-programmed, which can be expensive. Fortunately, several packaged software providers have recognized the problem and now include interface packages with their software. However, this feature is not normally available with low-end software packages. These cost issues may continue to keep EDI from being used for the bulk of business-to-business transactions.

EXHIBIT 4.3. Electronic Data Interchange Process Flow

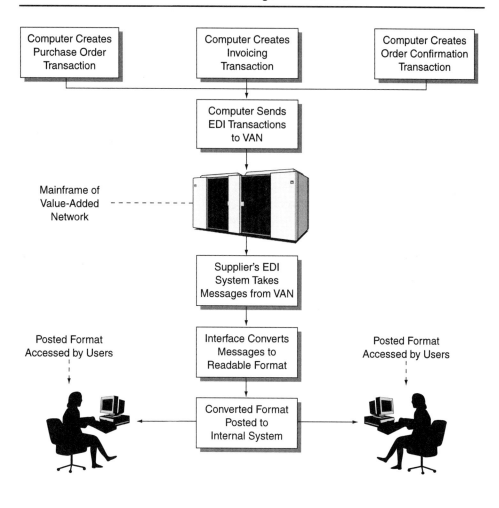

BACKFLUSHING

The preceding discussions have all focused on the uses of technology to make data collection easier. What about using a different production tracking system to eliminate the *need* for data entry? This system is called backflushing and is described in detail in Chapter 27. In this section we briefly touch on how it works and how it can be used to reduce the volume of data collection.

A traditional system, called the picking system, traces inventory as it moves from the warehouse, through the production process, and to the shipping dock. The picking system requires one to make an entry into the computer system for every transaction that occurs in the production process. If a component is moved from the warehouse to the production staging area, someone must make an entry in the computer that reduces the warehouse inventory account and increases the work-in-process account. Each time the component is moved through the production process to a new workstation, there must be another computer entry to ensure that the production control staff knows where the unfinished product is located and also so that the accounting staff can charge production costs to it. This is a clearly labor-intensive approach that is also highly prone to data entry error.

A different approach is used by the backflushing system. With this method no transactional entry is made until a product has been completed—there is no entry to show that anything has left the warehouse or that it has moved through the various stages of production. Instead, the computer system takes the final production figure entered, breaks it down into its constituent parts, and removes these items from the warehouse records.

This procedure can save a significant amount of data entry time, but it is useful only in certain situations. First, it should be used only when the production staff is fully capable of achieving accurate final production counts since miscounts result in incorrect changes to warehouse records. This is a particular problem for companies with high levels of production employee turnover or low educational levels, since such conditions result in poor levels of employee knowledge of procedures, which in turn leads to inaccurate data entry. Second, there must be accurate systems in place to trace any fallout from the production process, such as for scrap or rework. These items are not eliminated from the inventory database through the standard backflushing system and so must be accounted for separately. If this is not done, the reported inventory levels will be incorrect. Finally, the production process must be a short one, preferably completing products in a single day. If not, backflushing of components from stock may not occur for some time, which renders the inventory database inaccurate. It may state that inventory is on hand that is actually currently in production. This factor is also important from an inventory valuation perspective, for a rapid production process allows a company to flush out its production lines at the end of a reporting period so that there is no work in process to be valued by the cost accountant. If these factors have not been considered by the management team, it is probable that a backflushing system will lead to incorrect data in a company's materials management database, despite the greatly reduced level of data entry it requires. Consequently, the backflushing option should be used with care.

SUMMARY

There are a number of means available for making the data collection task much easier. Bar coding allows data entry errors to be avoided since information is transferred directly into a computer database from a bar code. Electronic data interchange sends information between companies with no data entry requirement, whereas document imaging attaches scanned documents to a database, providing more information to the cost accountant than would otherwise be the case.

Though all these technologies are attractive, they can be expensive, so a cost-benefit analysis is mandatory before purchasing the required equipment. Also, just because one of the technologies noted here does not make economic sense at the moment does not mean that this will be the case in the future—the price of technology is constantly being driven down, which may alter the economics of a new system acquisition. Given the downward trend of these costs, the cost accountant should keep all failed cost-benefit analyses on hand and review them occasionally to see if a purchase is warranted.

CHAPTER 5

Timekeeping and Payroll

In some industries labor costs are still such a large proportion of total costs that it is mandatory that they be carefully tracked and evaluated. In this chapter we explore the need for timekeeping, how to collect labor data, what costs should be assigned to the resulting data, and what kinds of reports can be generated for further analysis. We also consider the problems involved in timekeeping and how they can be avoided.

NEED FOR TIME TRACKING

Three types of costs are incurred by any organization—direct materials, overhead, and direct labor. Historically, the largest of these has been direct materials or labor, which has necessitated the creation of elaborate tracking mechanisms for these two cost categories while overhead costs have largely been ignored. However, with the advent of technology, the cost of overhead has skyrocketed and direct labor costs have shrunk. This has required a change in data tracking systems that favors the use of activity-based costing (Chapter 16) for the detailed analysis of overhead costs. Conversely, much of the accounting literature has advocated the complete elimination of direct labor cost tracking on the grounds that the tracking mechanism is much too expensive in relation to the amount of direct labor costs now incurred.

In reality a company's specific circumstances may still require the use of detailed direct labor tracking. This is certainly the case when the proportion of direct

EXHIBIT 5.1. Data Tracking Costs by Cost Type

Cost Type	Proportion of Total Costs (%)	Proportion of Total Tracking Costs (%)
Direct materials	40	15
Direct labor	10	65
Overhead	50	20
Total	**100**	**100**

labor to total company costs remains high, for example, 30% or more of total company costs. Given this large percentage, it is crucial that management know what variances are being incurred and how to reduce them. As another example, consider a company located in such a competitive industry that shifts in costs of as little as 1% have a drastic impact on overall profitability. In this instance there must be excellent data tracking mechanisms for *all* costs, no matter how small they are. Finally, the decision to use a detailed labor tracking mechanism can be driven less by the total direct labor costs and more by the level of efficiency of the tracking system. For example, when a company's data tracking costs bear the relationship to the proportions of total company costs shown in Exhibit 5.1, there is a strong need to reduce the labor tracking system.

In the exhibit the cost of direct labor is very low, whereas the cost of collecting all the associated data is much higher than for the other two types of costs, even when they are combined. The proportions shown here are quite common, and in this case the data tracking system for direct labor is probably not worth the cost of administration. However, if this data tracking system can be made more efficient, perhaps by employing the data collection methods noted in the next section, it may still be worthwhile to use a reasonably detailed timekeeping system.

In short, it makes sense to employ a relatively detailed time tracking system for direct labor if the proportion of total company costs is heavily skewed in favor of direct labor costs, if profit pressures are high, or if the cost of the timekeeping system is relatively low in proportion to the direct labor costs incurred.

DATA COLLECTION METHODS

In most cases a company's total direct labor cost is not high enough to warrant the creation of an elaborate data collection system. Instead, one can focus on a simple system that collects only the most basic data or install a system that utilizes a greater degree of automated data collection, thereby keeping costs low but still obtaining a high degree of detailed information.

If a simple data collection system is needed, the one most easily implemented is one in which employees are assumed to work 40 hours per week and the only need for the logging of hours is to keep track of any overtime. Overtime is recorded on an exception basis and forwarded to the payroll staff, who enter the additional costs into the payroll system and generate payments to employees. This approach is most useful when a company has a relatively fixed base of direct labor employees who rarely work any additional hours and who also rarely work less than a fixed number of hours per week. It is further justified when a company has such a small amount of direct labor cost that implementation of a more elaborate timekeeping system would not be worth the effort. This system yields no information whatsoever regarding how the cost of labor is being charged to various jobs. It has the singular benefit of being inexpensive to maintain, but at the cost of providing no costing information to management.

A slightly more complex system requires direct labor employees to fill out paper-based time cards that itemize the hours they work each week. These time cards are reviewed by their supervisors for accuracy and then forwarded to the payroll staff, which compiles the information and keypunches it into the payroll system. This approach is most useful when there is a significant amount of variation in the number of hours worked per week, resulting in continuing variations in employee pay from week to week. It requires considerably more administrative labor because of the large amount of data entry involved; additional labor is also needed to verify the entries made by employees and to investigate and correct any errors.

One step up from this entirely manual system is the addition of a time clock. In its simplest form, a $100 to $500 time clock can be mounted on a wall and employees can insert their time cards into it to have their "in" or "out" times punched. This approach makes time cards easier to read and also controls the recording of times worked so that there is less chance of any deliberate alteration of this data. This procedure is highly recommended since the additional cost is minimal and is easily justified by the increased level of data accuracy.

The next step up in system complexity involves the use of a computerized time clock. This device is also mounted on a wall for employee access; however, it has two additional features. One is the use of a bar-coded or magnetically coded employee card which is "swiped" through a channel on the side of the clock whenever an employee clocks in or out. This card contains the employee's identifying number so that the system records the person's identification, and all associated times worked, with complete accuracy. The second innovation is that the clock contains a computer linked back to a central payroll computer. This feedback mechanism allows the time clock to reject employee swipes made at the wrong times (such as during the wrong break times) or swipes made for employees who are not supposed to be working during specified shifts (which can occur if an employee brings in someone else's card and attempts to represent that person as being on the premises and therefore entitled to be paid). The system can reject swipes that fall into any number of violation parameters and require the override password of a supervisor in order to record these swipes. This innovation is a great improvement in a company's control over the timekeeping process. It provides a second major enhancement, which is that data swiped into it requires no further keypunching—all the information is sent straight into the payroll system where it is reviewed for errors and then used to pay employees. This practice eliminates the cost of extra data entry, as well as the risk of incurring data entry errors. However, all these innovations come at a price, which is typically in the range of $2000 to $3000 per automated time clock. A large facility may require several clocks if there are many employees who must use them, so the cost of this addition must be carefully weighed against the added benefits.

A larger volume of data can be obtained by using computerized time clocks at every workstation in the production area, or a modified version thereof. In this way employees can easily punch in information about the jobs they are working on at any given time without having to walk to a centralized data entry station to do so. These workstations can have time clocks directly linked to the payroll system, but since these clocks are so expensive, this option is not normally used, especially when many workstations are required. A more common approach is to purchase a number of "dumb" terminals with no internal error-checking capacity and link them to a central computer that does all the error-checking for employee and job codes as well as hours worked. This option is much less expensive, especially for large facilities. However, it has one significant flaw—if the central computer goes down, the entire system becomes nonfunctional. This problem does not arise when automated time clocks are used, for each one is a separately functioning unit that does not depend on the availability of a central computer. This problem is a particular issue in companies with large amounts of machinery that generate electric energy because the extra radiation can interfere with the transmission of signals from the workstations to the central computer, usually requiring the installation of either heavily shielded cabling or the use of fiber optics, both of which are expensive options.

An employee uses the dumb terminal to enter his employee number, the start time, and the job number. All time accrued from that point forward is charged to the entered job number until the employee enters a different job number. This data entry process may require a large number of entries per day, which introduces the risk of a high degree of data inaccuracy. However, this problem can be reduced by the use of bar-coded or magnetic stripe employee cards as previously described, as well as the use of bar code scanning of all current job numbers.

This last solution is clearly much more expensive than any of the preceding ones since the cost of a central computer can be anywhere in the range of $10,000 to $250,000 and the system also requires a large number of dumb terminals costing at least $500 each. What is the reason for incurring this expense? This system gives a company the ability to track the time worked on specific jobs. This is an important capability when customers are charged based on the specific number of hours employees work on their projects, especially when the customer has a right to examine the underlying hourly records and to protest billings that do not match these detailed records. For government work, where cost-plus contracts are still common and the government has a right to closely review all supporting labor records, this is a particularly important issue. It may also be a major concern for an organization for which the cost of direct labor is still a relatively large proportion of total costs; otherwise, managers would have no valid information about how a large proportion of company costs are being incurred. Nonetheless, the data entry system required to support collection of this information is expensive, so one should conduct a cost-benefit analysis to see if the value of the information obtained is worth the cost of the system.

It is also possible to have employees manually track the time they charge to each job on which they are working. This practice may seem much less expensive than the use of data entry terminals just described, however, this approach is not recommended unless the number of employees involved is small. The reason is that the level of data errors can be extremely high given the large number of jobs to which labor is charged each day: the time charged to a job may be wrong, as well as the job number to which the time is charged. As a result, the cost of administration time required to track down and correct these problems greatly exceeds the cost of installing an automated time tracking system; the cost of corrections is so high for a large facility that the comparable cost of an automated system is far lower.

A final timekeeping system not frequently used is backflushing—although it is not a real timekeeping system at all. Instead, the standard labor hours are stored in the labor routings database for each product and multiplied by the amount of production completed each day, yielding a standard amount of labor that should have been completed at each workstation in order to complete the total amount of production scheduled. This method is good only for developing an approximation of the amount of labor needed to complete each step in the production process, is of no use for spotting labor inefficiencies, and cannot be used to derive payroll (since it does not report hours worked at the employee level and, even if it did, these numbers would not be accurate). Thus, the backflushing method, though a simple way to derive approximate labor hours, does not yield accurate information for most purposes for which direct labor information is used.

It should be apparent from the discussion in this section that a higher degree of data accuracy and a lower cost of timekeeping on a per-transaction basis can be achieved only with a high degree of expensive automation—and the more information required from the system, the more expensive it is to collect it. Accordingly, one must first determine how badly a company needs every possible type of direct labor data and structure the type of data collection system based on the level of need. In order to make this decision, it is best to review the following section, which describes the various types of data that can be collected through a timekeeping system.

INFORMATION TO COLLECT THROUGH TIMEKEEPING

The most obvious item that must be collected through a timekeeping system is the number of hours worked by each employee. This single data element actually involves the collection of two other data items—the employee's name (or identification number) and the date on which the labor was worked. This minimal set of information is the smallest set of information required to do nothing more than calculate payroll for direct labor employees.

The next highest level of information that can be collected includes the identifying number of the job on which an employee is working. This additional data allows a company to accumulate information about the cost of each job. In some companies, where employees are assigned to a single workstation and perform work on a multitude of jobs that appear in front of them each day, the amount of data collected may be from 5 to 10 times greater than when only direct labor hours per day are collected. This level of data collection is most necessary when customer billings are compiled from the number of employee hours charged to their jobs and is least necessary in a process costing environment (Chapter 10), where there are no identifiable jobs.

A further level of detail can be collected from the workstation at which an employee works. This data is collected when a company wants to track the amount of time spent on each of its machines so that it can tell which ones are being used the most frequently. This information is of the most importance when a facility has bottleneck operations or expensive equipment whose utilization is an important factor in the determination of capital efficiency. However, this data can also be obtained by multiplying labor routings by production volumes, which yields an approximate level of machine use, or simply by visual examination of the flow of production through a facility. Thus, this additional level of detail is worth collecting only in selected situations.

Another possibility is to track the activity of each employee in the absence of an identifying workstation. For example, an employee can be employed when repairing faulty products, handling a machine as the primary operator, substituting for other workers during their lunch breaks, and sitting in on a quality circle—all in the same day. This added level of detail is useful if a company wants to track activities for an activity-based costing system, which in turn can be helpful activity-based management or the tracking of quality costs. However, this procedure represents a highly detailed level of data tracking that in many situations is not appropriate—picture a large number of employees moving through a facility and spending large parts of their day writing down what they are doing at any given moment or trying to locate a data entry terminal into which they can enter information. In many cases it is more efficient to conduct a study that results in estimates of employee time spent on various activities, which is a much more cost-effective way to collect information.

In short, a timekeeping system can collect information at four levels of detail:

1. Hours worked

2. Jobs on which hours are worked

3. Workstations used to work on jobs

4. Activities within each workstation used to work on jobs

Each of these levels of data collection represents an increasing level of detail that can overwhelm the timekeeping system. For example, at the first level there may be just one record per day that identifies the hours worked for one employee. At the next level an employee may work on five jobs in a day, which increases the number of records to 5. For each of these jobs the employee uses two workstations, which increases the number of records to 10. Finally, three activities are performed at each workstation, which results in a total of 30 records per employee per day. It is evident that each level of additional detail collected through the timekeeping system results in a massive jump in the amount of data that employees must enter into the system, as well as to be processed by it. A cost accountant must review the added utility of each level of data collected, compare this benefit to the cost of collecting it, and determine what level of data is sufficient for a company's needs. In many cases stopping at either the first or second level of data collection is more than sufficient.

TIMEKEEPING REPORTS

The reports issued from a timekeeping system should be directed toward the correction of data that has just been collected, comparisons to budgeted hours, and trends in hours. These reports should not include pay rates or the total dollar cost of direct labor since this information is more appropriately reported through the payroll system where all direct labor costs are stored.

A good timekeeping report designed to correct data entry errors should not present the entire (and likely voluminous) list of all employee times recorded in the current period but rather just those that clearly require correction. These can be times that are too high, any entry with missing information, overtime, or hours worked during a weekend. A computer program can be created to sort through all direct labor data, pick out possibly incorrect data, and present it in a report format similar to the one shown in Exhibit 5.2.

In addition to error correction it is also important to devise a report that lists expected direct labor hours for various functions and compare these hours to those actually worked. By doing so one can see where operations are being conducted inefficiently or where the underlying standards are incorrect. Budgeted labor information is most easily obtained through a manufacturing resources planning

EXHIBIT 5.2. Timekeeping Data Correction Report

Employee Number	Employee Name	Date Worked	Hours Worked	Job Number Charged	Comment
00417	Smith, J.	04/13/02	10	A-312	Overtime approval needed
00612	Avery, Q.	04/14/02	8	D-040	Invalid job number
00058	Jones, L.	04/13/02	8	—	No job number
01023	Dennison, A.	04/14/02	12	A-312	Overtime approval needed
03048	Grumman, O.	04/15/02	8	D-040	Invalid job number
03401	Smith, J.	04/16/02	8	A-310	Date is for a weekend
02208	Botha, T. L.	04/14/02	25	—	No job number

EXHIBIT 5.3. Comparison of Actual to Budgeted Time Report

Date	Work Center ID Number	Budgeted Hours	Actual Hours	Variance
04/14/02	PL-42	142	174	−32
04/14/02	PL-45	129	120	+9
04/14/02	RN-28	100	100	0
04/14/02	RN-36	140	145	−5
04/14/02	TS-04	292	305	−13
04/14/02	ZZ-10	81	80	+1
04/14/02	ZZ-12	40	60	−20

EXHIBIT 5.4. Trend of Hours by Employee Report

Department	Employee Name	Hours Worked			
		Week 1	Week 2	Week 3	Week 4
Drilling	Sanderson, Q.	40	40	40	40
Drilling	Underwood, C.	35	38	37	32
Drilling	Hecheveria, L.	32	32	32	32
Lathe	Anderson, B.	48	52	49	58
Lathe	Oblique, M.	47	45	50	52
Sanding	Masters, D.	40	40	40	40
Sanding	Bitters, I. M.	40	40	40	40

(MRP II) system, which for each workstation compiles from labor routings and the production schedule the hours that should be worked each day. Otherwise, the budgeted labor information for this report must be compiled manually. An example of the report is shown in Exhibit 5.3.

Normally there is no accounting system budget for the hours worked by each employee since an excessive amount of work is involved in compiling a budget that must be recompiled every time an employee leaves or joins the company. Instead, one can create a trend line report of hours worked by each employee, which is useful for determining any tendency to work an inordinate amount of overtime or to work less than a normal amount of hours. The example shown in Exhibit 5.4 covers only a few weeks, but this report can be reconfigured in landscape format to show the hours worked by an employee for each week of a rolling 12-week period. Another approach is to report employee hours by the month instead of by the week, which allows one to fit the hours worked for an entire year into a single report.

As in Exhibit 5.4, it is also useful to include a column that identifies the department in which an employee works, for overtime frequently varies considerably by department, given the different workloads and capacities under which each one operates. By sorting in this manner one can readily determine which departments are consistently under- or overutilized. In the exhibit it is readily apparent that the lathe department is being overworked, which will require the addition of more equipment, more personnel, or both.

COMPONENTS OF PAYROLL COSTS

No matter what type of timekeeping effort is used, some number of direct labor hours must be multiplied by the cost per hour of direct labor. But what cost per hour should be used?

The simplest and least accurate direct labor cost is the actual cost per hour paid to each employee. This cost is too low because it does not include a variety of taxes and benefits that can increase the cost per hour by 20% to 50%. Ignoring these extra costs has a marked effect on any financial analyses in which the cost of labor forms a large part of the total cost. However, the cost paid to each employee is easy to calculate and may be sufficient if the proportion of direct labor in a company's products is low—the lower level of reported labor cost per hour does not have a noticeable impact on any financial analyses.

The more common (and accurate) approach is to add the cost of all related payroll taxes to each employee's base pay when calculating the payroll cost per hour but not to include the additional cost of overtime or benefits. The reason for adding the cost of taxes is that these items—social security, Medicare, and unemployment taxes—vary directly with the amount of pay and so can be directly tied to the number of hours worked. The amount of these extra costs can be extracted from the payroll module of the accounting system and manually added to the base cost per hour for each employee to arrive at a burdened direct labor rate per hour that is a much more accurate representation of the true variable cost of payroll per hour.

Other payroll-related costs, such as the cost of workers' compensation, medical, dental, life insurance, and other benefits, are not normally included in the cost per hour of direct labor because they do not vary directly with the number of hours worked. For example, a company is charged a fixed amount per month by an insurance company for the medical cost of each employee, rather than being charged an amount that varies with the exact number of hours worked. Thus, benefit costs are incurred even if an employee works no hours at all. Given the loose linkage between the incurrence of benefit costs and the number of hours worked, these costs tend to be shifted to the cost of overhead instead.

The cost of overtime is also not normally added to the hourly cost of payroll. This item is treated separately because the amount of overtime cost incurred is essentially a scheduling or management decision that can be significantly altered from reporting period to reporting period rather than being a predetermined cost (such as base pay) that is incurred in a readily predictable amount when an hour of direct labor is worked by an employee. Accordingly, it is most commonly recorded in overhead rather than as a direct labor cost.

Having just noted that benefits and overtime are not normally charged to direct labor, we can also state that this can be done in a way that produces reasonably accurate results. By preparing a regression analysis (Chapter 38) comparing the quantity of direct labor hours to the cost of benefits or overtime, one can prove that there is indeed a positive relationship between these two items, resulting in an upward sloping regression line. This relationship exists in an imperfect form since there is a step costing relationship between the two. In other words, some benefits or overtime costs are very likely to be incurred as soon as an employee is hired, though the amount incurred does not precisely match the number of hours worked by each employee, which yields a moderately accurate relationship between the two types of data. Based on this information one can theoretically charge the cost of benefits and overtime to direct labor. Nonetheless, because of the imperfect relationship between the two types of data, these costs are more normally charged to overhead.

PAYROLL REPORTS

A complete set of payroll reports should not only note the cost per hour of each employee but also combine this information with the hours collected through the timekeeping system in order to derive the total cost per unit of work for each employee as well as (if necessary) the cost per job, workstation, and activity.

The most basic report is the one presented in Exhibit 5.5, which itemizes the cost per hour for each employee. This report clusters employees by department, which is useful for determining pay ranges for groups of people who perform the same basic tasks and also highlights any pay levels that are clearly too high or too low in comparison to the departmental average.

Another commonly used report is one that accumulates the labor costs for each job. The report can be at a summary level, where only a single labor cost total is recorded for each job, or it can be at a more detailed level that reveals the costs charged to a job according to employee name, job title, workstation, or department. A report listing the cost of each employee charged to a job is generally of limited usefulness, especially if there are so many employees working on the job that the information becomes overwhelming. However, this report format can be used to see if there are any employees who are incorrectly charging their time to a job. A better practice is to summarize job costs by job title, workstation, or department since this reduced level of detail is less overwhelming to the reader and also summarizes data at a level at which a job may have been assigned a budget. For example, the report shown in Exhibit 5.6 shows the direct labor costs assigned to a single job, summarized by work center, along with the associated budgets and

EXHIBIT 5.5. Pay Levels by Employee Report

Department	Employee Number	Employee Name	Rate per Hour ($)
Drilling	00417	Sanderson, Q.	13.28
Drilling	00612	Underwood, C.	12.75
Drilling	00058	Hecheveria, L.	15.11
Departmental average			**13.71**
Lathe	01023	Anderson, B.	9.00
Lathe	03048	Oblique, M.	9.25
Departmental average			**9.13**
Sanding	03401	Masters, D.	5.75
Sanding	02208	Bitters, I. M.	6.50
Departmental average			**6.13**

EXHIBIT 5.6. Labor Cost per Job Report

Job Number	Work Center	Direct Labor Actual Cost ($)	Direct Labor Budget ($)	Variance	Work Center Status
00542	Drilling	4,500	4,350	−150	Complete
00542	Lathe	12,200	8,500	−3,700	Complete
00542	Sanding	3,100	2,650	−450	Complete
00542	Assembly	3,050	3,800	+750	Complete
00542	Painting	1,550	1,475	−75	Open
00542	Packaging	2,725	2,000	−725	Open
00542	Inspection	1,100	1,500	+400	Open

variances for each of the work centers. This report also indicates whether work has been completed at each work center so that one can tell if costs may or may not continue to increase for each one. This is an excellent format to use when closely managing the labor costs incurred to complete a job because all status and variance information is clearly presented.

Another type of payroll report combines the hours reported at each workstation with the cost per hour of each employee who has charged hours to it and then runs a trend line of costs by workstation or compares it to a budgeted amount of labor cost per workstation. This information is most useful when management is trying to obtain quantification of the utilization of each work center, as well as during an activity-based costing review when the cost accountant wants to determine the cost of an activity, which is possibly represented by a work center. An example of such a report is shown in Exhibit 5.7, which lists the total machine run hours for a series of work centers as well as the total cost of all direct labor charged to them. In the last column the labor cost is divided by the machine hours, resulting in a cost per work center hour that can then be incorporated into an activity-based costing analysis.

The format of the preceding report can be altered to reveal the labor cost of various activities rather than work centers. The difference is that a work center is most closely related to machines (such as milling, sanding, or lathe work centers), whereas an activity is more closely related to a labor function, such as machine maintenance, product assembly, product rework, and inspection. Such a report is similar to the work center report and can also be used for activity-based costing analysis. An example of this format is shown in Exhibit 5.8.

A different report format is presented in this section for each of the levels of timekeeping information described earlier in Information to Collect Through Time-keeping. Though these are by no means the only payroll report formats that can be

EXHIBIT 5.7. Labor Cost per Work Center Report

Work Center	Work Center Hours of Utilitzation	Total Direct Labor Cost Charged to Work Center ($)	Direct Labor Cost Per Work Center Hour ($)
Drilling	328	4,500	13.72
Lathe	1,336	12,200	9.13
Sanding	253	3,100	12.25
Assembly	433	3,050	7.04
Painting	86	1,550	18.23
Packaging	330	2,725	8.26
Inspection	76	1,100	14.47

EXHIBIT 5.8. Labor Cost per Activity Report

Activity	Activity Hours of Utilization	Total Direct Labor Cost Charged to the Activity ($)	Direct Labor Cost per Activity Hour ($)
Receiving	40	420	10.50
Materials movement	80	980	12.25
Assembly	500	4250	8.50
Inspection	150	1463	9.75
Product rework	200	1700	8.50
Machine maintenance	120	2310	19.25
Billing	48	552	11.50

used to present these types of information, they do indicate how this information can be shown to its best advantage, revealing problem areas and trends that management can immediately act on to create a more profitable corporation. Also, none of the traditional payroll report formats are included here, such as those that itemize the gross pay, taxes, and deductions for each employee, since these reports have nothing to do with the cost of activities, jobs, or products. Here we are concerned only with report formats that are of direct interest to the cost accountant, not the payroll manager.

PROBLEMS WITH TIMEKEEPING AND PAYROLL

Despite one's best efforts to create an accurate timekeeping system, several errors arise from time to time and require special controls to avoid. One is charging time to the wrong job. This is an easy error to make, involving incorrect data entry by a direct labor person, such as a transposition of numbers or a missing digit. To keep this problem from arising, the timekeeping system can be an interactive one that accesses a database of currently open jobs to see if a job number entered matches one currently in use. If not, the entry is rejected at once, forcing the employee to reenter the information. This control can be made even more precise by altering the database to associate only particular employees with each job, so that only certain workers are allowed to charge time to specific jobs; however, this greater degree of precision requires additional data entry by the job scheduling staff, who must enter employee numbers into the database for all individuals scheduled to work on a job. If many jobs are running through a facility at one time, this extra data entry will not be worth the increase in data accuracy. If the existing data entry system is only a simple rekeying of data from paper-based time cards submitted by employees, the data must be interpreted and then entered by the data entry staff, which generally results in the least accurate data of all, for now there are two people entering information (the employee and the data entry person), which creates two opportunities to make a mistake. In short, the best way to avoid charging time to the wrong job is to have an interactive data entry system.

Another problem is that vastly inaccurate amounts of hours are sometimes charged to a job, usually through an inaccurate recording of numbers. For example, an 8-hour shift might be entered incorrectly as 88 hours. To avoid such obvious mistakes, the timekeeping system can be altered to automatically reject any hours that clearly exceed normal boundaries, such as the number of hours in a shift or a day. A more sophisticated approach is for the timekeeping system to automatically accumulate the number of hours already charged by an employee, during the current shift yielding an increasingly small number of hours that can still be worked during the remainder of the shift. Any excess can be rejected or require an override by a supervisor (indicating overtime being worked). This approach is not possible if employees record their time on paper since the information is entered after the fact and any correction of an incorrect number is a guess by the data entry person that may not be accurate.

Another possibility is that an employee charges an incorrect employee code to a job, resulting in the correct number of hours being charged to it, but at the labor rate for the employee whose number was used rather than the labor rate of the person who actually did the work. To avoid this problem, the timekeeping system should automatically access a list of valid employee numbers to at least ensure that any employee code entered corresponds to a currently employed worker. Though this is a weak control point, it at least ensures that hours charged to a job are multiplied by the hourly labor rate of *someone,* rather than by zero. A much better control is to require employees to use a bar-coded or magnetically encoded employee number that they carry with them on a card, which forces them to enter the same employee code every time. A lesser control is to post a list of bar-coded or magnetically encoded employee numbers next to each data entry station, but this is a less accurate approach since a worker can still scan someone else's code into the terminal. When a paper-based system is used, an employee normally writes his or her employee number at the top of a time report, and it is then entered into the computer by a data entry person at a later date. The problem with this practice is that the data entry person may enter the employee number incorrectly, which charges all the data on the time report to the wrong employee number. Once again, an interactive timekeeping system is crucial for the correct entry of information.

Yet another problem is that the cost per hour used by the timekeeping system may not be the same one used in the payroll system. This discrepancy arises when there is no direct interface between the timekeeping and the payroll systems, so that costs per hour are only occasionally (and manually) transferred from the payroll system to the timekeeping system. Then the resulting costs per hour on timekeeping reports are generally too low (on the grounds that employees generally receive pay *increases,* rather than *decreases,* so that any lags in data entry result in costs per hour that are too low). One way to correct this problem is to create an automated interface between the payroll and the timekeeping systems so that all pay changes are immediately reflected in any timekeeping reports that track labor costs. It is important that this interface be fully automated rather than one requiring operator intervention—otherwise there is still a strong chance that the cost data in the timekeeping system will not be updated as a result of operator inattention.

An alternative approach is to keep all labor costs strictly confined within the payroll system and to import timekeeping data into it rather than exporting payroll data to the timekeeping system. There are two reasons for taking this approach. First, exporting payroll data anywhere else in a company makes it easier for unauthorized employees to obtain confidential information. The second reason is that the payroll system cannot generate meaningful reports without data from the timekeeping system, whereas the timekeeping system can generate a number of reports that do not need labor cost data (see Timekeeping Reports). Thus, it may be better to leave the payroll data where it is and instead work on an automated interface between time-keeping data and the payroll system.

It is entirely possible that any of the problems described in this section will not only occur but will also go undetected for a substantial period of time. To avoid this situation, the internal auditing department should be asked to conduct a periodic review of the controls surrounding the timekeeping and payroll systems, as well as a test of transactions to see if any problems can be detected. The resulting audit report can be used to further tighten the controls around these data collection systems.

CASE STUDY

A routine analysis of the system costs of the General Research & Instrumentation (GRIN) Company has discovered that the cost of administering the company's direct labor timekeeping system appears to be inordinately high. Approximately 50% of the entire cost accounting function is devoted to the collection and interpretation of data related to direct labor. The controller asks Ms. Emily North, from the corporate cost accounting staff, to investigate the situation and recommend a revised system that will generate usable information while costing as little as possible to administer.

Ms. North finds that all GRIN Company facilities use the same timekeeping system, so she decides to go to the Atlanta production plant, investigate conditions there, and extrapolate her findings to all the facilities. Her plan for this analysis is to first determine the level of detailed information collected by the timekeeping system, then calculate the cost of collecting it, and then determine the benefit of using the resulting information. She will then see if costs can be reduced for the existing collection system so that no benefits from the system are lost. If this is not possible, or if costs can be reduced by only a modest amount, she will investigate the possibility of reducing the level of information gathered, which in turn will reduce the cost of data collection.

Her first step on arriving in Atlanta is to determine the level of detailed information collected by the timekeeping system. She interviews the facility's controller, Ms. MacCauley, who says that the timekeeping system requires employees to write down on a time sheet the hours they work each day on specific jobs, as well as the work centers where they work on each job. A typical time sheet looks like the one shown in Exhibit 5.9.

It is apparent from the time sheet that each employee must carefully enter a large amount of information during the course of a work shift. Also, the information entered by the employee in the example is not easy to read, which makes it likely that the data entry person who enters this information into the computer will have a difficult time entering it correctly. Further, many time sheets are submitted each day by the 412 direct labor personnel at the facility, some of which are lost by employees

EXHIBIT 5.9. Atlanta Facility Time Sheet

Employee Name: *Mort Dulspice*
Date of Time Card: 4/13/02

Time In	Time Out	Job	Work Center
08:00	08:45	004712	*Lithograph*
08:46	09:12	004712	*Etching*
09:13	10:48	004712	*Lamination*
10:49	12:00	004712	*Glue*
01:00	02:10	004799	*Lithograph*
02:11	03:04	004799	*Etching*
03:05	03:17	004799	*Lamination*
03:18	04:24	004799	*Glue*
04:25	05:00	004799	*Packaging*

or during the data entry process. This information must be re-created, which can be done only by estimating what work an employee completed during the period. Ms. North finds that these three issues give rise to three different types of costs.

The first cost is the time required by employees to enter their time worked on each time sheet and then transport this time sheet to the payroll office for data entry. The second cost is for the data entry staff to initially enter the data into the computer, and the third cost is to track down and correct any missing information or to correct data that was incorrectly entered. Ms. North calculates these costs for a typical month in this way:

- **Cost to initially record data.** She estimates that each employee requires 10 minutes per day to complete and deliver their time sheets. Since the average burdened cost per hour for all 412 employees is $17.92, this results in a monthly cost of $25,869 to collect the information, assuming 21 business days per month (412 employees × 21 days × $2.99/day).

- **Cost to enter data into computer system.** She finds that 1 ½ employees are required in the accounting department, on a full-time basis, to enter the information from all 412 time sheets into the computer system. These hourly employees earn a burdened wage of $12.05 per hour, so this represents a cost of $3037 per month (1.5 employees × 21 days × 8 hours/day × $12.05/hour).

- **Cost to correct data errors.** On average, the accounting staff spends 3 hours per day correcting mistakes that have been discovered on time sheets or created during data entry. These errors are investigated and corrected by a senior data entry clerk whose hourly burdened pay is $15.28 per hour. This results in a monthly cost of $963 (3 hours × 21 days × $15.28).

The grand total of all these costs is $29,869 per month, or $358,428 per year.

Ms. North's next task, determining the value of the benefits derived from the timekeeping system, is much more difficult. She finds that the daily hours worked are used by the payroll staff to calculate and pay weekly wages to direct labor employees. She describes this function as a mandatory one for which the system must provide sufficient data to calculate the payroll, but she cannot ascribe a monetary value to it.

Next, she looks at the benefit of tracking hours by job worked. This information is used by the cost accounting staff to develop an income statement for each job, which the sales staff uses to revise its pricing estimates for future jobs in order to verify that pricing levels are sufficiently high to ensure a targeted profitability level per job of 30%. The proportion of direct labor to all job costs is about one-third, so this is considered a significant cost that must be tracked for this purpose. The pricing staff assures Ms. North that they frequently alter their pricing strategies in accordance with the information they receive through job income statements. Once again, Ms. North finds herself unable to clearly quantify a benefit associated with the tracking of direct labor hours, this time in relation to job numbers, but it appears that obtaining the information is mandatory.

Ms. North's last benefits-related task is to quantify the benefit of tracking labor hours by work center within each job. She finds that this information is used only by the industrial engineering staff, which summarizes it into a report listing the total hours worked at each work center, by day, so that it can determine when capacity utilization levels are reaching such heights that new equipment must be purchased or when levels are so low that existing equipment can be sold. A brief discussion with the production scheduling staff reveals that standard capacity amounts per job are already stored in the labor routings of the facility's manufacturing resources planning (MRP II) system, which produces a similar report by multiplying the units in the production schedule by the hours per unit of production listed in the labor routings. This means that an alternative system can be used to provide the industrial engineering staff with the information it needs without resorting to additional data entry.

Ms. North then peruses a sample of time sheets submitted by employees and notes that an average of three work centers are referenced on each time sheet for each job on which work is performed. If she can convince management to eliminate the tracking of time by work center, she can cut the labor time spent on timekeeping by direct labor employees by two-thirds (as well as similar amounts of time expended by data entry clerks who would otherwise have to enter and correct this information) since these additional entries no longer have to be made. This works out to a cost savings of $19,912 per month ($29,869 × 2/3), which is $238,950 per year. The remaining cost of the timekeeping system has now been reduced to $119,478.

Ms. North realizes that the industrial engineering staff will agree to this change only if it can be proved that the data it receives from the MRP II system is sufficiently accurate to replace the work center capacity data it previously received from the timekeeping system. To ensure that the MRP II system maintains a high level of labor routing accuracy (which is the prime driver of the accuracy of capacity information produced by the MRP II system), she adds $50,000 back to her estimate of remaining timekeeping system costs, which will pay for an engineer whose sole purpose will be to continually review the accuracy of labor routings. This results in a timekeeping system cost of $169,478, which still represents a reduction of $188,950 in the cost of the earlier timekeeping system, a drop of 53%.

The cost accountant's key steps in this case study were to clearly define the procedure to be followed in determining the costs and benefits of the existing timekeeping system. By doing so she quickly found that three levels of timekeeping data were being collected, the third of which (work center data) was the most expensive to collect and also could be eliminated by using an alternative source of information. She did not have to resort to an expensive automated data collection system in this instance since the immediate savings from using the MRP II system to provide replacement data was so large. However, an additional project could involve the analysis of costs and benefits associated with the use of data collection terminals to input job-related data directly into the computer system, thereby largely avoiding the need for a data entry and correction staff.

SUMMARY

The timekeeping function is coming under increasing attack as cost accountants realize that the costs of administering a detailed timekeeping system are exceeding the value of the resulting information. This issue can be resolved by reducing the level of the timekeeping effort until the effort expended equals the utility of the resulting information (which may result in complete elimination of the timekeeping function) or by more fully automating the timekeeping and payroll functions so that the cost of the system administration is reduced to the point where it is once again a cost-effective means of tracking labor activities.

The choice of which direction to take is based not only on the portion of total corporate costs devoted to direct labor but also on how crucial it is to a company to wring out the highest possible profits from operations. Thus, the nature of the timekeeping system is driven not only by the total cost of direct labor but also by the level of profitability of the business.

CHAPTER 6

Chart of Accounts

The chart of accounts is the set of data entry buckets in the accounting system in which data is stored. It is important to set up the correct account code format to be used for each account in the chart of accounts since a company's data collection efforts may be hindered if account codes are not available. Also, the chart of accounts must be set up in such a manner that asset, liability, revenue, and expense entries can be readily stored in separate buckets and be easily available for later extraction for reporting purposes. This chapter describes the variations that can be used on the account code format, as well as the layout of the chart of accounts.

ACCOUNT CODE FORMAT

A crucial part of the data collection system is an account code format that allows an organization to store data in a manner that can be easily summarized into any reporting format required and at the same time can be easily used for data entry. In this section we look at the format of the account code and determine which one is best for different data collection situations.

When a packaged accounting computer program is being set up, an account code is one of the first items the user is asked to enter. Once the account code format has been entered into the system, the computer usually issues a warning that the code cannot be changed again without starting the accounting system over from the beginning. This is a major issue! If the cost accountant recommends an account code format that is inadequate for a company's needs, the entire accounting system will have to be started over again to accommodate any changes in the account code format. Thus, the following discussion is extremely important for the creation of a data entry system.

A simple account code for the smallest company can be a simple sequential set of numbers, from 000 to 999, which the founding managers feel is sufficient to cover all possible buckets into which money can be dropped—after all, this three-digit code can be used to describe a total of 1000 accounts. Surely that must be enough! Under this scenario, a prudent accounting manager might assign a number to an account, skip a few spaces to allow for future growth in the number of accounts, and then assign another number. The chart of accounts might look like this:

Account Number	Account Description
400	Salaries expense
410	Payroll benefits
420	Office Supplies
430	Telephones

By introducing gaps in the numbering of accounts, it is possible to add accounts close to similar existing accounts. For example, if there is a need to split payroll benefits into smaller accounts, such as federal income taxes, medical insurance, and workers' compensation, accounts can be added after account 410 with this result:

Account Number	Account Description
400	Salaries expense
410	Payroll benefits
411	Federal income taxes
412	Medical insurance
413	Workers' compensation

So far, so good. The account code structure is still easy to read, there is room for new accounts, and the accounting staff has such a small account code to deal with (just three digits) that it can easily memorize which accounts are used for each transaction.

Now let's add departmental accounting to the problem. To separately record the costs of each department, we must create a different set of account codes. However, when we try to insert these accounts into our three-digit account code structure, it no longer works. There are not enough spaces available. One way to get around this issue is to wait until the fiscal year is complete, create a new company in the computer system, restructure the chart of accounts so that all the accounts fit, and proceed from that point. The problem is that a large block of available account codes will be taken, so that further additions to the chart of accounts will be increasingly difficult. Also, there will be no way to compare the numbers stored in the current year's accounts to those from previous years since the account codes no longer match.

A better approach is to alter the structure of the account code by adding a second section that has a different meaning. For example, we can add two digits in front of the existing three-digit code and assign departments to the two digit codes. The chart of accounts then looks like this:

Account Number	Department	Account Description
10-400	Engineering	Salaries expense
10-410	Engineering	Payroll benefits
10-411	Engineering	Federal income taxes
10-412	Engineering	Medical insurance
10-413	Engineering	Workers' compensation
20-400	Sales	Salaries expense
20-410	Sales	Payroll benefits
20-411	Sales	Federal income taxes
20-412	Sales	Medical insurance
20-413	Sales	Workers' compensation

This format results in more organized data storage. However, what if we want to store the records for several divisions in the same chart of accounts? To do this, we add yet another set of codes in front of the account code structure that identify each company division. Then the chart looks like this:

Account Number	Division	Department	Account Description
30-10-400	Boston	Engineering	Salaries expense
30-10-410	Boston	Engineering	Payroll benefits
30-10-411	Boston	Engineering	Federal income taxes
30-10-412	Boston	Engineering	Medical insurance
30-10-413	Boston	Engineering	Workers' compensation
40-10-400	New York	Engineering	Salaries expense
40-10-410	New York	Engineering	Payroll benefits
40-10-411	New York	Engineering	Federal income taxes
40-10-412	New York	Engineering	Medical insurance
40-10-413	New York	Engineering	Workers' compensation

This type of account code structure has several advantages. First, it is *logical*—the largest unit of organization (company or division) is listed in the leftmost block, with the units gradually decreasing in size further to the right and ending in individual account codes. Second, it is *easy to understand*—a key point for the accounting department whose personnel typically memorize the most common account codes for its transaction entries. This is easy to do when the base-level account code is only three digits. Third, it is *consistent*—the same account codes apply to every department, and the same department codes are used for each company or division. Fourth, it is *expandable*—accounts, departments, and divisions can be easily inserted into this type of format.

There is no reason to use the exact account code structure listed here because a company may have slightly different needs that will result in a different structure. For example, a company may have a long history of buying and selling other companies, so it may want to use four digits instead of two digits to allow room for all the division codes it uses. Also, it may want to separate the types of customer revenues and expenses into different categories, which may call for an extra digit representing the customer type. Similarly, it may want to add a few digits so that revenues and expenses for individual products or product lines can be stored in separate accounts. Thus, the exact account code format depends on the particular needs of the organization.

If, as just noted, a company adds a number of additional digits to its account code structure, the resulting format might look like this:

$$XX\text{-}XX\text{-}XXX\text{-}XXX\text{-}XXX$$

This format represents these types of information:

Division-Department-Customer-Product-Account

Though certainly comprehensive, such a long account code is very difficult for anyone to enter into the computer system since there is a risk of misinterpreting each layer of information (such as swapping the codes at the department and customer levels) or of mistyping a code (the account code just mentioned has *13* digits). It is also difficult to automate the use of such a long account code with bar codes since the resulting bar code is so long that it might not fit on a document. Given these types of problems, it is best to always keep the account code structure as simple and as easy to use as possible. Otherwise, an attempt to pursue the ultimate level of refined data storage will just result in inaccurate data storage. Consequently, the previously described XX-XX-XXX format, which represents coding for divisions, departments, and accounts, is recommended for most situations.

CHART OF ACCOUNTS FORMAT

Now that we have some idea of the type of account code structure to be used, we can proceed to create of a chart of accounts. The layout of a COA is directly related to the account code structure, so the structure must be decided on before proceeding to the COA layout. Several examples of how the COA would look under different coding schemes were presented in the last section. In this section we assume that some type of account code structure has been used that breaks out company locations and departments from individual accounts and will see what the COA looks like in this format.

If the account code structure has a set of codes to identify different company locations or divisions, the accounting manager can assign each location to any numerical code that fits into the number of digits assigned to that part of the account code. They can be assigned in straight numerical sequence, or some digits can be skipped if locations are to be added later on. The exact system used is up to the individual company and does not have a significant bearing on the success of the COA.

A more important consideration is how department codes are to be used in the COA. These codes are itemized in the middle section of the account code structure and are shown in the underlined section of the code:

XX-XX-XXX

In this instance it is best to lay out all possible departments that will be used in any company division in advance and to assign a code to each one. The COA can then be quickly rolled out at any new company location even if the organizational structure of each one is a bit different. Over time, despite the best forecasting efforts of the accounting manager, it is likely that some new departments will be created, so there should be some gaps in the numerical sequence of the account code structure. The layout of this portion of the chart of accounts could look like this:

COA Code	Department Description
XX-10-XXX	Accounting department
XX-20-XXX	Administration department
XX-30-XXX	Computer services department
XX-40-XXX	Engineering department
XX-50-XXX	Marketing department
XX-60-XXX	Production department
XX-70-XXX	Quality department
XX-80-XXX	Sales department
XX-90-XXX	Warehouse department

There may be a need to record other subdepartments that roll up into a central departmental account. The most common case is the production department, which can be broken down into such areas as testing, machine centers, and packaging (this varies greatly by industry). The result may look like the following chart, which is the same as the last one except that we have used the numbers immediately following department 60 (production department) to itemize the subdepartments that roll up into it.

COA Code	Department Description
XX-10-XXX	Accounting department
XX-20-XXX	Administration department
XX-30-XXX	Computer services department
XX-40-XXX	Engineering department
XX-50-XXX	Marketing department
XX-60-XXX	Production department
XX-61-XXX	Material preparation
XX-62-XXX	Machine center 1
XX-63-XXX	Machine center 2
XX-64-XXX	Machine center 3
XX-65-XXX	Paint booth
XX-66-XXX	Finishing
XX-67-XXX	Packaging
XX-70-XXX	Quality department
XX-80-XXX	Sales department
XX-90-XXX	Warehouse department

Once the department codes have been configured, we must still figure out the best way to lay out the account codes that roll up into each department. The same expense accounts tend to be used for most departments, with just a few special items for specific departments, so the best approach is to block out the same set of expenses for each department and then reserve a block of numbers for special purposes. This example lists the most common expenses that can be used for most departments:

Account Number	Account Description
500	Salaries and wages
510	Benefits
520	Travel and entertainment
530	Office supplies
540	Training
550	Depreciation
560	Utilities
570	Dues and subscriptions
580	Overhead

Note that the account numbering starts at the 500 point, which leaves lots of available numbers both before and after it. The reason for using numbering in the middle of the numerical range is that this leaves room for asset, liability, revenue, and cost-of-goods-sold accounts near the top of the account numbering scheme (in case profit centers are to be used), as well as lots of trailing numbers that can be assigned to special expenses that are germane to only one or a few departments. When we combine all the elements of the account code structure into a complete format, the COA looks like this:

COA Code	Division	Department	Account Description
10-70-500	New York	Quality	Salaries and wages
10-70-510	New York	Quality	Benefits
10-70-520	New York	Quality	Travel and entertainment
10-70-530	New York	Quality	Office supplies
10-70-540	New York	Quality	Training
10-70-550	New York	Quality	Depreciation
10-70-560	New York	Quality	Utilities
10-80-500	New York	Sales	Salaries and wages
10-80-510	New York	Sales	Benefits
10-80-520	New York	Sales	Travel and entertainment
10-80-530	New York	Sales	Office supplies
10-80-540	New York	Sales	Training
10-80-550	New York	Sales	Depreciation
10-80-560	New York	Sales	Utilities

This type of COA format will likely result in excess accounts being made available in departments where they may never be used. In the last chart an example is a travel and entertainment account for the quality department, which may never use it. In these cases all but the most primitive accounting software packages allow one to block out the use of accounts by specific departments, and this feature can be extended to blocking out departments, too. For example, what if the New York division listed in the last chart has no sales department? Then, the entire set of accounts in the 10-80-500 through 10-80-560 series can be blocked from use. This useful tool keeps the number of accounts codes in use to a minimum.

If it is the intention of the management team to split apart variable and fixed costs so that they can keep better control over a company's break-even point, it may be necessary to identify which of the accounts are variable and which are fixed. The main problem is that some costs have variable and fixed components, which must be split into different accounts. For example, the cost of utilities for an entire building can be considered a fixed cost, but the cost of utilities for a specific production machine may be considered variable. Each of these costs has to be stored separately, which can greatly increase the number of accounts in use. It is also difficult for accounts payable and general ledger personnel to determine which costs go into which accounts. Given the extra level of complication and the effort that goes into maintaining such a system, the use of variable and fixed expense accounts is generally not recommended.

Different account coding may also be needed for government contracting purposes, which require costs to be tracked for individual contracts and contract line items. However, this cost storage is best handled through a separate job costing system that stores costs, as usual, in a normal chart of accounts, while also separately coding them to a specific contract file. Then there is no need to introduce contract codes into the chart of accounts, which would clutter it up.

When creating a chart of accounts, the main goals are to develop something that is orderly enough to be easy to understand and at the same time is simple enough that anyone using it will not be burdened by a vast number of accounts in which numbers can be stored.

SAMPLE ACCOUNTS

The cost accountant is not concerned with the vast majority of accounts typically found in a chart of accounts but only with those that have some direct application to the main cost accounting tasks, such as determining product profitability, project costs, or departmental costs. With these restrictions in mind, it is easier to recommend a small number of accounts that are of use in most situations. Here is a list of the accounts to use, as well as short discussions of the situations in which they are most useful:

- **Revenue by product.** If there is any need for profitability reviews by product, then this is a must. However, a company with a large number of products may find that its chart of accounts is completely snowed under by the number of accounts needed to keep track of all their products. It may be necessary to store the records in a subsidiary ledger, cluster product revenues together in product groups, or separately track revenues only on large-volume products and cluster all other revenues into a "miscellaneous revenue" account.

- **Raw materials inventory.** Nearly every company, even those oriented toward services instead of products, is likely to have a raw materials inventory account. This is because even some small quantity of materials is required for nearly every type of business activity. There are also many cases in which the largest cluster of assets in the company is stored in this account. If so, it may be necessary to break down the account into a set of smaller ones just to reduce it to more manageable pieces. However, this is generally not recommended because a good database reporting system can easily sort through all the components of the raw materials inventory and "slice and dice" it in every way imaginable without the need for additional accounts.

- **Work-in-process inventory.** This account is necessary only in production situations where there is a noticeable amount of production work that is incomplete at the end of each day. As is frequently the case, if all production is transferred almost immediately from raw materials to finished goods, there is no point in maintaining this account. Also, if a company has developed a just-in-time manufacturing system that works on a minimal amount of work in process at any one time, the amount of manufactured goods flowing across the production floor may be so small that there is no need to record them in this account. Yet another situation in which this account is not necessary is when backflushing is being used, since no record of production is made in the accounting system until a product is finished and transferred from the raw materials account to the finished goods account.

- **Finished goods inventory.** This account is needed if a company stockpiles completed production rather than shipping it immediately to customers. Since there are nearly always situations in which completed products are not ready for shipment at the end of an accounting period, there is a need for this account.

- **Variance, inventory counting.** There is always some kind of counting variance that arises when warehouse employees cycle-count their inventory, which may be caused by damage, shrinkage, theft, or paperwork errors. Then, it is useful to segregate the cost of all changes in the inventory balance into its own account. The contents of this account can be significant, especially if the transactions involving the raw materials inventory are faulty or if a backflushing system is being used without proper controls.

- **Variance, direct labor overtime.** The cost of extra labor for rush jobs or in situations where management has elected to increase capacity by having employees work longer hours, can be considerable. By segregating the cost of overtime, one can more readily identify this cost. The cost of shift differentials can also be stored in this account.

- **Variance, direct labor rate.** If a standard costing system is employed, or one in which labor routings are available and against which actual labor costs can be compared, this account should be used to accumulate labor cost variances. However, if the total amount of labor costs is minimal in comparison to other components of the cost of goods sold, it may not be necessary to use this account.

- **Variance, direct labor efficiency.** This account is also used when a standard costing system is installed, in order to track the differences between actual and expected labor usage. It is especially useful in situations where there is high turnover in the direct labor staff because this tends to lead to large amounts of labor inefficiency.

- **Variance, material price.** This account is used to track the performance of the purchasing staff. It can be used to compare buying performance against a preset standard but can be abused if large-quantity purchases are used to create favorable pricing variances. Accordingly, analysis of this account should be combined with a review of purchasing volumes in order to gain an informed perspective on the true nature of the variances.

- **Variance, material scrap—normal.** Most organizations incorporate an expected amount of scrap into the bill of materials for each item produced and do not bother to break out this cost separately from the direct materials expense account. However, for organizations that want to reduce their scrap costs to zero, it may be useful to itemize this cost in a separate account.

- **Variance, material scrap—abnormal.** This is a highly recommended account. One should itemize all scrap that is clearly in excess of standards. This account can also be used without a standard cost accounting system—just enter into it any scrap that is blatantly above the usual scrap level. This account must be thoroughly analyzed, so all entries should include the maximum possible amount of detail regarding each excessive scrap amount.

- **Variance, rework.** In situations where a significant amount of rework is required in the manufacturing process, it may be useful to split out this cost and store it in a separate account. However, this cost includes many types of expenses, such as labor, materials, and machine time, so the data collection effort required to segregate this information is considerable. One should be sure that the amount of expense is sufficient to warrant this effort before creating the account.

- **Variance, shipping.** A poorly organized materials management function requires a high frequency of rush shipments in order to ensure that the production staff has materials at scheduled production times. To determine the cost of these rush shipments, one should store their cost separately in this account. The amount of this expense can be surprisingly high. Use of this account is recommended.

- **Cost of quality.** The cost of quality has a large number of components (several dozen costs are defined in more refined systems—see Chapter 28). However, most organizations track only the costs of a few items for which they have tracking systems in place and ignore the others. These costs are clustered into subaccounts and rolled up into a single cost-of-quality account. An alternative is to set up a small number of cost-of-quality accounts, each of which traces the cost of a single major quality-related activity such as the cost of prevention or appraisal.

- **Variance, overhead volume.** This variance is used to demonstrate the amount of overhead that was either under- or overabsorbed in the latest reporting period. It is rarely used as a separate account because the same information can be calculated and presented alongside the financial statements without resorting to the use of a general ledger account.

- **Variance, overhead price.** This account records the variance from a preset standard of overhead costs, which may comprise costs for a number of different overhead categories. This account is rarely used since it is more precise to create a budget-versus-actual report for each overhead cost rather than dump them all into one account from which it is more difficult to extract useful information regarding the types of costs incurred and where they came from.

- **Cost of goods sold, direct material.** Typically the largest single account used by the cost accountant is the one that records the cost of materials. This is particularly important in direct costing (Chapter 11) and throughput (Chapter 14) costing applications, for which the direct material cost is the primary cost used for many decisions. If there are many products or locations for which management wants to track costs, this is the key account to subdivide since it constitutes the largest proportion of all costs. Consequently, there may be a number of subaccounts that roll up into it.

The main accounts used by the cost accountant have been listed here. A curious observation is that the bulk of the accounts are related to variances, which usually are not used unless there is a standard costing system in place (which requires their use to highlight variances from preset standard costs). Otherwise, the cost account is reduced to the use of just materials, labor, and overhead accounts, with perhaps some subaccounts to divide these accounts by specific company locations, departments, or product lines. In short, there are many instances in which one can function with a few accounts and subaccounts.

SUMMARY

It is very important for an accounting system to be designed with a correct chart of accounts and account code format. In this way, data is stored in a structure that is easy to access and with a coding system that is easy to understand. This makes it much easier not only to enter data into a computer system but also to extract information from it.

CHAPTER 7

Selecting and Installing Cost Accounting Software

The effectiveness of the cost accountant is to some extent determined by the ability of the in-house cost accounting system to collect, summarize, and issue information about various costing issues. Some of these systems comprise policies and procedures that are formulated and enforced internally, while other systems are primarily composed of computer software. This software has a major impact on the efficiency with which costing information is input into the accounting database, the need for duplication of data, the efficiency with which data is processed and stored, and the ability of system users to access various types of reports on costing topics.

In this chapter we explore how to select and install cost accounting software, including discussions of whether to use outside consultants, whether to use customized or packaged software, what features should be included in the software, and how to select, test, and implement software. This is a specialized, highly detailed topic that has been compressed into a small number of pages, so the reader is advised to also review other books that deal more comprehensively with this subject, such as Wilson et al. (1999).

NEED FOR OUTSIDE ASSISTANCE

The selection and implementation of a cost accounting system is a complex topic that requires a thorough knowledge of several disparate disciplines—cost accounting, systems analysis, programming, and project management. Few companies have all these areas of expertise available to them in-house, though some employees may be experts in a few of them. Rather than attempt to conduct the process with just its internal staff, whose time is also likely to be fully occupied with other matters, it is advisable for a company to engage the services of an outside consulting firm specializing in the selection or design of computer systems and in their implementation.

By doing so a company assures itself of having the undivided attention of a group of experts who can handle many of the most difficult technical issues as well as project management. If not quite such a comprehensive role is desired for the consultants, they can at least be used in an advisory role to ensure that key project issues are detected well in advance and dealt with before there is a risk of their stopping or delaying the project.

Consultants are certainly not inexpensive, but the alternative is to bear the risk of incurring massive cost overruns on a system installation, as well as the possibility of never being able to install the new software at all. The cost of even a junior-level staff consultant easily exceeds $100/hour, with many senior manager and partner-level consultants now earning $400/hour. If these rates appear too steep to justify any resulting benefits, a company should still consider the use of a small number of consultants in at least a high-level review or project management role in order to spot major problems as early as possible.

Consultants try to charge on a time-and-materials basis rather than a fixed fee, since they then have no cap on the level of fees they can charge. It is better for a company to insist on a fixed fee for a predetermined set of services and to closely inspect the resulting contract to see what services are guaranteed for this fixed fee. For a more detailed review of this topic, see Bragg (1998).

CUSTOMIZED VERSUS PACKAGED SOFTWARE

Some organizations may be tempted to write their own software for the cost accounting function or to modify the code of an existing software package to ensure that the precise requirements of the cost accounting staff are met. This is rarely a good idea. Only when a company wishes to gain a strategic advantage through the use of a specialized new cost accounting feature, such as better product pricing, or when the nature of the industry requires specialized costing systems, should any customization be undertaken. Some of the difficulties involved in using customized software are:

- **Cost.** Customization is always more expensive than purchasing a software package, for it includes the extra work associated with defining a new cost accounting system, programming it, and testing and documenting it. If the system is poorly defined at the start, all of the later costs will be multiplied while the software is rewritten.

- **Time.** All the added steps just mentioned require a great deal of time, almost certainly more than a year for a detailed cost accounting system. For many companies this is much too long a delay, given the importance and immediate use of the information that can be supplied by a cost accounting system.

- **Risk.** Given the high cost and time requirements of a customized cost accounting system, it is quite possible that the project will exceed the patience (and purse) of the management team, who will eventually withdraw funding from it.

- **Updating.** If a company elects to modify the software code of an existing software package, it will be locked into a particular version of that software since any new software versions released by the supplier will automatically erase any customizations by overwriting them.

- **Documentation.** A customized system may be much more poorly documented than a packaged one if there was not sufficient time or money to do a proper job of writing down how the software code functions. Then it will be difficult to trace through the code at any point in the future to determine where changes must be made. Thus, future alterations will be time-consuming.

- **Best practices.** A final reason for avoiding customized software is that it includes only features that the in-house cost accounting staff wants to include, whereas a packaged solution includes a number of best practices that have been recommended by other software users, which makes it a more efficient option.

For all these reasons a customized cost accounting system is a poor choice, except under the limited set of conditions mentioned earlier in this section. Despite these limitations it is still the course followed in organizations with a long tradition of supplying software to users that exactly meets their requirements—the users have a great deal of power within the organization and can force customization on those who decide which systems will be installed. In these cases the issue may devolve into a power struggle over which course to take, in which only a strong leader can force an organization in the direction of packaged software.

KEY FUNCTIONS OF A COST ACCOUNTING SYSTEM

When designing a cost accounting system from scratch or purchasing one, there are a number of functions that should be included in the system. Some are relatively generic ones that relate to the overall operability of the system and should include ease of navigation, clear and uncluttered screen layouts, and consistent and not excessively multilayered command structures. Additional generic features are the ability to drill down to underlying levels of transactional detail easily and excellent on-screen documentation and training features. However, these are basic functions that can be expected in any system. Of most concern to the cost accountant are the specialized functions that allow one to collect, process, and report information leading to better costing and pricing decisions. Some of these special functions are:

Additional records

- *Bill of activities.* Cost accountants who use an activity-based costing system appreciate a bill of activities, which itemizes the set of activities required to complete a product (or other user of costs).

- *Bill of materials.* Much of a cost accountant's most commonly used information is located in the bill of materials, which itemizes the specific quantities of materials used to construct a subunit or a complete product.

- *Labor routings.* Of particular importance to organizations that depend heavily on work centers or direct labor are labor routings, which record how much labor and/or machine time is required to complete each production step for a product.

- *Unit cost database at different volume levels.* Of great assistance in the costing of prospective products is an information set regarding the costs of various components at different volume levels, which the cost accountant can use to determine the cost of a completed product if it is produced in different volumes. This function is useful in modeling product costs at different volumes, which in turn can be used to develop product prices.

Additional fields

- *Alphanumeric storage fields.* With the advent of multiple allocation measures, it has become increasingly necessary for the cost accountant to collect information about many allocation measures (e.g., square feet, hours of machine time, kilowatt hours), all of which can be most efficiently stored in the accounting database through the use of alphanumeric fields.

- *Labor burdening percentage.* On arriving at the cost of direct labor, it is necessary to add to it a percentage that approximately represents the cost of all benefits and taxes that vary directly with the cost of direct labor, so that the full, burdened cost of labor is used. This percentage can be entered in a separate field.

- *Multiple units of measure.* An organization that allows access to unit-of-measurement records by all departments finds that some departments prefer to use different units of measure for the same component, resulting in endless bickering over the standard unit of measure to be used by everyone. This problem can be resolved by creating multiple unit-of-measure fields for each component, linked to a conversion table that shows the quantity of the component for each type of measure.

Functions

- *Activity-based costing functions.* Though many companies purchase separate software packages for this function, the cost accounting system can be designed to incorporate ABC functions, which should include the accumulation of costs into cost pools, the summarization of activity drivers, the calculation of activity costs, and the subsequent costing of and reporting on cost objects.

- *Cost layering.* The system should have the capability to layer costs in a variety of ways for inventory valuation purposes (Chapter 34). At a minimum there should be options available to layer costs using the first-in first-out (FIFO), last-in first-out (LIFO), and weighted average methods.

- *Direct and step-down allocations.* The system should allow not only for the automated allocation of overhead costs to any number of specified cost objects but also for step-down allocations of overhead costs into secondary cost pools from which they can again be allocated to cost objects.

- *Inventory disposition tracking.* It is most useful for a cost accountant to know how each item of inventory is disposed of that is not consumed through inclusion in a product. There should be a number of available codes in the system that users can enter to describe how they are eliminating various inventory items from stock, which the cost accountant can later compile and report on.

- *Job costing.* Most organizations record data by job, except for those with process costing systems. This requires the use of a job code field that acts as an index on which transactions can be sorted and grouped.

- *Inventory movement tracking.* When an organization moves materials through a large number of workstations, a large proportion of its product costs are assigned as they pass through each workstation, which requires an accurate inventory tracking system that notes which work centers a product has thus far passed through so that the cost accountant can accurately assign costs to work in process. This is not an issue in just-in-time manufacturing environments, where there is too little work in process to require the use of an elaborate inventory tracking system.

- *Rework tracking.* Many production operations require a significant amount of rework, which must be tracked and segregated in the accounting system so that management can tell what proportion of its costs are devoted to this activity.

- *Scrap tracking.* If a company operates in a production environment, the system should have the capability to separately store data for material scrap and summarize and report it with the associated costs.

- *Support backflushing.* The system should have the capability to automatically generate production costs by multiplying the standard costs of products by the amount actually produced. This is the main alternative to the picking system and is much more automated.

- *Support picking.* The system should have the capability to allow users to pick materials from each department in succession and move them to the next, thereby allowing the cost accountant to trace the buildup of product costs from department to department.

- *Target cost budgeting.* The system should allow the cost accountant to compile estimated product costs into product budgets, with associated estimates of component production and usage volumes, so that target costing teams can continually revise and improve on their estimates of product costs as they proceed with the design of new products.

- *Transfer pricing accumulations.* Though necessary only for a company with multiple divisions, all of which use the same accounting system, this is a useful feature for segregating the fixed and variable components of a product as it is transferred from division to division. The final (selling) division can then determine the grand total of the fixed and variable components of what it is selling, which allows it greater flexibility in marginal pricing decisions (Chapter 30).

- *Variance calculations.* Especially under standard costing methods, the system should calculate the volume, price, and efficiency variances as well as present detailed reports itemizing the precise causes of these variances.

Output
- *Data downloads.* The cost accountant should be able to extract data directly from the cost accounting files and convert it to a format that is readable by commonly used databases and electronic spreadsheets such as Access and Excel. This capability should include the option to merge data from multiple files with cross-indexing, rather than being limited to downloads from individual files, which results in a much more limited level of data access.

- *Report writing.* The cost accountant is constantly called on to analyze new situations, many of which call for the use of reports that are not in prepackaged formats. Instead, it is necessary to use a report-writing software package to extract just the needed information and format and summarize it into precisely the layout needed to provide the information for a specific analysis.

The above list of records, fields, functions, and outputs is by no means complete. To ensure that all key items are included in the requirements for a new cost accounting system, one should examine the existing cost accounting system to see what other features it contains and interview the employees who will use the system to see if they have any additional requirements. Other possibilities are to review the accounting literature and talk to consultants to see if there are any best practices that can be incorporated into the system.

INTERRELATIONSHIP OF COST ACCOUNTING SOFTWARE WITH OTHER SOFTWARE

Before proceeding to descriptions of the selection and implementation of software, it is important to note that one does not purchase or write software for a free-standing cost accounting system. Because it draws on information from so many other accounting and manufacturing systems, there is no way to create a truly free-standing system. Instead, the cost accounting software and related database tend to be merged into several other software functions, which makes it difficult to obtain a perfect cost accounting system.

As shown in Exhibit 7.1, cost accounting software cannot operate properly without direct input of data from other software systems. For example, a payroll system is required so that actual direct labor costs can be accessed. Similarly, general ledger and accounts payable modules are needed primarily for access to overhead and materials costs. The main linkage is with the materials management system, where the critical bill of materials and labor routing files reside, not to mention a wealth of other data such as scrap, production scheduling, and inventory. Without all these other sources of information, a cost accounting system cannot function properly.

Because of this close dependence on other software modules, it is virtually impossible to locate a cost accounting package in the marketplace. Instead, they are found as part of an accounting package or as part of an enterprise resources planning (ERP) system. The difference between these two types of systems is that a pure accounting system allows access only to data in the accounts payable, payroll, and general ledger areas; as indicated in Exhibit 7.1, the materials management module, which is the primary source of cost accounting data, is completely ignored. The ERP system, however, is a comprehensive set of software modules that address virtually all company functions and therefore is a much better source of data for a cost accounting system.

The cost accountant is rarely in a position to recommend a particular accounting or ERP system but rather just the limited set of features that relate to the cost accounting function, whereas employees in other parts of the company have input on the software features needed to run their parts of the company. As a result, the cost accountant may find that the features she needs are not part of the system that is finally purchased. This can even be a problem for in-house software projects that are completely custom-designed, since there may not be sufficient funding available to

EXHIBIT 7.1. Linkages between the Cost Accounting and Other Types of Software

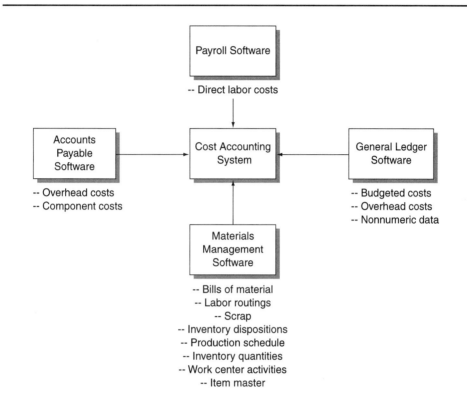

write code for every feature the cost accountant wants. Accordingly, it is important to itemize the most important cost accounting features needed and to vigorously promote their inclusion in any purchased package or customized system. Any other features that are less necessary run a higher risk of being excluded and may require manual work-arounds to accomplish.

We now proceed to the steps of software selection and implementation, which will likely encompass the installation of a larger computer system of which the cost accounting function is only a small part.

SOFTWARE SELECTION

This section describes the steps to be followed in purchasing software that includes cost accounting features. There are no hard and fast rules for the exact procedure to be followed, but the steps listed here are the ones most commonly employed and have generally been found to lead to more success in purchasing the most suitable software. They are:

1. *Obtain a project charter.* This is a document that has been approved by the senior management team and itemizes a project sponsor (who is responsible for periodically providing funding and any other type of high-level support for the project), a time frame during which the selection is to be completed, the key activities on which the project team is expected to work, and a budgeted dollar amount. It can also be described as a project outline that lays down the groundwork for successful project completion.

2. *Develop a plan.* The plan should fit within the outlines provided by the project charter, noting the exact, detailed activities to be followed, their start and stop dates, the resources to be expended on each one, milestones to be reached, and how various risks are to be approached and guarded against. For all but the smallest projects, there should be someone who is dedicated only to the ongoing maintenance of this plan, so that it can be constantly adjusted to reflect ongoing changes in the project.

3. *Define software requirements.* The project team should determine as precisely as possible the exact software features that will be included in the package to be purchased. It should prepare a complete itemization of the key record formats, features, and outputs required. Possible sources of information about these features are the existing system, key users, managers, and current literature (such as marketing materials) about the newest capabilities of other software currently on the market. Consultants can also be used since they sometimes maintain databases of software features.

4. *Investigate computer hardware options.* It is generally considered better to first select the software and then obtain whatever hardware is necessary to make it function properly. In reality many organizations cannot afford the extra hardware cost, and so they require that existing configurations be used to store any new software. Then the project team must find out what existing hardware is available, what its storage and processing capacity is, and whether or not the intended users of the cost accounting software currently have access to it.

5. *Determine the information technology capabilities of the existing staff.* If a company has a large, well-trained information technologies staff, it can feel free to purchase almost any type of software, including items that function only in unusual operating systems. However, and as is more commonly the case, a much weaker or a more specialized staff on hand may limit the project team's options in selecting software that is relatively robust and maintenance-free and that has a sufficient number of existing features to require no further customization.

6. *Document all required interfaces.* This can be a difficult activity to complete, for it is hard to document the full range of software interfaces that must be installed when the cost accounting software has not yet been purchased. Nonetheless, it may be possible, at least by reviewing the existing system, to determine the number of interfaces currently needed. This information is useful for budgeting funds for the later programming of interfaces for any new system purchased.

7. *Create a request for proposals.* Once all this information has been collected, the project team should write a request for proposals (RFP) whose purpose is to give potential software vendors a complete overview, as well as a detailed itemization, of the software the company would like to purchase. This means that the RFP should describe the who, what, when, and where of the project—who will use it, what features are needed, when is it expected to be installed, and where it will be located. The RFP must outline all key functions required and ask vendors to check off the ability of their software to provide each one.

8. *Compare vendor responses.* Once all RFPs have been returned, the project team must summarize the responses, in terms of prices, hardware requirements, and software features, in a comparative grid format. In particular, the grid should sort the desired software features in the order of those that are mandatory, those that are desirable, and those that are optional. It can then develop scores for each of these categories, thereby allowing it to determine the top three to five software packages in terms of meeting the company's prespecified needs. All other software packages can be dropped from consideration, and the team can then move on to a review of how these software packages actually work by contacting customers who currently have them installed.

9. *Conduct reference calls.* Though the software vendor may appear honest, it is best to corroborate not only the quality of support work provided by the vendor but also the general functionality of the software by calling and interviewing employees of other companies currently using it. This is not a situation where one needs to examine the performance of each aspect of the software, but rather to obtain a good overview of the quality of the vendor and its products. At the end of this process, it may be possible to further reduce the list of finalists, for it is not uncommon to find that at least one vendor has too few customers for references or that there is some general level of dissatisfaction with a product that is sufficiently pervasive to no longer warrant further investigation.

10. *Attend product demonstrations.* The next step is to arrange for a lengthy demonstration of all software modules by the vendor's sales and technical staff for the project team as well as for selected "heavy" users who will be

closely involved with the software on an ongoing basis. A demonstration staff is inclined to show off the software's "bells and whistles," so it is important to bring a list of key features to the demonstration and force the sales staff to carefully walk the project team through these features to ensure that they all exist and function as advertised. It may be possible to eliminate a few more vendors from the list of finalists after this step is completed.

11. *Complete site visits.* It is also important to see the software being used by a "real" company and to quiz its users about the specific problems they have had with various features and functions. This calls for advance preparation of a complete set of questions to be covered during site visits, as well as commitment of the project team to travel to locations that may be quite out of the way, if that is where user sites are located.

12. *Select software.* At this point there should certainly be enough information available to make an informed decision regarding which software package to purchase. Usually, it is quite clear that one package has the predominant scoring over its rivals in terms of features and functions. In some cases, however, there is no clear winner, and the project team may be forced to vote.

13. *Conduct negotiations.* Once a software package is selected, the team must conduct contract negotiations with the supplier. This involves a thorough analysis of any presented contract, with the addition of a number of adjustments specifying supplier delivery, warranty, and service commitments. If the supplier's contract appears to be too constrictive or one-sided, it may be necessary to compile a new contract from scratch.

Though all the steps mentioned here may seem expensive and prolonged (they are), they serve the dual roles of ensuring that the correct software is purchased and of obtaining acceptance of the purchased software by the key system users involved in the selection process. If these steps are avoided, there will be no organizational commitment to use the new system, which may be one that does not even contain the main features needed by a company to operate its business.

IMPLEMENTATION STEPS

Once the software package has been located (as described in the last section), there are still a number of steps to be followed to ensure that it is properly installed. If the rigorous implementation process described in this section is not followed, a company may find itself with a perfectly good piece of cost accounting software that is barely operable on the hardware on which it is installed, or else not fully utilized or accepted by its users. Only by crafting a careful implementation can a company avoid these pitfalls.

Some of the earliest steps mentioned in the last section in reference to the selection of a software package are applicable to the implementation phase as well. We initially note that it is once again mandatory to obtain a project charter, create a project plan, and then add these steps:

1. *Assemble a high-quality implementation team.* A great number of skills are needed to ensure that a software package is properly installed. It generally requires assembling several experts from various parts of the company to make certain that all the needed skills are properly focused on the success of the installation. If some skills are not available in-house, they should be obtained by hiring independent contractors or consultants. Some of the most important skills needed include project management, user training, software testing, hardware installation and operation, software programming, and system design.

2. *Initiate communications with users.* The largest single factor in the failure of any new system is a lack of acceptance by existing users. To keep this from happening, the project manager should immediately set up standard lines of communication with all users so that they are kept fully informed of the progress of the new system, as well as how they will fit into the installation process and be able to give feedback to the team.

3. *Assess project risks.* As early in the implementation as possible, the entire team should review the various types of risks to which the implementation will be subject. These can include human risks (such as problems caused by poor communication, minimal sponsorship, or a poor fit between the new system and the corporate culture), technical risks (such as problems caused by inadequate product testing, incorrect requirements analysis, or software that does not run on the available hardware), and project management risks (such as problems caused by inadequate planning assumptions or poor integration of work between teams). Each item considered significant should be carefully addressed and steps taken to mitigate the problem. For more information about this topic, see Willson et al. (1999).

4. *Install hardware.* Before any trial installations or testing can begin, the correct hardware must be installed, which should include the central processor and all peripherals and terminals used for common access to the database. The ability of the hardware to run the software with reasonable response times will be tested later, during volume testing.

5. *Install software.* Once the hardware has been tested and appears to be operating in the expected manner, one can install the operating system on which the software is designed to run. This system should be tested to ensure that a proper installation has been accomplished before continuing with installation of the software package itself. This is not a simple step because

there are usually many option settings that must be selected before the software can run properly—in the case of larger ERP packages, the number of available settings is in the hundreds. Given the complexity of this step, it is almost always necessary to bring in a consultant or (better yet) a representative from the software supplier who is knowledgeable about what the settings should be.

6. *Design interfaces.* If the new package is being integrated into a cluster of other software applications, it is possible that some data must be regularly transferred to and from them. If so, it will be necessary to design interfaces that automatically transfer the data. The programming team must analyze the data requirements and design, code, and test these interfaces to ensure that they operate properly. If the interfaces operate in batch mode, there must also be documentation for the system operator, who must initiate the batch processing.

7. *Test the software.* A major portion of the implementation process is system testing, which requires that several key steps to be followed. One may think that testing is necessary only for custom-designed software that may contain a number of bugs, but there are also several reasons for testing packaged software. For example, all custom-designed interfaces, add-on programs, and reports require thorough testing, as well as all data conversion routines that have been written. Also, if packaged software has had few previous users or has been newly released, it may be prudent to run it through a limited set of tests to ensure that it is reasonably free of errors. In addition, the system should be tested by users to ensure that it is acceptable for their needs and that it is durable enough to stand up under large volumes of transactions running through it simultaneously. These are all valid reasons to conduct testing. The main testing steps to follow are:

- *Create a test plan.* The number of tests that can be conducted on software is nearly infinite, but the available funding is not. Therefore, it is necessary to select tests that address what appear to be the areas of greatest possible system failure and which can be completed within the budgeted time and dollars. However, if the budget is too modest for any reasonable range of testing, one should attempt to have it increased rather than proceed with insufficient testing.

- *Write test documentation.* This is a set of documents that clearly state what is being tested, how to perform the tests, and what the expected results should be. They must be clearly written, for testers use them as the basis for their tests and any ambiguity will require additional testing for clarification.

- *Conduct software testing.* Testers use test documentation as the basis for verifying that software code functions as expected. If not, the circumstances of any failure must be clearly documented so that they can be repeated by the programmers assigned to correct the problem.

- *Log, prioritize, and assign defects for repair.* Once a software bug has been found, it must be logged into a database along with an identification number, a judgmental rating of its severity, a description, its cause, and its estimated repair date. The testing manager then reviews this record, as well as those for all other bugs that have not been fixed, and determines an order of priority for repair. Those that must be completed prior to the cut-over date are assigned the highest priority, whereas bugs with only a minor nuisance value are slotted for fixing at some later date. This procedure also applies to these other tests:

- *Retest.* Once a programmer completes an initial repair, the bug is scheduled for an additional test; the problem is cycled back through the documentation and error correction steps as long as it takes to resolve it. Then the record is marked as closed.

- *Conduct security testing.* As noted in the following section, there is a need to limit access to some data used by the cost accounting system. This requires several security features, such as restricted access to specified modules, screens, and fields. This function should be tested and repaired if necessary.

- *Conduct recovery testing.* All systems crash at some time and must be rebooted. To ensure that no data is lost when this happens, the team should conduct a series of intentional system crashes and make the system more robust if the crashes cause data to be lost or corrupted.

- *Conduct documentation testing.* Users consult the system documentation from time to time for assistance in using the system. If the documentation does not match the system features, the ability of users to process transactions through it is limited. Some testing should therefore be conducted to ensure that the documentation matches the actual system features and functions.

- *Conduct volume testing.* A system may appear to work well for a single user but have unacceptably slow response times or even lock up when a large number of users access it at the same time. To guard against this the testing team should determine the maximum number of potential users and run a test simulating this number of user accesses at the same time to ensure that response times are acceptable.

- *Conduct acceptance testing.* This is a test run by the system's prospective users, who must satisfy themselves that the system meets their operational requirements. The objective here is not to fix bugs but rather to ensure an adequate degree of functionality.

8. *Create policies and procedures.* Even if the software being installed already has its own set of on-line documents, there is still a need for written policies and procedures because there must be a linkage between the computerized portion of the cost accounting system and the manual systems that input data into it and extract information from it. Written policies and procedures are the means by which this linkage is accomplished. This task can be a complex undertaking, requiring a thorough knowledge of all manual systems and how they will be modified by the new computer system. It is also important to have the testing staff review all resulting documents for accuracy since the level of system complexity will probably introduce some errors into the procedures.

9. *Train users.* When the software and all related documentation are in place and have been tested, it is time to train all the users of the system. If this were done earlier, the users would probably forget a large part of what they just learned—the ideal training time is within a few days of giving users on-line access to the new system. The training method employed is critical and should involve hands-on use of the software by every user, allowing a separate terminal for each one and having a low instructor-to-student ratio. A ratio of no higher than 10:1 is recommended.

10. *Convert data.* A critical step that is frequently ignored until it is too late is the conversion of data from the old database to the data format required for the database used by the new software. There may be a rare case in which the new system provides a built-in utility that automatically converts data in the format currently used by the company. Far more frequently, however, the computer services staff must devise a customized data conversion utility that maps all data from the old format onto the new one, which requires extensive testing prior to the actual conversion. Only in the smallest systems is it realistically possible to manually keypunch all data from the old system into the new one, but (because of the number of data entry errors involved) this practice is not recommended.

11. *Cut-over to new system.* There are two ways to switch from the old system to the new one. The most dramatic is the "cold turkey" approach in which the old system is shut off and the new one turned on, with all users immediately switching over. This may appear to be the simplest approach, but it is difficult to achieve if system users access the old system at all times of the day or night—there is no time to convert data from the old to the new. Also, there is some risk that the new system will fail for a variety of reasons—database errors, excessive user volume, and minimal user training, to name a few. Many of these risks of failure can be avoided if the new system is instead brought on-line more gradually. This is done by switching over just one module of the system at a time, carefully ensuring that it runs properly, and then proceeding to the next module. It is usually necessary to code a

large number of temporary interfaces between each new module and the old software to which it is still connected so that data transfers properly to all portions of the system. Then these temporary interfaces are shut down as new modules are brought on-line. Though this is a much closer approach, it is a more methodical way to ensure that the cut-over to the new system is successful.

12. *Provide follow-up services.* After the system has been fully installed, there is a period of disruption that may last several months, during which users require assistance with some transactions and special problems arise that are related to special transactions ignored during the earlier system analysis stages. There may also be problems with system crashes or slow response times. The project team should be kept together long enough to deal with these problems and then gradually be dismantled as the volume of issues declines. It is also important to retain an ongoing training program, which can offer refresher classes to previously trained employees and system familiarization training to new ones. Unless the system is a small one, there will probably always be a need for some follow-up by the computer services department on an prolonged basis.

There are a number of steps in the implementation process, many of which require the services of expert help that may not be available in most companies, where computer expertise is limited to ongoing system operations rather than installations. Therefore, many organizations find it worthwhile to pay for the services of outside consultants and contractors who specialize in various stages of the implementation process. Though expensive, they give an implementation a much greater chance of success.

SOFTWARE SECURITY

Software security is a major issue for virtually any software function but is a key item for a cost accounting module in particular, as well as the many modules that feed into it. The reason is that alterations to seemingly minor fields, such as a unit of measure, can have a profound impact on the costs reported from the cost accounting system. For example, if a roll of tape is listed in the item master file with a cost of $5.00 per roll and someone changes the unit of measure to an inch (of which there are 1760 per roll), then the cost of the roll changes to $8800 (1760 × $5). Similarly, changes in the quantities of inventory in stock or on order must be tightly controlled, as well as the standard costs of products and the line items in bills of material and labor routings. Changes in any of these fields can cause massive alterations in product costs, all of which must be carefully investigated by the cost accountant and corrected.

The best way to prevent these problems is to require a detailed level of software security in the software modules related to cost accounting, production scheduling, materials management, and purchasing. Various degrees of security can be used. The least effective is terminal security, unless there are only a few heavily controlled terminals. Of more use is a security system that keeps users from accessing either entire software modules or specific screens. At the most advanced level, this can include the use of specific field restrictions, though this requires much more maintenance for the security system.

In general, a cost accounting system must be protected by high walls of security; if not, the number of errors and inaccuracies in the system will become widespread, resulting in inaccurate cost accounting information and requiring an enormous amount of system maintenance to correct the problems.

SUMMARY

The cost accounting function is usually not represented in a computer system by a separate software package. Instead it is part of a much larger system such as an accounting or enterprise resources planning system. Because it is a small part of a larger software system, the cost accountant has little more than an advisory role, requesting that certain cost-related features be included in any system created in-house or purchased as a package. This chapter has described the key features the cost accountant should ask for, ranging from special fields or records to functions, outputs, and security features. The cost accountant rarely obtains the full set of cost accounting features, so it is critical to clearly define and push hard for the approval of the most important features that are absolutely mandatory for the success of his work.

REFERENCES

Bragg, S. (1998). *Outsourcing.* New York: John Wiley & Sons.
Willson, J., Roehl-Anderson, J. M., & Bragg, S. (1999). *Controllership: The work of the managerial accountant* (6th ed.). New York: John Wiley & Sons.

CHAPTER 8

Paper-Based Documents in the Modern Costing System

Many larger companies have recently installed enterprise resource planning systems, replacing nearly all their existing systems with a highly integrated set of programs that can trace transactions through virtually every area of the organization. In these companies nearly every part of every transaction can be entered, altered, or accessed through a local computer terminal, and there is little need for paper-based documents at any point. However, the majority of companies do not have such a system. Instead, they have probably installed a stand-alone accounting computer system with no linkages to any other systems, of which there may be a few for specific functional areas, such as production planning. Some automated data collection and storage are available, but much of the data in the company is still on paper. In these situations how does the cost accountant work around the lack of automation or recommend that some paper-based documents be automated while others are left alone? This chapter covers these issues.

ISLANDS OF AUTOMATION

With the notable exception of ERP systems, most organizations can be described as having only "islands of automation," which can perhaps be more accurately referred to as "islands of computerization." Under this scenario various parts of a company have installed automated data gathering and storage systems that meet their specific needs but do not interact with the computerized systems elsewhere in the company. These islands of automation reflect a mind-set focused on the improvement of local operations within a single department rather than the operations of the company as a whole, which would have led employees to instead recommend the installation of an ERP system that integrates data from all locations into a single vast database.

A company with islands of automation finds that there are numerous locations where data is converted to a paper-based document as output from one system and must then be manually converted back to data if it is to be used in a different system. This is a problem particularly for the cost accountant, who is constantly in need of all types of information from all parts of the company. He must gain access to every island of automation within the company or (as is more common) collect paper-based documents related to any topic outside the accounting system and search through them in order to find needed information.

This is a particular problem when the cost accountant is attempting to drill down through multiple layers of information to find the specific record that will yield an answer to whatever question he is attempting to resolve. For example, a cost accountant is attempting to discover why the cost of goods sold is much higher than the standard costing system leads him to believe. He accesses the cost-of-goods-sold accounts in the general ledger, which is fully computerized, and finds that the variance appears to be arising in the account where inventory counting variances are stored. The software has a drill-down capability, which allows him to click on the account and view all the entries comprising its total. Unfortunately, he finds that there are no detailed records concerning the counting variances—only journal entries summarizing the results of manually calculated counting sheets prepared in the warehouse. For further information he must leave the computer terminal, walk over to the warehouse, and examine the counting sheets there.

This scenario might still arise even if a materials management computer system is in place, such as a manufacturing resources planning system (Chapter 26). This system could certainly track the causes of inventory adjustments and store this information in its central database (unless the system is *really* primitive), but there may be no linkage between this database and the one used by the accounting department. The cost accountant would then have to find a means of tracing entries appearing in the general ledger to the costs and related unit quantities shown in the materials management system, gain access to that system, and proceed with his investigation.

Here are the typical islands of automation found in many companies, along with notes on the types of information they contain:

- **Accounting system.** Though it may come as a surprise, the accounting system serves only the accounting department and so can be termed an island of automation. It handles accounts payable and accounts receivable, fixed-assets costing, job costing, payroll, and the general ledger. Though it is a valuable source of information for the cost accountant, there are many other sources, as are noted on this list.

- **Contracts tracking system.** The legal department should maintain a database of all unexpired contracts, which includes such information as contract termination dates, obligations, related pricing changes, and warranty periods. The range of information stored depends on the types of contracts. The cost accountant uses this information to track such items as scheduled changes in the prices of products to customers or components from suppliers.

- **Credit management system.** The finance department may have a system linked to an on-line credit tracking firm, such as Dun & Bradstreet, that reveals the creditworthiness of current or prospective customers. It may also be linked to the company's accounts payable system so that it can extract information about the payment histories of existing customers. The cost accountant uses this information to develop reports that itemize bad debt loss rates for existing customers, as well as the credit standards being applied in accepting new customers.

- **Engineering library.** The engineering staff maintains a voluminous set of computerized drawings of all existing components and completed products, which it can draw on when designing new products. This library also includes specifications for each component part. The cost accountant uses this information to report on the proportion of reusable parts being included in new product designs, as well as the number of redesigns initiated for existing components.

- **Engineering project tracking system.** The engineering manager uses a computerized project tracking system to determine the number of hours and related expenses incurred at each stage of an engineering project, as well as percentages of completion, milestone achievement, specific resources required for future project steps, and the nature of the work required to complete projects. The information in this system is mandatory for the cost accountant function, where it is needed to report on the progress and cost of projects.

- **Human resources system.** The human resources staff maintains a database containing data on every employee, such as a skills, history of pay rate changes, history of benefits received, history of workers' compensation claims, and so on—this database can cover a broad range of topics. The cost accountant uses this information for a variety of purposes, such as reporting on the efficiency of employees at a particular education level or on the cost of benefits for different types of employees.

- **Machine maintenance system.** The maintenance staff should have a computer database that tracks not only the maintenance histories of each machine but also the cost of all maintenance that has been performed on them. This information is valuable to the cost accountant, for it reveals maintenance trends that clearly indicate when an old machine should be replaced.

- **Materials management system.** This is a very comprehensive system containing operating information used by the purchasing, production scheduling, production, and warehousing departments. It traces inventory anywhere in these departments, as well as the status of orders, component parts and labor and machine requirements for each product, and the use of resources. This is the main database used by the cost accountant, more so than the accounting system, since some portion of it can be used for almost any analysis in which an accountant becomes involved.

- **Sales prospects system.** The sales staff needs to track its sales prospects so that it can manage a constant inflow of sales. This database usually includes contact names, the stage in the sales cycle for each customer, probabilities of sale completion, and probable dollar amounts for sales. The cost accountant can use this information to determine the effectiveness of the sales staff, as well as the stream of sales flowing in from different territories.

- **Treasury system.** The finance staff may have a small database system that has on-line linkages to various outside financial services and is used for monitoring cash flows and making investments. Given the risk of malfeasance associated with this system, it is usually kept separate from other company systems and has considerable security protection. Nonetheless, it can be a useful source of information for the cost accountant, who can find information here regarding the company's cost of funds (always useful for cost-of-capital calculations).

It is rare to find that all these computerized systems have been installed at a company. More commonly, a few progressive departmental managers have installed a system just for their areas, leaving other functional areas to work with paper-based systems. Thus, the cost accountant finds that researching various projects involves drilling down through a few layers of accounting data and then jumping to another department's computer system or continuing the search by manually reviewing reams of department-specific documentation.

However, having islands of automation is better than having no automation at all. When a computerized database is available, the cost accountant may be able to access the system from a desktop computer and view records directly, though this may require learning how to navigate the new system. As an alternative, she might have to physically travel to the department where the paper-based documents are located, quiz the staff about where to find the correct material, and then sort through it (or have the local staff do so, which may involve some queue time that seriously lengthens the investigation).

COST OF DATA COLLECTION

The implication so far has been that paper-based documents are the result of poor integration of islands of automation within a company, but this is not entirely the case. Some types of data are so infrequently used, or have such a minimal value when included in a computer database, that it is not worth the effort to install systems that would automatically collect and store the information. For example, a company with a comprehensive ERP system might find that one of its facilities still manually enters the weekly time card totals into the ERP system even though the system has preexisting software linkages supporting the use of bar-coded time clocks that can sweep detailed data directly into the central database. The cost accountant always has to call the facility and ask to have the time cards faxed to him for analysis, rather than just calling up the information on a computer terminal. And so he requests that a bar-coded time clock be installed at the facility. The cost of the clock, with installation and phone line linkages, would be $3000. Is it really worthwhile for the company to invest in this extra equipment to obtain access to more detailed information on 10 employees? Perhaps not.

In another situation the information may be so rarely accessed that there is little need to store it in the computer system even if there is some data volume involved. For example, a company conducts a single inventory count at year-end and compiles the inventory cost at that time for the year-end financial statements. The inventory is so small that the company does not bother to conduct more careful checks of its data over the course of the year. When the cost accountant needs to examine inventory records, he has to go to an index file and compare it to actual units on the warehouse shelves. Though this is a labor-intensive activity, the management group may make a reasoned decision that the inventory is just not very important and that the cost of maintaining an elaborate computerized inventory database is not worth the cost. Computer systems may be available, but the choice has been made not to use them.

COMMON PAPER DOCUMENTS

The use of automation to collect data is covered in detail in Chapter 4. In this section we address only the issues of what documents are available for automation and how to determine a cost-benefit analysis of their computerization.

Exhibit 8.1 shows the points in a company's systems where paper-based documents can most commonly be found. Automation methods can be used to eliminate the documents indicated in each of the areas in the exhibit. The documents and their associated methods of automation are:

- **Bills of material.** This document lists all the component parts used to construct a finished goods item, as well as the standard quantities of each component required. The cost accountant must access this document frequently for a number of costing applications, so some degree of computerization is mandatory. At its most primitive level this can be a separate electronic spreadsheet for each bill of material, which is readily accessible to those with proper access

EXHIBIT 8.1. Locations of Paper-Based Documents in Corporate Systems

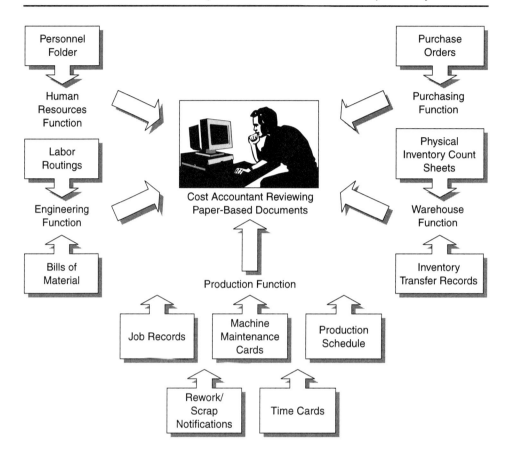

codes. However, this arrangement does not allow the bills to be used for automatic inventory valuations or other reports, so the best approach is to purchase a software package that not only allows users to update this information on-line but also to integrate it with other applications. This functionality is common in enterprise resources planning systems, as well as in manufacturing resources planning and material requirements planning systems.

• **Inventory transfer records.** These records trace the quantity of goods that have been received into or transferred out of the warehouse. When there is no computerized database to store these records, they are kept on index cards, with a running quantity total listed on each one. The cost accountant needs this information for inventory valuation purposes. Itemizing it in a computer system is such a basic need that nearly all companies have done so with some sort of computer software, unless they run just-in-time manufacturing systems that use no inventory or unless their inventory levels are so low that there is no need to compile a valuation.

- **Invoices.** When there is no computerized accounting system, invoices sent to customers must be written by hand. This is rare circumstance since accounting packages can be purchased quite inexpensively. However, there are a few cases, such as when sales personnel create handwritten invoices when they deliver goods to customers, where they are still used.

- **Job records.** This is a major source of information for the cost accountant, for it contains the labor hours and types and quantities of materials used to complete a job, as well as the names of the employees who charged hours to the job; in some cases the time spent on each machine can also be found in these records. This information is mandatory in investigating variances from expected job costs, which comprises a significant part of the cost accountant's job. This function is computerized in most accounting systems, though it still requires the job cost record to be entered into the computer. To avoid this data entry, one can have direct labor personnel enter job numbers when they swipe their bar-coded employee badges through automated time clocks that automatically charge the time worked against the indicated jobs. Material quantities and costs, as well as machine time, can be automated through the use of backflushing procedures (Chapter 4), which avoids the use of many transactions that would otherwise be added to a job record.

- **Labor routings.** The labor routing contains data about the quantity of labor needed to create a product, as well as the sequence of workstations at which this labor must be used. This information is of great use to the cost accountant, who can mine it to determine what workstations contain the largest amount of labor for a given product, which labor standards are being exceeded by actual costs, and related issues. This information can exist on paper, but then there is no way to roll it up into product costs or labor use forecasts. Consequently, it is now included in the computer systems of virtually all manufacturing resources planning systems.

- **Machine maintenance card.** Every machine in a production process should have information about it stored somewhere that itemizes the frequency and cost of all maintenance associated with it. This information is used by the cost accountant to determine trend lines of costs for machines in order to predict when they should be replaced with lower-maintenance successors. It is also useful for determining the impact of preventive maintenance programs. It is common to still find this information on paper since most fully integrated computer packages dealing with production are not really so integrated—they do not provide for the storage or manipulation of maintenance information. This problem can be avoided by creating custom software or by purchasing maintenance-specific software and then creating a custom interface between this software and whatever other production systems are currently in use.

- **Personnel folder.** The personnel folder contains information about every facet of every employee, such as important dates, benefits, performance reviews, and location changes. A cost accountant in the service industry, where personnel-related costs comprise the bulk of all costs incurred by a company, may have a considerable need for this information. If it is still paper-based, the research required to extract any useful cost accounting information can be a nightmare. The best alternative is to transfer the data in these documents into a broad-based human resources package, such as PeopleSoft, which categorizes it into databases, thereby allowing the costing staff to directly mine all the needed information at a much higher speed than would otherwise be possible.

- **Physical inventory count sheets.** The physical inventory counting process involves the recording of inventory counts on multiple copies of count sheets which are then numerically controlled and keypunched into the computer system for verification against on-line totals. The problem is that the cost accountant can have a hard time sorting through this data if she is attempting to determine the sources of sudden changes in inventory balances caused by possibly incorrect inventory counts. This task requires one to search through the inventory count sheets by hand, find the tags on which the counts were performed, and (even harder) try to determine exactly where in the facility these counts were made. Though control sheets can ease this task somewhat, the use of automation can eliminate the entire process. The best approach is to equip the counting staff with radio-frequency bar code scanners that directly access the central inventory database. This allows them to punch in each inventory location along with the count for each one and then have the computer immediately store this information, which includes the identification of the counter, the time when the count was taken, and the quantities entered (not to mention an immediate variance response to the counters if there is one). Though this is an expensive option, a sophisticated company will find that it is an excellent method for improving the physical inventory counting process.

- **Product rework/scrap notifications.** When a product is pulled out of the production process because of scrap or rework problems, the quality staff usually fills out a form itemizing the nature of the problem, the product number, and the quantity pulled. The accounting staff then keypunches this document into the computer system, which reduces quantities in inventory and in the production process. This is a difficult task because the scrap identification tags can be created anywhere in a facility and so can be lost anywhere in the facility. Though it is a complicated transaction to automate, one can affix bar codes to all products passing through the production process and then equip the quality staff with radio-frequency bar code scanners or install numerous fixed scanning stations so that defective items can be immediately recorded in the computer system. The difficulty is that many components do not have bar codes attached to them and users may forget to log in some items. Consequently, even an advanced level of automation may still present problems to the cost accountant in this area.

- **Production schedule.** This schedule is a constantly revised document that itemizes exactly what products are to be manufactured at any given time. The cost accountant uses this information to trace perpetual inventory records through the system since there should be drops in raw materials inventory levels when production for a specific product occurs, and jumps in finished goods inventory levels immediately following the completion of a production run. This scheduling function is computerized in all manufacturing resources planning and material requirements planning systems.

- **Purchase orders.** This document is used by the purchasing staff to officially authorize suppliers to send products and services to the company. Most organizations use some kind of packaged software to accomplish this task. If not, the cost accountant would be unable to trace purchase authorizations through the computer system. A purchase order capability may be available as an extension to some computerized accounting packages and is certainly a standard feature in all manufacturing resources planning systems, as well as in all material requirements planning systems.

- **Requisitions.** This is a document that is filled out by anyone who needs to purchase something. It lists the item, the quantity, when it is needed, and perhaps a suggested supplier. The purchasing department uses this information to place orders with suppliers, and the cost accountant sometimes uses this record to determine the source of purchase requisitions. On-line purchasing forms, set up on a computer network, can eliminate requisitions by having users type the information directly into a purchasing database.

- **Supplier check payments.** The cost accountant is not normally called on to locate information about a check a supplier has used to pay the company. This document lists the check number, the date it was issued, which bank cashed it, and when it was cashed. Finding this information requires one to sort through copies of received checks (assuming that copies are made) or to contact the supplier and request a copy. Either method is painfully time-consuming. A better approach is to encourage suppliers to make their payments by wire transfer and an associated electronic data interchange transaction so that the details of the money transfer are routed directly into the company's computer system through an interface module. This procedure eliminates all manual intervention in the recording of cash receipts and stores all the related payment information in the company's database for ready access. However, this system can be an expensive one to set up (especially the interface module, which may require customized programming), so many companies do not pursue this level of automation.

- **Time cards.** This is still a common paper-based document. A company stores time cards in a rack next to a punch clock; employees take their cards out of the rack and insert them into the clock when they are entering or leaving the office; and the clock then punches the time onto the cards. This information is then manually compiled by a payroll clerk, who enters the summary totals into the payroll system. The cost accountant sometimes needs to examine the original time cards when looking for potential errors in the summarization of time records. This form of paperwork can be completely eliminated with the use of bar-coded time clocks, as noted in Chapter 5.

Given the large number of paper-based documents mentioned here, it is obvious that in the modern corporation much information is still not readily accessible to the cost accounting staff. One way to make this information more accessible is to convert it to a computer database that can then be directly accessed by the staff. However, the cost of creating such a system may very well exceed the benefit to be obtained from doing so. Consequently, the best approach to determining whether a paper-based source should be switched to a computer database is to first determine the labor cost of continually researching the existing documents for costing studies. When doing this, one should be particularly careful to note the frequency of these accesses since a high degree of frequency is a good indicator of the need for a better information storage system. Alternatively, a one-time major review of data recorded on paper documents may leave everyone wishing that it was available on a computer system, but the cost cannot be justified if there is no prospect of needing the information again. The next step is to determine the purchase, installation and training, and ongoing maintenance costs of computer systems designed to replace paper-based documents. This cost may be inordinately high in comparison to the benefit in reduced labor costs derived from its use. By making this comparison one can readily determine if a conversion from paper to digital storage makes any sense. It may also be useful to conduct a net present value calculation (Chapter 24) of such an analysis to verify that there really is a justifiable reason for switching to a new system.

SUMMARY

It is evident from the discussion in this chapter that the cost accountant encounters varying degrees of difficulty in accessing data within a company since some of it is stored on paper, rather than in a computer. This problem may be due to the existence of several unlinked computer systems, which results in the creation of paper-based documents by each system rather than a seamless integration of functions. The problem also arises when there are areas in which the cost of converting data to a computer database is greater than the utility to be gained from doing so. In the first case the cost accountant must determine the benefit to be gained from linking disparate systems or (as in the second case) adding new systems. These benefits must then be compared to the reduction in research time required to access paper-based documents. A decision should be made to introduce computer storage only into areas where a solid cost-benefit relationship can be proven.

PART III

Costing Methodologies

CHAPTER 9

Job Costing

Job costing is the most common method for marshaling cost accounting information into a data structure containing usable information. Most cost accountants have experienced this system at some point in their careers, quite possibly at every facility where they have ever worked. In this chapter we consider the nature of job costing and why it is used so frequently. In addition, we present a graphical representation of how data flows through this system and then proceed to a discussion of the main control points to be aware of and how they can fail.

NATURE OF JOB COSTING

As the name implies, job costing is designed to accumulate the costs of small batches, or jobs, of products. This may mean that a single job is considered a single product created in volumes of one, or much larger batches produced for several weeks or months—it all depends on the production process.

In essence, job costing traces all material and direct labor costs directly to a batch and allocates overhead costs to batches as well. This is a simple rendition of the system. In reality it must first accumulate costs for any components or subassemblies stored in inventory and then shift these costs to specific jobs once the items are taken from stock and assigned to a job. It also requires direct labor employees to charge their time to specific jobs (which necessitates a good timekeeping system—see Chapter 5). In addition, overhead costs must be stored in separate cost pools and then allocated to each job. These overhead costs can be allocated using a standard overhead rate, which is called *normal* costing, or they can be allocated with actual costs, which is (predictably) called *actual* costing. The result is a computer file on each job that itemizes all the direct material, direct labor, and overhead costs that have been assigned to it. In the next section we consider the advantages and disadvantages of this method and then go on to present a more in-depth review of the transactions that flow through the system.

ADVANTAGES AND DISADVANTAGES OF JOB COSTING

One of the primary advantages of job costing is that the management team has ready access to all the costs incurred for each job being completed. This allows the team to examine each cost incurred, finding out why it happened, and determine how it can be controlled better in the future, thereby contributing to better ongoing levels of profitability. For example, a proper job record contains any special reworking costs, which a manager can then use to trace back to the specific reason why the rework was needed. Similarly, overhead allocations based on machine usage reveal problems with excess use, which might be the result of lengthy machine setups or breakdowns as well as longer-than-expected machine cycle times.

Another reason for using job costing is that it yields ongoing results for each job. In today's world of fully computerized production tracking databases, one can use a job costing system to track costs as they are added to a job rather than waiting until the job has been completed. This gives a company several advantages. One is that the accounting staff can monitor job accounts to see if costs are being posted to the wrong accounts and correct them right away, rather than waiting until the job closes and having to frantically review records to see why the results are different from expectations. Another advantage is that a company can monitor the costs incurred for longer jobs and have enough time to make changes before they close, based on the costing information revealed by the job costing system. For example, a lengthy new-product development project might be over budget after just 25% of the work has been completed; if the management team is made aware of this costing problem early in the project, it will still have 75% of the project in which to make corrections and bring costs back down to budgeted levels. Yet a third advantage is that changes in the cost of a job can result in negotiations with cost-plus customers who are paying for all the costs incurred, so that they are fully aware of cost overruns well in advance and are prepared to pay the additional amounts. All these factors are the main advantages of using job costing in a computerized environment.

There are also several problems with job costing. One is that it focuses attention primarily on products rather than on departments or activities. This is not an issue if there are supplemental systems in place that record information about these other cost categories but, it leaves management with inadequate information if this is not the case. Another difficulty is that overhead is generally allocated based on rates that are changed only about once a year. Considerable fluctuation in overhead costs over the course of a year can result in both over- and underallocation of overhead costs to jobs during that period. Another problem is specific to the use of normal costing. As noted in the last section, this practice involves the use of a standard overhead rate rather than one that is based on actual costs and requires adjustment from time to time. If it is management's intention to charge individual jobs for the variance between standard and actual overhead rates, this may not be possible if some jobs have already been closed by the time the variance allocation takes place. This is not just a technical accounting issue, for some jobs are fully reimbursed by customers who pay on a cost-plus basis; if the overhead variance is a positive one, a company may not be able to charge its customers for the added costs if the related jobs have already been closed.

Another issue is that job costing has little relevance in some environments. For example, the software industry has high development costs but almost zero direct costs associated with the sale of its products. The use of a job costing system to record these costs makes little sense if the associated costs represent only a few percent of the total revenue gained from each one. The same problem arises in service industries, such as retailing, where there is no discernible product. These situations limit the most effective use of job costing to two areas—production and professional services. The first case, production, is an obvious use for the concept since there are high material costs that can be specifically identified with a job. The same is true of professional services, but here the main cost is direct labor rather than direct materials. In most other cases job costing does not provide management with a sufficient quantity of information to be useful.

The most important problem with job costing is that it requires a major amount of data entry and data accuracy in order to yield effective results. Data related to materials, labor, overhead, indirect labor, scrap, spoilage, and supplies must be entered into a system capable of accurately assigning these costs to the correct jobs every time. In reality such systems are rife with mistakes due to the sheer volume of data transactions, keying errors, misidentification of jobs, and the like. Problems can be resolved with a sufficient amount of error tracing by the accounting staff, but there may be so many that there are not enough staff members to keep up with them. Though these issues can to some degree be resolved through the use of computerized data entry systems (Chapters 4 and 5), one may still have to determine whether the cost of maintaining such a system outweighs the benefits to be gained from it.

A final issue is that a large proportion of the costs assigned to a job, frequently more than 50%, comes from allocated overhead. When there is no fully proven method for accurately allocating overhead, such as through an activity-based costing system (Chapter 16), the results of the allocation yield meaningless information. This has been a particular problem for companies that persist in allocating overhead costs based on the direct labor used by each job, since a small amount of labor is generally being used to allocate a much larger amount of overhead, resulting in large shifts in overhead allocations based on small changes in labor costs.

Some companies avoid this problem by ignoring overhead for job costing purposes or by reducing overhead cost pools to include only overhead directly traceable at the job level. In this way, many costs are not allocated to jobs at all, but those that are allocated are fully justifiable.

Clearly, one must weigh the pros and cons of using a job costing system to see if the benefits outweigh the costs. This system is a complex one that is prone to error, but it does yield good information about product-specific costs.

JOB COSTING DATA FLOW

In this section we consider the most common transactions encountered when using a job costing system. These transactions are noted graphically in Exhibits 9.1 through 9.4, each of which indicates the journal entries used. In these exhibits, journal entries are contained within rectangles showing the accounts that are debited and credited, as well as transaction descriptions (in bold) at the bottom of each rectangle.

Three types of transactions flow through a job costing system. The first is related to direct materials and is shown in Exhibit 9.1. As noted at the top of the exhibit, materials are purchased by a company and stored in inventory on receipt. When they are pulled from stock and issued to a job, a second transaction shifts the cost of these materials out of inventory and into work in process ("WIP Inventory"). There should be a subledger in the accounting system that stores these material costs by specific job and then summarizes this information into a single lump-sum entry in the general ledger (thereby keeping the general ledger from becoming too cluttered with entries). As the materials are used in the production process for each job, there may be abnormal amounts of scrap or spoilage; if so, the cost of these quantities is charged directly to the cost of goods sold (as described further in Chapter 20). Alternatively, the cost of any expected, or normal, scrap and spoilage is charged to an overhead cost pool for later allocation back to jobs. These two transactions are noted on the left side of the exhibit. Once each job is finished, a transaction shifts its total cost from work in process to finished goods. Finally, when there is a sales transaction, the cost of the finished goods is shifted to the cost of goods sold and the sale is recorded in a separate journal entry. These transactions are noted at the bottom of Exhibit 9.1 and are the primary job costing transactions related to direct materials.

The second type of transaction that flows through a job costing system is for labor and is detailed in Exhibit 9.2. It begins with the incurrence of labor, for which there is a journal entry to wages expense and wages payable. The wages payable is eventually cleared with an offset to the cash account, but this issue falls outside the job costing system. The main problem is what happens to the wages expense. It comprises both direct and indirect labor. As noted on the right side of the exhibit, direct labor costs are shifted from the wages expense account to the work-in-

EXHIBIT 9.1. Job Costing Transactions for Direct Materials

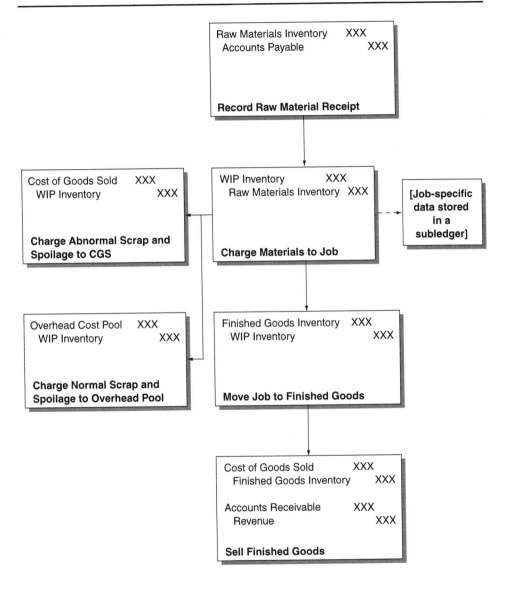

process account, where they are itemized by job in a subsidiary ledger. As was the case for direct materials, these individual job records are rolled up into a summary-level account in the general ledger. Indirect labor (i.e., any labor that cannot be directly ascribed to a specific job) is charged to an overhead cost pool as noted on the left side of the exhibit. These costs are later allocated back to jobs, as noted in Exhibit 9.3. Finally, at the bottom of Exhibit 9.2, we see the same transactions that

EXHIBIT 9.2. Job Costing Transactions for Labor

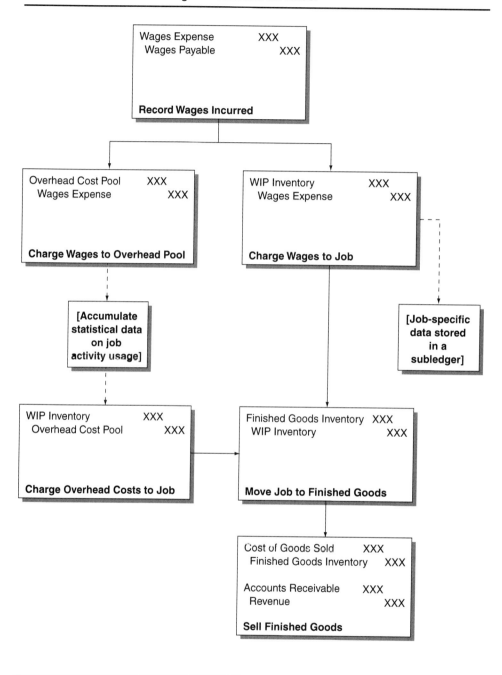

EXHIBIT 9.3. Job Costing Transactions for Actual Overhead Cost Allocations

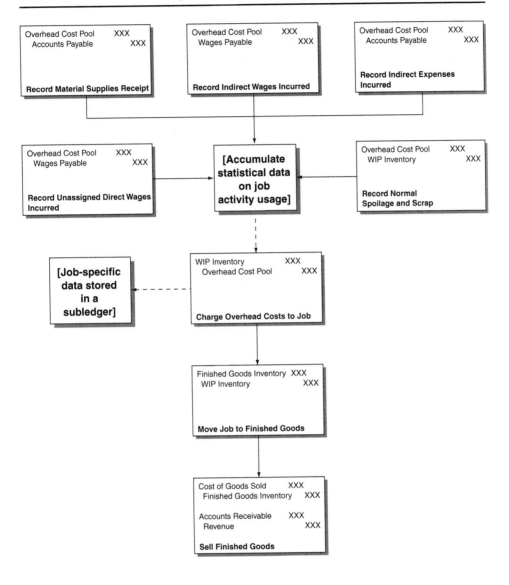

shift completed jobs from work in process to finished goods and then to the cost of goods sold. These are the primary job costing transactions related to labor.

The third type of job costing transaction is related to overhead costs. As indicated in Exhibit 9.3, overhead costs are summarized into one or more cost pools and then allocated to all open jobs based on some activity measure. Exhibit 9.3 presents the flow of transactions based on the assumption that actual costing is being used for the overhead allocation process; the normal costing process flow is presented in the next exhibit.

The transaction flow begins with the accumulation of costs into an overhead cost pool. There are a number of sources of these costs. Material supplies (i.e., materials not directly traceable to a specific job) are charged to an overhead cost pool as soon as they are purchased, since they are not stored in the inventory account. Indirect wages, as just noted, are also charged to an overhead cost pool. In addition, there are a number of other expenses, such as utilities and insurance, that are charged directly to a cost pool as soon as bills are received from suppliers. Likewise, several variances from direct labor and direct materials are charged to overhead. One is for direct labor that has not been specifically charged to a job, and another is any normal spoilage or scrap from direct materials. All these journal entries are noted in the top half of Exhibit 9.3. These costs can be accumulated into different overhead cost pools if the activity measures used to allocate them to jobs are substantially different. For example, a cost pool that accumulates all material handling costs can allocate costs based on the number of material moves required for each job, whereas another cost pool for machine-related expenses charges out its costs based on the minutes of machine use by each job. The number and type of cost pools used are based on the activity measures employed and the utility of the resulting increases in the accuracy of allocations. See Chapter 16 for a lengthier description of this topic.

The next step in the cost allocation process is to determine an activity measure to use for allocating the costs in each pool to the various open jobs (again, see Chapter 16 for a discussion of allocation methods). Next, one must accumulate statistics on the amount of each activity used by each job and then allocate costs from the cost pools to the jobs based on the amounts of each activity used. This results in the journal entry in the middle of Exhibit 9.3, where we debit the work-in-process account and credit the overhead cost pool account. We then finish with the usual transactions that shift costs from work in process to finished goods on completion of each job, and from there to the cost of goods sold when each job is sold.

An alternative to allocating direct costs is to use the normal costing approach as outlined in Exhibit 9.4. With this method, we create a standard allocation rate per unit of activity rather than using the actual cost. This is done in order to facilitate the allocation of costs, which may otherwise be delayed while actual costs are accumulated. As noted in the exhibit, this process starts by creating an allocation rate which is then used to charge costs to jobs. This standard rate is generally based on historical records, so it should not be too far from an allocation rate based on actual costs. In a separate step (as noted by the dividing line in the exhibit), we then accumulate all the actual costs incurred, just as in Exhibit 9.3, and store them in the overhead cost pool. Next we subtract the total amount allocated using the standard allocation rate from the actual amount of overhead costs. There should be a difference between the two types of allocation, which must then be disposed of.

There are three ways to eliminate a variance between the standard and actual allocation totals. One approach, as noted in the lower left corner of Exhibit 9.4, is to

EXHIBIT 9.4. Job Costing Transactions for Normal Overhead Cost Allocations

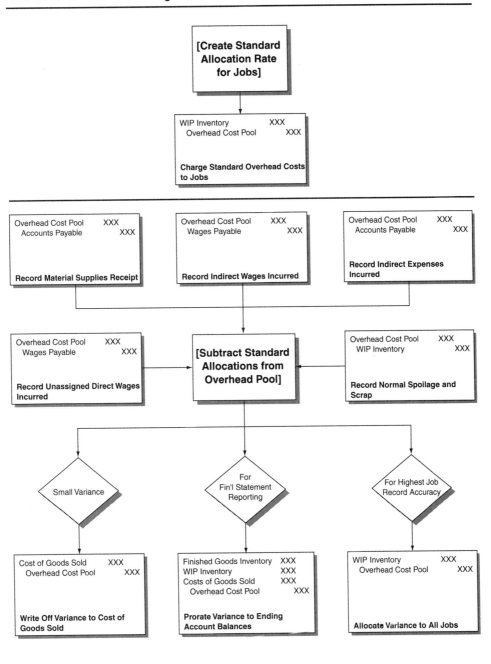

charge the entire variance to the cost of goods sold. This is the easiest approach, but it may skew the total cost of goods sold unless the amount of the variance is relatively small. The next option, as shown in the bottom center of the exhibit, is to prorate the variance among the cost of goods sold, work-in-process inventory, and finished goods inventory, based on the ending balances in each account. This option is most useful for external financial statement reporting, where such allocations are required, and is only slightly more difficult to calculate than the direct charge-off to the cost-of-goods-sold option. The final option, as noted in the lower right corner of the exhibit, is to charge the variance to each job that was open during the period when the overhead costs were being accumulated. This method is by far the most labor-intensive since there may be many jobs to which the variance must be allocated. It is recommended only if it is important to have the highest possible level of job record accuracy or if the variance is so large that the other two methods will yield inaccurate reporting results. To calculate this allocation costs are spread to jobs based on their use of whatever activity measures were originally compiled to allocate overhead costs to them.

The exhibits in this section show the general flow of transactions required to operate a job costing system. Though the basic steps are not difficult to follow, there are quite a few of them, which makes job costing a tricky system to operate and one that frequently results in odd-looking results, thereby forcing the cost accountant to engage in considerable account tracing and reconciliation to see where accounting transactions were incorrectly processed. To avoid these problems, anyone involved with job costing transactions should be thoroughly versed in the process flows noted here.

CONTROL POINT ISSUES

The job costing system requires a significant number of inputs, variance dispositions, and allocations and so is subject to problems at a number of control points. By being aware of these problems, one can revise the system to avoid control problems. This section contains a review of the most common issues.

Disposition of job costing variances is one of the most common control problems. If a manager is oriented toward improving reported profit levels (perhaps because his bonus would be increased), variances are never charged to the cost of goods sold even if they are due to abnormal scrap or spoilage situations. Instead, they are rolled into overhead or prorated among the period-end inventory and cost-of-goods-sold accounts, which keeps some of them from being recognized as expenses in the near term. The best solution to this problem is to periodically review the journal entries used to dispose of variances, as well as to investigate the nature of each one, which can be an ongoing task for the internal auditing department.

A manager who wants to increase profits also has an incentive to park as many jobs in work in process as possible, even if they have really been completed. This gives the manager one or more buckets in which to store extra costs that would otherwise be shifted to finished goods and from there to the cost of goods sold. One way to avoid this issue is to look for old jobs that have not yet been closed. However, a canny manager may shift costs from old jobs to newer ones as the old ones are closed, so it may also be necessary to look for transactions that shift costs between jobs.

Yet another way to pump up reported profit levels is to use indirect labor personnel for work that is really of the direct labor variety, so that these labor costs are shifted to an overhead cost pool rather than being charged straight to a job. If this is done, it is likely that some of the overhead costs will be stored in an inventory account at the end of the accounting period rather than being charged straight to the cost of goods sold. This practice can be avoided by running a trend line of direct labor costs to see if these costs are being reduced despite steady or upward trends in production volume.

An additional control problem occurs when a manager loads costs into a job not scheduled to be sold for some time, thereby keeping them from being charged to the cost of goods sold. This results in a bloated work-in-process or finished goods inventory. The best avoidance measure here is to compare actual job costs to budgeted levels to see if overages are occurring, especially if they are occurring on jobs that are not yet completed.

Another control problem is carrying job cost variances past the end of the fiscal year. A legitimate system always charges any remaining variances to the cost of goods sold. However, anyone wanting to increase reported profit levels tries to avoid this and so routes the variances into an inventory account, thereby hopefully escaping the attention of the auditors who review the year-end accounting records. Once the auditors are gone, the variance is taken back out of the inventory account and charged off in the next year. This issue requires a close examination of the variance accounts to see what journal entries are made to reduce variance levels. If there are many entries running in and out of these accounts, it can be quite a chore to spot such transactions.

Another control problem involves someone trying to add costs to overhead cost pools that are really period expenses and should therefore be charged to the current period. When they are stored in the overhead cost pool, some portion of the overhead is stored in inventory instead of being expensed, thereby increasing reported profits. This common problem can be detected by periodically tracing the origins of all costs added to cost pools, as well as by running trend lines of cost pool totals just to see if they are on a steadily increasing path (which may indicate the addition of unrelated costs).

Another problem arises in the area of allocation methodology. The most appropriate way to spread costs to jobs may be through a number of cost pools and allocation methods (such as through an activity-based costing system), which yields the most accurate allocations. If this is not done, perhaps through the excessive accumulation of costs into too few cost pools or through inappropriate allocation techniques, the amount of overhead costs charged to each job may be too low or too high. This issue can be avoided by using an activity-based costing system.

When there are many product lines in a facility, it is also possible that different job costing systems are set up for each one because different costing personnel are used to create each one or because there is some perceived justification for using different cost accumulation or allocation systems. In reality this creates confusion, leading to inefficient costing systems. It is better to force all production lines into the same job costing mold.

Allocations can be inaccurate if a company chooses to use a normal costing system without some historical basis for using standard costs. When this happens, the allocations vary significantly from actual costs, resulting in repeated adjustments to the allocation rates being used, which in turn results in inaccurate overhead costs being assigned to jobs. In such situations it is better to start with an overhead allocation system based on actual costs and then switch over to a normal costing system *after* there is a history of costs on which to base a set of valid overhead standards.

A final problem is that some companies feel compelled to update their cost allocation rates too frequently, perhaps every month. They may do this based on a feeling that allocation rates are not accurate if they are not regularly compared to actual costs. However, there can be considerable fluctuation in monthly costs, based on seasonal cost changes, based on the number of workdays in each month, or because the accounts payable staff erroneously records no expenses in one month and double the amount in the next month. Whatever the reason, it is common to see costs fluctuate from month to month, which results in allocation rates for jobs that fluctuate in a corresponding manner. It is better to wait a few months before updating allocation rates simply because a longer time period flattens out any monthly cost changes.

Clearly, there are many control issues related to the job costing system. This does not mean that job costing is an inefficient system, just that it incorporates so many transactions that there are many situations in which costs can be deliberately or accidentally skewed. Thus, one must keep a watchful eye on the overall process in order to ensure that transactions are appropriately processed.

SUMMARY

Job costing is one of the primary cost tracking systems employed by corporations today. Because it is commonly used, the cost accountant will probably encounter the transactions described in the chapter at some point and so should know how to operate the system and have a firm grasp of its problems and control issues. Because this system is frequently used does not mean that it is perfectly suited to all situations, however; on the contrary, it is too much work for many cost accountants in relation to the types of information it produces. Consequently, one should review the other costing systems described in this book to see if one of them will work better or if job costing can be combined with a different costing system to yield the best blend of efficiency and effectiveness.

CHAPTER 10

Process Costing

Process costing is used in many industries where there are such large quantities of similar products that it makes no sense to track the cost of either individual products or small batches of them. Instead, costs are averaged over large quantities of production, yielding the same unit costs for all items in a production run. This type of costing requires accounting calculations considerably different from those used for job costing in the last chapter, though the resulting transactions are similar. In this chapter we review the nature of process costing, the three most commonly used process costing calculations, and the advantages and disadvantages associated with this methodology.

NATURE OF PROCESS COSTING

Process costing is used in situations where job costing cannot be used; that is, for the mass production of similar products when the costs associated with individual units of output cannot be differentiated from each other. In other words, the cost of each product produced is assumed to be the same as the cost of every other product. Examples of industries where this type of production occurs include oil refining, food production, and chemical processing. For example, how would a cost accountant determine the precise cost required to create one gallon of aviation fuel when thousands of gallons of the same fuel are gushing out of a refinery every hour? The cost accounting methodology in this case is process costing.

There are three types of process costing. The first is based on weighted average costs and is described in the next section. It assumes that all costs, whether from a preceding period or the current one, are lumped together and assigned to produced units. It is the simplest version to calculate. The second type of process costing is based on standard costs. Its calculation is similar to that for weighted average costing, but standard costs are assigned to production units rather than actual costs; after total costs are accumulated based on standard costs, these totals are compared to actual accumulated costs and the difference is charged to a variance account. This calculation is described in Process Costing Data Flow, Standard Costing Method. Finally, one can use first-in first-out costing. This is a more complex calculation that creates layers of costs, one for units of production started in the previous production period but not completed, and another layer for production started in the current period. This calculation is described in Process Costing Data Flow, the FIFO Method. For a more detailed review of the FIFO concept, the reader should refer to Chapter 13, which covers cost layering concepts. Anyone already familiar with these concepts might ask why no costing formulation is presented here for last-in first-out cost layering. The LIFO concept is used to determine the cost-of-finished-goods inventory in situations where the last units of inventory added to a stockpile are the first removed from the pile and sold. Though the LIFO concept is perfectly valid for final sales to customers, it is not a reasonable system to use within a company, where production moves through the facility in a steady stream—the first production unit to enter a department is also the first one to leave it. Since the theoretical LIFO concept is not actually encountered in the majority of production situations, we do not include a costing example based on it in this chapter.

Why have three different cost calculation methods for process costing, and why use one version instead of another? Different calculations are required for different cost accounting needs. The weighted average method is used in situations where there is no standard costing system or where the fluctuations in costs from period to period are so slight that the management team has no need for the slight improvement in costing accuracy that can be obtained with the FIFO costing method. Alternatively, process costing based on standard costs is required for costing systems that use standard costs. It is also useful in situations where companies manufacture such a broad mix of products that they have difficulty accurately assigning actual costs to each type of product; under the other process costing methodologies, which both use actual costs, there is a strong chance that costs for different products will become mixed together. Finally, FIFO costing is used when there are ongoing, significant changes in product costs from period to period—to such an extent that the management team needs to know the new costing levels so that it can reprice products appropriately, determine if there are internal costing problems requiring resolution, or perhaps change manager performance-based compensation. In general, the simplest costing approach is the weighted average method, with FIFO costing being the most difficult. If there are no other factors impacting one's decision regarding which method to use, it is best to stay with the simplest system.

PROCESS COSTING DATA FLOW, WEIGHTED AVERAGE METHOD

The weighted average method is the easiest process costing system to understand because it uses actual costs and does not attempt to create layers of costs, as is the case with the first-in first-out method (described later in this chapter). The method is best illustrated with an example, which is shown in Exhibit 10.1.

Two types of costs are assigned to products during a process costing calculation. One is direct materials, and the other is all other conversion costs required to complete the processing of the product; conversion costs can include labor, overhead charges, and so on. Direct materials are generally added at the beginning of the production process, while other conversion costs are more commonly added throughout the process. For example, a furniture maker starts with a block of wood and continually adds labor to it for the remainder of the production process in order to arrive at a completed wooden bureau—the direct materials are added at the beginning of the process, and the conversion costs are added in a steady stream. In our example we assume that costs are added to the process flow in this manner. In Exhibit 10.1, the top section is devoted to the calculation of units of production based on the concept that direct materials are completed first. In this section, "Units Summary," we see that the production process has successfully completed 1000 units during the period. Since these units are fully completed and shipped out of the company, the number of units from the perspective of cost application are the same for both direct materials and conversion costs—1000 units. However, there are also some units that were still in the production process at the end of the accounting period, totaling 350 units. The treatment of these units is somewhat different. From a cost application perspective, we assume that all 350 units are present for direct material cost application since all 350 units had all the direct materials added to them at the beginning of the process. However, conversion costs have been only partially applied. According to the production manager, only 60% of all conversion costs have been applied to these units as of the end of the accounting period. We enter this number in the "Conversion Factor" field and multiply it by the total of 350 units that were in process, which gives us just 210 units for purposes of conversion cost application. Thus, the weighted average cost allocation method yields 1350 units of

EXHIBIT 10.1. Example of the Weighted Average Costing Method

Weighted Average Cost Allocation Method

Units Summary	Direct Material Units	Conversion Factor	Conversion Cost Units
Completed Units	1,000		1,000
		60%	
Ending Units in Process	350		210
Unit Totals	1,350		1,210

Unit Cost Calculation	Direct Materials		Conversion Costs	Totals
Beginning WIP Cost	$ 20,000		$ 15,000	$ 35,000
Current Period Costs	$ 28,000		$ 21,500	$ 49,500
Total Costs	$ 48,000		$ 36,500	$ 84,500
Unit Totals (see above)	1,350		1,210	
Cost per Unit	$ 35.556		$ 30.165	

Unit Cost Allocation	Direct Materials		Conversion Costs	Totals
Cost of Completed Units	$ 35,556		$ 30,165	$ 65,721
Cost of Ending WIP Units	$ 12,444		$ 6,335	$ 18,779
Totals	$ 48,000		$ 36,500	$ 84,500

completed production for the purpose of applying direct material costs, but only 1210 units for applying conversion costs.

Next we must determine the cost per unit. This calculation is shown in the middle of Exhibit 10.1 under "Unit Cost Calculation." In this section we enter the beginning work-in-process costs for both direct materials and conversion costs, which should be stored in the general ledger from the preceding accounting period. We then compile all costs added during the current period and enter them on the next line, which gives us total direct material costs of $48,000 and total conversion costs of $36,500, for a grand total of $84,500. We then enter the unit totals from the preceding section and divide them into the cost totals for direct materials and conversion costs, which yields a cost per unit of $35.556 for direct materials and $30.165 per unit for conversion costs.

Finally, we multiply the unit costs we have just calculated by the number of units of completed production and remaining work in process in order to determine which costs are assigned to the finished goods general ledger account and which to the work-in-process account. To do this, we proceed to the bottom of Exhibit 10.1 to the section "Unit Cost Allocation." There are four calculations in this section. To determine the amount of total direct materials to charge to the finished goods account, we multiply the completed units of 1000 at the top of the exhibit by the cost per unit to arrive at a total of $35,556. Similarly, we multiply 1000 completed units in the conversion cost column by the conversion cost per unit of $30.165 to arrive at a total conversion cost per completed unit of $30,165. This gives us a total completed unit cost of $65,721, as noted in the far-right column at the bottom of the page. We then perform the same calculations to determine the cost of the work-in-process inventory, but now we use units itemized under "Ending Units in Process" to perform the calculation with the same costs per unit. This results in total direct material costs of $12,444 and total conversion costs of $6335, for a grand total of $18,779 being charged to the work-in-process inventory account. To assist in the understanding of these calculations, arrows have been inserted into the exhibit to give a visual reference to the flow of each calculation. As a check on our calculations, we can see that the $84,500 of total costs used in the center of the exhibit to determine the cost per unit is the same amount that we have arrived at in the bottom section, so all costs incurred are being charged to the general ledger inventory accounts.

The explanation for weighted average costing has been a lengthy one, yet it is the simplest of the three process costing variations described in this chapter. The main reason for the complicated calculations is the split between costs for direct materials and conversion costs. Why not just combine the two costs, thereby cutting the total number of calculations in half? The reason is that costs could then be significantly skewed. For example, if one were to assume that all conversion costs are assigned at the *beginning* of the production process, thereby avoiding the need for a conversion factor in Exhibit 10.1, there would be a resulting increase in the ending work-in-process valuation of about $3000 and a drop in the finished goods valuation of the same amount. This may seem like a paltry change in the balances of the two inventory accounts, but what if all the finished goods are sold before the end of the accounting period? This would result in a $3000 reduction in the cost of goods sold during the period, which would increase profits by a corresponding amount. This altered calculation is shown in Exhibit 10.2 with all changes noted in boldface.

EXHIBIT 10.2. Costing Calculation with No Consideration of the Conversion Factor

Weighted Average Cost Allocation Method

Units Summary	Direct Material Units	Conversion Factor	Conversion Cost Units
Completed Units	1,000		1,000
Ending Units in Process	350	100%	350
Unit Totals	1,350		1,350

Unit Cost Calculation	Direct Materials		Conversion Costs	Totals
Beginning WIP Cost	$ 20,000		$ 15,000	$ 35,000
Current Period Costs	$ 28,000		$ 21,500	$ 49,500
Total Costs	$ 48,000		$ 36,500	$ 84,500
Unit Totals (see above)	1,350		1,350	
Cost per Unit	$ 35.556		$ 27.037	

Unit Cost Allocation	Direct Materials		Conversion Costs	Totals
Cost of Completed Units	$ 35,556		$ 27,037	$ 62,593
Cost of Ending WIP Units	$ 12,444		$ 9,463	$ 21,907
Totals	$ 48,000		$ 36,500	$ 84,500

Variance from Preceding Exhibit:	Preceding Exhibit Totals	This Exhibit Totals	Variance
Cost of Completed Units	$ 65,721	$ 62,593	$ 3,128
Cost of Ending WIP Units	$ 18,779	$ 21,907	$ (3,128)
Totals	$ 84,500	$ 84,500	$ -

As noted in Exhibit 10.2, we must separate the direct material cost and conversion cost calculations or run the risk of arriving at incorrect inventory valuation calculations that can result in an incorrect cost of goods sold.

PROCESS COSTING DATA FLOW, STANDARD COSTING METHOD

The costing solution noted in the last section may not be acceptable for companies that operate on a standard costing system (Chapter 12). These organizations use a standard, predetermined cost for each step in the production process and deal separately with any variances from these standards. We can accommodate these companies by altering the weighted average model from the last section so that standard costs are assigned instead of actual costs, with any differences being charged to variance accounts. This costing model is shown in Exhibit 10.3.

In the exhibit the numbers used are the same as in Exhibit 10.1, so that differences in calculations can be easily seen. The section "Unit Summary" at the top of the exhibit is identical to the format used for weighted average costing. The main difference is in the second section of the exhibit, where there is no calculation of total beginning work-in-process or current period costs, which are normally used to derive the cost per unit. Instead, preset standard costs are used. So far, this makes the calculations *easier* than in the weighted average model (though this soon changes). The next step is to assign the standard costs to the units of production, the calculation of which is identical to that in the weighted average costing system. At this point we would have completed our calculations for the weighted average model. Here, however, we must insert a fourth section into the model that summarizes actual costs during the period and subtracts them from the standard costs already calculated, yielding a variance for both direct materials and conversion costs. These variances are then charged to the cost of goods sold. This final step makes the standard costing method slightly more time-consuming than the weighted average method.

As noted in an earlier section, the standard costing approach is most useful for situations where a number of products are being manufactured, which increases the danger that the costs for different products will be mixed together, resulting in inaccurate product costing. By using standard instead of actual costs, a company can reliably assign costs to all products that are fully provable.

EXHIBIT 10.3. Example of the Standard Costing Method

Weighted Average Cost Allocation Method Using Standard Costs

Units Summary	Direct Material Units	Conversion Factor	Conversion Cost Units
Completed Units	1,000		1,000
Ending Units in Process	350	60%	210
Unit Totals	1,350		1,210

Unit Cost Calculation	Direct Materials		Conversion Costs
Standard Unit Cost	$ 32.000		$ 31.500

Unit Cost Allocation	Direct Materials	Conversion Costs	Totals
Standard Cost of Completed Units	$ 32,000	$ 31,500	$ 63,500
Standard Cost of Ending WIP Units	$ 11,200	$ 6,615	$ 17,815
Standard Costs Totals	$ 43,200	$ 38,115	$ 81,315

Period Variance			
Beginning Standard WIP Cost	$ 20,000	$ 15,000	$ 35,000
Current Period Actual Costs	$ 28,000	$ 21,500	$ 49,500
Total Period Costs	$ 48,000	$ 36,500	$ 84,500
Standard Cost Totals	$ 43,200	$ 38,115	$ 81,315
Cost Variance	$ 4,800	$ (1,615)	$ 3,185

PROCESS COSTING DATA FLOW, THE FIFO METHOD

The final method for calculating process costs is the FIFO method. This is a cost layering approach that requires more calculations than the previous two methods. Once again, we illustrate the method with an example, as shown in Exhibit 10.4. In

EXHIBIT 10.4. Example of the Process Costing Method

First-In First-Out Cost Allocation Method

Units Summary	Direct Material Units	Conversion Factor	Conversion Cost Units	Total Units
Units from Beginning WIP	-	75% [work not done]	225	300
New Units Finished in Period	700		700	700
Ending Units in Process	350	60% [work done]	210	350
Unit Totals	1,050		1,135	1,350

Unit Cost Calculation	Direct Materials		Conversion Costs	Totals
Current Period Costs	$ 28,000		$ 21,500	$ 49,500
Unit Totals (see above)	$ 1,050		$ 1,135	
Costs per Unit	$ 26.667		$ 18.943	

Unit Cost Allocation	Direct Materials		Conversion Costs	Totals
Beginning Work-in-Process Cost	$ 20,000		$ 15,000	$ 35,000
Costs Added to Beginning WIP Units	$ -		$ 4,262	$ 4,262
Costs Added to New Units Finished in Period	$ 18,667		$ 13,260	$ 31,927
Costs Added to Ending Work in Process	$ 9,333		$ 3,978	$ 13,311
Totals	$ 48,000		$ 36,500	$ 84,500

this instance we add extra calculations and separate the costs recorded in the general ledger for work-in-process units from the previous period.

In the example we no longer identify just the completed and work-in-process units of production in the "Units Summary" portion of the spreadsheet. Instead, we also separate the units that were in the work-in-process account at the end of the preceding period. By doing so, we can segregate the cost of work done in the previous period, which may be different from the costs per unit incurred in the current period. The result of this additional segregation in production units is that the unit totals are now lower, with only 1050 units appearing for direct material costing purposes and

1135 for conversion costing purposes. This is because we have split the 1000 completed units itemized in the preceding examples into 300 units that were not completed in the previous period and 700 units that were both started and completed in the current period. The FIFO system records units for costing purposes in the current period only if there are additional costs that must be added to the units. Accordingly, zero direct material units are shown in the "Units from Beginning WIP" row since the direct material costs were all added in the previous period. However, 75% of the conversion work has not yet been done on these units (as noted in the same row), so 75% of the 300 units (225 units) are shown in the "Conversion Cost Units" category. All other parts of the "Units Summary" portion of the analysis remain the same.

Next we move to the "Unit Cost Calculation" portion of the exhibit. Here we see that only costs incurred in the current period are used to calculate the cost per unit. The reason for excluding the cost of incoming work in process for the preceding period is that we are attempting to create a cost layer specific to the units of production in the current period *only*. The costs stored in inventory at the end of the preceding accounting period have not gone away but have just shifted to the "Unit Cost Allocation" section of the exhibit. Meanwhile, we calculate the cost per unit in the usual manner, obtaining a direct material cost per unit of $26.667 and a conversion cost per unit of $18.943. These unit costs are lower than the costs derived for the weighted average and standard costing methods because we have thus far excluded costs from the beginning work-in-process inventory. Once these costs are added back in (in the last part of the exhibit), we will see that all costs have been accounted for.

Finally, we must complete the "Unit Cost Allocation" at the bottom of the exhibit, which tells us what costs to assign to either finished goods or work-in-process inventory. First, we add all beginning work-in-process costs, which are shown in the first row. Next we add to them any additional costs incurred during the current period in order to complete units of production started in the previous reporting period. To do this, we multiply the units in the "Units from Beginning WIP" row at the top of the exhibit by the unit cost. This results in no additional cost allocation for direct materials but in an extra $4262 of conversion costs. At this point we have completed the costing for all the units of production started but not completed in the preceding period, which totals $39,262. This cost is then shifted to the finished goods account in the general ledger. Next we multiply the production units that were both started and completed in the current period by the cost per unit, which results in total direct material costs of $18,667 and conversion costs of $13,260. These costs are also shifted to the finished goods account. Finally, we multiply the ending units in process quantities by the unit costs to derive the cost totals that will be transferred to the work-in-process inventory account in the general ledger. These costs are $9333 for direct materials and $3978 for conversion costs, for a total ending work-in-process cost of $13,311. Six calculations are required to determine the numbers in the "Unit Cost Allocation" section, so arrows have been added to ease the task of tracing the flow of each one. Also, note that the total amount allocated is $84,500 (as shown in the lower right corner of the exhibit), which proves that we have allocated all the costs with which we started the calculation.

In essence, we have segregated the cost of work done in the previous period, added any costs incurred in the current period to complete unfinished work from the previous period, and run a separate set of calculations to charge costs to all other units of production that are based on costs incurred in the current period. Thus, we have effectively avoided merging costs from different periods. This does not have a large impact on a company's reported costs as long as costs do not vary much from period to period. However, if costs fluctuate considerably over time, it may make sense to use this more complicated calculation to ensure that cost changes are immediately reflected in the financial statements of the period in which they occurred.

ADVANTAGES AND DISADVANTAGES OF PROCESS COSTING

Process costing is the only reasonable approach to determining product costs in many industries. From the three costing methodologies just described in this chapter, a company can select the best one for determining costs in either a standard or actual costing environment. Process costing also uses most of the same journal entries found in a job costing environment, so there is no need to restructure the chart of accounts (Chapter 6) to any significant degree (with one exception, as noted below). This makes it easy to switch over to a job costing system from a process costing one if the need arises, or to adopt a hybrid approach that uses parts of both systems.

Despite these advantages there are several problems with process costing that one should be aware of. The most obvious is determining the percentage of completion. This percentage is needed to calculate the amount of costs to be assigned to units of production in each period. If the percentage is incorrect, resulting unit valuations will also be wrong. A canny manager aware of this problem can manipulate the percentage of completion to raise or lower unit costs, thereby changing the reported level of profitability. This problem is difficult to sidestep if the manager causing the trouble is in a position of authority. If not, cross-checking of completion percentages can be used to introduce some accuracy verification. Another solution is to establish a preset completion percentage, such as 50%, that is never changed in any reporting period no matter what the actual level of completion is. Unfortunately, this option can lead to manipulation also, for a manager could dump partially completed products into a department just to have extra costs automatically charged to them, or arbitrarily held in an upstream department, depending on what types of cost results are desired. A further option is to divide conversion costs into several cost pools, rather than one large cost pool, and separately determine the percentage of completion for each one, with a different person responsible for each determination. Though this approach can result in more accurate overall estimates, it is also a more complicated system to maintain.

Another problem arises with transfer costs if any of these process costing methodologies are used for individual departments. The trouble is that each successive department inherits the entire costs from the preceding set of departments that have charged costs to the products being manufactured and so have no idea which portion of the incoming costs are variable and which are overhead allocations. As discussed in Chapter 30, it is important to know the variable portion of one's costs since they can be used for incremental pricing decisions. The best way to avoid this difficulty is to use process costing only for the company as a whole, rather than for each of a series of departments, so that variable costs (e.g., direct material costs) can be more readily split off from the total costs. However, this is not possible in companies with long production cycles because process costs are spread over many units of production in many stages of completion, resulting in inaccurate per-unit costs.

Another difficulty is associated with the chart of accounts. Though the journal entries related to process costing are quite similar to those used for job costing, there is one difference. Job costing assigns costs to specific jobs within the work-in-process inventory account, whereas costs in a process costing environment can be shifted from department to department as products move through the production process. Thus, the focus of data collection shifts from jobs to departments. This change requires the addition of one or more digits to each account number in the chart of accounts, which identifies each department. This topic is discussed at greater length in Chapter 6.

A problem specific to the weighted average calculation with standard costing is the deliberate alteration of standard costs in order to create variances. If a manager wants to create an accounting profit in a given period, he can order the standard costs for products to be produced in the current period to be set somewhat high. In this way additional direct materials and conversion costs are stored in inventory. This variance results in a false increase in the reported level of profitability, a problem that can be partly corrected by giving the engineering staff tight control over standard cost changes. Nonetheless, someone at the level of general manager could still muster sufficient authority to overcome such controls.

Of the issues noted here the primary one is incorrect estimation of the percentage of completion. Consequently, the bulk of the cost accountant's efforts in this area should be directed toward creating a solid estimating system not subject to coercion.

SUMMARY

Process costing is a common cost summarization and allocation methodology, three variations of which are most heavily used. It tends to be a relatively inexpensive system to operate but also runs the risk of producing inaccurate outputs, especially if a company's systems are a mixture of job- and process-based production. Consequently one should carefully consider how this system fits into existing production systems, and what special cost system alterations are required to ensure that the collected data can be converted to the most useful set of costing information.

CHAPTER 11

Direct Costing

Direct costing is either highly favored or much maligned by cost accountants; those who favor it claim that it is helpful for a number of short-term decisions, while those against it point out that it does not include many of the costs to which today's overhead-heavy firms are subjected, and thereby leads to poor decisions. In this chapter we explore the nature of direct costing and how it can be used to improve management decision making. We also note its flaws and how to avoid them. Finally, we present brief discussions of what happens to financial reporting and inventory valuation when direct costing is used in their compilation.

DEFINITION OF DIRECT COSTING

There are several ways to define direct costs, so rather than create an amalgamated definition, we list several distinct ones:

- All costs left after period-specific costs have been eliminated

- All costs that can be directly attributed to an incremental change in production volume

- All costs that can be reasonably allocated to specific units of production

- All costs that would disappear if the related production volume were to stop

Though these definitions appear to be somewhat different, a common thread runs through them all—a direct cost must be one that is clearly attached to incremental changes in production volume. That is, the cost changes if the volume changes.

The obvious costs that can be readily considered direct costs are those for materials and direct labor used to construct a product or provide a service. There are a number of other lesser costs that can sometimes be added to these two major costs, such as the payroll taxes that accompany direct labor and incidental supplies needed to construct a product. For example, the bill of materials for a product may not include the cost of fittings or fasteners because corporate policy charges these costs to expense in each period under the category "shop supplies." Nonetheless, these costs are consumed during the manufacture of the product and are therefore direct costs.

The list of costs that can be considered direct costs changes as the volume of production increases. For example, when a cost accountant is reviewing an issue related to the incremental pricing of one additional unit of production, its direct cost is just its material cost since the direct labor staff is not sent home just to avoid the hours required to make one extra unit (assuming a small amount of labor per unit). Under this scenario the amount of direct labor cost goes down as the related unit volume decreases. However, when the same product is analyzed in terms of an entire batch of production, the direct costs include the cost of utilities incurred by any machines involved in the batch processing, as well as the cost of any labor needed to set up or break down the machinery for a production run. At high volume levels, direct costs can include the cost of an entire factory. Consequently, which costs to include in the direct cost category vary directly with the production volume addressed by the analysis being made.

Direct costs can also switch to being indirect ones (and vice versa), depending on management decisions. For example, if a company has a labor-intensive production process and management decides to switch its production process over to one that replaces much of the direct labor with automated machinery, the direct cost of each incremental unit of production declines by the cost of the direct labor that has been eliminated, while the period costs, which now include the cost of the automated machinery, increase.

Having noted that costs defined as direct vary based on the circumstances, we bring up the question of how a cost accountant is supposed to know when a cost is direct and when it is not. There are three ways to make this distinction. The first is to use one's judgment. As noted in the next section, the primary use of direct costing is for short-term, incremental decisions related to pricing, product mix, and contribution margins. Given these uses, the cost accountant must determine the production volume being considered in each individual analysis and use her knowledge of the company's costs to determine which ones should be classified as direct for the purposes of that analysis. Since this may require some specialized knowledge of how costs are incurred, the cost accountant should feel free to call on internal experts in company operations, such as industrial engineers or shift managers, for advice on how to classify costs. This is a quick and relatively accurate way to determine the nature of a cost and is the method most frequently used, especially when there is little time for either of the other two methods.

An alternative approach is to rely on the industrial engineering staff to conduct an engineering review of how each cost is incurred and what activities cause it to be incurred. Though an accurate approach, this is by far the most labor-intensive way to determine the nature of a cost and so is rarely used for ongoing cost accounting analyses.

The final method for determining a direct cost is through the use of statistical analysis. As noted in Chapters 29 and 38, regression analysis can be used to determine the "best fit" line that plots a set of costs at various levels of a supposedly related activity. When the slope of this line is steep, there is clearly a close relationship between the activity and the cost. For example, there is an obviously tight relationship between the cost of materials and production volume, whereas the cost of supervisory salaries and the level of production are not closely linked. Though this method requires less time to complete than an engineering study, it is still substantially longer than the first method and so is used only for the most detailed cost accounting analyses where a high degree of precision is required.

Now that we have a clear conception of a direct cost, what about all the costs that are *not* direct? How are they classified? These costs are known as period costs since their incurrence bears no relationship to future activities that fall outside the current accounting period. Examples of these costs are administrative salaries, research and development, machinery depreciation, maintenance, and utilities—essentially all the categories of overhead or general and administrative expenses that cannot be directly assigned to the manufacture of individual units of production.

Another way of looking at these period costs is to think of them as the cost of capacity during the period. They must be incurred in order to keep a company ready to fill a customer order, even if that order never arrives. When period costs are interpreted in this manner, management's attention is focused on whether or not it should maintain the current level of capacity. If it wishes to reduce period costs, then a likely result will be a diminution in the company's ability to process the same level of transactions; this may be acceptable if a smaller level of production is needed to fill customer orders.

The final element in the definition of a direct cost is the contribution margin. This is simply revenues minus direct costs. It is not the same as the gross margin, which requires the inclusion of all related overhead costs in its calculation, whereas the contribution margin calculation specifically excludes overhead costs. Consequently, the contribution margin is always higher than the gross margin. Its use is described in the next section.

The key points in this section were descriptions of direct costs, period costs, and the contribution margin, which are the primary components of the analyses discussed in the next section. It is also important to note that, because direct costing involves only a subset of a company's total costs, it is not a system that one should rely on for all of a company's costing needs. It is useful only for specific purposes, which will be defined in the next section.

USES OF DIRECT COSTING

Direct costing is used for a limited set of cost accounting analyses because it does not consider overhead (period) costs. However, the uses to which it can be put are the ones most commonly encountered by the cost accountant, and so it is still a valuable tool. In this section we describe how direct costing can be used. Examples of the various types of analyses are:

- **Which customers are most (un)profitable?** The majority of period costs bear no direct relationship to the costs incurred to service a specific customer, with a few exceptions, such as the cost of customer service, order taking, and shipment. Given the small number of costs involved, it is typically a simple matter to derive a customer profitability profile, such as the one noted in Exhibit 11.1, which summarizes all customer revenues and related direct costs, to arrive at contribution margins by customer. In the exhibit it is evident that the profitability of sales to customer Q is quite low because of high labor and order taking costs (which are classic signs of a customer who requires an excessive degree of support). Management can use this information to determine which customers should be charged more in order to increase profits, or dropped entirely so that available capacity can be used to sell to other, more profitable customers. The same format can also be used to determine the profitability of entire sales regions, individual products, or product lines.

EXHIBIT 11.1. Profitability by Customer, Using Direct Costs

	Customer B	Customer Q	Customer Z
Revenue ($)	12,598	23,042	100,782
Direct costs			
Materials ($)	6,250	11,500	51,432
Direct labor ($)	1,231	4,803	9,078
Commission of 5% ($)	630	1,152	5,039
Order taking cost ($)	126	3,050	1,008
Shipping cost ($)	252	461	2,016
Total direct costs ($)	8,489	20,966	68,573
Contribution margin ($)	4,109	2,076	32,209
Contribution margin (%)	33	1	32

- **What impact will automation have on our cost structure?** When automation is used to eliminate direct labor, the direct cost to produce an item inevitably goes down (since the direct labor element is reduced or eliminated), while the period cost goes up because of the increased cost of depreciation for the new equipment, as well as maintenance costs to keep it operational. From the perspective of direct costing, this means that a company has a smaller incremental cost of production and can sell at an even lower price and still turn a profit. However, this lower price must still generate a sufficient contribution margin to ensure that period costs are covered.

- **What profit can we expect at various volume levels?** Direct costing is very good for profitability modeling. As noted in Exhibit 11.2, one can set up a chart itemizing various levels of sales volume and calculate the direct costs for each one. Then the period costs, which are assumed to be constant, are added, resulting in estimated levels of profit.

- **Can I use direct costing for make-or-buy decisions?** This is an excellent use for the direct costing methodology, for only direct costs should be included in the make-or-buy analysis. If a company needs to decide if it should manufacture a product in-house, versus at a supplier, most overhead costs are considered sunk costs that do not affect the decision. This leaves just the costs that will disappear if a product is removed from the production line and given to a supplier. This decision is described in greater detail in the case study at the end of this chapter.

- **Can I use direct costing as the foundation for commission calculations?** Most commission systems are based on paying a percentage of a product's sale price to a salesperson after a sales transaction has been completed. However, this method does not factor in the possibility that salespeople are selling whatever products are easiest for them to sell, rather than those with the highest level of profitability, which can result in massive sales of the wrong products and no bottom-line profits. To avoid this problem a company can alter the commission calculation

EXHIBIT 11.2. Profitability Analysis at Different Volume Levels

	Number of Units		
	10,000	20,000	30,000
Direct cost/unit ($)	17.43	17.43	17.43
Price/unit ($)	50.00	50.00	50.00
Total revenue ($)	500,000	1,000,000	1,500,000
Total direct cost ($)	174,300	348,600	522,900
Total period cost ($)	300,000	300,000	300,000
Profit (loss) ($)	25,700	351,400	677,100
Profit (%)	5	35	45

system so that commissions are based on a product's contribution margin. Each product's standard contribution margin can be calculated once a year, and a standard commission payment generated based on this amount, which sales personnel will be awarded for selling each incremental unit of the product. Using the contribution margin as the basis for commission payments has the unique advantage of making it easy to explain to the sales staff, which may have a difficult time understanding how overhead costs can be applied to products.

- **Can I determine which product sales yield the highest profit mix when capacity is fully utilized?** When companies find that there are more customer orders on hand than they can possibly fill given the constraints of production capacity, they are left with the problem of which orders to turn away. Direct costing can be used to decide which orders are the least and most profitable so that management can pick and choose among them, maximizing the total amount of profit earned. However, "cherry picking" among customer orders may permanently turn away some customers, which can be a major problem if the company later experiences a drop in orders and has alienated too many customers to regain sales volume.

In addition to the specific issues mentioned here, there are also some general benefits associated with the use of direct costing. One is that users can make fast analysis calculations, for there are so few costs associated with the direct costing system that they are easy to assemble. This is in opposition to an analysis that uses full-absorption costing, where one must not only determine the correct amount of overhead costs to allocate but also field questions from users regarding the applicability of these overhead allocations to the analysis in question.

Another point in its favor is that it is easy for users to understand. Any direct costing analysis is extremely simple, with only a few costs listed along with a contribution margin—there is no allocation of general and administrative costs, no overhead charge from corporate headquarters, and no allocation of costs from any number of cost pools. Many of the recipients of direct costing information are located in the sales and marketing department, where employees are highly trained in areas other than accounting and do not have time to puzzle over allocation rates and absorption levels. They are greatly appreciative of the clarity of direct costing and how it can help them in setting short-term pricing levels.

It is evident that direct costing is of great value in making a number of incremental pricing and costing decisions. However, the initial enthusiasm for this technique must be tempered by a knowledge of its pitfalls, which are described in the next section.

PROBLEMS WITH DIRECT COSTING

The single largest problem with direct costing is that it ignores all indirect costs. Though these costs may appear to be irrelevant in short-term decision making, which is where direct costing works best, they are still costs that must be factored into a company's long-range profitability planning. For example, when any of a company's indirect costs are treated by a direct costing analysis as though they do not exist, short-term pricing decisions that cover direct costs but most certainly do not cover indirect costs may result. When the company continues to use direct costing as its primary method for determining prices, it runs the risk of accepting margins that are much too low to pay for all the indirect company costs not included in the direct costing analysis. This is a serious problem for organizations, such as software companies, whose costs are almost entirely related to overhead. For example, the direct cost of selling one additional unit of software is only the cost of the CD or floppy disk on which it is stored (and not even that if the software is downloaded from a Web site); a direct costing analysis for this type of product results in a recommendation to sell the software for almost no price at all, which would never come close to paying for all the associated overhead costs. Thus, an exclusive focus on short-term decisions, with direct costing serving as the basis for these decisions, can place a company in serious financial difficulty.

Another problem is that direct costing does not yield valid information when it is used to analyze cases that fall outside the current capacity situation. For example, a sales manager is considering a proposal by a customer to purchase an additional 10,000 units of Product Alpha. The direct costing analysis reveals that, at a price of $18 each, the company will realize a profit of $2 per unit, or $20,000. However, what the direct costing analysis does not show is that this proposal requires more production capacity than the company has available, so that extra overtime, costing $22,000, or the addition of more automated machinery, costing three times the amount of the profits from this prospective deal, will be required. In other words, direct costing does not consider the additional cost of capacity that must be added if an incremental pricing decision cannot be filled with the existing capacity. This shortcoming can be reduced by using expert opinion and/or a review by the industrial engineering staff to determine the added cost of any required capacity.

Another issue is that costs can switch between direct and indirect costs for a number of reasons, which must be carefully investigated when conducting a direct costing analysis. For example, the cost of utilities is generally considered an indirect cost but can be defined as a direct one when it is tracked for specific machines used in the production process. If such a machine is in operation to manufacture goods, then the associated utility costs are clearly a direct cost. Similarly, if the chart of accounts is structured so that indirect costs are coded for one specific manager and direct costs are coded for another (e.g., the vice president of administration and the vice president of production), shifting a cost to the responsibility of the person in the indirect costing area can convert a direct cost to an indirect one in the company's accounting system.

Another issue to be aware of is that the costs included in a direct costing analysis gradually increase as the volume of production included in the analysis goes up. For example, when the subject of an analysis is to produce only one extra unit of production, the only relevant cost is probably the associated material cost, and such a small change in unit volume does not even have an impact on the company's ability to reduce the amount of direct labor employed during the shift. However, when the unit volume included in the analysis increases, the ability to exclude or include additional direct labor is relevant to the analysis. At larger volume levels the cost of the use of specific machines, or of entire production lines, can be considered a direct cost. At high production volumes, the entire cost of a production facility can reasonably be considered direct costs. This is not really a problem with direct costing, but one must be aware of which costs are impacted by the production volumes considered during specific direct costing analyses—ignorance of this issue may result in the wrong costs being added to or excluded from a direct cost analysis.

The main point of this discussion is that direct costing is most relevant within a relatively narrow band of production volumes. As the number of units of production covered by an analysis mounts, one must continually verify that the set of costs identified for the analysis as being direct have not expanded to include additional costs that would otherwise be considered indirect.

USING DIRECT COSTING FOR COST CONTROL

Direct costing can be of great use in controlling costs, so much so that some organizations have converted their entire internal cost control systems to a direct costing basis.

The chief benefit of direct costing in the control of costs is that volume-based costs are split away from period costs so that each can be compared to budgeted cost levels in a different manner. For example, direct costs should be itemized on a per-unit budgeted cost basis and multiplied by the number of units manufactured to arrive at the budgeted total direct cost that should apply to a specific volume of production. An example of this is shown in Exhibit 11.3. This format is necessary because direct costs vary directly with volume, whereas period costs do not. Note

EXHIBIT 11.3. Cost Control Report for Direct Costs

Actual Volume Produced: 13,412			
	Actual Cost ($)	Budgeted Cost ($)	Variance ($)
Direct material unit cost	14.02	14.00	−0.02
Direct labor unit cost	3.12	3.00	−0.12
Direct other unit cost	4.00	3.50	−0.50
Total direct unit cost	21.14	20.50	−0.64
Extended total direct cost	283,530	274,946	8,584

in the example how there is no variance for the *volume* of production in this format since the budget is based on the cost per unit rather than the quantity produced.

Period costs are best compared to a fixed budget level for each period in the format shown in Exhibit 11.4. There is no need to convey to the reader what the production volume was in the period since the same cost amounts are incurred no matter what volume was generated. This is the standard format used for *all* costs by most companies but is really usable only when comparing period costs to a fixed budget.

Also, there may be a few costs that increase only when certain volume levels are reached, in a step-cost fashion. These require a mixed budget/actual reporting format, such as the one in Exhibit 11.5. This format allows the reader to select the most appropriate column of budgeted costs, based on actual production volume, and compare it to the actual costs column to see how well costs were controlled during

EXHIBIT 11.4. Cost Control Report for Period Costs

	Actual Cost ($)	Budgeted Cost ($)	Variance ($)
Auditing fees	35,000	35,000	0
Insurance	5,400	5,000	−400
Legal fees	13,098	13,000	−98
Salaries, administration	207,892	210,000	2,108
Salaries, supervisory	78,045	82,000	3,955
Security services	3,742	2,500	−1,242
Total	**343,177**	**347,500**	**4,323**

EXHIBIT 11.5. Cost Control Report for Mixed Costs

		Production Volume: 23,200		
	Actual Cost ($)	Budgeted Volume of 10,000 Units ($)	Budgeted Volume of 20,000 Units ($)	Budgeted Volume of 30,000 Units ($)
Maintenance	100,405	80,000	100,000	120,000
Production scheduling labor	48,250	45,000	47,500	50,000
Purchasing salaries	81,000	72,000	85,000	98,000
Utilities	71,381	48,000	60,000	72,000
Workers' compensation	14,501	12,000	15,000	18,000
Total	**315,537**	**257,000**	**307,500**	**358,000**

the period. Note that this report contains no variance column. Given the large number of budget columns that address the costs at different activity levels, it would require many extra columns to detail the variances from actual for each one, so the report reader is left to determine the correct variance on her own.

Instead of using the cost control reports presented here, many companies use one report format for all three types of costs. Then it becomes nearly impossible to determine how well costs have been controlled since there is no way to relate production volumes to costs. In addition, this merged format typically calls for the allocation of overhead costs, which shifts costs from the period cost category to the direct cost area; as a result, these costs are so commingled that it is difficult to determine when or why costs were incurred or what budget they related to. This format is of little use to managers who want to know how well their company is controlling costs.

Consequently, it is clear that the more detailed set of reports shown here, which is based on the direct costing method, provides management with much better information for control purposes than the traditional single report that combines a number of different types of costs and then worsens matters by shuffling costs around under the guise of overhead allocation.

IMPACT OF DIRECT COSTING ON REPORTED FINANCIAL RESULTS

Direct costing is not allowed when reporting financial results to external entities, such as the investing public or creditors. However, it is frequently used in some capacity for internal management reports. In this section we discuss how its use impacts the reported level of profitability, as well as how it can best be used.

One type of financial report is a comparison of budgeted to actual costs, which was covered in the last section. From that discussion it is apparent that using direct costing to divide costs into different types of variance reports makes it easier to see if a company is controlling its costs. Additional benefits are derived by not obscuring the expense line items by reallocating costs among them.

A different type of financial report is the format most commonly seen in external financial reports where revenues and expenses are compared to the results from previous reporting periods. If these reports are constructed with absorption costing, it is quite likely that a large number of costs will be carried over from month to month, on the assumption that they must be matched to revenues that have not yet occurred. In this way, the period-to-period financial results appear to be smoothed out—there are no sudden spikes in expenses. A different result appears when direct costing is used to create financial statements. In this case all period costs are expensed at once, rather than carrying them forward to a future period. This results in a uniform set of period expenses incurred in each reporting period, on the assumption that these costs are truly fixed or semifixed. When there are capacity costs associated with production, these costs are also charged to the current period rather than being rolled into the cost of finished goods or work in process. Accordingly, there are sudden jumps and dips in the reported level of profitability, depending on the amount of sales completed during the reporting period. An example is shown in Exhibits 11.6 and 11.7; the first exhibit shows a financial report that utilizes absorption costing, while the second reports the same financial and production volume information but uses direct costing principles. Note how the profitability level remains relatively steady from period to period in Exhibit 11.6 but varies widely in Exhibit 11.7.

The only difference in the information presented in the two exhibits is that Exhibit 11.6 shows the cost of overhead at a standard rate of $4.00 per unit sold, with any difference between this amount and the actual cost of overhead being rolled into the cost of inventory, which is presented at the bottom of the exhibit. The direct costing format in Exhibit 11.7 dispenses with this approach, instead electing to charge all current overhead costs to expense within the current period. As a result, the profitability level in the first exhibit has a high-low range of 14% and always shows a profit, whereas the second (direct costing) exhibit reveals a high-low profitability range of 25% and shows a loss in the final accounting period. These radical differences in reported results are due solely to the treatment of overhead costs.

The erratic financial results of the direct costing method do not mean that it creates incorrect results—on the contrary, an examination of the cash flow statement

EXHIBIT 11.6. Financial Reporting with Absorption Costing

	Period 1	Period 2	Period 3
Units produced	50,000	50,000	50,000
Units sold	40,000	60,000	30,000
Price per unit ($)	28.00	28.00	28.00
Direct cost per unit ($)	15.00	15.00	15.00
Standard overhead cost per unit ($)	4.00	4.00	4.00
Actual overhead cost/period ($)	200,000	200,000	200,000
Revenue ($)	1,120,000	1,680,000	840,000
Cost of goods sold			
Materials and labor ($)	600,000	900,000	450,000
Overhead (at standard) ($)	160,000	240,000	120,000
Total cost of goods sold ($)	760,000	1,140,000	570,000
Gross margin ($)	360,000	540,000	270,000
Sales and administrative costs ($)	225,000	225,000	225,000
Profit (loss) ($)	135,000	315,000	45,000
Profit (loss) (%)	12	19	5
Overhead capitalized into inventory ($)	40,000	−40,000	80,000

EXHIBIT 11.7. Financial Reporting with Direct Costing

	Period 1	Period 2	Period 3
Units produced	50,000	50,000	50,000
Units sold	40,000	60,000	30,000
Price per unit ($)	28.00	28.00	28.00
Direct cost per unit ($)	15.00	15.00	15.00
Standard overhead cost per unit ($)	4.00	4.00	4.00
Actual overhead cost/period ($)	200,000	200,000	200,000
Revenue ($)	1,120,000	1,680,000	840,000
Cost of goods sold			
Materials and labor ($)	600,000	900,000	450,000
Overhead (at actual) ($)	200,000	200,000	200,000
Total cost of goods sold ($)	800,000	1,100,000	650,000
Gross margin ($)	320,000	580,000	190,000
Sales and administrative costs ($)	225,000	225,000	225,000
Profit (loss) ($)	$95,000	$355,000	$35,000
Profit (loss) (%)	8	21	−4
Overhead capitalized into inventory ($)	0	0	0

for the same period would reveal that the direct costing method closely mirrors the actual cash flows of the company. Since there are no allocations or capitalizations of costs under the direct costing methodology, it closely reflects how cash actually moves through a company. If these cash flows happen to be erratic, then so be it—the system shows how the company actually operates.

Another reason why the financial results reported under direct costing are better than those using absorption costing is that the information presented yields more accurate trend lines of costs incurred. For example, if a manager wants to know the cost of machine maintenance incurred over a series of consecutive reporting periods, he might have a difficult time obtaining this information under an absorption costing system. The cost may have been rolled into a machine cost pool and then further allocated to the cost of production or capitalized into inventory—which can be a tortuous path to retrace to find out the monthly cost incurred. Direct costing, however, leaves costs in the accounts in which they were first incurred, so that it is a simple matter to accumulate costs and create trend lines that are accurate over long periods of time.

Another reason for using direct costing for financial reports is that it can be used to create rapid estimates of period profits. This is easy because the information is so clearly laid out, with no allocations between expense accounts, or costs being capitalized into (or out of) inventory. A financial statement based on absorption costing, however, would require considerable amounts of investigation before its information could be used as the foundation for a financial analysis.

An unusual reason for using direct costing instead of absorption costing for financial statements is that statements based on absorption costing do not yield costs that are quite so smooth from period to period as one might think. The reason for this is that costs in each period that cannot be charged to the current period (because of excessive volumes of production) are charged instead to inventory or (less directly) to a volume variance account itemized on the balance sheet as inventory; from time to time, the amount of costs charged to inventory or a volume variance are reviewed, and any excessive amounts are charged to the current period if the amount of inventory on hand no longer justifies the capitalization of so many costs. When this charge-off occurs, there is a sudden spike in costs, which skews the reported level of profitability for the period. This charge-off has more to do with the timing of accounting staff reviews of capitalized expenses than with any particular volume of production, so it cannot be explained by changes in the activity level of the company. Also, because the analysis tends to be a complicated one, any related charge-off is also difficult to explain to nonaccountants. Thus, though direct costing has a reputation for resulting in highly variable financial results, the same can be said for absorption costing.

A final argument in favor of direct costing for financial reporting is the theory that many overhead costs are more closely related to a facility's available capacity than to the manufacture of additional units of capacity. Based on this theory, there should certainly be fewer overhead costs capitalized into inventory than is currently the case under absorption costing, and perhaps the same number as under direct costing (which is to say, none at all).

This discussion strongly favors the use of direct costing for financial reporting, but the one clear issue running against it is GAAP—this method is not allowable for external financial reporting. Though this view may change in the future, it is current practice, and so the use of direct costing must perforce be confined to reports intended strictly for internal consumption.

IMPACT OF DIRECT COSTING ON INVENTORY VALUATION

Direct costing is not allowed for the valuation of inventory under generally accepted accounting principles. The reason for this is that direct costing assumes that all period costs are charged to expense during the period, whereas GAAP state that some period costs directly tied to the production process should be allocated to any incremental increase in inventory that occurs during the period. If direct costing were used instead of this cost absorption method (which is still possible for internal accounting purposes), there would be differences in the cost of goods sold and the value of inventory.

If the amount of inventory increased during an accounting period, the amount of period costs charged to expense during the period would be less than under a direct costing system since some portion of the costs would be applied to inventory. Alternatively, if the amount of inventory on hand declined during the period, the costs that had previously been applied to this inventory would also decline, thereby forcing it to be expensed in the current period. This means that costs would be higher than under the direct costing system. Only if the level of inventory remained perfectly stable from period to period (an unlikely occurrence) would the costs charged to expense in each period be the same, irrespective of the costing method used.

Given these differences, there are a few reasons why a company might want to use direct costing for internal reporting of the valuation of inventory. One is to guard against fraud. This problem arises when a company has a history of, or wishes to avoid, situations where plant managers authorize massive overproduction, which greatly increases inventory valuations and reduces the amount of expense charged to the current period, thereby making their production facilities look inordinately profitable. By eliminating the temptation to build inventories through the capitalization of overhead costs, corporate-level managers can determine which production facilities are doing the best job of controlling costs rather than storing them in inventory.

Direct costing can also be used for inventory valuation when the cost accounting staff is so short-handed, or the accounting system so primitive, that it is difficult to compile a reasonably accurate inventory analysis for management that can track how much inventory has been charged to or taken out of the warehouse in each period and exactly what the components of these costs are. This is a problem particularly if there are constant fluctuations in the valuation of inventory from period to period, resulting in wild swings in the reported level of profitability. As a result, managers may opt to entirely avoid applying overhead costs to inventory except at the end of the fiscal year and even then may leave this chore for the external auditors to complete or at least review in detail.

Though these are limited cases in which direct costing can be used for inventory valuation, they are surprisingly common, especially the second case. Many organizations that do not regularly issue financial reports to the public prefer to avoid absorption costing of their inventory until the end of the fiscal year, and then promptly revert back to direct costing at the beginning of the next fiscal year.

CASE STUDY

The Atlanta division of the General Research and Instrumentation Company manufactures a plastic casing for an electronic compass that is assembled at the same facility. A plastic injection molding supplier has visited the plant and made an offer to construct this casing for $1.42 per unit. Would this result in improved profits for the company?

The first step is to determine which costs are relevant to the decision. The cost of the product is listed on the company's accounting records as $2.48, which comprises:

	Cost
Batch setup costs	$0.32
Direct materials	1.20
Machine depreciation	0.09
Machine maintenance	0.20
Machine operator benefits	0.15
Machine operator labor	0.35
Machine utilities	0.04
Material handling labor	0.10
Scrap	0.03
Total	$2.48

Initially the decision appears to be an easy one, for the internal cost is well above the price the supplier is willing to charge. However, before we write the purchase order to the supplier, let us review the data in a different manner by stripping out costs that would disappear at both the unit level and batch level if the casing were no longer produced internally. This analysis reveals:

	Unit Costs	Batch Costs	Other Costs
Batch setup costs		$0.32	
Direct materials	$1.20		
Machine depreciation			$0.09
Machine maintenance			0.20
Machine operator benefits			0.15
Machine operator labor			0.35
Machine utilities			0.04
Material handling labor			0.10
Scrap	0.03		
Total	$1.23	$0.32	$0.93

This further analysis reveals a somewhat different picture of the internal cost of the casing. Now we see that most of the cost elements are overhead costs related to the injection molding machine or its operator, neither of which will be eliminated if the casing is withdrawn from production and given to the supplier. Since these costs will still be present under any scenario, they should not be considered when making the make-or-buy decision. However, we are still left with the remaining two elements of the casing cost, the direct materials and the related scrap, and batch setup costs. It is evident that the material cost varies directly with the number of units produced and so is relevant to the decision. But what of the setup cost? Machine setup in this instance is performed by a highly specialized injection molding technician who supervises the installation of a new mold in the machine and verifies that the correct clamping pressure and temperature are set to produce new products. This person is paid on an hourly basis, and goes home if there is no setup work to do. Under this scenario the setup cost is a direct cost and so is relevant to the decision. If the setup person had been a salaried employee who would be paid irrespective of the presence of the casing work, then this would not have been a relevant cost.

Based on the preceding analysis, we find that both the unit- and batch-level costs of producing the compass casing are direct costs, which total $1.55. Since this cost is higher than the cost charged by the supplier, the company elects to accept the supplier's offer and outsource the production of the compass casing.

This case study demonstrates that many of the costs charged to a product are nothing more than allocations and have no relevance in determining the incremental cost of producing it.

SUMMARY

There are many situations in which a direct costing analysis can be of use to a company. It is most useful in reviewing problems with a short-term time frame for which production volumes fall within the current range of capacity. However, if a company has a large proportion of overhead costs, is considering issues with a longer-term time frame, or is looking for solutions that require significant changes in the level of capacity, the direct costing methodology does not yield accurate results. Nonetheless, when used prudently, direct costing is a valuable tool that should be carefully stored in every cost accountant's tool chest.

CHAPTER 12

Standard Costing

This chapter covers an old topic—integrating standard costing into the accounting function. This practice gained popularity early in the twentieth century, both as a means for comparing actual operating results to a standard and as a way to reduce the accounting effort required to process transactions related to the production process. With the advent of ever more powerful computing systems, there is less need to use standard costing as a labor-saving approach to accounting; this view has spawned a movement that has advocated doing away with standard costs entirely, claiming that actual costs should be used for the majority of accounting applications.

In this chapter we consider the various functions in which standard costs can be used, as well as instances where this method is no longer valid. As the reader will see, there are still situations where standard costing can be of considerable benefit, though one must now be more selective in using it than was previously the case.

PURPOSE OF STANDARD COSTS

A standard cost has a number of potential uses. A company can design its standards to apply to just one of these uses or to many, depending on its needs. The main purposes of standard costs are listed here, along with a discussion of the situations in which each use is most applicable:

- **Budgeting.** A standard can be set for any type of cost that is the amount expected to be incurred in each accounting period in the future. It can be a total dollar amount per period or a cost per unit of output that varies in total, depending on the total amount of activity that occurs. It is especially useful when a company builds tables of information relating the incurrence of different costs to specific levels of activity, so that projected changes in activity levels can be related back to precisely defined standard costs. Actual activity can then be compared to these standard costs to determine where a corporation is not doing a good job of controlling costs.

- **Variance analysis.** An adjunct to the budgeting use of standard costs is their use in determining the variances from actual costs incurred and investigate the nature of these costs. A description of the types of variances and how they are used appears in Chapter 19. Much concern has been expressed in accounting circles that too much time and effort are spent in defining and investigating variances, especially in just-in-time manufacturing environments where rapid information feedback is required.

- **Pricing.** If there is a full set of standard costs on hand, one can quickly determine the projected price of a product rather than laboriously researching actual costs, resulting in an increase in the speed of price quoting.

- **Financial closing.** It is easier to compile costs for inventories and determine the cost of goods sold if standard costs per unit are used rather than actual costs, resulting in a faster closing of the financial books at the end of each accounting period. However, since nearly all companies have converted from manual to computerized accounting systems, this method is much less of an advantage than was previously the case.

- **Cost smoothing.** Standard costing includes the use of predetermined overhead rates, which results in the incurrence of a standard amount of overhead expense in each period that conforms to the level of activity. This practice is in opposition to the immediate expensing of all overhead costs as they are incurred, which tends to result in significant swings in expenses from period to period. When standard overhead costs are used, the amount of overhead expense recognized in any given period is much smoother than it would be otherwise. However, those favoring direct costing (Chapter 11) feel that this approach hides overhead costs more properly related to the current period and so should not be carried forward to a future period despite the resulting variability in the level of overhead expense recognized.

Thus, there are several reasons for using standard costing. Though concerns have been expressed about some of the purposes noted here, it is a rare company that finds no use at all for the standard costing concept in some of its accounting activities. However, to be sure of one's need for this approach, we next address in more detail the problems that have been encountered with standard costing.

PROBLEMS WITH STANDARD COSTS

The opposition to standard costing has grown more intense over the last few years. Though the problems outlined in this section do not herald the elimination of standard costing, one should keep in mind that some of the points noted here are valid ones; consequently, standard costing must now be selectively implemented only in particular situations rather than automatically installed at every company. Here are the main problem areas to be aware of:

- **Not useful in a continuous improvement environment.** Standard costs, as noted in the next section, are designed to be the expected cost of a product or activity for some period of time into the future. This means that the expected lifetime of a standard cost is generally considered to be at least a full year, and in many cases it is not expected to change at all unless the underlying processes are altered. However, in today's increasingly common environment of continuous improvement, a standard cost may be rendered invalid by the end of the month, thereby requiring the time-consuming formulation of a new standard. Given this rapid degree of change, a case can be made for eliminating standard costs entirely.

- **Not useful for short product lives.** It takes a fair degree of effort and time to compile a standard cost. This is a problem when a product has a short life span, since the standard cost may not even be available until the product has been on the market for a few months and will be useful for only a few more months before the product is rendered obsolete and replaced. This problem occurs particularly in the high technology arena, where products may last in the market for as little as a month.

- **Does not result in rapid feedback of cost information.** The traditional cost accounting system accumulates production quantities for an entire month, compiles their standard costs, and feeds this information back to the production staff shortly after the end of the month. This is too slow for many organizations with just-in-time manufacturing systems, for they need to have costing information immediately, before their short production runs are completed. For them, perusing standard cost variances a month after a production run is simply a waste of time.

- **Does not yield information at the batch level.** Most standard costing systems accumulate costs in total for an accounting period and churn out variances that apply to the entire manufacturing operation. This approach yields no information about problems at the batch production level, which is where most issues arise. The problem can be mitigated to some extent by accumulating costs at a more detailed level.

- **Results in contrary purchasing behavior.** One of the variances resulting from a standard costing analysis is the price variance, which determines the amount of excess materials cost a company incurred in manufacturing a product. The presence of this variance forces the purchasing staff to focus a large part of its attention on lowering the price of materials. Though this may seem like a rational use of purchasing time, it can be taken too far, so that excess quantities are purchased or inferior components are acquired—all to ensure that there is no unfavorable purchase price variance.

- **Results in contrary production scheduling behavior.** The labor efficiency variance also results from a standard costing system; it itemizes the cost of excess labor time incurred by an operation. This was a closely watched variance in the days of large batch runs and a large labor component to total costs, for it gave managers an incentive to operate long production runs that were cost-effective on a per-unit basis. However, now that production runs tend to follow just-in-time principles and are of short duration, the presence of this variance gives production schedulers an incentive to schedule long production runs when they are not called for—simply in an effort to improve labor efficiency, though this is no longer a major cost item.

- **Results in contrary labor scheduling behavior.** One of the most common ways to create a positive direct labor variance is to avoid the use of direct labor entirely by bringing in employees who are officially categorized as indirect labor. The workload stays the same, but the accounting system is distorted so that the situation appears to have improved. This practice also tends to be less efficient, since indirect labor personnel may not be as well trained in production methods.

- **Perpetuates inefficiencies.** When a standard cost is compiled, the industrial engineer doing the work determines the standard amount of labor and material inefficiency and scrap currently in the production process, or that expected in the near term, and includes these costs in the standard. Organizations driving toward zero inefficiency find that the use of standard costs distracts their focus because they want their employees to eliminate *all* inefficiency, rather than allowing some inefficiency to be included in the standards.

- **Labor standards are not accurate.** In many instances the accuracy of labor costs is substantially worse than that for material costs because the designer of a standard fails to take into account a number of additional factors, such as downtime, break time, and training. Consequently, the standard cost of labor does not accurately reflect reality.

- **Shifts management focus toward labor variances.** Several of the variances generated by a standard costing system are related to direct labor. Even though the quantity of this cost has gradually declined in many companies, to the point where it is one of the smallest costs included in the production process, the existence of these variances forces managers to investigate adverse variances even if their total dollar amount is relatively minor. This issue can of course be eliminated by not reporting direct labor variances.

One cannot help but notice that the list of problems associated with standard costs mentioned in this section is longer than the list of favorable items described in the last section. Despite this disparity, there are still situations where standard costs are of great use. The main point in favor of standard costing is that it creates a benchmark against which one can compare performance. Even if the standard carries with it the possibility of being inaccurate, it is still a basis of comparison. Also, if the adverse changes in management behavior caused by the existence of direct labor variances is a problem, one can always stop reporting them to management. Further, if the current manufacturing environment is one where continuous improvement practices constantly alter actual costs, it may still be possible to locate some aspects of the production process whose costs vary so little that standards can still be constructed for them. By making these adaptations to the existing production system, one can still selectively find a place for standard costing in most organizations.

FORMULATION OF STANDARD COSTS

A number of factors go into the formulation of standard costs. First, one must determine who creates these standards. The setting of material and labor standards for products is usually the job of the industrial engineering staff, though the cost accountant may assist this department in compiling costs for the standards. A representative from the purchasing department may also be assigned to this work, since the purchasing staff can determine how raw material costs are altered at different volume levels. If standards are being created for overhead costs, the lead designer is usually the cost accountant instead of an industrial engineer since there is no need to include details of the production process in the formulation of overhead standards.

Another issue is the timing of changes in the creation of standards. The decision to update a standard is based on several factors. For example, if a company's costs rarely change (an unusual circumstance), reformulation of a standard can be undertaken perhaps as rarely as once every few years. However, given the rapid rate of cost fluctuation with which most companies now deal, a more common situation is to at least update material cost standards whenever there is a significant change in the underlying actual material costs.

The same applies to labor standards. The labor price component of a labor standard is generally changed whenever there is a bulk alteration in actual labor rates, for example, when a new union contract goes into effect. In between these periods there is no reason to alter this standard at all. However, the labor efficiency portion of a standard may need to be changed more frequently. Whenever a labor-saving device or process is installed, there is a decrease in the amount of labor needed to complete a product, which justifies a change in the standard. Given the frequency of these incremental changes, before making a change in the labor standard, the industrial engineering staff usually waits until several efficiency changes have combined to produce a significant alteration in the amount of required labor. This reduces the work of the engineering staff, while still keeping the labor standards relatively accurate.

Overhead standards are generally adjusted with much less frequency than material or labor standards. Typically, they are altered at the beginning of each fiscal year, when the accounting staff reviews and adjusts overhead rates from the previous year.

An issue that impacts the timing of all types of standards is the amount of effort required to make adjustments. This includes not only the time of the cost accounting and engineering staff, who must analyze standards, but also that of the accounting staff, who must make changes in the accounting records and explain the resulting variances to management. This is a major problem for organizations without a sufficient number of staff. Thus, even if costs change continually, it is quite likely that a company simply does not have the resources to make timely updates to standards.

Another issue that impacts the timing of changes in standard costs is the use of these costs in inventory valuation. Though there is no specific accounting rule stating that standard costs cannot be used for inventory valuation, the standards must be close enough to actual costs that there is essentially no difference between the standard cost of an inventory item and its actual cost. To ensure that this is the case, a company that uses standard cost inventory valuation must make a large number of adjustments to standard costs over the course of a year. In this case accounting rules force one to update standards with greater frequency.

One last situation that impacts the timing of standards adjustment is their use as cost controls. If this is a major purpose of standards, then it is essential that they accurately reflect actual costs rather than be outmoded standards that have not been updated for some time. If a company neglects regular updates, its standard costs will not be useful as a basis for cost control.

Having discussed who creates and adjusts standards, as well as their timing, we next address *how* standards are created. In general, any type of standard is a carefully compiled cost that ignores all past inefficiencies and instead focuses on the short-term future cost of the item in question. In this way one sets a goal that a company can attempt to attain in the short run. Formulation of this standard cost should include a consideration of these factors:

• **Learning curve.** Labor efficiencies are driven by the level of experience the production staff achieves while creating a specific product. The staff becomes more efficient as the volume of the product manufactured increases. Thus, any projected increase in production volume can be expected to result in added labor efficiencies.

- **Production volume.** All types of standards—labor, materials, and overhead—are based to some extent on the volume of projected production. For example, increased production volume results in greater purchasing volumes, which drive down the unit price for components purchased.

- **Substitute materials.** In many instances there is some substitution of materials for those listed in a product's standard bill of materials. This may be a result of periodic material shortages. If the problem arises at regular intervals, it may be necessary to include an average cost of materials in a product's standard cost that is the combined cost of the regular material and its substitute.

- **Equipment layout.** The efficiency of the workforce is strongly influenced by the layout of equipment in the production facility. If the distances between machines are considerable, additional labor costs will be involved when materials are moved to the next machine in the sequence. This situation can also impact material scrap rates because materials are batched before they are moved the long distance to the next machine; scrap can build up in these batches before anyone discovers it and corrects the problem.

- **Equipment condition.** An old machine processes materials less efficiently than a new one if only because it requires more frequent adjustment. This impacts the efficiency of the labor force and may increase material scrap rates.

- **Inventory accuracy.** If the inventory system does not yield accurate inventory tracking information, there are likely to be material shortages from time to time that stop production. This in turn reduces the efficiency of direct labor, which must either wait for new materials to be found or shift to a different machine to perform other work.

- **Work instructions.** If there are no instructions attached to a job, or if these instructions are difficult to interpret, the direct labor staff may not be able to set up or run a job with the optimal level of efficiency.

- **Production scheduling system.** The method for scheduling jobs throughout the production facility has a major impact on the amount of production that can be run through a plant. For example, when there is a focus on producing small batches of products rather than on long runs, more time is devoted to setting up and breaking down jobs, which reduces the time available for production.

- **Speed of equipment setup.** Much of the time required for a production run is taken up by switching the tooling on a machine. A company that constantly works to reduce this setup time can devote more of the total time of a production run to actually producing product, which reduces its cost.

- **Test runs.** It may not be possible to estimate a standard for a new product without first operating a test run of the production process and estimating production times from this test. Other alternatives are to use engineering studies or an analysis of past experience, adjusted for future expected conditions.

- **Anticipated collective bargaining results.** The standard labor price can be reasonably estimated for companies with unions since there is a historical record of the rates that other companies have settled for in the past.

Clearly, there are many factors to consider when creating a standard cost. Though not all the information sources noted here will be used to develop a single standard, a combination of sources will probably be used for the creation of each one. By using multiple sources of information, such as an engineering study or historical records, one can compare and contrast information, which is helpful in finding and eliminating data that is clearly inaccurate or inconsistent.

A final factor to consider when generating a standard cost is the type of standard to be published. Should it be a theoretical standard, one that reflects past results, or perhaps one that is just attainable? Some issues related to each perspective are:

- **Theoretical standard.** This is a standard cost that can be reached only if the company runs its operations perfectly—machines never break down, the staff is always on hand, there is no scrap, and production volumes are maximized. While it is nice to know what the absolute lowest cost can be, using such a cost as a standard can frustrate the staff since it can never hope to match this standard, much less surpass it. Also, if only the standard costs of products are charged to inventory, all excess costs—which may be considerable with this type of standard—will be charged to the current period, skewing the reported financial results.

- **Historical standard.** This standard cost is essentially the average of costs actually experienced in the recent past. This type of standard closely reflects near-term costs, especially if there are no significant changes in the workforce or production systems. However, this standard has a great deal of inefficiency built into it, which gives employees no incentive to surpass it by achieving greater efficiency.

- **Attainable standard.** This standard cost is lower than the historical standard but not as low as the theoretical standard. It incorporates a reasonably achievable level of inefficiency, which roughly corresponds to the expected increases in efficiencies the facility can be expected to attain in the near term. With this standard employees have a reasonable cost goal as their target. Also, if attainable standard costs are used to compile the cost of inventory, the amount charged to inventory will be somewhat lower than in the case of historical standards but higher than for theoretical standards.

Of the various types of standards considered here, the recommended one is the attainable standard, for it represents a cost that the organization will not find hopelessly out of reach (i.e., a theoretical standard) nor will it be too easy to match (i.e., the historical standard). Instead, it is one that can be reached through the implementation of changes that are reasonably achievable.

STANDARD COSTS FOR PRICING

As noted at the beginning of this chapter, price quotes can be compiled much more quickly with standard costs than with actual ones because actual costs can require a great deal of research. For example, if a customer requests a quote on an order size of 20,000 units, the sales department must call for an emergency meeting with the cost accountant to lay out the volume requirements of the quote; the cost accountant must then find some evidence of previous component part purchase volumes in the same range or ask the purchasing staff to research this information for her. Then she must go to the production scheduling department to determine the typical setup time for the production run required to produce the requested product and consult the production manager or industrial engineering staff about the required machine and assembly effort required to create the product. Finally, she must go back to the accounting department to determine what the overhead charge will be. Then she compiles the collected cost estimates and takes them to the sales department—where everyone is wondering why it took so long to provide the quote.

A much simpler approach is to create a set of standard costs that are readily accessible by the sales department and which can be plugged into a standard quoting model that itemizes all the costs of the order. The salesperson answering the customer's request may even be able to keep the customer on the phone, while entering information in the quote model, and return a quote to the customer at once. This method reduces the price quoting time from days to minutes.

There are two key factors to consider when using this type of quoting model. First, any significant changes in actual costs must be updated in the standard costs fed into the quoting model as soon as possible so that quotes are not based on faulty data. This problem is most acute for products with a large proportion of purchased parts, since a modest change in a price charged to the company by a supplier will result in a significant change in profits if the cost change is not immediately passed on to the customer. The second and much larger problem is that the database of standard costs must include standards for different ranges of production volume. For example, the setup cost for any production run is the same, but the cost of the setup is spread over many more units when the run is a large one, thereby reducing the cost per unit. Similarly, the cost of purchased parts drops when they are purchased in large volumes for a large customer order. Also, labor efficiencies increase for a large production run since workers require less time per unit when many units are being produced. Given the impact of volume on standard costs, multiple standard costs for a broad range of potential volumes should be stored in the computer system. Without this information the sales staff is able to issue quotes for only a narrow range of order quantities, reducing much of the efficiency obtained by using standard costs for product pricing.

STANDARD COSTS FOR BUDGETING

The most obvious use of standard costs is in budgeting. A standard cost is used as the basis of comparison for actual costs incurred during an accounting period. This is an excellent use since there must be some standard against which an actual cost can be compared to ensure that incurred costs fall within a range predetermined to be satisfactory.

For budgeting purposes the existing standard cost for products and activities must be updated to reflect expected costs in the period against which the standard cost is matched. For example, if the current rental rate per month is $80,000 but the lease agreement clearly specifies that the rate will increase to $92,000 per month in the budget period, the budgeting standard set for that month must be $92,000. If numerous changes in the standard are expected during the budget period, the budget should reflect these changes. Another way to budget for this situation is to keep the standard amount the same for the entire set of budgeted periods but to add a budgeted variance for periods in which a change from the standard is anticipated.

The use of standard costs in a budget has a unique advantage in that these costs are not incorporated directly into accounting transactions through the use of variances, as can be the case for cost of goods sold or inventory transactions (as described in a later section). Instead, they are keypunched into a separate file containing only budget information. This file is not used in accounting transactions but is simply added to financial reports that compare actual costs to budgeted costs.

STANDARD COSTS FOR INVENTORY

A common use for standard costs is to apply them to a company's inventory. By doing so, one can rapidly determine the cost of inventory just by having a firm grasp on the quantities of inventory on hand rather than the individual actual cost of each item. This approach simplified the work of cost accountants for a number of years, especially before the advent of computer systems, which make it much easier to trace the actual cost of a purchased item. Despite the use of computers, this method is still a valid one, for tracing actual costs through work in process is quite difficult—using standard costs in this area is most helpful in quickly compiling costs that are reasonably accurate. The main issue here is that the speed and efficiency with which the accounting staff can value all portions of an inventory are greatly improved by the use of standard costs.

It may not be necessary to use standard costs for inventory valuation if a company has a small inventory or uses just-in-time systems. In both cases there is so little inventory on hand, or it passes through the facility so quickly, that its value is no longer a significant element of the balance sheet and so requires little attention. However, most companies still have thousands of parts in stock or have complex products that spend a great deal of time moving through the production process. For these organizations standard costs are still the best approach for valuing inventory.

One issue that arises when standard costs are used for inventory valuation is the frequency with which changes should be made in the standards. Changes should be made as often as is necessary to ensure that total actual costs closely approximate total standard costs. This rule is based on the requirement that standard costs can be used for external financial reporting purposes only if they closely match actual costs. Thus, many organizations undertake a comprehensive comparison of standard costs to actual costs as often as once a month. Since this level of frequency invalidates the reason for using standards—they require less work—a better approach is to determine which elements of a standard cost comprise the bulk of the total cost and then track these specific costs with great frequency while other costs are reviewed at greater intervals. For example, a piece of hard candy is made almost entirely of sugar and corn syrup, with all other materials comprising less than 2% of the total cost. Therefore, it is reasonable to adjust the standard cost of this product for just these two components at regular intervals and leave the remaining costs for an annual review.

Another way to save labor when changing standard costs is to cluster components by commodity code for reporting purposes and then review them at the commodity level with different amounts of frequency, depending on which commodities are the most volatile in price.

Once standards are in place, a company will find that variances from the standard that inevitably arise must be charged to the current period's cost of goods sold or stored in inventory. Which is the correct method? From an external financial reporting perspective, actual costs should be used to value inventory, and the actual cost is the standard cost plus (or minus) any related variances. From this point of view, variances should be rolled into the cost of inventory. However, any excess cost over a standard can be considered a wasted cost since the standard cost represents the amount that should be expended during purchasing and production. According to this view, waste should be charged to the current period. The decision of where to put variances is not a small one because charging variances to the current period alters the level of reported profits, which in turn impacts the amount of income taxes paid. The preferred method is to avoid charging variances to inventory. This reasoning involves not just avoiding taxes but also the efficiency of the accounting staff, for charging variances to inventory requires the maintenance of a separate variance inventory account, which must be reconciled in each reporting period. In short, it is easier to charge variances to the cost of goods sold.

The issue of whether or not to store variances from standards in the inventory can be reduced in scope by using standard costs only for certain stages of inventory. For example, raw materials can be carried on the accounting books at actual cost, while work-in-process costs are charged as standard costs. This is a particularly appealing way to handle the problem, especially if there is already a computer system in place that does an adequate job of tracking the actual cost of goods purchased. The reason for using only standard costs for work-in-process activities is that they involve many activities taking place over a short time frame, which results in a large quantity of cost-related information that must be handled by the cost accounting staff whenever something moves through the production process. By switching to standard costs for just this part of the inventory, a cost accountant can reduce the paperwork needed to determine the actual added cost of WIP activities.

Another method is to calculate the cost of all types of inventory using standard costs, but also to determine variances from the standard at all stages of the production process, and adjust the inventory balance continuously so that the total cost of inventory recorded on the books is essentially the same as its actual cost. For example, a component is purchased and received, at which point it is recorded at its actual cost. Before the component travels to the shop floor for inclusion in the production process, its standard cost is compared to the actual cost and a variance is immediately recorded. Once the component finishes running through the production process, any additional standard costs are compared to actual costs, and any further variances are disposed of. This may seem like a great deal of work, and it certainly is. However, it has the benefit of providing managers with immediate knowledge of variances and also makes it possible to issue accurate daily financial statements. These benefits are considerable but must be weighed against the substantial cost of conducting daily examinations of variances.

A special case sometimes arises when a standard cost is changed to such a large extent that the incremental difference in standard costs causes a significant change in the recorded value of inventory. For example, a new union contract is approved that increases the labor rate by 10%. When labor standards are increased to reflect this change, the value of the inventory suddenly jumps since much of the inventory contains some element of labor cost whose value has now increased. To offset this problem, one can determine the value of the inventory before making a standard cost change, calculate the difference after the change, and alter the recorded value of the inventory to offset the change caused by the alteration in standards. Since there may be many standard cost changes every month, it is not efficient to complete such an analysis for every change. Instead, the adjustment effort should be reserved for only the largest changes. All other alterations tend to be too small to warrant a special costing adjustment.

One case in which the use of standard costs is *not* acceptable is in the costing of a specific product that will be charged to a customer at a price having a direct relationship to the costs incurred to produce it. For example, the government may offer a company a cost-plus contract to create a customized item. The company must compile its actual costs, add a predetermined margin percentage, and bill this total to the government. There is no standard cost because the product is a unique one that requires the compilation of actual costs. Since actual costs must be tracked, it would be a duplication of labor to create standard costs, too.

In this section we have discussed the situations where standard costs can reduce the labor required to record the valuation of inventory, as well as the (more limited) instances where they do not result in an appreciable reduction in the accountant's work. We have also described the reasoning behind the treatment of variances from standard. One must carefully consider all these factors before deciding whether to use standard costs for inventory valuation and to what extent they should be used.

STANDARD COST ENTRY

How are standard costs incorporated into the accounting system? Thus far we have talked about swapping actual and standard costs into and out of an accounting system as though they are easily substituted car parts—the car runs, no matter which part is installed. In truth the methodology is somewhat different.

Standard costs are compiled in a separate file from all other accounting transactional data. For example, the cost of goods sold is compiled in the accounting system by accumulating the total cost of components purchased during the period, which is stored in the accounts payable file. Labor costs for the period are accumulated from the payroll system, while other overhead costs are drawn from accounts payable records. These are all actual costs and roughly match the amount of cash a company has expended to acquire the resources needed to manufacture its products. Meanwhile, standard costs are accumulated by engineering, purchasing, and cost accounting personnel in an entirely different set of files. At no time are the standard and actual cost files merged.

At the end of the reporting period, the number of units of production is accumulated and multiplied by the standard cost of each unit. The total is then compared to the accumulated actual cost of production (net of any inventory changes). If there is a difference between the two total costs, the total standard cost is assumed to be the correct amount of cost of goods sold; any shortfall or overage in actual costs compared to the standard amount is charged to a variance account. These variances are then broken down into efficiency, price, and volume variances, and further comparisons are then made between the actual costs incurred and the standard cost file. The mechanics of variance investigation is explored in more detail in Chapter 19.

This approach maintains the "purity" of accounting transactions since actual costs are always recorded for every transaction. It is only when these actual costs are compared to a baseline cost (the standard) that they are split into variances which are recorded in separate accounts.

SUMMARY

In this chapter we saw that there are a number of situations, primarily related to production lines with continuous improvement efforts in place or short product cycles, where actual costs cannot be used effectively. However, cases where it cannot provide some benefit, even if only in a limited form, are quite rare. Many cost accountants find that standard costs are still valuable for product quotes, inventory valuation, budgeting, and variance analysis. They are also beneficial in reducing the labor associated with the analysis and use of actual costs.

CHAPTER 13

LIFO, FIFO, and Average Costing

This chapter could also be called "Cost Flow Assumptions" because that is the essence of its content. Cost flows describe the order in which costs are incurred. The reason why cost flows are important is that the cost incurred for an item may change over time, so that different costs appear in the accounting records for the same item. In this situation, how does the cost accountant handle these costs? Are the earliest costs charged off first, or the later ones? Or is there an alternative approach that avoids the issue? In this chapter we look at the last-in first-out, first-in first-out, and average costing systems and how each one is used under a different assumption of cost flows.

LAST-IN FIRST-OUT METHOD

In a supermarket the shelves are stocked several rows deep with products. Shoppers walk by and pick products from the front row. If the stock clerk is lazy, he will then add products to the front row locations from which products were just taken rather than shifting the oldest products to the front row and putting the new ones in the back. This concept of always taking the newest products first is called last-in first-out. It is illustrated numerically in Exhibit 13.1, where we list a number of inventory purchases and usages on the first column and note various calculations across the top row.

In the first row of Exhibit 13.1, we purchase 500 units of a product with part number BK0043 on May 3, 2000 (as noted in the first row of data), and use 450 units

EXHIBIT 13.1. LIFO Valuation Example

LIFO Costing: Part Number BK0043

Date Purchased (1)	Quantity Purchased (2)	Cost per Unit ($) (3)	Monthly Usage (4)	Net Inventory Remaining (5)	Cost of 1st Inventory Layer ($) (6)	Cost of 2nd Inventory Layer ($) (7)	Cost of 3rd Inventory Layer ($) (8)	Cost of 4th Inventory Layer ($) (9)	Extended Inventory Cost ($) (10)
05/03/00	500	10.00	450	50	(50 × 10.00)				500
06/04/00	1000	9.58	350	700	(50 × 10.00)	(650 × 9.58)			6727
07/11/00	250	10.65	400	550	(50 × 10.00)	(500 × 9.58)			5290
08/01/00	475	10.25	350	675	(50 × 10.00)	(500 × 9.58)	(125 × 10.25)		6571
08/30/00	375	10.40	400	650	(50 × 10.00)	(500 × 9.58)	(100 × 10.25)		6315
09/09/00	850	9.50	700	800	(50 × 10.00)	(500 × 9.58)	(100 × 10.25)	(150 × 9.50)	7740
12/12/00	700	9.75	900	600	(50 × 10.00)	(500 × 9.58)	(50 × 9.58)		5769
02/08/01	650	9.85	800	450	(50 × 10.00)	(400 × 9.58)			4332
05/07/01	200	10.80	0	650	(50 × 10.00)	(400 × 9.58)	(200 × 10.80)		6492
09/23/01	600	9.85	750	500	(50 × 10.00)	(400 × 9.58)	(50 × 9.85)		4825

during that month, leaving 50 units. These 50 units were all purchased at a cost of $10.00 each, so we itemize them in column 6 as our first layer of inventory costs for this product. In the next row of data, we see that an additional 1000 units were bought on June 4, 2000, of which only 350 units were used. This leaves an additional 650 units at a purchase price of $9.58, which we place in the second inventory layer, as noted in column 7. In the third row we have a net decrease in the amount of inventory, so this reduction comes out of the second (or last) inventory layer in column 7; the earliest layer, as described in column 6, remains untouched since it was the first layer of costs added and will not be used until all the other inventory has been eliminated. The exhibit continues through seven more transactions, at one point increasing to four layers of inventory costs.

There are several factors to consider before implementing a LIFO system. They are:

- **Many layers.** The LIFO cost flow approach can result in a large number of inventory layers, as shown in the exhibit. Though this is not important when a computerized accounting system is used that automatically tracks a large number of such layers, it can be burdensome if the cost layers are manually tracked.

- **Alters the inventory valuation.** If there are significant changes in product costs over time, the earliest inventory layers may contain costs that are wildly different from market conditions in the current period, which could result in the recognition of unusually high or low costs if these cost layers are ever accessed.

- **Reduces taxes payable in periods of rising costs.** In an inflationary environment costs that are charged to the cost of goods sold as soon as they are incurred result in a higher cost of goods sold and a lower level of profitability, which in turn results in a lower tax liability. This is the principal reason why LIFO is used by most companies.

- **Requires consistent usage for all reporting.** Under Internal Revenue Service (IRA) rules, if a company uses LIFO to value its inventory for tax reporting purposes, it must do the same for its external financial reports. The result of this rule is that a company cannot report lower earnings for tax purposes and higher earnings for all other purposes by using an alternative inventory valuation method. However, it is still possible to mention what profits would have been if some other method had been used, but only in the form of a footnote appended to the financial statements. If financial reports are generated only for internal management consumption, any valuation method can be used.

- **Interferes with the implementation of just-in-time systems.** As noted in the last item, clearing out the final cost layers of a LIFO system can result in unusual cost-of-goods-sold figures. If these results cause a significant skewing of reported profitability, company management may be put in the unusual position of opposing the implementation of advanced manufacturing concepts, such as just-in-time, that reduce or eliminate inventory levels (with an attendant highly favorable improvement in the amount of working capital requirements).

In short, LIFO is used primarily for reducing a company's income tax liability. This single focus can cause problems, such as too many cost layers, an excessively low inventory valuation, and a fear of inventory reductions due to the recognition of inventory cost layers that may contain low per-unit costs, which result in high levels of recognized profit and therefore a higher tax liability. Given these issues, one should carefully consider the utility of tax avoidance before implementing a LIFO cost layering system.

FIRST-IN FIRST-OUT METHOD

A computer manufacturer knows that the component parts it purchases are subject to rapid rates of obsolescence, sometimes becoming worthless in a month or two. Accordingly, it is sure to use up the oldest items in stock first rather than running the risk of scrapping them a short way into the future. For this type of environment, the FIFO method is the ideal way to deal with the flow of costs. This method assumes that the oldest parts in stock are always used first, which means that their associated old costs are used first as well.

The concept is best illustrated with an example, which we show in Exhibit 13.2. In the exhibit we list the same data previously used for parts purchases and use in Exhibit 13.1, but now we account for the costs using FIFO instead of LIFO. In the first row we create a single layer of inventory that results in 50 units of inventory at a per-unit cost of $10.00. So far, the extended cost of the inventory is the same as under LIFO, but that changes as we proceed to the second row of data. In this row we have a monthly inventory usage of 350 units, which FIFO assumes will use the entire stock of 50 inventory units left over at the end of the preceding month, as well as 300 units purchased in the current month. This wipes out the first layer of inventory, leaving a single new layer composed of 700 units at a cost of $9.58 per unit. In the third row there are 400 units of usage, which again come from the first inventory layer, shrinking it down to just 300 units. However, since extra stock was purchased in the same period, we now have an extra inventory layer made up of 250 units at a cost of $10.65 per unit. The rest of the exhibit proceeds using the same FIFO layering assumptions.

Several factors must be considered before implementing a FIFO costing system:

- **Fewer inventory layers.** The FIFO system generally results in fewer layers of inventory costs in the inventory database. For example, the LIFO model in Exhibit 13.1 contained four layers of costing data, whereas the FIFO model in Exhibit 13.2, which used exactly the same data, resulted in no more than two inventory layers. This conclusion generally holds true because a LIFO system

EXHIBIT 13.2. FIFO Valuation Example

FIFO Costing: Part Number BK0043

Date Purchased (1)	Quantity Purchased (2)	Cost per Unit ($) (3)	Monthly Usage (4)	Net Inventory Remaining (5)	Cost of 1st Inventory Layer ($) (6)	Cost of 2nd Inventory Layer ($) (7)	Cost of 3rd Inventory Layer ($) (8)	Extended Inventory Cost ($) (9)
05/03/00	500	10.00	450	50	(50 × 10.00)			500
06/04/00	1000	9.58	350	700	(700 × 9.58)			6706
07/11/00	250	10.65	400	550	(300 × 9.58)	(250 × 10.65)		5537
08/01/00	475	10.25	350	675	(200 × 10.65)	(475 × 10.25)		6999
08/30/00	375	10.40	400	650	(275 × 10.40)	(375 × 10.40)		6760
09/09/00	850	9.50	700	800	(800 × 9.50)			7600
12/12/00	700	9.75	900	600	(600 × 9.75)			5850
02/08/01	650	9.85	800	450	(450 × 9.85)			4433
05/07/01	200	10.80	0	650	(450 × 9.85)	(200 × 10.80)		6593
09/23/01	600	9.85	750	500	(500 × 9.85)			4925

leaves some layers of costs completely untouched for long time periods if inventory levels do not drop, whereas a FIFO system continually clears out old layers of costs so that multiple costing layers do not have a chance to accumulate.

- **Reduces taxes payable in periods of declining costs.** Though it is unusual to see declining inventory costs, this sometimes occurs in industries where there is ferocious price competition among suppliers or high rates of innovation that in turn lead to cost reductions. In such cases, using the earliest costs first results in immediate recognition of the highest possible expense, which reduces the reported profit level and therefore reduces taxes payable.

- **Shows higher profits in periods of rising costs.** Since it charges off the earliest costs first, any recent increase in costs is stored in inventory rather than being immediately recognized. This results in higher levels of reported profits, though the attendant income tax liability is also higher.

- **Less risk of outdated costs in inventory.** Because old costs are used first in a FIFO system, there is no way for old, outdated costs to accumulate in inventory. Thus, the management group does not have to worry about the adverse impact of inventory reductions on reported levels of profit, either with excessively high or excessively low charges to the cost of goods sold. This avoids the dilemma noted earlier for LIFO, where just-in-time systems may not be implemented if the result will be a dramatically different cost of goods sold.

In short, the FIFO cost layering system tends to result in storage of the most recently incurred costs in inventory and higher levels of reported profits. It is most useful for companies whose main concern is reporting high profits rather than reducing income taxes.

AVERAGE COSTING METHOD

The average costing method is calculated exactly in accordance with its name—it involves a weighted average of the costs in inventory. It has the singular advantage of not requiring a database that itemizes the many potential layers of inventory at the different costs at which they were acquired. Instead, the weighted average of all units in stock is determined, at which point *all* the units in stock are accorded this weighted average value. When parts are used from stock, they are all issued at the same weighted average cost. If new units are added to stock, the cost of the additions are added to the weighted average of all existing items in stock, which results in a new, slightly modified weighted average for *all* the parts in inventory (both old and new).

This system has no particular advantage in relation to income taxes since it does not skew the recognition of income based on trends in either increasing or declining costs. This makes it a good choice for organizations that do not want to deal with tax planning. It is also useful for small inventory valuations, where there would not be any significant change in the reported level of income even if the LIFO or FIFO method were used.

Exhibit 13.3 illustrates the weighted average calculation for inventory valuations using a series of 10 purchases of inventory. There is a maximum of one purchase per month, with use (reductions from stock) also occurring in most months. Each of the columns in the exhibit shows how the average cost is calculated after each purchase and use transaction.

We begin the illustration with the first row of calculations, which shows that we have purchased 500 units of item BK0043 on May 3, 2000. These units cost $10.00 per unit. During the month in which the units were purchased, 450 units were sent to production, leaving 50 units in stock. Since there has been only one purchase, we can easily calculate (column 7) that the total inventory valuation is $500 by multiplying the unit cost of $10.00 (column 3) by the number of units left in stock (column 5). So far, we have a per-unit valuation of $10.00.

Next we proceed to the second row of the exhibit, where we have purchased another 1000 units of BK0043 on June 4, 2000. This purchase was less expensive since the purchasing volume was larger, so the per-unit cost for this purchase is only $9.58. Only 350 units are sent to production during the month, so 700 units are now in stock, of which 650 are added from the most recent purchase. To determine the new weighted average cost of the total inventory, we first determine the extended cost of this newest addition to the inventory. As noted in column 7, we arrive at $6227 by multiplying the value in column 3 by the value in column 6. We then add this amount to the existing total inventory valuation ($6227 plus $500) to arrive at the new extended inventory cost of $6727 (column 8). Finally, we divide this new extended cost in column 8 by the total number of units now in stock (column 5) to arrive at our new per-unit cost of $9.61.

The third row reveals an additional inventory purchase of 250 units on July 11, 2000, but more units are sent to production during that month than are bought, so the total number of units in inventory drops to 550 (column 5). This inventory reduction requires no review of inventory layers, as was the case for the LIFO and FIFO calculations. Instead, we simply charge off the 150 unit reduction at the average per-unit cost of $9.61. As a result, the ending inventory valuation drops to $5286, with the same per-unit cost of $9.61. Thus, reductions in inventory quantities under the average costing method require little calculation—just charge off the requisite number of units at the current average cost.

The remaining rows of the exhibit repeat the concepts just noted, alternatively adding units to and deleting them from stock. Though there are a number of columns in this exhibit to be examined, it is really a simple concept to understand and work with. A typical computerized accounting system performs all these calculations automatically.

EXHIBIT 13.3. Average Costing Valuation Example

Average Costing: Part Number BK0043

Date Purchased (1)	Quantity Purchased (2)	Cost per Unit ($) (3)	Monthly Usage (4)	Net Inventory Remaining (5)	Net Change in Inventory During Period (6)	Extended Cost of New Inventory Layer (7)	Extended Inventory Cost ($) (8)	Average Inventory Cost/Unit ($) (9)
05/03/00	500	10.00	450	50	50	500	500	10.00
06/04/00	1000	9.58	350	700	650	6227	6727	9.61
07/11/00	250	10.65	400	550	−150	0	5286	9.61
08/01/00	475	10.25	350	675	125	1281	6567	9.73
08/30/00	375	10.40	400	650	−25	0	6324	9.73
09/09/00	850	9.50	700	800	150	1425	7749	9.69
12/12/00	700	9.75	900	600	−200	0	5811	9.69
02/08/01	650	9.85	800	450	−150	0	4359	9.69
05/07/01	200	10.80	0	650	200	2160	6519	10.03
09/23/01	600	9.85	750	500	−150	0	5014	10.03

SUMMARY

An examination of a company's flow of costs will result in the decision to value its inventories based on the LIFO, FIFO, or average costing concept. The LIFO method is the most complex, resulting in reduced profit recognition and a lower income tax liability in periods of rising inventory costs. The FIFO method is almost as complex but tends to result in fewer inventory cost layers; it reports higher profits in periods of rising inventory costs and so has higher attendant tax liabilities. The average costing concept avoids the entire layering issue by creating a rolling average of costs without the use of any cost layers; it tends to provide reported profit figures between those that would be described using the LIFO and the FIFO methods. As more companies reduce their inventory levels with advanced manufacturing techniques such as material requirements planning (Chapter 26) and just-in-time (Chapter 27), they will find that the reduced amount of inventory left on hand makes the choice of a cost flow concept less relevant.

CHAPTER 14

Throughput Costing

Every now and then, a completely new idea comes along that can be described as refreshing, disturbing, or both. Within the accounting profession, throughput accounting is that idea. It originated in the 1980s in the writings of Eliyahu Goldratt, an Israeli physicist. It is based on the concept that a company must determine its overriding goal and then create a system that clearly defines the main capacity constraint that allows it to maximize that goal. The changes this causes in an accounting system are startling.

THROUGHPUT DEFINITIONS

A few new terms are used in throughput costing, so we define them before delving into the throughput model. They are:

- **Throughput.** This is the contribution margin left after a product's price is reduced by the amount of its totally variable costs (explained in the next item). There is no attempt to allocate overhead costs to a product nor to assign any semivariable costs to it. As a result, the amount of throughput for most products tends to be high.

- **Totally variable costs.** This cost is incurred only if a product is created. In many instances this means that only direct materials are considered a totally variable cost. Direct labor is not totally variable unless employees are paid only if a product is produced. The same rule applies to all other costs, so there are no overhead costs in the "totally variable cost" category.

- **Capacity constraint.** This is a very important concept in throughput accounting. It is a resource within a company that limits its total output. For example, it may be a machine that can produce only a specified amount of a key component in a given time period, thereby keeping overall sales from expanding beyond the maximum capacity of that machine. It may be the sales staff, which is not large enough to bring in all possible customer orders. It may even be a raw material of which there is not enough to ensure that all orders can be filled. There may be more than one capacity constraint in a company, but rarely more than one for a specific product or product line.

- **Operating expenses.** This is the sum total of all company expenses, excluding totally variable expenses. Of particular note is that throughput accounting does not care if a cost is semivariable, fixed, or allocated—all costs that are not totally variable are lumped together for the calculation model shown in the next section. This group of expenses is considered the price a company pays to ensure that it maintains its current level of capacity.

- **Investment.** This definition is the same as the one found under standard accounting rules. However, there is a particular emphasis on a company's investment in working capital (especially inventory), as we will see shortly.

We now use these definitions to create the throughput accounting model in the next section.

THROUGHPUT MODEL

The primary focus of throughput costing is on how to force the most throughput dollars as possible through the capacity constraint, pure and simple. It does this by first determining the throughput dollars per minute of every production job scheduled to run through the capacity constraint and rearranging the order of production priority so that the products with the highest throughput dollars per minute are produced first. The system is based on the supposition that only a certain amount of production can be squeezed through a bottleneck operation, so the production that yields the highest margin must come first in order of manufacturing priority to ensure that profits are maximized. The concept is most easily demonstrated in the example shown in Exhibit 14.1.

In the example there are four types of products a company can sell. Each requires some machining time on the company's capacity constraint, which is the circuit board manufacturing process (CBMP). The first item is a 19-inch color television, which requires 10 minutes of the CBMP's time. The television sells for $150.00

EXHIBIT 14.1. Throughput Model*

Maximum Constraint Time: **62,200**

Product	Throughput ($/min of constraint)	Required Constraint Usage (min)	Unit Demand/Actual Production	Cumulative Constraint Utilization	Cumulative Throughput/Product ($)
19-in. color TV	8.11	10	1,000/1,000	10,000	81,100
100-W stereo	7.50	8	2,800/2,800	22,400	168,000
5-in. LCD TV	6.21	12	500/500	6,000	37,260
50-in. high-definition TV	5.00	14	3,800/1,700	23,800	119,000
			Throughput total		$405,360
			Operating expense total		$375,000
			Profit		$30,360
			Profit percentage		7.5%
			Investment		$500,000
			Return on investment		6.1%

Note: Adapted from *Throughput Accounting* (p. 44), by T. Corbett, 1998, Great Barrington, MA: North River Press.

and has associated direct materials of $68.90, which gives it a throughput of $81.10. We then divide the throughput of $81.10 by the 10 minutes of processing time per unit on the capacity constraint to arrive at the throughput dollars per minute of $8.11 shown in the second column of Exhibit 14.1. We then calculate the throughput per minute for the other three products and sort them in high-low order based on which ones contribute the most throughput per minute. This leaves the 19-inch television at the top of the list. Next we multiply the unit demand for each item by the time required to move it through the capacity constraint point. We do not care about the total production time for each item; only the time required to push it through the bottleneck. Then we determine the total amount of time during which the capacity constraint can be operated, which in the example is 62,200 minutes and is noted at the top of the example. We then fill in the total number of minutes required to produce each product in the fifth column, which also shows that we do not have enough time available at the capacity constraint to complete the available work for the high-definition television, which has the lowest priority. Then, by multiplying the throughput per minute by the number of minutes for each product and multiplying the result by the total number of units produced, we arrive at the total throughput for the entire production process for the period, $405,360. However, we are not finished yet. We must still subtract from the total throughput the sum of all the operating expenses for the facility. After they are subtracted from the total throughput, we have achieved a profit of 7.5% and a return on investment of 6.1%. This is the basic throughput accounting model.

So far, this looks like an ordinary analysis of how much money a company can earn from the production of a specific set of products. However, there is more here than is at first apparent. The issue is best explained with another example. Let us say that the cost accounting manager arrives on the scene, does a thorough costing analysis of all four products in the preceding exhibit, and determines that, after all overhead costs are properly allocated, the high-definition television actually has the highest gross margin and the 19-inch television has the least. The relative positions of the other two products do not change. The cost accounting manager's summary of the product costs appears in Exhibit 14.2.

EXHIBIT 14.2. Fully Absorbed Product Costs

Product Description	Price ($)	Totally Variable Cost ($)	Overhead Allocation ($)	Gross Margin ($)
19-in. color TV	150.00	68.90	49.20	31.90
100-W stereo	125.50	65.50	18.00	38.00
5-in. LCD TV	180.00	105.48	41.52	33.00
50-in. high-definition TV	900.00	830.00	20.00	50.00

According to the cost accounting scenario, we should actually be producing as many high-definition television sets as possible. To test this theory we duplicate the throughput analysis shown earlier in Exhibit 14.1, but this time we move the high-definition television to the top of the list and produce all 3800 units that are on order, while dropping the 19-inch television to the bottom of the list and produce only as many units as are possible after all other production has been completed. All the other variables stay the same. This analysis is shown in Exhibit 14.3.

According to this analysis, which is based on best cost allocation principles, where we have carefully used activity-based costing to ensure that overhead is closely matched to actual activities, we have altered the mix of products and realized a net *reduction* in profits of $53,360! How can this be possible?

This outcome can be traced to three major problems with the traditional cost accounting method, all of which are corrected through the use of throughput accounting. All three factors contributed to the problem just noted in Exhibit 14.3. The first is that we cannot really allocate overhead costs to products and expect to use the resulting information in any meaningful way for incremental decisions of any kind. To do so would be to make the erroneous assumption that overhead costs vary directly with every unit of a product produced or sold. In reality the only cost that varies directly with a product is the cost of its direct material. That is all. Even direct labor is no longer so direct. In how many companies does the staff go home immediately after the last product is completed? Instead, the staff is employed on various projects during downtime periods so that experienced employees are available for work the next day. There is an even less tenuous linkage between machine costs and products. Does a company immediately sell a machine if there is one less unit of production running through it? Of course not. The machine sits on the factory floor and accumulates depreciation and preventive maintenance costs until some other job comes along that requires its services. In short, nearly all the costs of any company can be lumped into a general category called "operating expenses" or something similar. These are simply the costs that a company incurs to maintain a given level of capacity rather than a disaggregated group of costs that are closely tied to specific products. The reason why this concept has such a large bearing on Exhibit 14.3 is that the high-definition television was assumed to have a much higher margin than the 19-inch television on the basis of allocated costs. However, for the purposes of the production runs used in the throughput example, the overhead cost pools assigned to these two products still become valid expenses, whether or not either of the products is produced at all. Consequently, it is detrimental to use overhead as a factor in determining product throughput, no matter what traditional cost accounting principles state.

The second major problem with traditional cost accounting is that it completely ignores the concept of limited production capacity. Instead, the primary goal of a costing analysis is to determine which products have the highest gross margins and which have the least. This information is then used to pursue two

EXHIBIT 14.3. Throughput Analysis Using Priorities Based on Overhead Costs

Maximum Constraint Time: **62,200**

Product	Throughput ($/min of constraint)	Required Constraint Usage (min)	Unit Demand/ Actual Production	Cumulative Constraint Utilization	Cumulative Throughput/ Product ($)
50-in. high definition TV	5.00	14	3,800/3,800	53,200	266,000
100-W stereo	7.50	8	2,800/1,125	9,000	67,500
5-in. LCD TV	6.21	12	500/0	0	0
19-in. color TV	8.11	10	1,000/0	0	0

Throughput total $333,500
Operating expense total $375,000
Profit -$41,500
Profit percentage -12.4%
Investment $500,000
Return on investment -8.3%

goals—selling oodles of the high-margin products while dumping or improving the margins on the low-margin products. Unfortunately, the real world knows that production capacity is limited, so one must choose among the best customer orders available at the moment, only some of which can be run through the capacity constraint and possibly none of which are the highest-margin products the company is capable of producing. Therefore, a simple categorization of which products are "best" or "worst" has no meaning on a day-to-day basis. The real world forces one to choose among possible product sales, which requires one to continually reevaluate a mix of product orders for different products and quantities in relation to each other. In Exhibit 14.3 ignoring the capacity constraint would have led to the much higher profit of $177,360 (assuming that all production is completed for all four products), but of course this was rendered impossible by the capacity constraint.

The final problem, and the one that is clearly the largest inherent flaw in traditional cost accounting, is that it ignores the fact that a company is one large, interactive system and instead strives to achieve lots of local improvements in efficiency. The flaw revealed in the example in Exhibit 14.3 is that the cost accounting manager determined the fully absorbed cost of each product on its own, not realizing that to a significant degree each product shares in the use of many overhead costs. Any type of allocation system results in locally optimized profitability levels for individual products but does not address the fact that the overhead cost pool really services the capacity of the company as a whole, not an individual product. For example, the cost of a production scheduler's salary may be allocated to a product based on the amount of scheduling time required to insert it in the production schedule. But does this added cost really "belong" to the product? If the product were not produced at all, the scheduler would still be there, earning a salary, so it is evident that for the purposes of the throughput model, there is no point in assigning such overhead costs to products. This means that because so many costs are not assignable to products, it is valid to charge totally variable costs only to a specific product; all other costs must be paid for by the combined throughput of *all* the products produced since the overhead applies to all of them. In short, we cannot look at the individual profitability levels of products but rather at how the throughput of all possible product sales, when combined, can be used to offset the total pool of overhead costs.

What we have just seen is that traditional cost accounting methods make multiple mistakes; first, of applying overhead to products for incremental decision-making purposes; second, of ignoring the role of capacity constraints; and finally of not considering the entire set of products and related operating expenses a complete system for which various combinations of products must be considered in order to determine the highest possible level of profitability. However, we are still dealing with throughput accounting at an abstract level. We now work through a few examples to clarify the concepts presented thus far.

THROUGHPUT ACCOUNTING AND VOLUME PURCHASING DECISIONS

The sales manager of the electronics company in our previous example runs into corporate headquarters flush from a meeting with the company's largest account, Electro-Geek Stores (EGS). He has just agreed to a deal that drops the price of the 100-watt stereo system by 20% but which guarantees a doubling of the quantity of EGS orders for this product for the upcoming year. The sales manager points out that the company may have to hold off on a few of the smaller-volume production runs of other products, but no problem—the company is bound to earn more money on the extra volume. To test this assumption the cost accountant pulls up the throughput model on his computer, shifts the stereo to the top of the priority list, adjusts the throughput to reflect the lower price, and obtains the results shown in Exhibit 14.4.

To be brief, the sales manager has just skewered the company. By dropping the price of the stereo by 20%, much of the product's throughput was eliminated and so much of the capacity constraint was used up that there was little room for the production of any other products that might generate enough added throughput to save the company. This example clearly shows that one must carefully consider the impact on the capacity constraint when debating whether to accept a high-volume sales deal. This is a particularly dangerous area in which to ignore throughput accounting, for the acceptance of a really large-volume deal can hog all the time of the capacity constraint, eliminating any chance for the company to manufacture other products and thereby eradicating any chance of offering a wide product mix to the general marketplace.

THROUGHPUT ACCOUNTING AND CAPITAL BUDGETING DECISIONS

The production and cost accounting managers have been reviewing a number of workstations in the production area and find that they can speed up the production capacity of the circuit board insertion machine, which is the next workstation in line *after* the capacity constraint operation. The speed of this machine can be doubled if the company is willing to invest an extra $28,500. To see if this is a good idea, we once again look at the throughput model. In this instance the only number we change is the investment amount. The results are shown in Exhibit 14.5.

By making the extra investment, the only change in the company's situation is that its return on investment drops by fourth-tenths of a percent. The reason is that any investment used to improve any operation besides the capacity constraint is a waste of money. *The only thing that a company achieves by making such an investment is*

EXHIBIT 14.4. Throughput Model with Volume Discounts

Maximum Constraint Time: **62,200**

Product	Throughput ($/min of constraint)	Required Constraint Usage (min)	Unit Demand/ Actual Production	Cumulative Constraint Utilization	Cumulative Throughput/ Product ($)
100-W stereo	4.36	8	5,600/5,600	44,800	195,328
19-in. color TV	8.11	10	1,000/1,000	10,000	81,100
5-in. LCD TV	6.21	12	500/500	6,000	37,260
50-in. high-definition TV	5.00	14	3,800/100	1,400	7,000
			Throughput total		$333,500
			Operating expense total		$320,688
			Profit		$375,000
			Profit percentage		−$54,312
			Investment		−16.9%
			Return on investment		$500,000
					−10.9%

EXHIBIT 14.5. Throughput Model and Investment Analysis

Maximum Constraint Time: **62,200**

Product	Throughput ($/min of constraint)	Required Constraint Use (min)	Unit Demand/ Actual Production	Cumulative Constraint Utilization	Cumulative Throughput/ Product ($)
19-in. color TV	8.11	10	1,000/1,000	10,000	81,100
100-W stereo	7.50	8	2,800/2,800	22,400	168,000
5-in. LCD TV	6.21	12	500/500	6,000	37,260
50-in. high-definition TV	5.00	14	3,800/1,700	23,800	119,000
Throughput total					$405,360
Operating expense total					$375,000
Profit					$30,360
Profit percentage					7.5%
Investment					$528,500
Return on investment					5.7%

EXHIBIT 14.6. Throughput Model with Increased Constraint Time

Maximum Constraint Time: 70,000

Product	Throughput ($/min of constraint)	Required Constraint Usage (min)	Unit Demand/ Actual Production	Cumulative Constraint Utilization	Cumulative Throughput/ Product ($)
19-in. color TV	8.11	10	1,000/1,000	10,000	$81,100
100-W stereo	7.50	8	2,800/2,800	22,400	168,000
5-in. LCD TV	6.21	12	500/500	6,000	37,260
50-in. high-definition TV	5.00	14	3,800/2,257	31,600	157,990
			Throughput total		$444,350
			Operating expense total		$375,000
			Profit		$69,350
			Profit percentage		15.6%
			Investment		$500,000
			Return on investment		13.9%

that it improves the efficiency of an operation that is still controlled by the speed of the capacity constraint. In reality the situation is even worse, for any newly upgraded subsidiary operation now has greater efficiency and can therefore produce in even greater quantities—all of which turns into work in process that piles up somewhere in front of the bottleneck operation, which increases the company's work-in-process investment. Thus, an investment in a nonbottleneck operation may actually worsen the overall financial results of the company because the investment in inventory increases.

This is an important concept for investment analysis, for the typical cost accountant is trained to examine each investment proposal strictly on its own merits, with no consideration of how the investment fits into the entire production system. If the impact of the capacity constraint were also factored into investment analyses, few of them would ever be approved because they do not have a positive impact on the capacity constraint.

To look at this problem from a different angle, let us say that the company's engineering staff has determined that it can increase the speed of the capacity constraint from 62,200 available minutes per month to 70,000 minutes, but only if additional processing work is completed by the machining operation just before the constraint operation, which will cost $51,000 in operating expenses and reduce the available capacity of the preceding operation by 28%. As Exhibit 14.6 shows, this is a good idea, for much of the remaining production that we were unable to schedule can now be processed, creating an added profit of nearly $39,000; the added use of a nonconstraint operation makes no difference since it simply improves the rate of throughput at the capacity constraint. However, a traditional cost accounting analysis might have rejected this proposal because the cost of the additional machining time at the preceding workstation would have been added to the cost of any products running through it, which would have increased their fully burdened price, thereby making their margins supposedly too low to bother with.

These two examples clearly show that examining the cost of an *individual* investment is not sufficient. Instead, we must look at the impact of each new investment on the capacity constraint to see if it changes the throughput level of the system as a whole.

THROUGHPUT ACCOUNTING AND OUTSOURCING DECISIONS

One of the company's key suppliers has offered to take over the entire production of the 5-inch LCD television, package it in the company's boxes, and drop-ship the completed goods directly to the company's customers. The catch is that the company's cost will increase from its current fully burdened rate of $147.00 (as noted in Exhibit 14.2) to $165.00, which leaves a profit of only $15.00. A traditional cost

EXHIBIT 14.7. Throughput Model with an Outsourcing Option

Maximum Constraint Time: **62,200**

Product	Throughput ($/min of constraint)	Required Constraint Use (min)	Unit Demand/ Actual Production	Cumulative Constraint Utilization	Cumulative Throughput/ Product ($)
19-in. color TV	8.11	10	1,000/1,000	10,000	81,100
100-W stereo	7.50	8	2,800/2,800	22,400	168,000
5-in. LCD TV	6.21	12	500/500	N/A	7,500
50-in. high-definition TV	5.00	14	3,800/2,129	29,806	149,030
			Throughput total		$405,630
			Operating expense total		$375,000
			Profit		$30,630
			Profit percentage		7.5%
			Investment		$500,000
			Return on investment		6.1%

accounting review would predict that the company will experience reduced profits of $18.00 if this outsourcing deal is completed (the difference between the current and prospective costs of $147.00 and $165.00). To see if this is a good deal, we turn once again to the throughput model, which is reproduced in Exhibit 14.7. In this exhibit we have removed the number from the Cumulative Constraint Utilization column for the LCD television since it can now be produced without the use of the capacity constraint. However, we are still able to put a cumulative throughput dollar figure in the final column for this product since there is some margin to be made by outsourcing it through the supplier. By removing the LCD television's use of the capacity constraint, the company is now able to produce more of the next product in line, which is the high-definition television. This additional production allows it to increase the amount of throughput dollars, thereby creating $270.00 more profits than was the case before the outsourcing deal.

Once again, the traditional cost accounting approach would have stated that profits would be lowered by accepting an outsourcing deal that clearly costs more than the product's internal cost. However, by using this deal to release some capacity at the bottleneck, the company is able to earn more money on the production of other products.

THROUGHPUT ACCOUNTING AND UNPROFITABLE PRODUCTS

The company has just completed a lengthy activity-based costing analysis that has altered the allocation of overhead costs. It is now apparent that much more overhead must be charged to the high-definition television than was previously thought to be the case. This results in a clear loss for the product. Accordingly, the cost accounting manager writes a memo to the management team outlining his reasons for requesting that this product be immediately pulled from the company's production. To see what effect this will have on company profits, we return to the throughput model, as noted in Exhibit 14.8, and remove the line item for the high-definition television.

The model reveals that dropping only this product *reduces* the company's ability to create throughput that can be used to cover the existing pool of operating expenses, thereby creating a loss. This issue highlights a classic problem with traditional cost accounting—allocating overhead to a product does not mean that eliminating the product also eliminates the associated overhead. To ensure that overhead costs are really eliminated, one must carefully review each overhead line item and verify that it can indeed be dropped, as well as create a plan to ensure that actions are taken to eliminate it. Otherwise, the cost will be retained but there will be less throughput available to pay for it.

To take this issue to its logical extreme, the same pool of overhead costs are now allocated to the remaining (and smaller) set of products, which drives up their costs

EXHIBIT 14.8. Throughput Model without an Unprofitable Product

Maximum Constraint Time: **62,200**

Product	Throughput ($/min of constraint)	Required Constraint Use (min)	Unit Demand/ Actual Production	Cumulative Constraint Utilization	Cumulative Throughput/ Product($)
19-in. color TV	8.11	10	1,000/1,000	10,000	81,100
100-W stereo	7.50	8	2,800/2,800	22,400	168,000
5-in. LCD TV	6.21	12	500/500	6,000	37,260
			Throughput total		$286,360
			Operating expense total		$375,000
			Profit		−$88,640
			Profit percentage		−30.9%
			Investment		$500,000
			Return on investment		−17.7%

once again. Based on this new information, yet another product is dropped because of a lack of profits, which results in even larger losses and another iteration of cost increases. By focusing instead on the level of throughput that each product generates, one can avoid this overhead allocation trap.

THROUGHPUT AND TRADITIONAL ACCOUNTING COMPARED

In the last few sections we have addressed examples of how throughput accounting yields results different from those reached using more traditional cost accounting methods. In this section we cover additional differences in several other areas.

One of the most popular accounting methodologies is activity-based costing (ABC), which is covered in detail in Chapter 16. Though the author enthuses in that chapter about how ABC can be used to determine the exact causes of overhead (which can be used to tightly control costs), there is another side to this activity. The problem is that ABC reviews require an inordinate amount of time on the part of a number of employees to examine detailed costing information about every facet of a company's operations. Throughput accounting avoids all this work and instead focuses its attention on what it will take to force as much production volume as possible through the capacity constraint, which will increase profits. This laser beam focus requires much less analysis effort than for ABC, which yields more time for the accounting staff to complete other work.

Along similar lines, the management team (as well as the accountants) finds that its efforts are widely spread out over any number of projects when they rely on ABC information, since these analyses focus on the optimization of *all* resources rather than just the capacity constraint. This leaves less time to work on bottleneck-related issues. Throughput accounting, however, ignores problems in other parts of a facility in favor of a detailed analysis of only the capacity constraint, which tends to focus management's attention on improving throughput in this one area.

Another difference between traditional and throughput accounting is that most accountants are trained to report on overhead and direct costs, which in turn draws the attention of managers to tightly controlling these costs. Though this is still a concern in the throughput accounting arena, its primary focus is on increasing the flow of production through the bottleneck operation. Thus, the first method draws attention to reducing costs, while the other attempts to increase revenues.

Yet another difference is that a throughput accountant is interested in the ability of the organization to exactly meet the production schedule for all components that feed into the bottleneck operation, as well as the schedule for the bottleneck itself. Any interruption in this schedule has a direct and immediate impact on revenues. Thus, the throughput accountant delves into the reasons why these schedules are not met—missing materials, improper manning, machine downtime, and so on.

None of these activities are common pursuits of the traditional accountant, who is concerned only with the cost of activities and products.

Another significant difference is that a system that focuses on throughput requires a considerable amount of excess capacity at the work centers that feed the capacity constraint. The reason for this excess is that any shortage in production at a feeder operation reduces the amount of materials flowing to the bottleneck operation, which in turn impacts the amount of production that can flow through it. Accordingly, it is quite acceptable, if not mandatory, to have excess capacity in these feeder operations. When dealing with throughput capacity issues, one should divide the total amount of capacity at each work center into three parts. The first is productive capacity, which is the portion of the total work center capacity needed to process currently scheduled or anticipated production. The second is protective capacity, which is the additional portion of capacity that must be held in reserve to ensure that a sufficient quantity of parts can be manufactured to adequately feed the bottleneck operation. Any remaining capacity is called idle capacity. Only the last type can be eliminated from feeder work centers. The concept of protective capacity is completely foreign to traditional accounting theory, which holds that *all* excess capacity should be eliminated.

Another difference is that traditional cost accounting methodology clearly states that pricing should include fully absorbed costs plus an acceptable profit margin. The sales and marketing staff chafes under this formulation, since it is sometimes confronted with offers from customers to buy large quantities of product at reduced prices, but the accountants will not approve the lower prices. However, throughput theory holds that *any* price point that exceeds the totally variable cost of a product should be considered. To say the least, this offers the sales staff a much larger degree of flexibility! Now projected prices can be included in the throughput model presented several times earlier in this chapter in order to see whether the prices will increase the total throughput of the organization. If not, the proposed price will not be offered to customers. However, if it improves the mix, new price points may be acceptable. Also, the sales staff does not need to deal with a complex absorption costing formula for each product it needs to price. Instead, all it needs is the totally variable cost and the throughput model. The level of simplicity and ease of understanding make the throughput model the preferable device for pricing.

Another pricing issue treated differently in the traditional and throughput systems is the pricing of customer orders that involve small batch sizes. Under the ABC model the cost of setups is assigned to a product's cost, which can be an overwhelmingly large cost if the batch is sufficiently small. Not so under throughput accounting, which holds that the people doing the setups are employed (and paid) by the company even if they are not performing any setups—therefore the setup cost is a fixed cost that should not be assigned to a specific product. Given this assumption (a large one in some instances), the sales staff can still sell small batches to customers at prices not far above their totally variable costs. This tends to result in a company offering a much richer mix of order sizes and products to its customers, which can result in greater market share. However, this concept must be used with caution, for ignoring the cost of setups leads to larger operating expenses in the long run, as many more staff are hired to manage the larger number of production jobs and setups.

Since we are discussing the topic of setups and job lot sizes, this is yet another difference. Traditional accounting holds that one should run long jobs so that the cost of setting up each job can be spread over more units of production. Throughput accounting holds a mixed view of the situation. On the one hand, it prefers long production runs at the capacity constraint since this results in more throughput. On the other hand, all feeder work centers should have short runs since this tends to reduce the amount of lead time required to switch over to the production of parts that can be used immediately in the bottleneck operation.

A further difference is that traditional cost accounting focuses on determining a product's gross margin at the most common, or standard, price and recommending that this product be produced if the standard margin is positive. Throughput accounting prefers to review the throughput of each product at every possible price point. For example, if a product is selling to one customer for $10.00 and to another one for $9.50, there is a difference in throughput of $0.50, meaning that the second customer order is ranked lower in the throughput model of scheduled production than the first one and may not be produced at all if there are other products with better throughputs. Thus, it is crucial to examine the price point of *every* customer order.

Another issue is that throughput accounting places greater emphasis on scheduling work through the capacity constraint that can be sold immediately rather than parked in inventory. The reason is that sending products to inventory results in a drop in profits, which cannot be earned until the product is sold and shipped to a customer. Using the bottleneck to increase the size of the inventory is a waste of available capacity. Since the more traditional cost accounting methodology does not recognize the existence of capacity constraints in a system, it does not point out this problem to management.

An interesting difference is in the treatment of quality-related issues. Accountants have greatly increased their focus on the cost of quality over the last few decades, having realized that the cost of repairing products and customer relations damaged by quality issues is extremely expensive. A common result is the preparation of a lengthy cost-of-quality report that itemizes problem areas in every part of a company. Management then prioritizes these problems and works to reduce the overall cost of quality. As one might expect by now, the throughput approach cares only about the impact of quality on the capacity constraint. When a quality problem results in the bottleneck operation not being fed a sufficient quantity of materials or subcomponents, the company's total throughput drops, resulting in a loss of profits. Therefore, quality reporting under this scenario requires one to focus solely on work centers that feed the capacity constraint.

This issue rolls into a related one, the costing of scrap. Under traditional cost accounting the cost of any scrapped item is its fully absorbed cost. Under throughput accounting it is its totally variable cost—if the point at which the item is scrapped is prior to the capacity constraint. If after it, the cost of the scrap rises substantially. The reason for the increase is that the scrapped item must now be replaced with another one that will use up time being processed through the bottleneck operation. Thus, the cost of scrap that occurs after the bottleneck is really its totally variable cost plus the lost throughput that would have been realized if the item had been sold. This is a unique concept—the cost of scrap depends on where it occurs in the production process!

A final difference is the strategic placement of the capacity constraint. The bottleneck operation can be one that is not planned, but a wise management team carefully determines exactly where it should be and plans accordingly. The most typical location is at the most expensive work center. By placing it there managers can keep investment in new machinery at a minimum. Alternatively, a traditional costing system does not even know where the bottleneck operation is located. As a result, excess funds may be invested in increasing the capacity of a bottleneck operation, which may not result in a sufficient increase in throughput to justify the increased investment.

There are obviously a great many differences between traditional and throughput accounting. Clearly, it is very important to view a number of costing-related decisions in terms of the throughput accounting model to ensure that one's decisions do not change from this viewpoint. Next we review the problems with throughput accounting. The following information can be of use when determining the usefulness of information generated by this model.

PROBLEMS WITH THE THROUGHPUT MODEL

The chief problem with the active use of throughput accounting for short-range alterations in the mix of production is that it can *really* annoy customers. When throughput accounting is the driving force behind all production scheduling, a customer that has already placed an order for a product that will result in a suboptimal profit level for the manufacturer may find that its order is never filled. The order continues to fall to the bottom of the manufacturer's list of open orders until the mix of existing orders creates an opening at the capacity constraint that allows it to be produced. Theoretically, this means that some customers may never receive their orders. This issue can be resolved through the use of scheduling policies that require customer orders to be produced, no matter what profitability level will result, after a certain time period has elapsed.

A related problem is that a company's ability to create the highest level of profitability is now dependent on the production scheduling staff who decides what products are to be manufactured and in what order. Because this group has never been involved with profitability issues, there may be some confusion in the scheduling department in terms of how the daily production schedule is to be completed. Should the overriding priority be on throughput? Or must consideration also be given to how long some customers have waited for their orders to be completed? Or should the schedulers still rely on suggested scheduling criteria that can be extracted from the manufacturing resources planning system in the computer? Given the number of issues that must now be dealt with by the schedulers, the best approach may be to have daily schedule review sessions attended by all interested parties, in order to arrive at a production schedule generally agreeable to everyone.

Another issue is that, as noted in Chapter 29, all costs are totally variable in the long run since management then has time to adjust them to long-range production volumes. This being the case, the totally variable cost element of the throughput formula really should include far more than just direct materials if it is used for long-range planning. Otherwise, the management group will operate under the misconception that the entire block of operating expenses is fixed and immovable.

The problems noted here are relatively minor ones and can certainly be overcome with the correct supporting procedures. When balanced against the considerable benefits of this approach, it is apparent that throughput accounting is a major new tool for the cost accountant.

REPORTING WITH THE THROUGHPUT MODEL

When the throughput model is used for financial reporting purposes, the format appears slightly different. The income statement includes only direct materials in the cost of goods sold, which results in a "throughput contribution" instead of a gross margin. All other costs are lumped into an "operating expenses" category below the throughput contribution margin, yielding a net income figure at the bottom. All other financial reports stay the same. Though this single change appears relatively minor, it has one significant impact.

The primary change is that throughput accounting does not charge any operating expenses to inventory, so that they can be expensed in a future period. Instead, all operating expenses are realized during the current period. As a result, any incentive for managers to overproduce is completely eliminated because they cannot use the excess amount to shift expenses out of the current period, thereby making their financial results look better than they would otherwise.

Though this is a desirable result, such a report can be used only for internal reporting purposes because of the requirement of generally accepted accounting principles that some overhead costs be charged to excess production. Nonetheless, it may be worthwhile to use this format internally if it is used to rate the performance of managers.

SYSTEMIC CHANGES REQUIRED FOR ACCEPTANCE OF THE THROUGHPUT MODEL

Unfortunately, throughput accounting requires an entirely different view of the world, one that does not have a logical linkage with the more traditional forms of cost accounting. This will make it difficult for it to gain acceptance.

The main problem is that this method does not use cost as the basis for the most optimal production decisions; instead it uses throughput. This is entirely contrary to the teachings of any other type of accounting, which hold that the highest-margin products (with varying degrees of direct and overhead costs attached to them) should always be produced first. Given that the underpinnings of traditional cost accounting are threatened by throughput accounting, we come to an all-or-nothing decision—one uses either throughput or traditional costing exclusively. Or is there a way to merge the two? Here are some thoughts on the subject:

- **Inventory valuation.** Generally accepted accounting principles clearly state that the cost of overhead must be apportioned to inventory. Throughput accounting states that none of the overhead cost should be so assigned. In this case, since the rules are so clear, it is apparent that throughput accounting loses. The existing accounting system must continue to assign costs, irrespective of how throughput principles are used for other decision-making activities.

- **Inventory investment analysis.** Here there are fundamental differences between the two methodologies. Both hold that the objective is to always keep one's investment at a minimum. In the case of traditional cost accounting, this is because the return on investment is higher when the total dollar amount of the investment is forced to the lowest possible level. Throughput accounting, however, wants to shrink the amount of investment because it includes work-in-process inventory in this category; it tries to keep WIP levels down so that waste is reduced in the production system. In short, the first system advocates a small investment for financial reasons, while the later system favors it because it makes more operational sense. Despite the differences in reasoning, the same conclusion is reached by both methodologies. However, the throughput approach is still better, for it forces one to analyze all inventory reduction projects in light of how they together will impact the capacity constraint, rather than individually.

- **Capital investment analysis.** Because traditional cost accounting only analyzes each investment proposal on its own, rather than considering its impact on the production process as a whole, it tends to recommend investments that will result in an incremental investment but no overall change in the level of corporate capacity, which is driven by capacity constraint. Throughput accounting, however, has a tight focus on investments only in areas that impact the capacity constraint—

all other investment proposals are rejected. In this instance it is best to reject the traditional system and conduct analyses based on throughput principles.

- **Product costing.** Under throughput accounting a product has only a totally variable cost, which may be far lower than the fully absorbed cost that would be assigned to it under more traditional costing systems. This totally variable cost is almost always direct materials, which is an easily calculated figure. Full-absorption costing, however, requires a large amount of calculation effort before a detailed cost can be compiled for a product. Given the wide range in costing outcomes, there is a significant issue in terms of which one to use. For companies selling to the government under cost-plus contracts, there are lengthy, detailed requirements for what variable and overhead costs should be assigned to each product manufactured. These rules virtually require the use of absorption costing—throughput costing is not a viable option. For companies that do not require detailed costing justifications when selling their products, it may be possible to use the much simpler throughput accounting approach.

- **Production scheduling.** Existing production scheduling systems do not include any kind of throughput modeling that tells production planners which orders should be produced first. It may be possible to customize existing systems or to upgrade packaged software so that this option is available to planners. This would allow them to produce the items that result in the highest throughput per minute of the capacity constraint. However, despite the impassioned arguments of most advocates of throughput accounting, the author does not think that this "improvement" is useful. Any company that has already received a customer order has an obligation to fill it, even if the resulting sale will reduce its overall level of profit from the theoretical maximum that can be calculated with throughput accounting. Maximizing short-term profits by ignoring orders is tantamount to long-term suicide since customers will leave in droves. Consequently, production planners should be left alone to schedule production in the traditional manner, rather than basing their decisions on short-term profit maximization.

- **Long-term planning.** This is a prime usage area for throughput accounting. One can estimate the approximate sales levels for each product type over a long time frame, such as a year (as well as the price point at which each one will sell), enter it into the throughput model, and determine what mix of prospective sales will result in the highest level of profitability. This method is much superior to the use of throughput costing for short-term production decisions since long-term planning sidesteps problems by avoiding existing customer orders that will result in low profits. Long-term planning does not involve existing customer orders (since they have not been placed yet), so that decisions to produce various types of products at different price points can be made before the sales force goes out to obtain orders.

- **Price setting.** The sales and marketing staff favors throughput accounting because the margin on products is simple to obtain—just subtract totally variable costs from the price. This beats the often incomprehensible jargon and maze of allocations accompanying activity-based costing systems. Price setting in the throughput environment focuses more on what products can be inserted into the existing production mix at a price that will incrementally increase overall profits, rather than the painful accumulation and allocation of costs to specific products. Throughput is the clear choice here, based on ease of understandability and the speed with which information can be accumulated.

Existing corporate systems are not designed to work with throughput accounting because it uses such a startlingly different approach to determine what products to sell. There are some special cases where it cannot be used at all, such as for inventory valuation and cost-plus billings to customers. However, there are several optimal cases where throughput can bring immediate discernible value to a company. These areas are product pricing, long-term planning, and investment analysis.

SUMMARY

Throughput accounting is a fresh, unique view of how to handle decision making within a company. It has a multidecade battle on its hands to gain acceptance simply because it runs counter to so much established practice in the cost accounting field, an area that will be completely overthrown if throughput ever gains general acceptance. Whether or not other people take to it, the reader should give this approach a great deal of thought, find situations where it can be applied, work it into existing decision-making models, and use it during presentations to management. This method will result in different types of production and sales decisions that will lead to higher levels of profitability; if other people choose not to use it, the reader will have a competitive advantage over them until they choose to do so.

CHAPTER 15

Joint and By-product Costing

In many instances companies operate a single production process that results in several products, none of which can be clearly identified through the early stages of production. Examples of such merged production occur in the wood products industry, where a tree can be cut into a wide variety of end products, and in the meat-packing industry, where an animal carcass can be cut into a number of different finished goods. Up to the point in the production process where individual products become clearly identifiable, there is no clear-cut way to assign costs to products. We consider several cost allocation methods in this chapter that deal with this problem and also discuss the usefulness (or lack thereof) of these allocation methods.

NATURE OF JOINT COSTS

To understand joint products and by-products, one must have a firm understanding of the split-off point. This is the last point in a production process where it is impossible to determine the nature of the final products. All costs that have been incurred by the production process up until this point—both direct and overhead—must somehow be allocated to the products that result from the split-off point. Any costs incurred thereafter can be charged to specific products in the normal manner. Thus, a product that comes out of such a process has allocated costs from before the split-off point and costs that can be directly traced to it that occur after the split-off point.

EXHIBIT 15.1. Multiple Split-off Points for Joint Products and By-products

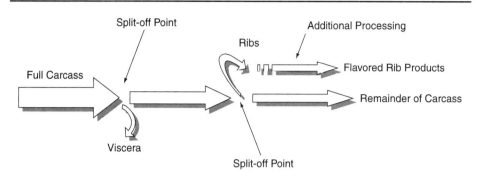

A related term is "by-product," which refers to an additional product that arises from a production process but whose potential sales value is much smaller than that of the principal joint products obtained from the same process. As we will see, the accounting for by-products can be somewhat different.

A complication of the joint cost concept is that there can be more than one split-off point. Exhibit 15.1 diagrams meat processing in a slaughterhouse, where the viscera are removed early in the process, creating a by-product. This is the first split-off point. Then the ribs are split away from the carcass at a second split-off point. The ribs may in turn be packaged and sold at once, or processed further to produce additional products such as prepackaged barbequed ribs. In this instance some costs incurred through the first split-off point may be assigned to the by-product viscera (to be discussed later), while costs incurred between the first and second split-off points are no longer assigned to the viscera but must in turn be assigned to the remaining products that can be extracted from the carcass. Finally, costs that must be incurred to convert ribs into final products are assigned directly to these products. This is the basic cost flow for joint products and by-products.

REASONING BEHIND JOINT AND BY-PRODUCT COSTING

As we will see in the next section, the allocation of costs to products at the split-off point is essentially arbitrary in nature. Though two standard methods are used, neither leads to information that is useful for management decision making. Why, then, must the cost accountant be concerned with the proper cost allocation method for joint products and by-products?

Because there are accounting and legal reasons for doing so. Generally accepted accounting principles require that costs be assigned to products for inventory valuation purposes. Though the costs incurred by a production process up to the split-off point cannot be clearly assigned to a single product, it is still necessary to find some reasonable allocation method for doing so in order to obey the accounting rules. Otherwise, all costs incurred up to the split-off point could reasonably be charged directly to the cost of goods sold as an overhead cost, which would result in enormous overhead costs and few direct costs (only those incurred after the split-off point).

The logic for allocating costs to joint products and by-products has less to do with a scientifically derived allocation method and more with finding a quick, easy way to allocate costs that is reasonably defensible (as we will see in the next section). The reason for using simple methodologies is that the promulgators of GAAP realize that there is no real management use for allocated joint costs—they cannot be used to determine break-even points, setting optimal prices, or figuring out the exact profitability of individual products. Instead, they are used for any of the purposes listed here, which are more administrative in nature:

- **Bonus calculations.** Manager bonuses may depend on the level of reported profits for specific products, which in turn is partly based on the level of joint costs allocated to them. Thus, managers have a keen interest in the calculations used to assign costs, especially if some of the joint costs can be dumped onto products that are the responsibility of a different manager.

- **Cost-plus contract calculations.** Many government contracts are based on reimbursement of a company's costs, plus some predetermined margin. In this situation it is in a company's best interests to ensure that the largest possible proportion of joint costs is assigned to jobs that will be reimbursed by the customer; the customer is equally interested, but because of a desire to *reduce* the allocation of joint costs.

- **Income reporting.** Many organizations split their income statements into sublevels that report on profits by product line or even individual product. In such cases joint costs may make up such a large proportion of total production costs that these income statements do not include the majority of production costs unless they are allocated to specific products or product lines.

- **Insurance reimbursement.** If a company suffers damage to a production or inventory area, some finished goods or work-in-process inventory may be damaged or destroyed. Then it is in the interests of the company to fully allocate as many joint costs as possible to the damaged or destroyed stock so that it can receive the largest possible reimbursement from its insurance provider.

- **Inventory valuation.** It is possible to manipulate inventory levels (and therefore the reported level of income) by shifting joint cost allocations toward products stored in inventory. This practice is obviously discouraged since it results in changes to income that have no relationship to operating conditions. Nonetheless, one should be on the lookout for the deliberate use of allocation methods that alter the valuation of inventory.

- **Transfer pricing.** As noted in the Chapter 30, a company can alter the prices at which its sells products among its various divisions so that high prices are charged to the divisions located in high-tax areas, resulting in lower reported levels of income against which these high tax rates can be applied. A canny cost accounting staff chooses the joint cost allocation technique that results in the highest joint costs being assigned to products being sent to such locations (and the reverse for low-tax regions).

Next we look at the two most commonly used methods for allocating joint costs to products, which are based on product revenues for one method and gross margins for the other.

JOINT COST ALLOCATION METHODS

Though several joint cost allocation methods have been proposed in the accounting literature, only two have gained widespread acceptance. The first is based on the sales value of all joint products at the split-off point. To calculate this value the cost accountant compiles all costs accumulated in the production process up to the split-off point, determines the eventual sales value of all products created at the split-off point, and assigns these costs to the products based on their relative values. If by-products are associated with the joint production process, they are considered too insignificant to be worthy of any cost assignment, though revenues gained from their sale can be charged against the cost of goods sold for the joint products. This is the simplest joint cost allocation method and is particularly attractive because the cost accountant needs no knowledge of any production processing steps that occur after the split-off point.

This different treatment of the costs and revenues associated with by-products can lead to profitability anomalies at the product level. The difficulty is that the determination of whether a product is a by-product or not can be quite judgmental; in one company, if a joint product's revenues are less than 10% of the total revenues earned, it is a by-product, while another company might use a 1% cutoff figure instead. Because of this vagueness in accounting terminology, one company may assign all its costs only to joint products with an inordinate share of total revenues and record the value of all other products as zero. If a large quantity of these by-products is held in stock at a value of zero, the total inventory valuation will be lower than another company would calculate, simply because of its definition of what constitutes a by-product.

A second problem with the treatment of by-products under this cost allocation scenario is that they can be sold only in batches, which may occur only once every few months. This can cause sudden drops in the cost of joint products in the months when these sales occur since these revenues are subtracted from their cost. Alternatively, joint product costs appear to be too high in periods when there are no by-product sales. Thus, one can alter product costs through the timing of by-product sales.

A third problem related to by-products is that the revenues realized from their sale can vary considerably based on market demand. In such cases these altered revenues cause abrupt changes in the cost of the joint products against which these revenues are netted. It certainly may require some explaining by the cost accountant to show why changes in the price of an unrelated product caused a change in the cost of a joint product! This can be a hard concept for a nonaccountant to understand.

The best way to avoid the three issues just mentioned is to avoid designating *any* product a by-product. Instead, each joint product should be assigned some proportion of total costs incurred up to the split-off point, based on their total potential revenues (however small they may be), and no resulting revenues should be used to offset other product costs. By avoiding the segregation of joint products into different product categories, we can avoid a variety of costing anomalies.

The second allocation method is based on the estimated final gross margin of each joint product produced. The calculation of gross margin is based on the revenue that each product will earn at the end of the entire production process, less the cost of all processing costs incurred from the split-off point to the point of sale. This is a more complicated approach because it requires the cost accountant to accumulate additional costs through the end of the production process, which in turn requires a reasonable knowledge of how the production process works and where costs are incurred. Though it is a more difficult method to calculate, its use may be mandatory in instances where the final sale price of one or more joint products cannot be determined at the split-off point (as is required for the first allocation method), thereby rendering the other allocation method useless.

The main problem with allocating joint costs based on the estimated final gross margin is that it can be difficult to calculate if there is a great deal of *customized* work left between the split-off point and the point of sale. Then, it is impossible to determine in advance the exact costs that will be incurred during the remainder of the production process. In such a case the only alternative is to make estimates of expected costs that will be incurred, base the gross margin calculations on this information, and accept the fact that the resulting joint cost allocations may not be provable based on the actual costs incurred.

The two allocation methods described here are easier to understand with an example, which is shown in Exhibit 15.2. In the exhibit we see that $250.00 in joint costs has been incurred up to the split-off point. The first allocation method, based on the eventual sale price of the resulting joint products, is shown beneath the split-off point. In it the sale price of the by-product is ignored, leaving a revenue split of 59%/41% between products A and B. The joint costs of the process are allocated between the two products based on this percentage. The second allocation method, based on the eventual gross margins earned by each of the products, is shown to the

EXHIBIT 15.2. Example of Joint Cost Allocation Methods

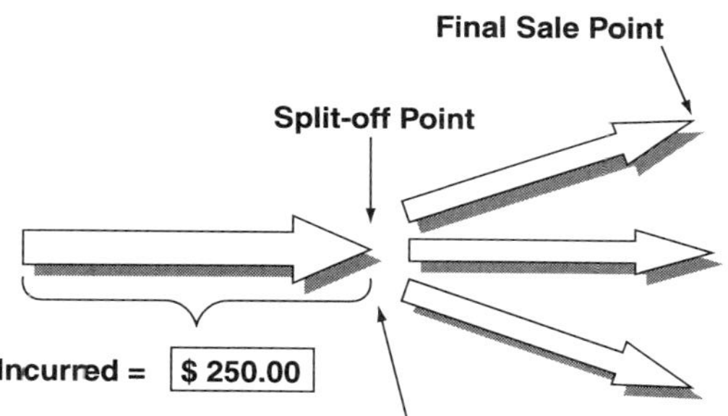

Final Sale Point

Split-off Point

Total Costs Incurred = $250.00

Joint Cost Allocation Based on Estimated Sales Value at the Split-off Point

Name	Type	Final Revenue	Percent of Total Revenues	Cost Allocation
Product A	Joint	$ 12.00	59%	$ 148.15
Product B	Joint	$ 8.25	41%	$ 101.85
Product C	By-product	$ -	0%	$ -
		$ 20.25	100%	$ 250.00

Joint Cost Allocation Based on Gross Margin After the Split-off Point

	Final Revenue	Costs After Split-off	Margin After Split-off	Percent of Total Margins	Cost Allocation
Product A	$ 12.00	$ 8.50	$ 3.50	39%	$ 97.22
Product B	$ 8.25	$ 3.00	$ 5.25	58%	$ 145.83
Product C	$ 0.25	$ -	$ 0.25	3%	$ 6.94
	$ 20.50	$ 11.50	$ 9.00	100%	$ 250.00

right of the split-off point. This calculation includes the gross margin on the sale of Product C, which was categorized as a by-product and therefore ignored in the preceding calculation. This calculation results in a substantially different sharing of joint costs among the various products than we saw for the first allocation method, with the split now being 39%/58%/3% among products A, B, and C, respectively. The wide swing in allocated amounts between the two methods can be attributed to the different bases of allocation—the first is based on revenue, whereas the second is based on gross margins.

PRICING OF JOINT PRODUCTS AND BY-PRODUCTS

The key operational activity in which joint cost allocations should be ignored is the pricing of joint products and by-products. The issue here is that the allocation used to assign a cost to a particular product does not really have any bearing on the actual cost incurred in creating the product—either method for splitting costs among multiple products, as noted in the last section, cannot really be proven to allocate the correct cost to any product. Instead, we must realize that all costs incurred up to the split-off point are sunk costs that will be incurred no matter what combination of products is created and sold from the split-off point forward.

Because everything prior to the split-off point is considered a sunk cost, pricing decisions are concerned only with the costs incurred *after* the split-off point because these costs can be directly traced to individual products. In other words, incremental changes in prices should be based on the incremental increases in costs that accrue to a product after the split-off point. This can result in inordinately low costs being assigned to products because so few costs are incurred after the split-off point. This can occur in response to competitive pressures or because it seems necessary to add only a modest markup percentage to the incremental costs incurred after the split-off point. If these prices are too low, the revenues resulting from the entire production process may not be sufficiently high for the company to earn a profit.

The best way to ensure that pricing is sufficient for a company to earn a profit is to create a pricing model for each product line. Such a model, as shown in Exhibit 15.3, itemizes the types of products and their likely selling points, as well as the variable costs that can be assigned to them subsequent to the split-off point. Thus far, the exhibit results in a total gross margin earned from all joint and by-product sales. Then we add up the grand total of all sunk costs incurred prior to the split-off point and subtract this amount from the total gross margin. If the resulting profit is too small, the person setting prices will realize that individual product prices must be altered in order to improve the profitability of the entire cluster of products. Also, by bringing together all the sales volumes and price points related to a single production process, one can easily see where pricing must be adjusted in order to obtain the desired level of profits. In the example we must somehow increase

EXHIBIT 15.3. Pricing Model for Joint and By-product Pricing

Product Name	Price/Unit ($)	Incremental Cost/Unit ($)	Throughput/ Unit ($)	Number of Sales Units	Total Throughput ($)
Viscera	0.40	0.10	0.30	1	0.30
Barbequed ribs	3.00	1.80	1.20	4	4.80
Flank steak	5.50	1.05	4.35	2	8.70
Quarter steak	4.25	1.25	3.00	4	12.00
Pituitary gland	1.00	0.48	0.52	1	0.52
			Total throughput		$26.32
			Total sunk costs		$30.00
			Net profit (loss)		−$3.68

the total profit by $3.68 in order to avoid a loss. A quick perusal of the exhibit shows us that two of the products—viscera and pituitary gland—do not generate a sufficient amount of throughput to cover this loss. Accordingly, the sales staff should concentrate the bulk of its attention on repricing the other three listed products in order to eliminate the operating loss.

This format can be easily adapted for use for entire reporting periods or production runs rather than for a single unit of production (as was the case in the last exhibit). Then we simply multiply the number of units of joint products or by-products per unit by the total number of units to be manufactured during the period and enter the totals in the far right column of the same format used in Exhibit 15.3. The advantage of this more comprehensive approach is that a production scheduler can determine which products should be included in a production run (assuming that more than one product is available) to generate the largest possible throughput. For a more comprehensive discussion of throughput costing and how it can be used to generate higher profit levels, the reader should refer to Chapter 14.

SUMMARY

The main point of interest in this chapter is that the allocation of costs through any method discussed here is essentially arbitrary in nature—it results in some sort of cost being assigned to a joint product or by-product, but these costs are useful only for financial or tax reporting purposes, not for management decisions. For the latter issues one should use direct costing from the split-off point onward as the only relevant costs and consider all preceding costs sunk costs.

CHAPTER 16

Activity-Based Costing

The cost structure of most organizations contains a small proportion of variable costs, as well as many other costs that are lumped together as overhead. The proportion of overhead to variable costs has gradually increased over the years, until there are now companies with three or more times the amount of their variable costs invested in overhead.

Overhead is an amorphous entity that is difficult to assign to any specific product, customer, product line, project, or activity. For this reason it is difficult for a company to allocate its overhead costs to anything. By default, overhead has been allocated based on the amount of direct labor incurred. This practice occasionally results in an allocation of overhead costs that accurately reflects actual overhead use, but most of the time the allocation is either too high or low, yielding incorrect costs that are useless for any kind of decision making.

Activity-based costing (ABC) was invented in order to introduce a logical system of overhead allocation that would result in better information and improved related management decisions.

SHORTCOMINGS OF TRADITIONAL COST ALLOCATION SYSTEMS

Activity-based costing was developed because of the shortcomings of traditional cost allocation systems. The chief problem with these systems is that they do not allocate overhead in a manner that truly reflects the use of overhead. This is because all overhead costs are lumped into one large overhead cost pool and because of the use of inappropriate allocation measures to spread the cost of this pool to products. The end result is incorrect product costing, which can lead to incorrect decisions based on these costs.

The problem is particularly obvious when the overhead cost pool greatly exceeds the size of the allocation measure, which is frequently direct labor. In some industries where considerable machinery or engineering staff are involved (such as the automotive, drug, and aerospace industries), the ratio of overhead to the allocation measure is frequently in the range of 300% to 400%. This means that a slight change in direct labor results in the application of an inordinate additional amount of overhead to a product, which in all likelihood is never justified by changes in its use pattern.

Another problem is that the overhead cost pool is allocated based on only one allocation measure. Many of the costs in the overhead cost pool do not have the slightest relationship to the allocation measure and should not be allocated based on it. Here are some of the costs stored in the overhead cost pool that have no relationship whatsoever to the most common allocation measure, direct labor:

- **Building rent.** A better allocation is based on the square footage of the facility used by the machinery and inventory storage areas related to a product line.

- **Building insurance.** A better allocation is square footage.

- **Industrial engineering salaries.** A better allocation is the total number of units expected to be produced over the lifetime of a product line.

- **Machinery depreciation.** A better allocation is the hours of machine time used.

- **Machinery insurance.** A better allocation is the hours of machine time used.

- **Maintenance costs.** A better allocation is the hours of machine time used.

- **Production scheduling salaries.** A better allocation is the number of jobs scheduled during the accounting period.

- **Purchasing salaries.** A better allocation is the number of parts in a product or the number of suppliers from whom parts must be purchased.

- **Utilities.** A better allocation is based on the hours of machine time used.

- **Warehouse salaries.** There are several better allocations, such as the number of receipts or shipments related to a product or the number of parts it has.

It is evident from the above list that most overhead costs lack the slightest relationship to direct labor and that a good cost allocation cannot depend on just one basis of allocation—several are needed to realistically portray the actual use of each element of overhead.

Another issue is that traditional cost allocation systems tend to portray products made with high levels of automation as being deceptively low in overhead cost. For example, when a high-technology company decides to introduce more automation into one of its production lines, it replaces direct labor with machine hours by adding robots. This shrinks the allocation base, which is direct labor, while increasing the size of the overhead cost pool, which now includes the depreciation, utilities, and maintenance costs associated with the robots. When the overhead cost allocation is performed, a *smaller* amount of overhead is charged to the now-automated production line because the overhead costs are being charged based on direct labor use, which has declined. This makes the products running through the automated line look less expensive than they really are. Furthermore, the increased overhead cost pool is charged to other production lines with large amounts of direct labor, even though these product lines do not have the slightest association with the new overhead costs. The end result is a significant skewing of reported costs that makes products manufactured with automation look less expensive than they really are, and those produced with manual labor look more expensive.

Traditional cost allocation systems also tend to portray low-volume products as having the highest profits. This problem arises because the overhead costs associated with batch setups and teardowns, which can be a significant proportion of total overhead costs, are allocated indiscriminately to products with both large and small production volumes; none of the special batch costs associated with a specific short production run are allocated to it. This results in the undercosting of products with short production runs and the overcosting of products with long production runs. This problem is one of the most common in cost accounting and leads to faulty management decisions to increase sales of short-run jobs and reduce sales of long-run jobs, which results in reduced profits as company resources are concentrated on the lowest-profit products.

Based on these examples, it is clear that there are serious problems with the traditional cost allocation system. It does not apportion overhead costs correctly, resulting in management receiving information about products that is correct only by accident and leads to decisions not based on factual data. Activity-based costing was developed in order to correct these shortcomings.

OVERVIEW OF ACTIVITY-BASED COSTING

Before describing an ABC system implementation, it is best to see how the system works, from a determination of project scope to a detailed costing of cost objects. This section presents a lengthy overview of the entire ABC system. For a numerical example illustrating how these concepts are converted to an ABC system, the reader should refer to the case study at the end of this chapter.

An ABC system begins with a determination of the scope of the project. This is a critical step, for creating an ABC system that encompasses every aspect of every department of all corporate subsidiaries takes an inordinate amount of time and resources and may never show valuable results for several years, if ever. We first determine the range of activities that the ABC system is to encompass and the results desired from the system. It is not usually necessary to create an ABC system for simple processes for which the costs can be readily separated and reported on. Instead, activities deserving of inclusion in an ABC system are those that involve numerous machines, complex processes, automation, many machine setups, or a diverse product line. These are areas in which it is difficult to clearly and indisputably assign costs to products or other cost objects. When creating a system scope to include these areas, it may be best to start with just a few of them on a pilot project basis so that the installation team and the affected employees can get used to the new system. The scope can later be expanded to include other areas of sufficient complexity to warrant the use of this system.

Scope considerations should also be expanded to include the level of detailed information the system should produce. For example, an ABC system designed to produce information only for strategic analysis is considered satisfactory if it issues high-level information. This system requires a much lower level of detailed information handling and calculation than one used for tactical-level costing of products, activities, or customers. Thus, the level of detailed information analysis built into the project's scope depends entirely on how the resulting information is to be used.

Another scope issue is the extent to which the ABC system is to be integrated into the existing accounting system. If the project is to be handled on a periodic recalculation basis, rather than being automatically updated whenever new information is introduced into the accounting system, all linkages can be no more than a manual retyping of existing information into a separate ABC system. However, a fully integrated ABC system requires extensive coding of software interfaces between the two systems, which is both time-consuming and expensive. These changes may include some alteration of the corporate chart of accounts, the cost center structure, and the cost and revenue distributions used by the accounts payable and billing functions. These are major changes, so the level of system integration should be a large part of any discussion regarding scope.

A final scope issue is a determination of how many costs from nonproduction areas should be included in the system. For companies with proportionately large production departments, this may not be an issue; but for service companies or those with large development departments, such costs can be a sizable proportion of total costs and should be included in the ABC system. These costs can come from areas as diverse as the research and development, product design, marketing, distribution, computer services, janitorial, and administration functions. Adding each new functional area increases the administrative cost of the ABC system, so a key issue in scope determination is whether or not the cost of each functional area is large enough to have an impact on the activity costs calculated by the system. Those with a negligible impact should be excluded.

Once we have determined the scope, we next separate all direct materials and labor costs and set them to one side. These costs are adequately identified by most existing accounting systems already, so it is usually a simple matter to locate and segregate the general ledger accounts in which they are stored. The remaining costs in the general ledger should be ones that can be allocated.

Next, using our statement of the scope of the project, we identify the costs in the general ledger that are to be allocated through the ABC system. For example, when the primary concern of the new system is to determine the cost of the sales effort on each product sale, finding the sales and marketing costs is the primary concern. Alternatively, if the purpose of the ABC system is to find the distribution cost per unit, only costs associated with warehousing, shipping, and freight must be located.

With the designated overhead costs in hand, we proceed to store costs in secondary, or resource, cost pools. A secondary cost pool is one that provides services to other company functions without directly supporting any activities that create products or services. Examples of resource costs are administrative salaries, building maintenance, and computer services. The costs stored in these cost pools will later be charged to other cost pools with various activity measures, so the costs should be stored in separate pools that can be allocated with similar allocation measures. For example, computer services costs can be allocated to other cost pools based on the number of personal computers used, so any costs that can reasonably and logically be allocated based on the number of personal computers used should be stored in the same resource cost pool.

In a similar manner we store all remaining overhead costs in a set of primary cost pools. There can be a large number of cost pools for the storage of similar costs, but one should consider that the cost of administering the ABC system (unless it is a rare case of full automation) increases with each cost pool added. Therefore, it is best to keep the number of cost pools under 10. A few standard cost pool descriptions are used in most companies. They are:

- **Batch-related cost pools.** Many costs, such as purchasing, receiving, production control, shop floor control, tooling, setup labor, supervision, training, material handling, and quality control are related to the length of production batches.

- **Product line–related cost pools.** A group of products may have incurred the same research and development, advertising, purchasing, and distribution costs. It may be necessary to split this category into separate cost pools when there are several different distribution channels and the costs of the channels differ dramatically from each other.

- **Facility-related cost pools.** Some costs cannot be directly allocated to specific products because they relate more closely to the entire facility. These include building insurance, building maintenance, and facility depreciation costs.

Other cost pools can be added to these three basic cost pools if the results will yield a significantly improved level of accuracy or if the extra cost pools will lead to attainment of the goals and scope set at the beginning of the project. In particular, the batch-related cost pool can be subdivided into several smaller cost pools depending on the number of different operations within a facility. For example, a candy-making plant has a line of cookers, the cost of which can be included in one cost pool, while the cost of its candy extruding machines can be segregated into a separate cost pool, and its cellophane wrapper machines into yet another. Costs can be allocated quite differently, depending on the type of machine used, so dividing this category into a number of smaller cost pools may make sense. The various sources of product costs are noted in Exhibit 16.1.

Costs cannot always be directly mapped from general ledger accounts into cost pools. Instead, there may be valid reasons for splitting general ledger costs into different cost pools. An allocation method that does this is called a resource driver. Examples of resource drivers are the number of products produced, the number of direct labor hours, and the number of production orders used. Whatever the type of resource driver selected, it should provide a logical, defendable means for redirecting costs from a general ledger account into a cost pool. There should be a minimal number of resource drivers because time and effort are required to accumulate each one. In reality, most companies use management judgment to arrive at a set percentage of each account to be allocated to cost pools, rather than use a formal resource driver. For example, the cost of computer depreciation may be allocated 50% to a secondary cost pool, 40% to a batch-related primary cost pool, and 10% to a facility-related primary cost pool because these percentages roughly reflect the

EXHIBIT 16.1. Sources of Product Costs

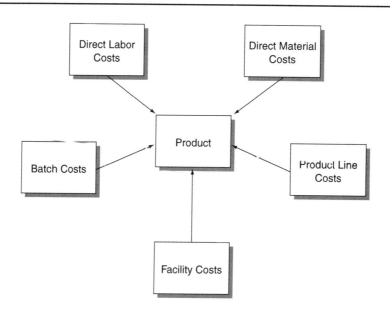

210

number of personal computers located in various parts of the facility. This in turn is considered a reasonable means of spreading these costs among different cost pools.

There are varying levels of detailed analysis that one can use to assign costs to cost pools. The level of analysis is largely driven by the need for increasingly detailed levels of information; when there is less need for accuracy, a less expensive method can be used. For example, if there are three cost pools in which purchasing department salaries can be stored, depending on the actual activities conducted, the easiest and least accurate approach is to make a management decision to send a certain percentage of the total cost to each one. A higher level of accuracy requires that the employees be split up into job categories, with varying percentages being allocated from each category. Finally, the highest level of accuracy requires time tracking by employee, with a fresh recalculation after every set of time sheets is collected. The level of accuracy needed, the size of the costs being allocated, and the cost of the related data collection drive the decision to collect information at progressively higher levels of accuracy.

The next step is to allocate all the costs stored in secondary cost pools to primary cost pools. This is done with activity drivers, which we will explain shortly. Allocating these cost pools to primary cost pools causes a redistribution of costs that can then be further allocated from the primary cost pools, with considerable accuracy, to cost objects. This subsidiary step of allocating costs from resource cost centers to primary cost centers can be avoided by sending all costs straight from the general ledger to the primary cost pools, but several studies have shown that this more direct approach does not do as good a job of accurately allocating costs. The use of resource cost centers reflects more precisely how costs flow through an organization—from resource activities such as the computer services department to other departments, which in turn are focused on activities used to create cost objects.

Now that all costs have been allocated to primary cost pools, we must find a way to accurately charge these costs to cost objects, which are the users of the costs. Examples of cost objects are products and customers. We perform this allocation with an activity driver, a variable that explains the consumption of costs from a cost pool. There should be a clearly defined cause-and-effect relationship between the cost pool and the activity so that there is a solid, defensible reason for using a specific activity driver. This is important because the use of specific activity drivers changes the amount of costs charged to cost objects, which can raise the ire of the managers responsible for these cost objects. Exhibit 16.2 itemizes a number of activity drivers that relate to specific types of costs.

The list of activities presented in Exhibit 16.2 is by no means comprehensive. Each company has unique processes and costs that may result in the selection of activity drivers different from the ones noted here. There are several key issues to consider when selecting an activity driver. They are:

- **Minimize data collection.** Few activity drivers are already tracked through the existing accounting system since few of them involve costs. Instead, they are

EXHIBIT 16.2. Activity Drivers for Specific Types of Costs

Cost Type	Related Activity Driver
Accounting costs	Number of billings
	Number of cash receipts
	Number of check payments
	Number of general ledger entries
	Number of reports issued
Administration costs	Hours charged to lawsuits
	Number of stockholder contacts
Engineering costs	Hours charged to design work
	Hours charged to process planning
	Hours charged to tool design
	Number of engineering change orders
Facility costs	Amount of space utilization
Human resources costs	Employee head count
	Number of benefits changes
	Number of insurance claims
	Number of pension changes
	Number of recruiting contacts
	Number of training hours
Manufacturing costs	Number of direct labor hours
	Number of field support visits
	Number of jobs scheduled
	Number of machine hours
	Number of machine setups
	Number of maintenance work orders
	Number of parts in product
	Number of parts in stock
	Number of price negotiations
	Number of purchase orders
	Number of scheduling changes
	Number of shipments
Marketing and sales costs	Number of customer service contacts
	Number of orders processed
	Number of sales contacts made
Quality control costs	Number of inspections
	Number of supplier reviews
Storage time (e.g., depreciation, taxes)	Inventory turnover
Storage transactions (e.g., receiving)	Number of times handled

more related to actions, such as the number of supplier reviews or the number of customer orders processed. These are numbers that may not be tracked anywhere in the existing system and so require extra effort to compile. Consequently, if there are few differences between several potential activity drivers, pick the one that is already being measured, thereby saving the maintenance work for the ABC system.

- **Pick low-cost measurements.** If it is apparent that the only reasonable activity measures must be collected from scratch, then—all other factors being equal—pick the one with the lowest data collection cost. This is a particularly important consideration if the ABC project is operating on a tight budget or if employees believe that the new system is consuming too many resources.

- **Verify a cause-and-effect relationship.** The activity driver must have a direct bearing on the incurrence of costs in the cost pool. To test this relationship perform a regression analysis (Chapter 29); if the regression reveals that changes in the activity driver have a considerable direct impact on the size of the cost pool, it is a good driver to use. It is also useful if the potential activity driver is one that can be used as the basis of measurement for further improvements. For example, if management can focus the attention of the organization on reducing the quantity of the activity driver, a smaller cost pool will result.

Once an activity driver has been selected for each cost pool, we then divide the total volume of each activity for the accounting period into the total amount of costs accumulated in each cost pool to derive a cost per unit of activity. For example, assume that the activity measure is the number of insurance claims processed and that there are 350 in the period. When they are divided into a human resources benefits cost pool of $192,000, the resulting cost per claim processed is $549.

Our next step is to determine the quantity of each activity used by the cost object. To do this, we need a measurement system that accumulates the quantity of activity driver used for each one. This measurement system may not be in existence yet and so must be specially constructed for the ABC system. If the cost of this added data collection is substantial, there will be considerable pressure to reduce the number of activity drivers, which represents a trade-off between accuracy and system cost.

Finally, we have reached our goal, which is to accurately assign overhead costs to cost objects. We multiply the cost per unit of activity by the number of units of each activity used by the cost objects. This should flush out all the costs located in the cost pools and assign them to cost objects in their entirety. Now we have found a defensible way to assign overhead costs in a way that is not only understandable but, more importantly, can be used by managers to reduce these costs. For example, if the activity measure for the overhead costs associated with the purchasing function's cost is the number of different parts ordered for each product, managers can focus on reducing the activity measure, which entails a reduction in

EXHIBIT 16.3. ABC Allocation Process

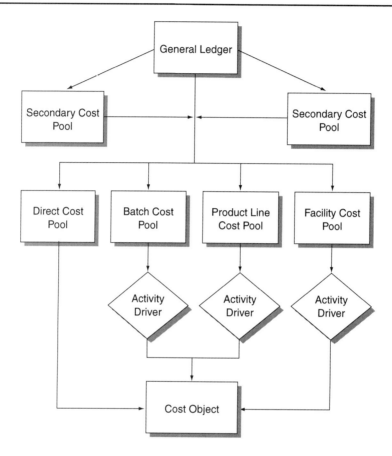

the number of different parts included in each product. Then the amount of purchasing overhead will indeed be reduced, for it is directly associated with and influenced by this activity driver. Thus, the ABC system is an excellent way to focus attention on costs that can be eliminated.

The explanation of ABC has been a lengthy one, so let us briefly recap it. After setting the scope of the ABC system, we allocate costs from the general ledger to secondary and primary cost pools, using resource drivers. We then allocate the costs of the secondary cost pools to the primary cost pools. Next we create activity drivers closely associated with the costs in each of the cost pools and derive a cost per unit of activity. We then accumulate the number of units of each activity used by each cost object (such as a product or customer) and multiply this number by the cost per activity driver. This procedure completely allocates all overhead costs to the cost objects in a reasonable, logical manner. An overview of the process is shown in Exhibit 16.3. The case study at the end of this chapter provides a numerical example of this process.

PROBLEMS WITH ACTIVITY-BASED COSTING

Though an ABC system can resolve many difficulties, it has several attendant problems that have resulted in many system installation failures. To ensure a higher degree of success, one should be aware of the problems described in this section and solve as many of them as possible in the earliest stages of an ABC system installation.

An underlying problem is that company managers hear about the wonders of ABC and demand that it be installed at once—without considering whether or not their organization actually needs it. ABC is most useful in situations where cost accounting information is muddied by the presence of multiple product lines, machines used to process different products, complex routings, automation, and numerous machine setups. If a company does not meet any of these criteria, it may not need an ABC system. For example, a company with a single product line, one production facility, and a small number of customers can probably generate reasonably accurate costing information from its existing general ledger system without resorting to a lengthy ABC installation. Companies that persist in installing ABC under these circumstances may find that they have achieved only a minor improvement in accuracy at the price of having a second accounting system layered over the existing one.

Another issue is the time required to create an ABC system. This undertaking can be a lengthy one, especially if the desired system is a comprehensive one that straddles multiple product lines and facilities. A project of this magnitude can easily require more than a year to complete. For work of this duration there is a greater chance that opponents of the project will start sniping at it after a few months have passed without any tangible results. In short, the longer the project's duration, the greater the chance that it will be terminated prior to completion. This problem can be avoided by limiting the scope of the ABC project to an area that can be completed, at least as a pilot project, within a much smaller time frame. By taking this approach one can show concrete, valuable results in short order, which builds enthusiasm for a continuing series of ABC projects that will gradually cover the main areas of a company's operations.

A major problem in many instances is that an ABC system extracts information from and reports on the activities of many departments, which draws their ire. If a sufficient number of department managers are irritated by the reports issued by the ABC system, they can use a variety of methods to withhold information from it so that the system no longer yields a sufficient amount of information to make it worthwhile. To avoid this problem, one should ensure that a high-level manager takes personal responsibility for the project so that any interdepartmental problems can be dealt with both quickly and in favor of the ABC system. This also means that great care must be taken to hand off this project sponsor position to succeeding individuals who have an equally high degree of enthusiasm for ABC.

A further issue is that an ABC system almost always involves construction of a set of data separate from the general ledger. If this second database becomes so massive that it is unwieldy, or if the data it contains diverges sharply from the information in the general ledger, the accounting department will offer significant resistance. This conflict arises because staff time must be spent on maintenance—very likely including the hiring of extra cost accounting staff—and the results from the system may be difficult to trace back to the company's financial reports, entailing additional effort by the accounting staff. Thus, an increase in the workload can produce resistance within the accounting department. To avoid this problem, it is necessary to properly design the ABC system so that it collects the minimum possible amount of extra information in addition to what is already stored in the general ledger. In this way data collection and maintenance requirements are reduced, and it is easier to trace ABC numbers back to the general ledger. System simplification is an important factor here.

Reporting is also a problem. The users of accounting reports may have become accustomed to seeing the same accounting reports for a number of years and do not want to put any effort into learning to read new ones. Instead, they continue to use the old reports and ignore the new ones. The obvious solution to this problem is to phase out or restrict access to the old reports, while providing training in the use of the new reports. Follow-up training is crucial since users may not at first understand the concept of activity-based costing.

The trade-off between the number of cost pools used and the level of accuracy obtained is another issue. When costs are summarized into too few cost pools, the resulting level of information accuracy is reduced, whereas an increase in the number of cost pools (and therefore a finer level of overhead allocation) results in more accurate costing. The trouble is that an ABC system becomes much more expensive and complex to operate when there are too many cost pools. To resolve this issue it is useful to create an analysis of the incremental cost required to maintain each additional cost pool added to the ABC model and to stop when the cost exceeds a preset threshold or when the level of complexity appears to have become excessive.

A final issue is that the ABC system is frequently set up to be repeated on a project basis, which means that it requires continual reauthorization to reiterate. Because it is a project, it can be killed by reduced funding or staffing whenever the next project renewal review occurs. ABC information is frequently derived on a project basis because it is too expensive to collect and process on a continuing basis. To avoid this issue one can alter the ABC system so that some parts of it are designed into the existing cost accounting system, with some ABC information constantly being updated and only a small part of it still obtained on a project basis.

Any ABC information that is easy to collect and interpret, or yields immediate and continuing information of importance, can be included in the ongoing ABC system. More peripheral ABC information can be collected on a project basis. This format retains the most crucial ABC information even if the ancillary ABC project that collects secondary data is dropped.

It is apparent that a number of issues can impede or stop the development or ongoing functioning of an ABC system. However, by using the suggestions noted here, they can all be anticipated and sidestepped, resulting in a strong, well-run ABC system that yields important accounting information.

IMPLEMENTING AN ACTIVITY-BASED COSTING SYSTEM

Though a small ABC installation can be completed by a single person in a few days, the much more likely scenario is that the installation requires a great deal of analysis, dedicated resources for a number of months, and its own budget. For this second scenario, here is a list of standard implementation steps:

1. *Obtain high-level support.* An ABC project involves the procurement of funding and dealings with multiple departments. To make these chores easier, there should be a high-level supporter of the project on the management team who can give it enough "push" through the corporate bureaucracy to ensure that it is completed in a timely manner.

2. *Obtain a project schedule and budget.* The project team leader should work with the high-level project sponsor to obtain a project schedule and funding that is sufficient for completion of the system. For organizations not familiar with ABC, this can be split into two steps, with the first step given only enough funding for a pilot project, and full funding contingent on the results of the pilot.

3. *Assemble the ABC team.* This team does not consist of just accountants. Instead, because of the wide array of knowledge required to formulate an ABC system, it should include employees from the engineering, marketing, materials management, computer services, and production departments. They may have to be assigned to the project on a full-time basis if the installation is sufficiently large.

4. *Train the team.* Many team members may never have heard of ABC before or have only a passing familiarity with it. An in-house expert or a consultant can be brought in to conduct an intensive review session with the team.

5. *Gather information.* The project team needs to gather data in order to identify activities, costs, relationships between activities and costs, and types of

cost drivers. The best information is usually obtained through interviews. Additional sources of information are the general ledger, financial statements, and a detailed review of all costs. The project team can also obtain general operational information by observing operations in action.

6. *Conduct modeling and analysis.* With all the information in hand, the team should use flowcharting to determine how activities occur and flow through departments. It is at this point that resource drivers, cost pools, and activities are identified and documented.

7. *Select and purchase a software package.* It may be necessary to purchase a third-party ABC software package, which typically makes it easier to conduct analysis and ad hoc inquiries; it also makes it easier to control the system since all ABC-related files are kept in one place. The project team must assemble a detailed list of software functionality requirements and compare this list to the functionality of several possible software packages. The team should then pick the package that most closely meets its requirements.

8. *Create software linkages.* It may be possible to create automated linkages between the ABC system and other systems, such as the general ledger, that allow one to save time by streamlining the flow of information into the ABC system. These interfaces should be carefully tested to ensure their operability.

9. *Test the software.* The team should create a set of sample ABC transactions and run them through the ABC software. This step is designed not just to see if the software works as advertised but also to ensure that the team understands how the ABC system works.

10. *Design reports.* An ABC system usually requires an entirely new set of reports. These must be constructed with the ABC package's report writer, or customized, or written with the aid of a third party's software package. The team should create sample reports with test transactions to be certain that the reports function as planned.

11. *Design policies and procedures.* Once the software is determined to be acceptable, the team must prepare a set of policies and procedures to integrate the operation of the ABC system and the software into the existing operations of the accounting department. These should be tested with the people who will be using the system, and retested after the system has been installed, to ensure that they are constructed correctly.

12. *Implement the system.* The team should coordinate the training of all ABC system users just prior to the "go live" date, be present on the day the system is made operational, and for several weeks subsequent to this date, provide a help desk to answer all user questions. Other tasks may be required during this stage, such as revisions to software code, reports, or procedures

that reflect problems found subsequent to the implementation.

13. *Follow up on the installation.* An ABC system rarely works exactly as expected. Instead, there are problems that are caused by improper or inadequate training, missing procedures, or faulty analysis. To detect these problems, the project team should return to the ABC system a short time after the installation and review each of the processing steps. These problems can then be documented and corrected. Further reviews can be spread out over longer periods as the new system gradually "settles down."

Though not all these steps apply in all cases, they form a rough guide for the implementation of an ABC system. Steps can be added to or subtracted from this list to arrive at the most functional set of activities for a particular ABC installation.

BILL OF ACTIVITIES

An important outcome of an ABC system that deserves a separate discussion is the bill of activities (BOA). This document is similar to a bill of materials (BOM) in that it itemizes all the components of a product; however, it lists only the overhead components as defined through an ABC system, rather than the direct material and labor costs most commonly found in a BOM.

When combined with the costs listed in a BOM, the BOA yields a high level of detail for all costs associated with a product. These two documents then become the core of almost any cost-based analysis involving products. For example, one can use the BOA to determine the exact overhead costs to apply to a product in a full costing situation, while also assigning costs based on only certain cost pools, depending on the analysis issue being reviewed. If there is a question regarding the development cost per unit of production, the BOA has this information. If managers are curious about the overhead cost per batch, the BOA contains this information, too.

An example of a BOA is shown in Exhibit 16.4. Note that there are different line items for each cost pool, so that one can clearly differentiate the overhead costs based on batch-level, product line–level, and facility-level activities. Also, note that the cost pool quantities are divided by the activity volumes associated with these pools. For example, the product engineering cost pool is divided by the total number of units expected to be produced over the life of the product since this quantity bears a valid relationship to the research and development costs required to create it.

EXHIBIT 16.4. Bill of Activities

Overhead Cost Pool	Total Pool Cost ($)	Activity Measure	Relevant Volume	Cost per Unit ($)
Product engineering	300,000	Units produced	50,000/life cycle	6.00
Process planning	175,000	Units produced	50,000/life cycle	3.50
Batch-specific	90,000	Batch size	12,000/batch	7.50
Marketing and distribution	120,000	Annual volume	10,000/annually	12.00
Total Costs				**29.00**

USES OF ACTIVITY-BASED COSTING

Now that we have an ABC system, how are we going to use it? There are many questions it can answer, such as:

- **How do we increase shareholder value?** When an ABC analysis is combined with a review of investment costs for various tactical or strategic options, one can determine the return on investment to be expected for each investment option.

- **How much does a distribution channel cost?** An ABC system can accumulate all the costs associated with a particular distribution method, which allows managers to compare this cost to the profit margins earned on sales of products sold through it. One can then determine if the distribution channel should be reconfigured or eliminated in order to improve overall levels of profitability.

- **How do product costs vary by plant?** An ABC analysis itemizes the costs of each plant and correctly allocates these costs to the activities conducted within them, which allows a company to determine which plants are more efficient than others.

- **Should we make or buy an item?** An ABC analysis includes all activity costs associated with a manufactured item, providing a comprehensive view of all costs associated with it and can then be more easily compared to the cost of a similar item that is purchased.

- **Which acquisition is a good one?** By using internal ABC analyses to determine the cost of various activities, a company can create a benchmark for these costs in potential acquisition targets. When the targets have higher costs than the benchmark levels, the acquiring company knows that it can strip out costs from the acquisition candidate by improving its processes, which may justify the cost of the acquisition.

- **What does each activity cost?** An ABC analysis can reveal the cost of each activity within an organization. The system is really designed to trace the costs of only the most significant activities, but its design can be altered to itemize the costs of many more activities. This information can then be used to determine which activities are so expensive that they will be the main focus of management attention or can be profitably combined with other activities through process centering. This is a primary cost reduction activity.

- **What price should we charge?** An ABC analysis reveals all the costs associated with a product and so is useful for determining the minimum price that should be charged. However, the actual price charged may be much higher since it may be driven by the ability of the market to absorb a higher price rather than the underlying cost of the product.

- **What products should we sell?** An ABC analysis can be combined with product prices to yield a list of margins for each product sold. When sorted by market, product line, or customer, it is then easy to see which products have low or negative returns or yield such low margin volumes that they are not worth keeping.

- **Where are the non-value-added costs?** An ABC analysis can reveal which activities contribute to the completion of products and which do not. Then, by focusing on those non-value-added activities that do not create value, a company can create significant improvements in its profitability.

- **Where can we reduce costs?** An ABC analysis reveals the cost of anything a management team needs to know about—activities, products, or customers—which can then be sorted to see where the highest-cost items are located. Combining this with a value analysis, one can determine what costs return the lowest values and structure a cost reduction effort accordingly.

- **Which customers do we want?** An ABC analysis can itemize the costs specific to each customer, such as special customer service or packaging, as well as increases in warranty claims or product returns. When combined with the margins on products sold to customers, this analysis reveals which customers are the most profitable after *all* costs are considered.

The number of uses to which an ABC system can be put is limited only by the imagination of the user. However, it is necessary to address this issue *before* the system is installed, for the design of the system (as noted earlier) is heavily dependent on the uses to which it will be put. To ensure that the correct system use is determined in advance, it is critical that the input of system users (especially senior-level managers) be obtained during the earliest phases of the ABC system design.

ACTIVITY-BASED MANAGEMENT

Though we have just considered the uses to which ABC can be put, they do not describe a formal methodology for using the information. This is provided by activity-based management (ABM). In essence, it begins where ABC stops by using ABC information to make changes in corporate activities that result in greater streamlining of activities.

The starting point for ABM is to determine the ratio of primary to secondary activities within an organization. A primary activity is one that contributes directly to the production of a product or service for a customer, while a secondary activity is a supporting function, such as filling out forms, entering data, calculating payroll, or issuing financial statements. It is common to see a ratio of 50:50 between these two types of activities, indicating that a large part of a company's resources are not being used in a manner that contributes to revenue production. It is the goal of ABM to drive this ratio in the direction of 100:0 (clearly impossible), usually settling for 80:20 as an indication that a company is efficient in its operations and effective in completing primary tasks.

The next step is to focus the attention of a project team on the secondary activities taking up a large part of the company's resources in terms of cost or time; time is a crucial factor if there is a significant delay in shipping products. The team carefully reviews each phase of the targeted activity, looking for wasteful steps that can be eliminated or reduced. It then works with the users of the system to see if the proposed changes will work and then designs policies and procedures that can be used as training tools and ongoing guidelines for altering the system.

Finally, the project team conducts training sessions with system users, to educate them about all the changes to be made, and then oversees the system conversion that results in a more streamlined process. The project team then lists recommended audit review steps for the internal audit team to use when it conducts its periodic audits; these steps are valuable for ensuring that the recommended changes have been firmly adopted by the system users. If not, the project team can be called in at a later date to reinforce user knowledge of the new system, perhaps with added training or slight modifications that will make it easier to operate.

This general process briefly represents how ABM works; the exact process varies by company, the composition of the project teams, and the type of system.

ROLE OF THE COST ACCOUNTANT IN AN ABC SYSTEM

The cost accountant is positioned squarely in the center of any ABC system purchase, installation, and operation. This is because the purpose of using ABC is to obtain better costing information, which is the business of the cost accountant.

The cost accountant's role in the selection of ABC software centers on the creation of a requirements definition—a listing of all the features needed in the software packages to be reviewed. The cost accountant gains this knowledge of the requirements by interviewing other employees to see what they need, as well as from their theoretical knowledge of cost accounting, knowledge of how other companies use ABC, and what the company's strategy requires in the way of costing information. This information is then assembled on a checklist which the cost accountant uses to review all prospective software selections. The best approach is to design a sample transaction that tests the presence of each requirement and then run the transaction through the sample software to see if it functions as per the itemized requirements. Because of this detailed review process, the opinion of the cost accountant is frequently the deciding factor in determining which ABC package is purchased.

Another task for the cost accountant is to structure the flow of costs through the ABC system. This involves determining what costs are to be consolidated into which costs pools and how they are to be allocated to various activities. This is information that the cost accountant deals with every day and which he has the best knowledge of. Also, the cost accountant should determine the boundaries of what will (and will not) be included in the ABC system, so that it measures only what is needed and does so within the cost budgeted for the system.

Once the system has been created, the cost accountant becomes its chief user. He determines whether any allocations require alteration, what reports it should issue, how the information is used, what employees receive information, and how this information can support strategic and tactical decisions. Since these activities nearly match a cost accountant's job description, it is evident that he must become its most expert user in order to complete his job. The ABC system and the cost accountant are closely intertwined.

CASE STUDY

The board of directors of the General Research and Instrumentation Company has completed a benchmarking comparison of the company's costs to those of its competitors and finds that the company is expending a significantly higher proportion of its revenues on production scheduling activities than anyone else in the industry; the department's costs appear to be one-third higher than they should be. It suspects that the company is running a large number of small production runs, which requires an extra scheduling effort, but wants to find out for certain before discussing operational changes with the CEO. This demand trickles down through the organization to Mr. Albert Goizueta, who is in charge of ABC analysis at the corporate headquarters. He recognizes that his main task is to determine the activities in which the production scheduling staff is involved. To do so, he assembles a planning document for an ABC system and obtains approval from the CFO, who becomes the project sponsor. Since this is a small ABC project, he requires no staff, and only a time budget for himself, so there is no need for a reallocation of resources to the project.

The next step is to construct cost pools for production scheduling. A brief review of the departmental income statement for the production scheduling department reveals that there are no costs other than payroll and benefits, which are all segregated into two separate accounts in the general ledger. Now that he knows where the underlying costs are stored, he must determine the range of activities conducted by the production schedulers and allocate these payroll costs to those activities, which are stored in separate cost pools. To locate this information he interviews the production scheduling manager, who itemizes the daily tasks along with the proportion of time spent on each one:

Activity	Proportion of Time Spent (%)
Job scheduling	32
Job under run investigation	15
Review of material shortages	53
Total	**100**

To be certain that this proportion applies to the entire production scheduling staff, Mr. Goizueta interviews the entire department and finds general agreement on the stated proportions. Then he creates a separate cost pool for each of the three main activities and allocates the salaries and benefits for the department, as itemized in the general ledger, to them. The calculation is:

Total General Ledger Cost ($)	Proportion (%)	Cost Pool Description	Allocation to Cost Pool ($)
480,000	32	Job scheduling	153,600
	15	Job investigation	72,000
	53	Material shortages review	254,400
Total	100		**480,000**

Further discussion with the production scheduling staff reveals the most appropriate activity drivers for the three cost pools. The job scheduling cost pool is entirely related to the *number of jobs* scheduled for production since a specific amount of work is required for each job to determine which machines are available, when they can be used, and how this scheduled production fits the customer's expectations. The cost pool for the investigation of jobs that were run over or under the desired quantities is most closely tied to the *number of scrapped units,* for an excessively high scrap rate results in production shortages that require the scheduling of additional production runs to complete. Finally, the material shortage review is directly tied to the *number of parts in a product;* those with a large number of component parts require much more investigation into component quantities to ensure that there are enough parts on hand for a scheduled production run. A regression analysis calculation (Chapter 29) confirms that there is a strong relationship between the activity drivers and the costs stored in the cost pools.

Mr. Goizueta's next task is to determine the total quantity of each activity driver that occurs during a standard accounting period. First, he learns that the production scheduling staff maintains a database of all production jobs, so he is easily able to compile from it a total number of scheduled jobs for the accounting period. Next he obtains from the quality assurance department the total number of scrapped units for the same period and then goes to the engineering department to obtain the number of parts required to build each product, which he then multiplies by the total number of different parts produced during the period to obtain the total number of different parts used. He then compiles this information in a table and extends it to determine the activity cost per unit of each activity driver.

Activity Driver	Activity Volume	Related Cost Pool	Total Cost in Related Cost Pool	Cost per Unit of Activity Driver ($)
No. of jobs	625	Job scheduling	153,600	245.76
No. of scrapped units	15,204	Job investigation	72,000	4.74
No. of parts in product	1,204	Material shortages review	254,400	211.30

He then needs to determine the impact of these activity costs on individual products and decides to apply the cost of each activity driver to a representative product that was running during the month under review—a wrist-mounted global positioning system (GPS). The product has direct costs of $225 and was manufactured in a production run of 450 units. The overhead costs applied to it through the ABC system are:

Activity Driver	Activity Volume in Job	Number of Units in Production Run	Cost per Unit of Activity Driver ($)	Total Unit Costs ($)
No. of jobs	1	450	245.76	0.55
No. of scrapped units	51	450	4.74	0.54
No. of parts in product	18	450	211.30	8.45
Direct cost per unit				225.00
Total				**234.54**

The last table clearly shows that the impact of the number of jobs at the current volume level per scheduled job has a negligible impact on the cost of the unit produced, as is also the case for scrapped parts that cause additional production jobs to be scheduled. The real issue is that far too many parts shortages are impacting the ability of the company to schedule and successfully complete production runs, as shown in the table by the $8.45 scheduling charge based on the number of parts contained in the product.

Armed with this ABC-based information, Mr. Goizueta can return to the board of director's original question—Why is the cost of the production scheduling department so high? The answer is contained in his report to the board:

> The primary reason for the excessively high cost of production scheduling is not the size of the production runs but rather the amount of material shortages in the materials management system. The production scheduling staff must spend approximately half of its time manually verifying that materials are on hand before they can schedule production runs, which absorbs the bulk of all departmental costs. To correct this problem I recommend two steps: first, improve the materials management system with the installation of a manufacturing resources planning system that will improve the accuracy of our in-house materials records, and second, reduce the number of parts designed into our products, so that there are not only fewer components for the production scheduling staff to investigate but also fewer materials to be handled by the materials management system.

This case study shows that the use of an ABC system can reveal that the causes of costs are diffcrent than one might initially think, resulting in different management activities that can eliminate the underlying reasons for the incurrence of costs. Also, of particular interest in this case is the extremely limited nature of the study—it was designed specifically to answer a particular question, which it did in an efficient manner. Thus, implementing a broad-based, companywide ABC system may not be the answer if only specific management questions must be answered with the system—a more focused effort is more appropriate in these situations.

SUMMARY

An ABC system provides much better information about the uses of overhead costs than a traditional overhead allocation system. Though its installation must be carefully thought out to ensure that various pitfalls are avoided, an ABC system can result in a considerable improvement in the quality of cost accounting information available to a company, especially those with complex systems and multiple product lines, where costs tend to become obscured and difficult to trace to specific products, customers, or activities.

CHAPTER 17

Target Costing

The majority of costing systems are focused on the control of labor and raw material costs and on the manner in which overhead costs are applied to production activities. However, only target costing has a tight focus on the activities that occur *before* production commences—the product design process. In this section we describe target costing and delve into the types of data it requires, as well as the situations where it can be most usefully employed. We also cover special implementation issues, points at which target costing can be most easily controlled, and the extent of its potential impact on profitability.

DESCRIPTION OF TARGET COSTING

The concept behind target costing is based on the realization that the bulk of all product costs are predetermined before a product ever reaches the production floor. This is because the types of materials used are determined during the design stage, as are the types of production methods used to shape and assemble the parts into a completed product. Consequently, the cost reduction focus of any company that designs its own products should be to closely review the costs of products while they are still in the design stage and do everything possible to keep these costs to a minimum.

The target costing method addresses the costs designed into a product with a four-step process:

1. *Conduct market research.* This involves reviewing the competitive landscape to see what other products are in the marketplace, as well as the types

of new products that competitors say they are about to release into the market. It also involves a review of which customers may buy future products, what their needs are, and what prices they are likely to pay for selected product features. Further, one should determine the size of the market into which the new products are to be released and the amount of market share that can likely be obtained. This gives a company the general outlines of a revenue plan in terms of the probable number of units that can be sold and the price at which they will sell.

2. *Determine margin and cost feasibility.* This involves clarifying what product features customers want, based on the information gathered in the first step, and translating this into a preliminary set of product features that will be part of the anticipated product design. We then determine a price point, again based on the preceding market research, at which the product is likely to sell. Then we determine the standard margin to be applied to the product (which is commonly based on the corporate cost of capital, plus an additional percentage), which results in a cost figure that the product cannot exceed. We then conduct a preliminary review of anticipated product costs to see if the product design is in the cost "ballpark." If not, we cancel the design project as being unfeasible.

3. *Meet margin targets through design improvements.* This involves the completion of all value engineering needed to drive down the product's cost to the level at which the target price and margin can be attained, as well as confirming the viability of the material and process costs with suppliers and other parts of the company impacted by these design decisions. The design is then finalized, and the resulting bill of materials is sent to the purchasing staff for procurement, while the industrial engineering staff proceeds to install all required changes to the production facility needed to implement lower-cost production processes.

4. *Implement continuous improvement.* This involves the product launch at the manufacturing facility, first through a pilot production run and then at full production volumes. Also, the cost accountant begins the regular review of all supplier costs that contribute to the cost of the product and reports variances to management to ensure that targeted cost levels are maintained subsequent to the design phase. There is also an ongoing continuous improvement program, known as kaizen costing, that focuses on the reduction of waste in the production process, thereby further lowering costs below the initial targets specified during the design phase.

These target costing steps are shown graphically in Exhibit 17.1.

A concept called value engineering was mentioned in phase 2 of the preceding process. This is a collective term for several activities used to lower the cost of a

EXHIBT 17.1. Target Costing Process

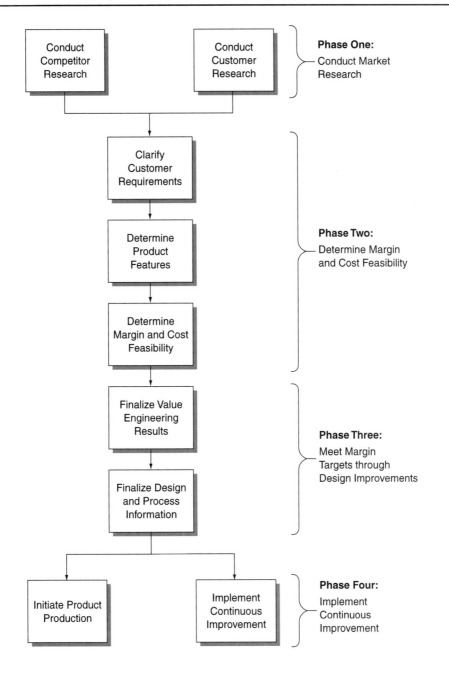

product. Here are some of the issues that are dealt with during a value engineering review:

- **Can we eliminate functions from the production process?** This involves a detailed review of the entire manufacturing process to see if there are any steps, such as interim quality reviews, that add no value to the product. By eliminating them, one can take their associated direct or overhead costs out of the product cost. However, these functions were originally put in for a reason, so the engineering team must be careful to develop work-around steps that eliminate the need for the original functions.

- **Can we eliminate some durability or reliability?** It is possible to design an excessive degree of sturdiness into a product. For example, a vacuum cleaner can be designed to withstand a 1-ton impact, although there is only the most vanishing chance that such an impact will ever occur; designing it to withstand an impact of 100 pounds may account for 99.999% of all probable impacts, while also eliminating a great deal of structural material from the design. However, this concept can be taken too far, resulting in a visible reduction in durability or reliability, so any designs that have had their structural integrity reduced must be thoroughly tested to ensure that they meet all design standards.

- **Can we minimize the design?** This involves the creation of a design that uses fewer parts or has fewer features. This approach is based on the assumption that a minimal design is easier to manufacture and assemble. Also, with fewer parts to purchase, less procurement overhead is associated with the product. However, reducing a product to extremes, perhaps from dozens of components to just a few molded or prefabricated parts, can result in excessively high costs for these few remaining parts, since they may be so complex or custom-made in nature that it would be less expensive to settle for a few extra standard parts that are more easily and cheaply obtained.

- **Can we design the product better for the manufacturing process?** Also known as design for manufacture and assembly (DFMA), this involves the creation of a product design that can be created in only a specific manner. For example, a toner cartridge for a laser printer is designed so that it can be successfully inserted into the printer only when the sides of the cartridge are correctly aligned with the printer opening; all other attempts to insert the cartridge will fail. When used for the assembly of an entire product, this approach ensures that a product is not incorrectly manufactured or assembled, which would call for a costly disassembly or (even worse) product recalls from customers who have already received defective goods.

- **Can we substitute parts?** This approach encourages the search for less expensive components or materials that can replace more expensive parts currently used in a product design. It is becoming an increasingly valid approach since new materials are being developed every year. However, sometimes the use of a different material impacts the types of materials that can be used elsewhere in the product, which may result in cost increases in these other areas, for a net increase in costs. Thus, any parts substitution must be accompanied by a review of related changes elsewhere in the design. This step is also known as component parts analysis and involves one extra activity—tracking the intentions of suppliers to continue producing parts in the future; if parts will not be available, they must be eliminated from the product design.

- **Can we combine steps?** A detailed review of all the processes associated with a product sometimes reveals that some steps can be consolidated, which may mean that one can be eliminated (as noted earlier) or that several can be accomplished by one person, rather than having people in widely disparate parts of the production process perform them. This is also known as process centering. By combining steps in this manner, we can eliminate some of the transfer and queue time from the production process, which in turn reduces the chance that parts will be damaged during these transfers.

- **Is there a better way?** Though this step sounds rather vague, it really strikes at the core of the cost reduction issue—the other value engineering steps previously mentioned focus on incremental improvements to the existing design or production process, whereas this one is a more general attempt to start from scratch and build a new product or process that is not based in any way on preexisting ideas. Improvements resulting from this step tend to have the largest favorable impact on cost reductions but can also be the most difficult for the organization to adopt, especially if it has used other designs or systems for the production of earlier models.

Another approach to value engineering is to call on the services of a company's suppliers to assist in the cost reduction effort. These organizations are particularly suited to contribute information concerning enhanced types of technology or materials, since they may specialize in areas that a company has no information about. They may have also conducted extensive value engineering for the components they manufacture, resulting in advanced designs that a company may be able to incorporate into its new products. Suppliers may have also redesigned their production processes, or can be assisted by a company's engineers in doing so, producing cost reductions or decreased production waste that can be translated into lower component costs for the company.

A mix of all the value engineering steps noted above must be applied to each product design to ensure that the maximum permissible cost is safely reached. Also, even if a minimal amount of value engineering is needed to reach a cost goal, one should conduct the full range of value engineering analysis anyway, since this can result in further cost reductions that improve the margin of the product or allow management the option of reducing the product's price, thereby creating a problem for competitors who sell higher-priced products.

Another term mentioned in the earlier explanation of the target costing process is "kaizen costing." This is a Japanese term for a number of cost reduction steps that can be used subsequent to issuing a new product design to the factory floor. Some of the activities in the kaizen costing methodology include the elimination of waste in the production, assembly, and distribution processes, as well as the elimination of work steps in any of these areas. Though these points arc also covered in the value engineering phase of target costing, the initial value engineering may not uncover all possible cost savings. Thus, kaizen costing is really designed to repeat many of the value engineering steps for as long as a product is produced, constantly refining the process and thereby stripping out extra costs. The cost reductions resulting from kaizen costing are much smaller than those achieved with value engineering but are still worth the effort since competitive pressures are likely to force down the price of a product over time, and any possible cost savings allow a company to still attain its targeted profit margins while continuing to reduce costs. This concept is illustrated in Exhibit 17.2.

Of particular interest in Exhibit 17.2 is the use of multiple generations of products to meet the challenge of gradually reducing costs. In the example the market price continues to drop over time, which forces a company to use both target and kaizen costing to reduce costs and retain its profit margin. However, prices eventually drop to the point where margins are reduced, which forces the company to develop a new product with lower initial costs (Version B in the example) and for which kaizen costing can again be used to further reduce costs. This pattern may be repeated many times as a company forces its costs down through successive generations of products. The exact timing of a switch to a new product is easy to determine well in advance since the returns from kaizen costing follow a trend line of gradually shrinking savings and prices also follow a predictable downward track; plotting these two trend lines into the future reveals when a new generation of product must be ready for production.

The type of cost reduction program used for target costing has an impact on the extent of cost reduction, as well as on the nature of the components used in a product. When a design team elects to set cost reduction goals by allocating specific cost reduction amounts to major components of an existing product, it tends to focus on finding ways to make incremental cost reductions rather than focusing on entirely new product configurations that might both radically alter the product's design and lower its cost. This approach is most commonly used during the redesign of products already on the market. Another cost reduction approach is to allocate cost reductions based on the presence of certain product features in a product design. This method focuses the attention of the design team away from using the same components that were used in the past, which tends to produce more radical design changes that yield greater cost savings. However, the latter approach is also a riskier one, since the resulting product concepts may not work, and also requires so much extra design work that the new design may not be completed for a long time. Therefore, the second method is generally reserved for situations where a company is trying to create products at a radically lower cost than previously.

EXHIBIT 17.2. Stages of Cost Reduction

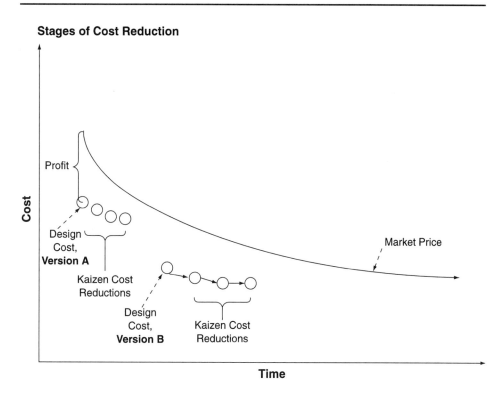

All the changes noted in this section that are necessary for the implementation and use of the target costing methodology represent a massive change in mind-set for the product design personnel of any company because they require the constant cooperation of many departments and rapid, voluminous communications between them, not to mention heightened levels of trust in dealing with suppliers. All these concepts run counter to the traditional approach, as indicated in Exhibit 17.3.

It is no coincidence that the traditional design process shown in Exhibit 17.3 uses castles to define each of the departments that take part in the process. These departments tend to guard their turf jealously, which is a major impediment to realizing a smoothly functioning set of product development teams. Only the most active support from senior management can enforce the new approach of drawing product design team members from all these castles and having them work together amicably.

Having described the key elements of target costing, value engineering, and kaizen costing, we now turn to a variety of related topics to flesh out the reader's understanding of target costing, including target costing problems, control points, and data flows, as well as its impact on profitability and the key steps required to install it.

EXHIBIT 17.3. Traditional Product Design Process

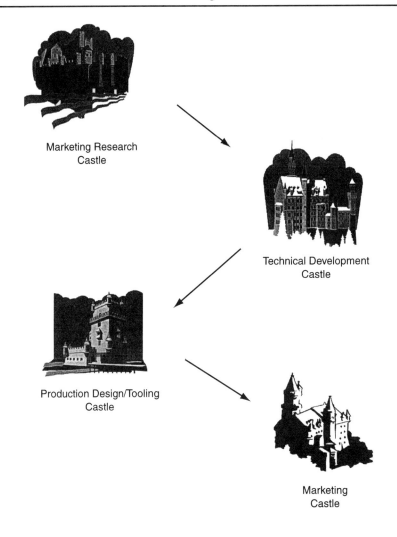

Marketing Research
Castle

Technical Development
Castle

Production Design/Tooling
Castle

Marketing
Castle

PROBLEMS WITH TARGET COSTING

Though the target costing system results in clear, substantial benefits in most cases, it has a few problems that one should be aware of and guard against.

The first problem is that the development process can be lengthened to a considerable extent since the design team may require a number of design iterations before it can devise a sufficiently low-cost product that meets the target cost and margin criteria. This occurrence is most common when the project manager is unwilling to "pull the plug" on a design project that cannot meet its costing goals within a reasonable time frame. Usually, if there is no evidence of rapid progress toward a specific target cost within a relatively short amount of time, it is better to either ditch a project or at least shelve it for a short time and then try again, on the assumption that new cost reduction methods or less expensive materials will be available in the near future that will make the target cost an achievable one.

Another problem with target costing is that a large amount of mandatory cost cutting can result in finger-pointing in various parts of the company, especially if employees in one area feel they are being called on to provide a disproportionately large part of the savings. For example, the industrial engineering staff will not be happy if it is required to completely alter the production layout in order to generate cost savings, while the purchasing staff is not required to make any cost reductions through supplier negotiations. Avoiding this problem requires strong interpersonal and negotiation skills on the part of the project manager.

Finally, having representatives from a number of departments on the design team can sometimes make it more difficult to reach a consensus on the proper design because there are too many opinions regarding design issues. This is a major problem when there are particularly stubborn people on the design team who are holding out for specific product features. Resolving this difficulty requires a strong team manager, as well as a long-term commitment on the part of a company to weed out those who are not willing to act in the best interests of the team.

For every problem area outlined here, the dominant solution is retaining strong control over the design teams, which calls for a good team leader. This person must have an exceptional knowledge of the design process, good interpersonal skills, and a commitment to staying within both time and cost budgets for a design project.

COST ACCOUNTANT'S ROLE IN A TARGET COSTING ENVIRONMENT

Given the strong cost orientation in a target costing environment, there is obviously a considerable role for the cost accountant on a design team. What are the specific activities and required skills of this person?

The cost accountant should be able to provide for the other members of the design team a running series of cost estimates based on initial design sketches, activity-based costing reviews of production processes, and "best guess" costing information from suppliers based on estimated production volumes. Especially in the earliest stages of a design, the cost accountant works with vague cost information and so must be able to provide estimates within a high-low range of costs, gradually tightening this estimated cost range as more information becomes available.

The cost accountant should also be responsible for any capital budgeting requests generated by the design team since he or she has the most knowledge of the capital budgeting process, how to fill out the required forms, and precisely what types of equipment are needed for the anticipated product design. The cost accountant also becomes the key contact on the design team for answers to any questions from the finance staff regarding issues or uncertainties in the capital budgeting proposal.

The cost accountant should work with the design team to help it understand the nature of various costs (such as cost allocations based on an activity-based costing system), as well as the cost-benefit trade-offs of using different design or cost options in the new product.

In addition, the cost accountant is responsible for tracking the gap between the current cost of a product design and the target cost that is the design team's goal, providing an itemization of where cost savings have already been achieved and where there has not been a sufficient degree of progress.

Finally, the cost accountant must continue to compare a product's actual cost to the target cost after the design is completed, and for as long as the company sells the product. This is a necessary step because management must know immediately if costs are increasing beyond budgeted levels and why these increases are occurring.

Given the large number of activities for which a cost accountant is responsible under the target costing methodology, it is evident that the job is a full-time one for all but the smallest costing projects. Accordingly, a cost accountant is commonly sent to a design team as a long-term assignment and may even report to the design team's manager, with few or no ties back to the accounting department. This may even be a different career track for a cost accountant—permanent attachment to a series of design teams.

There are particular qualifications that a cost accountant must have to be assigned to a target costing team. Certainly, one is having a good knowledge of company products as well as their features and components. Also, the cost accountant must know how to create an activity-based costing system to evaluate related production costs, or at least interpret such costing data developed by someone else. Further, he or she must work well in a team environment, proactively assisting other members of the team in constantly evaluating the costs of new design concepts. In addition, he or she should have good analytical and presentation skills, since the ongoing costing results must be continually presented not only to other members of the team but also to the members of the milestone review committee (see Target Costing Control Points). Thus, the best cost accountant for this position is an outgoing person with several years of experience within a company or industry.

IMPACT OF TARGET COSTING ON PROFITABILITY

Target costing can have a startlingly large positive impact on profitability, depending on the commitment of management to its use, the constant involvement of cost accountants in all phases of a product's life cycle, and the type of strategy a company follows.

Target costing improves profitability in two ways. First, it places such a detailed continuing emphasis on product costs throughout the life cycle of every product that it is unlikely that a company will experience runaway costs; also, the management team is completely aware of costing issues since it receives regular reports from the cost accounting members of all design teams. Second, it improves profitability through precise targeting of the correct prices at which the company feels it can field a profitable product in the marketplace that will sell in a robust manner. This is opposed to the more common cost-plus approach under which a company builds a product, determines its cost, tacks on a profit, and then does not understand why its resoundingly high price does not attract buyers. Thus, target costing results not only in better cost control but also in better price control.

Target costing is really part of a larger concept called concurrent engineering, which requires participants from many departments to work together on project teams rather than having separate departments handle new product designs only after they have been handed off from the preceding department in the design chain. Clustering representatives from many departments together on a single design team can be quite a struggle, especially for older companies that have a history of conflict between departments. Consequently, only the most involved, prolonged support by all members of the senior management group can ensure that target costing, and the greater concept of concurrent engineering, will result in significant profitability improvements.

The review of product costs under the target costing methodology is not reserved just for the period up to the completion of design work on a new product. On the contrary, there are always opportunities to control costs after the design phase is completed, though these opportunities are fewer than during the design phase. Therefore, cost accountants should not be pulled from a design team once the final drawings have left the engineering department. Instead, they should regularly monitor actual component costs and compare them to planned costs, warning management whenever significant adverse variances arise. Also, cost accountants should take a lead role in the continuing review of supplier costs to see if they can be reduced, perhaps by visiting supplier facilities, as well as constantly reviewing existing product designs to see if they can be improved, and by targeting for elimination waste or spoilage on the production floor. Therefore, the cost accounting staff must be involved in all phases of a product's life cycle if a company is to realize profitability improvements from target costing to the fullest extent.

A company's strategy can also impact its profitability. If it constantly issues a stream of new products, or if its existing product line is subject to severe pricing pressure, it must make target costing a central part of its strategy so that the correct price points are used for products and actual costs match those originally planned. However, there are other strategies, such as growth by geographical expansion of the current product line (as is practiced by retail stores) or growth by acquisition, where there is no particular need for target costing—these companies make their money in other ways than by a focused concentration on product features and costs. For them, there may still be a role for target costing, but it is strictly limited by the reduced need for new products.

If the issues presented here are properly dealt with by a management team, it should find that target costing is one of the best accounting methods available for improving profitability. It is indeed one of the most proactive systems found in the entire range of accounting knowledge.

TARGET COSTING DATA FLOW

The typical accountant is used to extracting data from a central accounting database carefully stocked with the most accurate, reliable data from such a variety of sources as accounts payable, billings, bills of material, and inventory records. However, the cost accountant assigned to a target costing project must deal with much more poorly defined information, as well as data drawn from sources much different from those he or she is accustomed to using.

In the earliest stages of product design, the cost accountant must make the best possible guesses regarding the costs of proposed designs. Information about these costs can be garnered through the careful review of possible component parts, as well as a comparison to the costs of existing products with designs similar to those now under review. No matter what the method, it results in relatively rough cost estimates, especially during the earliest stages of product development. To operate in this environment a cost accountant must have a wide-ranging view of costing systems and a willingness to start with rough estimates and gradually refine them into more concrete information as designs gradually solidify. Therefore, cost accountants with a narrow focus should not be assigned to a product design team.

Though cost estimates are admittedly rough in the earliest stages of a new product design, it is possible to include with the *best* estimate an additional estimate of the *highest* possible cost that will be encountered. This additional information lets management know whether there is a significant degree of risk that the project may not achieve its desired cost target. Though this information can result in outright termination of a project, it is much more common for senior management to interview the project director in some detail to gain a better understanding of the variables underlying an excessively high cost estimate, as well as the chances that these costs can be reduced back to within the targeted range. Only after obtaining this additional information should a company make the decision to cancel a product design project.

There are also new sources of data a cost accountant can access. One is competitor information collected by the marketing staff or an outside research agency. This database contains information about the prices at which competitors are selling their products, as well as the prices of ancillary products and perhaps also the discounts given at various price points. It can also include market share data for individual products or by firm, the opinions of customers regarding the offerings of various companies, and the financial condition of competitors. This information is mostly used to determine the range of price points at which a company should sell its existing or anticipated products, as well as the features that should be included at each price point. The information about the financial condition and market shares of competitors can also be of use, since a company can elect to alter the pricing of its products to obtain a better market position. This database is of value to the cost accountant in determining the price at which products should be released to the market.

Another database used by the cost accountant is one that details the cost structure of competitors. This information is compiled by a combined effort of the marketing and engineering staffs through a process called reverse engineering. Under this methodology a company buys a competitor's product and disassembles it in order to determine the processes and materials used to create it, and their costs. This information is of value in determining the greatest allowable cost of a new product design since a company can copy the methods and materials used by a competitor, and see if a reduction in costs will be achieved. The information is also of use from a pricing perspective since it gives management some idea of the profits a competitor is probably obtaining from sales of its products; management can then aggressively price some or all of its competing products low enough to take away some of the competitor's profits.

Cost data can be found in yet another database that the cost accountant should peruse. This is not the inventory or bill of materials data already available in the typical accounting database but rather costs associated with specific product features or the production functions involved in manufacturing them. This type of information is not commonly found in the accounting system. Instead, the engineering staff may have compiled, over the course of numerous design projects, a set of tables itemizing the cost of components or clusters of components used to create a specific product feature. Also, the cost of specific production functions generally requires an in-depth analysis that can be obtained only through a prolonged activity-based accounting review. If none of this information is available, an enterprising cost accountant assigned to a product design team may take it upon herself to conduct this research, thereby not only improving the costing database of the current product design team but also providing a valuable information base for future design teams.

Yet another database is one containing engineering data. This information does not stop with the usual bills of material and also includes notes on upcoming technological changes that can be used to enhance the features of existing products. There should also be information about the interaction of various components of a product, so that one can predict what cost changes are likely to arise in the subsystem of a product if a part is reconfigured in a different subsystem. Further, there should be information available about the changes in costs that will arise from the use of a smaller or larger number of fasteners, different materials, different product sizes or weights, or a host of other factors. All this information is not easily reduced to a standard database format, and so it tends to be partly paper-based and not as well organized as the information stored in other databases. Nonetheless, this is a valuable tool for the cost accountant since it yields many clues regarding how costs can be altered as a result of changes in product design.

The final database available to the cost accounting member of a design team contains information regarding the previous quality, cost, and on-time delivery performance of all key suppliers, as well as the production capacity of each one. It may even reach a sufficient level of detail to include assumed profitability levels for each supplier. The cost accountant can use this information to determine which standard parts are no longer acceptable for future product designs, based on a history of high cost, poor quality, or inadequate on-time delivery. Also, if suppliers clearly show inadequate profits, it may signal their inability to obtain further cost reductions through capital asset purchases, which may necessitate switching to a different supplier.

Based on the wide variety of data sources mentioned in this section, it is evident that the cost accountant who is an integral member of a product design team has access to a considerable amount of information that is of great use in determining product prices and costs. However, few of these data sources are those that the typical accountant is used to accessing, nor do they contain the high level of data accuracy more common in an accounting database. Consequently, the cost accountant who collects this information must be well trained in its uses, as well as its shortcomings, and be able to use it to realistically portray expected cost and margin levels, given its imprecise nature.

MOST USEFUL SITUATIONS FOR TARGET COSTING

Target costing is most useful in situations where the majority of product costs are locked in during the product design phase. This is the case for most manufactured products, but few services. In the services arena, such as consulting, the bulk of all activities can be reconfigured for cost reduction during the "production" phase, which is when services are being provided directly to the customer. In the services environment the "design team" is still present but is more commonly concerned with streamlining the activities conducted by the employees providing the service, which can continue to be enhanced at any time, not just when the initial services process is being laid out.

For example, a design team can lay out the floor plan of a fast-food restaurant, with the objective of creating an arrangement that allows employees to cover the shortest possible distances while preparing food and serving customers; this is similar to the design of a new product. However, unlike a product design, this layout can be readily altered at any time if the design team can arrive at a better layout, so that the restaurant staff can continue to experience high levels of productivity improvement even after the initial design and layout of the facility. In this situation costs are not locked in during the design phase, so there is less need for target costing.

Another situation where target costing results in less value is the production of raw materials, such as chemicals. In this case there are no design features for a design team to labor over; instead, the industrial engineering staff tries to create the most efficient possible production process, which has little to do with cost reduction through the improvement of customer value by creating a product with a high ratio of features to costs.

TARGET COSTING CONTROL POINTS

A target costing program eventually results in major cost reductions if design teams are given an unlimited amount of time to carry out a multitude of design iterations. However, there comes a point where the cost of maintaining the design team exceeds the savings to be garnered from additional iterations. Also, most products must be released within a reasonably short time frame or they will miss the appropriate market window when they can beat the delivery of competing products to the market. To avoid both these cost and time delays, we use milestones as the principal control point over the course of a target costing program.

Several milestone reviews should be incorporated into a target costing program. Each one should include a thorough analysis of the progress of the design team since the last review, such as a comparison of the current cost of a design with its target cost. The main issue here is that the amount of cost yet to be worked out of a product must shrink, on a dollar or a percentage basis, after each successive milestone review, or else management has the right to cancel the design project. For example, there may be a standard allowable cost variance of 12% for the first milestone meeting, 10% at the next meeting, and so on until the target cost must be reached by a specific future milestone date. If a design team cannot quite reach its target cost, but comes close, the management team should be required to make a "go/no go" decision at that time which overrides the cost target and sends the design into production, allows time for additional design iterations, or terminates the project.

A milestone can be based on a time budget (e.g., one per month) or on the points in the design process at which specific activities are completed. For example, a milestone review can occur as soon as each successive design iteration is completed, when the conceptual drawings are finished, when the working model has been created, or when the production pilot has been run. In the last-mentioned case, there are many more steps that the management group can build into the milestone review process so that cost analyses become a nearly continual part of the target costing regimen.

IMPLEMENTING A TARGET COSTING SYSTEM

A target costing initiative requires the participation of several departments. Because there are so many participants in the process from so many departments, some of whom have different agendas in regard to what they want the program to produce, it is quite common for the results obtained to be less than stellar. Design projects can be delayed by squabbling or by an inability to drive down design or production costs in a reasonably efficient manner. This delay may lead to serious cost overruns in the cost of the design team itself, which can lead to abrupt termination of the entire target costing system by the management team. However, these problems can be mitigated or completely eliminated by ensuring that the steps listed here are completed when the target costing system is first installed:

- **Create a project charter.** The target costing effort should begin with a document, approved by senior management, that describes its goals and what it is authorized to do. This document, known as the project charter, is essentially a subset of the corporate mission statement and related goals as they pertain to the target costing initiative. Written approval of this document by the senior management group provides the target costing effort with a strong basis of support and direction in all subsequent efforts.

- **Obtain a management sponsor.** The next step is to obtain the strongest possible support from a management sponsor. This should be an individual who is well positioned near the top of the corporate hierarchy, believes strongly in the goals of target costing, and will support the initiative in all respects—obtaining funding, lobbying other members of top management, working to eliminate roadblocks, and ensuring that other problems are overcome in a timely manner. This person is central to the success of target costing.

- **Obtain a budget.** The target costing program requires funds to ensure that one or more well-staffed design teams can complete target costing tasks. The funding should be based on a formal allocation of money through the corporate budget, rather than a parsimonious suballocation grudgingly granted by one or more departments. In the first case the funds are unreservedly given to the target costing effort, whereas in the latter case, they can be suddenly withdrawn by a department manager who is not fully persuaded of the need for target costing or who suddenly finds a need for the money elsewhere.

- **Assign a strong team manager.** Because the typical target costing program involves so many people with different backgrounds and represents so many parts of a company, it can be difficult to weld the group together into a smoothly functioning team focused on key objectives. The best way to ensure that the team functions properly is to assign to the effort a strong team manager skilled in dealing with management, the use of project tools, and working with a diverse group of people. This manager should be a full-time employee, so that his or her complete attention can be directed toward the welfare of the project.

- **Enroll full-time participants.** A target costing team member puts the greatest effort into the program when he or she is focused only on target costing. Thus, it is essential that as many members of the team as possible be devoted to it full-time rather than also trying to fulfill other commitments elsewhere in the company at the same time. This may call for the replacement of these individuals in the departments they are leaving so that there are no emergencies requiring their sudden withdrawal back to their "home" departments to deal with other work problems. It may even be necessary to permanently assign them to a target costing program, providing them with a single focus on ensuring the success of the target costing program because their livelihoods are now tied to it.

- **Use project management tools.** Target costing can be a highly complex effort, especially for high-cost products with many features and components. To ensure that the project stays on track, the team should use all available project management tools, such as Microsoft Project (for tracking the completion of specific tasks), a company database containing various types of costing information, and a variety of product design tools. All these items require assured access to many corporate databases, as well as a budget for whatever computing equipment is needed to access this data.

The main focus of the steps described in this section is to ensure the fullest possible support for target costing by all available means—management, money, and staff. Only when all these elements are in place and concentrated on the goals at hand does a target costing program have the greatest chance for success.

CASE STUDY

The GetLost Company is a manufacturer of global positioning systems used in a variety of applications to determine a user's precise position on the surface of the planet. The founder of the company, Mr. Larry Ost, is concerned that the price point for hand-held recreational GPS units has plummeted from more than $500 to about $100 in the past 5 years in response to severe pricing pressure from competitors. He decides to attack the problem by creating a target costing team.

The team conducts a number of marketing surveys to determine what features a prospective GPS unit should include. It finds that a key complaint of potential users is that all GPS units currently on the market are too bulky, which is a major concern for hikers and hunters who want to reduce the size of anything they carry with them into the outdoors. In a major insight the marketing personnel on the team decide to combine the GPS unit with a standard walkie-talkie, which many outdoorsmen also carry. The resulting device can then be marketed as a major space saver compared to the alternative, which is to carry both devices.

On initial review, the target costing team compiles a set of costs for a device that will cost $200, well above the $125 that surveys reveal is the most realistic price point for this type of device. Also, since the company wants to attain a 25% margin on this product, the team arrives at a cost reduction goal of $106 in this manner:

Target market price	$125
Target margin	25%
Target margin	$ 31
Target cost	$ 94
Current cost	$200
Target cost	−$ 94
Cost reduction goal	$106

To meet the cost reduction goal, the team begins its value engineering effort by reviewing combined functions in the radio and GPS parts of the product. It finds that both share an antenna and a receiver; by merging these two components the company can save $45. Also, by working with a supplier the team finds that a new liquid crystal display (LCD) is now available that can cut the price of the existing LCD by $40. Finally, a design review of the circuitry in the product reveals that microminiaturization will result in a $2 cut in the price of the circuit board, while also creating a board that is half the size of its predecessor. This allows the design team to create a much smaller plastic case for the device, reducing both the molding cost for the case and the cost of creating the injection mold used to create the case. The cost reduction from these two innovations is $19. All these changes yield a new product cost of $94, which allows the GetLost Company to produce an innovative new product in a highly competitive market—and one that carries with it a reasonable profit.

As a final measure, the target costing team assigns several staff members to review the production process with the objective of eliminating enough production waste to further reduce costs by 3% per year on a continual basis. Achieving this goal will allow the company to continue to reduce prices in the future, in the face of a heightened level of expected competition, while still retaining a reasonable degree of profitability.

SUMMARY

Target costing is one of the few "proactive" costing activities an accounting department performs. Most other costing work done by accountants involves an after-the-fact review of costs that have already been incurred. Only in this case does the cost accountant form an active part of the new product design team, constantly apprising the design team of the current cost of a design, as well as the impact of contemplated design changes on costs. These activities have a major direct impact on the profitability of products, which makes target costing, and the cost accountant's role in it, one of the most valuable activities a company can pursue.

In this chapter we discussed the various steps a target costing program typically follows, as well as the types of value engineering that can be used to remove costs from a product design and the production processes used to manufacture it. We also noted the situations in which target costing is most useful, how it impacts profitability, where to install control points over the process, and how to implement the methodology.

CHAPTER 18

Costing Systems Summary

So far in this part of the book, we have looked at nine methods for summarizing and interpreting costing information. Each one can be effectively used in specific circumstances, but may provide useless, or incorrect, information in others. In this chapter we briefly review each of these costing systems and then discuss the situations in which each one should be used.

BRIEF REVIEW OF COSTING SYSTEMS

This section presents a summary of each of the costing systems discussed in the last nine chapters of this book. Each summary includes a description of the system, the cost accountant's role in its use, and how the resulting information is generally used.

Job costing is one of the most common systems used to track a company's costs. As many costs as possible are directly tied to specific jobs on which a company is working, while most other costs are summarized into cost pools and then allocated to the jobs. This approach makes up the bulk of a company's data collection systems since most costs must be tracked in some way to an overhead cost pool or to a job; this requires the use of job tracking for employee labor hours and material costs. The cost accountant is responsible for setting up and maintaining the job costing system, as well as for investigating any unusual cost amounts charged to specific jobs. This method is useful for determining the full cost of each production job, especially when these costs can be billed directly to a customer.

Process costing is used almost as frequently as job costing. It requires the collection of data for long production runs in which individual units cannot be readily distinguished from fellow products (such as in oil refining) or for production runs that are so long that it is difficult to determine the start and stop intervals for a specific job within an accounting period. It involves the aggregation of cost data into cost pools, which are then spread across the total volume of production during a specified period. As was the case for the job costing system, the cost accountant must set up and maintain the system, as well as investigate any apparent discrepancies in cost accumulations or allocations. This approach is used for generating approximate per-unit costs, as well as inventory valuations.

Direct costing deals with only a portion of a company's total costs. It collects data only about costs that can be directly and indisputably assigned to a specific product or activity and charges all other costs to the current period. This makes for a simpler data collection system since there is no need to compile or allocate overhead costs. The cost accountant's role in its use is similar to that for job and process costing. It is most commonly used for determining the minimum price point at which an item can be sold.

Standard costing assumes that actual costs vary only slightly from period to period, thereby allowing standard costs to be substituted for them. In this way actual costs can be compared to the standards, and variances generated and investigated. The cost accountant has considerable work to do in this system because the job expands to include variance investigation. This system works best in cases where a company has been in business for some time and therefore has a cost structure that does not vary much from period to period.

LIFO, FIFO, and average costing are all different ways to model the flow of costs through a company. When the correct calculation method is used, a slightly more accurate view of how costs flow can result. Since each of these costing methods is automatically maintained by the accounting computer system, the cost accountant's role is limited to investigating any unusual changes in costing layers. Each of these systems is most commonly used to value inventory for external reporting purposes.

Throughput costing differs substantially from every other costing system in that it does not involve *any* costs—it focuses only on the incremental gross margin generated by a company's bottleneck operation. It assumes that changes in costs elsewhere in a company do not have a substantial impact on bottom-line profits, so only decisions regarding the product mix at the bottleneck point have any relevance. In this system, the cost accountant's role is altered substantially, to that of a capacity analyst. This method has many uses, particularly for determining incremental changes in the production mix.

Joint and by-product costing is a set of allocation methods used to assign costs to two or more products jointly created by the same production process. Being strictly an allocation system, it is best used only for inventory valuations or external financial reporting where *some* sort of cost allocation is required. The cost accountant performs the allocation calculations and justifies their formulation with a company's outside auditors.

Activity-based costing is a complex system that charges direct materials and labor to specific products, while also charging overhead costs to a series of cost pools; these pools are then allocated to various activities in the production process, which are in turn used as the basis for cost allocations to specific products. The focus of the ABC system is generally on product costing, but it can be refocused on specific company processes, customers, or anything else about which costing information is required. It is a highly detailed system that seeks to allocate *all* costs in as comprehensive a manner as possible so that the recipients of the resulting information have the best possible information about the complete set of costs incurred by a product. The cost accountant is deeply involved in the setup and maintenance of this system, which requires many detailed analyses, data collection systems, and calculations.

Target costing involves the ongoing accumulation of costs for new products currently under development and the use of this information to determine if such products can be manufactured at a target cost that will generate sufficient profit to make the development effort worthwhile. This system may not result in perfectly accurate costs since many of them are estimates, obtained internally or from suppliers, that may vary somewhat as each development project proceeds. However, the costs should become more accurate over time as the costing information for each development project becomes more certain. Thus, the cost accountant must continually refine the accuracy of the costing information supplied to the design team. This information can be used to make a decision to abandon or to proceed with a project, as well as to focus on the specific parts of a development project that require cost reductions in order to meet the cost target.

Having briefly described each of the costing methodologies, we now proceed to review the situations in which each one is most useful.

APPLICATIONS OF COSTING SYSTEMS

There are a number of decisions to which a cost accountant can contribute valuable information—information that can be derived from a combination of the various costing systems. In this section we itemize the most important cost-related decisions and point out which of the various systems can be best used to support them. The results are also listed in a table in Exhibit 18.1, which highlights the particular uses of each costing system. The main costing decisions involve:

- **Capacity utilization.** From the perspective of capital investment, the management team needs to know what assets are under- or overutilized so that it can change the mix of equipment being employed on the shop floor. This is particularly important for bottleneck operations since sales cannot be increased to a higher level than can be run through the operation. Only the throughput costing system targets this issue. It assumes that the main focus of management attention should be the amount of revenue that can be rammed through the bottleneck operation, so it pays close attention to which work center is the bottleneck and how well this machine is used. However, even throughput costing is really concerned only with the bottleneck operation rather than with the capacity utilization of all other work centers, so a special data gathering system must typically be constructed to track this information.

- **Capital budgeting.** The main goal of capital budgeting is to determine the cash inflows and outflows associated with a specific capital purchase. The direct costing system is particularly useful for this function since it focuses specifically on costs that can be directly traced to a single activity (in this case, a machine), while excluding all other nonrelevant costs. Other systems, such as job, process, and activity-based costing, all allocate overhead costs, which may not be relevant to a capital budgeting decision. Thus, these other systems are less likely to reveal relevant information for this purpose.

- **Cost reductions.** The perennial favorite question asked by all managers is, How can the company save money? Several systems can be used to answer this question, depending on the precise nature of the question. For example, if the question is oriented toward how to save money on manufactured products, the best method to use is target costing; this system closely tracks costs as a product is being developed and so can influence final product costs considerably. If the question is oriented more toward nonproduct costs, the best alternatives are job and activity-based costing. Job costing is (as the name implies) oriented toward costs incurred to complete a job and so provides good costing detail at that level. An ABC system, however, focuses on overhead costs and how they are used by various activities. When employed properly, the ABC system can provide a wealth of detail in this area. Finally, throughput costing can be used to determine whether changes in costs will impact the ability of a bottleneck operation to manufacture more or fewer products—in some instances this system results in recommendations to increase rather than decrease costs on the grounds that an incremental cost increase may result in a higher level of throughput and therefore a higher gross margin (Chapter 14).

- **External financial reporting.** This item has less to do with supporting management decisions and more with following a fixed set of accounting rules in order to issue a reliable, accurate set of financial statements. For this purpose a cost flow system such as LIFO, FIFO, or average costing, should be used to create a legally correct inventory valuation. We should also use the job, process, joint and by-product, or ABC system to allocate overhead in a legally valid manner. We cannot use the direct costing system because it does not provide for overhead allocation, nor can throughput or target costing be used since they are specialized applications not oriented toward this use.

- **Internal management reporting.** This is a broad topic that may require a wide range of systems to ensure that valid information is provided to solve numerous possible problems. Generally speaking, the costing systems employed to generate external reports are *not* the ones to use for internal reports because the overhead allocations needed for external reporting are less useful for internal reporting. Thus, we favor direct, throughput, ABC (the one system that is useful for both internal and external reporting because of the accuracy of its overhead allocations), and target costing systems for internal reports.

- **Inventory valuation.** The valuation of inventory requires the allocation of costs to inventory items because this is required by generally accepted accounting principles. This requirement immediately reduces our choices to a few systems that incorporate allocation methodologies, namely, the job, process, cost flow (e.g., LIFO, FIFO, and average costing), joint and by-product, and activity-based costing systems. Indeed, some systems, such as joint and by-product costing, are designed almost entirely for this use.

- **Outsourcing decisions.** Any decision to shift an in-house function to an outside supplier requires an incremental analysis of how this change will affect a company's costs. For incremental analysis there is nothing better than direct costing since this system avoids the use of all costs that do not directly pertain to a cost object. Another good system for outsourcing decision making is throughput costing because it can tell if outsourcing will alter the total amount of product that can be pushed through a company's primary bottleneck operation, thereby impacting gross margins.

- **Pricing.** One area in which the cost accountant is likely to become involved is the setting of product prices. Sales and marketing managers, who set prices, want to know the fully burdened cost of each product so that they can determine a price point that will cover all costs over the long term. For this purpose one can use the job, process, standard, and activity-based costing systems. In addition, there are incremental pricing situations in which they want to know the minimum price that can be charged—for this, the direct costing system is the best alternative. Also, if there is a problem with pricing products that must flow through a bottleneck operation, the throughput costing approach is the best methodology. Finally, if product pricing is a methodical process in which new products are carefully designed to meet a specific price point, the best alternative is target costing. Unfortunately for the cost accountant, nearly every costing system can be used for pricing simply because there are so many variations on how to set a price.

- **Process improvement.** Three systems can be used for process improvement analysis, though each one is employed for entirely different purposes within this category. First, direct costing is used to determine the incremental cost of a particular process activity. It is used to develop a minimum cost for a process step that will change if a process improvement is implemented. This is the most common costing method for this purpose. The second system is throughput costing, which can be employed to determine what gross margin changes can be expected if any process improvements are made that will impact a bottleneck operation. This procedure is used the least because many process improvement efforts bear no relationship to a bottleneck operation, which means that throughput costing is indifferent to them. Third, activity-based costing is used to improve processes that require a large amount of overhead costs. It is ideal for this purpose because it carefully tracks how overhead costs are used by various activities—by reducing the activities the related overhead costs can (theoretically) also be eliminated. Thus, different systems can be used for different purposes under the general heading of "process improvement."

- **Product design.** Without a doubt the only costing system to use for product design analysis is target costing. This system was specifically created to trace the ongoing costs of new product designs in relation to target cost levels and so is the perfect vehicle for conveying product design costing information to the management team.

- **Product mix.** The decision to manufacture a specific mix of products is the primary purpose for creation of the throughput costing system, which clearly identifies how changes in the production mix influence the total gross margin that can be expected. Other costing systems do not yield such excellent results because they "muddy the waters" by using overhead cost allocations, which usually have no direct relevance to the product mix decision.

- **Product profit.** There are many ways to determine how much of a profit a product has earned. If a fully burdened profit is the objective, then the job, process, standard, joint and by-product, or activity-based costing system should be used. However, if the incremental profit earned from product sales is the desired result, direct costing is the preferred alternative. Finally, if the management team simply wants to verify that the planned profit for a new product is being met in the marketplace, target costing can be used. Thus, one must be conversant with many different costing systems to know how to properly report product profitability.

- **Scrap costing.** Different systems yield entirely different costing results in the valuation of manufacturing scrap. On the one hand, an activity-based costing system values it based on the amount of overhead it has absorbed, as well as all direct costs. On the other hand, a throughput costing system places a higher value on scrap downstream from a bottleneck operation because it must be replaced with good production that must be run through the expensive bottleneck

EXHIBIT 18.1. Uses of Costing Systems

Costing System	Capacity Utilization	Capital Budgeting	Cost Reduction	External Financial Reporting	Internal Management Reporting	Inventory Valuation	Outsourcing Decisions	Pricing	Process Improvement	Product Design	Product Mix	Product Profitability	Scrap Costing
Job costing				X		X		X				X	
Process costing				X		X		X				X	
Direct costing		X			X		X	X				X	
Standard costing								X	X			X	X
LIFO, FIFO, average costing				X	X	X							
Throughput costing	X		X				X						
Joint and by-product costing			X	X		X		X	X		X	X	X
Activity-based costing			X		X			X	X	X		X	
Target costing			X		X			X				X	X

252

operation again. Finally, a standard costing system works best for segregating excess scrap from a standard use rate, which makes it easier to determine where high scrap levels are occurring. The most commonly used of these systems is standard costing because it gives higher visibility to scrap costs. However, throughput costing is recommended as an ancillary system because it highlights the increased cost of downstream scrap.

A graphical view of the preceding costing system applications is presented in Exhibit 18.1, where the various costing systems are displayed in the first column and the various costing decisions just discussed are shown as column heads.

A key issue to remember from this discussion of system applications is that no one system can be used in all situations since each one is designed for a different purpose. If a single system were used, its results would be correct for some applications but seriously incorrect for others. Not only would this constantly cause trouble for the management team, which would make incorrect decisions based on incorrect costing reports, but it would also reduce the perceived effectiveness of the cost accountant within the organization.

SUMMARY

As previously indicated in Exhibit 18.1, there are many uses to which costing information can be put. No single costing system can meet all these demands. Some are good at costing for a single purpose, while others have broader applicability. However, it is simply not possible to use one system for all of a company's costing needs. Consequently, the cost accountant must have a broad knowledge of all the systems mentioned here and know when to use different systems in different situations.

PART IV

Using Costs in Pricing, Variance, and Operational Analysis

CHAPTER 19

Cost Variances

Earlier, in Chapter 12, we discussed the use of standard costs, which are predetermined costs that can serve as benchmarks for performance. In this chapter we discuss a consequence of using standard costs—the cost variance. A cost variance is the difference between the actual cost incurred and the standard cost baseline against which it is measured. This may seem like an easy issue to deal with, but in reality there are several subcategories into which a cost variance can be broken down. We cover the main variance types in this chapter—volume, price, and efficiency variances. The bulk of the text is devoted to descriptions of variances, what causes them, and to whom they should be reported. The case study at the end of the chapter presents a numerical example of their use.

OVERVIEW OF COST VARIANCES

A cost variance is any cost that departs from an expected value. For example, a controller notices on the financial statement that the cost of goods sold is higher than the expected cost, as noted in the budget, by $100,000. How does the controller go about splitting up this variance into smaller pieces so that it is easier to investigate? Variance analysis is the answer.

There are three main categories of cost variances into which one can divide a total cost variance. One is the *price variance*. This is the difference between the expected, or standard, cost of an item and the cost actually incurred, multiplied by the number of units actually used. This variance is typically divided into three subcategories of price variance: one for purchased materials, one for direct labor, and one for variable overhead. To continue with our example, the controller determines that the budgeted total of direct labor for the period was $50,000 but finds there was an increase in the hourly wage paid, which accounts for $10,000 of the total variance. Similarly, the price paid to suppliers for three key parts was $12,000 more than the standard price for these items, while the variable overhead cost of machine maintenance contracts was priced $2000 higher than the budgeted cost. All these issues involve price variances, which account for $24,000 of the total cost variance.

Another type of variance is the *efficiency variance*. This is the difference between the actual quantity of resources consumed to manufacture an output, minus its budgeted quantity, multiplied by its standard cost. This variance is usually subdivided into three categories: direct labor efficiency, materials (or yield) efficiency, and variable overhead efficiency. Many companies do not use the variable overhead efficiency measure, instead preferring to lump all variable overhead costs into the fixed overhead category; however, this practice reduces the amount of information available to management, revealing that some overhead costs do indeed vary with changes in underlying activity levels, as can be proven with the use of activity-based costing (Chapter 16). To return to our example, the controller finds that an excessive number of hours were required by the production staff to complete production, which translates into a direct labor efficiency variance of $12,000. Also, there was a significant amount of material scrap incurred during the production process, which works out to $8000 more than the amount of material use listed in the standard for the level of actual production. Finally, an excessive amount of outsourced quality analysis time was needed for the production process; this was listed in the product standards database as 1 hour for every 50 units produced but turned out to be 1 hour for every 30 units. The excess number of outsourced hours required for this task was categorized as a variable overhead efficiency variance of $2000. The total efficiency variance sums to $22,000. The controller finds that combining this figure with the cumulative price variance of $24,000 accounts for $46,000 of the total cost variance.

The final variance contributing to the total cost variance is the volume variance. This applies only to fixed overhead costs since all the other cost categories (e.g., materials, direct labor, and variable overhead) fluctuate directly with the volume of activity. Fixed overhead is charged to the cost of goods based on a budgeted total amount per period rather than a rate per unit of activity. Consequently, when the level of activity during the period varies substantially from the level assumed when the total overhead allocation was determined, there is a cost variance due to the volume of activity that did (or did not) occur. This *volume variance* is determined by multiplying the fixed overhead component of the overhead rate by the number of units of activity that actually occurred, and subtracting this amount from the total fixed overhead cost pool. To return to our example, the controller finds that the production volume in the period was well below expected levels, resulting in $52,000 of fixed overhead costs being charged to the current period, rather than absorbed into inventory as had been anticipated in the budget. This calculation accounts for the remaining portion of the total cost variance.

All three of the variances just described are needed to describe how all the various costs included in a total cost variance are derived. The three variances are noted in Exhibit 19.1. This exhibit contains a matrix itemizing which variances can be used for each of the four major types of costs—materials, direct labor, variable overhead, and fixed overhead. Given the number of variance types and cost types, a total of eight variances can be calculated, which is perhaps too many for some companies to investigate, given their limited resources. How can this number of variances be reduced to a manageable size?

One way to reduce the number of variances calculated is to eliminate those over which a company has little control and concentrate instead on the few that are controllable, recurring, and involve a sufficient amount of potential dollar savings to be worth the investigatory effort. For example, it is difficult to reduce the labor price variance because it is mostly based on predetermined labor rates that are hard to change. However, material price variances should be the chief focus of attention in the purchasing department, one of whose primary tasks is to ensure that materials are located that match their standard costs. Efficiency variances are generally a good focus of attention since their underlying causes tend to involve product scrap, quality issues, and ineffective process manning—all issues that the management team should be eager to address. However, the volume variance is simply based on the number of units produced, which a company is not likely to alter over the long run in order to eliminate the variance. Thus, selected types of variances are more worthy of a company's attention and so should be calculated with more regularity and in more depth than other variances that are less controllable.

EXHIBIT 19.1. Summary-Level Review of Variance Components

		Material	Labor	Variable Overhead	Fixed Overhead
(Total Actual Cost)	Price Variance	Yes	Yes	Yes	Yes
minus	Efficiency Variance	Yes	Yes	Yes	No
(Total Budgeted Cost)	Volume Variance	No	No	No	Yes

The last point implies that a company does not need to calculate every possible variance from standard. Though a precision-minded cost accountant may be inclined to calculate and report on every possible variance, it is usually not worth the effort to analyze each one, even if the accounting system can be reconfigured to automatically calculate many of the variances. Part of the reason for ignoring selected standards is efficiency—some manual investigation of the underlying details of any variance is required, no matter how much automation is used to compile the data. For example, it is not enough to have a computer system dredge up all the reported scrap items that make up the material yield variance for a given period—the cost accountant must also review this data for trends or any oddities that may require immediate attention, summarize and repackage it for further consumption, and present it to the recipient. All these steps require considerable effort for which there may not be sufficient accounting resources available.

It also may not be necessary to further "slice and dice" variances into smaller degrees of precision. For example, the material efficiency variance can be further refined to include a material mix variance, which describes how much of the yield variance from the budget for the period is attributable to the mix of production being different. Though there may be a few cases where this is needed, it is usually sufficient to stop at one of the three main variance *types* and proceed to the investigation of major variance *causes*.

A final reason to reduce one's analysis of variances is that there is little action a company can take to improve on its overhead variances. For example, the major components of the fixed overhead cost pool include rent, machine depreciation, and utilities. All three of these costs require massive amounts of effort to change—such as moving the business and replacing machinery. Thus, in the short term, a manager has few reasonable options for changing overhead costs, no matter how bad the variances may be. The only alternative may be to change the overhead standards to reflect the reality of actual costs.

The three main types of variances—price, efficiency, and volume—are easy to calculate and can result in an adequately detailed report for management review, but it is important for a cost accountant not to become bogged down in variance analysis since many variances are not controllable in the short term. Instead, it is best to focus most closely on the few variances that are readily controllable and can result in significant cost reductions.

VOLUME VARIANCES

From a costing perspective the volume variance can be used only for fixed overhead. The reason is that all other variances are related to the pricing or efficiency of individual units of activity, and so, as noted in Exhibit 19.1, there is no excess or shortage of units compared to the standard from which a variance can be generated.

The volume variance calculation for fixed overhead is a simple one: the standard overhead cost per unit of activity multiplied by the difference between the actual and budgeted quantities of the activity. An example of the volume variance calculation is presented in the case study at the end of this chapter. The only problem that may arise in explaining this variance to managers occurs when there are many different activities to which fixed overhead costs are tied, as is the case in an activity-based costing system. For example, the fixed overhead cost pool may be split up into a subset of cost pools, each of which is allocated with different activity measures such as square footage, number of machine hours, or (the old standby) direct labor hours. Each one of these allocations requires a separate volume variance, so there may be quite a few, depending on the number of activities used to allocate fixed overhead.

The volume variance can be used in a different arena than costing—sales reporting. If the reported level of actual sales in a given period is different from the budget, then it can be due to a difference in the price per unit sold (as described in the next section) or to differences in the volume of sales. This second situation can be more fully described with the volume variance calculation. For this purpose the calculation subtracts the budgeted sales quantity from the actual quantity and multiplies the difference by the standard price per unit sold. This calculation is made more complicated by the number of products that a company sells since it must be repeated for each one. If the resulting list of volume variances is excessive, the number can be reduced to just those that exceed a predetermined variance percentage, such as 10%. The resulting report can then be sent to the responsible person, the sales manager.

PRICE VARIANCES

One of the three main elements of a variance, as noted in Exhibit 19.1, is the price variance. This is the difference between the standard and actual prices paid for anything, multiplied by the number of units of each item purchased. The same calculation can be applied to the prices charged for products sold. In this section we look at the derivation of price variances for materials, wages, variable overhead, and fixed overhead and digress briefly to discuss the same issues for the sales price variance. They are:

- **Material price variance.** This is based on the actual price paid for materials used in the production process, minus the standard cost, multiplied by the number of units used. It is typically reported to the purchasing manager. This calculation is a bit more complicated than it at first seems since the "actual" cost is probably either the LIFO, FIFO, or average cost of an item, as disgorged from the inventory tracking system (Chapter 13). The LIFO and average costs tend to be close to the current market price of a purchased part, but the FIFO cost may be derived from an old inventory layer whose cost is considerably different from the current market rate. It may be necessary to raise this issue in the notes accompanying the variance analysis if the cost differential is a large one. Here are some additional areas to investigate if there is a material price variance:

- The standard price is based on a different purchase volume.

- The standard price is incorrectly derived from a different component.

- The material was purchased on a rush basis.

- The material was purchased at a premium because of a supply shortage.

- **Labor price variance.** This is based on the actual price paid for the direct labor used in the production process, minus its standard cost, multiplied by the number of units used. It is typically reported to the production manager, who is responsible for staffing jobs with personnel with the correct wage rates, and to the human resources manager, who is responsible for setting the allowable wage rates that employees are paid. This tends to be a relatively small variance as long as the standard labor rate is regularly revised to match actual labor rates at the production facility. Since most job categories tend to be clustered into relatively small pay ranges, there is not much chance that a labor price variance will become excessive. Here are some situations to investigate if there is a labor price variance:

  - The standard labor rate has not been recently adjusted to reflect actual pay changes.

  - The actual labor rate includes overtime or shift differentials not included in the standard.

  - Jobs are being staffed with employees whose pay levels differ from those used to develop standards for these jobs.

- **Variable overhead spending variance.** Though the name of this variance sounds different, it is still a price variance. To calculate it, subtract the standard variable overhead cost per unit from the actual cost incurred and multiply the remainder by the total unit quantity of output. This variance is very similar to the material and labor price variances since some overhead costs are directly related to the volume of production, as is the case for materials and labor. The detailed report on this variance is usually sent to the production manager, who is responsible for all overhead incurred in the production area. This variance can require considerable analysis, for a number of costs may fall into this category, all of which can be hiding significant variances. Here are some areas to investigate if there is a variable overhead spending variance:

  - The cost of activities in any of the variable overhead accounts has been altered by the supplier.

- The company has changed its purchasing methods for the variable overhead costs to or from the use of blanket purchase orders (which tend to result in lower prices because of higher purchase volumes).

- Costs are being misclassified between the accounts, so that the spending variance appears too low in one account and too high in another.

- **Fixed overhead spending variance.** This is the total amount by which fixed overhead costs exceed their total standard cost for the reporting period. Notice that, unlike the preceding price variance, it is not multiplied by any type of production volume. There is no way to relate this price variance to volume because it is not directly tied to any sort of activity volume. The detailed variance report on this topic can be distributed to a number of people, depending on who is responsible for each general ledger account number it contains. Investigations of variances in this area generally center on a period-to-period comparison of prices charged to suppliers, with particular attention to those experiencing recent price increases. It may be beneficial to link this investigation to a summary of all contractual agreements with suppliers since these documents will reveal any allowable pricing changes—only those *not* allowed by such agreements will still require further investigation.

- **Selling price variance.** Though the selling price variance is not strictly a cost variance, it is included here to show how a company's sales can also be divided into variances. In this case the variance is the actual selling price, minus the standard selling price, multiplied by the number of units sold. This variance is usually reported to the sales manager. This can be a key variance in investigating why a company's sales are not meeting expectations. Here are some of the areas to investigate if the selling price variance is significant in size:

  - Discounts were given to customers.

  - Customers have paid lower prices than stated on invoices issued to them.

  - Customers have ordered in sufficiently large volumes to warrant lower prices.

  - The standards do not reflect price points for different options sold with each product.

Of the different types of pricing variances noted here, the one whose investigation usually yields the most fruitful results is the material price variance. This is because there are several key areas, such as rush materials purchases and incorrect purchasing quantities, that cause the variances and are highly correctible if acted on promptly. The labor pricing variance results in fewer positive changes by management because it usually is not a large dollar volume and because it is tied to internal labor rates, which are not easily altered. The overhead price variances can be large but may be difficult to improve in the short run since many are tied to long-term contracts.

EFFICIENCY VARIANCES

The efficiency variance is the most important of the three main types of variances. The reason is that efficiency is entirely within the control of the company and can be greatly improved through close management attention to internal processes. For example, the material yield variance shows the excess amount of material used to create a product. Managers can examine this excess level of use to determine why the excess occurred and alter such variables as raw material quantity, machine set-ups, and operator training to ensure that the yield improves in the future.

The efficiency variance applies to materials, labor, and variable overhead, as noted in Exhibit 19.1. It does not apply to fixed overhead costs because these costs are incurred independently of any resource use. Here is a closer examination of the efficiency variance as applied to each of these areas:

- **Material yield variance.** Though its traditional name is slightly different, this is still an efficiency variance. It measures the ability of a company to manufacture a product using the exact amount of materials allowed by the standard. A variance arises when the quantity of materials used differs from the preset standard. It is calculated by subtracting the total standard quantity of materials that are supposed to be used from the actual level of use and multiplying the remainder by the standard price per unit. This information is usually issued to the production manager. Here are some of the areas that should be investigated to correct the material yield variance:

  - Excessive machine-related scrap rates.

  - Poor material quality levels.

  - Excessively tight tolerance for product rejections.

  - Improper machine setup.

  - Substitute materials that cause high reject rates.

- **Labor efficiency variance.** This measures the ability of a company's direct labor staff to create products with the exact amount of labor set forth in the standard (actually the labor routing, as noted in Chapter 26). A variance arises when the quantity of labor used is different from the standard; note that this variance has nothing to do with the cost per unit of labor (which is the price variance), only the quantity of it that is consumed. It is calculated by subtracting the standard quantity of labor consumed from the actual amount and multiplying the remainder by the standard labor rate per hour. As was the case for the material yield variance, it is most commonly reported to the production manager. Here are the likely causes of the labor efficiency variance:

  - Employees have poor work instructions.

- Employees are not adequately trained.

- Too many employees are manning a workstation.

- The wrong mix of employees is manning a workstation.

- The labor standard used as a comparison is incorrect.

- **Variable overhead efficiency variance.** This measures the quantity of variable overhead required to manufacture a unit of production. For example, if the machine used to run a batch of product requires extra time to produce each item, there will be an additional charge to the product's cost based on the price of the machine, multiplied by its cost per minute. This variance does not involve the machine's cost per minute (which is examined through a price variance analysis) but the number of minutes required for the production of each unit. It is calculated by subtracting the budgeted units of activity on which the variable overhead is charged from the actual units of activity, multiplied by the standard variable overhead cost per unit. Depending on the nature of the costs that make up the pool of variable overhead costs, this variance can be reported to several managers, particularly the production manager. The causes of this variance are tied to the unit of activity on which it is based. For example, when the variable overhead rate varies directly with the quantity of machine time used, the main causes are any action that changes the rate of machine use. When the basis is the amount of materials used, the causes are those just noted for the materials yield variance.

The true test of a management team is its ability to create products with the minimum possible level of efficiency variance. All types of efficiency variance noted here—labor, materials, and variable overhead—are totally controllable by managers, so they should be held completely responsible for these variances from standard.

ANALYSIS AND FEEDBACK OF VARIANCE INFORMATION

Once you have calculated a variance, what do you do with it? In its initial form it does not reveal a great deal of information—it is just a single number—so the first step is to delve into the reasons behind its occurrence. With this information in hand one can then feed back a much more detailed set of information to the management team. This is a major value-added activity for the cost accountant. Without the underlying investigative work so critical to the understanding of why variances occur, the cost accountant cannot begin to explain variances to managers or suggest corrective actions.

As an example of the required level of investigation one should complete, the ABC Company experienced a material price variance of about $4000 in the preceding month. By itself, this information is not sufficient for management's use, so the cost accountant compares the standard cost of each item purchased during that month to the actual cost at which it was purchased. This information is shown in the table in Exhibit 19.2.

This investigation reveals that seven of the eight components used in the product (a cordless phone) have negative price variances. Should the cost accountant issue a report to management itemizing all seven pricing problems noted in the exhibit? Only if the managers have a great deal of time on their hands. The problem is that the cost accountant is now giving managers too much information; they do not need to know about the small pricing problems that the bulk of the line items noted in the example. Instead, the accountant should use the Pareto principle and report only the 20% of items that cause 80% of the pricing variance. In the exhibit this means that we report only that portion of the variance caused by the top and bottom plastic cases.

However, having decided to limit the report to just two items, is it sufficient to itemize the variation from standard costs for each one? Not at all. The management group still does not know why the variance occurred and likely does not have time to find out. A better approach is to delve deeper into the problem before issuing a report to management. To continue the example, we know that the problem has arisen from the purchase of two plastic parts from a supplier. The supplier's invoice to the company reveals only the unit price and total price, which are accurately reflected in the report. Since this is of no use, the cost accountant decides to look further and contacts the purchasing manager, who is new to the position, to discuss the situation. She explains that the company orders these parts in quantities sufficient to match production levels for a full month, which results in 12 orders per year, or

EXHIBIT 19.2. Detailed Comparison of Standard to Actual Material Prices

Part Description	Standard Cost ($)	Actual Cost ($)	Variance ($)	Unit Volume	Extended Variance ($)
Antenna	1.20	2.00	−0.80	500	−400.00
Speaker	0.50	0.70	−0.20	375	−75.00
Battery	2.80	3.10	−0.30	201	−60.30
Plastic case, top	0.41	0.50	−0.09	14,000	−1,260.00
Plastic case, bottom	0.23	0.41	−0.18	11,000	−1,980.00
Base unit	4.00	4.25	−0.25	820	−205.00
Cord	0.90	0.91	−0.01	571	−5.71
Circuit board	5.78	4.00	+1.78	1,804	+3,211.12
Total	—	—	—	—	**−774.89**

roughly 14,000 units per month. The supplier has always offered the same pricing for this dollar volume of purchase. As a cross-check, the cost accountant goes back to the previous year's accounting records and finds that the price charged by the supplier was much lower—it matched the standard cost. Additional investigation reveals that the purchasing staff did indeed order in monthly quantities during the past year; however, these orders were releases under a blanket purchase order that committed the firm to a full-year order quantity of 168,000 units, qualifying it for a substantial price break. The new purchasing manager was not aware of this pricing agreement, which expired shortly before her arrival, and so she proceeded to order the parts based on lower monthly volumes and a higher per-unit price. The mystery was finally solved.

The level of detailed analysis just described is far beyond simple calculation of and reporting on variances by the cost accountant. Instead, considerable persistence is required to root through a company's transactions and ferret out the exact reasons why variances arise. This also results in a report to management that contains far fewer numbers and much more verbiage than one might expect. For example:

> The company experienced a negative materials price variance of roughly $1,000 for the January reporting period. Investigation of the problem revealed that the plastic case components were responsible for the bulk of the variance. This was caused by the lapsing of a blanket purchase agreement at the end of the last year, under which the company committed to full-year purchase quantities and received in return price breaks that allowed it to match the standard cost for these parts. The issue has been brought to the attention of the new purchasing manager.

Note that this short explanation of the price variance contains only one number—everything else relates to the reason for the problem. By using this descriptive approach one can reveal a great deal of added information to the management team.

Clearly, this approach to variance analysis requires much more effort than a cost accounting manager usually spends on variance analysis. One way to reduce the workload is to assign certain accounting personnel to the same types of variances month after month. These employees gradually build up experience in the best way to investigate each type of variance, which may include consulting particular reports or specific individuals in the company who are familiar with certain kinds of information.

Also, it rapidly becomes apparent that the same types of problems arise over and over again when these variances are investigated. After a few months of detailed variance analysis, it becomes a simple matter to determine the top dozen or so variance causes and cluster them in a standard report such as the one shown in

Exhibit 19.3. By using this format, the cost accounting staff can easily group its findings into a format that managers can quickly scan to determine continuing causation issues.

There is no particular need to include subtotals or totals in the report shown in Exhibit 19.3, for few people see all the numbers on the report. Instead, the report is customized to show only variances that are the responsibility of a particular recipient. Adding totals to a partly completed report is misleading, so it is better not to include them at all.

This reporting format lacks one key item, a detailed explanation for the causes of variances. Though it is an efficient format for the cost accounting staff to use in summarizing its variance information, it is best issued with accompanying notes, such as those used in the example for the ABC Company earlier in this section. Combining the two report formats results in a good summarization of variance information, as well as detailed explanations of each one.

Another issue regarding feedback is its frequency. Should variance reports be issued at the time-honored rate of once a month, or is a more frequent rate necessary? As usual, the answer is, it depends. Top-level managers do not have the time to peruse reports more frequently than once a month, given the small portion of their time that is available for this task. However, lower levels of management may indeed require more frequent notice of variance issues. At the shop floor level, managers expect to hear from the cost accounting staff every day regarding problems that occurred the day before. Only by such continual review can a company be assured of keeping its variances down to a minimum. The trouble with such frequent reporting is that it eats up the time of the cost accounting staff. To keep this information from becoming too excessive, the amount of daily reporting should be limited to a small number of items—perhaps just two or three—so that the cost accountant can spend a sufficient amount of time on each one and still have time to complete other tasks.

Another problem with the analysis of variance information is what to do with variance problems that arise continually. For example, what if a specific machine breaks down to an inordinate extent or the price of a major purchased part continually exceeds its standard cost? This information can be summarized separately from accounting system reports, for example, in an electronic spreadsheet. However, such tools are subject to error and may not be regularly reconciled to the general ledger, so that the information is not entirely reliable. A different approach to the problem is to set up separate accounts for the largest long-term variance problems in the general ledger and store the costs in this location. This method has the advantage of storing fully traceable information in the general ledger, where supporting journal notations can also be itemized. However, an excessive number of special variance accounts can clutter up the chart of accounts, so this approach should be used sparingly.

EXHIBIT 19.3. Standardized Variance Reporting Form

Variance Description	Variance ($)	Responsible Manager	Comment
Pricing variances, labor			
Staffing changes	4,302	M. Maspero	Two extra staff on hand
Overtime	10,030	J. Morgan	Overtime on third shift
Pay raises	129	M. Maspero	Overbudget pay raise to L. Lintro
Shift premium	2,002	R. Jervis	Work done on third shift
Pricing variances, material			
Rush order	12,250	O. Henry	Air freight on resin purchase
Order size	5,407	J. Morgan	Resin order quantities too small
Substitute material	500	M. Maspero	Switched oak for pine wood
Efficiency variances			
Broken tool	240	R. Jervis	Insert snapped on machine 03-32
Inadequate work procedures	319	J. Morgan	No procedures for Baines job
Inadequate worker training	5,038	O. Henry	New employees not usable in foundry area
Incorrect standard	420	O. Henry	Standard based on incorrect calculation for wing nut holder
Machine breakdown	905	M. Maspero	Work flow stopped when machine 17-01 failed
Machine manning	2,067	O. Henry	Excessive staffing on feeder machine
Material quality	8,178	J. Morgan	Stopped work when sugar extrusions were found to be tainted
Missing materials	682	R. Jervis	Boxes missing for Templeton job
Missing tool	0	—	—
Old standard for new machine	900	M. Maspero	New machine runs slower than standard set for 13-13 machine
Old standard for new process	671	J. Morgan	New assembly process runs slower than standard set for previous process
Old standard for new tools	0	—	—
Run time	340	M. Maspero	Incorrect setting on machine 04-21
Setup time	0	—	—
Substitute materials	4,067	J. Morgan	Replacement resin takes longer to cure

The key points to remember for variance analysis and feedback are to conduct detailed investigations of only the largest variances and to report these findings only to those who are in a position to act on the information.

RESPONSIBILITY FOR COST VARIANCES

Once a cost variance has been calculated and its causes examined, what do you do with this information? One option is to assemble the entire package of analyses into a large tome and issue it to every manager in the company. However, its sheer size will keep anyone from reading it in detail, thereby negating its greatest value—being a tool for improving internal company operations. A better approach is to determine which managers are responsible for particular types of variances and issue selected data to them that relates to their areas of responsibility. This reduces the information overload that would otherwise occur, resulting in a higher level of corrective action.

When determining which variance information to issue in a report, it is best to strip out any variances that cannot be controlled *by the recipient.* For example, the production manager does not know what to do with a report itemizing the price variance for purchased components because he or she has nothing to do with the acquisition of materials. Alternatively, the purchasing manager should be the recipient of this information, but not of a report on efficiency variance itemizing the use of the materials—this is the responsibility of the production manager. Of course, a few managers, such as the controller and the chief financial officer (CFO), will want to see the entire range of variances, but only because they should have complete knowledge of the sizes, types, and causes of variances in all areas of the organization.

Though the just-noted rule for distributing variances seems simple enough, here are some specific situations to clarify the issue further:

- **Responsibility for a continuous service.** An example of a continuously available service is the electricity generated by a company's internal power plant. In this instance cost variances must be sent to two responsible managers. One is the manager of the department that uses this service, on the grounds that excess use of the resource will eventually require expansion of existing levels of capacity, which will require a capital investment on the part of the company as a whole. The second recipient is the manager of the resource—in the example the manager of the power plant. This individual is directly responsible for the efficiency with which the service is created.

- **Responsibility for an on-demand service.** An example of an on-demand service is outsourced copying at the local print shop. The cost is not incurred at all unless it is specifically asked for by a department. This type of cost is easily traceable to a specific individual, so that person, or the manager of the department in which that person works, should receive variance information.

- **Responsibility for deviations.** An example of a deviation from standard practice is an authorization to use a substitute product. When the substitute is used, it may result in related variances, such as labor inefficiencies caused by more difficult manufacturing processes related to the material, or perhaps a higher scrap rate. In such cases the responsible person is the one who authorized the deviation. However, tracking down this individual can be quite difficult, especially if there are many deviation authorizations in a typical accounting period and many people involved in the decisions.

- **Responsibility for price variances.** A price variance occurs, for example, when the cost of a component is increased by a supplier. Though the obvious party to whom this information is sent is the purchasing manager, assigning responsibility for this variance can be difficult. The price variance is based on an original expectation of what a price should be, and that standard may have been compiled by, or influenced by, someone besides the purchasing manager. For example, the sales vice president may inform the purchasing manager that the sales expectation for product ABC is 100,000 units in the upcoming year. The purchasing manager accordingly determines the unit price of the product's component parts on the assumption that large volumes of parts will be purchased. When the actual sales volume turns out to be 10,000 units, the purchasing manager is forced to buy much smaller quantities at a much higher price. In this instance both the purchasing manager and the sales vice president should be sent the same purchase price variance information since they are both responsible for the problem.

- **Responsibility for external factors.** Some variances are not under the control of anyone inside the company. For example, oil-producing countries may unexpectedly decide to raise the price of oil, driving up the price of jet fuel. This in turn increases the cost of airline tickets and impacts passenger traffic at an airport, which loses revenue from its concessions. These concessions suffer a decline in sales that represents an uncontrollable volume variance. Though there is no specifically responsible person to whom this variance must be sent, it is reasonable to issue it to members of the management team who are concerned with external conditions, such as the CEO, CFO, controller, and manager of strategic planning.

- **Responsibility for efficiency variances.** It is easiest to assign responsibility for the efficiency variance. This generally relates to a specific department, work center, or production line, so it is sent to the person responsible for these areas.

The key issue to remember when reviewing the ground rules for variance responsibilities is that the number of variances ascribed to any one person should be thoroughly investigated in advance to ensure that the recipient truly has some control over the variance. If he cannot improve the underlying performance that caused a variance, the report should not be issued to him.

A special variance case that bedevils all accountants at some point in their careers is the purchase price variance. The purchasing manager is generally held responsible for deviations from the standard price of all purchased parts. This individual frequently avoids responsibility for the variance by becoming involved in the initial setting of standards and ensuring that they are set at levels that are easy to attain. Then all subsequent purchases generate a positive variance, which makes the purchasing manager look good. Alternatively, whenever there is a negative price variance, the purchasing manager complains that the issue is beyond her control because she cannot influence supplier pricing. In short, she looks good on the upside and avoids blame on the downside. What can one do to avoid this situation?

The answer is to create expectations for no variance of any kind. The purchasing manager's job is not to beat the standard by unfairly setting price standards too low but rather to lock in pricing on all key components for the entire year (or longer), with long-term contracts or blanket purchase orders, and then simply monitor the situation to ensure that actual purchase prices match the standard exactly. If there is a positive variance, it should be attributed to a lack of management by the purchasing manager, rather than considered an improvement over the standard. This mind-set must be reinforced by altering the purchasing manager's compensation plan to give her an incentive to lock in purchase prices rather than to fudge standards. This is a difficult practice to enforce and requires the full cooperation of the purchasing manager's supervisor to ensure that it takes place.

CASE STUDY

Ms. Deborah MacCauley is the controller of the Atlanta production facility of the General Research and Instrumentation (GRIN) Company. Despite the company's cheerful acronym, she is not in a happy mood, for the total variance of actual manufacturing costs from standard for the last reporting period is much worse than she normally expects to see. She is looking at the cost variance report for product line 400GL3, which is reproduced in the upper left corner of Exhibit 19.4.

This report reveals that there is a negative variance of more than $61,000. To collect more information, she goes to the general ledger, which itemizes in separate accounts the four types of costs in which manufacturing costs are incurred. As noted in the large block in Exhibit 19.4, these cover direct materials, direct labor, variable overhead, and fixed overhead. By comparing the costs in the general ledger to the budget, she can see that there are negative variances for all four costs, with direct materials having the single worst variance at $26,000.

At this stage she still does not have enough information about any of the cost variances to determine where she should concentrate her investigations, so she calculates all the price, efficiency, and volume variances noted in Exhibit 19.4. All the

EXHIBIT 19.4. Cost Variance Report

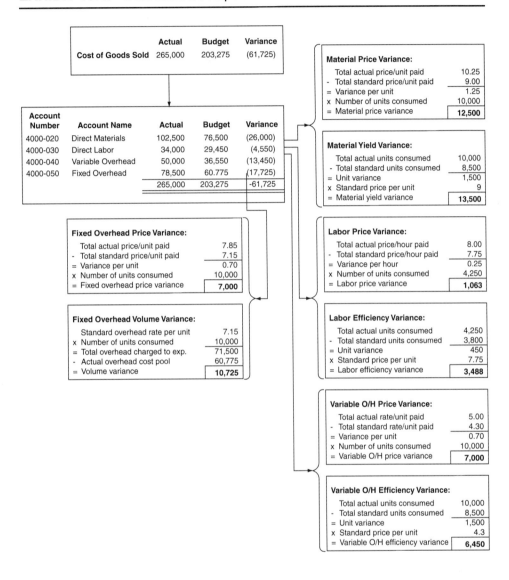

required calculations are shown in the exhibit. Here are her sources of information for these calculations:

• **Standard prices and quantities.** This information comes from the company's standards database, which is located in its manufacturing resources planning system.

- **Actual prices paid.** This information comes from the purchasing database, which is linked to the accounts payable portion of the accounting system.

- **Actual units consumed.** This information comes from the production control system's files, in which are recorded all production quantities used as well as scrapped and reworked items; this file is also part of the MRP II system.

- **Actual overhead cost pool.** This information comes directly from the general ledger.

Having compiled the various variances, Ms. MacCauley wants to know which ones are small enough to ignore. She finds that approximately 71% of the variance total consists of the variances related to fixed overhead and materials. Since this represents the bulk of the variance, she elects to ignore the labor and variable overhead variances and concentrate her attention on the other two. She takes these steps to uncover more information about them:

- **Material price variance.** She prints a report that compares actual to standard costs for all items purchased during the period and extracts the 20% of line items that cause 80% of the variance. This may be a sufficient level of detail to report to management, or she can continue to another level of detail, and see if the variances are caused by rush orders, small orders, and so on.

- **Material efficiency variance.** She prints a report that compares actual to standard units consumed during the period, and, as in the case of the material price variance, extracts the few items that caused the bulk of the variance. She can report to management at this point or talk to the production manager about specific reasons for excess use levels, such as incorrect machine settings or low-quality raw materials.

- **Fixed overhead price variance.** She compares the actual overhead costs paid to the amounts budgeted for the period and sorts the list of variances in order of size. For variances of sufficient size, she may choose to talk to the responsible managers or even call suppliers to determine why costs have increased.

- **Fixed overhead volume variance.** She compares the standard cost applied to the cost of goods sold to the pool of actual costs incurred to determine how much of the variance is caused by changes in the volume of the underlying production processes. She then compares the actual volume during the period to long-term trends to see if the standard needs to be changed. She can then make a recommendation regarding standard changes, management actions to reduce fixed overhead expenses, or a combination of the two.

A key issue in this case study is the logical process Ms. MacCauley goes through in investigating variances. She starts at the highest possible level of variance summarization and proceeds downward through increasing levels of detail, throwing out smaller variances as she goes. This method allows her to quickly zero in on the largest variance causes, which avoids wasting time on minor issues. Also, as we saw in the last set of steps, she can go in a variety of directions even after investigating variances in some detail; she can conduct further analysis if this seems necessary, or stop when the quality of information collected appears to be sufficient and convey it to management. Efficiency and effectiveness are crucial here—she should continue to investigate only if such extra labor will result in more valuable information than if she shifts the information to the management team, which may be in a better position to conduct further investigations.

SUMMARY

The primary linkage between a standard and an actual cost is the set of variances considered in this chapter. Of the three main variances described, the cost accountant must know which ones can be reported to various levels of management for further action (such as the efficiency variance) and which ones can be left out of variance reports because they are caused by factors that managers cannot control (such as the volume variance). Not only is it necessary to determine who is responsible for each variance but also the level of variance-related detail each recipient needs to deal with the variances for which they are responsible. In short, calculating a variance is only the starting point for the cost accountant—repackaging the variance information into a format that can be used by the management group is even more important.

CHAPTER 20

Waste: Spoilage, Rework, and Scrap

Accumulating data related to waste, as well as reporting it to management, are part of any cost accountant's job. Doing this work properly leads to a clear understanding of where waste occurs, how much it costs, and what causes it; this information can then be used by managers to ensure that the most significant areas of waste are tightly controlled.

In this chapter we review spoilage, rework, and scrap, which are the three main areas of waste that are encountered in a manufacturing environment. In addition, we examine how waste impacts several special areas—backflushing, just-in-time systems, and reported financial results.

SPOILAGE

Spoilage is defective production. It occurs in all manufacturing processes where the range of acceptable manufacturing tolerances is sometimes exceeded. For example, a machined part may be acceptable if its width is off by no more than 1/10 inch. Therefore, a part that is off by 1/9 inch is rejected and called spoilage. This situation can also occur at the beginning of a production run, when the setup staff produces a few products that are well outside the acceptable range of tolerances; this is an expected cost of the production process, since the spoilage must be incurred in order to set up the machinery. Spoilage can be a considerable cost if a company has poor control over its manufacturing processes or if setups are lengthy.

This type of waste cannot be reworked, so it is scrapped or sold off at a reduced rate. If it is scrapped, some payment may be received in exchange. For example, any parts with metal components can be sold to a scrap reseller; however, the return from these sales tends to be quite low. A more profitable approach is to clearly label it as rejected goods and then sell it off at a reduced rate.

There are several ways to treat the expenses and revenues resulting from spoilage. If the spoilage is in the range of quantities expected in the normal course of production, it is (predictably) considered normal spoilage and is included in the cost of the product. For example, it can be included as a standard spoilage percentage in the bill of materials for a standard product, or it can be included as a separate line item in the job costing file for a specially made product. It can also be included in the overhead cost pool and allocated to all products. In all these cases the cost of this normal spoilage is included in the value of month-end inventory if the completed products have not yet been sold off by that time.

When the amount of spoilage is considered to be abnormally large, the excess amount over the normal spoilage rate is charged off at once. This means that it is not factored into a product's bill of materials nor is it charged to the cost of a specific job. Instead, it is recorded as a spoilage variance and charged to the cost of goods sold in the current period. If the amount is large enough, it can be stored in a separate account in the general ledger.

If there is revenue to be gained from the sale of spoiled stock, the cost accountant can handle it in one of two ways. One is to record it separately as a revenue line item. This method works best if the revenue resulting from the sale of spoiled stock is large and therefore worthy of separate itemization. However, in most cases the revenue to be gleaned is so small that it is better to net it against the cost of the spoilage, which gives management a better idea of the true cost of the spoiled items. Taking this concept a step further, one could also include in the cost of the spoiled items the lost profit from their sale if they had been sold at full market price. This approach informs managers of the opportunity cost of the spoiled items, which may be considerably larger than the cost of the underlying goods.

Another issue is which costs should be assigned to an item considered spoiled. Does it cost as much as a fully burdened product, or do we avoid overhead costs? And do we charge the full cost of a completed product or some lesser figure? The standard practice is to assign the fully burdened cost of a normal product to a spoiled product up to the point in the production process where the spoilage is detected. For example, if the spoilage is found near the beginning of the production process, a minimal amount of labor and overhead is added to the material cost of the spoiled item for costing purposes. Alternatively, if the spoilage is found at the end of the production process, the full cost of the product is assigned to the spoiled item. Based on this rationale, a cost accountant should determine which production processes are most likely to result in spoilage and position an inspector immediately after these processes to prevent the spoiled parts from further processing before being removed from the production line. This keeps additional costs from being added to a product that is already either worthless or substantially reduced in value. Of course, the cost of inspection may exceed the cost saved by spotting spoiled goods more quickly, so a cost-benefit analysis must be performed to see how many inspection stations are needed for an overall minimization of both spoilage and inspection costs.

A different approach to the valuation of spoiled items is promulgated by advocates of throughput accounting (Chapter 14). Under this methodology the focus is on the bottleneck operation; if a product is run through this operation and then found to be spoiled, the profit that would otherwise have been gained on the sale of this product is lost. Therefore, the lost profit from the sale of a good unit is charged to the spoiled item. However, a product that is found to be spoiled prior to reaching the bottleneck work center does not impact the total throughput of the company and so should be charged only with its direct cost. Thus, the cost of spoilage depends on its precise location within the production process.

REWORK

Rework is any defective product that is subsequently fixed and sold off at regular or reduced price. This is a particularly important topic in light of the amount of extra work required to fix such items. In many organizations rework is allowed to pile up during periods of greatest activity and completed only during slack periods. This practice can result in the accumulation of a great deal of rework, which is subject to damage while it is lying about the facility. It can also greatly increase the amount of recorded inventory, since managers may record it at its full value even though extra work must be completed to ensure that it reaches that level of valuation. To avoid these problems the cost accountant should highlight them by creating a report that specifies how much rework there is to be done, where it is located, and the projected cost to complete it. An example of such a report is shown in Exhibit 20.1. In this exhibit, which is from a telescope manufacturer, the columns show the series of work centers, in sequence, that a company uses to complete its products. The number of rework items not yet completed are shown in each of these columns, along with their current valuation as indicated in the far right column.

This format is used so that the production scheduling staff can see where time must be allocated at each of the work centers in order to complete the rework and send it along to the next stage of production. The valuation column is useful for the production manager, who can use it to determine the potential valuation of all the rework currently located in the system—the greater the valuation, the more likely the manager is to be motivated to prepare it for immediate sale.

An alternative reporting format is one that itemizes each batch of rework items, the specific problem that must be corrected, the estimated labor required to complete the work, and the date this work is expected to be completed. The reason for

EXHIBIT 20.1. Rework Report

Product	Glass Grind	Tube Paint	Assembly	Calibration	Valuation ($)
4-in. reflector	38	0	0	40	8,000
8-in. reflector	0	100	22	0	12,412
12-in. reflector	41	0	80	10	6,051
2-in. refractor	0	0	400	0	3,090
6-in. refractor	8	13	49	72	7,906
6-in. Schmidt-Cassegrain	90	0	0	48	19,654
Total	**177**	**113**	**551**	**170**	**57,113**

this alternative format is that some rework does not need to be fed through the entire production process again; it just needs a little work at selected work centers and can then be considered complete. This type of report, as shown in Exhibit 20.2, is much easier to maintain since the quality control staff or a single production scheduler is usually assigned to track the rework as it moves through the facility. It is treated as a special entity, rather than as products that are mixed back into the regular WIP, because it undergoes only a small amount of work at a specific work center and is then pulled out of the production process. This special handling requires special oversight, hence a special reporting format.

Though these are excellent reporting formats, a substantial amount of work is required to maintain the information. The production staff must make entries into the computer system or send information to the production control staff that moves regular production into the rework category and then enters additional information into the system to record the work center locations of each item. This means that an entry must be made whenever a work-in-process item is shifted to the next work center in line. The problem is further complicated by the need of some accountants to accumulate additional costs for rework items, since they are, in essence, sent through the production process twice—the first time, when they are completed incorrectly, and the second time, for repairs. However, this added cost tracking effort is rarely worth the effort unless there is an inordinate quantity of rework to be tracked.

Rework can become the sand in the production system that keeps it from operating more smoothly because it tends to accumulate in work areas, may not be included in the production scheduling system, or may be rammed through the production system on an expedited basis. All three of these problems make rework an irritation that managers are happy to integrate into their operations more smoothly. The preceding reporting format gives managers the information they need by identifying precisely where rework is located in the system, and production schedulers can then use it to schedule the remaining steps required for completion.

EXHIBIT 20.2. Rework Issues by Rework Batch

Product	Rework Batch Number	Problem Description	Estimated Rework Cost ($)	Estimated Completion Date
4-in. reflector	0051	Regrind mirrors	1,200	05/01/02
8-in. reflector	0102	Tubes scratched / repaint	4350	05/10/02
12 in. reflector	0157	Shipment damaged—all-stage review	10,080	04/29/02
2-in. refractor	0217	Redrill spotter scope mounts	800	05/05/02
6-in. refractor	0300	Shipment dropped in warehouse—all-stage review	9,010	05/14/02
6-in. Schmidt-Cassegrain	0301	Loose intermediary mirror mount—regrind and reaffix	4,600	05/20/02

Another issue is how to record the added cost of rework. This involves a number of costs, such as the identification of rework products, removing them from the production system, tagging them as defective, determining the work required to repair them, and managing their subsequent reintroduction into the production process. These costs are spread throughout the facility and so are difficult to accumulate, summarize, and report on regularly. A better approach is to conduct a periodic special review of the issue using staff personnel to do the work. This practice keeps the production staff from having to fill out paperwork related to rework costs (always a plus), while allowing for a short period of intensive review that should give managers a reasonably accurate idea of the ongoing cost of the problem.

SCRAP

Scrap is the excess material left over after a product has been completed. For example, a sheet metal stamping machine punches out a number of parts from a single sheet of metal; any areas of the sheet that are not stamped into parts are considered scrap.

Scrap is similar to spoilage in its accounting treatment. One can include a material percentage in the bills of material for all products, identifying a proportion of expected scrap to be included in the cost of each product. Alternatively, it can be added to the overhead cost pool and allocated to the various products, usually on the basis of the amount of raw materials used by each one. Another method is to manually track the cost of all scrap as it is incurred and then charge it to the jobs where it occurred (most useful for cost-plus projects). It can also be charged directly to the current cost of goods sold rather than being allocated. The last approach is the preferred one since it avoids any possibility of overestimating the cost of inventory, in which the cost of scrap would otherwise be accumulated.

The revenues gleaned from scrap sales tend to be small, since the only value left is in the underlying raw materials because no value has been added to the product (as is the case with spoiled goods). Given the small size of scrap-related revenues, it is customary to not record it as a separate source of revenue in the general ledger; instead, it is netted against the cost of goods sold or against the overhead cost pool (if scrap costs are stored there).

There can be a timing issue related to the sale of scrap. The problem is that scrap is usually piled up until there is a sufficient quantity of it on hand to be picked up by a scrap supplier. This may be several months after the scrap occurred. Therefore, no offsetting revenue from scrap can be recorded against the original cost during the period when the scrap cost was incurred. In most cases the amount of scrap revenue is so small that this issue is of little import. However, it may be an issue for cost-plus job costing situations where customer billings are based on a complete compilation of all costs and revenues associated with their projects. In such cases the easiest approach is to estimate a likely revenue amount from actual scrap cost figures, record this as revenue in the job cost records, and list the offsetting debit as a liability on the balance sheet. This liability is drawn down when the sale is actually recorded at a later date, and any difference is written off to the cost of goods sold in the current period. However, this procedure is much too complicated for most situations and is not recommended unless the accuracy of job costing records is paramount.

As just noted, scrap can pile up for some time before a supplier purchases it. During this waiting period there may be a sufficient amount on hand to result in a value that is material for financial reporting purposes. If so, the value of the scrap can be recorded as part of inventory. The value of this inventory must be an estimate since there is no way to determine a precise valuation for each scrapped item, nor it is worth the effort to do so. The best way to make this estimate is to base it on the current market rates for similar types of scrap or, if these rates are not available, on the scrap value used by the supplier who purchased the last lot of scrap. In many instances the amount of scrap that accumulates is so small that it is not worth the time of the cost accounting staff to count it all, research the market rate, and calculate a value for inventory. Instead, they assume that it has no value for inventory purposes and exclude it from the detailed inventory valuation database.

Though it may not be necessary to closely track the value of on-hand scrap, it may be necessary to track its physical quantities. The reason is that scrap is commonly stored in an open area where anyone has ready access to it and so can steal it. Though scrap has a small value, the theft of a sufficient quantity can have a noticeable impact on profits. To prevent this the production manager can install physical controls over the scrap area. In addition, the cost accountant can measure a trend line of scrap revenue to see if there are unaccountable drops that may have been caused by theft. Though this is not a major problem, running this measure occasionally keeps management apprised of potential problems.

ADDING DISPOSAL COSTS TO WASTE ANALYSES

A typical costing analysis for any type of waste includes the cost of lost materials and perhaps the cost of the labor needed to rework it, if rework is possible. More comprehensive analyses may also include the overhead items associated with waste, such as inspection personnel, waste handling, and related paperwork. However, an important issue rarely addressed is the disposal cost of waste. In some instances this is simply the fee charged by the trash company to haul away the items. In other cases involving hazardous substances, it may include the additional fees charged by an environmental disposal company. In the latter case this cost can be substantial. However, there is a further cost that is nearly impossible to quantify— the impact of waste storage on the environment. Though there may be no directly attributable cost associated with this issue, a more enlightened board of directors may recognize that a company would do well to be "environmentally friendly," if only from a community relations perspective. This may result in a waste minimization policy conceived by the board. If so, the cost accountant may find herself compiling a report for board review that details the trend of waste quantities over time; this document may even be released to environmental or community organizations, so it needs to have a firm basis in factual backup information in case the presented figures must be proven.

IMPACT OF WASTE ON BACKFLUSHING SYSTEMS

Waste presents a particular problem for any company that uses a backflushing system. In this system the total amount of production is carefully tracked and then entered into the computer system, which automatically determines how much of each component part was supposed to be used, based on standard quantities, and removes this amount from inventory and charges it to the cost of goods sold. Backflushing is a more automated approach than its counterpart, picking, which requires manual removal from the computer system of every part as it is sent to the production floor.

The difficulty encountered by a backflushing system is that it is designed to remove from stock only the *standard* quantity of any material for a part that has just been produced. Any additional waste incurred is not removed from inventory records, which results in an inaccurate inventory whose recorded quantities are higher than their actual amounts.

To resolve this problem a company using such a system must institute waste recording systems that separately extract the excess amount of waste from the inventory and charge it to the cost of goods sold. This can be done by manually compiling the amount of spoilage, scrap, and rework at all stages of production and sending this information to the accounting or production control department where it can be removed from the inventory database. If the shop floor is equipped with a sufficient number of terminals, it may also be possible to create a simplified data entry screen for use of the production staff and have the information entered into the computer (though having inexperienced users do this can lead to errors).

A key problem with this separate entry of waste information is that the standard quantities the backflushing system uses probably already include some allowance for waste. For example, the bill of materials for a product may assume that 5% of the raw materials are scrapped during the production process, and so the system backflushes 5% of the materials from stock; however, the total scrap turns out to be 6%. How does anyone know that only the incremental increase of 1% of scrap should be removed from stock? They do not. Consequently, if the amount of waste is significant, it is best to remove all waste allowances from the standard records and instead record all of it separately.

Even if a company creates an effective waste reporting system, it is likely that the inventory and cost-of-goods-sold records will gradually diverge from their actual values. This problem arises because waste can occur anywhere in a facility and is easy to lose sight of. Employees may neglect to record it, may steal it, or are not well trained enough to realize that it must be recorded in the computer system and throw it away without another thought. Whatever the reason, waste occurs that is not accounted for throughout the system. The only way to ensure that inventory records are kept accurate in this situation is to conduct a rolling inspection of the inventory on a frequent basis and adjust inventory records based on these findings.

Backflushing is used successfully at many companies that understand the effect that waste tracking can have on the accuracy of their inventory records. The key is to set up an effective waste tracking and recording system that supplements the backflushing calculations to ensure that record accuracy is maintained.

TRACKING WASTE THROUGH A JIT SYSTEM

The just-in-time manufacturing methodology stresses the immediate correction of any type of waste. In this way, it keeps waste from building up in the production system and thereby reduces it to a small fraction of total production costs. Given the need for a JIT system to have immediate feedback regarding waste-related problems, it does not make much sense for the accounting staff to require production personnel to keep a log of each wasted item, which is then fed back to the management team at the end of the month; the information would be irrelevant because the underlying problems would have been fixed days before the report was received.

Instead, we must split the need for waste-related information into two parts. First, it is used as a feedback mechanism for the production staff. These employees do not have time to enter waste information into a log or a computer and would probably forget to make entries from time to time, rendering the waste records incomplete. A better approach is to have anyone discovering waste signal a maintenance team or supervisor, perhaps with a buzzer or overhead light, so that they can address the problem immediately—no feedback loop is required here! At most, the maintenance team that corrects the problem may want to keep a log of what issues it has resolved, so that managers can see if there are recurring problems that require a more permanent solution.

Second, waste-related information is used to determine the cost of waste. There are several ways to do this. One is to conduct periodic surveys of the manufacturing process using nonproduction personnel who measure waste levels at the time of their visit. This method has the advantage of only temporarily disrupting the work of the production staff and gives managers a periodic view of waste levels, which can be plotted on a trend line. Another approach is to determine that the JIT system is reducing scrap levels to such a low point that the cost of tracking it exceeds the cost of the resulting information; then there is no need to separately record any kind of waste. When this method is used, the cost cannot be segregated into overhead for allocation purposes and instead is usually dumped into the cost of goods sold for recognition in the current period. Both of these approaches are minimally intrusive at best and are recommended. The worst approach is to require a full-scale tracking of every type of waste throughout the facility, since this interferes with the activities of the production staff which would be better occupied actively eliminating waste-related activities, as is taught through the JIT methodology.

IMPACT OF WASTE ON REPORTED EARNINGS

The method the controller chooses to use when reporting the cost of waste can have an impact on a company's reported financial situation. It is perfectly allowable to include in a product's standard cost the amount of all normal waste—scrap, spoilage, and even rework. This is permitted because some waste arises in the course of any production process, thereby making it acceptable to consider this cost directly related to the manufacture of a specific product. Thus, one finds that a percentage of waste is included in the bill of materials for many products. This cost can then be used to compile the value of inventory if there is any on hand at the end of the reporting period. When there is inventory, the cost of normal waste is added to it, which increases the total inventory valuation and thereby increases the level of reported earnings.

Reported earnings can be manipulated by altering the level of scrap included in the bills of material. For example, the ABC Company has a long-standing tradition of adding 4% to material use on the bills of material for its furniture products. The company is expecting to show below-par financial results in the current quarter, so the controller accesses the bill of material records and adjusts the waste percentage upward, to 5%. This change adds 1% to the cost of materials for all furniture products currently stored in the warehouse, as well as for all new products being added to it. When the company later has a quarter in which results are better than expected, the controller reduces the waste percentage back to its previous level, which results in the 1% of added material costs being charged to the cost of goods sold.

This method is not acceptable because it results in modifications to earnings that are not even slightly related to actual corporate transactions—it is simple manipulation. An alternative is to implement tight security controls over access to the bill of material records in the computer and to require signed authorizations to update waste percentages in the bill of materials. Another acceptable approach is to charge all waste costs directly to the cost of goods sold at all times, so that there is no temptation to modify earnings.

An alternative method frequently used is to store the cost of waste in inventory by including it, or some portion of it, in the overhead cost pool from which it is charged out through an increased overhead allocation rate. This method too is subject to manipulation by altering the amount of waste costs charged to this account. Once again, the preferred approach is to remove the temptation to modify waste costs by simply excluding them from the cost pool.

Of the two methods mentioned here for charging waste to inventory, the one that is more difficult to trace is the addition of a waste percentage to bills of material. This is because changes can be spread over a large number of bills, altering each one only slightly, so that only a sharp auditor notices the changes. For this reason it is important that access to bill of material records be especially tightly controlled.

SUMMARY

Recording information about waste is important, for the management team must be aware of why waste occurs so that it can be controlled. However, the same cannot always be said for the importance of recording the *cost* of waste. Though it is necessary to determine what types of waste are the most expensive, it can be a considerable waste of time to determine the precise cost of all types of waste and to charge them to various jobs, overhead cost pools, or directly to inventory. These allocations can be manipulated to misrepresent the level of a company's profits when there is no defendable reason for doing so. In short, finding the cause of waste is more important than allocating its cost.

CHAPTER 21

Cost-Volume-Profit Analysis*

There is usually a narrow band of pricing and costs within which a company operates in order to earn a profit. If it does not charge a minimum price to cover its fixed and variable costs, it will quickly burn through its cash reserves and go out of business. During the early stages of development of a new product, when pricing can be high, it is difficult *not* to cover all possible costs, and making a profit is easy. However, when competition intensifies, prices drop to the point where they only barely cover costs, and profits are thin or nonexistent. When competition reaches this level of intensity, only companies with a good understanding of their own break-even points, and those of their competitors, are likely to make the correct pricing and cost decisions to remain competitive.

In this section we review break-even analysis, which is also known as the cost-volume-profit relationship. This is one of the most important concepts in cost accounting, so the following sections go into some detail regarding how the methodology works, what happens to the cost-volume-profit relationship when all possible variables are altered, and how to use it in a variety of analysis situations. Break-even charts are used liberally in this chapter, beginning with the most elementary examples and then progressing through a variety of additional variables that reveal how complex this topic can be.

*This chapter is adapted with permission from *Financial Analysis: A Controller's Guide,* (Chapter 8), by S. Bragg, 2000, New York: John Wiley & Sons.

BASIC BREAK-EVEN FORMULA

The break-even formula is an exceedingly simple one. To determine a break-even point, add up all the fixed costs for the company or product being analyzed and divide the total by the associated gross margin percentage. This results in the sales level at which a company neither loses nor makes money—its break-even point. The formula is:

Total fixed costs gross margin percentage = Break-even sales level

The uses to which this simple formula can be put are legion. A sample of them, along with examples of how to modify the formula to attain the desired results, are shown later in this chapter in Case Studies in Break-even Analysis.

For those who prefer a graphical layout to a mathematical formula, a break-even chart can be quite informative. The sample chart in Exhibit 21.1 shows a horizontal line representing the fixed costs that must be covered by gross margins, irrespective of the sales level. The fixed cost level fluctuates over time and in conjunction with extreme changes in sales volume, as noted in the next section, but we assume no changes for the purposes of this simplified analysis. Also, there is an upward-sloping line beginning at the left end of the fixed cost line and extending to the right across the chart. This is the percentage of variable costs, such as direct labor and materials, needed to create the product. Once again, the variable cost rate is assumed not to vary with volume, though this is not always the case, as discussed in Impact of Variable Cost Changes on the Breakeven. The last major component of the break-even chart is the sales line, which begins at the lower left corner of the chart and extends to the upper right corner. The sales volume in dollars is noted on the vertical axis, while the production capacity used to create the sales volume is noted along the horizontal axis. Finally, a line extending from the marked break-even point to the right, which is always between the sales line and the variable cost line, represents income tax costs. These are the main components of the break-even chart.

It is also useful to look between the lines on the graph and understand what the volumes represent. For example, as noted in Exhibit 21.1, the area beneath the fixed costs line is the total fixed cost to be covered by product margins. The area between the fixed cost line and the variable cost line is the total variable cost at different volume levels. The area beneath the income line and above the variable cost line is the income tax expense at various sales levels. Finally, the area beneath the revenue line and above the income tax line is the amount of net profit to be expected at various sales levels.

We have described the simplest version of the break-even formula and how to understand a break-even chart. In the following sections, we explore the vagaries of all three break-even components—fixed costs, variable costs, and sales volume—to see how special circumstances can further impact this powerful analysis tool.

EXHIBIT 21.1. Simplified Break-even Chart

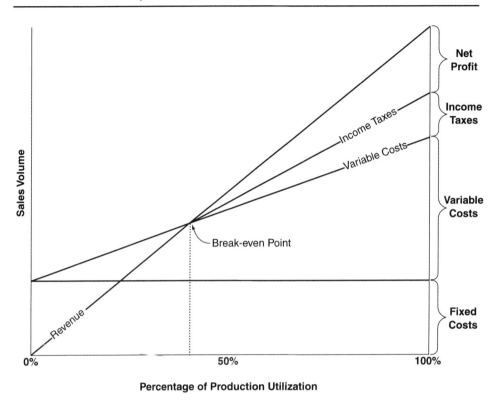

Percentage of Production Utilization

IMPACT OF FIXED COST CHANGES ON THE BREAKEVEN

Though the break-even chart in Exhibit 21.1 appears quite simplistic, there are additional variables that can make a real-world break-even analysis a much more complex endeavor to understand. In this section we look at one of these variables—changes in the level of fixed costs.

"Fixed cost" is a misnomer, for any cost can vary over time or outside a specified set of operating conditions. For example, the overhead costs associated with a team of engineers may be considered a fixed cost if a product line requires continuing improvements and enhancements over time. However, what if management decides to gradually eliminate a product line and milk it for cash flow rather than keep the features and styling up-to-date? When this happens, the engineers are no longer needed and the associated fixed cost goes down. Any situation

EXHIBIT 21.2.   Break-even Chart Including Impact of Step Costing

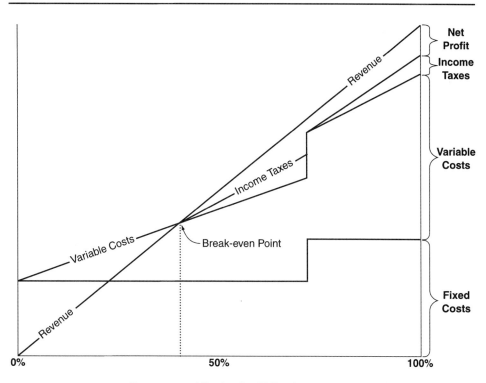

where management is essentially abandoning a product line in the long term will probably result in a decline in overhead costs.

More commonly, fixed costs are altered when additional personnel or equipment is needed in order to support an increased level of sales activity. As noted in the break-even chart in Exhibit 21.2, the fixed cost steps up to a higher level (an occurrence known as step costing) when a certain capacity level is reached. An example of this situation is when a company has maximized the use of a single shift and must add supervision and other overhead costs such as electricity and natural gas expenses in order to run an additional shift. Another example is when a new facility must be brought on-line or an additional machine acquired. Whenever this happens, management must take a close look at the amount of fixed costs that will be incurred, because the net profit level may be less after the fixed costs are added despite the extra sales volume. In Exhibit 21.2, the maximum amount of profit a company can attain is at the sales level just *prior to* incurring extra fixed costs because the increase in fixed costs is so high. Though step costing does not always involve such a large increase in costs as indicated in Exhibit 21.2, this is certainly a major point to be aware of when increasing capacity to take on additional sales volume. In short, more sales do not necessarily lead to more profits.

IMPACT OF VARIABLE COST CHANGES ON THE BREAKEVEN

The next variable in the break-even formula is the variable cost line. Though one would think that the variable cost is a simple percentage composed of labor and material costs that never varies, this is not the case. This percentage can vary considerably and frequently drops as the sales volume increases. The reason for the change is that the purchasing department can cut better deals with suppliers when

EXHIBIT 21.3.   Break-even Chart Including Impact of Volume Purchases

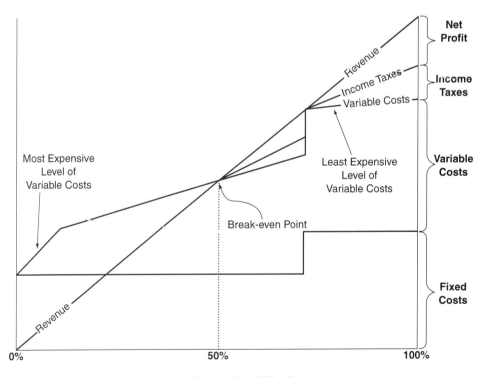

Percentage of Production Utilization

it orders in larger volumes. In addition, full truckload or railcar deliveries result in lower freight expenses than would be the case if only small quantities were purchased. The result is shown in Exhibit 21.3, where the variable cost percentage is at its highest when sales volume is at its lowest, and gradually decreases in concert with an increase in volume.

Because material and freight costs tend to drop as volume increases, it is apparent that profits increase at an increasing rate as sales volume goes up, though there may be step costing problems at higher capacity levels, as is the case in Exhibit 21.3.

Another point is that the percentage of variable costs does not decline at a steady rate. Instead, and as noted in Exhibit 21.3, there are specific volume levels at which costs drop. This is because the purchasing staff can negotiate price reductions only at specific volume points. Once such a price reduction has been achieved, there will not be another opportunity to reduce prices further until a separate, distinct volume level is reached once again. In short, suppliers do not charge lower prices just because a customer's sales volume goes up incrementally by one unit—they reduce prices only when there are increases in the volume of purchases of thousands of units.

IMPACT OF PRICING CHANGES ON THE BREAKEVEN

The changes in fixed costs and variable costs in the break-even analysis are relatively simple and predictable, but now we come to the final variable, sales volume, which can change for several reasons, making it the most difficult of the three components to predict.

The volume line in the break-even chart can vary because of the mix of products sold. A perfectly straight sales volume line, progressing from the lower left to the upper right corner of the chart, assumes that the same mix of products is sold at all volume levels. Unfortunately, this is a rare situation, since one product is bound to become more popular with customers, resulting in greater sales and a variation in the overall product mix. When the margins for the different products being sold are different, any change in the product mix results in a variation, either up or down, in the sales volume achieved, which can have either a positive or a negative impact on the resulting profits. Since it is difficult to predict how the mix of products sold will vary at different volume levels, most analysts do not attempt to alter the mix in their projections, thereby accepting the risk that some variation in mix can occur.

The more common problem impacting the volume line in the break-even calculation is that unit prices do not remain the same when volume increases. Instead, a company finds that it can charge a high price early on, when the product is new and competes with few other products in a small niche market. Later, when management decides to produce a larger unit volume, unit prices are lowered in order to secure sales to a larger array of customers or to resellers who have a choice of competing products to resell. For example, the price of a personal computer used to hover around $3000 and was affordable for less than 10% of all households. As of

EXHIBIT 21.4. Break-even Chart Including Impact of Variable Pricing Levels

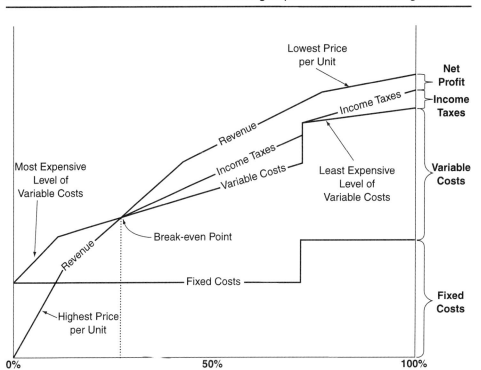

Percentage of Production Utilization

this writing, the price of a personal computer has dropped to as little as $400, resulting in more than 50% of all households owning one. Thus, higher volume translates into lower unit prices. The result appears in Exhibit 21.4, where the revenue per unit gradually declines despite a continuing rise in unit volume, which causes a much slower increase in profits than would occur if revenues rose in a straight, unaltered line.

The break-even chart in Exhibit 21.4 may make management think twice before pursuing a high-volume sales strategy, since profits will not necessarily increase. The only way to be sure of the size of price discounts is to begin negotiations with resellers or to sell the product in test markets within a range of lower prices to determine changes in volume. Also, in some cases the only way to survive is to keep cutting prices in pursuit of greater volume because there are no high-priced market niches in which to sell. For example, would anyone buy a color television set for more than a slight price premium? Of course not. The market is so intensely competitive that all competitors must continually pursue a strategy of selling at the smallest possible unit price.

The break-even chart previously noted in Exhibit 21.4 is a good example of what a break-even analysis really looks like in the marketplace. Fixed costs jump at different capacity levels, variable costs decline at various volume levels, and unit prices drop with increases in volume. Given the fluidity of the model, it is reasonable to periodically revisit it in light of continuing changes in the marketplace in order to update assumptions and make better calculations of break-even points and projected profit levels.

CASE STUDIES IN BREAK-EVEN ANALYSIS

There are many ways in which an innovative cost accountant can use the break-even model to obtain useful results. This section contains eight examples that are representative of the broad range of situations in which the model can be used. In each case the situation is described, followed by an analysis of how to use a break-even calculation to come up with a desired result. They are:

• **What level of extra revenue is needed to cover the costs of a capital acquisition?** In this case the Letdown Window Blind Company is considering the purchase of a $100,000 machine to replace an old one that is still functional but moderately inefficient. The old machine has long since been fully depreciated. To see what impact this decision has on the break-even point, refer to the modified break-even chart shown in Exhibit 21.5. Here, the dotted lines show how the break-even chart originally developed in Exhibit 21.1 is altered. The fixed cost line rises because the new machine cost has been added. Without any other changes to offset the increased cost, the break-even point shifts to a much higher level, where company utilization levels are at approximately 70%. Because the break-even point is so much higher, the company can make a profit only at the highest utilization levels, which gives it little chance of making any money and a significantly higher risk of *not* making any money. Therefore, the decision to buy the machine is a bad one unless management can show that there are other mitigating factors, such as an offsetting reduction in variable costs that will keep the break-even point where it is.

• **How do I know if a new business forecast is accurate?** When reviewing a business forecast, it is difficult to extract from the morass of detail the essentials of the forecast, which are the break-even point and the risk of not achieving it. The break-even calculation for a forecast follows that of a typical calculation and has the usual components—volume, fixed costs, and variable costs. As long as these items are listed somewhere in the forecast, it is a simple matter to derive the break-even point. If not, the forecast should be rejected at once and not reviewed

EXHIBIT 21.5. Break-even Chart Including Impact of Extra Fixed Costs

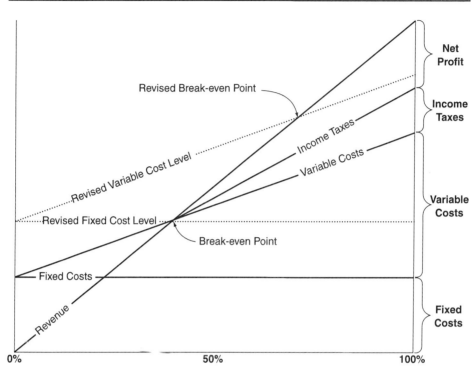

Percentage of Production Utilization

again until the requisite information is supplied. The *real* issue is determining the risk of the forecast. This risk is the range of break-even points associated with the sales targets most likely to be achieved, which are the highest, median, and lowest values. A forecast must contain these ranges of sales values to allow for a risk analysis with the break-even formula. If any of these values result in a break-even level that will yield no profit or a loss, there is some risk in using the business forecast as the basis for running a company. In such a situation it is up to management to determine the probability that the forecasted scenario will result in the projected loss. An example of this risk analysis is noted in Exhibit 21.6, where three forecasted sales levels are shown. Note that the minimum sales level results in a loss, which may be of concern to management.

- **At a specified sales level, what cost reductions are needed to earn a specific profit?** This is an analysis that should be reviewed whenever pricing changes in

EXHIBIT 21.6. Risk Analysis of a Business Forecast

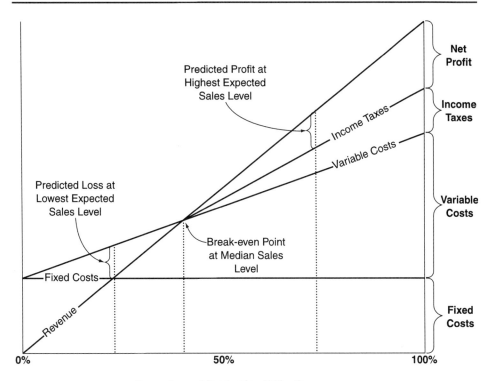

Percentage of Production Utilization

a commodity market force a company to change its pricing levels, resulting in a modification of profitability. An example of how to calculate this measure is to first set a target sales level. We use $1000. Let us then set a target profit figure of $150. These two numbers remain constant throughout the remainder of the calculation. We then progress to the remaining two elements of the break-even equation, which are variable costs and fixed costs. We can change either one to achieve a targeted profit level. Since either or both numbers can be altered, theoretically there are an infinite range of changes that will result in the target profit of $150 at the targeted sales level of $1000. However, to make the range of alternatives easier to understand, we use a chart to outline the different costs that will result in the target profit. For our example such a chart is shown in Exhibit 21.7. The chart notes the expected sales level in the first column, a range of variable cost percentages in the second column, and a range of fixed costs in the third column that will always result in the target profit, which is in the last column.

EXHIBIT 21.7. Table of Cost Variations That Achieve a Specified Profit Level

Target Sales Level ($)	Variable Costs (%)	Fixed Costs ($)	Target Profit Level ($)
1000	50	350	150
1000	45	300	150
1000	40	250	150
1000	35	200	150
1000	30	150	150
1000	25	100	150

Some analysts assume that fixed costs cannot change in the short term and focus their attention only on changes in variable costs. But fixed costs can be altered over time, so it is more accurate to use both costs as variables in the calculation.

- **What is the effect of a change in product mix on overall profits?** Product mix has an enormous impact on corporate profits, except in the rare cases where all products happen to have the same profit margins. To determine how the change in mix impacts profits, it is best to construct a chart, like the one shown in Exhibit 21.8, containing the number of units sold, the standard margin for each product or product line, and the resulting gross margin dollars. The resulting average margin impacts the denominator in the standard break-even formula. For example, if the average mix for a month's sales results in a gross margin of 40% and fixed costs for the period are $50,000, the break-even point is $50,000 ÷ 40%, or $125,000. If the product mix for the following month were to result in a gross margin of 42%, the break-even point would shift downward to $50,000 ÷ 42%, or $119,048. Thus, changes in product mix alter the break-even point by changing the gross margin number that is part of the break-even formula.

- **What is the effect on profits of a specific increase in sales?** We can use the break-even calculation to provide this information. However, when doing so, always remember that there are usually extra fixed costs associated with an increase in sales that reduce the actual profit level to one lower than that predicted by the formula. For example, there may be a need for more order entry or sales staff, or perhaps machinery maintenance or utility costs will go up to reflect the increased use of machinery. If these situations are likely, it is best to factor in a higher level of fixed costs (if the changes are in the category of cost) or increased variable costs (if these costs are those most likely to rise). To calculate the change in profits that will result from a change in sales, multiply the expected sales level by one minus the anticipated variable cost percentage to obtain the gross margin. Then subtract the expected fixed costs from the gross margin to

EXHIBIT 21.8. Calculation Table for Margin Changes Due to Product Mix

Product	Unit Sales	Margin (%)	Margin ($)
Flowmeter	50,000	25	12,500
Water collector	12,000	32	3,840
Ditch digger	51,000	45	22,950
Evapo-Preventor	30,000	50	15,000
Piping connector	17,000	15	2,550
Total	**160,000**	**36**	**56,840**

arrive at the projected profit. For example, if sales are expected to increase to $250,000, the variable cost percentage is 55%, and fixed costs are $100,000, the calculation is:

$$\$250,000 \times (1 - 0.55) = \$112,500$$
$$\$112,500 - \$100,000 = \$12,500$$

- **What is the increased volume needed to offset a reduced selling price?** The Kleaner Klothes Bleach Company is considering a promotion to sell more of its product. The promotion is a coupon for $0.50 off the retail price of the product, which normally sells for $2.00. Currently, the company breaks even on this product when sales reach $188,888 per month, which is due to fixed costs of $85,000 and a gross margin of 45%. It is currently earning $27,500 on sales of $250,000. The calculation needed to determine the new sales volume that will ensure the identical profit level first requires one to determine the new gross margin, which dropped when the price was reduced. Since the previous margin was 45% on a unit price of $2.00, this translates into a cost of goods sold of $1.10 [or $2.00 × (1 − 45%)]. Since the cost of goods sold is assumed to stay the same even though the price drops, the new gross margin percentage will be 27% (or $1.50 − $1.10). We then add the desired profit of $27,500 to the existing fixed costs of $85,000 to sum to $112,500, which is the amount that the gross margins from sale of the product must equal. The final calculation is to divide the new margin of 27% into $112,500 to determine that an enormous jump in sales, to $416,667, is needed to ensure that profits from the product will remain the same after the promotion is implemented. Given the size of the sales increase needed, management should perhaps reduce the size of the promotional discount.

- **What is the range of profits I can expect, given current market conditions?** In some industries, especially the most competitive ones, pricing varies in the short run within a fairly predictable range. For example, crop levels at the time of harvesting create a glut that drives prices down, while there are shortages just prior to the harvest since only stocks remaining from the previous year are available. In such cases a company knows that prices will be variable and that they will travel within a reasonably predictable range. Then, it is useful to know the range of profits to expect. A break-even analysis can determine the high-low profit points, but it cannot determine the amounts of time that market conditions will keep profits at one end of the spectrum or the other—that is for the user to determine. To calculate this measure, determine the lowest expected revenue level, multiply by the gross margin percentage, and subtract the expected fixed costs to determine the minimum profit level. Then run the same calculation for the highest expected sales level. For example, if the lowest and highest sales levels are expected to be $500,000 and $800,000, respectively, the gross margin percentage is 31%, and fixed costs are $150,000, the calculation for the range of profits is:

	Lowest Sales	Highest Sales
Sales level ($)	500,000	800,000
Gross margin percentage (%)	31	31
Gross margin ($)	155,000	248,000
Fixed costs ($)	150,000	150,000
Profit (loss) ($)	5,000	98,000

• **What is the unit cost at different sales levels?** The cost of a product includes both fixed and variable costs. The fixed cost component varies with the number of products sold because the cost can be spread over more or fewer units. For example, a software package with $100,000 of fixed programming costs has a unit cost of $100,000 if only one copy of it is sold but has a unit cost of only $1 if the cost is spread over 100,000 copies sold. Based on this example, it is obvious that product costing is highly dependent on the volume produced, especially if the proportion of fixed costs to total product costs is high. To calculate this measure determine the variable cost, divide the total number of units sold by the total fixed cost to determine the per-unit fixed cost, and add these two costs together to determine the total unit cost. For example, if a product has a variable cost of 62% and a unit price of $5.16, the variable cost is:

$$\$5.16 \times 0.62 = \$3.20$$

If the fixed cost for all production is $275,000 and 75,000 units are sold, the fixed cost component is:

$$\$275,000 / 75,000 = \$3.67$$

EXHIBIT 21.9. Table of Product Cost Changes at Different Volume Levels

Unit Volume	Unit Variable Cost ($)	Unit Fixed Cost ($)	Total Unit Cost ($)
55,000	3.20	5.00	8.20
65,000	3.20	4.23	7.43
75,000	3.20	3.67	6.87
85,000	3.20	3.24	6.44
95,000	3.20	2.89	6.09

Thus, the total cost of the product at a sales level of 75,000 units is:

$$(\$3.20 \text{ of variable costs}) + (\$3.67 \text{ of fixed costs}) = \$6.87$$

To clarify this information for a large range of volume levels, it may be useful to present the information in a chart like the one in Exhibit 21.9 that lists a number of unit volumes and the fixed and total cost changes resulting from these different volumes. In Exhibit 21.9 the cost and volume assumptions used are the same as those just noted in the costing example.

SUMMARY

This chapter explained how break-even analysis works and gradually built on the basic model by adding explanations and discussions of ways in which the fixed cost, variable cost, and volume components of the calculation can be modified to arrive at a variety of real-world break-even scenarios, several of which were covered in the preceding section. A brief perusal of the break-even case studies makes it apparent that paying constant attention to this form of analysis in the daily running of a business yields a better understanding of how and at what volume level a company can be expected to turn a profit.

CHAPTER 22

Analysis Reporting

The director of strategic planning for a Fortune 500 company claims that she spends 25% of her time formulating her view of the company's strategic direction and 75% of her time figuring out how to present this information to the management team. Seventy-five percent of her time! How much time does the typical cost accountant spend creating and presenting reports on various costing topics? Five percent? Ten percent?

The key point addressed by this chapter is that a cost accountant's research is of little use unless the management team takes some action as a result of it—and this happens only if these findings are presented in a such a manner that is clear and forceful enough to ensure that a decision takes place. In this chapter we look at how to ensure that cost accounting data is verified, summarized, formatted, and presented in such a way that cost accounting research always results in a useful decision by management.

DATA VERIFICATION

When an employee starts a new job, there is a "honeymoon period" during which coworkers usually give him the benefit of a doubt regarding his job performance because they have no reason to think otherwise. However, if he produces shoddy work over time, this period will end abruptly and be replaced by a well-founded belief that his work cannot be trusted. If this belief continues, not only does it become difficult to reverse, but it also results in minimal effectiveness of the reports issued by him—simply because no one believes the information.

This is a particularly deadly problem for a cost accountant, who continually provides management with a series of costing reports crucial to a variety of management decisions. If this person's credibility is questionable, it will be difficult to persuade managers that the reports they have received contain valid information and recommendations, which in turn will likely lead to a transfer to some other position or to a dead-end job. To avoid this situation it is mandatory for a cost accountant to verify all information contained in all reports issued.

One way to avoid this problem is to have someone else in the accounting department review all the information compiled before it is sent outside the department. This allows an independent, unbiased person to review material when the cost accountant has become too deeply involved to see any obvious problems. This approach is particularly useful for detecting "high-level" problems, such as missing facilities, incorrect dates, and the like. However, such a reviewer may not have the time or inclination to review report information in any degree of detail, so it is still likely that computational errors will not be caught.

To correct detail-level problems, such as incorrect computations, it is best to leave a prospective report alone for at least a few hours, and then come back and review it with a fresh perspective. Then attempt to run through the data without a calculator, just rounding off the numbers and performing general range estimates to ensure that the results of the report are reasonable. This type of review can detect major computational errors. For example, if a report adds the numbers 5.1067 and 11.409 together, one can quickly round off the two numbers and expect to find a total of between 16 and 17. If the report actually shows a number outside this range, a more detailed review of the calculations is certainly in order.

It may also be possible to create a procedure for error checking, perhaps including a short checklist of the standard features that every report should contain before it is released for general consumption. For example, managers may be particular about receiving reports that include the date on which the report was printed, since they may receive many versions of the report and otherwise cannot tell which one is the most recent. Another checklist item is the name of the facility to which the report applies— this is mandatory for companies that use standard reports for all their subsidiaries. Similarly, there may need to be a company-standard header at the top of the report, or perhaps a standard format requiring an executive summary, a detailed section, and a recommendations section. Whatever the case may be, a short checklist is invaluable for ensuring that a report meets a company's minimum standard requirements.

If the report under review has particularly important consequences in terms of the management decisions that hinge on it, the level of detail review should be correspondingly higher. If, however, it is a standard daily report on costing information, it is usually sufficient to quickly compare it to the previous day's report to ensure that the results are approximately the same. The circumstances determine the level of required review.

The speed with which a report is needed should be a warning signal that extra care should be taken concerning the accuracy of the information it contains. Reports needed immediately are those on which management needs to make a decision at once. The cost accountant should realize that any such report is therefore particularly important and must undergo a quality review no matter how much pressure is being brought to bear to complete it.

Given the volume of information with which the cost accountant deals every day, it is almost impossible to avoid an error somewhere in a report. Constant vigilance is needed to keep mistakes from degrading one's perceived reputation for creating accurate reports.

DATA SUMMARIZATION

After completing a study a cost accountant may be tempted to submit all the data that went into it, if only to impress the recipient with the amount of work required to arrive at a conclusion. However, it is not advisable to do this because it detracts from the primary objective of the report, which is to issue a recommendation to the reader—who may have trouble finding it in the midst of all the other data presented. Instead, the objective should be to present the *minimum* amount of data supporting the report's conclusion and to spend lots of time writing the conclusion.

For example, let us say that the sales manager has asked for a report itemizing the profitability of each product sold by the company. The main reason the sales manager wants this report is to determine which products have excessively low profit levels. The cost accountant prepares a spreadsheet that indicates, in separate columns, the price of each product, its direct material, labor, and overhead cost (assuming that overhead charges are relevant for the analysis). The spreadsheet also reveals the gross margin and margin percentage for each item. At this point, she could simply issue the report to the sales manager, but there is more information in it than the sales manager needs. It would be better to omit all the columns except the gross margin percentage since this is the only information required. Also, the report should be sorted so that the worst margins appear at the top. The end result is that five-sixths of the data required to produce the report is eliminated because the recipient does not need it.

The written conclusion accompanying any numerical analysis is at least as important as the numbers. There are several reasons for this. One is that the recipient may have no aptitude for numbers and needs to have the analysis explained in writing. Another reason is that the numerical analysis may not be so clear that a conclusion immediately presents itself. Yet another reason is that the numerical analysis may be so detailed, possibly covering a variety of alternatives or scenarios, that the only way to present conclusions quickly is through a written summary. In addition, the numerical analysis may be valid for only a specific range of volumes (see the following example), which should be identified clearly. Finally, when properly presented, a written summary is more forceful than a block of numbers.

Here is an example of a written conclusion that can greatly assist the reader in making a decision:

> The attached report addresses the problem of what minimum price to charge for product ABC. As noted in the analysis, the direct material cost of the product, when purchased in volumes of less than 10,000 units, is $15.50. Since this is the only truly variable cost associated with the product, the price must not drop below this level. If the purchase volume were to increase past 10,000 units, the cost per unit would drop to $14.25, which in turn would become the new price floor. If one were to develop a price based on the impact on bottleneck operation Alpha, however, the price point would increase considerably. At the moment, the least profitable item running through Alpha creates a profit of $4.00 and requires exactly the same processing time per unit in that operation as would be needed for product ABC. Consequently, the price of ABC must be increased by at least $4.00 over the cost of direct materials to ensure that the company as a whole generates the same or greater profit than is currently the case.

This example of a conclusion presents several topics that would be difficult to insert into a numerical analysis—it notes the relevant volume range within which a certain price is valid, mentions the impact on a bottleneck operation, and concludes with a recommended minimum price point. This type of summarization is necessary to ensure that all relevant information is included in a costing report.

REPORT GRAPHICS

There are many instances where the inclusion of graphics in a costing report results in a much more vivid, understandable presentation. As long as the use of graphics transfers information more readily to the report recipient, it should be included.

Exhibit 22.1 includes six different types of graphics that can be used for reporting purposes. Each one is useful for a different situation, as described here:

- **Pie chart.** The first graphic in the exhibit is a three-dimensional pie chart. This format shows the proportion of parts relative to a whole. It is most commonly used when no more than six items make up the total. Any additional items would clutter the presentation. It is not usable for trend lines or comparisons unless a series of pie charts are used.

- **Bar chart.** The second graphic in the exhibit on the left side is a bar chart. This is used for comparison purposes so that one can see relative levels for numbers

EXHIBIT 22.1.   Samples of Report Graphics

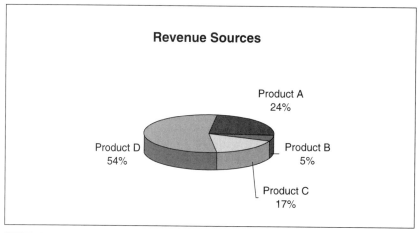

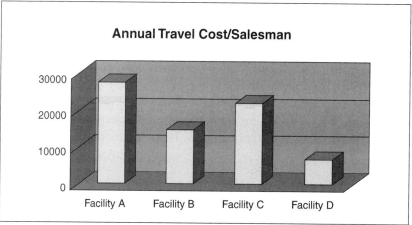

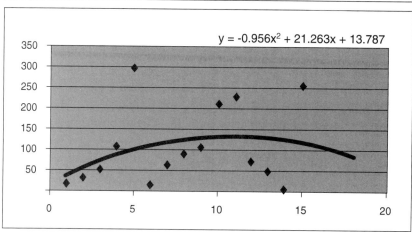

EXHIBIT 22.1.

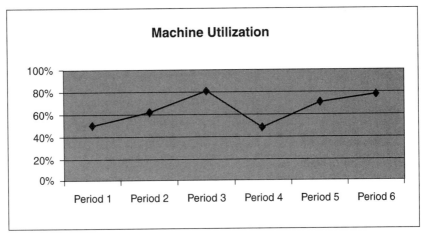

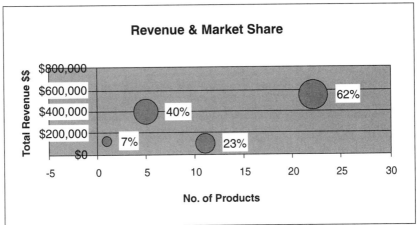

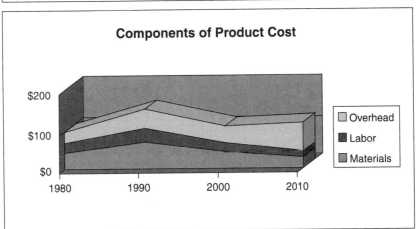

for different entities. For example, the exhibit compares the cost of a specific expense for several facilities. This format tends to be employed with too many types of data, leading to cluttered graphics. If there are numerous comparisons to be made, it is better to break the data apart into several different graphs in order to improve readability.

- **Scattergraph.** The third graphic in the exhibit is a scattergraph. This format is particularly useful to a cost accountant, who needs it to determine the presence of patterns in raw data. A trend line has been added to the exhibit along with its equation, which can be useful when determining the variability of various data points on the chart.

- **Trend line.** The fourth graphic in the exhibit is a trend line. It can also be shown in three dimensions but tends to be less easy to read in that format. The trend line is one of the best graphical tools for the cost accountant since it is a good way to show cost changes over time, which are a common reporting item. It is best not to use several different trend lines in one chart because it makes the graphic much less readable.

- **Bubble chart.** The fifth graphic in the exhibit is a bubble chart. Though this format conveys a great deal of information, it is really usable only for showing market share and revenue levels, which limits its use by the cost accountant. It requires three sets of information to generate—x and y coordinates and a market share (or some similar) percentage for each coordinate in the graphic.

- **Area chart.** The final graphic in the exhibit is an area chart. It is similar to a stacked bar chart in that numbers can be stacked on top of each other, but it adds the capability of showing the information on a trend line so that one can see changes in the relative proportions of numbers over time. This can be an effective way to convey trend information, but the graphic can become cluttered if too many types of data are included.

REPORT FORMATTING

The layout and formatting of the final report also has a lot to do with the degree to which the recipient understands its contents. If a report is issued that contains raw data, the reader must try to determine which parts are important and which can be ignored. However, when font sizes and types, underlining, shading, blocking, and arrows are used appropriately, the essence of the information leaps off the page.

Report formatting is best described with an example. In Exhibit 22.2 we see a report constructed in response to the question, Why does the downtime vary so much on machine MD-100? The report is a simple compilation of information that includes the maintenance cost by month, the months when preventive maintenance was performed, production volumes by month, and the percentage of downtime for

EXHIBIT 22.2. Unformatted Report Layout

Month	Cost ($)	Month	Preventive	Month	Production	Downtime (%)
Jan	5,402	Jan	X	Jan	1,000	0
Feb	1,003	Feb		Feb	15,000	30
Mar	7,512	Mar		Mar	1,000	5
Apr	500	Apr	X	Apr	4,000	8
May	1,750	May		May	6,000	12
Jun	3,000	Jun		Jun	10,500	20
Jul	5,250	Jul	X	Jul	13,000	24
Aug	6,000	Aug		Aug	11,000	26
Sep	5,500	Sep		Sep	4,500	10
Oct	2,000	Oct	X	Oct	25,000	38
Nov	12,005	Nov		Nov	1,500	2
Dec	1,000	Dec		Dec	5,000	10
Total	**50,922**		**4**		**97,500**	

each month. Though the answer to the question is contained within the information presented, it is not easily extracted.

In Exhibit 22.3 we take the information used in Exhibit 22.2 and reformat it into a better presentation. First, a brief examination reveals that the months in which high maintenance costs occur are always preceded by a month of heavy production. Accordingly, we group the maintenance costs and production volumes together and offset the months so that the production volumes are shown 1 month later, thereby revealing the cause-and-effect relationship between the information. Next we use this block of information to create a line graph that clearly reveals the relationship between these two items. To ensure that the reader knows where the data in the graph comes from, we add arrows and data labels. Though we have established and proven a data relationship, we have not yet shown why the downtime percentage varies by month. A brief review reveals that the maintenance cost is highest in the same months that downtime is highest. To show this relationship, we place the maintenance costs column next to the downtime percentage so that the reader can directly compare this information. In addition, we add small graphs showing the trend line for each column. Since one set of information is in whole numbers and the other is in percentages (less than 1), it is not possible to show them together on one graph. Instead, we create separate line graphs for each one and stack them one over the other; this makes it clear that there is a direct relationship between maintenance costs and the amount of downtime incurred. Though the layout of the report is much better, there is still no conclusion. We then add a text box at the bottom of the report, stating that high maintenance costs and downtime are caused by high production volumes in the preceding month. In order to keep this downtime from occurring, it is best to

EXHIBIT 22.3. Enhanced Version of Report Layout

Cause of Maintenance Downtime on Machine MD-100

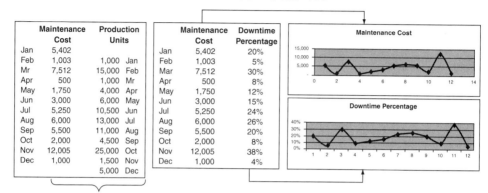

	Maintenance Cost	Production Units	
Jan	5,402		
Feb	1,003	1,000	Jan
Mr	7,512	15,000	Feb
Apr	500	1,000	Mr
May	1,750	4,000	Apr
Jun	3,000	6,000	May
Jul	5,250	10,500	Jun
Aug	6,000	13,000	Jul
Sep	5,500	11,000	Aug
Oct	2,000	4,500	Sep
Nov	12,005	25,000	Oct
Dec	1,000	1,500	Nov
		5,000	Dec

	Maintenance Cost	Downtime Percentage
Jan	5,402	20%
Feb	1,003	5%
Mar	7,512	30%
Apr	500	8%
May	1,750	12%
Jun	3,000	15%
Jul	5,250	24%
Aug	6,000	26%
Sep	5,500	20%
Oct	2,000	8%
Nov	12,005	38%
Dec	1,000	4%

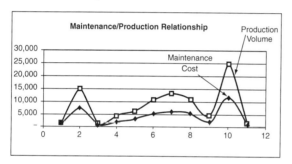

Problem: Determine why there is so much machine downtime.

Answer: Production volume is causing machine maintenance work, and related expenses, to fluctuate from month to month. High production in one month results in a heavy maintenance burden in the following month, with resulting downtime for the maintenance. Recommend that preventive maintenance be scheduled immediately before and during heavy production periods, so that less maintenance downtime will be required in the following periods.

schedule preventive maintenance immediately before and during high-production periods, so that the equipment is in the best condition when it is most needed. Finally, we clean up the report by centering and underlining the column heads, increasing the font size of the report title (as well as making it more explanatory), and enclosing the data columns in boxes. We also clear out any extraneous data; in this case the listing of preventive maintenance dates was not relevant, so it was removed.

Though it may seem that a considerable amount of extra time is required to complete the type of report formatting advocated in this section, it is also evident from the briefest comparison of the two report formats shown here that the reader obtains far more information from a properly formatted report. Consequently, this step should be considered one of the most important a cost accountant takes when issuing information.

REPORT PRESENTATION

It is not sufficient to send an e-mail to a report recipient that merely attaches a copy of the report file. This method of report presentation does nothing to give the recipient a clear view of the issues and recommendations being made, especially if the written report is a thick one requiring a major time commitment to read. Instead, a key report should always be presented in person, with a quick overview of the salient points and allowing extra time to answer follow-up questions from the recipient. If the cost accountant feels the report has a major impact on some issue, it may be worthwhile to summarize the key points in a PowerPoint presentation and use it to make a formal presentation to several members of the recipient's staff. This presentation does not have to be excessively long, but it must touch on the data that has led the cost accountant to a conclusion, a precise statement of this conclusion, and a set of recommendations based on this conclusion. In this instance the written report becomes a handout that recipients may only peruse for key information—it becomes an adjunct to the information used in the presentation.

Other reports do not require so much presentation work. For example, daily reports can be issued via whatever medium results in *immediate* receipt of the report by the bulk of recipients, whether it be written, spoken, or electronic. Standard reports, such as financial statements, can be issued with a brief executive summary on the lead page; these reports are seen by recipients so much that they have long since become aware of the main issues and need only informational updates—formal presentations are certainly not needed.

Thus, the nature of the report dictates the method of presentation. If the information presented is unique, or can lead to significant management decisions, the cost accountant should allocate a significant amount of time to its formal presentation.

REPORT FOLLOW-UP

Reports are all too frequently filed on a shelf and forgotten. Though the cost accountant is not in a sufficiently high management position to make other employees act on costing reports, other parts of the company can be forced to at least see if any actions have been taken. For example, it is possible to indicate in the plan of action for a new report that the internal auditing staff will be asked to conduct a periodic review of any actions taken based on the report and send the results of this study back to the audit committee (which usually consists of members of the board of directors). Another approach is to treat any completed costing reports as "old business" on departmental committee agendas so that they are continually relisted as action items until some action is taken. In addition, the cost accountant can ask that a project review for an issued report be included in her future activities so that she is "forced" to conduct an examination of how previous information has been used. The results of such examinations can be particularly useful when the controller is scheduling work requests from other departments and finds that previous reports issued to them have not been used. If the cost accountant can point this out, the departments that have failed to take advantage of costing information in the past may find that they now are less likely to receive any additional information. In short, those who have proven that they use cost accounting information can be assured that they will receive more of it—those who have not, will not.

SUMMARY

One cannot overemphasize the importance of issuing costing reports that are properly verified, summarized, and formatted. Without such reports all the detail work a cost accountant puts into creating a report is wasted. One must remember that a successful report is one that provokes some response on the part of the reader; if not, the presentation was not sufficiently convincing to spark some action. Every section in this chapter is crucial to the achievement of a top-notch report. Be sure to include all the recommended actions in the next report issued and see what a difference it makes in the results obtained!

PART V

Managing Costs

CHAPTER 23

Cost Controls and Feedback Loops

Much of the discussion in the preceding chapters centered on how to collect and marshal costs into a format that can then be summarized to reveal a company's hidden cost structure. What should one do with this information? In this chapter we look at how to control the costs that have been discovered—the various formats to use when presenting this information and the feedback loops that can be used to ensure that issues are rapidly sent back to those parts of the company where they can be quickly addressed and resolved.

PLANNING: SOURCE OF CONTROLS

Before delving into the types of controls and how they can be fashioned into feedback loops, it is important to determine the source of the baseline information against which costs are compared. Without some kind of a baseline, it is impossible to tell if a cost, by itself, is too high or too low. There are several sources of baseline information, which are:

- **Strategic plan.** Ultimately, the control point against which all of a company's operations are measured is its strategic plan. The purpose of this document is to describe such issues as entry into new markets, new types of research projects, efficiencies to be gained through automation, and the like. Given the high-level nature of its contents, it should be no surprise that the "hard" numbers it generates are usually limited to a small number of financial and operational performance targets. Consequently, it is of limited use in creating numerical standards for control, which instead are generated through the next item.

- **Tactical plan.** This is a group of plans that are directly derived from the strategic plan and which itemize the exact targets to be achieved in each functional area of a company. These plans typically yield anywhere from a few dozen to several hundred performance measures, which can be used as control points. However, many costs still are not individually addressed at this level, which calls for yet another source of control information, as noted in the next item.

- **Budget.** This is the monetary plan for all line items in the chart of accounts, in terms of both revenues and expenses. This information is based on historical revenue and cost patterns or on a detailed examination of the sales prospects for the upcoming accounting period, as well as on the costs required to attain these sales. Though the budget creates a cost standard against which general ledger line items can be controlled, it still does not itemize standards for individual components, labor types, products, or machines. These items are addressed in the next category.

- **Engineered standards.** This is a cluster of databases maintained by both the engineering and purchasing departments. They include the item master, which lists the standard cost of each component (if standard costing is used), the labor routings database, which contains the time required to complete work at each work center, and the bill of materials, which identifies the components and scrap levels required to manufacture each product.

All four sources of information noted here are used to create controls. The high-level measures described in the strategic plan are usually included only in monthly operational and financial reports, so that long-term trend lines in overall company performance can be measured. The standards set in the tactical plans are more commonly included in a statistical comparison page that accompanies the monthly financial reports. The standards derived from the budget are usually transferred directly to the financial statements, where they occupy the "budget" column and are used to derive the actual-to-budget variance. Finally, the engineered standards are not normally contained in the accounting system at all—instead, they are stored in files located in the materials management and engineering databases. These records are not normally accessible to a cost accountant, unless the accounting system is closely integrated with these other files. This is the case when a company has installed a manufacturing resources planning system or an enterprise resources planning system, which brings together the computer files of many different company functions for ready access by all. If either of these systems is available, the cost accountant can use it to compare actual labor, component, and machine costs to the engineered standards that reside in these files. This activity is still possible even if there is no MRP II or ERP system in a company, but the cost accountant is forced to collect and compare data manually, which greatly reduces his level of effectiveness.

It is apparent that many sources of information are needed to derive the comparison data used to ascertain whether a company's actual costs and revenues are too high or too low. It is important that all the data sources listed here be tapped for comparison data; if only a small set of tactical measures is available, without any supporting budgeted or engineered comparisons, the bulk of all company costs will not have a firm basis of comparison. Similarly, if many budgeted and engineered standards are available but no strategic plan, one must question how all these low-level standards relate to each other to form a cohesive set of companywide controls that will result in consistent, long-term profitability.

In the following sections we see how these bases of comparison can be used to create control systems and feedback loops to ensure that a company consistently meets its revenue and cost targets.

VOLUME-BASED COST CONTROLS

Volume-based controls apply only to costs incurred in direct proportion to changes in the level of activity. The obvious example of such costs is the direct materials costs incurred when each incremental unit of a product is manufactured. This can apply to other areas as well, such as the cost of life insurance that a company pays for each incremental employee kept on staff.

A volume-based control is a standard cost that is estimated in advance and which is incurred for each additional unit of volume change. For example, the standard cost for each unit of production might be $141.03, while the standard cost for the annual amount of life insurance per employee is $505.00. In these cases we do not attempt to create a total cost for all the related volume that might be incurred during the reporting period because our concern is only with the standard cost for *each* incremental unit. Once the actual volume for the period has been determined, we simply multiply this amount by the standard cost per unit and compare that total to the total cost actually incurred. The report format used for volume-based cost controls is shown in Exhibit 23.1, where we itemize the related activity volume and cost per unit of activity at the top of the report and then compare the standard cost (based on these two figures) to the actual costs incurred immediately below it. There is no comparison of actual to standard activity volume because that is not the purpose of the report; we are only trying to multiply a standard cost per unit by whatever activity volume occurred and then compare this to the total actual cost incurred.

EXHIBIT 23.1. Volume-Based Control Report

	Actual Cost	Standard Cost	Variance
Activity volume	20,000		
Unit cost ($)	141.03		
Total ($)	**3,004,017**	**2,820,600**	**−183,417**

The standard cost derived through this control report may not match the total actual costs incurred. If so, the variance between the two can be explained with several variance analyses, which are described in Chapter 19.

The source of the standard cost per unit usually is engineered standards, as noted in the last section. These costs are carefully reviewed by the industrial engineering and purchasing staffs, who determine the exact cost incurred for each unit of production at different levels of purchasing and production volume. The results of their research are contained in the item master, bill of materials, and labor routing files, from which they are taken to construct volume-based control reports similar to the one just shown in Exhibit 23.1.

Volume-based cost controls cannot be used for the majority of costs because they do not vary directly with volume. Instead, it is more common to see costs that are totally fixed within set volume ranges or are only partly influenced by volume considerations. The cost controls that address these two types of costs are discussed in the next two sections.

FIXED COST CONTROLS

The most common cost controls are for fixed costs. Examples of these costs are salaries, payroll taxes, and rent payments. They do not change in size within normal operating parameters, though they can change if the size of a company's activity volumes change to an inordinate degree. For example, the number of employees in the accounting department may be sufficient for current operating levels, but a doubling of production volume would probably call for the hiring of additional clerks. Thus, within normal, expected levels of operation, these types of costs are relatively fixed in size and are readily predicted.

These costs are relatively easy to control, for one can extract predicted costs from the annual budget and compare them to actual results to see if the actual costs incurred are approximately the same as those in the budget. The sole source of this comparative information is the budget; the level of detail needed is not normally found in the strategic or tactical plans, while the data contained in engineered standards is almost always used just for variable cost items.

EXHIBIT 23.2. Fixed Cost Control Report

	Actual Cost ($)	Standard Cost ($)	Variance ($)
Engineering salaries	408,320	425,000	+16,680
Payroll taxes	31,240	32,513	+1,273
Benefits	41,490	43,800	+2,310
Training	40,000	38,000	-2,000
Travel	28,420	24,000	-4,420
Supplies	12,993	10,000	-2,993
Totals	**562,463**	**573,313**	**+10,850**

An example of a fixed cost control report is shown in Exhibit 23.2, where we see the costs for the engineering department, which are generally considered to be entirely fixed. There is no need to itemize activity levels, as was the case in the last exhibit, for these costs are incurred irrespective of the level of activity. Actual costs are then matched to budgeted costs, which yields a dollar variance in the final column.

The largest problem with fixed cost controls is that companies have a bad habit of trying to apply them to costs that vary directly with activities, such as production volumes. The most common mistake is considering the cost of goods sold a fixed cost and comparing it to a fixed level of production costs that bears no relationship to the level of production that actually occurred. This results in a large variance, for which the blame is alternately shifted among the sales, production scheduling, and production departments. In reality, there should not be a large variance if the control point used was only a variable standard that fluctuated with production volume rather than one that was frozen throughout the reporting period.

CONTROL OF SEMIVARIABLE COSTS

The most incorrect cost control in nearly all organizations involves semivariable costs. These are costs that vary somewhat with different types of activity volume but which also have a fixed cost component that is always incurred. For example, a company's telephone costs consist of a flat monthly fee for the use of local phone lines, plus variable costs for long-distance charges. The flat fee is incurred every month, whereas the variable cost of long-distance calls fluctuates in relation to the number of employees in the company. Despite the presence of both fixed and variable elements in this cost, it is most common to see it treated in cost control reports as a fixed cost, so that actual telephone costs are compared to a fixed budgeted amount in each reporting period. As a result, there is a variance from the budget every month, which managers choose to ignore or shift back to the cost accountant for a thorough analysis.

EXHIBIT 23.3. Semivariable Cost Control Report

Expense Type	50,000 Sq Ft	100,000 Sq Ft	150,000 Sq Ft
Salaries ($)	63,000	84,000	100,000
Taxes and benefits ($)	6,700	10,100	14,900
Supplies ($)	3,500	7,200	9,100
Depreciation ($)	10,000	10,000	12,000
Training ($)	500	750	800
Totals ($)	**133,700**	**212,050**	**286,800**

There are two ways to control semivariable costs, both of which are better than the approach just described. One is to split these costs into their variable and fixed components and track them separately through the general ledger. This is possible in our example, where the telephone company usually itemizes the cost of the phone lines separately from long-distance charges. In other cases the split between these two types of costs is not so apparent. Then, the next best approach is to create a table that itemizes the expected cost of each item within a preset range of activities. An example is shown in Exhibit 23.3, where we see an itemization of the costs of the janitorial department, which vary in proportion to the number of square feet of building that must be cleaned. To use this table for cost control, one must compile the activity volume for the reporting period, locate this volume on the table, and transfer the costs related to it to the budget file used for comparison purposes in the financial statements. It is a rare accounting system indeed that contains the table shown in Exhibit 23.3 for semivariable costs. Instead, one must store this information off-line, perhaps in an electronic spreadsheet, and manually transfer it into the accounting system. Though this is a labor-intensive approach, it yields relatively accurate results for cost control purposes.

RESPONSIBILITY ACCOUNTING

Now that we have determined a reasonable method for reporting on costs in comparison to a standard, how should we use it to make sure that costs are incurred in accordance with expectations? This is best done through the concept of responsibility accounting, which is the assumption that every cost incurred by a company is the responsibility of one person somewhere in the company. For example, the cost of rent can be assigned to the person who negotiates and signs the lease, while the cost of an employee's salary is the responsibility of that person's direct manager. This concept also applies to the cost of products, for each component part has a standard cost (as listed in the item master and bill of materials), and it is the responsibility of the purchasing manager to obtain each part at the correct price. Similarly, scrap costs incurred at a machine are the responsibility of the shift manager.

By using this approach the cost control reports presented in the last three sections can be tailored for each recipient. For example, the manager of a work cell receives a financial statement that itemizes only the costs incurred by that specific cell, whereas the production manager receives a different one that itemizes costs for the entire production department, and the president receives one that summarizes costs for the entire organization.

In the following sections we cover the various types of responsibility centers used to report cost controls. The simplest of these is the cost center, which (as the name implies) reports on all expense line items for which an individual is responsible. A similar responsibility center is the revenue center, which holds a person responsible for just revenues. At a more sophisticated level is the profit center, which holds an employee responsible for both revenues and costs. Finally, there is the investment center, which adds to the responsibilities of profit center an additional responsibility for incremental investments and the return on these investments.

As one moves upward through the increasingly complex, sophisticated forms of responsibility centers, it is also common to find fewer of them being used. For example, each person in a department may be placed in charge of a separate cost, and so each one receives a report itemizing their performance in controlling that cost. However, when the more complex profit center approach is used, these costs are typically lumped together in a group of costs that can be directly associated with revenues from a specific product or product line, which therefore results in fewer profit centers than cost centers. Then, at the highest level of responsibility center, the investment center, one makes investments that may cut across entire product lines, so the investment center tends to be reported at a minimal level of an entire production facility. Thus, there is a natural consolidation in the number of responsibility reports generated by the accounting department as more complex forms of responsibility reporting are used.

Because a company has succeeded in shifting its cost control structure to the highest levels of profit center and investment center reporting does not mean that all revenue and cost center reporting systems have been abandoned. On the contrary, people within each functional area are still responsible for individual costs and revenues, so it is entirely appropriate for them to continue to receive custom-tailored reports. Also, some cost centers (such as maintenance and janitorial departments) have no associated revenues of any kind and so they will continue to be treated as cost centers and receive cost center reports, even if the facility within which they are located is treated in general as a profit or an investment center.

In the following sections we explore the differences between the various types of responsibility centers and look at the differences between the reports used for each one.

COST CENTERS

The most elementary form of responsibility center is the cost center, which is mirrored by the revenue center (as noted in the next section). The cost center itemizes all the expenses incurred to run a specified function but ignores the cost of capital invested in it, as well as any associated revenues. The primary form of control in a cost center is against a fixed or semivariable budget determined at the beginning of the year. It is not common to see a variable budget being used in a cost center since purely variable costs tend to be most closely associated with production, for which there are associated sales—this relationship means that variable budget costs are more commonly found in profit centers than in cost centers. An example of the cost center reporting format is shown in Exhibit 23.4, where all the expense line items for the janitorial department are listed. There is also a subtotal for costs directly attributable to the department, followed by an overhead allocation for administrative costs (which is not controllable by the janitorial manager). This general format can be used for any cost center.

Though this is a good start for a company that wants to implement controls over its expenditures, it suffers from one main flaw—those responsible for cost centers are concerned only with the tight control of costs, rather than other key company goals such as customer service, creating new products, or acquiring new customers. This can lead to counterproductive behavior. For example, the manager of the computer services department, which is operated as a cost center, is determined to avoid any cost overruns. The sales manager, who is trying to increase profits, asks that a customized report be created that lists the margins for each existing customer, so that the sales team will know which customers are the best ones to sell to. However, the computer services manager refuses this request, for it will result in extra costs that will exceed her budget. This problem occurs regularly when a company is structured into many cost centers, each of which

EXHIBIT 23.4. Sample Cost Center Report

Expense Type	Actual Expenses ($)	Budgeted Expenses ($)	Variance ($)
Wages	58,000	60,000	+2,000
Personnel benefits	6,000	5,500	−500
Equipment depreciation	2,400	2,000	−400
Supplies	4,800	3,200	−1,600
Expense subtotal	**71,200**	**70,700**	**−500**
Overhead allocations	6,100	6,100	0
Total expenses	**77,300**	**76,800**	**−500**

looks out for its own self-interest. To avoid this problem, many cost centers are converted to profit centers, which are described in a later section.

REVENUE CENTERS

As the name implies, a revenue center is one where the employees located in a specific functional area are solely responsible for attaining preset revenue levels. The sales department is sometimes considered a revenue center. In this capacity employees are essentially encouraged to obtain new sales without regard to the costs involved. This can be a dangerous way to run a function unless strict guidelines are set up to control the overall spending limits allowed, the size and type of customer solicited, and the size and type of orders obtained. Otherwise, the sales staff will obtain orders from all kinds of customers, including those with poor credit records or histories of returning goods, not to mention orders that are so small that the cost of processing them exceeds the profit gained from the sale. Other counterproductive activities associated with revenue centers are the inordinate use of travel funds to meet with customers, selling products at large discounts from the standard price, offering special promotional guarantees to customers, allowing credits for previously purchased products if the price subsequently declines, and offering to extend payment terms. All these activities are surefire ways to increase revenues, but only at considerable additional cost, which will eat into, if not eliminate, profits. For all these reasons, revenue centers are not recommended without the addition of stringent controls to ensure that the sales staff obtains only revenues that will result in adequate levels of profitability. Here are some of the controls that should be required for a revenue center:

- **Travel policies.** Create policies for salesperson trips that encompass the types of expenses that are allowable, as well as the maximum amounts of expenditures that can be incurred for various cost categories such as hotel rooms, meals, and car rentals.

- **Centralized airline ticket procurement.** This allows company managers to control the cost of airline tickets bought by the sales staff and avoids the indiscriminate purchase of first-class seating or seat upgrades.

- **Credit approvals.** Ensure that customer credit approvals are made only by the finance department. By shifting credit approvals to someone outside the sales staff, it is much easier to dispassionately weigh a prospective customer's ability to pay for their accounts receivable. This policy can even be extended to prior credit approval of customers before they are contacted by a salesperson for an initial sales call.

- **Commission basis.** Compensation should be based on the profitability of product sales, rather than revenue volume. When product profitability is used as the key determinant of the size of commissions, sales personnel push the sales of high-profit items. This also solves a host of other problems, such as the granting of discounts, which can cut into profit margins.

- **Product returns.** A company should tightly control the ability of its customers to return quantities of unused product without prior authorization. This function should certainly not reside in the sales department since the sales staff tends to agree to most requests made by their customers. Also, there should be a policy that cuts off sales to customers who have a history of returning so many products that the cost of processing them has driven the customer's profitability below a minimum acceptable level.

- **Promotions.** The ability to grant advertising allowances to customers should be strictly controlled by the marketing department rather than by the sales staff, which would be tempted to use them as a tool to obtain more sales rather than for their intended purpose, which is to increase customer awareness through carefully targeted advertising and related promotions.

- **Order size.** At some point a customer's order size may become so small that the cost of processing and shipping it exceeds the profit to be gained from the sale. There should be a strictly followed policy in place preventing the sales staff from selling below this minimum point.

Though this may seem like a considerable number of restrictions to place on a revenue center, they must be used to ensure that the personnel at that center are tightly focused not only on bringing in new revenue but also on doing so at the lowest possible cost, while ensuring that only the most profitable revenues are solicited.

PROFIT CENTERS

The profit center resolves many of the problems just described for the cost and revenue center concepts by combining the two. Now, the manager of a profit center is primarily responsible for generating the highest possible profit (or least possible loss). This provides a strong incentive to pursue only sales with a sufficient margin, while also incurring expenses only if they will result in an incremental increase in revenue. An example of a profit center report is shown in Exhibit 23.5. This format is similar to the one used for a cost center, except that it includes a revenue line at the top and a profit amount at the bottom.

The profit center concept is highly recommended since it results in the strongest possible management attention to profitability. However, there are some cases where it is difficult to convert a cost center to a profit center because there is no way for it to gain revenues by directly selling its services. Examples of such cost centers are the computer services, engineering, and production departments. These

EXHIBIT 23.5. Sample Profit Center Report

Account Type	Actual Expenses	Budgeted Expenses	Variance
Revenue ($)	90,000	92,000	−2,000
Expenses			
Wages ($)	58,000	60,000	+2,000
Personnel benefits ($)	6,000	5,500	−500
Equipment depreciation ($)	2,400	2,000	−400
Supplies ($)	4,800	3,200	−1,600
Expense subtotal ($)	**71,200**	**70,700**	**−500**
Overhead allocations ($)	6,100	6,100	0
Total expenses ($)	**77,300**	**76,800**	**−500**
Profit ($)	12,700	15,200	−2,500
Profit (%)	14	17	−3

groups are all involved in the production or support of products, but it can be difficult to attribute sales directly to them. One way around this problem is to have each department charge other departments for its services. A good example is the computer services function, where many organizations create a programming cost per hour that is charged to all other departments that request changes in computer programs; it is also common to charge for the processing time used by each department's programs, as well as the cost of report processing, generation, and distribution. These are valid charges to make, for departments now have the option of outsourcing some functions, such as computer services, so that suppliers provide the same services that were previously performed internally. If a department can find a better deal outside the company, it should go ahead and purchase the outside services. By using this method a company can force many of its cost centers to pay much more attention to costs incurred and services rendered to other departments—if they drop below the level of outside service providers, there will be no call for their services and the employees in these departments will lose their jobs. This approach can be used for many functions besides computer services, such as engineering, production, and accounting. If the function can be outsourced, it can be treated as a profit center. For more information on outsourcing, see Bragg (1998).

When determining revenues for profit centers, it may be necessary to allocate revenues based on the cost of services or materials added to a product as it moves through a department. This allocation process is described in detail in Chapter 30. If there are cases where it becomes difficult to justify a revenue allocation, or it is impossible to prove that any value is added to a product or service, it may be better to leave the function as a cost center rather than attempt to convert it to a profit center.

A final issue involving profit centers is that the income statement format used no longer involves the use of just fixed cost targets that do not vary with volume;

instead, there are likely to be some semivariable and variable costs that change in direct proportion to the level of activity experienced by the profit center. If so, the income statement format should be similar to the "flex" format discussed earlier in Chapter 11, which deals with direct costing. By altering the income statement budget levels to match the exact volume level experienced during the reporting period, it becomes much easier to generate a standard for comparison purposes, yielding accurate variance analysis for a profit center.

Thus, the profit center approach represents a clear improvement over the cost and revenue centers through its modification of manager behavior to focus attention on profits rather than just costs or revenues.

INVESTMENT CENTERS

A step beyond the profit center in level of sophistication is the investment center. It is the same as a profit center, but the responsible manager is also held accountable for any investments in the business. This added responsibility means that one additional measure is added to the normal set of measures used for a profit center—return on investment. This measures the ability of a manager not only to generate a profit but also to create one at a sufficiently high level to offset the cost of capital for any newly invested funds.

The investment center is particularly appropriate for cases where investment decisions must be made rapidly in order to take advantage of changes in local business conditions. This is a particularly important issue for companies in rapidly expanding markets or where consumer needs change rapidly, where waiting for investment approval from a central authority may result in lost sales.

Though the investment center seems like the most sophisticated of all the various types of responsibility accounting, given its incorporation of revenues, costs, and invested funds, it is still rarely used. The reason is that the manager of an investment center could obligate a corporation into a large investment and never generate a sufficient return to pay off the investment, thereby worsening the financial condition of the corporation as a whole. Though a valid concern, this problem can be restricted by adding some form of investment oversight. For example, an investment committee at the corporate headquarters or division level can be used to approve all investments greater than a certain amount. This approach gives the managers of investment centers total leeway to invest smaller amounts of money while still reducing the overall corporate risk of a bad investment by requiring a more detailed analysis for large investments.

Another way to control the risk of a poor investment is to use a standard methodology to examine all prospective investments (Chapter 24). By doing so one can be assured that all relevant information is included in an analysis, that all key measures (e.g., net present value, internal rate of return, payback period) have been calculated, and that this review has been compared to the cost of capital to ensure that this minimum investment hurdle has been surpassed.

The one instance where the investment center probably does not work is when there is a highly centralized corporate management structure in place. In this instance few decisions are left for the local manager, and certainly not investment-related decisions. These are strictly controlled by a central capital investment review function and usually require approvals from all levels of management before an investment can be finalized. The alternative corporate structure, decentralization, merely *requires* the use of investment centers since the corporate management staff goes out of its way not to become involved in operational issues at the local facility level. Thus, the overall management structure is a strong driver of the level of use of investment centers.

As long as the controls noted here are put in place, there is no reason why many profit centers cannot be converted to the more advanced investment center concept, though this is highly dependent on the willingness of the top management group to push investment decisions far down into the corporate hierarchy.

SAME-DAY FEEDBACK LOOPS

The one area in which cost accountants can provide the greatest amount of added value in terms of cost controls and feedback loops is in increasing the quantity of information cycled back to the organization every day. Historically, the cost accountant has been required to issue only a single monthly report itemizing the costs of various activities and their variances from preset standards. However, managers can use this information much more frequently to make minor daily adjustments to their operations that increase efficiencies immediately, while problems are fresh in their minds. This approach also keeps problems from festering for an entire month. For example, if a member of the purchasing staff buys an inordinate amount of a component in order to take advantage of a price discount, it does no good for the purchasing manager to be made aware of this problem a month after the purchase was made—instead, immediate action is needed to spot the issue, remonstrate with the buyer, and return the excess amount of components to the supplier. This prompt action not only provides instant feedback to the employee that he has done something wrong but also gives the manager a chance to correct the problem immediately. Thus, the short-term feedback loop is of great value to a company. How do we create and operate one?

The first step is to determine what information to send back to managers each day. A major problem is that the cost accountant may overreact to this plan and assemble a vast pile of data for transmission. However, managers have little time each day to peruse so much data and may end up missing the key nuggets of information buried in the report. A better approach is to review with the recipients in advance the main items of information they are interested in receiving. This list changes over time, as a company emphasizes or deemphasizes certain activities, so it is important to review the list of data several times a year. Another approach is for the cost accountant to transmit to managers only those variances significant enough in size to be worth review and to exclude all other data. These actions ensure that managers receive only the information they need to make immediate corrections to operations.

The type of information sent to managers is only partly financial in nature. It is much more common to include operational data in these reports because it can result in immediate changes in operations that will improve financial results. Examples of operational information that can be included in daily feedback reports are scheduled shipments that did not ship on time, excessive scrap rates for specific production operations, inventory shortages, and machine bottlenecks. There are also some financial statistics that are worthy of immediate feedback to managers, such as month-to-date sales and specific accounts receivable that are overdue; this information can be acted on to improve financial results in the short term. Thus, short-term feedback loops tend to include a mix of financial and operational information, with the preponderance of the information being of the operational variety.

The next step is to determine the timing with which the information will be run through the feedback loop. It may be every day or by a certain time of day; for example, the author has a standard policy of posting daily financial statements on the company's intranet site before 8 A.M. every day. Other information may not be quite so necessary and so is issued only once a week or every other week. The day of the week may also be important since the information may be used for meetings held on specific days of the week. For example, if there is a manager's committee meeting each Monday, the participants may want to receive a variance report early on the preceding Friday so that they have sufficient time to investigate the variances prior to the meeting. The timing of the feedback loop is entirely dependent on the need for the information.

A third issue is the format of data presentation. This is not a place to issue a complex report that is difficult to read. A manager wants to quickly extract a few key points from the report and act on them. An example is the following canned voice mail message used to convey to managers the amount of sales volume billed so far during the month—the intent is to compare the period-to-date actual billings to expectations so that everyone knows if there is a billing problem. Any other information is extraneous. The message is:

Good morning. This is the daily sales report. Our month-to-date billings are $_____, as opposed to a month-to-date budget of $_____. This leaves us with a positive/negative variance of $_____.

The message is quick and to the point. Managers can quickly listen to it, understand the billing situation, and determine what billings actions are expected of them. Another approach is to create a standard electronic spreadsheet that itemizes a few key statistics, compares them to a forecast or budget, and is included in a daily e-mail or intranet posting. This format allows one to quickly update any information that has changed since the previous day and to immediately send it out to users for perusal.

The final issue to decide on is the method of data transmission. This can take a variety of forms, depending on the level of technology available to the company. Some alternatives for transmission methods are:

- **Voice mail.** This method is good for the transmission of a small set of information; anything too long requires too much time to listen to. If group voice mail transmissions are available, the sender can quickly read through a canned text, insert the few items of data that have changed since the last voice mail, and punch a single button to issue the data to a preset group of recipients. Since this is a highly standardized process, it is not as suitable for the transmission of data to groups of recipients whose members change for each report.

- **Orally.** If there is an immediate problem, it can be conveyed in person in order to impart the urgency of the information. This approach is best used for single items, since a lengthy review of information is a waste of time for both the sender and the recipient. This is also a good approach if there are several recipients who have no access to phones or e-mail (such as production workers) and for whom this is the only way to receive information. A good example of this is a morning production meeting at which the cost accountant reads a list of key items from the previous day's production.

- **Electronic mail.** This is one of the best ways to transmit information since there is no transmission cost and a report can be sent to a group of recipients with a few keystrokes. This approach does not work well, however, when many of the intended recipients do not have ready access to e-mail, either because they have no computer or because they are located in outlying areas with no linkage to e-mail.

- **Posted messages.** In a small company one can simply post information in a central location. Though a quick and easy approach, this technique forces users to find the information, rather than having it pushed into their offices as is the case with e-mail and voice mail deliveries. Also, because of its excessively public method of transmission, the data in the report can be examined by anyone, which is not good if the information is intended to be confidential.

- **Intranet postings.** If a company possesses an intranet site and employees are accustomed to accessing it, information can be posted on that site for them to peruse at their leisure. This allows large quantities of information to be posted. However, it suffers from one major problem, which is that users must go to the site to obtain the information rather than wait passively for it to be sent to them. Because there is a lack of "push" behind the information, some employees may never receive critical information because they never access the intranet site.

When handled correctly, the short-term feedback loop is an excellent tool for providing managers with the key information they need to run their parts of the company. However, careful attention to the content, format, and timing of the feedback loop is required, as well as to the method of transmission.

LONGER-TERM FEEDBACK LOOPS

As accounting is taught in business schools, much of the accounting reporting function is centered on long-term feedback loops. Under this approach the accounting staff accumulates financial information over the course of a month, summarizes it during the month-end closing process, and issues a set of financial statements to the management group shortly thereafter. The reports most commonly included in these financial statements are:

- Executive summary
- Current month and year-to-date budget versus actual income statement
- Current month balance sheet
- Current month and year-to-date statement of cash flows
- Monthly trend of income statement results
- Monthly trend of balance sheet results
- Monthly trend of key statistics

It is also common to add supplemental information tailored to the needs of the business. Such information may involve customer or subscription turnover, time to complete specific jobs, employee turnover, detailed itemizations of budget variances, sales volume by customer, and insurance claims.

Nearly all the information listed in these long-term feedback loops tends to be financial in nature. This is partly because of the long tradition of issuing financial statements once a month practiced virtually everywhere and also because operational information requires much more rapid feedback in order to be effective and so tends to be included in faster feedback loops. The one place in these reports where one can include a reasonable quantity of operational information is on the statistics page of the financial statements. Examples of typical operational statistics are:

- Average cycle time
- Customer return levels
- Employee turnover

- Inventory turnover

- Proportion of on-time shipments

- Proportion of production schedule completed

- Proportion of rush orders in production schedule

- Scrap rates

These operational statistics are more summary-level in nature and are most useful for reporting on the combined results of a number of activities that occur every day. A manager would have to request additional information or be tied into daily feedback loops in order to obtain more detailed information about each statistic.

The reason for including operational information in long-term feedback loops is not so that specific operational changes can be made—which is the reason for short-term feedback—but rather to inform management of the success of its overall policies in driving operational changes. If the summary-level statistics do not show adequate levels of period-to-period improvement, managers must take steps to alter the underlying processes in order to effect the changes they are seeking.

Another reason for adding operational information to long-term feedback loops is so that this information can be used for performance reviews. For example, when a production manager's bonus is based on improvements in the average cycle time, he or she is keenly interested in the reported results and tracks them avidly.

Though there is some opportunity to include operational information in long-term feedback loops, the bulk of such information is best included in short-term loops, where it can be acted on immediately. Financial information, which rarely requires such rapid feedback, is the primary element in any long-term feedback report.

SPECIAL ISSUES

Managers who find themselves targeted by a cost control system's results fight back against their occasional poor showing with several arguments intended to shift the blame for poor operational and financial results from the manager to the system. Some of these arguments are valid, but in other cases managers are "blowing smoke" to divert attention away from the real problem areas. In either event the cost accountant should be aware of the various problems that can arise through a cost control and feedback system and be prepared for them in advance. Here are the most common issues:

- **Charged costs are not controllable by the responsible manager.** This is the most common (and valid) argument presented. It most commonly arises when control reports include some kind of overhead allocation, such as for corporate or local overhead costs, to specific departments or divisions. The person responsible for the operating results of each department or division has virtually no control over the incurrence of these overhead costs and so can make a reasonable argument against being judged on this number. The best way to avoid this issue is to exclude overhead charges from the responsibility financial statements or to subtotal all other financial results prior to adding in overhead charges, so that the total of all other costs is easy to determine.

- **Costs have been inherited.** It is quite likely that the cost structure of a function has been largely created by the last manager of that function through the hiring of staff, creation of long-term strategies, and signing of various contracts. If so, a manager has a valid point in claiming that the function's results are less than expectations. However, rather than absolving the manager of all blame, a better approach is to revise the budgeted revenue and cost levels against which he or she is measured in order to reflect the long-term costs of the function; this still allows one to judge a manager's performance. Also, this reduced standard of performance should gradually be made more difficult to achieve over subsequent periods, on the assumption that the manager can gradually strip away some of the long-term costs associated with the function.

- **Costs are shared.** Another argument is that the costs listed as being the responsibility of one manager are actually shared with several other people. For example, if the engineering department shares a computer system with the purchasing staff, the manager of the engineering department cannot arbitrarily increase or decrease the size of this system (and its related cost) without the agreement of the purchasing manager. One resolution of this problem is to give ultimate authority over and responsibility for a shared cost to one manager, who is then held totally accountable for it; however, this may result in decisions that do not benefit the organization as a whole. Another approach is to separate all shared costs on each function's income statement so that all other expenses that are clearly the responsibility of a specific manager can still be identified.

- **Costs do not belong in the recorded period.** A common complaint is that a cost itemized on an income statement has been recorded in the wrong period, because of delays in the recording of the receipt or because the matching revenues have not yet been earned. This problem can be resolved by issuing a preliminary income statement to each manager so that they have an opportunity to request corrections prior to issuance of the completed reports to the full management team. An alternative approach is to create a standard set of accruals for all major expenses so that any significant expense is included, even if the supplier's invoice has not yet arrived.

- **The report never arrived.** As a last line of defense, a manager can always state that he has never received the income statement for his functional area and therefore cannot comment on any problems. This feedback issue can be resolved by having managers sign for reports received, but this is a time-consuming way to eliminate the problem. A better approach is to e-mail the reports and then have the computer system determine whether the e-mail was ever opened by the recipient.

Most of the problems noted here are due to specific issues managers attempt to use to invalidate an entire financial statement that reports on their performance. The best way to resolve these issues is to segregate the problem areas on the income statement, so that the areas under dispute do not impact all the other revenues and costs reported, for which managers should be held entirely responsible.

FUTURE OF CONTROLS AND FEEDBACK LOOPS

Given the wide array of cost controls and feedback loops already in existence, can we foresee any additional changes in the future? Several factors impacting the business world are most likely to bring about some changes. They are the further advance of computer systems, increased use of just-in-time production systems, and greater market penetration of enterprise resources planning systems.

As computer systems become more prevalent in the workplace, we can look forward to having the ability to feed back information to all company employees through a company's intranet, so that all the control information they need is sent straight to their computers. This can take the form of a simple e-mail message or perhaps a linkage back to a posting on the company's intranet site that itemizes all variances and related information. It is also likely that financial reports will be converted to electronic files and sent through the intranet to employees, rather than following the tortuous (and slower) path of a paper-based report. This feature is already available at many companies but will become more applicable as more departments gain access to computers.

Just-in-time systems still do not enjoy a large market penetration, despite considerable publicity. Nonetheless, the nature of controls will be radically altered for organizations that implement this system. Under JIT the bulk of an organization's operating problems are dealt with immediately on the production line, where there is no need for feedback loop. Given the speed of response in this system, it is likely that the cost accountant will not have any short-term controls to measure at all and instead will calculate only periodic financial results that follow the normal distribution channels.

The increasing use of ERP systems allows employees anywhere in a company to access information about virtually any activity anywhere in the company—even at a multitude of other locations. This allows a cost accountant to spend more time determining what information employees should see and packaging this information for them in a manner they can access as soon as transactions of any kind are updated. This approach eliminates nearly all of the time lag so common in feedback loops, as well as the need for most paper-based reports. This is a major shift in the focus of the cost accountant from preparing reports to analyzing information requests from users who call with questions about transactions that may have happened just moments before and require answers immediately.

In short, the future of cost controls and feedback loops is tending in the direction of faster information turnaround time. This will be a major competitive advantage for companies who have invested in companywide computer systems and train their employees to mine data to yield up-to-the-minute information that can result in fixes for problems as they occur rather than months later.

SUMMARY

It should be apparent from this discussion that many steps must be taken before a company can be assured of having an adequate set of cost controls and feedback loops. Baseline cost and operational benchmark figures must first be established in a number of different areas, which are then used in a combination of accounting and operational reports to send results back to the various functional areas of the company. Further, these areas must be structured into responsibility centers so that the information can be targeted at specific individuals. When even one element of this chain of events is missing, it is difficult to ensure that employees will receive the correct control information or that they will receive it on a timely basis.

REFERENCE

Bragg, S. (1998). *Outsourcing*. New York: John Wiley & Sons.

CHAPTER 24

Capital Budgeting

One of the most common issues a cost accountant is asked to render an opinion on is the need to acquire additional capital assets. Though higher-level managers are usually the ones who make the final purchasing decision, the opinion of the cost accountant is given considerable weight. The reason for so much reliance on the cost accountant is that capital budgeting is a complex issue to review properly and may involve financial information spanning a number of years with which the cost accountant is familiar.

In this chapter we review the overall process for selecting capital projects, as well as the various criteria for doing so, the most common financial analysis measures used, and the use of postcompletion audits to investigate the reasons for any variances in the performance of completed capital projects.

PROJECT SELECTION PROCESS

The capital expenditure decision usually begins at the facility level. The reason is that the facility manager is the one with the best knowledge of what assets are needed to replace existing capacity, expand it, or comply with a variety of regulatory requirements that may involve the upgrading or replacement of equipment. Capital expenditures can also begin in the corporate engineering department, for this group is responsible for building entirely new facilities which may not yet have facility managers with equipment requests. The top-level corporate managers also have a say in what capital items are purchased, for they develop the strategic plan, which itemizes what products and capacity levels will be needed for a number of years into the future—the facility managers and engineers use this document as a guide in determining what general categories of equipment must be obtained.

Whoever initiates a capital proposal then goes to the corporate or facility cost accountant for assistance in creating a capital expenditure request form. This form itemizes the type of capital expenditure, the timing of expected cash inflows and outflows, and the results of various financial analyses. The most common types of capital investments are:

- **Capacity expansion.** This is equipment needed to expand the current level of production at an existing facility. In particular, it may refer to the acquisition of equipment needed to resolve a production bottleneck.

- **Cost reduction.** This is equipment that replaces existing equipment, resulting in more efficient operations.

- **Profit.** This is equipment that will increase profits through the production of new products or line extensions.

- **Regulatory/environmental.** This is equipment required by the government. The usual reason is environmental, and it can include smokestack scrubbers, chemical storage and disposal facilities, and even wastewater cooling equipment.

- **Replacement.** This is equipment that replaces existing equipment without any improvement in efficiency. The usual reason for replacement is that the original equipment is no longer operable or is too expensive to maintain.

- **Safety.** This is equipment needed to address safety concerns that have been raised either internally or externally, usually by employee input or by a safety audit.

The cost accountant then forwards these forms to the corporate budgeting manager who assembles them into a preliminary budget. This early budget itemizes capital expenditures if they exceed a certain amount and lumps all others into a single capital line item if they are too small to be worth the attention of those reviewing the budget.

The finance staff then becomes involved, for it must determine if there are sufficient funding sources available to pay for the capital expenditures being requisitioned. This group can recommend a lump sum of available cash for capital purchases, if there is a strict limitation on funds, or devise different payment methods, such as the leasing of equipment and facilities, that will allow the company to go forward with the entire group of projects. If the first option is the case, then the finance staff can review the various requisitions and recommend that those with high risk levels or low returns on investment be canceled for the current budget period. These recommendations and the preliminary budget are then sent to the senior management team.

This group reviews the capital expenditures based on their impact on the ability of the company to achieve its strategic plan. For example, any project that is key to the success of a strategic plan is approved, even if its return on investment is problematic, while other projects that are not clearly tied to strategy are approved only if there is a sufficient level of funding available. The senior management team can encourage the submission of strategy-related project requests by allowing a reduced hurdle rate (see the next section) for any projects tied to the overall strategic direction, while using a higher rate for all other projects such as those that replace or enhance existing equipment or facilities. This group may also accept or reject projects based on the divisions in which they originate, for divisions with high levels of profitability or a track record of completing their projects on time and within planned budget levels enjoy a "most favored division" status and can be safely entrusted with additional projects.

Once all approvals are in place, the final set of capital projects is included in the final budget and approved. However, this does not mean that an individual capital project has been approved for immediate installation; on the contrary, the company has only approved the allocation of a large block of cash for a number of capital projects. When it comes time to actually start up a capital acquisition, most senior management teams conduct a final review and approve it again before allowing the acquisition and installation to proceed. The reason for this second approval is that the first one tends to deal with each project on a summary-level basis since there are many projects under consideration during the budget preparation period and there is no time for a more detailed analysis. Also, the availability of cash may have changed by the time the project is to begin, which may delay it. Similarly, the underlying economics of the project may have changed since the budget was created, so a second review of the acquisition application must be conducted. Despite these issues, some wealthier companies with unrestricted access to cash sometimes avoid a secondary review and let projects proceed as soon as the annual budget is approved.

For companies that conduct a secondary approval, there is usually a set of approval signatures required that varies with the amount of funding. A sample of required approvals is:

- Plant manager—up to $25,000

- Division manager—from $25,001 to $100,000

- Group vice president—from $100,001 to $250,000

- President—from $250,001 to $1,000,000

- Board of Directors—above $1,000,000

The exact amount of funding that can be approved by each signatory varies dramatically depending on the size of the firm and the level of decentralization. For example, a small firm may drop a zero from each of the above recommended approval levels, while a large firm may add one. Also, high levels of corporate decentralization push the decision-making process for capital acquisitions further down in the corporate hierarchy, with most decisions possibly being centered on the plant manager. Conversely, a highly centralized organization may require corporate-level approval for virtually all capital projects.

It is also a common occurrence for new projects to arise that were not originally included in the capital budget, perhaps because of a sudden shift in strategy, the failure of existing equipment, or the passage of new legislation requiring new equipment in order to bring the company into compliance. Whatever the reason, these new projects will need more funding than was originally planned for. One way to deal with these situations is to institute a rule requiring the company to substitute the new project for one at a similar funding level that was already included in the budget, thereby preserving the overall capital allocation for the year. Another approach is to require much more stringent approvals for any unbudgeted projects, including approval by the CFO, who must determine if additional funding can be found.

Once all approvals are in place, the accounting department assigns a project code to each project, under which all expenditures for the project are accumulated in the general ledger. This information is regularly compiled into a report that the project manager summarizes and formally presents to the management team for review. The reason for these interim reports is to ensure that each project is meeting its expected milestone dates and expenditure levels. If not, the management group can decide if it must assign more project management resources to the project and if it wants to fund any cost overruns. Some organizations allow a certain percentage of cost overruns to be incurred without further management approval, while others want a more stringent analysis conducted, even if only one additional dollar is needed for completion. The former case is the more common, with allowable overages in the range of 3% to 5% being the most common. However, as projects become more expensive, the allowable cost overrun tends to become lower, in the 2% to 3% range, because this overage can become a great deal of money. For example, a 5% cost overrun on a $10,000 project is only $500, but the same percentage overrun on a $1,000,000 project is $50,000.

Once a capital project has been completed, many organizations prefer to conduct an audit of the final results in order to determine where cost or revenue projections were incorrect, why these problems occurred, and what to do in the future to avoid similar problems. This can be an extensive process, and many organizations do not have a sufficient number of internal auditors to complete the work. As an alternative, they may pick a small number of projects out of the full set of capital projects for review, or they may complete a brief audit overview of all projects and conduct an in-depth review only if the brief review finds evidence of significant problems. A key issue concerning these audits is how long to wait before initiating them. Some companies like to conduct them as soon as projects are completed, but this carries with it the risk that some costs may not yet have been recorded; this problem can be exacerbated if project managers deliberately delay the submission of supplier invoices to the accounting department on the grounds that these invoices will not be recorded until after the audit. A better approach is to wait at least 3 months before starting the audit, which tends to flush out all missing supplier invoices. Some organizations wait as long as a year, on the grounds that they also want to see if any related revenues are occurring, which may not be the case if production levels are still ramping up for some months after completion of the capital asset installation.

The results of the postcompletion audits are presented to the audit committee, which is a subset of the board of directors. Based on the presented information, this group decides if policies or procedures must be changed in order to improve the results of the capital acquisition process. These changes are sent back down to the finance and accounting departments, which administer the bulk of the process.

The steps noted here may seem quite lengthy and involved—they are. However, a great deal of money is involved in these projects, so corporate managers have a fiduciary responsibility to ensure that it is wisely invested in assets that will generate a return that cumulatively exceeds the corporate cost of obtaining the invested funds. We next explore how to calculate the cost of these funds, which is known as the cost of capital.

COST OF CAPITAL

A company needs some basis for determining the minimum allowable return on its investment in a new capital project. It does this by calculating its cost of capital.

The cost of capital is the average cost of all debt and equity currently outstanding or expected to be outstanding during the period, weighted for the various components of debt and equity. For example, if an organization has $42,000,000 of outstanding debt of various kinds and $58,000,000 of outstanding common stock, its cost of capital might look like the mix shown in Exhibit 24.1.

In the exhibit we see that the cost of all debt is tax-deductible, which reduces the cost of the debt. However, this is not possible for the cost of equity, which is not tax-deductible. Also, the cost of equity is much higher than the cost of debt because investors have much higher expectations for their return on investment. A company could take the short-term view that its equity is free, but if it did not provide a sufficient return to investors, they would sell the stock, lowering its price on the open market and reducing the value of the firm. Consequently, few managers deal with the return on equity in a cavalier manner.

EXHIBIT 24.1. Calculating the Cost of Capital

Description	Amount Outstanding ($)	Cost after Tax[a] ($)	Weighted Average Cost of Capital
Debt—10%, 30 years	9,000,000	558,000	
Debt—8%, 12 years	21,000,000	1,041,600	
Debt—14%, 2 years	12,000,000	744,000	
Equity, common[b]	58,000,000	11,600,000	
Total	**100,000,000**	**13,943,600**	**13.9%**

[a]Assumes 38% tax rate.
[b]Equity holders expect a 20% return on their investment.

A significant problem for anyone creating a cost-of-capital calculation is how to derive the cost of capital for equity. It is simple enough for debt since creditors specify a precise rate of return in the debt documentation. However, no such document is signed by investors. Instead, it must be derived by determining the long-term price/earnings (P/E) ratio for the company or industry, which yields the return that investors want in exchange for paying a certain amount for their shares of stock. For privately held companies, there is no price/earnings ratio because the stock is not publicly traded. In this instance once can use the P/E ratio of publicly held companies in the same industry as a reasonable indicator of the cost of equity for the company.

The numbers shown in Exhibit 24.1 realistically portray the difference in cost between debt and equity. Because of the much lower cost of debt, it is no surprise that many managers want to increase the proportion of debt in their debt/equity structure since this reduces their cost of capital. This is true, but debt requires a fixed repayment schedule, while equity does not, so there is an increased risk of bankruptcy for firms that go too far and create a high proportion of debt to equity.

One issue to consider when calculating the cost of capital is whether to use the current cost of capital or a projected cost for the period during which the capital projects will require funds. This is not normally an issue, for most organizations do not alter their capital structures so radically that there is a significant change in the cost of capital. There may even be loan covenants that require a company to avoid a preset debt/equity level, which force it to stay close to a certain debt/equity ratio. However, if there is a significant planned change, the planned amount will more closely match the cost of capital for new capital projects than the existing cost of capital.

The frequency of recalculation may also be a concern. For most organizations, reviewing the cost of capital once a year is more than sufficient, for changes in the underlying capital structure are so infrequent that any more frequent review would not result in a significant change in the cost of capital. Even for companies that are constantly adding funding through new debt or equity offerings, these changes are usually not hard to forecast and so can be incorporated into an annual recalculation of the cost of capital.

Once the cost of capital has been calculated, it can be used as a minimum return on investment for new capital investments. In this role it is called the "hurdle rate," for it is the minimum return that a project must hurdle in order to be accepted as a viable project. This hurdle rate can be varied by corporate management if it wants to encourage the installation of a particular kind of project. For example, an internal equipment replacement may involve a hurdle rate of 30% on the grounds that it is not a project that creates new opportunities for the company. Alternatively, new product production lines may have much lower hurdle rates assigned to them, so that division managers have more of an incentive to create capital acquisition proposals in this area. Another way in which the hurdle rate can be altered is by division. Many companies have a number of divisions, each of which may have its own equity and debt. If so, the cost of capital may vary by significant amounts by division and so justifies the use of separate cost of capital calculations. Even if subsidiaries do not have separate capital structures, corporate managers may feel that there are significantly different levels of operating risk for each division, which warrants the use of a different hurdle rate for each one. For example, a highly risky fiber optic cabling venture may have such a high risk of failure that the corporate headquarters staff sets a hurdle rate of 50% on all projects originating in that division, while the hurdle rate for a staid manufacturing division that produces automobile brakes is given a hurdle rate of 15%. This policy has much more to do with perceived levels of risk than the actual underlying cost of capital but is considered a valid alternative for situations where there are major differences between divisions in operating risk.

The cost of capital is of particular importance when used in conjunction with such cash flow discounting methods as internal rate of return (IRR) and net present value (NPV). We will cover these topics shortly but first address the issue of how to construct a project cash flow, from which the IRR and NPV calculations are derived.

CONSTRUCTING PROJECT CASH FLOWS

The key piece of information needed to conduct a financial analysis of a capital requisition is a summary of all cash flows associated with it. This format should cluster all cash flows by year, with the initial cash outflows to pay for the project usually being itemized within year 0 and subsequent cash inflows and outflows being entered under years 1 through 5. Few cash flow analyses extend more than 5 years into the future since later flows are considered to be too difficult to project; they also result in small net present values, given the time value of money.

A number of line items are included in a project cash flow. They can be summarized into just a few line items on the final cash flow analysis sent to management for approval, but a detailed listing of all line items must be kept as backup information in case there are questions about the exact nature of a cash flow. Key items to include are:

Cash Outflows

- **Equipment cost.** Any equipment to be used for the project must be listed as a cash outflow. If advance payments are required that are well in advance of the equipment installation date, they should be noted in the cash flow analysis separately, along with the date when cash will be paid out for them.

- **Market value of existing equipment.** Some companies also include as a cash outflow the market value of any existing equipment that will be incorporated into a capital project. Their reason for doing so is twofold: first, the alternative use of the equipment would be to sell it, so the opportunity cost of selling it (at the market value) would indeed be a cost of the project; and, second, any project making heavy use of existing equipment would otherwise show a much better return on investment than a project requiring the use of all-new equipment, which makes it impossible to generate comparisons between different projects.

- **Working capital cost.** If there is an incremental change in working capital, either up or down, it should be included as a cash inflow (if the investment goes down) or a cash outflow (if the investment goes up). For example, a new project may result in a significant increase in sales, which will require an extra investment in accounts receivable for support.

- **Research and development expenditures.** Some projects require research, perhaps to complete a pilot installation or because the company is undertaking the risk of shifting directly from the development stage to full production mode. If so, the cost (and therefore the risk) of these activities should certainly be included in the cash flow analysis. When this is done, the cost of the associated research and development drives down the net cash flows from the project, which is an appropriate way to focus attention on the extra risk of such projects.

- **Sales and marketing costs.** Any incremental sales and marketing costs directly associated with a capital project that would not otherwise be incurred should be included in the cash flow analysis. This is not an issue for many projects, since any sales resulting from their installation are sold through the existing sales and marketing apparatus and do not result in the incurrence of any new costs.

- **Income taxes.** A capital project will hopefully create income, and this income will be taxed. The tax rate used for the analysis can be the marginal one incurred on each extra dollar, usually assumed to be the maximum income tax percentage, or the average tax rate paid by the company, which tends to be lower. The marginal rate reflects reality somewhat better than the average rate; the main point is to be consistent in using the same tax rate for all projects so that they are all comparable. Some companies do not include income taxes in their cash flow analyses at the divisional level, on the grounds that the divisions are responsible for only before-tax returns on investment.

Cash Inflows

- **Revenue.** The most obvious cash inflow is the incremental increase in cash flows that can be directly attributed to the installation of new capital equipment. This should not include the revenue stream from an existing piece of equipment that is being replaced since no resulting increase in cash flows is obtained by replacing it.

- **Depreciation.** The depreciation charge associated with any capital item does not directly affect cash flow, because depreciation is only an accounting journal entry. However, any incremental increase in the amount of depreciation that appears on a company's tax return reduces the amount of income taxes paid—which *does* have a direct impact on cash flows. Consequently, the tax impact of depreciation should be noted in the cash flow analysis as a cash inflow.

- **Investment tax credit.** A federal, state, or local tax credit may be available for new investments. If so, the cash inflow should be recorded in the accounting period when tax payments are reduced by it.

- **Return of working capital.** When capital equipment is to be dismantled at the end of its useful life, there is no longer a need for any associated working capital, such as accounts receivable or inventory. One should therefore assume that these values are liquidated into cash at the end of the project. However, it is wise to assume that some of the inventory cannot be liquidated, on the grounds that some is either obsolete or cannot be sold at its book value. Accordingly, the cash inflow from the return of working capital should be reduced by an estimate for nonliquidating inventory.

- **Residual asset value.** There may be some market value left in the capital equipment when the project no longer has a useful life. This value can be estimated by an appraiser or by using the company's past experience with sales of similar equipment. The net amount realized from a sale should be reduced by the cost of dismantling and transporting the equipment to the buyer. Also, the timing of the sale may be well after the project termination date, given the extra time required to dismantle and sell it. Some organizations do not bother to estimate a residual value on the grounds that it is too small (especially in terms

EXHIBIT 24.2. Sample Cash Flow Layout

	Year 0	Year 1	Year 2	Year 3
Incremental revenue ($)		2,500,000	2,600,000	2,850,000
Incremental cost ($)		−1,250,000	−1,300,000	−1,425,000
Capitalized cost ($)	−2,050,000			
Pretax cash flow ($)	−2,050,000	1,250,000	1,300,000	1,425,000
After-tax cash flow (35% tax rate) ($)	−2,050,000	812,500	845,000	926,250
Depreciation (%)		5	10	10
Cash recovered from depreciation ($)		35,875	71,750	71,750
Incremental investment in inventory ($)		−300,000		300,000
Equipment resale value ($)				400,000
Total after-tax cash flow	**−2,050,000**	**548,375**	**916,750**	**1,698,000**

of its present value), its value cannot be estimated, or the cost of dismantling it will match or exceed any expected revenue. The valuation method used must fit the circumstances.

These various types of cash flows can be included in a simple cash flow layout, such as the one shown in Exhibit 24.2. The purpose of this format is to provide a summary of the general cash inflows and outflows associated with a specific capital project, which is then used (as noted in the following sections) to construct various financial measures of payback, internal rate of return, and net present value.

In the exhibit the cost of constructing or buying the asset is assumed to occur at the beginning of the project and so is noted under "Year 0." All other cash flows are assumed to occur at the end of years 1, 2, and 3; their timing is really much more variable, but we assume this cash flow timing not only to standardize the timing of all cash flows but also because it results in more conservative discounted cash flows. We then reduce the net cash flows by the average or marginal corporate tax rate because these cash flows will result in either taxable income or losses. Then we calculate the cash recovered from depreciation, which in the example is 5% or 10% of the capitalized cost in each year, multiplied by the tax rate. We then note the increased cash investment required for working capital at the start of the project and the return of these funds at the project's end. We conclude with an estimate of the equipment's resale value at the end of the project, which is assumed to be in year 3. This simple format is generally sufficient for all but the largest capital investments, which may require more detailed information but which still follow the same general guidelines.

PROBLEMS WITH CASH FLOW PROJECTIONS

Before we proceed to the use of cash flow projections with various analysis tools, it is useful to be aware of the problems with constructing an accurate cash forecast. One is the difficulty of determining a realistic residual value. Most projects are given a time line of at least 5 years, with a projected sale of all equipment at the end of that period (or later). Because of the variability of resale values so far in the future, one can have great difficulty creating a residual value estimate that has any meaning. This is less of an issue if the equipment to be sold has a ready market and has had one for many years already. An example of this is any manufacturing equipment in an "old line" industry, such as metal pressing, plastics, or furniture production, where the equipment used evolves only slowly and there is a good after-market for it. The problem is at its worst for high-technology equipment, which may become so outmoded that it can only be junked at the end of the project and may have to be replaced even before then. The most conservative way to deal with this issue is to record no residual value at all; this is a particularly valid approach in two cases: when the project termination date is so many years in the future that the discounted value of any residual sale price is near zero anyway, and when the cost of removing the equipment offsets any price to be gained from its sale. A less accurate approach is to use the remaining book value on the assets to be sold. This method is not recommended because the book value may bear no relationship to the market price, which is what the cash flow projection needs. The best (though most expensive) approach is to use the services of a professional appraiser to determine a likely future market value for the equipment and to include this value in the cash forecast.

Another issue is likely cost overruns. Many companies do not install equipment on a regular basis and so do not have an industrial engineering staff devoted to completing such work on a regular basis. Instead, installations tend to be inefficient and completed much later than expected, resulting in increased project costs. It is difficult to include in a cash flow report an expected overage in project installation costs, because it would reflect poorly on those who install the equipment. Nonetheless, the report will be inaccurate without it, so the cost accountant should attempt to include a reserve for extra installation costs in the forecast. It may be easier to include this reserve if the cost accountant can prove that there is a consistent history of similar problems with preceding capital acquisitions.

Another issue is that the actual operational life of a project may be shorter than listed in the cash flow projection, resulting in greatly reduced or even negative cash flows. One way to avoid this problem is to press for a standard policy of cutting off all cash flows at 5 years, on the grounds that project performance is too difficult to predict past that point. An additional approach is to carefully review the estimates of various project sponsors, which may reveal which ones consistently overestimate cash flows; this information can be used to further discount the value of selected capital acquisition proposals. A final option is to allow many years of estimated cash flows in capital proposals, but to greatly increase the discount rate on all cash flows predicted past a certain number of years, on the grounds that these estimates are so far off in the future that they are too risky to estimate with the standard company discount rate.

Another problem is that the timing of cash outflows may vary significantly from those itemized in the cash flow forecast. For example, advance payments may be required for the purchase of large industrial equipment well in advance of the purchase of other capital equipment. These problems are difficult to spot without a detailed review of each cash flow forecast with an expert who is deeply involved in each proposed capital expenditure. Accordingly, the cost accountant should set aside a large block of extra time to review the largest capital requests, preferably with the company's industrial engineering staff, to verify the timing of the most expensive line items.

A final issue is that some management groups completely ignore the results of a cash flow analysis no matter how negative they are. The reason is that they are more interested in the pursuit of long-range company goals, which may call for investments in new areas that will generate losses for a number of years, with an eye toward expanding into a new market at some point in the future and gathering profits at a later date. This is an entirely valid approach for companies that are far-sighted and aggressive enough to pursue such goals. In this instance the job of the cost accountant is strictly to advise the management team of the likely extent of losses if capital projects are implemented, so that they are fully aware of the cost of their actions in pursuing long-range strategic goals.

FINANCIAL APPRAISAL WITH THE PAYBACK CALCULATION

The simplest measure of a capital project's anticipated financial performance is payback. This is not a measure of expected return on investment but rather of liquidity. It is designed to calculate the time period from the initiation of a project until the point where it generates enough cash to pay off the original investment, without using any discounted cash flows. The calculation is:

$$\frac{\text{Net initial investment}}{\text{Average annual cash flow}}$$

For example, if a project requires an initial investment of $300,000 and spins off $100,000 in cash flows each year thereafter, the calculation is:

$$\frac{300,000}{100,000} = 3.0 \text{ years to pay back investment}$$

This method has the singular advantage of being extremely easy to understand. It requires no difficult or convoluted calculations, and the results are clear. This makes it the most heavily used capital investment performance measure in business today. However, it also has several problems, which are:

- **Does not use the time value of money.** There is no discounting of future cash flows, so the resulting measure of payback becomes increasingly inaccurate if the inflation rate is high or if cash flows extend out for many periods into the future. This is a major flaw.

- **Does not include cash flows after payback is achieved.** The calculation is the same if there is only enough cash flow from the project to just pay back all expenses incurred, or if it results in an unending stream of rich cash flows. The only way to obtain this information is through an additional IRR or NPV calculation (see the next two sections).

- **Incorrectly calculates payback if cash flows are uneven.** The formula assumes that exactly the same amount of cash is generated by the project each successive year. In reality, cash flows may vary considerably. As a result, the calculated payback term may not be accurate. For example, if a project requires an expenditure of $300,000 and then experiences cash inflows of $25,000, $50,000, $125,000, and $250,000 in years 1, 2, 3, and 4, then the payback period, assuming average period-to-period cash flows, is 2.67 years ($300,000 investment divided by $112,500 average annual cash flows). However, the example contains a significant ramp-up in cash inflows over the 4-year period, which skews the calculation. Instead, we must use the following *cumulative* calculation, which recalculates the payback period at the end of each year and then determines the precise payback month during the final year of the calculation:

Year	Annual Cash Flow ($)	Cumulative Cash Inflow ($)	Amount Not Paid Back ($)	Payback Period
0	−300,000			
1	25,000	25,000	−275,000	
2	50,000	75,000	−200,000	
3	125,000	200,000	0	**3.0 years**
4	250,000	450,000		

The reason for the difference between the payback periods calculated using the average annual cash flow and using the more detailed cumulative method is that the averaging method includes cash flows that may lie outside the actual payback period, thereby skewing the result. In our example the skewing is caused by inclusion of the fourth year's cash flow in the averaging, when in fact the payback period was achieved after just 3 years, rendering the fourth year of cash flows irrelevant for the purposes of this calculation.

A final point is that, rather than castigate the payback method for its lack of discounted cash flows, we can alter the technique to *include* them, thereby removing the most important problem with this method. This modified format is called the discounted payback method. As an example of its use, we take the preceding block of payback calculations and add a column indicating the discount rate. We assume that the discount rate is based on a corporate cost of capital of 10%. We then multiply each year's cash flows by the discount rate to determine a discounted level of cash flow and calculate the payback in the usual manner. This calculation is slightly more complex but results in a much more accurate measurement. It is shown in Exhibit 24.3, where the altered cash flows result in a payback period that has been extended from the 3.0 years in the preceding example to 3.8 years when discounting is used.

EXHIBIT 24.3. Discounted Payback Example

Year	Annual Cash Flow ($)	10% Discount Rate	Discounted Cash Flow ($)	Cumulative Cash Inflow ($)	Amount Not Paid Back ($)	Payback Period
0	−300,000	1.0000	−300,000			
1	25,000	0.9091	22,728	22,728	−277,272	
2	50,000	0.8264	41,320	64,048	−235,952	
3	125,000	0.7513	93,913	157,961	−142,039	
4	250,000	0.6830	170,750	328,711	0	**3.8 years**

FINANCIAL APPRAISAL WITH THE IRR CALCULATION

One of the best ways to determine the return on investment of a capital project is to use the internal rate of return calculation. This method derives the interest rate at which a project's stream of future cash flows must be discounted in order to arrive at a net present value of zero. It can be achieved by manually calculating the net present value with different interest rates and using high and low interest rates to gradually bracket the target value of zero net present value. The concept is shown in Exhibits 24.4 and 24.5, where we use discount rates based on interest rates of 7% and 9% to determine that the IRR lies somewhere in between. Since the lower estimated interest rate of 7% in Exhibit 24.4 results in a positive net present value of $13,740 and the higher rate of 9% results in a negative net present value of $517, we can assume that the actual IRR is closer to 9% than to 7%. Additional calculations would show that the actual IRR is 8.92%.

A quicker way to calculate the IRR is with an electronic spreadsheet, such as Excel, Lotus 1-2-3, or the excellent FCPlus Professional, which runs on the Palm computing platform. An example of the IRR calculation on the Excel spreadsheet is presented in Chapter 38.

This method has the particular advantage of not requiring any knowledge of a company's cost of capital, thereby avoiding the need to devise a second cost of capital calculation. However, there is still a need for a cost of capital, since there is otherwise no way to determine if the rate of return on a project exceeds the associated cost of funds. Still, the IRR can at least be used to categorize a set of capital projects in terms of their returns, so that one can easily determine which are most likely to be approved.

One problem with the IRR method is that one cannot cluster a group of projects together to derive a group IRR without first summarizing all the cash flows into a single cash flow and then recalculating them. This is not an issue when the net present

EXHIBIT 24.4. Internal Rate of Return Calculation, Low Estimate

Year	Cash Flow ($)	7% Internal Rate of Return	Present Value ($)
0	−250,000	1.000	−250,000
1	55,000	0.9345	51,398
2	60,000	0.8734	52,404
3	65,000	0.8163	53,060
4	70,000	0.7629	53,403
5	75,000	0.7130	53,475
		Net present value	$13,740

Note: From *Financial Analysis: A Controller's Guide,* by S. Bragg, 2000, New York: John Wiley & Sons. Reprinted with permission.

EXHIBIT 24.5. Internal Rate of Return Calculation, High Estimate

Year	Cash Flow ($)	9% Internal Rate of Return	Present Value ($)
0	−250,000	1.000	250,000
1	55,000	0.9174	50,457
2	60,000	0.8417	50,502
3	65,000	0.7722	50,193
4	70,000	0.7084	49,588
5	75,000	0.6499	48,743
		Net present value	−$517

Note: From *Financial Analysis: A Controller's Guide,* by S. Bragg, 2000, New York: John Wiley & Sons. Reprinted with permission.

value method is used, since this method does not calculate a percentage but rather a total amount of positive or negative cash that is left after discounting is completed; these cash totals can be quickly added together to derive the net present value of a group of projects.

The IRR also does not indicate the amount of cash flow that will be realized if a project is implemented—only the percentage return. Thus, the IRR is not of much use if a project has a fabulous return of $5 on an investment of $2, which ignores the fact that another project will return $1 million on an investment of $3 million. The first project has a better IRR, but the second results in vastly more positive cash flow. This problem is resolved by the analysis method described in the next section, which is the net present value.

FINANCIAL APPRAISAL WITH THE NET PRESENT VALUE CALCULATION

The net present value method calculates the discounted cash flows from a capital project using the corporate cost of capital. If the result is a positive number, then the project will produce cash flows that exceed the cost of capital and therefore is worth funding. If the discounted amount is negative, then the stream of cash flows will not exceed the cost of financing the project, and it should be rejected. The method is shown in Exhibit 24.6, where we assume that the cost of capital is 8%. The discount rate of 8% results in a positive cash flow of $6894 after paying for the cost of capital, so this project is worth funding.

The discount factor in the third column of the exhibit was derived from a standard net present value table (also known as a "present worth table—single future payment"), which can be found in many accounting textbooks. If such a reference is not handy, the present value can also be calculated with the formula:

$$\text{Present value of future cash flow} = \frac{\text{Future cash flow}}{(1 + \text{discount rate})^n}$$

where n is the number of periods of discounting.

Another approach to the calculation is to use an electronic spreadsheet, which can instantly return a NPV. This calculation is shown in Chapter 38.

The NPV calculation has several advantages. First, it is easy to understand and explain. Also, it calculates an amount of discounted cash flow, rather than a percentage return on investment, that tells a manager which of several projects will return the largest amount of cash. Also, it is easy to combine the NPV results of

FIGURE 24.6. Simplified Net Present Value Example

Year	Cash Flow ($)	Discount Factor[a]	Present Value ($)
0	−100,000	1.000	−100,000
1	25,000	0.9259	23,148
2	25,000	0.8573	21,433
3	25,000	0.7938	19,845
4	30,000	0.7350	22,050
5	30,000	0.6806	20,418
		Net present value	6,894

[a]Discount factor is 8%.

Note: From *Financial Analysis: A Controller's Guide,* by S. Bragg, 2000, New York: John Wiley & Sons. Reprinted with permission.

several projects in order to determine the total NPV of a group of capital projects, which is of particular use when a group of linked capital investments must be made. All these factors make the NPV form of analysis the preferred one of the three presented here. The more common approach is to calculate and present all three—payback, IRR, and NPV—so that managers can gain some additional understanding from the extra information presented to them.

INCLUDING INTANGIBLE ISSUES IN THE PROJECT APPRAISAL

A common problem that the reviewer of a capital project must deal with is how much credence to give to any number of intangible issues associated with a purchase. For example, an acquisition may result in better community relations by reducing particulate emissions in the vicinity of the production plant, or it may improve the flow of materials through the plant—important issues, but not ones to which a dollar value can be assigned. Do we ignore these items or find some way to incorporate them into the capital purchasing decision?

A variety of methods have been devised for assigning weights to various intangible values so that they can be prioritized and balanced against the weightings assigned to other projects. Some of these schemes are quite elaborate. However, they all suffer from one fatal flaw, which is that there is no way to convert the resulting numerical scores to a dollar value that can then be added to the cash flows expected to arise from a project.

The best and simplest way to deal with cash flows is to address them only if a project's discounted cash flows are not quite sufficient to overcome the corporate hurdle rate. If so, the financial analysis staff should determine the exact amount of additional cash flow needed to meet the hurdle rate and forward this information to the management group that reviews capital proposals along with a list of all intangible benefits. This group can then make a management decision as to whether or not the perceived value of the extra intangible items associated with a project is worth the missing cash flow that would otherwise lead to rejection of the proposal. Though this approach is crude, it gives a company a simple means for including intangible items in the capital budgeting process.

INCLUDING RISK IN APPRAISAL TECHNIQUES

When a capital budgeting request is received by the management team, there is frequently some cause for skepticism, for the projected cash flows for all the years listed on the request are remarkably smooth or rise to dramatic heights a few years into the future. Experienced managers know that actual cash flows vary dramatically from year to year and that major upward swings in projected cash inflows may just as easily turn into significant downward spirals instead. In addition, here are a number of other risks that can arise as part of a capital project:

- New competing products
- New substitute products
- New technological innovations
- Unexpected additional costs
- Unexpected changes in the length of the project's revenue stream
- Unexpected changes in the project completion date
- Unexpected changes in the salvage value of the equipment

Given the number of potential risks, how can one gain some measure of comfort with the cash flow assumptions so important in the preceding discounted cash flow analyses?

One approach is to increase the hurdle rate (or discount rate) used to construct discounted cash flows. A project must then show such an inordinately high return on investment in order to be accepted that the corresponding risk becomes much easier to accept. The hurdle rate can be increased to as high a level as required to reduce the number of projects down to a few with large returns on investment. The main problem with this approach is that it cannot be used as a blanket increase in the hurdle rate for *all* capital projects, for then even the least risky ones would be required to show enormous returns on investment. Instead, an increased rate should be applied only to projects that clearly have a high level of risk.

Another approach is to reduce the number of years of cash flow in the capital expenditure proposal, perhaps to as little as 2 or 3 years. Then, the analysis eliminates any cash inflows that are so far in the future that they can be predicted with only the greatest difficulty. By cutting back on the duration of estimated cash flows, this method also eliminates some portion of the reported return on investment, which makes it critical for a risky investment to show a high level of return on investment during just its first few years of operation. However, this approach automatically goes against any project that may require a few years to build up its level of cash flows, which may eliminate from consideration projects that would be quite valuable to a company if given enough time to mature.

A more judgmental approach is to compile the usual IRR and NPV calculations and then let the management team decide for itself if the results are sufficiently high to offset any perceived level of risk. This is, of course, as far from a quantitative approach as one can get, but it may work well if the managers doing the evaluating are a seasoned group with considerable experience in the completion of similar projects.

For companies with less-experienced managers, or those having a low comfort level with qualitative decisions, several other options are available. One is to use high-medium-low cash flow estimates. This requires the construction of three separate IRR or NPV calculations, so some additional time is required for this analysis. Part of the work can be eliminated by throwing out the high-end estimate since the main point of the analysis is how low the cash flows can go in the lowest estimate. If this estimate reveals the possibility of significant losses, the management team can use its judgment to decide if the project should proceed or not.

Along similar lines, one can construct a number of cash flow estimates and assign to each one a probability of occurrence, which can then be summarized into a single cash flow estimate derived from all these individual estimates. An example is shown in Exhibit 24.7. In the exhibit there is a strong chance of substandard cash flows, but the offsetting chance of obtaining large returns results in a combined estimated cash flow still near the middle estimate of cash flow results. One can then show both the summary and individual estimates to the managers reviewing projects, providing them with the best guess regarding a project's final actual cash flow and the set of assumptions used to derive it.

A final option for reviewing risk is the use of sensitivity analysis. This means that one can examine a project and determine the few key factors likely to have a major impact on cash flows, assume that each of these factors in turn is reduced to a low level, and then calculate new cash flows based on this low level. For example, if the price of coal is a key cost for a coal-fired electricity-generating plant, one can create a model that shows the cash flows from this facility if the price of coal increases by some maximum amount, such as 25%. Similarly, if a newspaper is considering the purchase of a new printing facility, the main variable it should conduct a sensitivity analysis on is the level of capacity utilization at which the new facility will pay for itself. If the model shows that a high utilization level is required in order to justify the facility, then it may be a poor decision to build it.

There is no single correct answer to the problem of how to determine the risk of a capital project. The method selected varies, depending on the time available, the amount of funds that may be lost if an incorrect decision is made, and the impact

EXHIBIT 24.7. Probability Distribution for Project Cash Flows

Cash Flow ($)	Probability (%)	Extended Probability ($)
−250,000	30	−75,000
10,000	20	2,000
650,000	25	162,500
1,200,000	15	180,000
2,000,000	10	200,000
Total	**100**	**469,500**

on overall corporate strategy. Generally, projects with a greater degree of fallout from a bad decision should require the use of several of the risk analyses described in this section, whereas the review of a conservative, inexpensive investment requires only the most perfunctory of risk reviews.

POLICIES AND PROCEDURES FOR CAPITAL BUDGETING

Only a few policies and procedures are needed to keep a reasonable level of control over the capital budgeting process. They are designed to ensure that the proper steps are completed to support the process and that the correct timing and steps are used to ensure that projects flow through the standard budgeting process, rather than fall outside it and thereby require special handling. The most common capital budgeting policies are:

- **The cost of capital shall be recalculated once a year.** This ensures that the discount rate used for all cash flow discounting calculations is based on the most recent financial information.

- **The hurdle rate shall be based on the corporate cost of capital, and can be adjusted for divisional or project-specific risks only with approval of the CFO.** This policy is designed to ensure that project sponsors are prevented from using low hurdle rates to ensure that their projects are approved.

- **Capital approvals shall be required by the plant manager for purchases up to $25,000, additionally by the division vice president for purchases up to $100,000, additionally by the president for purchases up to $250,000, and approval by the board of directors for any larger purchases.** This policy is designed to set forth the standard approval levels for a capital budget request.

- **Any capital purchases not flowing through the annual budget process must be approved by the president.** This policy recognizes that there may be a sudden, unplanned need for new equipment, which must be rushed around the usual process, and ensures that high-level approval is obtained for this exception.

Only three procedures are needed to ensure a smooth flow of capital proposals through the capital budgeting process. One involves the use of a standard application form, the second governs the overall timing of the process, and the third describes the postcompletion audit, which covers the entire capital budgeting work flow. They are:

- **Use of a standard application form.** A standard form is needed for all capital budgeting applications. Otherwise, there is too much or too little information for the cost accountant to analyze, resulting in wasted time while all the proper information is reformatted. A typical format is shown in Exhibit 24.8.

EXHIBIT 24.8. Sample Capital Investment Proposal Form

Capital Investment Proposal Form

Name of Project Sponsor: *H. Henderson*   **Submission Date:** *09/09/01*

Investment Description:

Additional press for newsprint

Cash Flows:

Year	Equipment	Working Capital	Maintenance	Tax Effect of Annual Depreciation	Salvage Value	Revenue	Taxes	Total
0	−5,000,000	−400,000						−5,400,000
1			−100,000	800,000		1,650,000	−700,000	1,170,000
2			−100,000	320,000		1,650,000	−700,000	1,170,000
3			−100,000	320,000		1,650,000	−700,000	1,170,000
4			−100,000	320,000		1,650,000	−700,000	1,170,000
5		400,000	−100,000	320,000	1,000,000	1,650,000	−700,000	2,570,000
Totals	−5,000,000	0	−500,000	2,400,000	1,000,000	8,250,000		1,850,000

Tax Rate:	40%
Hurdle Rate:	10%
Payback Period:	4.28
Net Present Value:	(86,809)
Internal Rate of Return:	9.4%

EXHIBIT 24.8. Sample Capital Investment Proposal Form (*continued*)

Type of Project (check one):

Legal requirement	_____
New product-related	_____
Old product extension	Yes _____
Repair/replacement	_____
Safety issue	_____

Approvals:

Amount	Approver	Signature
<$5,000	Supervisor	_____
$5,000–19,999	General Mgr	_____
$20,000–49,999	President	_____
$50,000	Board	_____

Note: From *Financial Analysis: A Controller's Guide*, by S. Bragg, 2000, New York: John Wiley & Sons. Reprinted with permission.

This format provides space to briefly describe a project, the key elements of all related cash flows, and the resulting financial performance measurements. There is also room in the middle of the report to itemize the type of capital project, as well as spaces at the bottom for various levels of approval. No matter what format is used, the key point is to keep the informational presentation as succinct as possible; the worst case is to require the completion of so many pages of information that division managers avoid new projects when the alternative is increased paperwork.

- **Process timing.** Division managers must begin to gather information about their prospective capital purchases well in advance of the time when they will be approved, given the number of analyses that may take place prior to final approval. Consequently, there should be an annual time line for capital project submissions that gives enough time to proposal formulation, financial analysis, and manager reviews to ensure that each item is included in the annual budget. This schedule can be altered if a company uses an alternative to the annual budget, such as a rolling capital budget that is updated each quarter.

- **Postcompletion audit.** This procedure (described at greater length in the next section) should note the timing of when an audit should be conducted after project completion, how many projects should undergo this review, the format of the resulting report, who should receive the report, and what actions are required thereafter, such as follow-up reviews covering problem areas.

The exact policies and procedures used for capital budgeting vary by company, based on such factors as the speed with which such projects must be approved, the period of time required to obtain project funding, and the level of decentralization. However, the core items covered here should be addressed in all cases.

POSTCOMPLETION PROJECT ANALYSIS

Once a project has been installed, the cost accountant has one last task to complete—verifying that the projections noted in the original capital acquisition proposal have actually been achieved. This is a difficult issue to evaluate if the postcompletion audit is performed too soon after the project is installed, for a period of extra months must pass during which extra costs are incurred to fine-tune the installation and associated revenues begin to ramp up to their anticipated levels. For these reasons the audit should not be started until at least 3 months after the official project completion date. At that time these issues should be explored:

- **Did the timing of cash flows match expectations?** There may have been deposits on purchases that were well in advance of budgeted cash outflows, or cash

EXHIBIT 24.9. Comparison of Actual to Projected Capital Investment Cash Flows

Description	Actual ($)	Projected Actual ($)	Budget ($)	Actual Present Value[a] ($)	Budget Present Value[a] ($)
Cash outflows					
Capital items	1,250,000		1,100,000	1,250,000	1,100,000
Working capital	750,000		500,000	750,000	500,000
Total outflows	2,000,000		1,600,000	2,000,000	1,600,000
Cash inflows					
Cash inflows					
Year 1	250,000		250,000	229,350	229,350
Year 2	375,000		400,000	315,638	336,680
Year 3	450,000		500,000	347,490	386,100
Year 4		450,000	500,000	318,780	354,200
Year 5		450,000	500,000	292,455	324,950
Total inflows	1,075,000	900,000	2,150,000	1,503,713	1,631,280
Net present value				−496,287	+31,280

Note: From *Financial Analysis: A Controller's Guide,* by S. Bragg, 2000, New York: John Wiley & Sons. Reprinted with permission.
[a]Uses discount rate of 9%.

flows may have occurred at different times within the year than were anticipated in the original project budget.

- **Did the amount of cash flows match expectations?** There may be significant differences from the project budget in terms of overall expenditures for assets or working capital, and there may also be major variances in the size of cash inflows.

  The results of this investigation can be summarized into a report form similar to the one shown in Exhibit 24.9, where we see a project that incurred an extra $400,000 in cash outflows, as well as a modest drop in expected cash inflows for all years except the first one, resulting in a net present value that is substantially negative rather than the modestly positive one that had been projected.

This financial information should be released only with an accompanying report itemizing the exact reasons for any problems that caused adverse cash flows to occur, as well as recommended changes for the evaluation of future projects that might keep these issues from arising again. In this way one can forestall the management team from conducting its own "witch hunt" into each completed project and turn the audit experience into a positive one that results in improvements to the entire capital evaluation system.

Finally it should be noted that one cannot effectively review a project if the accounting system does not do a good job of segregating all cash inflows and outflows related to it. The best way to ensure that this information is properly stored is to set up a separate account number for each capital project as soon as it is approved and store all revenues and expenses related to it in this account. This approach is preferable to the less precise practice of storing project-related financial information in a separate database, where there is a danger that it will be less complete than if it were stored in the general ledger. Only by using the most complete accounting information can a project be properly evaluated.

SUMMARY

Capital budgeting is a tremendously important topic for companies that tie up a significant proportion of their assets in equipment and facilities. They are faced with the problem of trying to determine which investments will generate a sufficient return to justify the initial and ongoing cash expenditure. The cost accountant can use the tools outlined in this chapter to provide the answers—calculate the cost of capital to determine the hurdle or discount rate, construct a cash flow, and discount it to find out if there is an adequate return on investment. In addition, the policies and procedures noted here can assist the cost accountant in formalizing the process of submitting, evaluating, and approving capital requests. Only by following these steps can a company mitigate the risk of investing valuable funds in the wrong capital projects.

CHAPTER 25

Capacity Management

At first glance a cost accountant might think that capacity issues fall entirely within the area of responsibility of the industrial engineering staff. These individuals determine when to bring in new machines, obtain top-management approval, and acquire and install the machinery. The cost accountant then incorporates the new machine into depreciation cost pools to adjust for a changed cost of overhead, and life goes on.

This is a seriously incorrect view of how a cost accountant can impact the management of a company's capacity. Capacity management is an issue that has a profound impact on an organization's profitability, break-even level, and pricing and acquisition decisions—all matters about which a cost accountant is regularly called on to render an opinion. In this chapter we will see how the proper accounting for and measurement of capacity utilization can have a major impact on a company.

IMPACT OF CAPACITY ON OPERATIONS

Before we delve into the mechanics of how to manage capacity, it may be prudent to ask what happens from an operational standpoint when capacity is not managed properly. The answer may motivate us to find better ways to manage capacity.

Capacity is the ability of an organization to produce at a specific volume level. This involves not just machinery but also the number of employees and their ability to handle a specific number of transactions. It can also include the ability of a company's warehouses to store product, its computer systems to process information, and even its telephone system to handle the volume of customer orders. All these items and more make up an organization's ability, or capacity, to conduct business.

The great challenge for all organizations is to stretch a company's current ability to produce while adding the smallest possible number of expensive assets to assist in the production process. The reason for this behavior is that few organizations are so well funded that they can purchase significant additional quantities of new assets or hire new employees whenever there is the slightest chance that production levels will not be met. Instead, managers try to improve the reported level of return on assets and profitability per employee, which improves shareholder value by squeezing more productivity out of the existing asset and employee base. In most cases there is also a limited amount of funding available, which restricts the amount of purchasing and hiring.

The end result is that managers are constantly trying to find new ways to make a company more efficient, while adding capacity only when there is a clear, immediate need to do so. Sometimes they fail in this endeavor. When this happens, an organization finds itself operating too near its maximum theoretical level of capacity, which results in the problems listed here by functional area:

- **Product design capacity is overwhelmed.** If the organization's prime strategic direction is to grow by creating and selling new products, a prime potential bottleneck is located not in its factories, but in the design lab. A lack of qualified engineers is a critical issue in this instance. The result of this issue will be a dearth of new products, encouraging customers to flock to other organizations that sell more "leading edge" products.

- **Purchasing capacity is overwhelmed.** If a company intends to grow by reselling a wide array of items, it must rely heavily on the ability of its purchasing staff to procure a varied, low-cost array of new products. A shortage of purchasing staff can severely impact this strategy and result in a narrow range of product offerings. This is also a problem if a company uses just-in-time purchasing to feed components to its production lines. If there are not enough purchasing agents on hand to coordinate the flow of components, there will be production shortfalls.

- **Production capacity is overwhelmed.** The traditional capacity problem occurs when there is not a sufficient quantity of operable machinery available to work on all scheduled production, with the inevitable result that shipping deadlines are missed.

- **Distribution capacity is overwhelmed.** Even if a company has an efficient production facility that can churn out all scheduled production in a timely manner, this does little good if the distribution system is not capable of delivering the goods to consumers. This may result from a combination of excessively short scheduled delivery times and (more likely) a dearth of transportation equipment for delivering items. The last problem is most common when a company has a sudden surge in volume that its in-house fleet is ill-prepared to handle.

- **Computer system capacity is overwhelmed.** Processing an order involves not just running materials through a machine but also ensuring that the information related to a transaction, such as procurement, scheduling, and delivery issues, is routed through the system in a timely manner. However, if the computer system supporting this flow of information is incapable of processing transactions on time, this will contribute to a reduction in the capacity of a facility.

- **Customer service capacity is overwhelmed.** The first point of contact for a customer is the customer service/order entry department. The inability of this department to receive and enter orders promptly may constitute the prime bottleneck in the organization—and, as in a bottle, the choke point is at the top, before any other departments even see the customer order. If orders are lost or delayed at this point, customers will desert in droves.

- **Accounting capacity is overwhelmed.** Though this may not seem like an area where a bottleneck can cause problems, the accounting department may not be equipped to handle increased levels of activity related to accounts payable and accounts receivable, which may result in unpaid (and unhappy) suppliers, as well as unbilled (and happy) customers. The end result may be conflicts with business partners and a potential for reduced cash flows that can put a large crimp in a company's overall ability to transact business.

The reader may peruse this list of potential capacity problems and find only one that applies to his company. This can still be a major issue, for it takes only one capacity problem anywhere in the chain of design, production, and distribution to greatly reduce an organization's ability to deliver goods to customers in the expected quantities and at the expected times. If there are several apparent capacity issues, then the combination of problems is probably sufficient to give a company severe product delivery problems, perhaps to the extent that customers are driven away—not by the lack of a quality product but by the lack of a shippable product that arrives on time.

THE BASELINE FOR CAPACITY MEASUREMENT

Having discovered that a multitude of problems can arise from capacity-related issues, we next need to consider what level of available capacity is either too little or too much. To do so we must determine the capacity baseline against which we are measuring. For example, if a company that operates on one shift, Monday through

Friday, claims it is operating at maximum capacity, is it truly at such a level or is it really ignoring the possibility of adding additional shifts? What about available time on weekends or holidays? And what about using every single hour of every day of every week as the baseline? Is it realistic to assume that a company really has 168 hours of available capacity every week of the year? What is the correct baseline to use? There are several options available.

The most extreme capacity baseline is called *theoretical capacity*. This baseline assumes that a company operates for every minute of every day, around the clock, with no downtime for anything. It is aptly named, for it is virtually impossible for any organization to operate in such a manner without some downtime for a variety of reasons, such as holidays, machine maintenance, break time, or pauses due to acts of God, such as power outages, floods, or lightening. This method is most commonly used by organizations that operate on three shifts and have sufficiently well-run operations that they can come close to the theoretically attainable limit of capacity utilization. Other companies, such as those employing professionals who refuse to work on the second or third shift, do not feel that this baseline is appropriate for their needs.

A variation on theoretical capacity is called *practical capacity*. This baseline uses the same underlying assumptions as the theoretical capacity formulation, but it is then reduced by unavoidable situations such as machine maintenance time and company holidays. This capacity represents the maximum that is achievable over the long run. However, this baseline suffers from manipulation, for a manager whose performance is based on an ability to produce at the practical capacity level attempts to increase the amount of deductions in order to reduce the baseline against which he or she is being measured.

So far, we have reviewed two baselines based on a company's ability to supply the maximum amount. These baselines are best used in situations where a company is struggling to churn out as much product as possible. If this scenario is not correct and the real issue is just to meet demand, then the *normal capacity* baseline may work best. This baseline uses the long-term average level of production needed to satisfy demand, which may be much less than the baseline used for either theoretical or practical capacity, perhaps revealing as little capacity as would be used on just one shift. This variation is of the most use when valuing inventory, as we will see in a later section.

A final type of capacity baseline is for *budgeted capacity,* which is the same as normal capacity but which may vary substantially in order to project the exact amount of capacity needed in each month of the current budget year. This baseline is best used for budgeted versus actual comparisons of capacity usage, which tells managers how closely they are matching expected levels of capacity. This is a common baseline in situations where capacity levels vary widely from month to month, which is a typical occurrence in seasonal industries.

Of the four baseline capacity measures identified here, there is no one best baseline. Each one can be used in specific circumstances. For instance, theoretical capacity is most useful for comparison against actual utilization levels in an environment where a company works around the clock, so that managers can determine how closely they can come to the theoretical maximum. This baseline is used in Exhibits 25.1 and 25.2 later in this chapter. The practical capacity level is most profitably used in situations where a company is barely keeping up with strong demand levels and the performance reviews of managers are tied to their ability to operate as close to maximum capacity levels as possible. The normal capacity baseline assumes that capacity levels are only high enough to meet long-term demand, which usually translates into a much lower capacity level, though one that also matches a company's most realistic capacity use experience. Because this variation tends to mimic actual experience, accountants like to use it as the basis for assigning overhead costs to inventory and the cost of goods sold (to be discussed later). Finally, the budgeted capacity level is the best one for developing comparisons between budgeted levels and actual performance on a month-to-month basis, for it reflects the utilization levels of the people who created the budget—if managers are achieving utilization levels close to the budgeted level, then there should be no need to spend excess amounts of capital on new equipment beyond the amounts already anticipated in the budget.

Thus, there are different uses for all the capacity baselines mentioned in this section. It is possible that a larger company can find uses for all of them, depending on its particular needs.

We now proceed to a review of how capacity can be measured. To be consistent all the reports covered use a theoretical capacity baseline; any of the baselines could have been used, but the assumption for these reports is that the target company operates 24 hours every day and at close to maximum capacity levels, which makes this the best choice.

MEASURING CAPACITY

The most common report of capacity utilization is a single line item in the financial statements, tucked into the operating statistics, that reveals the aggregate utilization level in the past month. This information is of little use to anyone since it does not indicate what machines were running at full tilt and which were not, or the uses to which the machines were put when they were not productively employed, and it certainly does not give managers timely information since it is revealed some time after the end of the month in which the operations occurred. There are several reporting formats that correct these deficiencies.

The most common capacity utilization reporting format is shown in Exhibit 25.1. It itemizes the productive use of each machine in a plastic injection molding and blow molding facility (the same format can be used for any type of production facility and can also be used to report employee utilization instead of machine use). It gives a history of utilization for the past 3 months of operation, as well as for each

EXHIBIT 25.1. Measuring Capacity by Individual Machine

Machine ID	Machine Description	Week of				Month of		
		5/22–5/29 Run Hours	5/15–5/21 Run Hours	5/8–5/14 Run Hours	5/1–5/7 Run Hours	Mar. Avg. Weekly Run Hours	Feb. Avg. Weekly Run Hours	Jan. Avg. Weekly Run Hours
01–50	50 Ton	129	77	111	139	112	122	104
02–55	55 Ton	136	114	120	132	114	154	119
03–55	55 Ton	93	132	94	112	138	125	111
04–65	65 Ton	125	54	138	122	117	132	144
05–65	65 Ton	100	124	142	104	126	111	120
06–100	100 Ton	121	141	167	137	142	167	147
07–120	120 Ton	158	117	147	152	125	109	102
08–150	150 Ton	128	101	163	114	133	139	133
09–150	150 Ton	136	113	59	154	122	124	127
10–150	150 Ton	154	127	125	119	114	132	54
Subtotal		76%	65%	75%	76%	74%	78%	69%
11–310	310 Ton	102	116	109	126	117	101	113
12–310	310 Ton	84	97	102	132	97	106	91
13–310	310 Ton	78	106	147	138	148	125	148
14–355	355 Ton	77	91	162	125	135	142	129
15–355	355 Ton	102	168	133	111	93	125	100
16–355	355 Ton	124	133	139	152	128	136	154
17–400	400 Ton	101	125	137	117	101	78	102
18–400	400 Ton	116	148	133	137	78	77	120
19–475	475 Ton	78	148	152	132	52	62	50
20–475	475 Ton	120	79	122	144	107	142	96

		58%	72%	80%	78%	63%	65%	66%
	Subtotal							
BM–01	Blow Mold	166	143	124	164	103	111	119
BM–02	Blow Mold	137	135	127	129	161	96	106
BM–03	Blow Mold	113	142	133	126	146	128	89
	Subtotal	83%	83%	76%	83%	81%	66%	62%
	Grand Total	69%	71%	77%	78%	70%	71%	67%

week of the current month, and also calculates an average capacity utilization for each group of machines. This format is particularly useful for noting at a glance any variations in the utilization levels of entire departments, which may allow one to determine if there is over- or undercapacity in some areas. It is also good for determining trends in utilization levels over a number of months and reveals patterns in the use of individual pieces of equipment. Further, the report is released weekly, so that managers receive more rapid feedback about key information. This reporting format is an advancement over the single utilization line item so common in financial reports, but it suffers from a few drawbacks. First, it does not tell managers what is happening to machines when they are *not* being productive. This is a key issue if some of the nonproductive activities can be eliminated, thereby creating more hours that can be used productively. Second, it does not provide feedback more rapidly than on a weekly basis, which may not be sufficient in some rapid response environments requiring high levels of hands-on management. The next two supplemental reports solve these two problems.

Another report that creates another level of detail is one that shows the exact activities performed by each machine (or employee). An example of this format is shown in Exhibit 25.2, where we see the same machines used in the preceding example but now focus on just the hours for the last week of the preceding report, May 22 through May 29. For this week the report lists not only the productive hours noted in Exhibit 25.1 but also how the remaining hours were used. This means that we can now see if a machine was just lying idle for lack of work or if maintenance or setup time prevented it from being used to create new products. In the example it is painfully clear that a number of machines require continual and extensive maintenance, which reduces the overall capacity level of the facility by 11%. In particular, machines 6-100, 12-310, and 19-475 were being repaired for one-fourth of the past week. If the level of maintenance could be improved, perhaps through the use of preventive maintenance or the replacement of old machinery, the facility would realize a net increase in available capacity. Another issue revealed by this report is the amount of time required to set up machines for new production runs. This appears to occupy about 10% of the total time during the week in question. By focusing on rapid setups and teardowns, managers can reduce the time devoted to this activity as well, thereby effectively increasing the available capacity of the facility. The report can also include other categories that break down the types of nonproductive activities further, such as machines running scrap, running for process development, and running for product development activities.

The remaining problem we have not yet addressed is the timeliness of information provided to managers. Reports are most commonly issued on a weekly basis, but capacity issues may arise every minute of every day, for example, prolonged setup times that managers cannot fix because they are not aware of the problem. The report shown in Exhibit 25.3 resolves this last issue. It is not really a paper-based report but rather a computer screen tied to data entry terminals next to each machine in the facility. Operators keypunch in the current status of their equipment,

EXHIBIT 25.2. Detailed Analysis of Capacity Usage

		Week of 5/22–5/29				
Machine ID	Machine Description	Productive Hours	Setup Hours	Maintenance Hours	Idle Hours	Total Hours
01-50	50 Ton	129	10	14	15	168
02-55	55 Ton	136	4	15	13	168
03-55	55 Ton	93	8	28	39	168
04-65	65 Ton	125	11	25	7	168
05-65	65 Ton	100	29	22	17	168
06-100	100 Ton	121	7	40	-	168
07-120	120 Ton	158	10		-	168
08-150	150 Ton	128	29	10	1	168
09-150	150 Ton	136	13	12	7	168
10-150	150 Ton	154	5	5	4	168
11-310	310 Ton	102	20	30	16	168
12-310	310 Ton	84	12	50	22	168
13-310	310 Ton	78	15	11	64	168
14-355	355 Ton	77	5	24	62	168
15-355	355 Ton	102	10	25	31	168
16-355	355 Ton	124	2	17	25	168
17-400	400 Ton	116	14	18	20	168
18-400	400 Ton	101	22	19	26	168
19-475	475 Ton	78	19	41	30	168
20-475	475 Ton	120	25	3	20	168
BM-01	Blow Mold	166		2	-	168
BM-02	Blow Mold	137	15	16	-	168
BM-03	Blow Mold	113	51	4	-	168
Total Hours		2,678	336	431	419	3,864
Percent of Total		69%	9%	11%	11%	100%

which then appears on the screen in a summarized format that immediately tells anyone accessing the screen the exact operational status of each piece of equipment in the facility. The screen shows a layout of the facility, with each machine coded with dots or cross-hatching according to its capacity utilization status. In the example the user can determine at a glance which machine is currently undergoing setup or maintenance, so that someone can draw additional resources down on it in order to ensure that the issue is resolved as quickly as possible. This format can also use color coding to achieve the same result. This report requires an expensive set of data entry terminals, as well as custom programming of the screen that pulls together all the status information, so the perceived value of such a system must be readily apparent before a company decides to develop it.

EXHIBIT 25.3. Graphical Layout of Capacity Use

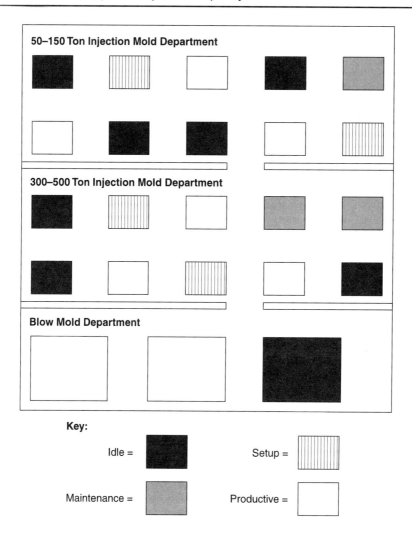

The problem with all three of the reports presented here is the considerable amount of time and effort needed to set up data collection systems that feed information into them. There must be either manual or automated data tracking at every machine in a facility in order to have sufficient data available for reporting purposes. Given the level of effort required, one should be sure of a company's need for the resulting information before creating the system. The benefit gleaned from the reports must outweigh the cost of preparing them.

None of the three reports presented here should be substituted for another because they are intended to be a package of information. The first report shows the long-term use by machine, the second reveals specific use by machine over the short term, and the third is designed to give immediate feedback regarding utilization issues at the current moment. These represent three different types of information, and they should all be provided to management in order to present the most complete package of capacity-related information.

IMPACT OF CAPACITY ISSUES ON PRODUCTION

Capacity management has a major impact on the methods used to run a production department. A company that tries to keep tight control over its investment in assets must alter a number of production activities in order to ensure that production is maximized while the asset base is kept as low as possible.

One such activity involves spreading production over many periods to avoid sharp increases in production demand caused by seasonal changes in customer demand. For example, the demand for lawn chairs by furniture retailers is high in the spring but nonexistent at most other parts of the year. A company that tries to maintain a steady level of capacity utilization must schedule its production of lawn chairs well in advance of the demand period in order to avoid a sudden flood of orders that it cannot fill by the required dates. This practice of leveling production demand calls for more skill in production scheduling, not to mention a much higher investment in inventory that may not be sold for many months. The cost accountant can be of great assistance in weighing the offsetting costs of carrying inventory for extra months against the risk of lost orders, as well as the costs of production overtime incurred during the peak production period.

Another method used to increase the level of available capacity is to concentrate management attention on the activities that occur when assets are not being productive. These activities can include maintenance, setup and breakdown time, downtime due to missing materials, and a multitude of other factors. By reducing the time devoted to these activities, one can effectively increase the total amount of practical capacity available without having to invest in additional assets. This requires the use of a report similar to the one shown earlier in Exhibit 25.2, which details the various types of nonproductive capacity utilization. The report shown in Exhibit 25.3 is also useful, for it tells managers what activities are currently taking place on the shop floor, allowing them to bring to bear the largest amount of personnel onto immediate capacity-related problems.

Yet another production activity is the continuing focus on and resolution of bottleneck operations. Nearly all companies have at least one operation that is incapable of keeping up with production demands, even if capacity levels are relatively low. By using a report like the one in Exhibit 25.1, managers can quickly determine which equipment is continually overworked. By selectively adding assets to these bottlenecks, the overall capacity level of the entire production operation can be increased. The same principle applies to a service organization where specific employees represent bottleneck operations. By adding additional employees to increase the capacity of selected bottleneck operations, the overall capacity of the entire service area is increased.

Another practice is to avoid any additional asset investments by predicting the demand levels at which production requirements will exceed the ability of the production line and then outsource this incremental increase to a supplier specializing in outsourced production. This activity calls for the analysis skills of a cost accountant who can offset the savings from not investing in more assets against the incremental cost increase per unit charged by the supplier.

A final production activity heavily influenced by the level of utilization is the selective acceptance or rejection of customer orders based on which ones will incrementally yield a higher profit. For example, if only 10% of available capacity is left at the facility and there is a choice of using this capacity to produce an item with a 20% margin or with a 50% margin, the production scheduler always picks the one with a 50% margin. This approach can be used to review all the orders a plant accepts and not just the last few orders that will fill up the last iota of available capacity. Though this approach doubtlessly leads to higher profits in the short term, it does not do much to enhance relations with customers whose orders have been rejected.

All the activities noted here are directly influenced by the issue of capacity utilization and can be best managed with a detailed knowledge of capacity levels by facility, department, machine, and individual employee, which requires use of the reports described in the last section.

IMPACT OF CAPACITY ISSUES ON PRICING DECISIONS

The level of pricing a company adopts is directly impacted by its level of available capacity, not to mention how it accounts for and recognizes this capacity.

The sales and marketing staff is fully cognizant of the laws of supply and demand; if the production facility is fully loaded with work, they not only will refuse low-priced offers for company products but will also be tempted to raise prices all around in order to maximize profits. However, their actions will be predicated on what kind of capacity information they are given. For example, they may be given capacity utilization information based on the budgeted or normal capacity that reveals a 100% utilization level, when in fact there is a considerable amount of additional capacity left that would have been revealed if the same report had been based on either theoretical or practical capacity. Thus, the type of capacity baseline used in calculating capacity can have an impact on the unit prices a company charges for its products.

The reverse situation occurs when the sales and marketing staff knows that there is a great deal of available capacity. In this instance they attempt to maximize marginal profits by accepting any customer order as long as the price exceeds the variable cost of the product. Though the resulting sales may not cover fixed costs, the company does not care—for foregoing these sales will still result in unused capacity. As was the case for a high-capacity utilization scenario, the type of capacity baseline used to report utilization has an impact on these pricing decisions. For example, if the theoretical capacity baseline is used as the foundation for a utilization report, it may reveal that there is a large amount of unused capacity available, when in fact the excess occurs only if the company resorts to a third shift, which will cost it extra in terms of more management salaries, shift premiums, and added maintenance. Even if a third shift is already in place, a theoretical capacity report will not reveal capacity that is not available because of a variety of systemic problems, such as machine downtime. A better baseline for reporting information in a low-utilization situation is the practical capacity baseline, which factors out all systemic issues related to downtime. Thus, the utilization reporting baseline can alter a company's pricing policies in a low-utilization situation.

The type of utilization baseline used can also impact prices if they are directly based on a product's reported level of fully absorbed cost. This may occur in cost-plus pricing situations, perhaps for government contracts, where the buyer accepts any price as long as it has a logical costing basis. In this instance it is to the advantage of the company to avoid the use of both the theoretical and practical capacity baseline models and instead to favor normal or budgeted baseline calculations. The reason is that the theoretical and practical baselines assume that a company is producing the absolute maximum volume of product, which means that the cost of factory overhead is spread over many more products, reducing the amount of overhead cost charged per unit actually produced. However, if the normal or budget baseline is used, this means that overhead costs are spread over fewer units of production, leading to a higher cost per unit and therefore a higher price.

To expand on this concept, when a company allocates its overhead costs based on the theoretical capacity baseline, overhead costs can be charged at a much lower rate per unit. This overhead rate is recorded in a product's bill of materials, which is the standard compilation of costs for each product. The sales and marketing staff can use this BOM document to determine a product's cost and also to establish its minimum price. However, when the overhead cost pool is allocated based on the theoretical capacity baseline, only under unusual full-utilization circumstances can a company actually produce enough units to totally absorb the cost of the overhead cost pool. A much more likely scenario is that the company cannot produce at the theoretical level, meaning that the number of units produced falls short of the amount required to absorb all the overhead costs. The end result is that the company must charge the remaining amount of cost in the overhead cost pool to the cost of goods sold in the current period. This means that the overhead cost charged to each product in the BOM was insufficient. Therefore, the overhead cost per unit that the sales and marketing staff sees is not really as high as it should be, so this group does not realize that its pricing decisions are based on fully absorbed costs set too low. The best way to avoid this problem is to use the normal capacity baseline, which approximates a company's actual history of production volume over the long run.

The problem with using an incorrect capacity baseline to calculate the amount of overhead charged to a product is not an issue from a pricing perspective for companies who sell at a fixed market–based rate, as is common for producers of generic and indistinguishable products like corn and wheat. However, companies that have some degree of control over the prices they charge and who use fully absorbed product costs as the basis for their pricing calculations find that an incorrect overhead calculation can have a deleterious impact on pricing decisions.

IMPACT OF CAPACITY ISSUES ON REPORTED PROFITS

A concept that was brought up in the last section can have a significant impact on a company's reported level of profitability. To reiterate, if a theoretical or practical capacity baseline is used to calculate the standard overhead amount charged to products in each period, there will be excess overhead that is not charged to products in periods where actual production volume does not match the amount used in the baseline. This problem can still occur even if normal or budgeted capacity baselines are used; however, the production quantities assumed to arise under the two latter baseline calculations are usually much less than are assumed for the theoretical and practical capacity baselines, and so the amount of excess overhead left unallocated tends to be much less.

This issue is best illustrated with an example, as shown in Exhibit 25.4. In the example we assume that a company has the option of using any of the four standard capacity baselines for its calculation of overhead costs per unit. These baselines range from 100,000 units per month at the high end to 50,000 at the low end. The example shows a total estimated overhead cost pool of $500,000 that should be allocated to production that occurs during the month. When the theoretical capacity baseline is used, $5 is allocated to each unit of production during the month ($500,000 / 100,000 units). When the budgeted capacity baseline is used, this figure rises to $10 per unit ($500,000 / 50,000 units). If the latter overhead cost per unit is used and if actual production turns out to be 50,000 units, then all the overhead will be properly allocated to every unit manufactured. However, when the theoretical capacity baseline is used, only $5 is allocated to each of the 50,000 units produced, which leaves the company with $250,000 of unallocated overhead cost. The company then has the choice of manually allocating this extra overhead cost

EXHIBIT 25.4. Impact of Capacity Baseline on Reported Earnings

	Theoretical Capacity	Practical Capacity	Normal Capacity	Budgeted Capacity
Production estimate	100,000	90,000	60,000	50,000
Overhead cost pool ($)	500,000	500,000	500,000	500,000
Cost per unit ($)	5.00	5.56	8.33	10.00
Actual production	50,000	50,000	50,000	50,000
Overhead charged to produced units ($)	250,000	278,000	416,500	500,000
Remaining overhead charged to the cost of goods sold ($)	250,000	222,000	83,500	0

to the produced items or of charging the entire amount to the cost of goods sold in the current period. If the latter course is taken, then the reported level of profitability will drop by $250,000.

Though this may seem like a remarkably large amount by which reported earnings can be skewed, it is actually possible only under circumstances where the bulk of all production is stored in inventory at month-end, rather than sold off (and therefore charged to the cost of goods sold). When production is stored, the associated cost of goods is capitalized into inventory until the items are eventually sold. Alternatively, if the products are sold at once, it makes no difference if the overhead allocation method charges costs to the products or directly to the cost of goods sold, for the overhead cost will still be charged to the current period, with no skewing of reported profitability.

As more companies shift their mode of operation to just-in-time manufacturing, overhead will generally be charged to the current period (since there is no inventory to allocate it to), which makes this peculiar accounting anomaly much less of an issue than for companies operating under systems that require high levels of inventory.

Many companies reconcile their overhead cost pools to actual production volumes in each reporting period and so always charge exactly the correct amount to each unit of production that results in no leftover costs in the overhead cost pool to be charged directly to the cost of goods sold. However, many other organizations feel they do not have the time to conduct such a reconciliation every month and so are content to use the standard overhead cost per unit, which is partly derived from a specific capacity baseline methodology. For these companies there is always some positive or negative amount left over in the overhead cost pool at the end of each period that must be charged off to the cost of goods sold, simply because no capacity baseline method can exactly predict the actual level of production in any given month.

IMPACT OF CAPACITY ISSUES ON BREAK-EVEN ANALYSIS

As noted in the last section, there is a possibility that the choice of capacity utilization baseline can have an impact on the reported level of profitability in a reporting period. The main factor is the size of the difference between the actual amount of production in a given month and the amount assumed in the capacity baseline. If the baseline is much higher, then a large proportion of overhead costs will be dumped directly into the cost of goods sold, rather than allocated to individual units of production, where they may sit in inventory for some time before being sold, thereby keeping them from being expensed.

This issue can result in an incorrect break-even calculation for a product, which may lead to incorrect management decisions concerning it. The point is best described with an example. We continue to use the information presented earlier in Exhibit 25.4 and show the break-even point for all four of the capacity baselines used in that example. Under this scenario we assume that only 25,000 units were sold during the month and that every other unit produced was stored in inventory at the end of the reporting period. Also, we assume that there is a $10 variable cost associated with each unit produced, that each unit sells for $22, and that there are $200,000 of fixed costs associated with the product line that are charged to expense each month. The results are noted in Exhibit 25.5.

The example shows a massive disparity between the reported break-even levels for each of the capacity baseline methods. When a manager sees a break-even report based on information using the theoretical capacity baseline, it appears that the product is a hopeless one, with a tiny margin and enormous sales volumes required in order to achieve break-even. However, the same calculation using the budgeted capacity baseline results in a break-even level that is seven times lower! Though the numbers in this example were stretched beyond what is normally seen in practice, the point is clear—the choice of capacity baseline has a direct impact on a product's break-even level.

There are several instances in which the severity of the break-even analysis problem is not as great. One is when a company is able to sell all its production during the month when it is manufactured or is at least able to keep its finished goods inventory at a steady month-to-month level. In either case the full amount of overhead cost incurred during a month flows straight through to the cost of goods sold, irrespective of whether it was directly charged to the cost of goods sold or was first charged to an inventory item and then charged to the cost of goods sold at the time of sale. In this instance the type of capacity baseline used is irrelevant.

Another case where the break-even analysis problem can be ignored is when the cost accounting staff ignores the standard amount of overhead to be charged to production in each month and instead allocates only the *actual* overhead costs incurred during the period. When actual costs are used, there are no leftover overhead costs that have not been allocated, and so there are no extra expenses to charge to the cost of goods sold. This is an excellent way to deal with overhead but is more labor-

EXHIBIT 25.5. Impact of the Capacity Baseline on Reported Break-even Levels

	Theoretical Capacity	Practical Capacity	Normal Capacity	Budgeted Capacity
No. of units sold	25,000	25,000	25,000	25,000
Variable cost per unit ($)	10.00	10.00	10.00	10.00
Total variable cost ($)	250,000	250,000	250,000	250,000
Add: excess overhead costs charged to the cost of goods sold (see Exhibit 25.4) ($)	250,000	222,000	83,500	0
Total product cost ($)	500,000	472,000	333,500	250,000
Total cost per unit sold ($)	20.00	18.88	13.34	10.00
Selling price per unit ($)	22.00	22.00	22.00	22.00
Margin per unit (%)	9	14	39	55
Total fixed costs ($)	200,000	200,000	200,000	200,000
Break-even point (fixed cost/percent margin) ($)	2,222,222	1,428,571	512,821	363,636

intensive than the standard costing approach that requires the use of a capacity baseline and so is more typically used only at the end of the fiscal year, when more precision is needed for external reporting purposes.

The problem is also reduced if the capacity baseline used is the normal or the budgeted baseline. These two baselines are based on the long-run history of actual production volume (normal capacity baseline) or on expected production volume by month (budgeted capacity baseline). Because both measures are based on actual demand for production, rather than on the theoretical amount that can be produced, they tend to track much closer to actual production experience. This means that, when using either of these two methods, the standard amount of overhead dollars allocated to production tends to account for most of the costs that have accumulated in the overhead cost pool, leaving little remaining to be charged to the cost of goods sold.

A final and important issue is why the overhead costs that can cause a break-even analysis to be skewed so badly are even listed as variable costs in the break-even formula—after all, they are overhead costs and so by definition do not vary directly with the volume of production. The reason is that generally accepted accounting principles require overhead to be allocated to units of production; most companies meet this requirement by including overhead costs as a line item in their bills of material. The trouble with this approach is that many accounting systems are unable to differentiate between the variable and fixed costs itemized in a bill of materials, and so managers tend to think of the entire cost of a bill of materials as variable rather than as a mix of fixed and variable elements. When this happens, the overhead cost pool is treated as though it is a variable cost rather than a fixed one.

The problem described in this section is limited only to specific circumstances—to companies that use break-even analysis, use a theoretical or a practical capacity baseline, and do not sell off all their production during the month in which manufacturing occurs. Though these are tightly limiting circumstances, the results are important for organizations that fall within these parameters, for the wild swings in reported break-even levels noted in Exhibit 25.5 are possible in these cases.

IMPACT OF CAPACITY ISSUES ON ACQUISITION ANALYSIS

Capacity management can be an issue even when a company is looking into the acquisition of another organization. The reason is that the buyer may need additional capacity in a hurry, because of additional demand from customers, but cannot purchase the necessary machinery in a sufficiently short period of time; its best alternative is to obtain the capacity by purchasing another company that already has the equipment. Acquisitions take a considerable amount of time to complete, so this is a good alternative only when the equipment to be obtained has a long lead time, which is sometimes the case for heavy machinery of a specialized nature. This alternative is especially attractive when the acquiree also has a sufficiently large management infrastructure to run the newly acquired capacity.

This issue is also a valid excuse to make an acquisition when the assets involved are not equipment, but employees. A company may find that it is less expensive to buy a company with a department full of valuable employees, such as engineers in specialized areas who could be replaced only after an inordinate amount of recruiting. This option is not as certain as when a company is buying a load of inanimate equipment, since equipment cannot walk out the door, but employees who are being acquired can.

If a company is being acquired for its equipment or employee capacity, the cost accountant is likely to be called in to advise on how the new capacity should be used. This can be a difficult issue, for the acquiree is unlikely to have built up a large amount of excess capacity without some level of demand from its customers to justify the expansion—in other words, if there is not a sufficient amount of capacity between the two organizations to service the needs of all existing customers, then the cost accountant must delve into the acquiree's financial records, determine the profitability level of each one, and recommend that the company drop customers with the lowest profitability until there is just enough demand left to be adequately met by the combined capacity of the two organizations.

This strategy works best when the acquiring company has a significantly higher margin on its products or services than those of the acquiree, as well as an excessive amount of customer demand, so that it can replace at least some of the acquiree's low-margin sales with its own, thereby improving the profitability and cash flow of the newly combined entity.

OTHER TYPES OF CAPACITY

The bulk of this chapter has dealt with the collection of information about the capacity of machines and how this information can be used to utilize them as efficiently as possible. Though machinery is certainly an important factor in many organizations, if only from the perspective of being a large capital investment, there are even more organizations that have few or no machines but who still have capacity-related issues. These companies fall into the broad category of service industries and can include auditors, consultants, programmers, bankers, and architects, as well as advertising agencies, engineering firms, and many similar organizations. Their capacity issues are related much more closely to their human capital than to their equipment.

The same principles noted in the preceding sections apply in force to a services company. For example, if the management of a programming company thinks that there is no way to increase capacity beyond a single day shift (because of the reluctance of professional staffers to work evening shifts), there are numerous examples of companies that have perfected the art of transmitting work between different time zones, so that there is always a day shift of programmers somewhere in the world that is available for work. A recent example of this is Microsoft, which used teams of programmers located around the world to develop the Windows 2000 operating system. As each shift ended, the work group that had just completed its shift transmitted its programs to the next group, wherever it was located, so that the work could continue. The same principle applies to customer service centers, which can be located anywhere in the world and so can use day shift employees at all times. Because of these innovations, it is possible for service companies to use the same types of capacity baselines used by manufacturers.

Two of the three reports presented earlier in Exhibits 25.1 through 25.3 can also be used by services companies. The two reports in Exhibits 25.1 and 25.2 can be easily adapted to track the capacity utilization of employees simply by swapping the names of equipment for the names of employees or departments and by using daily or weekly time sheets to accumulate the information they contain. The third report, which notes real-time capacity utilization, is not of much use for services companies since employees cannot be expected to report their utilization frequently enough to make the report worthwhile.

The key aspect in which the capacity of a services firm varies from that of a manufacturing one is that the volume of available employee capacity must closely match immediate demand levels, whereas a manufacturer usually has the option to produce items in advance to avoid having to procure extra equipment capacity to cover high-demand periods. A services firm does not have this luxury. For example, a tax preparation firm must have a large staff on hand to meet the needs of its clients, who must have their tax returns completed by April 15 of each year. As soon as April 16 arrives, there is a much smaller demand for tax work and therefore a need for fewer staff. The tax firm can avoid this problem to some extent by using part-time workers and by offering discounts to clients if they can bring in their tax information at the beginning of the tax season. However, there is no way to complete tax returns throughout the year and let them sit in a pile until April 15 and then mail them all out, for the returns cannot be completed until corporate or individual year-ends have been completed. Accordingly, a services firm in a seasonal industry must pay especially careful attention to the flow of customer demand and promptly change employee capacity levels to match this demand as closely as possible. If they do not match these two factors, they will be unable to meet customer demand or will have to pay the salaries of employees who are not being used. For these companies it is more important to carefully track changes in capacity than is the case for many manufacturing organizations.

A key factor that allows services companies to off-load their work in periods of high demand is outsourcing. This is the practice of shifting some of the work of a company's internal departments to a supplier who performs the work instead. The concept is particularly useful in services industries where it is difficult to rapidly change the level of employment to match demand. For example, it is unwise to churn through a staff of engineers since these people are difficult to locate and hire and will not return if laid off. Accordingly, a reasonable capacity management solution for many services firms is to keep a core staff on hand at all times to handle the minimum level of expected demand and outsource the surplus to a supplier, thereby avoiding the problem of ramping up capacity to meet sudden surges in demand.

PROBLEMS WITH CAPACITY MANAGEMENT

The analysis of capacity thus far sounds something like a game of swapping assets in and out of a company if the supporting analysis dictates such changes. The reality is somewhat different, for there are several operational issues that keep an organization from constantly reshuffling its assets.

One such problem is the age of the existing base of equipment. If it is very old, it is more likely to break down than newer machinery. When this is the case, it is wise to retain a few extra machines that would not normally be needed because the company may need to shift production capacity to the extra machines if the primary machines break down. Thus, a set of old equipment calls for some additional capacity, even though a capacity analysis may reveal that there is excess capacity on hand. To see if this is a problem, the capacity analysis can include the age of each piece of equipment, as well as the hours of maintenance downtime, in each reporting period.

Another problem with trying to incrementally shrink capacity levels to closely match current usage is that this approach does not allow for any prospective increase in sales. By reducing capacity a company effectively keeps itself from growing. For example, if a new customer suddenly appears with an immediate order, a company with strictly controlled capacity will not be able to complete the order and so will lose the customer. For this reason tight capacity control is not a key strategy to pursue for a company experiencing strong revenue growth. However, it may be quite applicable for companies experiencing declining sales or locked into industries where there are significant long-term cyclic swings in the level of demand.

Yet another issue is that selling off capacity may result in a significant accounting loss on sale of assets. This problem occurs when a company's depreciation method is not expensing off an asset as rapidly as its actual value is declining on the open market. The cost accountant is then faced with the difficult choice of recommending that a nonperforming asset be kept to avoid reporting a loss or that it be sold to gain the resulting cash, but having to accept the loss at the same time.

An increasingly common problem with capacity management is that companies are no longer faced with simple replacement of the oldest machinery but also with replacement of the largest, most efficient machines with smaller, more flexible ones. This change is caused by the increasing use of just-in-time manufacturing layouts, which force an organization to replace its large, efficient machines that require lengthy setups and long run times with much smaller machines that are easier to configure and move (see Chapter 17 for more information about just-in-time). This change in philosophy means that one can no longer peruse a capacity report and simply recommend elimination of the oldest machine on the list if there is excess capacity. Instead, one must review the situation with the production manager and industrial engineers to see if they want to reconfigure the facility for JIT production, which may require retention of the oldest machine and replacement of a newer one that does not fit into their floor layout plans.

A final issue is that equipment capacity is not a fixed figure. By making a variety of production scheduling and related changes, one can increase a production facility's actual level of capacity. For example, when a company runs a large number of small production jobs through its equipment, an inordinate amount of its available production time is consumed by machine setups and teardowns. By accepting only larger production runs or by concentrating employee attention on the reduction of machine setup times, the time taken up by this activity can be reduced, thereby giving a company more production capacity than it had before even though it has not added any equipment. Another way to improve capacity is to implement a schedule of preventive maintenance so that machines do not break down. The same approach can be taken to the pre-positioning of materials near machines in order to ensure that the production run is not stopped for lack of raw materials. All these techniques can result in an increase in a facility's capacity.

Given the number of issues pointed out here, it is readily apparent that a cost accountant cannot just compile the monthly capacity report, examine it, and immediately recommend the elimination or purchase of assets in order to bring actual production use in line with available capacity. Instead, she must investigate a number of related issues in detail, such as the age of the equipment, the maintenance history of each machine, any planned shift toward a JIT manufacturing environment, expected changes in sales volume, planned scheduling and management techniques that may change the level of reported capacity, and the amount of depreciation taken on each machine. To obtain this level of additional knowledge requires someone who is intimately familiar with the production process and who has regular conversations with all members of the management team involved in sales forecasts, production forecasts, and engineering changes in the facility. These requirements point toward the need for a great deal of experience in the cost accounting position when changes in capacity are contemplated.

CASE STUDY

Ms. Emily North is a cost accountant working for the General Research and Instrumentation Company. She regularly monitors the use of production equipment at the company's various facilities and notes that the capacity utilization level of the Boston plant's assembly department has been consistently low for the last 6 months. The department uses five automated assembly machines, which are noted in Exhibit 25.6.

From the information in the exhibit, it is apparent to Ms. North that the operation has far too much equipment on hand for its available workload and that she should recommend that some of it be sold off. Based on the basic principle of eliminating old equipment first, she assumes that she will recommend the sale of the

EXHIBIT 25.6. Sample Capacity Utilization Percentages at the GRIN Company

Description	Year of Purchase	June	May	Apr.	Mar.	Feb.	Jan.
Whitby 100	1995	20	40	30	35	25	18
Warner F-100	1992	5	10	0	8	4	0
Mod 215	2001	75	73	75	74	62	75
Whitby 200	2000	60	55	40	50	29	45
Warner F-350	1999	85	80	90	82	86	90
Average		**49**	**52**	**47**	**50**	**41**	**46**

Whitby 100 and Warner F-100 machines, which are the oldest and least-utilized equipment in the department.

She then travels to the Boston facility and interviews the sales manager, Mr. Drew Jarvis, regarding any possible changes in sales volume that could require more equipment use in the assembly department. He states that this is not an issue and that the product assembled by that department is one with a long history of steady sales levels spread over several dozen customers—it is the epitome of consistent sales. So far, her initial recommendation appears to be the correct one.

During her walk through the plant to reach her next appointment, at the office of the industrial engineer, Mr. Harvey Drexler, she notes that the inventory levels of finished assembled products appear to be extremely high. At her subsequent interview Mr. Drexler affirms that inventory levels for that department have always been high because of the number of product variations offered for sale—the company cannot guess exactly which features will be ordered, so it keeps large stocks of all items on hand at all times. This has become a major concern for the plant manager, who has $2 million invested in the inventory. The manager has instructed Mr. Drexler to find a new production method that will eliminate some of the inventory. He has chosen the just-in-time methodology to achieve this, which involves short production runs and quick setups. He produces a report that reveals the following setup information about each of the five machines in the assembly department:

Machine	Average Setup Time
Whitby 100	15 min
Warner F-100	15 min
Mod 215	2.0 hr
Whitby 200	1.0 hr
Warner F-350	4.5 hr

Ms. North compares her chart of capacity utilization by machine and the list of average setup times and realizes that the Warner F-350, which has the longest setup time, is the most highly utilized machine in the department. This makes no sense to her, for a true JIT manager would want to run jobs through the machines with the shortest setup times. This supposition is valid, explained Harvey, but there is a significant difference in the mix of jobs entering the department. Approximately one-half of the assembly jobs are large enough to require long production runs and are direct orders from customers, so it is acceptable to run them on the most efficient machines, the Mod 215 and the Warner F-350.

There appeared to be a good opportunity to meld her recommendation for a reduction in machinery with the plant manager's goal of reducing inventory levels—but to be sure of her recommendation, she walked to the warehouse and asked for a list of all the items currently in the assembly department's inventory, along with the extended cost of each item. Ms. North took this report to the production scheduling department and reviewed the largest dollar items with the schedulers. She found that the items that had piled up in inventory were those produced by the machines with shorter setup times, rather than those with longer setups. She investigated the items that had been scheduled in the past 6 months for the long-setup machines and found that few of them were still retained in inventory. Based on all the information collected so far, she had no grounds for recommending the sale of the Mod 215 or the Warner F-350. But which of the remaining three machines should be eliminated?

With her inventory report in hand, Ms. North returned to the sales manager to discuss which products were sold as soon as they were assembled and which were built to stock. Mr. Jarvis agreed with her previous discovery that the largest assembly jobs were sold directly to customers, resulting in little on-hand inventory. He noted, however, that this was not the case for small production runs of specialty items, for the company had a specific strategy of charging high prices for the quick delivery of these items to customers. Accordingly, most products were assembled, stored, and then sent by overnight express mail to customers as soon as they were ordered. The markup on these sales was roughly 150%. Clearly, this was a strategy that yielded significant profits, but at the price of a large investment in inventory.

Ms. North pondered these conflicting issues over lunch and decided that the key issue was that the company needed to keep machines with short setup times in order to respond to customer demands as quickly as possible. Of the three machines still under consideration for elimination, this meant that she should recommend keeping the two oldest machines, because of their short setup times, and instead eliminate the Whitby 200 machine, which had a setup period of 1 hour. Because it was sandwiched between the two strategies of quick setups (adequately filled by the quick-setup machines) and longer-term, high-efficiency production runs (now filled by the Mod 215 and Warner F-350 machines), it could not be well utilized despite being the second *newest* machine in the department.

To test her recommendation Ms. North traveled to the order entry department and requested a list of customer orders that required overnight delivery. The volume was consistently in the range of 10 orders per day, with a maximum order volume over the past 6 months of 16 orders. None of the orders required more than a 30-minute production run. A quick calculation revealed that for 16 orders the setup time on the short-setup machines was 4 hours per day, with a maximum production run time of 8 hours. This meant that the two machines combined could easily handle all prospective sales volume under the JIT approach and could do so during one shift per day. Because of their advanced age, it made sense to retain both machines in case one machine broke down and required a backup.

For verification of her recommendation, Ms. North spoke briefly with the maintenance foreman, who assured her that there was a sufficient history of breakdown with the older machines to require the retention of a backup machine. The industrial engineer, Mr. Drexler, also approved of her recommendation, which she then took to the plant manager, who promptly sold off the Whitby 200 machine, thereby reducing the company's asset base by $200,000.

A key point in this case study was the number of contacts the cost accountant made before making her recommendation. She visited the sales manager, industrial engineer, production scheduling staff, warehouse staff, order entry staff, and maintenance foreman, before arriving at a solution—one that was different from her first expectation. The decision to change a company's equipment base is one that requires significant investigation and frequently results in a different resolution than what one might expect without first gaining input from a number of functional areas within a company.

SUMMARY

In this chapter we saw how the type of method selected to apportion the cost of capacity to products can have a significant impact on reported levels of profitability, and we also noted how the same issue can skew the reported break-even level for a product, product line, or company. Further, capacity reporting can alter the cost basis on which prices are set, which in turn can alter the levels of profitability and cash flow. Thus, it is apparent that appropriate use of the correct capacity costing method is critical to the understanding of managers who must use this information to manage the level of production capacity, as well as capacity of other types throughout the organization.

CHAPTER 26

Impact of Manufacturing Resources Planning on Cost Accounting

In this chapter we present a brief overview of the manufacturing resources planning system and then consider its impact on the accounting and measurement systems a cost accountant uses, as well as on product costs. Because the MRP II system is a widely used one, this information is applicable to the work of many cost accountants.

DESCRIPTION OF THE MRP II SYSTEM

The MRP II system was a gradual development of computer systems designed to bring the advantages of computerization to the manual manufacturing systems in existence prior to the 1960s. It began with the creation of databases that tracked inventory. This information had historically been tracked with manually updated index cards or some similar device and was highly prone to error. By shifting it to a computer system, companies could make it available to the purchasing department, where it could be readily consulted when determining how many additional parts to purchase. In addition, the data could now be easily sorted and sifted to see which items were being used the most (and the least) and which yielded valuable information about which inventory should be kept in stock and which should be discarded.

The purchasing staff now had better information about the amount of inventory on hand but did not know what quantities of materials were going to be used without making a series of tedious manual calculations. To alleviate this problem the MRP II system progressed another step by incorporating a production schedule and a bill of materials for every item listed on it. This was an immense step forward, for then the computer system could multiply the number of units listed on the production schedule by the number of component parts for each item, as listed on the bills of material, and arrive at the quantities that had to be purchased in order to meet production requirements. Prior to placing orders for more materials, this total amount of purchases was netted against the available inventory to see if anything in stock could be used. The lead times for the purchase of each part were also incorporated into the computer system so that it could determine for the purchasing staff the exact dates on which orders for parts must be placed. This new level of automation was called material requirements planning (MRP), since (as the name implies) it revealed the exact quantities and types of materials needed to run a production operation.

However, the computer programmers were not done yet. As the 1960s gave way to the next decade, the MRP system evolved into the manufacturing resources planning (MRP II) system. This newer version contained all the elements of the old MRP system along with several new features. One was the use of labor routings, which itemized the exact amounts of labor required to complete a product and identified the machines on which this work must be done. By multiplying labor routings by the production quantities listed on the production schedule, the computer system could report on the number of laborers required for a production facility for each day of production and even itemize the skill classifications needed. This was of great assistance in planning head-count requirements for the production floor. Of even greater importance was the use of the same information to determine the capacity use of each machine in the facility. When the MRP II system revealed that the scheduled production would result in a machine overload in any part of the plant, the production schedulers could reshuffle the schedule to shift work to other machines, thereby avoiding bottlenecks that would keep the company from meeting its production targets. The main features of the MRP II system are shown in Exhibit 26.1.

This capacity planning feature was of particular concern as the attention of companies shifted from simple material planning to ensuring that customers received their shipments on the promised dates. By verifying in advance that customer orders would be completed on time, there was no longer any last-minute scrambling to ship out orders for which there was no available machine time. Another benefit was that customers could be told at or near the time of order placement when their orders would be shipped. Also, if problems of any kind arose, the computer system notified the production planners, who could reschedule customer orders and tell customers as far in advance as possible of changes in their shipping dates. All these

EXHIBIT 26.1. Flow of Information in an MRP II System

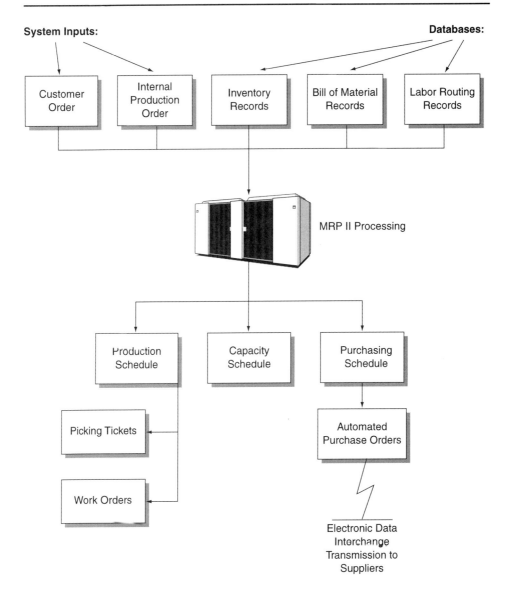

changes led to a major advance in the levels of customer service that companies could offer.

Though this is an extremely abbreviated description of MRP II, it touches on the highlights of how the system functions and what kinds of results are obtained by using it. The underlying software is exceedingly complex and requires lengthy hands-on training and course work to fully understand. However, the basic operating principles are the same, no matter what type of software is used, so expert MRP II practitioners do not have great difficulty in learning new MRP II software packages.

STRATEGIC AND TACTICAL IMPORTANCE OF THE MRP II SYSTEM

The MRP II system is essentially an enormous scheduling tool. It was originally intended to bring structure to the chaos of the manufacturing floor, which it certainly has done in many cases. However, the system was designed to track and plan for *existing* manufacturing practices rather than to attempt to impose a new production methodology on a company. As a result, the same old methods of production still underlie the system—only now everyone knows exactly how these inefficient methods work and can plan around them. The MRP II system still allows suppliers to ship in low-quality goods, requires periodic quality inspection points, allows work in process to build up, scrap to occur, and machines to have excessively long setup times—all factors that are directly addressed and reduced by the just-in-time manufacturing methodology. Consequently, the MRP II system is much more of a tactical weapon for a company than a strategic one—it does not allow an organization to make great improvements in cost reduction or invested capital, though it can certainly allow it to improve inventory turnover to a significant degree and leads to a much smoother production process.

For an overview of a system that has much more dramatic results and can alter a company's strategic positioning, see Chapter 27 for a discussion of the JIT system.

IMPORTANCE OF DATABASES IN AN MRP II SYSTEM

The foundation of the MRP II system is the three databases that feed it information. The most important is the bill of materials database. It contains a separate record for each product manufactured, with each record itemizing the exact quantities of components as well as their standard anticipated scrap rates. If there are large subassemblies, they are usually listed in a separate record and only referenced in the main record; this practice keeps bills down to a tolerably short length. The bill of materials database is the driving force behind the material requirements planning portion of the MRP II system, and so its accuracy is of the highest importance. An accuracy level of 98% is generally considered the bare minimum that allows the MRP II system to generate accurate information. To attain such a high level, access to the database is closely guarded, and the engineering, purchasing, and production staffs are actively encouraged to warn of problems originating from it. Without a sufficient level of accuracy in this database, employees can experience a number of problems with the information produced by the system, such as incorrect or missing purchased quantities that can rapidly lead to production shutdowns caused by missing materials.

The bill of material database is also an outstanding tool for the cost accountant since it contains accurate information about product components. With this information in hand it is usually a simple matter to reference the most current costs for each item and derive a product cost for anything in the database, which can then be used for a variety of variance and margin analyses.

Another key database contains labor routings. Each record in this database includes a detailed list of the exact amount of time each labor position needs to complete a product and usually indicates the required machine time as well. Accuracy levels in this database are expected to exceed 95%. Some small inaccuracies here cannot bring down a production facility, but work stoppages are occasionally created by inaccurate labor or capacity calculations that cause bottlenecks to arise.

The cost accountant can use the labor information in these records to determine the standard labor cost of each product, which has applications in the reporting of variances and margins. The information in this database is best used in concert with the bill of materials database, since between them they include all the direct costs applied to a product.

The final database is for inventory. It records the exact quantity of all items in stock. Better inventory databases also keep exact track of the use patterns of inventory for several years. Once again, the accuracy level must be extremely high, in the 95% range, or else the system will yield inaccurate reports that can lead to production shutdowns. For example, if the inventory database says there are 10 units of a gasket in stock but there are really only 5, the MRP II system will not place an order for additional gaskets when production is scheduled that calls for 10 gaskets. As a result, the production line uses all 5 remaining gaskets and grinds to a halt because the other 5 are not in stock. The purchasing staff then places a rush order for the extra gaskets to be delivered by expensive overnight mail.

The cost accountant finds that this database is also a gold mine of information, since one can extract from it the last dates when inventory items were used and thereby determine component or product obsolescence. It is also useful for sorting the inventory by total cost (always of concern to auditors), as well as for calculating the amount of inventory on hand (which highlights any excessive ordering practices by the purchasing department).

The key factor to consider here is the high degree of accuracy required of these databases so that the MRP II system can create accurate reports. If any one of them falls short of the highest accuracy standards, the production department will quickly fall into disarray, missing its shipment deadlines. There will also be a great deal of finger-pointing between this department and the purchasing staff since the blame will be placed on the buyers, who are not bringing in the correct parts at the right time or in the correct quantities—however, the real culprit is the accuracy of the databases, which are skewing the system's outputs. Consequently, the greatest possible attention must be paid to creating and maintaining an exceptional level of accuracy in these databases.

MRP II REPORTS

An MRP II system is capable of creating an enormous number of reports, some of which are useful to a cost accountant. In this section we examine a few reports having the most accounting applicability.

- **Capacity report.** This report lists the prospective utilization level of every piece of machinery in the facility. By tracking this report over time, one can see if there is an excessive amount of capacity in some machines and a shortfall in others, which would lead the cost accountant to recommend changes in the mix of machinery being used.

- **Production variance report.** This report lists the production quantities that were planned but not actually manufactured. It is a good starting point for the cost accountant who is investigating why the facility is not producing planned quantities, though other information is necessary in order to determine the exact causes.

- **Receiving date variance report.** This report notes the dates when components were supposed to have been received from suppliers, the dates when they actually were received, and the time variance. Combining this information with the receiving rejections report, a company can create a comprehensive supplier "report card" that can lead to replacement of the worst suppliers with new ones.

- **Receiving rejections report.** This report reveals all the parts, and the suppliers who provided them, that were rejected at the receiving dock and lists the reasons for rejection. It is an excellent tool for ranking the performance of suppliers.

- **Scrap variance report.** This report itemizes the excess quantities of scrap, by the identifying component number, that have been generated during the production process and which can be used to track down the causes of the scrap.

- **Shop floor variance report.** This report compares the planned quantities that should have been completed by each machine with the actual amounts completed for a specific time period. It is a telling indicator of labor inefficiencies or of planned machine capacity levels that do not match reality.

- **Where used report.** This report itemizes every component part listed in the MRP II database and lists the products in which each one is used. It is particularly valuable when determining which parts are *not* included in any products and hence are subject to disposition in order to reduce the overall investment in inventory.

The MRP II system certainly cannot be accused of generating an insufficient quantity of information for the cost accounting team, as the preceding report list reveals. This system collects and stores information about virtually all the activities in a production facility and so is a gold mine for the cost accountant, who can probably find any kind of information in the MRP II database by probing deeply enough.

IMPACT OF MRP II ON WASTE COSTS

An MRP II system is good at itemizing the waste in a purchasing and production system, but it is up to management to use this information to reduce it. Here are some examples of the types of waste identified by the system:

- **Labor variances.** The system stores inputted information about direct labor used at all stages of the production process and can compare it to the standard labor quantities listed in the system's labor routings to generate variances at every workstation in the production process, which management can use to investigate significant inefficiencies.

- **Late deliveries by suppliers.** The system records all information entered into it from the receiving dock that notes the dates on which suppliers deliver products to the company. The system can compare these actual receipt dates to the requested dates listed on company purchase orders to see if any suppliers consistently deliver late. Management is interested in this information, since late component deliveries can halt a production line.

- **Length of machine setup times.** This information is a basic component of the MRP II database and is required to properly schedule the amount of time needed to switch over to a new production run. By identifying the current length of each setup, management can determine which ones are excessively long and work to shorten them.

- **Part rejections by supplier.** The system records all information entered into it from any point in the production line where supplier parts are rejected, which can be at the receiving dock, at any quality control station, or at various points in the production process. The system can summarize this information for management review so that suppliers with consistently low-quality records can be identified and replaced.

- **Production run lengths.** A production run that is too long generates finished goods inventory that may stay in the warehouse for a long time before being sold. This is a form of waste since a company must invest in the working capital needed to support the extra inventory. One can create a report from the MRP II system itemizing the length of each run, which can be compared to actual finished goods use to see if there are any excessively long production runs that should be shortened in the future.

- **Production variances by machine.** The shop floor reporting module of the MRP II system compares the actual inputs to and outputs from each work center in the production facility, which allows management to home in on the production areas that consistently produce at less than expected levels.

- **Scrap produced by each machine.** The system records any input from the production floor regarding scrapped materials, so that it can schedule additional production to make up for missing products and generate additional supplier purchase orders to bring in extra materials. By reviewing scrap information by work center, managers can determine where there are excessive scrap levels and investigate the underlying causes.

- **Work-in-process quantities.** An excessive amount of work-in-process inventory is a major source of waste since it requires an extra working capital investment to maintain, can contain large amounts of defective parts that may not be discovered for some time, and clogs the production floor. The MRP II system tracks how much of this inventory is located on the shop floor, as well as the amounts of it that are scrapped for various reasons, which allows management to pinpoint the areas in the production flow where inventory tends to build up and where low-quality parts are being produced.

Management can use all this information to reduce or eliminate waste from the production system. However, this activity is totally up to the management team, for there is no component of the MRP II system that forces an organization to improve itself. The system merely works with the existing production inefficiencies.

IMPACT OF MRP II ON DIRECT COSTS

Since it is an excellent scheduling tool, the reports available through an MRP II system tell management whether it has a surplus or a shortage of direct labor staff on hand to deal with the scheduled production, and it can reveal this information for as far forward into the future as there is a production schedule listed in the computer system. Given this information, management can more closely tailor its staffing needs to actual requirements, which will result in a reduction in the direct labor cost. However, in companies where a large proportion of the direct labor staff is kept on the payroll even if there is not enough work (generally because they are too highly skilled to let go), this additional information does not result in a labor cost reduction. Also, the MRP II system requires considerable data recording at a multitude of points throughout the facility (to trace material movements, as well as to record labor time use); because this extra recording activity is usually done by the direct labor staff, it can reduce their overall level of productivity. Thus, the impact of this system on direct labor costs is somewhat muted in most cases.

The MRP II system does not have a direct impact on the cost of materials charged to a product, for it only allows for tighter control over the purchasing and scheduled movement of materials through a facility, as opposed to actively reducing the amount used. However, it is helpful in reducing the occasional expensing of obsolete inventory to cost of goods sold, for it gives the purchasing staff much better control over the amounts of materials purchased so that fewer materials tend to pile up in the warehouse. Also, its scrap reporting capabilities can be used by management to reduce overall scrap levels, which can eventually bring about a reduction in direct material costs. Nonetheless, the impact of MRP II on material costs is not clearly identifiable or is quite small and delayed in its effect.

In short, the total impact of the MRP II system on direct costs tends to be minor unless there is an extraordinary amount of wasted direct labor that can be scheduled out of a production operation. The main benefits of MRP II tend to lie elsewhere than in direct costs.

IMPACT OF MRP II ON OVERHEAD COSTS

To understand the impact of MRP II on overhead costs, it is important to first understand the types of activities that go on in a less structured environment. For example, with no control over the quantities or types of products being manufactured, there are numerous expediters who walk specific jobs through the production process, shunting aside other work in favor of the jobs they are shepherding. Also, there are extra purchasing employees who constantly call suppliers to alter the priority level of deliveries to be shipped, as well as to alter their size as production requirements constantly shift. In addition, there are costs associated with the management of large amounts of excess inventory, such as warehouse and materials handlers, supervisors and staff, storage racks, forklifts, damage to products, obsolescence, insurance coverage for inventory, overhead fire suppression systems, and repair to products damaged while in storage. These are significant costs that make up a large proportion of inventory.

When an MRP II system is installed, production expediters are banned from the shop floor, while the work of the purchasing staff is reduced to the daily monitoring of automated purchasing reports. Further, the just-enumerated overhead costs of inventory decline in direct proportion to the amount of inventory reduction achieved by using the system. These are significant reductions in overhead costs and are sometimes enough to justify an MRP II purchase and installation without even reviewing any other cost savings.

IMPACT OF MRP II ON WORKING AND FIXED CAPITAL REQUIREMENTS

By using an MRP II system a company can attain a much higher level of control over its purchases of raw materials since the system tells buyers when to buy parts and in what quantities. This is an improvement over a manufacturing process that has no such scheduling system. Consequently, the raw materials portion of a company's inventory balance declines after an MRP II system is installed, which represents a significant drop in the level of working capital invested in the business.

Also, the shop floor scheduling system within the MRP II software tells machine operators exactly what components to produce and when to do so, which prevents work-in-process inventories from accumulating. This is a considerable improvement over the typical shop floor, where machine operators frequently produce the wrong parts or the wrong quantities, resulting in an excessive amount of inventory. Thus, the level of work-in-process inventory also drops, which reduces the level of investment in working capital.

An MRP II system has no direct impact on the level of fixed asset investment in a company since it is designed to work with whatever equipment is currently installed. However, its capacity planning system informs managers if there is any equipment that is severely underutilized; these machines can then be eliminated, or the work done on them can be outsourced. This additional step is a management decision and falls outside the normal workings of an MRP II system, but at least the information it provides can lead to better capital investment decisions.

IMPACT OF MRP II ON PRODUCT PRICES

Companies that install an MRP II system have much better control over their ability to ship products in the quantities and on the dates that customers demand. They are also able to contact customers well in advance if the system indicates that a product will not be shipped on its previously projected date. Both these capabilities allow a company to provide better service to its customers. If the current service level in an industry is relatively low, this capability may be worth a price premium to customers. However, if a company has installed MRP II merely to keep pace with its competitors, the higher level of customer service will only keep its competitive capabilities level with those of its opposition, and so it will not be able to increase its prices.

After installing MRP II a company's inventory levels should drop substantially, reducing a number of inventory-related costs. When a company sees its costs drop, it has the option of reducing its prices to pick up additional business since it can now absorb the price decline and still maintain healthy margins.

PERFORMANCE MEASUREMENTS IN AN MRP II SYSTEM

Given the large amount of information created and stored by an MRP II system, the cost accountant has access to a particularly rich set of data from which to obtain performance measurements of various types. In this section we explore the most common and useful measurements for this system. They are:

- **Bill of material accuracy.** The most important database that drives the calculations of the MRP II system is the one containing all bill of materials records. To ensure that this database contains accurate information, the cost accountant should regularly measure its accuracy. This can be done by taking a sample of the bills and comparing them to actual material requirements. Any inaccuracies, such as in quantities, missing components, or units of measure, are counted as errors.

- **Inventory accuracy.** Another database needed by the MRP II system is one containing the quantities and types of inventory currently in stock. Because of its importance, the cost accountant may be called on to measure its accuracy as frequently as once a week. This is done by taking a sample of the inventory records and tracing them back to the physical items in the warehouse, noting any location, quantity, description, or unit-of-measure inaccuracies as errors. It is also important to take a sample of items in warehouse bins and trace them back to the database, to guard against missing records. If found, such inaccuracies should also be recorded as errors.

- **Labor routings accuracy.** The final database needed to run an MRP II system contains the labor routing records; to ensure that the system runs properly, one should determine the accuracy of these routings at least once a month. This can be done by taking a sample of routing records and comparing them to actual activity within the plant—this means that only records for which there is actual activity at the time of the review can be examined.

- **Number of expedited jobs.** A properly functioning MRP II system contains only work orders that march through the production facility in perfect lockstep. If there are any expedited jobs in the system, it is because there has been an MRP II system failure. Consequently, it is worthwhile to determine not only the number of these jobs but also the specific reasons why they are being processed. A production manager should take a dim view of expediting activity since it seriously disrupts an MRP II system.

- **Number of schedule changes.** A properly maintained MRP II system freezes the production schedule as it gets close to the date of actual production so that the purchasing staff has a sufficient amount of time to buy all the necessary parts. However, when there are many schedule changes, it is difficult to bring in materials in a timely manner. Consequently, this measure should be based on the changes in the production schedule inside the scheduling date on which material deliveries will be impacted (a date that varies by industry).

- **Percentage of delivery releases with full lead time.** An MRP II system is theoretically capable of scheduling 100% of all production work so that all deliveries are made to customers on the dates originally promised. However, difficulties sometimes arise that cause shipments to be missed. Since these problems directly impact customers, a discerning manager requires a detailed rendering of the specific deliveries that were late, as well as the reasons why, which should be included in this report.

- **Supplier delivery performance.** Production cannot take place if suppliers do not deliver the correct quantities of high-quality parts in a timely manner. To measure the ability of suppliers to do so, the receiving staff must track the number of parts rejected at the receiving dock for each supplier, as well as the dates on which deliveries are made (and hopefully entered into a central computer database for ease of access). The cost accountant can then summarize the data into a report card showing the performance of each supplier. This measurement can be used to see if some suppliers should be replaced with more reliable ones.

- **Work center input/output versus target.** An MRP II system may have been supplied with data about the ability of each work center to perform work at a certain rate. If this information is inaccurate, the system will schedule an amount of work that is either too high or low. To keep this from happening, the cost accountant can summarize information in the MRP II database to determine the scheduled and actual production for each machine, which can then be used to follow up with machine operators in regard to their efficiency or to adjust the capacity data used by the MRP II system to schedule machines.

None of the measurements described here are directly related to the costs of products, so the information revealed is somewhat outside the usual cost accountant's area of familiarity. Nonetheless, an MRP II system runs properly only if certain data inputs and activities are maintained or conducted properly, so the cost accountant must examine and report on these items to ensure that management knows if there are problems with its MRP II system.

COST-BENEFIT CASE STUDY ON MRP II

In this section we review a case study that itemizes the costs and benefits to be obtained by installing an MRP II system. As usual, we use for our study the General Research and Instrumentation Company. The person in charge of reviewing the switch to this system is Ms. Alice Weatherly, who runs the purchasing department. Because of the significant benefits to be enjoyed by her department if the system is installed, Ms. Weatherly has volunteered for the assignment. She first determines the cost of an MRP II system and its installation. After an extensive review she finds that the cost of a midrange system that could run on the company's existing mini-computer is about $400,000. (Note: Larger firms must budget several times this amount if they need to purchase software that incorporates all possible options and can be used for multiple locations, thousands of products, and more than a million component parts, such as that provided by Oracle, J. D. Edwards, and SAP.) Ms. Weatherly also knows that the installation cost of the system (which includes extensive staff training) typically costs five times more than the software. Consequently, she budgets $2,400,000 for the MRP II system.

Ms. Weatherly must now see if there are sufficient benefits to offset these costs. First, she determines that the current inventory turnover rate of two times per year can be improved to eight times by using the system. She gathers this information by talking to the references provided by the software supplier. Next she itemizes the overhead costs associated with inventory, such as insurance, extra staffing, facility storage space, and obsolescence, and decides that this cost is about 10% of the total inventory value. (Note: Some studies have shown that this cost is actually closer to 25% of the inventory valuation.) Another study reveals that one purchasing agent is currently needed for each $4,000,000 of cost of goods sold, but that automated purchasing will cut this number in half when the MRP II system is installed. A typical buyer is paid $60,000 per year. Also, she finds that the amount of direct labor should drop by 10% as a result of better production scheduling and manning; the current annual direct labor cost is $1,000,000. Knowing that the current cost of goods sold is $16,000,000 and that the company borrows money at the prime rate, which is currently 9%, she is now in a position to calculate the cost savings shown in Exhibit 26.2.

According to the exhibit, costs appear to go *up* as a result of buying the MRP II system. However, we have been mixing apples and oranges in the analysis, for a one-time purchasing and installation cost is being offset by the resulting cost savings for only the first year. Ms. Weatherly realizes that a more appropriate analysis is the one shown in Exhibit 26.3, where she itemizes all costs and benefits over a 4-year period and uses a discount factor of 10%, based on the corporate cost of capital, to arrive at a current period net present value for the entire project that does a better job of comparing costs with benefits.

By itemizing expenses and cost savings over a period of years and then factoring in the time value of money (e.g., the "Discount factor" line item), Ms. Weatherly arrives at a different outcome, which is that the MRP II installation shows a positive cash flow of $1,700,000 over a 4-year period. Note that this analysis also shows an extra expense that did not appear in the first exhibit because it is incurred only in subsequent years—namely, a 15% annual software maintenance fee charged by the software supplier. Because MRP II software has a good track record for being usable for many years, a company can extend this analysis out for a num-

EXHIBIT 26.2. Cost-Benefit Calculation for the Purchase of an MRP II System

Cost Type	Incremental Cost Changes with an MRP II System	Calculation Notes
Cost of software	+400,000	Software purchase price
Cost of implementation	+2,000,000	Five times the software purchase price is the estimated installation cost
Direct labor cost	−100,000	Current direct labor cost of $1,000,000, reduced by 10%
Buyer salaries	−120,000	50% reduction in the number of buyers, times $60,000 per person
Interest expense	−540,000	Improvement in inventory turns from 2 times to 8 times results in an inventory reduction of $6,000,000, times the 9% prime interest rate
Overhead expenses	−600,000	Improvement in inventory turns from 2 times to 8 times results in an inventory reduction of $6,000,000, times 10% (which equates to the corresponding drop in related overhead costs)
Net change in costs	+1,040,000	

ber of additional years and still be reasonably confident that the associated benefits will still be available well into the future. Accordingly, one can conclude that purchasing an MRP II system can be easily justified by using the analysis format presented in this section.

An interesting issue is that many companies do not bother with a cost-benefit analysis at all, or give it only the most cursory attention, because they are in such a poor competitive position without the system that they simply *must* buy it. They cannot effectively compete without it because of snarled purchasing, production, and delivery problems, and so make a rush decision to install it right away and worry about the cost consequences later. This is not a recommended approach because a company may opt to buy a software package that is so much more expensive than the one used in this analysis that the associated benefits do not cover the cost. It is better to at least determine the expected benefits and then verify that a software package exists that does not offset the sum total of the benefits.

EXHIBIT 26.3. Net Present Value Calculation for an MRP II System Purchase

Cost Type	Initial ($)	Year 1 ($)	Year 2 ($)	Year 3 ($)	Year 4 ($)
Cost of software	+400,000				
Cost of implementation	+2,000,000				
Annual maintenance fee		+60,000	+60,000	+60,000	+60,000
Direct labor cost	−100,000	−100,000	−100,000	−100,000	
Buyer salaries	−120,000	−120,000	−120,000	−120,000	
Interest expense	−540,000	−540,000	−540,000	−540,000	
Overhead expense	−600,000	−600,000	−600,000	−600,000	
Annual subtotal	+2,400,000	−1,300,000	−1,300,000	−1,300,000	−1,300,000
Discount factor[a]	**0.0000**	**0.9091**	**0.8264**	**0.7513**	**0.6830**
Annual net present value	+2,400,000	−1,181,830	−1,074,320	−976,690	−887,900
Total net present value	−1,720,740				

[a]Uses a 10% discount rate.

SUMMARY

The cost accountant must be cognizant of several key factors when using an MRP II system. One is that it is primarily a scheduling tool for all aspects of the production process—it does not purport to alter the underlying system, only to place tighter controls over it. Because of the need for accurate information to make the system work, the cost accountant's main focus in using this system is to measure the accuracy of the data going into and flowing through it, as well as the resulting outputs. Management is interested in finding sources of inaccurate data and fixing them, so the accountant must find this data and report it. Finally, the MRP II system is rich in data, for it is capable of tracing every production job from the point where it arrives at the receiving dock, travels through individual workstations, and is shipped out of the warehouse; this massive database allows the cost accountant to extract almost any type of data imaginable and convert it to a wide range of analyses that can further management's understanding of the flow of costs through the system.

A completely different approach to the production system is the active reduction of waste by altering the underlying system, which is covered in Chapter 27.

CHAPTER 27

Impact of Just-in-Time Systems on Cost Accounting

A just-in-time system is actually a collection of ideas that streamline a company's production activities to such an extent that waste of all kinds (time, material, and labor) is systematically driven out of the process. When completely implemented and used properly, JIT has a decisive, positive impact on product costs. In this chapter we review the various components of the JIT system and then delve into how its use impacts a variety of different costs, capital investments, and measurements. We complete the chapter with a case study that shows the extent to which costs change when a JIT system is used.

DESCRIPTION OF JUST-IN-TIME SYSTEMS

A JIT system has a number of subcomponents, which are described in this section. A complete JIT system begins with production at supplier facilities, includes deliveries to a company's production facilities, continues through the manufacturing plant, and even includes the types of transactions processed by the accounting system.

To begin, a company must ensure that it receives products from its suppliers on the exact date and at the exact time when they are needed. For this reason the purchasing staff must investigate and evaluate every supplier, eliminating those that do not measure up to the exacting delivery standards that will now be used. In addition, deliveries are sent straight to the production floor for immediate use in manufactured products, so there is no time to inspect incoming parts for defects. Instead, the engineering staff must visit supplier sites and examine their processes, not only to see if they can reliably ship high-quality parts but also to provide them with engineering assistance to bring them up to a higher standard of product quality.

Once suppliers have been certified for their delivery and product quality, a company must install a notification system, which may be as simplistic as a fax machine or as advanced as an electronic data interchange system or linked computer systems, that tells suppliers exactly how much of which parts to send to the company. Drivers then bring small deliveries of product to the company, possibly going to the extreme of dropping them off at the specific machines that will use them first. So far, we have described a process that vastly reduces the amount of raw materials inventory and improves the quality of received parts.

Next, we shorten the setup times for company machinery. In most factories equipment is changed over to new configurations as rarely as possible because the conversion is both lengthy and expensive. When setups take a long time, company management authorizes long production runs, which spreads the cost of the setup over far more units, thereby reducing the setup cost on a per-unit basis. However, with this approach too many products are frequently made at one time, resulting in product obsolescence, inventory carrying costs, and many defective products (because problems may not be discovered until a large number of items have already been completed). A JIT system takes a different approach to the setup issue, focusing instead on reducing the length of equipment setups and thereby eliminating the need for long production runs to reduce per-unit costs. To do this a videotape is made of a typical setup, and then a team of industrial engineers and machine users examine the tape, spotting and gradually eliminating steps that contribute to a lengthy setup. It is not unusual, after a number of iterations, to achieve setup times of minutes or seconds when the previous setup times were well into hours. By taking this step a company reduces the amount of work in process, while also shrinking the number of products that can be produced before defects are identified and fixed, thereby reducing scrap costs.

It is not sufficient to reduce machine setup times because there are still problems with machines not being coordinated properly so that there is a smooth, streamlined flow of parts from machine to machine. In most companies there is such a large difference between the operating speeds of different machines that work-in-process inventory builds up in front of the slowest ones. Not only does this create an excessive quantity of work-in-process inventory, but defective parts produced by an upstream machine may not be discovered until the next downstream machine operator works his way through a pile of work in process and finds them. By the time this happens the upstream machine may have created more defective parts, all of which must now be destroyed or reworked. There are two ways to resolve both problems. The first involves a "kanban card,"[1] which is a notification card that a downstream machine sends to each machine that feeds it parts, authorizing the production of just enough components to fulfill the production requirements being authorized in turn by the next machine further downstream. This is also known as a "pull" system, since kanbans are initiated at the *end* of the production process, pulling work authorizations through the production system. With this approach, there is no way for work-in-process inventory to build up in the production system, since it can be created only with a kanban authorization.

The second way to reduce excessive work-in-process inventory and defective parts is to configure machines into work cells. A work cell is a small cluster of machines that can be run by a single machine operator. This individual takes each part from machine to machine within the cell, so there is no way for work in process to build up between machines. Also, since the operator can immediately see if a part is defective, it is difficult for anything but a perfect product to be created by such a machine layout. This configuration has the additional benefit of lower maintenance costs since the smaller machines used in a machine cell are generally much simpler than the large, automated machinery they replace. Also, because the new machines are so small, it is much easier to reconfigure the production facility when it comes time to produce different products, avoiding the large expense of carefully repositioning and aligning equipment.

Both kanbans and machine cells should be used together—they are not mutually exclusive. By doing so a company can achieve extremely low product defect rates, as well as vanishingly small investments in work-in-process inventory.

Before the preceding steps are completed, it becomes apparent that a major change must also be made in the workforce. The traditional approach is to have one employee maintain one machine, which is so monotonous that workers quickly lapse into apathy and develop a complete disregard for the quality of their work. Now, with full responsibility for a number of machines, as well as product quality, workers become much more interested in what they are doing. To enhance this situation the human resources staff must prepare and implement training classes that teach employees how to operate a multitude of different machines, perform limited maintenance on the machines without having to call in the maintenance staff, spot product errors, understand how the entire system flows, and when to halt the production process to fix problems. In short, the workforce must be completely retrained and focused on a wide range of activities. This usually results in a reconfiguration of the compensation system as well, because the focus of attention shifts away from performance based on high production volumes and in the direction of performance based on high product quality.

A major result of having an empowered workforce is that employees are allowed to stop their machines when they see a problem, and either fix it on the spot or immediately call in a repair team. In either case the result is immediate resolution of the bulk of performance problems. This one step has a profound impact on much of the manufacturing variance analysis that cost accountants have been called on to perform for decades. Historically, they compile all kinds of variance information at the end of each month, investigate problems in detail, and then present a formal problem analysis report to management a few weeks after the end of the month. However, because the production staff resolved the underlying issues within a few minutes of their occurrence, the variance report becomes a complete waste of time. Management no longer cares what happened a month in the past because it is presently dealing with current problems that will not appear on cost accountant reports for weeks to come. In short, the quick response capabilities of a JIT system allow the cost accountant to omit a large amount of the variance reporting that was previously such a central job function.

Finally, the massive changes caused by the switch to a JIT system also require several alterations in the supporting accounting systems. Because of the large number of daily supplier shipments, the accounting staff faces the prospect of wading through a large pile of accounts payable paperwork. To make the problem worse there is no receiving paperwork, because the suppliers deliver parts directly to the production operation, so there is no way to determine if deliveries have been made. To avoid the first problem, accountants can switch to making a single consolidated monthly payment to each supplier. The second problem requires a more advanced solution. To prove that a supplier has delivered the part quantities it claims it has, the accounting system can determine the amount of finished products created during the period and then multiply these quantities by the parts listed on the bill of materials for each product, obtaining a total quantity for each part used. The accountants then pay suppliers based on this theoretical production quantity, which is also adjusted for scrap during the production process (otherwise suppliers—unfairly—will not be paid for their parts that are scrapped during the company's production process). This approach also means that there is no need for suppliers to send invoices, since the company relies solely on its internal production records to complete payments.

Clearly, the changes imposed by a JIT system are profound and can greatly improve company operations when installed and operated correctly. They can also have a profound effect on product costs, as explained in the following sections.

IMPACT ON WASTE COSTS

A characteristic of the JIT system is its relentless focus on eliminating all waste from a system. This can be a waste of assets, in the case of unneeded inventory. It can also be a waste of time, in the case of assets that are unused for long periods of time (e.g., work-in-process inventory held in a production queue). It can also be a waste of materials, such as unnecessary levels of obsolete inventory, defective products, rework, and the like. When fully installed, a JIT system vastly reduces all these types of waste. When this happens, there is a sharp drop in several aspects of a product's costs.

For example, by reducing the amount of work in process, machine operators can tell immediately if an incoming part from another workstation is defective and can notify the preceding workstation of the problem before it makes any more parts, which reduces the quantity of rework that must be done. Since a standard quantity of rework labor is frequently included in a product's labor routing, a reduction here lowers the amount of labor cost charged to a product. Similarly, any material that would have been scrapped because of improper rework is no longer lost, so the standard amount of scrap noted on a product's bill of materials can now be reduced. This also decreases a product's cost.

Overhead costs charged to a product also go down as other types of waste decline. For example, by clustering machines into cells, the materials handling costs previously incurred in shifting materials between widely scattered machines can be eliminated. This reduces the amount of materials handling costs that used to be charged to overhead. Also, machine cells tend to reduce the amount of floor space needed since there is no longer a need for large aisles for the materials handling people to drive their forklifts through; by reducing floor space, one can also reduce facility costs, which no longer appear in the overhead cost pool. Another form of waste is the quality inspections once performed on many machines. Under the JIT system machine operators conduct their own quality checks, so there is less need for a separate group of inspectors; accordingly, the cost of their pay can be eliminated from overhead costs. All these costs (and more) do not directly add value to a product, so they are wasteful costs that are subject to elimination. By doing so with a JIT system, there are fewer costs left to charge to a product.

A key focus of any JIT system is on reducing various kinds of wasted time so that the entire production process is concentrated on the time spent actually producing products. For example, all inspection time is stripped from the system by having operators conduct their own quality checks. Similarly, all move time, which involves shifting inventory and work in process throughout various parts of the plant, can be eliminated by clustering machines together in logical groupings. Third, queue time is eliminated by not allowing inventory to build up in front of machines. Finally, one can eliminate storage time by clearing out excess stocks of inventory and having suppliers deliver parts only as needed. By shrinking the amount of wasted time out of the manufacturing process, a company effectively eliminates activities that do not contribute to the value of a product, which in turn reduces the costs associated with them.

Another way in which waste is eliminated in a JIT system is to charge cost drivers to wasteful activities that accumulate costs. For example, overhead costs can be charged out based on the number of components in a product (since more parts require more purchasing activity and materials handling), the number of material moves (which is not a value-added activity), or the number of units scrapped. In this way the cost of these activities becomes apparent to management, and as a result, there will be considerable focus on reducing these cost drivers since the accounting system places so much emphasis on their total burdened costs. Then, when these cost drivers have been reduced to insignificant levels, the cost accountants can find other wasteful cost drivers and shift the allocation system to place the most emphasis on them. This directs management's attention toward their elimination, too. And so on. In this way the cost accounting system can be continually altered so that it has a direct, active role in reducing wasteful activities.

IMPACT ON OVERHEAD COSTS

As just noted, the costs of material handling, facilities, and quality inspection decline when a JIT system is installed. In addition, the reduction of all types of inventory results in a massive shrinkage in the amount of space required for the warehouse facility. Since all costs associated with the warehouse are assigned to the overhead cost pool, the amount of overhead is reduced when the costs of staff, equipment, fixed assets, facilities, and rent associated with the warehouse are sharply cut back.

There is also a shift of costs from the overhead cost pool to direct costs when machine cells are introduced. The reason for this change is that a machine cell generally produces only a small range of products, making it easy to assign the entire cost of each machine cell to these items. This means that the depreciation, maintenance, labor, and utility costs of each cell can be charged straight to a product, which is preferable to the traditional approach of sending these costs to an overhead cost pool from which they are assigned to products in a much less identifiable manner. Though this change does not represent a cost increase or reduction, it *does* increase the reliability of allocation for many more costs than was previously the case.

Despite the shift of many overhead costs to direct costs, there is still an overhead cost pool left over that must be allocated to products. However, given the large number of changes implemented as part of the JIT system, cost accountants may find that there are now better allocation bases available than the traditional direct labor allocation. For example, the amount of time a product spends in each work cell may be a better measure for allocating costs, as may be the amount of space taken up by the work cells that create each product. No matter what allocation system is used, it is somewhat different from the old system, so there is a shift in the allocation of costs between different products.

In short, overhead costs decline as some costs are eliminated, while other costs shift between products as more costs are charged directly to products and the remaining overhead costs are charged out using different allocation methods.

IMPACT ON OTHER COSTS

When a JIT system is created, the amount of inventory retained in a company drops precipitously. Raw materials inventory is reduced because suppliers deliver only small quantities of parts as they are needed. Work-in-process inventory drops because the conversion to machine cells and the use of kanban cards greatly reduces the need to pile up inventory between machines. Finally, finished goods inventory drops because inventory is produced only when there are orders in hand from customers (though finished goods inventories are allowed to build if a company experiences high seasonal sales). Consequently, the cost of maintaining inventory declines, which in turn reduces the overhead costs associated with inventories that are charged to products. Some of these inventory-related costs are:

- Interest cost related to the debt that funds the inventory investment
- Cost of inventory that becomes obsolete over time
- Cost of rent for inventory storage facilities
- Cost of all equipment used in the warehouse
- Cost of warehouse utilities
- Cost of warehouse employees
- Cost of insurance needed to cover the possible loss of inventory
- Cost of taxes on the inventory

Many estimates put the annual cost of inventory at 25% of the total inventory investment. By eliminating inventory a company experiences not only a decline in its inventory investment but also the elimination of all associated costs.

Besides a reduction in the level of working capital and inventory-related costs, a company can also reduce its investment in capital assets. This occurs when a company with a few large machines replaces them with a larger number of much smaller, more easily configured machines. Then, equipment setup times become shorter, which in turn makes it profitable to have shorter production runs, thereby eliminating an excess investment in inventory that would have been created by excessively long production runs. There is frequently a savings to be had when this change occurs, which releases cash for other uses while also reducing the amount of depreciation charged to overhead.

A potentially significant one-time cost that many companies do not consider involves the cost layers in their inventory costing systems. When a JIT system is installed, there is an immediate focus on eliminating inventory of all types. If a company uses some kind of layering method to track the cost of its inventory, such as last-in first-out or first-in first-out, it will find itself burrowing down into costing layers that may have been undisturbed for many years. Then, some unusually high or low costs may be charged off to the cost of goods sold when these inventory items are finally used up. For example, if the current market cost of a piston is $50, but a company has some old (but serviceable) ones in stock from 20 years ago that cost $20, then only the $20 unit cost is charged to the cost of goods sold when these units are finally used as a result of clearing out the inventory. Because of the unusually low cost of goods sold, the gross margin is higher than usual until these early cost layers are eliminated. Because of the lower-of-cost-or-market rule (under which the cost of excessively expensive inventory must be reduced until it is no higher than the current market value), this problem tends to be less of an issue when early cost layers are *too high,* though the costs charged are still somewhat different from those for newer layers of inventory. Once all cost layers have been used up, the only costs that management sees being charged to the cost of goods sold are those currently charged by suppliers.

Thus, the cost reductions and reduced capital requirements of JIT systems have a significant impact on the levels of fixed assets, working capital, and inventory needed to run a business, which in turn reduces the associated overhead costs charged to products.

IMPACT ON PRODUCT PRICES

When a company achieves a higher level of product quality, not to mention an increased ability to deliver products on the dates required, customers may be willing to pay a premium. This is particularly true in industries where quality or delivery reliability is low. If customers are highly sensitive to these two factors, it may be possible to increase prices substantially. Alternatively, if these factors are not of great importance, or if customers place a higher degree of importance on other factors, then there will be no opportunity for a price increase.

In industries where many companies are adopting JIT systems at the same time, or have already installed them, an improvement in product quality and delivery times does not differentiate a company from its peers. Instead, since everyone else is offering the same level of quality and service, it just keeps a company from losing sales to its competitors. In such a situation it is more likely that all companies remaining in the industry will use their new-found lower costs to initiate a price war that will result in a drop in prices.

Consequently, the impact of a JIT system on product pricing is primarily driven by customers' perceived need for higher product quality and reliable delivery times, as well as the presence of competitors with JIT systems, the same installation, and operational base.

JIT COST ALLOCATION DIFFERENCES

The chief difference between the types of cost allocations in a JIT environment and a traditional one is that most overhead costs are converted to direct costs. The primary reason for this change is the machine cell. Because a machine cell is designed to produce either a single product or a single component that goes into a similar product line, all the costs generated by the machine cell can be charged directly to the only product it produces. When a company completely converts to the use of machine cells in all locations, the costs related to all the cells can now be charged directly to products, which leaves few costs of any kind to be allocated through a more traditional overhead cost pool. The result of this change is much more accurate product costs and little debate over where allocated costs should go—since there are not enough of them left to be worth the argument.

Specifically, the costs that can now be charged directly to a product are:

- **Depreciation.** The depreciation cost of each machine in a machine cell can be charged directly to a product. It may be possible to depreciate a machine based on its actual use, rather than charging off a specific amount per month, since this allocation variation shifts costs to a product more accurately.

- **Electricity.** The power used by the machines in a cell can be separately metered and then charged directly to the products that pass through the cell. Any excess electricity cost charged to the facility as a whole still has to be charged to an overhead cost pool for allocation.

- **Material handling.** Most materials handling costs in a JIT system are eliminated since machine operators move parts around within their machine cells. Only costs for materials handling between cells should be charged to an overhead cost pool for allocation.

- **Operating supplies.** Supplies are used mostly within the machine cells, so the majority of items in this expense category can be separately tracked by individual cell and charged to products.

- **Repairs and maintenance.** Nearly all the maintenance costs a company incurs are for machinery, and they are all grouped into machine cells. By having the maintenance staff charge their time and materials to these cells, these costs can be charged straight to products. Only maintenance work on the facility is still charged to an overhead cost pool.

- **Supervision.** If supervision is by machine cell, the cost of the supervisor can be split among the cells supervised. However, the cost of general facility management, as well as of any support staff, must still be charged to an overhead cost pool.

As noted in several of the preceding items, a few remainder costs are still charged to an overhead cost pool for allocation. However, these represent a small percentage of the costs, with nearly everything now being allocable to machine cells. Only building occupancy costs, insurance, and taxes are still charged in full to an overhead cost pool. This is a vast improvement over the amount of money the traditional system allocates to products. A typical overhead allocation pool under the traditional system can easily include 75% of all costs incurred, whereas this figure can be dropped to less than 25% of total costs by switching to a JIT system. With such a higher proportion of direct costs associated with each product, managers then have much more relevant information about the true cost of each product manufactured.

PERFORMANCE MEASUREMENTS IN A JIT SYSTEM

Many of the measurements used in a traditional accounting system are not useful in a JIT environment, while new measures can be implemented that take advantage of the unique characteristics of this system.

One of the key measurements in a traditional system is machine utilization. This is used to ensure that every asset a company purchases is being thoroughly utilized. It is particularly important in cases where there has been a large investment in automation or large, high-speed machinery, since these items are quite expensive and should be used to the utmost. However, making machine utilization a key measurement forces production managers in the direction of manufacturing as much product as possible in order to show a high level of machine utilization, which can result in large amounts of inventory piling up in the warehouse. This is not a desirable end result in a JIT environment, where producing only what is actually needed is the underlying rule. Also, machine cells in a JIT system tend to be smaller and less costly than the highly automated (and expensive) juggernauts used in more traditional systems, so there is less need to justify the investment in these smaller machines by proving that they have been heavily used. In short, machine utilization measurements can be thrown out the back door when JIT comes in the front door.

Another inappropriate measurement is any type of piece rate tracking for each employee. This is a common measure in the textile industry, where employees are paid extra if they exceed certain production volume targets. However, a JIT system focuses on producing only what is needed, so an employee who has incentives to create vast piles of parts is producing contrary to the rules of the system. Accordingly, any piece rate system must be eliminated and replaced with measures that focus instead on the quality of output or the number of employee suggestions for improving the system, which are much more important outcomes in a JIT system.

Any type of direct labor efficiency tracking is highly inappropriate in a JIT system. It is a key measurement in more traditional systems, where employee time and productivity are closely monitored and measured. However, a JIT system does not focus on how fast an employee works—only on the quality of the products manufactured. Also, labor variance measurements require considerable employee time tracking, which forces workers to fill in a time sheet, punch a clock, or use a bar coding system to track what they are doing and what job they are working on. All this labor tracking is a non-value-added activity, which is something a JIT system strives to avoid as an unnecessary activity. Consequently, the cost accounting staff should advocate the complete elimination of all labor variance measurements.

However, installing a JIT system does not mean that there should be a wholesale elimination of variance or operational measures. There are still several measures that are highly relevant to operations. Some of them are:

- **Inventory turnover.** Those who have installed JIT systems emphasize the extraordinarily high inventory turnover that they now experience, which is the case in most instances. The turnover levels of such well-known JIT companies as Toyota have been known to exceed 70 per year, as opposed to the levels of 2 to 10 per year that are more common for companies with other types of manufacturing systems. This measure is best subdivided into smaller parts, so that one can determine the turnover levels for raw materials, work in process, and finished goods.

- **Setup time reduction.** Of great importance is the average setup time per machine, which can be measured periodically and plotted on a trend line. The shortest possible setup intervals are crucial to the success of short production runs, so this is a major JIT measurement. It is best to measure it by machine, rather than in the aggregate, since an aggregate measure does not reveal enough information about which equipment requires more setup time reduction work.

- **Customer complaints.** A JIT system is partly based on the premise that product quality will he superb. Consequently, any hint from customers that there are product problems should be greeted with the gravest concern and investigated immediately. The accumulation of customer complaints and their dissemination to management should be considered a major JIT measure.

- **Scrap.** Little waste should be generated by a JIT system, which means that material scrap should be driven down to exceedingly low levels. The cost of scrap (especially when supported by a detailed list of items that were scrapped) is of particular concern as a JIT system is being implemented, since it helps to identify problem areas requiring further management attention.

- **Cost of quality.** One focus of JIT is on creating high-quality products, so it is reasonable to keep track of the full cost of quality (which comprises defect control costs, failure costs, and the cost of lost sales) on a trend line. Managers want to see the details behind this measure, so that they know where the largest quality costs still reside in the company and can then work to reduce them.

- **Customer service.** This measure really has several components—delivering products on the dates required by customers, shipping full orders to customers, and not having products returned because of poor quality. This measure can be summarized in a variety of ways or reported at the component level, but the main issue is to measure and post the information for all to see, so that the company focuses strongly on providing the highest possible degree of customer service.

- **Ideas generated.** A JIT system works best when employees pitch in with hundreds of suggestions for improvements that, when taken in total, result in a vastly improved, efficient operation. The amount of idea generation going on can be measured by the number of ideas per worker, the number of ideas suggested in total, the number of ideas implemented, or the proportion of ideas suggested that are implemented.

The common theme that unites all the JIT measures just listed is that they are not financial in nature (with the exception of the cost of quality)—they are operational measures that focus attention on the nuts-and-bolts details of creating and running a JIT system. A cost accountant involved in the calculation and reporting of these measures may feel that this is quite a departure from the more traditional cost variance measures, but the end result will be a much more efficient JIT process that churns out and delivers high-quality products.

BACKFLUSHING IN A JIT SYSTEM

When a JIT system is installed, management finds that it is inundated with paperwork stemming from use of the time-honored picking system. This is a method for tracking parts as they flow through a manufacturing facility that involves making a separate inventory entry at all key steps in the production process—when an item is received, when it is stored in the warehouse, when it is picked and sent to the manufacturing floor, when it moves from machine to machine, when it returns to the warehouse for storage, and when it is sold. Because of the large number of moves of small quantities (and the large number of related transactions recorded), a picking system is difficult to maintain in a JIT environment. Instead, companies use the backflushing system.

Backflushing requires no data entry of any kind until a finished product is completed. At that time the total amount finished is entered into the computer system, which multiplies it by all the components listed in the bill of materials for each produced item. This yields a lengthy list of components that should have been used in the production process and which is subtracted from the beginning inventory balance to arrive at the amount of inventory that should now be left on hand. Backflushing is technically an elegant solution because data entry occurs only once in the entire production process. Given the large transaction volumes associated with JIT, this is an ideal solution to the problem.

However, there are some serious problems with backflushing that must be corrected before it will work properly. They are:

- **Production reporting.** The total production figure entered into the system must be absolutely correct, or else the wrong component types and quantities will be subtracted from stock. This is a particular problem when there is high turnover or a low level of training in the production staff that records this information, which leads to errors.

- **Scrap reporting.** All abnormal scrap must be diligently tracked and recorded; otherwise these materials will fall outside the backflushing system and will not be charged to inventory. Since scrap can occur anywhere in a production process, a lack of attention by any of the production staff can result in an inaccurate inventory. Once again, high production turnover or a low level of employee training exacerbates this problem.

- **Lot tracing.** Lot tracing is impossible under the backflushing system. It is required when a manufacturer needs to keep records of which production lots were used to create a product in case all the items in a lot must be recalled. Only a picking system can adequately record this information. Some computer systems allow picking and backflushing systems to coexist, so that pick transactions for lot tracing purposes can still be entered in the computer. Lot tracing may then still be possible if the right software is available; however, this feature is generally present only on high-end systems.

- **Inventory accuracy.** The inventory balance may be too high at all times because the backflushing transaction that relieves inventory usually does so only once a day, during which time other inventory is sent to the production process; this makes it difficult to maintain an accurate set of inventory records in the warehouse.

Of all the issues noted here, the worst is any situation where the production staff is clearly incapable of providing sufficiently accurate scrap or production reporting for the backflushing system. If there is an easily traceable cause, such as less capable workers on a particular shift, moving a few reliable employees into these positions can provide immediate relief from the problem. It may even be possible to have an experienced shift supervisor collect this information. However, where this is not possible for whatever reason, computer system users experience backflushing garbage in, garbage out (GIGO)—entering inaccurate information rapidly eliminates any degree of accuracy in the inventory records, requiring many physical inventory counts to correct the problem. Consequently, the success of a backflushing system is directly related to a company's willingness to invest in a well paid, experienced, well-educated production staff that undergoes little turnover.

CASE STUDY: COST-BENEFIT FOR A JIT SYSTEM IMPLEMENTATION

This section presents a case study on the change in costs that occurs when a JIT system is installed. As usual, we use the mythical General Research and Instrumentation Company as the subject of our analysis. Mr. Alan Grumpy, the production manager of the GRIN Company, is contemplating a switch from the current material requirements planning system (just installed in the last chapter!) to a JIT system. Before doing so he wants to determine if this is a cost-effective proposal. He divides the analysis into two parts, the first one reviewing just the costs and benefits of JIT purchasing, and the second dealing with JIT manufacturing.

There are a number of components to consider in this analysis. First, the cost of purchasing parts on a per-unit basis will clearly be higher when using JIT purchasing since suppliers must make far more deliveries and may have to deliver in odd quantities that require repackaging. For this analysis Mr. Grumpy assumes that the in-bound shipment cost will be an extra 5% for JIT purchasing (this varies considerably in reality, depending on the delivery distances and unit volumes involved). Next, the purchasing staff will have to place far more orders with suppliers, since there will now be more deliveries to be made. We assume that GRIN Company has not yet installed any automated order placement systems that would eliminate this cost. Accordingly, Mr. Grumpy assumes that deliveries will change from one per month to one per business day (assuming 21 per month) for each part, at an additional cost of $2 per order. So far, the cost of JIT purchasing appears to be quite a bit higher than under the traditional format. However, we have not yet considered the benefits of this approach.

The first benefit that Mr. Grumpy calculates is the considerable reduction in inventory at both the raw materials and work-in-process levels. He assumes that inventory levels will drop from the current (and not discreditable) 8 turns to 20 turns. When this reduction occurs, the company can extract the funds invested in inventory and use them to reduce debt. The GRIN Company currently borrows at the prime rate, which is 9%. Next, Mr. Grumpy can eliminate a considerable number of costs incurred as a result of having inventory, such as insurance coverage, material handlers, forklifts, and rented warehouse space. He believes that these costs are roughly 10% of the total inventory valuation.

Mr. Grumpy now has sufficient information to conduct a cost-benefit analysis on the applicability of JIT purchasing. On the assumption that the inventory level prior to implementing JIT is $2,000,000, inbound shipment costs are currently running at an annual rate of $300,000, and 200 parts are ordered each month, he creates the calculation shown in Exhibit 27.1.

Though the cost-benefit analysis shows a clear reduction in costs, Mr. Grumpy is suspicious of the findings because there is no doubt that the additional costs will be incurred at once, whereas the savings will occur only after inventory reductions have been completed. Consequently, he may call for a more elaborate analysis of cash flows over several years that itemizes the cost savings at various points in the future and discounts these cash flows down to a reduced current value.

Another issue is that the increased cost of ordering is really a step cost, rather than an incremental increase in costs of $2 for each additional order placed. Therefore, it may be more realistic to determine at what point an additional purchasing

EXHIBIT 27.1. Cost-Benefit Calculation for JIT Purchasing

Cost Type	Incremental Cost Changes with JIT Purchasing ($)	Calculation Notes
Inbound shipment cost	+15,000	($300,000 annual cost) × (5% surcharge)
Ordering cost	+96,000	(20 additional orders placed per month) × (200 parts) × (12 months) × ($2 per order)
Interest savings on inventory investments	−108,000	(Reduction in inventory of $1,200,000) × (9% interest rate on debt)
Inventory-related costs	−120,000	(Reduction in inventory of $1,200,000) × (10% inventory-related costs)
Net cost reduction	−117,000	

agent must be hired and substitute the burdened salaries of all these extra positions for the incremental ordering cost information noted in Exhibit 27.1.

Mr. Grumpy now moves on to an analysis of the costs and benefits associated with a JIT manufacturing system. He notes that the per-unit cost of each product manufactured will increase since the smaller machines in the machine cells are not configured for optimum efficiency, unlike larger, more fully automated machines. This also will increase the direct labor cost per unit since the staff is less efficient in processing smaller product batches and in constantly setting up machines. Mr. Grumpy estimates that this will increase the cost of each product by 14%.

Offsetting the increase in product costs will be a sharp decline in scrap costs, from the current level of 8% down to 2%. Also, the cost of rework will be completely eliminated, which is an extra 5% of total product costs. Both these declines are large but are justifiable in light of the direct focus of the JIT system on waste reduction and high product quality. Another offshoot of the improvement in quality will be the projected elimination of one-half of the quality inspection stations in the facility, which will reduce product costs by an extra 2%.

In addition, Mr. Grumpy expects a sharp drop in machine maintenance costs because the current set of large, automated machines that require intensive maintenance will be replaced by a number of smaller machines whose maintenance can be largely completed by the machine operators themselves. This will result in the elimination of three maintenance technician positions paying $45,000 each. Also, utility costs will drop by $50,000 because the smaller machines require much less energy than the large, automated equipment that they are replacing.

EXHIBIT 27.2. Cost-Benefit Calculation for JIT Manufacturing

Cost Type	Incremental Cost Changes with JIT Manufacturing ($)	Calculation Notes
Direct product	+2,240,000	($16,000,000 cost of goods sold) × (14% increase)
Scrap	−960,000	($16,000,000 cost of goods sold) × (6% decrease)
Rework	−800,000	($16,000,000 cost of goods sold) × (5% decrease)
Quality inspection	−320,000	($16,000,000 cost of goods sold) × (2% decrease)
Maintenance	−135,000	Elimination of three maintenance positions at $45,000 each
Utilities	−50,000	Substitution of large machines for smaller ones
Floor space	−100,000	Subletting of unused factory space
Production planning staff	−100,000	Elimination of two production planning positions at $50,000 each
Net cost reduction	−225,000	

Further, converting to machine cells will pack machines together much more tightly, eliminating 25% of all floor space, which the company will sublet to another organization for $100,000 per year.

Finally, Mr. Grumpy has less need for the large production planning team employed to manage the material requirements system, and so he expects to eliminate two of these positions, for an annual cost savings of $100,000.

Knowing that his current cost of goods sold is $16,000,000, he now has enough information to construct the cost-benefit table shown in Exhibit 27.2.

Though this cost-benefit analysis reveals a net cost savings, Mr. Grumpy is once again concerned with the results because the same problem has arisen: the cost increase associated with the change (less worker and machine efficiency on a per-unit basis) will occur as soon as the switch to a JIT manufacturing system takes place, however, the anticipated savings will be realized only after the new system is fully installed and operational, which lends some risk to the proceedings. This is a particularly difficult endeavor to justify when a company's workforce has been employed there for a long time, is used to a certain way of manufacturing products, and is not convinced of the need to make such a drastic change as a JIT system will entail. In this type of environment a company runs the real risk of attempting a JIT installation, having product costs leap to much higher levels as a result of the ensuing inefficiencies, and then accrue none of the advantages because of worker resistance to the changes. In such cases it may be wiser to adopt JIT on a pilot basis, so that employees can see it working in part of the facility, while educating them in depth regarding how the system works and why it is so important to install it.

SUMMARY

The JIT system is being installed in an increasing number of companies, so the changes outlined in this chapter related to costing, systems, and measurements will become of increasing importance to many readers. Of particular concern is the use of backflushing, the implementation of which must be carefully discussed to ensure that the resulting information is accurate enough to yield reliable conclusions. From the perspective of the cost accountant, the standard list of cost variances will require a great deal of revision (and elimination!) in order to work with the reduced set of information generated by a JIT system. The key issue to remember when working with this system is that its emphasis is on reducing waste—which means that little time is available to record the data a cost accountant is accustomed to using.

ENDNOTE

[1] A kanban is described in this text as a card, but it can actually be any form of notification. A common alternative is a container of a particular size. When an upstream machine receives this container, it means that the machine operator is authorized to fill it with parts—no more, no less—and then send it back to the downstream machine for immediate use.

CHAPTER 28

Cost of Quality

As the level of competition has gradually risen over the past few decades, the ability of an organization to produce a low-priced product is no longer a sufficient determinant of success. Instead, the minimum qualification for entry into an industry also includes the ability to produce products with an extremely high level of quality. Now, high quality is not only a competitive requirement but also a way to reduce costs from a company's processes. For both these reasons the pursuit of high quality levels throughout an organization has become one of the fundamental ongoing activities in which employees now engage. The cost accountant plays a key role in this process, as outlined in this chapter, which also describes the cost of quality, how to set up reporting systems for it, and how to create measurements encompassing it.

DEFINITION AND USE OF PRODUCT QUALITY

The definition of product quality is of particular concern to a company setting up quality control systems, for it has a major impact on the types, cost, and complexity of systems created, as will shortly become apparent.

Product quality is a product's conformance to customer expectations. It can also be defined as a product's fitness for a specific use. These are critical definitions to explore because they are useful for defining a product's level of quality. For example, if a company produces an injection-molded plastic stopper for the top of a milk jug, the stopper must have a size tolerance that allows it to properly seal the milk jug every time—it does not require perfect coloration, complete freedom from flaws, or size tolerances accurate to within 1/10,000 inch—it just has to seal the milk jug every time. Accordingly, in the eyes of the customer, the level of quality conformance that results in a quality product is relatively low, which allows the producing company to reduce its level of testing to the level where only the one key feature is reviewed. Any other quality factors are of no importance and have no impact on the customer's perception of the product. Thus, a product's quality is strictly defined by its ability to perfectly perform a designated function—and nothing more.

This definition allows a company to design its entire production process around the customer's product needs. By doing so it can avoid many additional quality costs that might otherwise go into creating a product that is of excessively high quality. This keeps the company from spending an undue amount on quality-related costs, which in turn reduces its overall cost structure and makes it more competitive in relation to other companies in the industry. And all these actions are driven by the definition of quality.

The definition of product quality can be broken down into two sublevels, which are of considerable use in creating quantitative quality performance measures. The first is a product's *quality of design.* This refers to the ability of the engineering staff to create a product that is precisely tailored to the quality perceptions of the customer. This may mean that a "quality" car has three cup holders, nonscratchable paint, tires that resist punctures, and an engine that always starts up within 2 seconds. If the engineering staff does not create a design perceived to contain a sufficiently high level of quality, there is nothing that the rest of the organization can do to improve that level of quality, even if it does a superlative job of production, shipping, customer service, and training. This is a difficult area to measure because the engineering staff converts *qualitative* customer perceptions of quality into a product. The quality of this area may become apparent only after customers have had a chance to review preliminary designs and render their opinions about them.

The second sublevel of the definition of quality is *quality of conformance,* which is the ability of the organization to produce, deliver, and support the product design. This is an easily measured item, because it involves determining the variance from a *quantitative* standard (e.g., the product design). For example, if the production process creates a part that varies from the design specification, this variance can be measured and reported. The high level of measurement possible under this quality definition greatly exceeds that for the quality of design. By separating the two quality measures, one can create measuring systems that address the qualitative (in the case of quality of design) and the quantitative (in the case of quality of conformance) issues peculiar to each one.

As an example, the General Research and Instrumentation Company has decided to manufacture a radar detector. In terms of quality its first order of business is to determine which features customers associate with a high level of quality. They are:

- The ability to detect radar emissions at the greatest possible distance
- The ability to screen out all emissions that cause false alarms
- The smallest possible product size
- Minimal power requirements

With this information in hand the design team now needs more specific quality measurements that give it concrete quality-of-design goals to achieve. It conducts a combination of customer surveys and reviews of the existing capabilities of products now on the market—if it can exceed the specifications of existing products, it will have achieved a new quality standard in the eyes of customers. For example, customers want radar detection at any range higher than what can be currently met by products now available. Since the current highest detection range is 400 yards, the design team shoots for a new detection limit of 500 yards (which is also supported by customer survey information). Next, the design team runs tests on the top three competing models to determine the proportions of alarms caused by stray electronic signals and finds that 8% is the best figure. It decides to set a 4% goal for the proportion of stray signals causing alarms, thereby doubling the performance of the best competing model. Next, it uses a customer survey to determine the smallest product size that customers want and supports the findings by determining the measurements of all competing products. This allows it to arrive at a target specification of 2 inches by 4 inches by 1/4 inch. Finally, the customer survey reveals that customers are tired of having to replace the battery in their detectors every 24 hours and would prefer one that lasts a month. The design team finds that one alternative is to incorporate a motion sensor into the product that automatically turns on and shuts off the device without a manual switch adjustment. This feature prolongs the estimated battery life to 3 months, which is well beyond the point at which customers consider the product a quality product. Thus, the GRIN Company design team has developed product specifications (and hopefully can actually create a working design!) that will yield a high level of quality of design.

Next, the GRIN Company production staff must attain a high quality of conformance by creating products that consistently and reliably achieve the measures created by the design team. To do this the quality assurance staff decides to create a testing process to verify that 99.5% of all radar detectors manufactured can detect radar emissions at the requisite distance of 500 yards, with the same reliability percentage being applied to the ability of these products to adequately screen out stray emissions. To achieve these two overriding goals, a variety of additional actions are needed that can correct the underlying problems that would cause the primary measures to fail. These include automated testing of all circuit boards going into the detectors to ensure that they are functional, postassembly testing and follow-up training to ensure that operators correctly assemble the final products, and development of new padded containers for shipment of the finished goods, to ensure that there is no product damage in transit. By taking these steps the GRIN Company assures itself of a high level of quality of conformance.

It is evident that close attention to the two types of product quality ensures that customers will be well satisfied with a company's products. This may allow an organization to charge higher prices, especially if competing products have a much lower level of quality. It also results in greater customer retention, because customers whose needs have been satisfied by a product have no need to search elsewhere— this results in reduced sales, marketing, and promotional costs. Despite these evident benefits, the managers of many companies need further proof before they embark on a campaign to improve product quality. This proof can be provided by the cost accountant, who compiles a cost-of-quality report as evidence that quality-related changes have a major impact on corporate profitability. In the next section we review the types of quality costs, followed by a discussion of the types of measurement and reporting systems required to properly inform managers of the cost of quality.

TYPES OF QUALITY COSTS

There are four types of cost categories into which quality costs fall. It is useful to split quality costs into these categories, for there are so many subcategories that it can be difficult to track them all without this method of organization.

The first category of costs is *prevention costs*. These are the costs a company incurs to ensure that product failures of various kinds do not occur during the production process or in the hands of a customer. These costs can also be incurred to ensure that there are fewer process-related failures. They are discretionary costs, for a company's management can choose not to expend any funds on prevention activities (though there will be an offsetting increase in failure costs). Examples of prevention costs are:

- **Administration of quality-related activities.** Some staff time is required to plan for and administer quality prevention activities. The cost of this labor should be supplemented by the cost of related benefits and payroll taxes.

- **Education.** A significant expense includes the preparation of training materials, the cost of trainers and training facilities, and (the largest expense of all) the labor cost of all employees attending the training. This is a key prevention activity and is one of the largest costs in the prevention category.

- **New product trial costs.** For organizations releasing new products, having customers test product designs is a central method for ensuring a high quality of design (see the last section). Accordingly, the costs of products given to customers and survey administration can be clustered into this subcategory.

- **Preventive maintenance.** Ensuring that machinery is capable of running when needed is a key prevention activity. This includes the costs of maintenance personnel engaged in preventive maintenance, as well as any related material and administrative costs.

- **Preventive maintenance scheduling software.** The preventive maintenance activities just mentioned can be more easily accomplished if maintenance software is available to track the last time such maintenance was conducted, determine how heavily a machine has been used since that time, and schedule additional maintenance based on these two factors.

- **Procedure and instruction development.** A major prevention activity is the creation of machine operation instructions and other procedures that give employees complete information about how to perform their jobs. With this information in hand there is much less chance that a step in the production process will be mishandled, resulting in quality problems. The costs of the initial investigation of activities, procedure development, and distribution of the resulting materials are in this subcategory.

- **Supplier qualification assessments.** Products cannot have a high quality level unless the supplier of their components has high quality standards. The cost of all employee time spent in reviewing and assessing the output of suppliers falls into this category.

- **Tool design reviews.** If a company uses a number of custom tools to create products, these tools must be carefully reviewed in terms of their ability to produce parts at minimum specification levels, as well as their ability to do so consistently and with minimal failure rates. The costs of these reviews and any resulting tool revision costs are in this category.

- **Warranty reviews.** One form of prevention is to closely review all customer warranty claims in order to obtain clues regarding what product problems can be prevented at the company before they reach customers. The cost of this review and any subsequent investigation of possible problems falls into this subcategory.

The second category of costs is *appraisal costs.* These are the costs incurred to measure products, the material components used in products, and the processes used to manufacture products. These activities are designed to reduce the number of defective products shipped to customers. They are different from prevention costs in that they attempt to improve quality strictly through increased inspection activities. They are also discretionary costs, for a company is not required to use any appraisal activities whatsoever—though eliminating them increases the number of low-quality products shipped to customers. Examples of appraisal costs are:

- **Incoming component testing.** If there are particularly troublesome problems with materials received from suppliers, a company may have to initiate an extensive effort to review a large proportion of these materials, which results in costs not only for testing personnel but also for any materials destroyed during the testing process.

- **Material appraisal.** It is common for the quality control staff to remove items from various stages of the production process for testing purposes. When the removed materials are destroyed during testing, the cost of these materials is recorded as an appraisal cost.

- **Outsourced laboratory testing.** Some of the tests conducted on materials are of such a specialized nature that a company finds it to be more cost-effective to send them to an outside laboratory for review. The fees of such laboratories are charged to this cost subcategory.

- **Process appraisal.** The appraisal process is not confined to material reviews. It is also necessary to periodically analyze how well the production and supporting processes are functioning; the staff time devoted to this activity is charged to this cost subcategory.

- **Prototype appraisal.** The quality staff can spot problems with new products before they are produced by examining a variety of quality-related issues for prototype products. The costs of testing and of destruction of prototypes are grouped into this cost subcategory.

- **Testing equipment calibration.** The testing equipment used by the quality staff must be periodically recalibrated to ensure its accuracy. This task is frequently performed by certified outside calibration services, which makes it easier to identify their fees and charge them to this cost subcategory.

- **Testing equipment.** Depending on the kinds of quality tests performed, the types of testing equipment needed can be expensive. When the cost of this equipment falls below a company's capitalization limit, the entire cost is charged straight to this subcategory. When it is higher, the associated depreciation expense is charged here.

The third category of costs is *internal failure costs.* These are costs incurred when product defects are discovered prior to shipment. At that time products can be taken out of the production or warehouse area, repaired and placed back in the production process if possible, or scrapped. The numerous related costs accompanying these activities make this an expensive cost category. Examples of internal failure costs are:

- **Correction of related paperwork.** When a product failure occurs internally, resulting in rework or scrap, various paperwork activities are required. The production scheduling staff must schedule new production to replace the items removed from production, and the eliminated items must be reported to the purchasing staff so that they can order replacement materials. Further, the accounting staff must determine the cost of the scrap or rework and record it in the financial records. The staff time required to complete all these activities is recorded here.

- **Lost profit on products sold as seconds.** When a company finds that it has products of a sufficiently low quality that they cannot be sold through normal sales channels, it can elect to sell them at a discount rather than expend extra rework effort to bring them up to a higher quality standard. Then, the loss in profits that occurs when these products are sold at the lower price point should be recorded in this subcategory as a cost or a sales discount.

- **Machinery downtime.** The discovery of internal product failures can lead to machinery downtime for two reasons. The machines are now needed to rework defective products, which keeps them from being used to create new products. Also, the cause of the internal failures may be the machinery, which requires some downtime while it is being investigated and repaired. In either case the cost of the machinery downtime should be charged to this cost subcategory.

- **Redesign.** If a product continues to have high quality error rates over time, the problem may not be in the manufacturing process but rather in the underlying product design. If so, the engineering staff will require extra time to develop a new design and test it to ensure that all quality problems have been resolved. The engineering time charged to this work should be summarized in this cost subcategory, as well as the costs of any inventory that will become obsolete as a result of design changes.

- **Reinspection and testing.** Once a product has been reworked, it must be inspected and tested to ensure that it now meets quality specifications, which requires extra staff time.

- **Repurchasing.** When products are scrapped, the purchasing staff may need to repurchase the components needed to create replacements. The cost of the time needed to do this can be recorded separately here, or in the "Correction of related paperwork" subcategory appearing earlier in this list.

- **Rework.** Depending on the extent of product rework required, a separate staff may be needed for this activity. If not, production workers must be drawn from the production line (thereby taking time away from the production of other products) to perform this work. In either case the cost of their time is charged to this account. There may also be a charge for the use of any machinery required to perform rework tasks.

- **Safety stock.** If there is a significant volume of internal product failure, the management team may find it necessary to keep on hand large quantities of extra components to make up the shortfall of components that occurs because of the scrapping of low-quality products. An interest cost is associated with the investment in this extra inventory, as well as storage, insurance, and obsolescence costs that can be accumulated in this cost subcategory.

- **Scrap.** Some products may be of such a low quality level that they cannot be reworked and so must be thrown away. However, some of these costs may be recouped by selling the scrap (if this is possible). For high-cost products, this is an expensive subcategory of internal failure costs.

- **Supplier claims processing.** When internal failure costs are traced to supplier quality problems, a company must not only ship back defective supplier parts but also process claims against the offending suppliers so that it does not have to pay for the low-quality parts. This claims-processing step can be an administrative headache, as well as an expensive one when there are many supplier-caused quality problems.

The final category of costs is *external failure costs.* These are costs incurred when low-quality products are shipped to customers. This tends to be the most difficult quality cost area to measure because it is hard to quantify some customer-related costs (as noted in the following list). There is general agreement among quality experts that these costs make up the most expensive of all the various cost-of-quality categories, for the loss of customers because of low-quality products can have a catastrophic impact on an organization's profitability. Examples of external failure costs are:

- **Customer surveys.** A company may conduct customer surveys for the sole reason that it needs feedback about the quality of products sold to them. If this is the only reason for creating and operating a survey (as opposed to one used by the marketing department for product positioning and pricing purposes), then the cost of the survey can be charged to this account.

- **Customer-imposed penalties.** Customers who use a company's output in their products may have considerable concerns about the quality of incoming components and reinforce these concerns with their suppliers by charging penalties for poor-quality production. If so, these penalties should certainly be segregated into a separate account so that management can easily determine their extent.

- **Invoice adjustments.** Processing changes in customer invoices can be time-consuming, especially when there is a large volume of customer returns, for each transaction tends to be a unique one that requires a considerable amount of time. If this activity requires too much time, the associated cost can be stored separately in this account; if not, it can be rolled into the "Processing customer returns" account (as noted later in this list).

- **Loss of customers.** This is potentially the largest cost in the external failure cost category. It can be quantified by contacting ex-customers to determine whether low quality influenced their decision to purchase elsewhere, and then calculating the lost profit based on sales to these customers in the preceding year. Though the resulting figure cannot be tied to any cost recorded through a traditional accounting system, the opportunity cost of sales lost should still be itemized in this account because of its potential size.

- **Loss of reputation.** A potentially large expense is the decline in a company's reputation that occurs when it continually sells low-quality products. This is a difficult cost to calculate or even estimate, so most companies do not use this cost account, preferring instead to simply itemize the potential for this cost in the narrative sections of their quality cost reports.

- **Processing customer returns.** Whenever a customer returns a product, the receiving staff must complete special paperwork on it, store it in a special location, have it reviewed by a quality control team, and disposition it in accordance with their instructions, while the accounting staff must process a credit to the customer. The costs of all these activities should be charged to this account.

- **Product recall insurance.** If a company has a history of conducting product recalls, it may be necessary to reduce its risk of incurring further recall-related costs by procuring a product recall insurance policy. However, this can be an expensive policy to obtain, especially if there is a recent recall history. The cost is certainly high enough to be placed in its own separate account.

- **Product recall.** If a company finds that products have sufficiently extensive quality problems, it can recall them. Many costs arise when this happens, including payment for inbound freight costs for returned products, the cost of reworking defective products, the cost of issuing replacement products, and the administrative overhead associated with these tasks. This can be an inordinately expensive cost subcategory.

- **Supplier warranty claim processing.** When customers return products, there is a good chance that their complaints involve product components sold to the company by its suppliers. If so, the company must expend considerable effort in filling out warranty claim forms to send to its suppliers in order to obtain reimbursement for shoddy components. These administrative costs should be charged to this account.

- **Warranty claim administration.** When there are many product returns from customers, a company may find it necessary to create a full-time warranty claims department. The cost of the staff for this department, as well as all associated overhead costs, should be charged to this account.

The list of quality-related costs presented here is a long one and can be extended for additional costs that are specific to certain industries. However, a cost accountant should not think that he or she must create a new measurement system for tracking all these items—that would be a Herculean job since most of the cost categories noted here are not currently included in any normal accounting measurement system. Instead, as discussed in the next section, the specific quality costs to be measured and reported are only those needed to assist in the reduction of quality costs.

CREATING A QUALITY MEASUREMENT AND REPORTING SYSTEM

Now that we have some idea of the types of quality-related costs that can be tracked, we need to decide which costs to accumulate, how to organize them into a data storage system, how to measure them, and what reports to generate.

The most important factor to consider is the first one—which costs to track. Giving this first step a great deal of thought before setting up tracking systems saves time and money and ensures that only necessary information is reported. For example, if a cost accountant decides that each quality cost line item should be tracked in detail, this would require the formation of a large, cumbersome reporting system that would likely demand time card tracking by all employees, new measurement devices for machinery, extra accounting staff to input all the information into a database, and investment in new software to mine and interpret the data stored in the database. This would be an expensive way to create a quality cost tracking system. A better approach is to consider these items when determining the types of costs to be tracked:

- **Ability to measure an activity.** Some activities are extremely hard to measure. For example, the accounting staff does not have a good method for determining the time it takes each day to issue credits to customers for low-quality products that have been returned, nor does the production staff usually track the time it takes to rework low-quality products. An extremely difficult quality cost to measure is the cost of lost sales from customers who take their business elsewhere. The cost accountant must evaluate the ability of the organization to collect such information and then determine if it is sufficient to report estimated costs in lieu of "real" data.

- **Available resources.** The resources required to set up and maintain a complete quality cost tracking system may exceed the investment in a company's normal accounting systems because of the in-depth nature of the information that must be obtained. Few organizations have the staffing or financial wherewithal to achieve such a task. Accordingly, one must determine the cost required to collect each type of quality cost information and offset it with the benefits of the uses to which the information can be put. This usually results in a much smaller number of quality cost items being tracked with any degree of regularity.

- **Continuing need for information.** Many organizations prefer to reduce quality costs through short-term projects with tightly defined beginning and ending points. They do not require cost information after a project is completed, just a summary report that itemizes the success (or failure) of each project. In such cases there is no need to continually report on issues that have long since been resolved, though it may be useful to review costs from time to time to see if there have been subsequent cost increases requiring follow-up activities to correct.

- **Nonfinancial measures.** Financial measures are most commonly used by senior management, which must compare the results obtained from its investments in quality-related projects to the related investments. However, lower levels of the organization require measurements based primarily on units, such as percentages of scrap reduction or parts per million of rework. These measures are more relevant to their activities. Accordingly, the preponderance of information gathered by the cost accountant may be nonfinancial in nature.

- **Quality objectives.** The quality cost tracking system should primarily support a company's quality cost reduction efforts. This means that if management wants to focus its attention on a few specific quality issues, the measurement system should be designed to provide the highest possible level of detail about just these areas. The next highest level of accuracy should be for measurements of areas that management has on its agenda for near-term improvements. Low-priority areas can be measured less precisely. Thus, the level of detail for quality cost measurements varies in accordance with the current and short-term quality cost reduction goals of management.

- **Speed of feedback loop.** Most quality cost reduction efforts require immediate feedback of information to those most closely involved in the project. This may require an information feedback loop of only a few minutes, whereas other improvement projects may operate well with feedback times of a week or a month. The type of information collected and the manner in which it is collected depend greatly on the speed with which it is needed. This also impacts the nature of the reports used since an elaborate report requiring days of effort is of little use if the information is needed immediately. This is a prime consideration when constructing a quality cost measurement system.

- **Types of reports needed.** Different types of reports are needed, depending on the management level of the recipient and the activities in which each one is involved. A cost accountant must be mindful of the need for information by each employee and tailor the reports issued to the needs of the recipient. For example, an exhaustively detailed quality cost report is of minimal use to senior management, which is more interested in a few key summary measures; alternatively, a department manager may require exceptional detail about a few key activities currently targeted for improvement. Also, the need for reports changes over time, so old reports must be discarded in favor of new ones, or altered to meet new reporting needs. Being mindful of these changes allows a cost accountant to avoid spending time on the wrong reports and ensures that the information issued is put to the best use.

These are the key factors in determining what information to collect and how to report it. After considering these items the cost accountant nearly always finds that only a portion of all quality costs must be measured at any one time. By constantly reevaluating an organization's information needs, one can continually tweak the cost measurement system to ensure that employees receive the correct information as soon as they need it.

The next issue is how to organize the selected quality costs into a data storage system. The central issue here is the structure to be used for the chart of accounts, so that these costs can be properly recorded in the general ledger. An example of such a chart of accounts is shown in Exhibit 28.1, where a three-digit code represents each of the four types of quality costs. In the example there are additional spaces in the chart-of-accounts numbering system in case the cost accountant decides to further subdivide the costs. For example, when using the code for equipment preventive maintenance costs (which is 120), we may decide to further subdivide costs for each machine in the facility; so if we assign a subcode of 27 to a specific machine, then the maintenance cost for that machine becomes 120-27. We can further subdivide the costs if it seems necessary to further refine the cost tracking system. For example, if we want to break down the materials, labor, and other maintenance costs for each machine, we can add a few more digits to the account code; to trace the labor cost of preventive maintenance for machine 27, we can use the code 120-27-01. By using an increasingly detailed chart-of-accounts codes in which to store the cost of quality data, a cost accountant can subdivide the information in more ways, allowing her to create and issue a greater variety of reports.

The main problem with using a highly detailed chart of accounts is that the data tracking systems that feed information into it are more difficult to maintain. To use our preceding example, the maintenance technicians repairing machine 27 must track their labor time and all other costs when working on that machine and then turn it in to the accounting staff for data entry into the general ledger. If the accounting staff wants to do a thorough job of tracing all maintenance costs, they will spend more time comparing the total payroll costs of the maintenance staff, as well as other costs they may have incurred during the reporting period, to the costs charged to specific machines and then report an additional variance composed of costs that were *not* charged to specific machines; additional work may be required to allocate these costs to specific preventive maintenance activities, if necessary. All these tasks are further complicated by the large number of account codes for which data must be collected and entered.

EXHIBIT 28.1. Cost of Quality Chart of Accounts

Account No.	Description
100-00-00	**Prevention costs**
105-00-00	Quality administration costs
110-00-00	Quality training costs
115-00-00	Supplier qualification review costs
120-00-00	Equipment preventive maintenance costs
125-00-00	Instruction design costs
130-00-00	Other prevention costs
200-00-00	**Appraisal costs**
205-00-00	Receiving inspection costs
210-00-00	Testing equipment calibration costs
215-00-00	Outsourced testing costs
220-00-00	Inspection labor costs
225-00-00	Test equipment depreciation costs
230-00-00	Other appraisal costs
300-00-00	**Internal failure costs**
305-00-00	Rework costs
310-00-00	Scrap costs
315-00-00	Repurchasing costs
320-00-00	Downtime costs
325-00-00	Cost of processing claims against suppliers
330-00-00	Other internal failure costs
400-00-00	**External failure costs**
405-00-00	Product liability insurance costs
410-00-00	Product liability costs
415-00-00	Warranty costs
420-00-00	Field service costs
425-00-00	Customer complaint processing costs
430-00-00	Other external failure costs

Setting up a complicated chart-of-accounts structure can be time-consuming, especially at the start of a cost-of-quality project when the cost accounting staff is not certain which costs need to be tracked. At this stage, because of the high uncertainty level, it is better to conduct a preliminary data collection and store the information in an electronic spreadsheet rather than use a more formal method that stores it in the general ledger. Once the initial quality cost review has been completed and everyone has a better idea of what information is wanted, the accounting staff can create a set of general ledger accounts and dispense with the spreadsheet storage system.

Having completed the structure of the underlying data storage system, we must now create procedures for collecting the information. This can be a difficult chore, for few of the costs itemized in the sample chart of accounts in Exhibit 28.1 can be extracted directly from the existing accounting system. Instead, new measurement systems must be constructed for each one. The typical sequence of steps to follow when creating such measurement systems is:

1. *Use the existing accounting system.* Do not reinvent the wheel. If quality costs are already being accumulated and stored in the accounting system, then extract and use them for the quality cost reporting system.

2. *Itemize required measurements.* Completion of the first step reduces the list of new measurements that must be created. Create a formal list of the remaining measures.

3. *Determine the cost of measurements.* Estimate the cost of setting up and operating measurement systems for each of the measures on the list. This may include the cost of automated measurement equipment, additional data entry clerks, new software, and the time required for existing employees to complete reports on the time they spend performing various activities.

4. *Create estimation alternatives for expensive or difficult measurements.* Some estimated measurement costs are extremely high. For these items specify alternative measurement systems that are less expensive, noting any reductions in the quality of information that will result from these trade-offs. For example, an alternative to a cumbersome new measurement system may be the use of a simple percentage estimate that is updated every few months.

5. *Gain approval for measurements.* Present the list of measures and their costs to the management team. They can pick the appropriate measurement systems from the list, choosing from among various alternatives, and perhaps eliminating some from the list entirely if they feel that certain measures are not important or too expensive to operate.

6. *Create procedures.* Create procedures for all measures approved by management. These should be sufficiently detailed that a user can learn a complete measurement system simply by reviewing a procedure.

7. *Test procedures.* Review all procedures with the employees who will be actively using them to collect measurement information. Correct the procedures with the resulting feedback to ensure that they are accurate. Also, be sure to create a feedback loop from employees to the people responsible for

updating the procedures, so that ongoing systemic changes quickly result in updates to the procedures.

8. *Roll out measurements and adjust as needed.* Use the completed procedures as the basis for a training program for all employees who will be involved in the measurement process. The level of training should be intensive to ensure that workers are thoroughly versed in their new measurement tasks. Be sure to have a trainer remain on-site with employees through their first few hours of measurement activity and conduct regular follow-up visits to ensure that all employee questions are promptly answered. If the training period is a lengthy one and not enough trainers are available to roll out the entire measurement program in a short period, it is usually acceptable to roll it out over a longer time frame, which results in a gradual increase in the number of quality cost line items reported as more and more measurement systems are enabled.

9. *Conduct postcompletion follow-up.* When the entire system is complete, compare its actual cost and the quality of the resulting information to the original estimates. Any significant variances should be reported back to the management team and also kept in the permanent project file for future reference, in case this information is needed when other quality cost measures are added in the future.

Having determined what costs to compile, created a rational cost accumulation system for them, and built a measurement system that accumulates the desired costs, we are now in a position to use the resulting information to prepare a number of different quality cost reports. Though the creation of reports may seem like the simplest step in the entire process, one must be careful to issue the correct types of reports, with just the right amount of information on each one, or else the recipients will be unable to use them. The amount of detail should be at a summary level in reports issued to top-level managers, who do not have time to root through a lengthy document and who are primarily interested in the bottom-line financial impact of the quality cost reduction program. However, reports sent to lower-level managers, those responsible for reducing these costs, should be chock-full of many kinds of detail, including not only financial information but also some operational statistics. They need such voluminous reports so that they can determine and correct the precise causes of quality costs. In reality, a mix of both types of reports is regularly issued, so that all parts of a company receive the information they need in a format that is of most use to each area. Throughout the remainder of this section, we review a number of quality cost reporting formats, noting the advantages and disadvantages of each.

At the highest possible level of summarization, the costs accumulated by the quality costing system can be lumped together in a pie chart, an example of which is shown in Exhibit 28.2. This format has the advantage of being easy to read, so

EXHIBIT 28.2. Pie Chart of Quality Costs

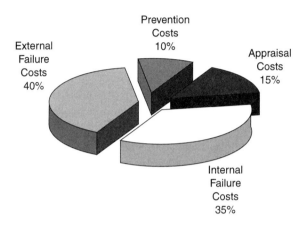

Costs of Quality Pie Chart

that the information it contains can be readily imparted to the viewer. This type of report is generally used during the earliest stages of a quality cost reduction project, when employees are just learning about the extent and types of quality costs. However, because it does not reveal cost trends or the total amount of costs involved and certainly contains no detailed breakdown of costs, it is of little use for ongoing reporting purposes. It is then discarded in favor of the other formats listed in this section, which contain more relevant, detailed information.

A greater level of detail is provided by the summary cost-of-quality report shown in Exhibit 28.3. This format itemizes the various costs that roll up into each of the four main cost categories. Its primary uses are to communicate costs to senior management and to show what cost line items are the largest—and therefore worthy of more in-depth discussion. For example, the exhibit shows that scrap and rework costs are by far the largest internal failure costs, while field service and customer complaint processing expenses are the largest external failure costs. However, this report format does not break down the cost line items into a sufficient level of detail to be of much use to lower levels of management where cost reports are scrutinized most intensively. They need information broken down by department or location.

For organizations with multiple locations or divisions, the format shown in Exhibit 28.4 is a more detailed one that reveals much more information. In this example we attribute the costs noted in the preceding exhibit to separate operating divisions. Then, we can see that the primary focus of quality cost reduction efforts should be the New York location because it accounts for 52% of total quality costs.

EXHIBIT 28.3. Summary Cost-of-Quality Report

GRIN Company Cost-of-Quality Report for February 2002

Cost Type	Detail	Summary
Prevention costs		
Quality administration costs	$7,500	
Quality training costs	2,500	
Supplier qualification review costs	4,000	
Equipment preventive maintenance costs	21,000	
Instruction design costs	2,400	
		$ 37,400
Appraisal costs		
Receiving inspection costs	$5,900	
Test equipment calibration costs	2,300	
Outsourced testing costs	5,000	
Inspection labor costs	15,000	
Test equipment depreciation costs	8,100	
		$ 36,300
Internal failure costs		
Rework costs	$51,000	
Scrap costs	43,000	
Repurchasing costs	1,900	
Downtime costs	3,500	
Cost of processing claims against suppliers	900	
		$100,300
External failure costs		
Product liability insurance costs	$8,000	
Product liability costs	88,000	
Warranty costs	29,500	
Field service costs	60,200	
Customer complaint processing costs	43,000	
		$228,700
Total quality costs		**$402,700**

EXHIBIT 28.4. Cost of Quality Reported by Location

GRIN Company Cost-of-Quality Report by Location
February 2002

Cost Type	Boston	New York	Portland	Summary
Prevention costs				
Quality administration costs	$900	$5,000	$1,600	$7,500
Quality training costs	500	1,250	750	2,500
Supplier qualification review costs	750	2,200	1,050	4,000
Equipment preventive maintenance costs	2,500	11,400	7,100	21,000
Instruction design costs	400	1,400	600	2,400
	$5,050	$21,250	$11,100	$37,400
Appraisal costs				
Receiving inspection costs	$600	3,000	$2,300	$5,900
Test equipment calibration costs	300	1,500	500	2,300
Outsourced testing costs	800	2,500	1,700	5,000
Inspection labor costs	1,500	7,500	6,000	15,000
Test equipment depreciation costs	950	4,350	2,800	8,100
	$4,150	$18,850	$13,300	$36,300

EXHIBIT 28.4. Cost of Quality Reported by Location (*continued*)

GRIN Company Cost-of-Quality Report by Location
February 2002

Cost Type	Boston	New York	Portland	Summary
Internal failure costs				
Rework costs	$4,500	$26,000	$20,500	$51,000
Scrap costs	6,000	22,000	15,000	43,000
Repurchasing costs	200	1,000	700	1,900
Downtime costs	350	2,000	1,150	3,500
Cost of processing claims against suppliers	150	500	250	900
	$11,200	$51,500	$37,600	$100,300
External failure costs				
Product liability insurance costs	$1,000	$4,200	2,800	$8,000
Product liability costs	5,500	47,000	35,500	88,000
Warranty costs	3,000	14,000	12,500	29,500
Field service costs	5,000	33,000	22,200	60,200
Customer complaint processing costs	3,500	21,500	18,000	43,000
	$18,000	$119,700	$91,000	$228,700
Total quality costs	$38,400	$211,300	$153,000	$402,700
Percentage of total costs	10%	52%	38%	100%

EXHIBIT 28.5. Report on Components of Cost of Quality

GRIN Company Cost-of-Quality Report for *New York Facility*
February 2002

Cost Type	Materials	Labor	Other	Summary
Prevention costs				
Quality administration costs	$0	$5,000	$0	$5,000
Quality training costs	0	1,000	250	1,250
Supplier qualification review costs	0	1,750	450	2,200
Equipment preventive maintenance costs	1,200	10,200	0	11,400
Instruction design costs	0	1,400	0	1,400
	$1,200	$19,350	$700	$21,250
Appraisal costs				
Receiving inspection costs	$0	$3,000	$0	3,000
Test equipment calibration costs	0	0	1,500	1,500
Outsourced testing costs	0	0	2,500	2,500
Inspection labor costs	0	7,500	0	7,500
Test equipment depreciation costs	0	0	4,350	4,350
	$0	$10,500	$8,350	$18,850

continued

Conversely, there is little point in addressing issues at the Boston plant, where quality costs make up a mere 10% of the total costs for the company. This format can be easily modified so that it itemizes these costs for departments instead of divisions. This report is most useful for managers at the department or division level, who need the extra information to see where quality costs are arising within their areas of responsibility.

Though the preceding report format is useful for telling senior managers where quality costs are being incurred at the facility level, it provides nothing at a more detailed level that would be of use to managers within each facility who require more information. This can be gleaned from the next report, shown in Exhibit 28.5. It covers the quality costs of only a single facility and is more specific about the types of costs incurred—materials, labor, or other (these costs categories can be swapped with others, depending on a company's specific needs). One can also add

EXHIBIT 28.5. (*continued*)

Cost Type	Materials	Labor	Other	Summary
Internal failure costs				
Rework costs	$10,000	$16,000	$0	$26,000
Scrap costs	22,000	0	0	22,000
Repurchasing costs	0	1,000	0	1,000
Downtime costs	0	2,000	0	2,000
Cost of processing claims against suppliers	0	500	0	500
	$32,000	$19,500	$0	$51,500
External failure costs				
Product liability insurance costs	$0	$0	$4,200	$4,200
Product liability costs	0	0	47,000	47,000
Warranty costs	0	14,000	0	14,000
Field service costs	8,000	22,000	3,000	33,000
Customer complaints	0	20,000	1,500	21,500
Processing costs				
	$8,000	$56,000	$55,700	$119,700
Total quality costs	$41,200	$105,350	$64,750	$211,300
Percentage of total costs	19%	50%	31%	100%

many more columns if it seems necessary to itemize the report for more types of costs. This extra level of detail allows managers at the facility level to more easily track down and reduce quality costs.

The preceding quality cost reports provide sufficient cost-related information for companies ramping up their first year of quality cost reduction activities. However, companies that have passed through their first year of such activities have accumulated a history of costs for each quality cost category; these organizations can create budget expectations for each cost category and use this extra information to construct reports itemizing the budgeted and actual quality costs for each period, as well as the variance between the two figures. In Exhibit 28.6 the report also includes additional columns for year-to-date information. This type of report structure is essential for organizations with enough historical budgeting information to conduct comparisons and a plan to use this information as the basis for long-range quality cost reductions. It is also useful for conducting performance evaluations of managers who are responsible for controlling quality costs.

EXHIBIT 28.6. Cost of Quality Versus Budget

GRIN Company Budgeted Versus Actual Costs Report
February 2002

Cost type	This Month Actual	This Month Budget	This Month Variance	Year-to-Date Actual	Year-to-Date Budget	Year-to-Date Variance
Prevention costs						
Quality administration costs	$7,500	$7,000	-$500	$16,000	$14,000	-$2,000
Quality training costs	2,500	3,000	+500	5,200	6,000	+800
Supplier qualification review costs	4,000	3,200	-800	8,500	6,400	-2,100
Equipment preventive maintenance costs	21,000	20,000	-1,000	44,500	40,000	-4,500
Instruction design costs	2,400	2,000	-400	5,000	4,000	-1,000
	$37,400	**$35,200**	**-$2,200**	**$79,200**	**$70,400**	**-$8,800**
Appraisal costs						
Receiving inspection costs	$5,900	$6,000	+100	$12,000	$12,000	$0
Test equipment calibration costs	2,300	4,000	+1,700	7,000	8,000	+1,000
Outsourced testing costs	5,000	2,500	-2,500	6,100	5,000	-1,100
Inspection labor costs	15,000	10,000	-5,000	30,700	20,000	-10,700
Test equipment depreciation costs	8,100	8,100	0	15,500	16,200	+700
	$36,300	**$30,600**	**-$5,700**	**$71,300**	**$61,200**	**-$10,100**

EXHIBIT 28.6. Cost of Quality Versus Budget (*continued*)

GRIN Company Budgeted Versus Actual Costs Report
February 2002

Cost type	This Month Actual	This Month Budget	This Month Variance	Year-to-Date Actual	Year-to-Date Budget	Year-to-Date Variance
Internal failure costs						
Rework costs	$51,000	$50,000	−$1,000	$99,900	$100,000	+100
Scrap costs	43,000	40,000	−3,000	78,700	80,000	+1,300
Repurchasing costs	1,900	3,000	+1,100	6,900	6,000	−900
Downtime costs	3,500	2,100	−1,400	6,500	4,200	−2,300
Cost of processing claims against suppliers	900	1,000	+100	2,050	2,000	−50
	$100,300	$96,100	−$4,200	$194,050	$192,200	−$1,850
External failure costs						
Product liability insurance costs	$8,000	$7,250	−$750	$17,100	$14,500	−$2,600
Product liability costs	88,000	65,000	−23,000	167,000	130,000	−37,000
Warranty costs	29,500	30,000	+500	60,000	60,000	0
Field service costs	60,200	60,000	−200	119,600	120,000	+400
Customer complaint processing costs	43,000	41,000	−2,000	87,200	82,000	−5,200
	$228,700	$203,250	−$25,450	$450,900	$406,500	−$44,400
Total quality costs	$402,700	$365,150	−$37,550	$795,450	$730,300	−$65,150

EXHIBIT 28.7. Cost-of-Quality Report by Operation

	Prevention Cost ($)	Appraisal Cost ($)	Internal Failure Cost ($)	External Failure Cost ($)	Total Cost ($)
Mold setup	0	0	3,500	0	3,500
Machine preparation	500	750	3,000		4,250
Injection mold	1,020	80	4,200	8,720	14,020
Processing					
Part trimming	500	500	2,200	500	3,700
Labeling				500	500
Hot stamping	250		500		750
Assembly	500	600		3,000	4,100
Boxing	0	0	0	0	0
Total	**2,770**	**1,930**	**13,400**	**12,720**	**30,820**

The preceding reports have focused on splitting specific accounting categories of costs into finer levels of detail. These formats are useful for locating and reducing specific types of costs. However, they do not draw management's attention to the specific processes within an organization that are causing problems. An example of a format that resolves this problem is shown in Exhibit 28.7, where we have sorted the four main types of quality costs by the steps in an injection molding production process. With this approach managers can quickly tell which production steps are incurring the majority of quality-related costs and focus their attention on the major offenders. In the exhibit the injection molding process incurs the majority of costs, while the assembly operation is a distant runner-up. This reporting format is most useful for employees directly involved in the improvement of quality costs. Its main weakness is that it does not give as sufficient a level of detail regarding the specific types of quality costs incurred as can be found in the preceding reports.

As employees dig deeper into the causes of various quality costs, they require more than a fine itemization of these costs. Instead, they need an analysis that shows the specific underlying reasons for each one. This problem is resolved by the format shown in Exhibit 28.8. This is a root case analysis report that lists a single expense line item (in the example, we use the $51,000 of product rework costs shown earlier in Exhibit 28.3) on the left side and then proceeds to define each incorrect activity leading up to the summary-level cost. Next to each incorrect activity is its estimated or actual cost. Though this type of report requires considerable investigation to complete, it tells managers precisely what problems are causing costs and which activities to correct in order to improve these costs. Because it can be used to reduce many quality costs, this is the most valuable cost-of-quality report for employees who are most directly involved in quality cost reduction.

EXHIBIT 28.8. Root Causes Report

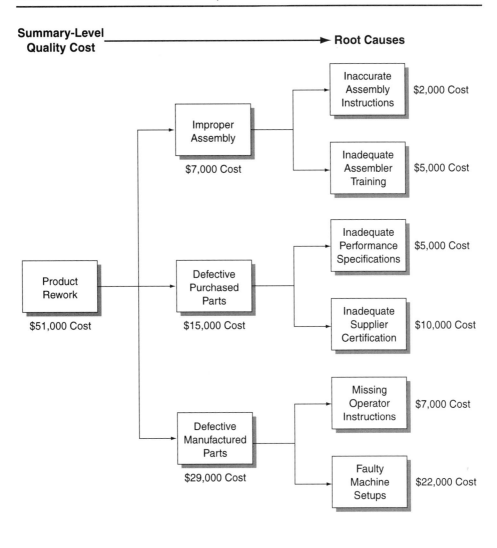

The preceding report is useful for telling employees which activities are causing expenses to occur, but it does not tell them what it will cost to make corrections. By comparing the costs of problems and the costs required to correct them, management can determine which corrections will result in the largest net increase in profits. The report also tells them if corrective activities will be so expensive that prevention will cost more than the quality problem to be fixed, so that they can avoid these corrective activities. An example of the reporting format that includes the cost-benefit trade-off for each corrective activity is shown in Exhibit 28.9. The

EXHIBIT 28.9. Cost-Benefit Trade-off Report

Root Causes	Corrective Activities	Quality Cost ($)	Associated Quality Cost ($)	Net Change in Costs ($)
Inaccurate assembly instructions	Audit and reissue assembly instructions	24,000	13,500	+10,500
Inadequate assembler training	Create training materials and conduct classes	60,000	27,000	+33,000
Inadequate performance specifications	Revise purchasing specifications for all purchased parts	60,000	42,000	+28,000
Inadequate supplier certification	Create certification program, screen suppliers, and drop those with poor performance	120,000	120,000	0
Missing operator instructions	Correct and reissue operator instructions	84,000	50,000	+34,000
Faulty machine setups	Create training program for all machine operators, with periodic updates	264,000	110,000	+154,000
Total		**612,000**	**362,500**	**+249,500**

example lists all the root causes noted earlier in Exhibit 28.8 in the first column along with corrective activities for each one. Then the costs of each root cause are reduced by the cost of each corrective activity to determine the net change in costs. However, this report format compares only the single-year costs of each root cause to the same single-year cost of each corrective activity; a more accurate approach would be to separately calculate the net present value of each set of activities over a long time period and discount it by a company's cost of capital to arrive at a more accurate net change in costs. These net present value calculations can be determined separately and the results included in this report format.

No matter what report format is used, there should be notation indicating which quality costs listed are only estimates. When this information is included, the reader will know that some information, on which decisions are being made, may require additional investigation. For example, if the cost of scrap is shown in a report as being $200,000, a manager may find this to be a sufficiently large number to initiate a massive scrap reduction campaign; this decision may turn out to be the wrong one if he finds out that the number was only an estimate and that he has initiated a campaign to reduce what is actually a much smaller cost.

There are several other reporting formats that may be of interest in selected situations and can be incorporated into any of the preceding formats. They are:

- **Report quality costs per share of stock.** Though this may seem like an unusual informational item to include in a report, it can be of use in a publicly held company for reports to the senior management team because this information points out the direct impact on earnings reported to the public if reductions in specific quality costs can be achieved.

- **Break down manufacturing variances into their quality cost components.** Many traditional manufacturing companies have used the same price and volume variance reports for decades and see no reason to stop just because the emphasis on cost controls has now changed to quality cost reports. To work with managers who have this mind-set, the quality cost reports can be inserted into the existing variance reporting structure to some extent by itemizing the various quality cost components that roll up into the traditional variance costs. However, there must still be additional reports that itemize the other quality costs that cannot be shoehorned into the old reporting formats.

- **Convert line items to a percentage of sales.** When reporting on quality costs over a number of reporting periods, the information presented will be skewed if the company is experiencing any shifts in sales volume. The skew arises because quality costs vary directly with changes in sales volume. To keep report readers from thinking that the management team cannot keep quality costs from varying wildly between periods, the information presented can be switched to a percentage of sales, thereby eliminating all volume-driven changes in quality costs from the reports.

- **Note the labor calculation method.** It is rarely practical to determine the exact labor cost associated with each type of quality cost because the cost accountant must determine precisely whose time was involved with each cost, as well as the pay rate for each person, and then summarize this information into the reported labor cost. A better way is to develop an average labor rate for each department and update it periodically. Since the averaging method used may result in some inconsistencies in the reported information, it is best to include a footnote with each quality report itemizing the averaging method used to determine the cost of labor listed in the report, so that readers can adjust the reported information based on the method used.

This section has covered a number of topics that will lead a cost accountant through the steps of determining what quality information is important and how to organize it, measure it, and convert it to reports that will be of use in reducing these costs. These are the core activities performed by the cost accountant when a company decides to reduce its quality costs. We now move on to a discussion of the profit impact of reductions in the cost of quality, emphasizing the need for a good cost-of-quality reporting system to support the people most closely involved in the reduction of quality costs.

IMPACT OF REDUCTIONS IN THE COST OF QUALITY

Having spent a great deal of time discussing the types of quality costs, as well as the types of measurement systems and reports that can summarize and itemize these costs, it is reasonable to ask why these issues are important. What is the point in investing a considerable amount of time in constructing such elaborate cost tracking systems?

The reason this question is asked only *after* detailing the types of quality costs is that the reader should have been struck by the sheer number of cost types related to quality—they cover issues involving transaction processing, material problems, production, warranty difficulties, suppliers, and problems with machinery—in short, quality costs are an insidious problem that permeates an organization. Without a cost reporting system that can itemize at least the largest quality-related costs, managers have no idea of how much these problems cost a company.

The costs revealed by a quality cost tracking system are enormous. A variety of studies have concluded that quality costs account for a minimum of 20% of a company's total revenues, with some revealing a proportion closer to 40%. If even a modest portion of this total can be eliminated from a company's operations, there will be an immediate impact on profitability. Given the size of possible savings, many organizations have targeted the reduction of quality costs as the premier way to improve profits. Because quality cost reduction is a totally internal process completely within the ability of a company's employees to improve, it is also a reliable, measurable way to do so. In contrast, a company that tries to improve profits by increasing its sales volume must depend on the whims of its customers to ensure sales growth, which is a much less reliable way to improve profits.

Thus, given the inordinate size of quality costs and the ability of companies to reduce them through internal activities, it is no surprise that corporate managers are so eager to construct cost-of-quality measurement systems so that they can use this information to target specific quality-related improvements. We will see in the next section how this information is used to assist in a cost-of-quality reduction activity.

QUALITY COST REDUCTION PROCESS

With a complete or more-targeted quality cost tracking system in place, a company is in a position to make informed decisions about which quality costs should be reduced first. In this section we review the key steps needed to complete a quality cost reduction project, as well as how a cost accountant fits into the process, how various quality costs change as a result of such projects, how managers can create short-term profits by making incorrect quality-related decisions, and how to plan for the disposition of assets released as a result of completing a quality cost reduction.

If a manager jumps directly into a quality cost reduction project without any pre-planning, it is likely that the project will not succeed because of problems caused by his failure to lay any groundwork in advance. For example, a cost reduction project may require the cooperation of a department over which the manager has no control, or it may need funding that is not currently available, or the results may not be those originally anticipated or promised to higher-level managers. One should follow these steps in order to avoid such problems:

1. *Select a target.* The first step is to determine which of the myriad of quality costs are most worthy of reduction. With the plethora of reports described earlier, one can sort the cost categories by size and pick one of the larger ones so that the results of the cost reduction project will be of a corresponding size. An alternative approach is to select a small cost category for which the solution is relatively obvious and easy to implement; by quickly completing a few of these easy projects, a manager can gain greater support for implementing a project that targets larger and more difficult to reduce cost categories.

2. *Create an overview document.* The next step is to obtain the support of a high-level manager within the company. This person will want to see a brief summary-level description of the proposed project—a document describing the project, estimated costs and benefits, risks, and the number of departments

that will be impacted. The purpose of this document is to sell a specific manager on the idea of becoming the project sponsor, so it should be structured to match the preferences of the recipient.

3. *Get a sponsor.* The project manager needs a high-level manager who is respected within the organization and who has the political skills to convince the managers of any departments that will be impacted by the project that it is a useful item to support. The sponsor's help is of more importance when a quality cost reduction project impacts many departments and is less critical if the project can be completed within a single department since the project manager has to deal with only one department manager.

4. *Create a project file.* Collect all available information about the problem area to be fixed. This should include an itemization of costs, a trend line of changes in these costs, notes from interviews with affected employees, and suggested problems and solutions. This documentation should be organized into a case file that will form the core of the project team's database for the project.

5. *Determine root causes.* By reviewing the available documentation in the project file and conducting more detailed investigations, determine the root causes that lead to the incurrence of quality costs. These may be buried below a number of other, more superficial causes and require some digging to uncover.

6. *Precisely define quality costs to be reduced.* By targeting the elimination of root causes, it is possible to calculate what cost savings will arise as a result of eliminating or mitigating these causes. These cost reductions can be wide-ranging, including downstream cost reductions in the areas of internal and external failure costs. This analysis is a key component of the cost-benefit study, which is described in the next step.

7. *Complete a cost-benefit study.* The cost accountant can play a key role in comparing the total cost savings from the project (as calculated in the last step) to the total costs required (including those incurred by the project team) to bring about the reduction. This analysis should be structured as a net present value calculation that offsets the positive and negative cash flows arising from the project over several years, discounted at the company's cost of capital.

8. *Determine risks.* With all numerical information now in hand, one must determine the risks that the project will not achieve its desired goals. These risks are rarely quantifiable but should be itemized in detail, so that the managers who review the project proposal can compare the financial benefits to the associated risks. These risks can include resistance from other departments, new technology that does not work as advertised, or improper

staffing that results in the loss of key personnel, as well as a range of other problems highly specific to the type of project under review.

9. *Create a budget.* Determine the payroll, travel, supplies, and training costs of the project staff, as well as the capital costs of computer or other equipment required by the team, plus new equipment needed in the production process to bring about quality improvements. The depreciation cost of any new capital equipment should be included in the budget. It should note the timing of all expenditures, as well as the milestone dates when final approval must be obtained for all capital purchases.

10. *Obtain funding approval.* With the project budget in hand, the manager can request funding approval. These funds may be allocated from a general cost improvement budget pool included in the annual budget or may require additional funding not included in the budget; this is generally harder to obtain since it goes around the established budgeting system. The support of the project sponsor can be invaluable in obtaining funding approval.

11. *Obtain final approval.* The project may need more than budget approval because it may also require the services of a number of employees who must be pulled from their departments and assigned to the project for its duration. Therefore, the project manager must make a presentation to a senior management group to obtain these approvals.

12. *Complete the project.* Using the allocated funds and personnel, correct the root causes, create procedures and use them to train employees in corrective methods, and set up a measurement system to ensure that the corrective actions are being followed.

13. *Measure the results.* Conduct a postcompletion comparison of the actual costs and benefits experienced, noting the reasons for any differences from the original estimates. This document is not used just as a verification of the project team's original cost and benefit estimating capacity—it is more useful as a tool for determining what original estimates were wrong, so that future estimating methods used on upcoming projects can be refined to achieve a higher level of estimation accuracy. The cost accountant is responsible for conducting this review.

14. *Report back to the sponsor.* Once the project is complete and its results measured, create a before-and-after comparison report itemizing all the changes made and the total costs and benefits. Also, itemize recommendations for permanent system changes that will keep the project's results from being lost over time. This is a key document, for a successful, well-publicized project will result in the organization being more receptive to further quality cost reduction projects.

Though the preceding list may appear to be a lengthy one, many of the steps require little time to complete; for a small quality cost reduction project, the majority of these steps can be completed in one day. For larger projects the time needed to complete them may be extensive, but the time taken will be paid back many times over if only because the responsible manager will be fully backed by an informed, committed project sponsor, know what costs and time are needed to complete the project, and is aware of potential risks that may keep the project from succeeding. These advantages are so crucial that any manager who wants to ensure the success of such projects should feel compelled to complete them.

When a quality cost reduction program is initiated, managers may be surprised to find that some types of quality costs increase as a result of their activities, rather than the reverse. This is because some prevention and appraisal costs must be increased in order to reduce internal and external failure costs. This is not a bad cost trade-off because appraisal and prevention costs are proportionally much less expensive than internal and external failure costs, resulting in a net reduction in overall quality costs. The concept is illustrated in Exhibit 28.10, where we see both prevention and appraisal costs gradually increasing at the start of a quality cost reduction program. Internal failure costs continue to rise for the first few months of the program because there is a lag of a few months before the additional quality

EXHIBIT 28.10. Trend Line of Quality Costs

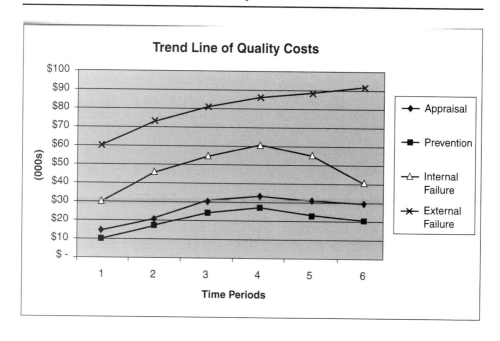

cost activities have a noticeable impact on them. External failure costs may not begin to decline for a few months because low-quality products that have already been sold to customers continue to cause problems for many months. Also, once the quality program has fully taken hold within the company, managers can selectively prune some appraisal and prevention costs, which brings about a small decline in these costs. By explaining these timing issues to management, one can set expectations for when quality costs will begin to decline, and the timing and extent of those that will rise. Proper management understanding of these issues also allows for easier approval of budgeted expense increases in the quality cost appraisal and prevention areas in order to reduce internal and external quality-related failure costs. This is an important issue to cover since managers may react strongly if quality costs do not drop immediately after the initiation of a quality cost initiative, and proceed to scrap the whole program.

As additional prevention and appraisal activities are added to the quality cost program, the cost accountant should conduct a review of the projected benefits to be obtained so that managers can determine when it is no longer cost-effective to keep adding new quality improvements. Though some companies continue to pursue a goal of zero quality problems, the reality, as shown in Exhibit 28.10, is that there comes a time when all the low-cost quality improvements have been instituted and all subsequent quality improvements require changes that are more expensive to implement than the benefits to be gained from the resulting quality increases. However, this does not mean that the quality improvement program should grind to a halt at the point (as noted in Exhibit 28.11) where quality cost increases bisect failure cost decreases. Instead, the management team should switch its attention to the latest enhancements in technology to determine what improvements would allow it to further reduce quality failure costs. As these new types of technology become available, a company can continue to lower its quality costs in a cost-effective way. Also, by keeping a company focused on these technology-driven improvements, the emphasis on quality is not lost—which might otherwise be the case if a company decides to halt all further quality improvement goals.

A key issue for a cost accountant to watch for and report on is the deliberate reduction of appraisal and prevention costs. These changes are forced on an organization by managers seeking short-term profitability improvements. For example, by cutting back on quality control training, which is a prevention cost, a company experiences an immediate reduction in its training costs, which can improve profits in the current period; however, this also brings about a gradual increase in internal and external failure costs over the long term because employees are less knowledgeable about the available quality control techniques that would have prevented the increase in failure-related costs. This is a particular problem in situations where a company is being readied for sale, so that immediate profits are of great value to the seller, as well as in cases where managers are given bonus incentives primarily based on short-term profit results. A cost accountant can report on these

EXHIBIT 28.11. Quality Cost-Benefit Analysis

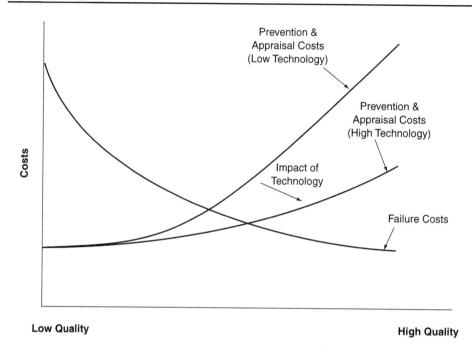

changes by issuing the trend line analysis noted earlier in Exhibit 28.9, which reveals reductions in appraisal and prevention costs and the resulting rise in failure costs of all types.

A final quality cost issue in which a cost accountant might become involved is the disposition of assets and employees no longer needed because of quality cost reductions. For example, when prevention activities result in a reduced number of customer complaints, there is less need for personnel in the customer service department. Does a company let these employees go or use them elsewhere in the company in different positions? The release of such assets can be predicted well in advance, based on trend lines in quality cost improvements in various cost categories. By helping to create or review these projected asset reductions, a cost accountant can assist in the orderly liquidation or redisposition of key assets in the most efficient manner.

It is apparent that the cost accountant plays a major role in the entire quality cost reduction effort. This can be limited to quality cost reporting, which is a major effort by itself, or it can extend into an active role in the day-to-day identification of cost reduction opportunities, project analysis, and implementation phases. By assisting in these projects, a cost accountant can have a major impact on corporate profitability. The next section more precisely defines the exact role of the cost accountant in this process.

ROLE OF THE COST ACCOUNTANT

Having considered the types of quality-related costs, how they are accumulated and reported, and how the quality cost reduction process works, it should be apparent that the cost accountant is an integral part of the entire quality process.

The cost accountant is responsible for creating quality cost measurement systems. This requires meetings with other employees involved in the quality cost reduction effort to determine what kinds of costs they need to track, as well as in the development and testing of cost accumulation and summarization systems. Further, the cost accountant must determine the best types of quality cost reports into which this information should be compiled, based on the needs of employees at various levels of management within the organization.

In cases where other parts of an organization have created their own quality cost tracking systems, it is customary for them to hand over the administration of these systems to the accounting department after the systems have been set up, the management of which may fall on the cost accountant. This hand-over takes place because some of the quality costs are already accumulated by the accounting department, the accounting staff already knows how to make cost estimates and allocations, and it has extensive practice in setting up control systems to keep information accurate. Thus, accountants are viewed as the systems management professionals within most organizations and therefore are placed on the receiving end of any informal cost tracking systems that other parts of an organization may create but not want to administer.

It is also customary for the cost accountant to examine quality cost reports and advise the various cost reduction teams about which costs will be most affected by their activities, which ones can be most significantly impacted by their activities, and the cost of projected new cost reduction activities. It may also be necessary to help the teams create capital purchasing proposals for any equipment they need to reduce quality costs because the cost accountant deals with these proposals constantly and is therefore better able to prepare them with minimal effort. This is an expert advisory role likely to require a cost accountant to attend the majority of planning meetings of every quality cost reduction team in a company.

For companies that have made a serious commitment to reducing quality costs, the activities noted here will probably require the full-time services of an entire cost accounting department. The cost of so many accountants is well worth the investment, however, when one considers that the cost of quality in many organizations can reach 20% to 40% of total sales. Given the size of the potential savings, adding a few cost accountants to the staff is one of the better investments a management team can make.

SUMMARY

The cost accountant plays a key role in the development of measurement systems and reporting on the cost of quality. This involves the determination of what costs require measurement, the extent of efforts needed to trace them in an accurate manner, and the creation of controls over the measurement process. Further, the cost accountant must determine the types of reports to use, what levels of the organization should receive each one, and whether or not the reports should contain operational as well as financial data.

These are especially difficult decisions to make, for many of the component costs summarized into the cost of quality are not precisely tracked by existing accounting systems, which calls for extensive revisions to existing systems as well as the creation of entirely new ones. Because these alterations and improvements require a great deal of time and funding to implement, the cost accountant should keep in mind one major consideration when developing them—create a measurement system tailored only to an organization's quality objectives. Otherwise, the resulting systems may provide the wrong information, along with an excessive level of detail that not only is not needed but is also a waste of time and money to obtain.

Given these constraints, the cost of a quality system set up by each company is a unique one tailored to the specific circumstances in which a firm finds itself. Accordingly, the best use of a cost accountant's efforts is in the design of this system rather than in data collection or reporting.

CHAPTER 29

Cost Variability

When a person first takes on the role of a cost accountant, the question she is asked most frequently is, How much does this cost? The item in question is almost always a finished product or a component that rolls into a finished product. The cost accountant then accesses the bill of materials for the item in question, which lists the cost of every component that goes into the finished product, and supplies the answer. This information can then be used to develop prices, determine break-even levels, justify a capital purchase, or calculate a product's profitability. Unfortunately, the resulting analyses might be wrong because the cost information used does not turn out to be correct. If so, the cost accountant will be told quite forcibly that there is a problem and instructed to find out the amount of the "real" cost.

The problem is not that the cost accountant has made a mistake in accessing information but rather in its interpretation. Costs are fixed only within a tightly defined set of parameters and can vary widely outside that range. In this chapter we review the multitude of factors that cause costs to vary, as well as how to predict changes in costs.

VARIATIONS IN COST BASED ON FIXED AND VARIABLE COSTS

One factor that can cause costs to vary is that they contain both variable and fixed elements. The cost of most products is itemized on a bill of materials that lists all the components assembled into it. An example of a bill of materials for a desk light is shown in Exhibit 29.1. All the line items on this BOM are variable costs, for each

EXHIBIT 29.1. Bill of Materials

Component Description	Quantity	Per-Unit Cost ($)	Total Cost ($)
Base	1	17.00	17.00
Switch	1	0.75	0.75
Spring	4	0.25	1.00
Extension arm, lower	1	3.75	3.75
Extension arm, upper	1	4.25	4.25
Adjustment knob	2	0.75	1.50
Bulb holder	1	0.30	0.30
Bulb	1	2.15	2.15
Bulb lens	1	1.50	1.50
Overhead costs		6.20	6.20
Total cost			**38.40**

one is incurred only when a desk light is created—that is, the costs vary directly with unit volume.

In this format the BOM is simple; we see a quantity for each component, a cost per component, and a total cost for each component that is derived by multiplying the number of units by the cost per unit. The only line item on this BOM that does not include a cost per unit or number of units is the overhead cost, which is situated near the bottom. This line item represents a variety of costs being allocated to each desk lamp produced. The costs included in this line item represent the fixed costs associated with lamp production. For example, there may be a legal cost associated with a patent that covers some feature of the desk lamp, the cost of a production supervisor who runs the desk lamp assembly line, the cost of a buyer who purchases components, the depreciation on any equipment used in the production process— the list of possible costs is lengthy. The key factor that brings together these fixed costs is that they are associated with the production of desk lamps, but they do not vary directly with the production of each incremental lamp. For example, if one more desk lamp is produced, there will be no corresponding increase in the legal fees needed to apply for or protect the patent that applies to the lamp.

This splitting of costs between variable and fixed costs can occupy the extremes of entirely fixed costs and entirely variable ones, with the most likely case being a mix of the two. For example, a software company that downloads its products over the Internet has entirely fixed costs; it incurs substantial costs to develop the software and set up a Web site for downloading purposes but then incurs zero costs when a customer downloads the software from the Web site (though even in this case, there is a small credit card processing fee charged for each transaction). Alternatively, a custom programming company charges customers directly for every hour of time its programmers spend on software development, so that all programming costs are variable (though any administrative costs are still fixed). To use a variation on the software example, a software developer that sells its products by storing the information on CDs or diskettes, printing instruction manuals, and mailing the resulting packages to customers incurs variable costs associated with the mailed packages, and fixed costs associated with the initial software development. All three variations on the variable-fixed cost mix are illustrated in Exhibit 29.2, where the first graph shows a straight horizontal line, indicating that there is no incremental cost associated with each additional unit sold. The second graph shows a steeply sloped line that begins at the X-Y intercept, which indicates that all costs are incurred as the result of incremental unit increases in sales. Finally, the third graph shows a sloped line beginning partway up the left side of the graph, which indicates that some (fixed) costs are incurred even when no sales occur.

To return to the BOM listed earlier in Exhibit 29.1, the format does a good job of itemizing the variable costs associated with the desk lamp, but a poor job of describing the fixed costs associated with the product; there is only a single line item for $6.20 that does not indicate what costs are included in the overhead charge or how it was calculated. In most cases this number is derived by summarizing all overhead into a single massive overhead cost pool for the entire production facility, which is then allocated to the various products based on the proportion of direct labor charged to each product. However, many of the costs in the overhead pool may not be related in any way to the production of desk lamps, nor may the use of direct labor hours be an appropriate way to allocate the fixed costs.

This is a key area in which the costing information provided by cost accountants can result in incorrect management decisions of various kinds. For example, if the purpose of a costing inquiry by management is to add a standard margin to a cost and use the result as a product's new price, the addition of a fixed cost that includes non-relevant costs will result in a price that is too high. Similarly, using the same information but without any fixed cost may result in a price that is too low to cover all related fixed costs unless enormous sales volumes are achieved. One of the best ways to avoid this problem with the proper reporting of fixed costs is to split the variable and fixed cost portions of a product's cost into two separate parts and report them as two separate line items to the person requesting the information. The variable cost element is reported as the cost per unit, while the fixed cost element is reported as the entire fixed cost pool, as well as the assumed number of units over which the cost pool is being spread. For the desk lamp example the report could look like this:

> In response to your inquiry regarding the cost of a desk lamp, the variable cost per unit is $32.20 and the fixed cost is $6.20. The fixed cost pool on which the fixed cost per unit is based is $186,000 and is divided by an assumed annual sales volume of 30,000 desk lamps to arrive at the fixed cost of $6.20 per unit. I would be happy to assist you in discussing this information further.

We do not know the precise use to which our costing information will be put by the person requesting the preceding information, so we give her the key details regarding

EXHIBIT 29.2. Graphs of Fixed Costs, Variable Costs, and Mixed Costs

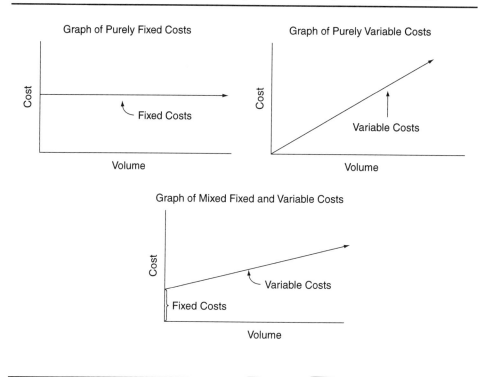

the fixed and variable cost elements of the desk lamp, from which she can make better decisions than would be the case if she received only the total cost of the desk lamp. This approach yields better management information, but—as we will see in the following sections—there are many other issues that can also impact a product's cost, which a cost accountant should be aware of before issuing costing information to the rest of the organization.

VARIATIONS IN COST BASED ON DIRECT LABOR

One of the larger variable costs on a product's bill of materials is direct labor. This is the cost of all labor directly associated with the manufacture of a product. For example, it includes the cost of an assembly worker who creates a product or of a machine operator whose equipment stamps out the parts later used in a product. However, it does not include a wide range of supporting activities, such as machine maintenance, janitorial services, production scheduling, or management, for these activities cannot be quite so obviously associated with a particular product. Conse-

EXHIBIT 29.3. Bill of Materials with a Direct Labor Component

Component Description	Unit of Measure	Quantity	Per-Unit Cost ($)	Total Cost ($)
Base	Each	1	17.00	17.00
Switch	Each	1	0.75	0.75
Spring	Each	4	0.25	1.00
Extension arm, lower	Each	1	3.75	3.75
Extension arm, upper	Each	1	4.25	4.25
Adjustment knob	Each	2	0.75	1.50
Bulb holder	Each	1	0.30	0.30
Bulb	Each	1	2.15	2.15
Bulb lens	Each	1	1.50	1.50
Fabrication labor	Hr	2.5	18.00	45.00
Assembly labor	Hr	2.0	12.50	25.00
Overhead costs			6.20	6.20
Total costs				**108.40**

quently, direct labor is itemized separately on the BOM (as noted in Exhibit 29.3), while all other indirect labor elements are lumped into the fixed cost line item.

In the exhibit we have now switched from just one type of unit-based cost, as in Exhibit 29.1, to two types of costs; one is still based on a cost per unit, but now we have included direct labor, which is based on a cost per hour. Accordingly, there is now a "Unit of Measure" column on the BOM that identifies each type of cost. The two types of direct labor itemized on the BOM are listed as a cost per hour and the fraction of an hour required to manufacture the desk lamp.

The trouble with listing direct labor as a separate variable product cost is that it is not really a variable cost in many situations. Companies are not normally in the habit of laying off production workers when there is a modest reduction in production volume and sometimes retain many key employees even when there is no production to be completed at all. This is hardly the sort of behavior that would lead a cost accountant to treat a cost as variable. The reason why companies retain their production employees irrespective of manufacturing volume is that the skills needed to operate machinery or assemble products are so valuable that a well-trained production worker can achieve much higher levels of productivity than an untrained one. Accordingly, companies are reluctant to release production employees with proven skills. While this issue may simply result in the layoff of the least-trained employees, while retaining the most experienced personnel at all times, the more common result is a strong reluctance by managers to lay off anyone; the level of experience lost with even a junior employee is too difficult to replace, especially in a tight job market where the pool of applicants does not contain a high level of quality.

Direct labor can also be forced into the fixed cost category if there is a collective bargaining agreement that severely restricts the ability of management to lay off workers or shut down production facilities. This issue is exacerbated by some national laws, such as those of Germany, that place significant restrictions on the closing of production facilities.

Managers are also forced by the unemployment tax system to avoid layoffs. The unemployment tax is based on the number of employees from a specific company who applied to the government for unemployment benefits in the preceding year. When there is a large layoff, the unemployment tax rises. Managers who are cognizant of this problem do their best to avoid layoffs in order to avoid an unemployment tax increase, though layoffs are still the most rational approach for a company that faces massive overstaffing with no near-term increase in production foreseen. In this instance the cost of the unemployment insurance increase is still less than the cost of keeping extra workers on the payroll.

The primary impact of these issues on the bill of materials is that the BOM identifies direct labor as a variable cost when in reality it is a fixed cost in many situations. Therefore, it may be best for a cost accountant to itemize this cost as fixed if there is no evidence of a change in staffing levels as production volumes vary.

VARIATIONS IN COST BASED ON BATCH SIZE

A major issue that can significantly affect a product's cost in the size of the batches in which parts are purchased, as well as manufactured. For example, if the purchasing department buys a trailer load of switches for the desk lamp in our ongoing example, the per-unit cost will be low since the switch manufacturer can produce a lengthy production run of switches with minimal setup costs. The per-unit cost will also be lowered because of the reduced cost of packaging and transportation, given the benefits of bulk shipping. However, if the purchasing staff buys only one switch, the manufacturer will charge a premium amount for it, either because a single production run must be set up for the single unit of output or (if the item is already stored in the manufacturer's warehouse) because the switch must be pulled from stock, individually packaged, and shipped. All these manufacturing, shipping, and handling costs cannot be spread over many switches since only one unit has been ordered. Accordingly, the per-unit cost is much higher for small-volume orders.

This is a particular problem when a company orders in odd-lot volumes. When this happens, the manufacturer of the part must repackage the items ordered into a new shipping configuration, possibly having to re-create the correct size shipping containers, just to satisfy the company's order size.

Another way of looking at the volume-related cost issue is that the proportion of fixed costs to variables costs within a product increases as the production volume drops. For example, if a product has $10 of variable costs and a one-time machin-

EXHIBIT 29.4. Proportion of Fixed to Total Costs as the Volume Changes

Volume	Total Variable Cost ($)	Total Fixed Cost ($)	Percentage of Fixed Cost (%)
2,000	20,000	4,500	18
1,000	10,000	4,500	31
500	5,000	4,500	47

ery setup cost of $4500, then the proportion of variable to fixed costs will change with the production volumes as noted in Exhibit 29.4.

A cost accountant must be cognizant of the proportional increase in fixed cost as the volume drops since this means that the full cost per unit increases as the volume declines. To use the example in Exhibit 29.4, at a volume of 2000 units produced, the full cost per unit is $12.25, but this cost per unit increases to $19.00 as the volume drops to 500 units.

To ensure that the most accurate information possible is assembled regarding order size, it is best to specify a volume range on the BOM within which the per-unit costs are accurate. An example of this format is shown in Exhibit 29.5, where we have included an extra column denoting the batch range for each line item. This range is also useful for labor since there is a learning curve (covered in a later section) associated with longer production runs that results in greater labor efficiency.

The cost accountant may need to supply a copy of the BOM with any reports that itemize batch sizes, since the reader may need to know the specific volumes within which the costs of certain line items are valid.

An additional problem related to batch size involves sudden jumps in costs incurred when production volumes surpass a specific level; these are known as step costs. An example of a step cost is the purchase of a new machine to relieve a production bottleneck. If the machine were not obtained, there would be no way to increase production capacity. The machine must be purchased in order to increase production volume by just one additional unit, so this represents a considerable incremental cost if the unit volume is to be increased by only a small amount. This concept is particularly important if a company is operating at production levels close to the maximum possible with existing equipment and personnel, for nearly any subsequent decision to increase production may result in the incurrence of a step cost. Other types of step costs are those for the addition of a supervisor if a new shift is opened up, for a new building if a production line must be built elsewhere, for a new warehouse to store the additional volumes of material needed for a new production line. A cost accountant must be particularly cognizant of this volume-driven issue since the costing information he issues may be relied on to increase production to levels where new step costs will take effect, thereby rendering the initial cost report irrelevant. A good way to ensure that a cost report is used correctly

EXHIBIT 29.5. Bill of Materials with Batch Range

Component Description	Unit of Measure	Batch Range	Quantity	Per-Unit Cost	Total Cost ($)
Base	Each	500–1,000	1	17.00	17.00
Switch	Each	1,000–2,000	1	0.75	0.75
Spring	Each	5,000–8,000	4	0.25	1.00
Extension arm, lower	Each	250–500	1	3.75	3.75
Extension arm, upper	Each	250–500	1	4.25	4.25
Adjustment knob	Each	400–800	2	0.75	1.50
Bulb holder	Each	1,000–5,000	1	0.30	0.30
Bulb	Each	2,000–2,500	1	2.15	2.15
Bulb lens	Each	500–1,000	1	1.50	1.50
Fabrication labor	Hr	250–500 units	2.5	18.00	45.00
Assembly labor	Hr	250–500 units	2.0	12.50	25.00
Overhead costs				6.20	6.20
Total cost					**108.40**

is to list on it the volume range within which the stated costs are accurate and to further note that the cost accountant should be consulted if volumes are expected to vary beyond this range.

An excellent competitive tool for companies that want to adjust their prices to match different production volumes is a separate database of unit costs for a wide range of production and purchasing volumes. The marketing staff can use this information to conduct "what if" analyses for a specific level of sales volume, so that it can estimate, with a fair degree of precision, the profits to be expected at each volume level. Unfortunately, such databases are usually custom-designed, and a great deal of research is required to assemble data for all the relevant volume ranges. Some Japanese companies have taken more than a decade to create such systems.

VARIATIONS IN COST BASED ON QUALITY

Various studies have shown that the cost of quality can make up as much as 20% to 40% of total revenue, which allows it to have an enormous impact on product costs. As noted in Chapter 28, there are a number of costs that can be included in the cost of quality, such as the costs of appraisal, prevention, internal failure, and external failure. Many of these costs are most closely identified with overhead costs and so cannot be easily allocated to a specific product. However, one element is easily attributed to a product, and that is scrap. Scrap is material that is lost during the manufacturing process for any of these reasons:

EXHIBIT 29.6. Bill of Materials with Scrap Percentage

Component Description	Unit of Measure	Batch Range	Scrap %	Quantity	Per-Unit Cost	Total Cost
Base	Each	500–1,000		1	17.00	17.00
Switch	Each	1,000–2,000		1	0.75	0.75
Spring	Each	5,000–8,000		4	0.25	1.00
Extension arm, lower	Each	250–500	8	1	3.75	4.05
Extension arm, upper	Each	250–500	8	1	4.25	4.59
Adjustment knob	Each	400–800	5	2	0.75	1.58
Bulb holder	Each	1,000–5,000		1	0.30	0.30
Bulb	Each	2,000–2,500	1	1	2.15	2.17
Bulb lens	Each	500–1,000	2	1	1.50	1.53
Fabrication labor	Hr	250–500 units		2.5	18.00	45.00
Assembly labor	Hr	250–500 units		2.0	12.50	25.00
Overhead costs					6.20	6.20
Total cost						**109.17**

- Excess amounts of material trimmed from raw materials (such as leftover sheet metal when parts are stamped from a metal sheet)

- Component parts thrown out at the receiving dock because they are defective

- Component parts thrown out in the warehouse because they are either obsolete or damaged

- Component parts thrown out during the material handling stage because they have been damaged while being moved through the production facility

- Work in process rendered unusable by incorrect manufacturing processes

- Work in process damaged by incorrect assembly

- Finished goods damaged while being stored, packaged for shipment, or transferred to a customer

Given the multitude of activities during which scrap can occur, it is no surprise that scrap levels can reach into the double-digit range for many products. This can therefore be a significant cost and is listed on the BOM as a separate column, denoted "Scrap %." This percentage is then factored into the cost per unit to yield a larger total cost for each line item, as shown in Exhibit 29.6. In the exhibit no scrap percentage is assigned to purchased parts since these tend to have a small scrap percentage, while manufactured items have significant scrap levels assigned to them.

A cost accountant does not normally have to itemize the cost of quality separately from the rest of a product's cost when reporting total product costs. The one exception is when the report recipient needs the information in order to target specific reductions in the cost of quality and therefore must know where the largest scrap costs are located.

VARIATIONS IN COST BASED ON OVERHEAD

The line item on a BOM that continually raises the most questions from recipients of cost reports is the one for overhead cost. They ask if this cost is relevant, what makes up the number, and how it is allocated.

The relevance of overhead costs is dependent entirely on the use to which the cost information will be put. If the report recipient is concerned only with pricing a product at a level near its variable cost, then there is certainly no need for the overhead cost, which can be ignored. However, if the issue is what price to set over the long term in order to cover all fixed costs, then the overhead figure must be included in the calculation.

If the latter situation is involved, the cost accountant must delve deeper into the manner in which overhead costs are calculated and allocated to ensure that only relevant overhead costs are charged on the BOM. There are two factors that go into the production of the overhead number. One is the compilation of the overhead pool, which yields the grand total of all overhead costs that will subsequently be allocated to each product. The second is the allocation method used to determine how much of the fixed cost is allocated to each unit.

The overhead cost pool can contain a wide array of costs related to the production of a specific product in varying degrees. For example, there may be machine-specific costs, such as setup, depreciation, maintenance, and repairs, that have some traceable connection to a specific product at the batch level. Other overhead costs, such as building maintenance and insurance, are related more closely to the building in which the production operation is housed, which has a much looser connection to a specific product. The overhead cost pool may also contain costs for the management or production scheduling of an entire production line, as well as the costs of distributing product to customers. Given the wide-ranging nature of these costs, it is evident that a hodge-podge of costs are being accumulated into a single cost pool, which almost certainly will result in inaccurate allocations to individual products.

The most common allocation method is based on the amount of direct labor dollars used to create a product. This method can cause considerable cost misallocation because the amount of labor in a product may be so much smaller than the quantity of overhead cost to be allocated that anywhere from $1 to $4 may be allocated to a product for every $1 of direct labor cost in it. Given the high ratio of overhead to direct labor, it is easy for the amount of overhead charged to a product to swing drastically in response to a relatively minor shift in direct labor costs. A classic example of this problem is what happens when a company decides to automate a product line. When it does so, it incurs extra costs associated with new machinery, adding to the overhead cost pool. Meanwhile, the amount of direct labor in the product plummets because of the increased level of automation. Consequently, the increased amount of overhead—which is directly associated with the newly automated production line—is allocated to other products whose production has not yet been automated. This means that the overhead cost of a product created by an automated production line does not have enough overhead cost allocated to it, while the overhead cost assigned to more labor-intensive products is too high.

There are solutions to the problems of excessively congregated cost pools and allocations based on direct labor. One is to split the single overhead allocation pool into a small number of overhead cost pools. Each of these pools should contain costs closely related to each other. For example, there may be an assembly overhead cost pool (as noted in Exhibit 29.7) containing only overhead costs associated with the assembly operation, such as janitorial costs, depreciation and maintenance for assembly equipment, and the supervision costs of the assembly area. Similarly, there can be another cost pool (as also noted in Exhibit 29.7) that summarizes all fabrication costs. This pool can contain all costs associated with the manufacture and procurement of all component parts, including the costs of machinery setup, depreciation, and maintenance, as well as purchasing salaries. Finally, there can be an overall plant overhead cost pool containing the costs of building maintenance, supervision, taxes, and insurance. It may not be useful to exceed this relatively limited number of cost pools, for the complexity of cost tracking can become excessive. The result of this process is a much better summarization of costs.

Each of the newly created cost pools can then be assigned a separate cost allocation method with a direct relationship between the cost pool and the product being produced. For example, the principal activity in the assembly operation is direct labor, so this time-honored allocation method can be retained when allocating the costs of the assembly overhead cost pool to products. However, the principal activity in the fabrication area is machine hours, so this becomes the basis of allocation for fabrication overhead costs. Finally, all building-related costs are best apportioned through the total square footage of all machinery, inventory, and related operations used by each product, so square footage becomes the basis of allocation for this cost pool.

EXHIBIT 29.7. Bill of Materials with Multiple Overhead Costs

Component Description	Unit of Measure	Batch Range	Scrap %	Quantity	Per-Unit Cost ($)	Total Cost ($)
Base	Each	500–1000		1	17.00	17.00
Switch	Each	1000–2000		1	0.75	0.75
Spring	Each	5000–8000		4	0.25	1.00
Extension arm, lower	Each	250–500	8	1	3.75	4.05
Extension arm, upper	Each	250–500	8	1	4.25	4.59
Adjustment knob	Each	400–800	5	2	0.75	1.58
Bulb holder	Each	1000–5000		1	0.30	0.30
Bulb	Each	2000–2500	1	1	2.15	2.17
Bulb lens	Each	500–1000	2	1	1.50	1.53
Fabrication labor	Hr	250–250 units		2.5	18.00	45.00
Assembly labor	Hr	250–500 units		2.0	12.50	25.00
Assembly overhead	Assembly labor hour	500–1000		2.0	3.25	6.50
Fabrication overhead	Fabrication machine hour	625–1250		2.5	1.20	3.00
Plant overhead	Sq ft	5000		1	1.75	1.75
Total cost						**114.22**

The result of these changes, as noted in Exhibit 29.7, is an altered BOM that replaces a single overhead cost line item with three different overhead costs, each one allocated based on the most logical allocation measure.

A final issue related to overhead is the frequency with which the overhead cost per unit is calculated. When the cost accountant adds the overhead cost to a BOM, the typical procedure is to calculate the overhead cost pool, apply an allocation formula, and enter the cost—and not update the resulting figure again for a long time. The updating process can be as laborious as manually accessing each BOM to make an update or entering a dollar cost for each unit of allocation (such as per dollar of direct labor, hour of machine time, and so on) into a central computer, which the computer system then uses to automatically update all BOMs. In either case the overhead cost in each BOM is not updated unless specific action is taken by the cost accountant to update the overhead figures. Consequently, the overhead cost on a BOM must be regularly updated to ensure its accuracy.

By using this more refined set of overhead allocation methods, the accuracy of cost reports can be increased. In particular, it tells managers which cost pools are responsible for the bulk of overhead costs being assigned to specific products. This is information they can use to target reductions in these cost pools, thereby reducing overhead charges.

VARIATIONS IN COST BASED ON ACTIVITY CHANGES

In a few rare cases companies have even restructured their bills of material to include activity costs charged to products. This is technically possible under the rules of activity-based costing (Chapter 16) but tends to be difficult to implement in practice. One issue is that because so many cost pools are being allocated, the BOM requires several dozen additional line items to include every cost that can be allocated; a less complicated approach is to use just a few overhead line items, as noted previously in Exhibit 29.7. Another issue is that more BOM line items require more maintenance; as activity-related costs change over time, someone must access the multitude of BOMs and alter each one to reflect the changes in costs, which can be time-consuming. This is a particularly irksome task if the activity-related costs are derived through an occasional cost study that does not delve into a sufficient degree of detail to yield consistently reliable cost information.

Yet another issue is that activity-based costing spreads costs based on an object's use of an activity—but many products do not directly use activities, so it is sometimes difficult to trace activity costs back to a specific product. The final issue is that for some activities, such as market-related costs like advertising, there is only a weak linkage between cost incurrence and the product being costed; as a result, the cost accountant can have a difficult time splitting such costs into variable or fixed costs. The recipient of a costing report may end up with a large number of cost line items listed as being mixed in nature since the cost accountant cannot determine how variable they really are. This results in extreme difficulty in creating break-even measures for a product.

For all these reasons it is generally best to not try to shoehorn the results of an activity-based costing system into a bill of materials. Instead, use the ABC information to reduce the costs of various non-value-added activities with activity-based management (as noted in Chapter 16), which indirectly reduces the total amount of overhead over time, thereby lowering the costs reported on the bill of materials for the overhead line items.

VARIATIONS IN COST BASED ON TIME

An old adage points out that in the long run, nothing is certain except death and taxes. This is not precisely true. Also, virtually all costs are variable in the long run. Accountants are good at classifying costs as fixed or variable, but they must remember that *any* cost can be eliminated if enough time goes by during which a change can be effected. For example, a production facility can be eliminated, as can the taxes being paid on it, as well as all the machinery in it and the people employed there. Though these items may all seem immovable and fixed in the short run, a determined manager with a long-term view of changing an organization can eliminate or alter them all.

Some fixed costs can be converted to variable costs more easily than others. There are three main categories into which fixed costs can fall. They are:

- **Programmable costs.** These are costs generally considered to be fixed but which can be eliminated relatively easily and without the passage of much time, while also not having an immediate impact on a company's daily operations. An example of such a cost is machine maintenance. If a manager needs to hold down costs for a short period, such as a few weeks, eliminating machine maintenance will probably not have much of an impact on operations (unless the equipment is subject to continual breakdown!).

- **Discretionary costs.** These are costs considered not to vary with production volume and which frequently are itemized as administrative overhead costs. Again, these are costs that can be eliminated in the short run without causing a significant impact on operational efficiencies. Examples of discretionary costs are advertising costs and training expenses.

- **Committed costs.** These are costs to which a company is committed over a relatively long period, such as costs for major capital projects. Because of the amount of funding involved, the amount of sunk costs, and the impact on production capabilities, these are costs that can be difficult to eliminate.

A manager looking into a short-term reduction in costs most profitably focuses his or her attention on the reduction of programmable and discretionary costs since they are relatively easy to cut. If the intention is a long-term reduction, especially if the size of the reductions contemplated is large, the best type of fixed cost to target is committed costs.

If the person requesting costing information is undertaking a long-term cost reduction effort, the cost accountant should go to great lengths to identify the exact nature of all fixed costs in the costing analysis so that the recipient can determine if these costs can be converted to variable costs over the long term or even completely eliminated.

VARIATIONS IN COST BASED ON RELEVANT COSTS

In addition to all the other factors previously mentioned, there are also a number of small ancillary costs that are frequently overlooked when compiling the cost of a product or service. If a company is faced with a tight profitability situation, where a change of just a percent or two can impact its decision to carry a product, then the inclusion or exclusion of these extra costs will have a significant impact on the decision to be made.

One cost that is frequently overlooked is freight—the freight charge for delivering raw materials to a company, as well as the freight charge on products sent out to customers (if they are not charged to the customers). Freight costs incurred for the delivery of raw materials are frequently charged to a separate freight account rather than being included directly in the unit cost of each item delivered. This separate charge-off occurs because few accounting systems automatically spread the freight cost of a shipment over the number of units delivered, which means that this chore must be completed manually. Given the difficulty of this task, most accounting departments opt to record the cost separately—but the trouble is that, once it is separated from a component's cost, it is never added back again. The best way to address this issue is to periodically review the average cost of freight charges for each component delivered to a company and then enter a line item on the bill of materials for the average freight cost.

Another issue involves the taxes and insurance charged on inventory, which can take three forms. One is the sales tax on purchased products, though a well-run company obtains sales tax exemption status for all purchased components being used for resale to customers—so there is no tax liability. Nonetheless, sometimes the sales tax is inadvertently paid, or special circumstances may require its payment. If so, it is generally not charged to a specific purchased part, especially when a lump-sum sales tax is charged on an invoice containing a number of line items. Another type of tax is the annual personal property tax, which in some locales includes the value of inventory at the end of the calendar year. Since this tax is based on the cost of inventory, it is an easy matter to determine the property tax cost per dollar of inventory and then include this cost on the BOM. Similarly, the cost of insurance coverage for inventory can be entered on the BOM as a separate line item.

The same situation frequently arises when customs duties are paid for components shipped in from outside the country to a manufacturing facility. These costs tend to be charged to the freight account rather than to individual components, which shifts the cost from a variable one to an overhead account. Once again, the solution is to include this cost as a line item on the BOM.

The costs just described are also included in the overhead cost pool cost accountants allocate to products. So why bother to shift the costs from the overhead category to line items on the BOM? The reason is that when the cost accounting staff issues costing information, it frequently does so by breaking down the cost of each product into its fixed and variable cost components, which are used by the recipients of this information to make decisions. If these costs are described as fixed costs instead of variable ones, this may change the decision of the person who has just received the costing information. For example, if the sales manager is trying to decide whether to accept an offer from a customer to sell a large block of merchandise at a price that is slightly more than the variable cost of the product, his decision will be impacted if these small ancillary costs have been hidden in the overhead cost (which is considered to be fixed), rather than included in the variable cost category. The sales manager may accept the customer's offer and end up selling at a price a few percentage points below the variable cost—all because he was not aware of the additional variable costs of taxes, insurance, and duties.

VARIATIONS IN COST BASED ON THE EXPERIENCE CURVE

Yet another factor that impacts a product's cost is the experience curve. This term refers to the idea that an organization gradually improves its ability to produce a product for a lower cost as the volume of production rises. For example, when a worker is asked to produce a single unit of a new product, the time required to peruse any associated instructions, learn how to use any necessary equipment, and then manufacture the product is very high. However, when the same worker is asked to produce two units, the time required to create the second unit is far less than the amount needed for the first, since the worker acquired additional skills during the original production process. This drop in production time continues as production volume grows, though the rate of time reduction for each incremental unit rapidly drops because of a reduced level of learning for each extra unit produced. A graph illustrating how the learning curve impacts the cost of a product is shown in Exhibit 29.8, which reveals a sharp drop in costs during the earliest stages of volume increase and then progressively smaller incremental reductions as production reaches high volume levels. This exhibit uses the combined fabrication and assembly labor cost noted earlier in Exhibit 29.7 for the desk lamp at a production volume level of 500 units and shows how the total labor cost declines by nearly half if the production volume can be increased from 500 units to 16,000 units.

The formula that best represents the experience curve concept states that the time required to produce a unit drops by a set percentage every time the unit volume doubles. For example, if the time required is 100 minutes per daily production volume of 500 units, then a learning rate of 10% will result in a drop to just 90 minutes per unit if the unit of the production volume increases to 1000 units per day. If the production volume doubles again, to 2000 units per day, then the time per unit will drop by an additional 10%, resulting in a time per unit of 81 minutes. A learning rate of 10% is conservative in many instances, with rates of 20% being more common in many applications. Given the significant cost reductions that can result from the learning curve, it is apparent that the cost of a product can be heavily influenced by this issue. Accordingly, it is best to present cost data with labor costs

EXHIBIT 29.8. Experience Curve

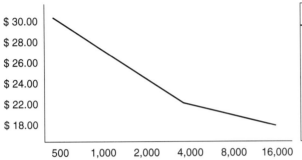

Data Table		
Unit Volume	Cost per Unit	Learning Rate
500	$ 30.50	10%
1,000	$ 27.45	10%
2,000	$ 24.71	10%
4,000	$ 22.23	10%
8,000	$ 20.01	10%
16,000	$ 18.01	10%

per unit that specify the production volume range within which the costs can be achieved. If cost reports are issued that contain experience curve assumptions well outside expected production volumes or learning rates, then the cost per unit will be wrong.

The assumption thus far has been that the impact of changes in the experience curve is primarily on direct labor costs. However, a number of indirect labor costs are also affected, such as the time required to set up a machine and the time needed to maintain one so that it can operate within a production run. These costs also drop as employees learn how to manage supporting equipment in the most efficient manner. Consequently, anticipated cost reductions can extend into the indirect labor category.

The experience curve concept is a powerful one for organizations that attempt to gain market share by pricing their products on the assumption that their costs will drop as volumes rise. By doing so, they use the experience curve to anticipate how costs will be lowered at higher production volumes and set their prices lower in expectation of achieving reasonable margins after the increased volume levels (caused by the lower prices) are reached. This approach can result in losses until the requisite production volumes are achieved, but it is an aggressive way to pull market share away from competitors who are not as aware of how their costs will decline as unit volumes increase.

A cautionary issue here is that the experience curve is not as effective if the production of a specific item is sporadic. In this case employees may forget how they originally produced an item and must spend time reacquiring the knowledge that first allowed them to produce at a lower cost. If there are long intervals between these periods of production, the beneficial impact of the experience curve may be lost. The same problem arises if the production staff has a high rate of employee turnover since some experience is lost with each person who departs. Though these issues may not entirely negate the positive impact of the experience curve, they can reduce its beneficial effect.

COST ESTIMATION METHODS

We have covered a number of issues that impact cost. After reviewing the preceding list, one might wonder how anyone ever estimates a cost with any degree of accuracy, given the number of issues that can impact it. In this section we cover a number of methods, with varying degrees of accuracy and difficulty of use, that can be used to derive costs at different levels of unit volume. These methods are of most use in situations where the costs listed on a BOM are not reliable because of the effect of outside variables (as noted in the preceding sections) that have caused costs to vary to an excessive degree.

The first and most popular method by far is to have experienced employees make a judgment call regarding whether or not a cost is fixed or variable and how much it will change under certain circumstances. For example, a plant manager may decide that the cost of utilities is half fixed and half based on the number of hours machines are operated in the facility, with this number becoming totally fixed when the facility is not running at all. This approach is frequently used because it is easy to make a determination and because in many situations the result is reasonably accurate—after all, there is something to be said for lengthy experience! However, costs may be much more or less variable than an expert estimates, resulting in inaccurate figures. Also, experts tend to assign costs to the fixed or the variable category without considering that they may really be mixed costs (as in the last example) that have both fixed and variable portions. The problem can be resolved to some degree by pooling the estimates of a number of experts or by combining this method with the results obtained from one of the more quantitative approaches to be covered shortly in this section.

A more scientific approach is the engineering method, which involves having a qualified industrial engineer team and a cost accountant conduct exact measurements of how costs relate to specific measurements. For example, this approach may use time-and-motion studies to determine the exact amount of direct labor required to produce one unit of finished goods. The result is precise information about the relationship between a cost and a specific activity measure. However, this approach is extremely time-consuming and so is difficult to use when there are many costs and activities to compare. Also, the cost levels examined are accurate only for the specific volume range being used at the time of the engineering study. When the study is conducted at a different volume of production, the original costing information per unit produced may no longer be accurate. However, since many businesses operate only within relatively narrow bands of production capacity, the latter issue may not be a problem. A final issue with the engineering method is that it cannot be used to determine the per-unit cost of many costs for which there is no direct relationship to a given activity. For example, there is only a tenuous linkage in the short run between the amount of money spent on advertising and the number of units sold, so the engineering method is of little use in uncovering per-unit advertising costs. Despite these problems, the engineering method can be a reasonable alternative if confined to costs that bear a clear relationship to specific activities and for which there are no significant changes in the level of activity from period to period.

An alternative approach that avoids an intensive engineering review is the scattergraph method. Under this approach the cost accounting staff compiles activity data for a given period and then plots it on a chart in relation to the costs incurred in the same period. An example of a scattergraph is shown in Exhibit 29.9. In the exhibit we plot the relationship between the number of units produced and the total variable material cost for the period. The total material cost is noted on the Y axis, and the number of units on the X axis. Though there is some variability in the positioning of costs per unit at different volume levels, it is clear that there is a significant relationship between the number of units produced and the total variable material cost. After completing the scattergraph the cost accountant manually fits a line to the data (as also noted in the exhibit). Then, by measuring the slope of the line and the point where the line intercepts the Y axis, one can determine not only the variable cost per unit of production but also the amount of fixed costs that will be incurred, irrespective of the level of production. This is a good quantitative way to assemble relevant data into a coherent structure from which costing information can be derived but suffers from the possible inaccuracy of the user's interpretation of where the average slope and placement of the line should be within the graph. If the user creates an incorrect Y intercept or slope angle, the resulting information pertaining to fixed and variable costs will be inaccurate. However, this approach gives the user an immediate visual overview of any data items that are clearly far outside the normal cluster of data, which allows her to investigate and correct these outlying data points or at least to exclude them from any further calculations on the grounds that they are extraneous. Further, the scattergraph method may result in a shapeless blob of data elements that clearly contain no linearities, which indicates that there is no relationship between the costs and activity measures being reviewed and means that some other relationship must be found. There are two ways to create a more precise determination of the linearity of this information—the high-low method and the regression calculation.

Since the manual plotting of a "best fit" line through a scattergraph can be quite inaccurate, a better approach is to use a mathematical formula that derives the best fit line without the risk of operator error. One such method is the high-low method. To conduct this calculation, we take only the highest and lowest values from the data used in the scattergraph and determine the difference between them. When the

EXHIBIT 29.9. Scattergraph Chart

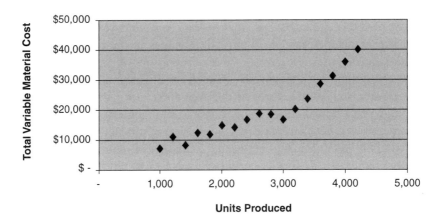

Scattergraph

same data noted in the scattergraph in Exhibit 29.9 is used, the calculation of the differential is:

	Total Variable Material Cost ($)	Units Produced
Highest value in data set	40,000	4,250
Lowest value in data set	8,000	1,000
Difference	32,000	3,250

The calculation of the cost per unit produced is $32,000 divided by 3250, which is the net change in cost divided by the net change in activity. The result is $9.85 in material costs per unit produced.

There may also be a fixed cost component to the trend line, indicating that costs will be present even if no activities occur. This is not the case in the example since we are focusing on variable material costs. However, it may well be the case in many other situations. For example, if the preceding trend line were the result of an analysis of machine costs per unit produced, we would intuitively know that some machine costs will still occur even if no units are produced. These costs can include depreciation on equipment, preventive maintenance, and personal property taxes. We can still use the high-low method to determine the amount of these fixed costs.

To do so we continue to use the $9.85 per unit in variable costs derived in the last example but increase the cost for the lowest data value observed to $11,000. We then multiply the variable cost per unit of $9.85 by the total number of units produced at the lowest observed level, which is 1000 units, obtaining a total variable cost of $9850. However, the total cost at the lowest observed activity level is $11,000, which exceeds the calculated variable cost of $9850 by $1150. This excess amount of cost represents the fixed costs that will be incurred irrespective of the level of activity. This information can be summarized into a formula describing the line, which is:

Y intercept = $1150
Slope of line = $9.85 × (number of units produced)

or

$Y = \$1150 + \$9.85 \times$ (number of units produced)

The obvious problem with the high-low method is that it uses only two values out of the entire available set of data, which may result in a less accurate best fit line than would be the case if all the scattergraph data were included in the calculation. The problem is particularly acute if one of the high or low values is a stray figure caused by incorrect data and is therefore so far outside the normal range of data that the resulting high-low calculation is significantly skewed. This problem can be avoided to some extent if the high and low values are averaged over a cluster of values at the high and low ends of the data range, or if the data is visually examined prior to making the calculation, and clearly inaccurate data is either discarded or corrected.

A formulation that avoids the high-low calculation's problem of using too few data items is called linear regression. It uses every data item in a data set to calculate the variable and fixed cost components of an activity within a specific activity range. This calculation is best derived on an electronic spreadsheet, which can quickly determine the best fit line on the scattergraph that comes the closest to all data points. It does so by calculating the line for which the sum of all squared deviations between the line and all data elements results in the smallest possible figure. The calculation of this process is described in detail in Chapter 38, and the result is shown in Exhibit 29.10, where a line has been plotted through the scattergraph by the computer. A variation on the process is shown in the same graph, which includes a curvilinear regression line that matches the data more closely. The curvilinear approach does not force the computer program to determine a straight line from the available data, thereby revealing trends in the data that may not otherwise be immediately apparent, such as higher or lower variable costs per unit at different volume levels.

EXHIBIT 29.10.   Linear and Curvilinear Regression Analysis

Scattergraph

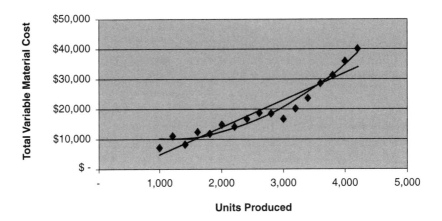

The regression calculation method is the most accurate of all cost prediction models but has several problems that one must be aware of when creating regression calculations. They are:

- **Verify a valid cause-and-effect relationship.** Even though the regression analysis may appear to find a solid relationship between an activity and a cost, be sure to give the relationship a reality test to ensure that it is valid. For example, there is a long-running, completely irrelevant relationship between the height of women's skirts and variations in the stock market. Even though there is a statistically valid relationship, there is no factual reason for it to exist, and so there is no reason to believe that changes in the activity can accurately predict stock market volatility in the future. Similarly, make sure that the activity measure being included in a regression analysis bears a reasonable relationship to the cost being reviewed.

- **Pick a cost driver with a statistically strong relationship to the activity being measured.** No matter how obviously a cost driver appears to relate to an activity from a commonsense standpoint, it may not be suitable if the measured data does not support the relationship. A tight relationship is one where the trend line in the regression analysis has a steep slope, and about which the data points are tightly clustered. If this is not the case, another cost driver should be found that results in a better statistical relationship.

- **Verify the accuracy of data collection methods.** A regression analysis may result in a weak correlation between a cost driver and an activity—not because there is in fact a weak correlation but because the data collection system compiling the activity data is not functioning properly. To correct this problem one should examine the procedures, forms, training, and data entry methods used to accumulate all activity data, and have the system periodically audited to ensure that the correct information is being reported.

- **Include all relevant costs.** When comparing an activity to a cost, a common problem is to not include costs because they are recorded in the wrong account or in the wrong time period. In the former case better attention should be paid to how costs are compiled and stored in the accounting system. In the latter case the easiest way to ensure that costs are included in the correct time period is to lengthen the time period used for the study—for example, from a month to a quarter. In this way interperiod changes in costs are eliminated and the sample size is so much larger that any remaining problems with the timing of costs are rendered statistically insignificant.

- **Ensure that the time required is worth the effort.** A regression analysis involves the determination of a cost driver, data collection, plotting on a scatter-graph to find and correct outlying data items, and (finally) the actual regression calculation. If the benefit of obtaining this information is less than the not inconsiderable cost of the effort required to obtain it, one should switch to a less accurate, less expensive prediction method that will yield a more favorable cost-benefit ratio.

No matter which of the preceding methods are used, there is still the potential for errors in costing predictions, given the various problems inherent in each method. To counteract some of these problems, it is useful to combine methods. For example, the linear regression method can derive an accurate formulation of fixed costs and variable costs per unit, but only if the data used is accurate; by preceding the regression analysis with a review of the data by an expert who can discard or adjust inaccurate data, the resulting regression analysis can be significantly improved. This same principle can be applied to any of the quantitative measures discussed here—if the underlying data is reviewed by experienced personnel prior to running the calculations, the results will be improved.

PROVIDING THE CORRECT COST INFORMATION TO MANAGEMENT

The preceding sections make it quite obvious that there are many factors that can alter a product's cost. Given this level of variability, the cost accountant will have difficulty reporting costing information unless he or she knows the precise use to which the information will be put. Otherwise, the recipient may use the cost information to take actions that fall outside the parameters within which the costs were developed, resulting in incorrect actual costs in comparison to the originally reported cost levels. This is the case all too often, and it results in accusations that the accounting staff is not supplying accurate information to the rest of the company, which in turn results in a defensive review of the data by the accounting staff and a general waste of time all around.

A better way to ensure that the management team is provided with the correct cost information is to walk them through a checklist of costing parameters, which the cost accountant can then use to compile costs relevant to the activity range being contemplated by management. A sample of such a checklist is:

- **To what use will this costing information be put?** This blanket question may illicit a great deal of extra information that will allow the preparer to create a more relevant document.

- **Is full or direct costing needed?** If the user needs only direct costs, the report can exclude any fixed costs that would otherwise cloud the issue the report requester is trying to resolve.

- **Will direct labor employees be laid off as a result of this costing report?** If not, the direct labor cost noted in the cost report should be treated as a fixed cost that will not decline as the unit volume drops.

- **What is the volume range for the purchased and manufactured component parts?** If the report's user is contemplating a large change in production volumes for an item, the cost report must be adjusted to reflect the costs that will be encountered within that volume range.

- **Will there be associated changes in quality costs?** If there is an ongoing or contemplated program of quality cost reduction, any changes in costs should be reflected in the cost report. However, if these costs cannot be quantified, it may be better to err on the side of caution and not itemize these cost reductions.

- **Are changes in overhead costs contemplated?** A cost report can be requested so that managers can determine what types of overhead costs are associated with specific products, which they can then use to target overhead cost reductions. If so, the cost report must include a much higher degree of detail about overhead costs than is normally itemized.

- **Are changes in activities contemplated?** The management team may be targeting reductions in the costs of specific activities associated with a product; if so, the cost report should itemize the various costs of such activities, as described in detail in Chapter 16.

- **Over what time period will this information be used?** If the management team will use a cost report over a long time period, such as the next budget year, the cost accountant can include some text describing how some fixed costs in the report can be eliminated or reduced over this longer time period, and what effect this change will have on the product cost.

- **What costs are considered relevant?** The person requesting a cost report may not need a complete set of cost information, but rather a short analysis of some portion of a product's costs. If so, the cost accountant can strip away a considerable amount of excess cost information.

- **Is production expected to be continuous or sporadic?** The impact of the experience curve on a product's cost is largely negated if production runs are widely separated in time since workers must relearn the manufacturing process every time. The cost accountant can use this information to alter the costs in the cost report accordingly.

The responses to all these questions should be attached to the costing report, so that any future problems with the information can be quickly researched. All costing reports should be filed in whatever manner will result in easy access to the information at some later date. Not only is this filing system a good one for assisting the cost accounting staff in defending its costing assumptions, but it also is useful for later comparison to actual results in case the original assumptions being used are modified (based on experience) in future analyses.

It may also be useful to have the report recipient sign the document containing all costing assumptions so that there is evidence of general agreement regarding them. This may seem like an excessive administrative step, but it can be useful in situations where there is a history of strong negative reactions to costing reports perceived to be inaccurate.

This detailed approach to documenting the assumptions used to create costing reports is a good way to ensure that the costing information disseminated to management is relevant to that group's specific needs.

CASE STUDY

Ms. Emily North is a cost accountant with the General Research and Instrumentation Company. She has just received a request from the product manager for the company's line of wrist-mounted global positioning systems to provide him with the cost of the product. The product has been produced for a year, so there is a good cost history on it compiled in a bill of materials that shows a fully burdened cost of $270 per unit. However, she hesitates to issue this information without learning more about the uses to which it will be put. Accordingly, she quizzes the product manager and finds out that the company wants to increase the marketing effort for this product from its current summer-only sales period (targeted at recreational enthusiasts), with a volume of 25,000 units, to a worldwide effort that can target the summer period in both the northern and southern hemispheres, with an estimated annual production volume of 50,000 units. This means that production can be increased from the current small batch run in the spring of each year to a continuous production run maintained at a moderate volume level throughout the year. Ms. North realizes that this single change can have a significant impact on the cost of the product, for a continual production process is likely to enjoy benefits not only from an experience curve but also from reduced scrap related to continuing refinement of the production process that would not otherwise occur in the current short-term production run environment. Offsetting these improvements will be the need for a quality control staff person to monitor improvements in quality processes in the production line.

Armed with this extra information, Ms. North searches through the company's other product lines and finds a comparable product that has experienced a drop in costs of 10% after 1 year because of the experience curve. It also lowered scrap costs as a percentage of the total cost by 5%, which took 2 years to accomplish. She also discusses purchasing volumes with the purchasing manager and discovers that a key component can be reduced in cost by 25% when production volumes reach the new, higher levels. This will result in an overall improvement in costs of 8%.

She then constructs a cost time line for the product manager that lists the current cost, less the 8% reduction due to the drop in purchasing costs, plus the fixed cost of the quality control person, as the appropriate cost for the first year of production. Then she reduces the cost by the estimated impact of the learning curve and scrap rate in the subsequent 2 years. This information results in the format shown in Exhibit 29.11.

Ms. North's analysis shows that there will be a significant drop in costs when production volumes are doubled. She could have added an additional cost savings in the year 2004 due to another 10% reduction in costs related to the experience curve; however, not having enough information about the likelihood of this occurrence from experience with similar product lines, she elects to leave the further cost reduction out of her analysis and merely points out the possibility in the footnotes that accompany her report.

This format tells the product manager that there are substantial opportunities for profitability improvements if this increase in sales is successfully completed, possibly enough to make it worth the company's efforts to pay for expansion into the new markets by purchasing or setting up distributorships. If Ms. North had not inquired into the uses to which the cost information would be put, the product manager would only have received a copy of the current bill of materials, which would not have indicated the possibility of a significant cost reduction. In this case the type of cost information reported had a profound impact on a company's decision to pursue a new sales strategy.

EXHIBIT 29.11. Sample Cost Report

	2002	2003	2004
Current full cost	$270.00	$270.00	$270.00
− Purchase cost reduction	21.60	21.60	21.60
− Experience curve cost reduction	0.00	27.00	27.00
− Scrap cost reduction	0.00	6.75	6.75
= Revised unit cost	$248.40	$214.65	$214.65
Number of units produced	50,000	50,000	50,000
Total cost of units produced	$12,420,000	$10,732,500	$10,732,500
+ Quality control staff person	$40,000	$40,000	$40,000
Grand total cost of production	$12,460,000	$10,772,500	$10,772,500
Divided by number of units produced	50,000	50,000	50,000
Cost per unit	**$249.20**	**$215.45**	**$215.45**

SUMMARY

Costs can vary based on a large range of factors, such as time, experience, volume, and quality. The cost accountant must be aware of the impact of all these factors on costs, so that he or she can properly formulate cost estimates in response to specific requests for information. Without adjusting for these factors, a cost estimate used for pricing, capacity, or break-even analysis may be so significantly incorrect that the underlying analysis is rendered useless. Consequently, this chapter should be continually used by cost accountants as a reminder of the factors that will directly impact costs and which should be included in many analyses.

PART VI

Pricing Issues

CHAPTER 30

Transfer Pricing

Many organizations sell their own products internally—from one division to another. This is especially common in vertically integrated situations, where a company has elected to control the key pieces of its supply chain, perhaps to "lock down" the supply of key components. Each division sells its products to a downstream division that includes these items in its own production processes. When this happens, management must determine the prices at which components are sold between divisions. This is known as transfer pricing. The transfer price is important, for the managers of each division use it to determine if they should sell to an internal division or externally, on the open market. If the transfer price is set too low, managers will have an incentive to sell outside the company, even if the organization as a whole would benefit from a greater volume of internal transfers. Similarly, an excessively high transfer price will result in too many internal sales, when some external ones would yield a higher overall profit. Because of its impact on the operational behavior of corporate divisions, care must be taken in selecting the most appropriate transfer price.

This chapter considers a wide range of transfer pricing methods and several special issues involving them. It concludes with a summary and comparison of all transfer pricing methods, as well as a case study involving the use of the more common ones.

IMPORTANCE OF TRANSFER PRICING

Transfer pricing levels are important in companies with any of the following three transfer or operational characteristics:

- **High volumes of interdivisional sales.** This is most common in vertically integrated companies, where each division in succession produces a component that is a necessary part of the product being created by the next division in line. Any incorrect transfer pricing under this scenario can cause considerable dysfunctional behavior, as noted later in this section.

- **High volumes of segment-specific sales.** Even if a company as a whole does not transfer much product between its divisions, this does not mean that specific departments or product lines within each division do not have a much greater dependence on the accuracy of transfer pricing for selected products.

- **High degree of organizational decentralization.** When an organization is arranged under the theory that divisions should operate as independently as possible, they are not motivated to work together unless the transfer prices used are set at levels that give them an economic incentive to do so.

Alternatively, the theoretical foundation for the calculation of transfer prices is of little importance for organizations with a high degree of centralization, for individual divisions are ordered to produce and transfer products to other divisions by the headquarters staff, irrespective of the prices charged. This is also the case for companies that rarely transfer any products among their divisions, for such transfers, when they occur, are typically approved at the highest management levels if they are large, or are so small that their impact is minimal.

For organizations with the first set of conditions noted above, it is crucial to be aware of the key factors that are influenced by the level of transfer pricing used. One is the overall level of corporate profitability, another is its use in determining the financial performance of each division, and yet another is the ease of use of the transfer pricing method selected. Each of these factors is discussed below.

The chief issue for any corporation is how to maximize its overall level of profitability. To do so, it must set its transfer prices at levels that will result in the highest possible profits, not for individual divisions but rather for the entire organization. For example, if a transfer price is set at nothing more than its cost, the selling division would rather not sell the product at all; however, the buying division can sell it externally for a huge profit that more than makes up for the lack of profit obtained by the division that originally produced it. A typical division manager selects product sales that result in the highest level of profit only for his division since he has no insight into (or interest in) the financial condition of the rest of the organization. Only if a way is found for the selling division to also realize a profit will it have an incentive to sell its products internally, thereby resulting in greater over-

EXHIBIT 30.1. Example of an Incorrect Transfer Price

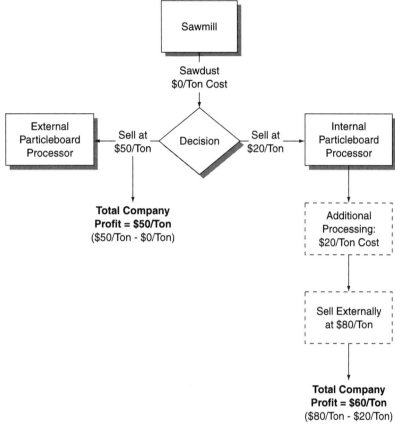

all profits. An example of such a situation is when a selling division creates a by-product that it cannot sell but which another division can use as an input for the products it manufactures. The selling division scraps the by-product because it has no incentive to do anything else with it. However, when the selling division is assigned a small profit from the sale of the by-product, it has an incentive to ship it to the buying division. Such a pricing strategy assists a company in deriving the greatest possible profit from all its activities. If such steps are not taken, then the situation noted in Exhibit 30.1 can arise. In the exhibit a sawmill is currently selling its sawdust to an outside company for $50 per ton. It does this because the internal transfer price for selling the sawdust to another division is only $20 per ton. The sawmill manager's actions in selling the sawdust externally are entirely rational from the perspective of the sawmill. However, since the internal division that would otherwise buy the sawdust could convert it to particleboard and sell it for a total company profit of $60 per ton, the profits of the company as a whole are reduced by $10 per ton; this problem is due entirely to the use of an incorrect transfer price.

Another factor is that the amount of profit allocated to a division through the transfer pricing method used impacts its reported level of profitability and therefore the performance review for that division and its management team. When the management team is compensated in large part through performance-based bonuses, its actions are heavily influenced by the profit it can earn on intercompany transfers, especially if such transfers make up a large proportion of total divisional sales. When transfer prices are set at high levels, this can result in the manufacture of far more product than needed, which may lock up so much production capacity that the selling division is no longer able to create other products that can be sold for a profit. Conversely, an excessively low transfer price results in no production at all, as long as the selling division has some other product available that it can sell for a greater profit. The latter situation frequently results in late or small deliveries to the buying divisions since the managers of the selling divisions see fit to produce low-price items only if there is spare production capacity available that can be used in no other way. Thus, improper transfer prices motivate division managers in accordance with how the prices impact their performance evaluations.

Yet another factor to consider is that the method used should be simple enough for easy calculation on a regular basis—some transfer pricing methods appear to yield elegant solutions but require the use of such arcane accounting methods that their increased utility is more than outweighed by their level of formulation difficulty. This is a particularly thorny problem when the pricing method requires constant recalculation. For everyday use a simple, easily understandable transfer pricing method is preferred.

Finally, altering the transfer price used can have a dramatic impact on the amount of income taxes a company pays if it has divisions located in different countries with different tax rates (this issue is discussed separately in Chapter 39). All these issues must be considered when selecting an appropriate transfer pricing method.

Companies that are frequent users of transfer pricing must create prices based on a proper balance of the goals of overall company profitability, divisional performance evaluation, simplicity of use, and (in some cases) reduction of income taxes. Attainment of all these goals by using a single transfer pricing method is not common and should not be expected. Instead, managers must focus on achieving the most critical goals, while keeping the adverse affects of not meeting other goals at a minimum. This approach may result in the use of several transfer pricing methods, depending on the circumstances surrounding each interdivisional transfer.

The following sections are divided into two main groups. The first cluster of topics covers transfer prices that are directly or indirectly related to transfer prices derived in some manner from market-based prices. The second group covers transfer prices that are instead based on product costs, usually because no reliable market price is available. The advantages and disadvantages of each transfer pricing method are noted in the relevant sections, so that one can find the most appropriate method that most closely meshes with his or her pricing requirements.

TRANSFER PRICING BASED ON MARKET PRICES

The most commonly used transfer pricing technique is based on the existing external market price. Under this approach the selling division matches its transfer price to the current market rate. By doing so a company can attain all the goals outlined in the last section. First, it can achieve the highest possible corporatewide profit. This happens because the selling division can earn just as much profit by selling all its production outside the company as it can by selling it internally—there is no reason to use a transfer price that results in the incorrect behavior of either selling externally at an excessively low price or selling internally when a better deal can be obtained by selling externally. Second, using the market price allows a division to earn a profit on its sales, no matter whether it sells internally or externally. By avoiding all transfers at cost, the senior management group can structure its divisions as profit centers, thereby allowing it to determine the performance of each division manager. Third, the market price is simple to obtain—it can be taken from regulated price sheets, posted prices, or quoted prices and applied directly to all sales. No complicated calculations are required, and arguments over the correct price to charge between divisions are kept to a minimum. Fourth, a market-based transfer price allows both buying and selling divisions to shop anywhere they want in buying or selling their products. For example, a buying division is indifferent as to where it obtains its supplies, for it can buy them at the same price whether or not that source is a fellow company division. This leads to a minimum of incorrect buying and selling behavior that would otherwise be driven by transfer prices that do not reflect market conditions. For all these reasons companies are well advised to use market-based transfer prices whenever possible.

Unfortunately, many corporations do not use this type of pricing, not because they do not want to but because there are no market prices available. This happens when the products being transferred do not exactly match those sold on the market. For example, wheat is a product that is exactly like the wheat sold by other companies; however, a dishwasher may not be exactly like the dishwashers made elsewhere—their features are sufficiently different that the market rate does not apply. Also, many transfers are for intermediate-level products that have not yet been converted to final products, so there is no market price available for them. When such situations arise, the transfer price must be obtained by other means, as described in the following sections.

Another problem with the use of market prices is that there must truly be an alternative for a selling division to sell its entire production externally. This does not work if the market for the product is too small, for dumping an excessively large quantity of product on the market at one time depresses its price; when this happens, the selling division may find that it could have obtained a better price if it had sold its production internally. This is a common problem for specialty products, where the number of potential buyers is small and their annual buying needs are limited in size.

Another problem with market pricing is that the market price may not accurately reflect the somewhat reduced cost of selling a product to another division. A selling division may find that internal sales are slightly more profitable than external ones because of reductions in selling costs, bad debt expenses, and a reduced investment in accounts receivable. With such incentives available, a selling division ignores the possibility of selling externally and pushes as much of its production onto the buying division as possible, which may result in more shipments to the buyer than it needs. This is dealt with in more detail in the next section.

A final issue is that market-based pricing can work against the objectives of the senior management team if it drives selling divisions to sell their production outside the company. This problem arises in tight supply situations, where a buying division cannot obtain a sufficient amount of parts from a selling division because it is selling them externally, and outside manufacturers cannot produce sufficient quantities to make up the difference. In this case the selling division maximizes its own profit at the expense of divisions that need its output. This is particularly important when the buying division adds so much value to the product that it can then sell it externally at a much higher margin than the selling division could. These problems may require the corporate headquarters staff to require all or a specified portion of divisional output to be sold internally.

For all the reasons noted here, the majority of corporations find that they cannot use a purely market-driven transfer pricing system. It is still the best approach for the limited number of situations in which it can be used, but other techniques must be considered if the problems with market-based pricing outweigh its associated benefits. In the next section we look at the applicability of adjusted market prices to the transfer pricing problem.

TRANSFER PRICING BASED ON ADJUSTED MARKET PRICES

Though market pricing is generally the best way to derive a transfer price, there are many cases where such prices must be altered slightly to account for slight anomalies in the external market prices or for internal factors.

When market prices are heavily dependent on the volume of products purchased, there may be a wide array of prices, all of them valid but only for a set range of product quantities. For example, a single car battery may sell for $60, but when sold by the trailer load, the price drops to $45. Which price should a division use when setting its transfer price? If it uses a wide range of transfer prices to reflect different sales volumes to buying divisions , it will achieve a reasonable correspondence between market prices and internal unit volumes. However, this may lead to a large number of transfer prices to keep track of, which can be difficult if a company transfers many products between its divisions. A simple approach is to determine the average shipment size once a year and set transfer prices based on that volume, thereby allowing a division to use just one transfer price instead of many. If a buying division turns out to have purchased in significantly different quantities than the ones assumed at the time prices were set, then a company can retroactively adjust transfer prices at the end of the year; or it can leave the pricing alone and let the divisions do a better job of planning their interdivisional transfer volumes in the next year. The latter method is generally the better one because the alternative of a multitiered transfer pricing formula tends to be difficult to calculate, not to mention mediate—division managers like to argue over the correct pricing to use when they have a number of choices.

There are also several internal factors that may require a company to adjust its market-based transfer prices. One is the complete absence of bad debt. When a company sells externally, it reserves a small proportion of each sale for accounts receivable that will never be collected. However, when sales are made internally, there is no reason to believe that other divisions cannot pay their bills. Accordingly, this expense can be eliminated from the price charged to internal customers. Another such cost is for the sales staff. If sales arrangements have already been made between divisions, the purchasing staffs and production planners from the selling and buying divisions (respectively) can bypass the sales staff of the selling division to place orders. Accordingly, the cost of the sales staff does not need to be apportioned to internal sales, which further reduces transfer prices. There may also be opportunities to reduce freight costs if product shipments can be handled by a company's internal transportation fleet (assuming that this cost is less than what would be incurred by using a third-party shipper to deliver to an outside party). Finally, when divisions pay each other promptly, the cost required to support the selling division's investment in accounts receivable can be reduced. All these factors can result in a respectable reduction in the transfer price charged to a buying division.

When the external sales price is adjusted downward to account for all these factors, the difference may be sufficiently large that divisions find themselves increasing their sales to one another to a considerable extent. This is just what the headquarters management team of an integrated corporation wants to see, as long as the adjusted prices are not so low that the internal transfer prices result in behavior skewed in favor of sales transactions that do not lead to optimal levels of corporate profitability.

A major issue to be aware of when using this pricing method is that there can be arguments between divisions over the exact reductions in external sale prices to be made. If there are aggressive managers running each division, those operating the selling divisions will resist any reductions in the external sale price, while those managing the buying divisions will push hard for greater reductions. These squabbles can devolve into prolonged arguments that can seriously affect the management time available to each division's management team. Also, if the negotiations for price adjustments excessively favor one division over another, the "losing" division may either sell its production or purchase its components elsewhere rather than conduct any further internal dealings. The corporate headquarters staff should watch out for and intervene in such situations to ensure that adjusted market pricing results in optimal internal transfer pricing levels.

TRANSFER PRICING BASED ON NEGOTIATED PRICES

Market-based pricing is generally the best way to structure transfer prices. However, there are many cases where external market prices are highly volatile or where the volumes being transferred between divisions are so variable that it is difficult to determine the correct transfer price. In these special situations many organizations use negotiated transfer pricing.

Under this technique the managers of the buying and selling divisions negotiate a transfer price between themselves, using a product's variable cost as the lower boundary of an acceptable negotiated price and the market price (if one is available) as the upper boundary. The price agreed on, as long as it falls between these two boundaries, should provide some profit for each division, with more profit going to the division with the better negotiating skills. This method has the advantage of allowing division managers to operate their businesses in a more independent manner and not have to rely on preset pricing. It also results in better performance evaluations for managers with better negotiation skills.

Unfortunately, there are several issues that relegate this approach to only a secondary role in most transfer pricing situations. First, when the negotiated price excessively favors one division over another, the losing division searches outside the company for a better deal on the open market and directs its sales and purchases in that direction; this may result in suboptimal companywide profitability levels. Also, the negotiation process can take up a substantial proportion of a manager's time, not leaving enough for other management activities. This is a particular problem if prices require constant renegotiation. Finally, interdivisional conflicts over negotiated prices can become so severe that the problem is kicked up through the corporate chain of command to the president, who must step in and set prices that the divisions are incapable of determining by themselves. For all these reasons the negotiated transfer price is the method generally relegated to special or low-volume pricing situations.

TRANSFER PRICING BASED ON CONTRIBUTION MARGINS

What should a company do if there is no market price for a product? It has no basis for creating a transfer price from any external source of information, so it must use internal information instead. One approach is to create transfer prices based on a product's contribution margin.

Under the contribution margin pricing system, a company determines the total contribution margin earned after a product is sold externally and then allocates this margin back to each division, based on their respective proportions of the total product cost. There are several good reasons for using this approach. They are:

- **Converts a cost center to a profit center.** Without this profit allocation method a company must resort to transfer pricing based on only product costs (as noted in later sections), which requires it to use cost centers. By using this method to assign profits to internal product sales, a company can force its divisional managers to pay stricter attention to their profitability, which helps the overall profitability of the organization. Also, when an organization has profit centers, it is easier to decentralize operations since there is no longer a need for a large central bureaucracy to keep watch over divisional costs—the divisions are now in a position to do this work themselves.

- **Encourages divisions to work together.** When every supplying division shares in the margin when a product is sold, it stands to reason that they will be much more anxious to work together to achieve profitable sales, rather than bicker over the transfer prices to be charged internally. Also, any profit improvements that can be brought about only by changes that span several divisions are much more likely to receive general approval and cooperation under this pricing method, since these changes increase profits for all divisions.

These are powerful arguments that make the contribution margin approach the most popular transfer pricing method next to the market price approach. Despite its useful attributes, it has a number of problems a company must guard against in order to avoid behavior by divisions that will lead to less than optimal overall levels of profitability. They are:

- **Can increase assigned profits by increasing costs.** When the contribution margin is assigned based on a division's relative proportion of total product costs, it does not take long for the divisions to realize that they will receive a greater share of the profits if they can increase their overall proportion of costs. This problem can be counteracted by allocation based on a standard cost that is carefully reviewed and agreed on once a year, rather than an actual cost that requires constant oversight to avoid the loading of unrelated costs.

- **Must share cost reductions.** If a division finds a way to reduce its costs, it will only receive an increased share of the resulting profits in proportion to its share of the total contribution margin distributed. For example, if Division A's costs are 20% of a product's total costs and Division B's share is 80%, then 80% of a $1 cost reduction achieved by Division A will be allocated to Division B, even though it has done nothing to deserve the increase in margin. This problem can be avoided by basing the contribution margin allocation on standard costs once a year; this approach allows each division to reduce its costs below their standard levels and retain all the resulting profit savings.

- **Difficult to allocate among many divisions.** Some highly vertically integrated organizations have dozens of divisions selling each other products of various kinds. In these cases it is difficult to determine the correct margin allocations simply because of the number of transfers. This task can be achieved, but it requires a large accounting staff to calculate the distributions.

- **Requires involvement of the corporate headquarters staff.** The contribution margin allocation must be calculated by someone, and since the divisions all have a profit motive to skew the allocation in their favor, the only party left that can make the allocation is the headquarters staff. This may require the addition of cost accountants to the headquarters staff, which will increase corporate overhead.

- **Results in arguments.** When costs and profits can be skewed by the system, there are inevitably arguments between the buying and selling divisions, which the corporate headquarters team may have to mediate. These issues detract from an organization's focus on profitability.

The contribution margin approach is not a perfect one, but it does give companies a reasonably understandable, workable method for determining transfer prices. It has more problems than market-based pricing but can be used as an alternative, or as the primary approach if there is no way to obtain market pricing for transferred products.

TRANSFER PRICING BASED ON MARGINAL COST

A transfer pricing technique supported more in the classroom than in corporations is based on marginal costs. Under this methodology a company should continue to sell a product up until the point where the incremental increase in costs for each additional unit is exactly matched by the transfer price. In this way a division can earn the maximum amount of profit by selling the largest possible quantity of a product that still earns a profit. This concept is illustrated in Exhibit 30.2.

As noted in the exhibit, a cost that a company incurs to produce a product gradually declines as it reaches optimum production volumes, which tends to be when a manufacturing facility is producing in the range of 50% to 80% of its total capacity. In this zone the production staff does not need to incur overtime hours, nor does the maintenance staff have to work during odd shifts to repair failed machinery, since there is enough slack time in the production schedule to complete any tasks during the normal workday. However, as production volumes rise past this optimum point and the company enters the upper reaches of its maximum capacity

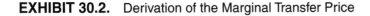

EXHIBIT 30.2. Derivation of the Marginal Transfer Price

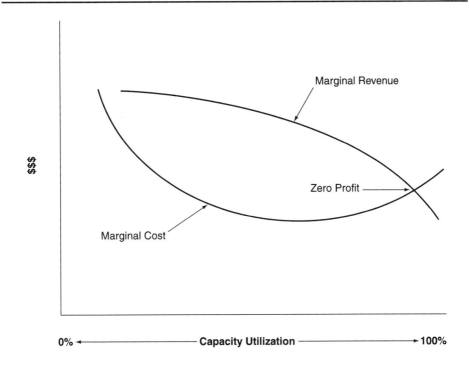

levels, it becomes more expensive to create each additional unit of product; the staff must work overtime or during late shifts that require a pay premium, while the machines require immediate repairs that may call for maintenance at any time of the day or night and the procurement of spare parts on a rush (and expensive) basis. For these reasons the incremental cost to produce one additional unit of production gradually declines as production volumes go up but then becomes more expensive as high levels of capacity utilization are reached.

As long as the transfer price is higher than the incremental cost required to make each additional unit of production, a division should continue to produce more parts (assuming that there is a willing buyer in the buying division for the extra units). However, once the marginal increase in costs forces a product's cost up to the point where there is no profit to be made on the sale of one more unit, then a division should sell no additional products. Though this approach works fine in theory, it is not simple to operate in practice. These problems make it a difficult transfer pricing system to use:

- **Lack of marginal cost information.** Few organizations have such a fine-tuned knowledge of their marginal costs that they can determine the exact point where marginal costs equal the transfer price. Most organizations operate their manufacturing facilities only within a narrow band of capacity utilization (opting for production consistency) and so have no idea of what additional costs will be incurred if more capacity is used. Instead, the cost accounting staff can only specify a range of production volumes somewhere within which the marginal cost will equal the transfer price. Because of this lack of precision, a division may find itself producing additional units at a loss.

- **Lack of marginal price information.** As production volumes increase, it is possible that so many units of the product will become available to buyers that they will begin to bid the price downward. If so, the point at which the marginal increase in product cost matches the marginal decrease in prices may come much sooner than expected. Since it is difficult to predict how prices will change as volumes increase, this makes it hard to predict the exact point at which additional production of a product will result in no further profits.

- **Impact of step costing.** In reality, costs do not increase by small amounts as each marginal unit of production is added. Instead, they tend to remain steady within certain ranges of production and then undergo sudden jumps in cost. These jumps are known as step costs and are caused by the acquisition of new assets or the need for additional activities that are required as soon as production levels reach a certain level of intensity. For example, if a production line cannot produce at a higher level without the addition of a band saw at a bottleneck operation, the cost of acquiring this band saw is a step cost. Similarly, moving additional production to a weekend shift requires the payment of a shift premium that represents a permanent increase in costs at the higher level of production. It is difficult to estimate the size or timing of these step costs, which makes it hard to ascertain the exact increases in marginal costs as production volumes go up.

- **Incentive problem.** As a division approaches the point at which its marginal costs nearly match its marginal revenue on the sale of each additional unit, its incentive to continue to churn out more products declines. This happens because its profit return approaches zero as it approaches this point. The manager of the selling division sees costs escalating and profits declining on additional sales and so prefers to stop production well short of the point where profits equal zero. The reason for stopping short is not based on just the diminishing size of profits per unit but also on the manager's uncertainty regarding the actual cost of each incremental unit; cost information is not exact, and the manager prefers to err on the side of caution.

Though the marginal cost concept appears to be a good one on paper, it is difficult to calculate marginal costs and to estimate matching declines in marginal revenues. Also, as profits begin to decline, there is no incentive for selling divisions to produce additional product. For all these reasons transfer pricing based on marginal costs has found little real-world application.

TRANSFER PRICING BASED ON COST PLUS

In situations where a division cannot derive its transfer prices from the outside market—perhaps because there is no market for its products or because it is small—the cost-plus approach may be a reasonable alternative.

The cost-plus approach is based on its name—just accumulate a product's full cost, add a standard margin percentage, and this becomes the transfer price. It has the singular advantage of being easy to understand and calculate and can convert a cost center to a profit center, which may be useful for evaluating the performance of a division manager.

Unfortunately, the cost-plus approach also has several serious flaws. They are:

- **Arbitrary margins.** The margin percentage added to a product's full cost may have no relationship to the margin that would actually be used if the product were sold externally. When a number of successive divisions add a standard margin to their products, the price paid by the final division in line, the one that sells the completed product externally, may be so high that there is no room for its own margin, which gives it no incentive to sell the product (see Impact of Profit Buildup later in this chapter).

- **Incentive to increase costs.** When the selling division increases the cost of the product it is transferring, the margin assigned to it is even larger (assuming that the margin is based on a percentage of costs rather than on a dollar amount). This is a particularly dangerous incentive to give to a division that sells some products externally, for it will then shift reported costs away from products meant for immediate external sale and toward costs that can be shifted to buying divisions. In this situation not only is the buying division's cost increased (perhaps preventing it from later selling the product at a reasonable profit), but the cost basis for external sales by the selling division is also artificially lowered (since the costs are shifted to internal sales), possibly resulting in the lowering of prices to external customers to a point below the product's variable cost. In short, changes in costs caused by the cost-plus system can result in reduced profits for the company as a whole.

Because of these issues, the cost-plus transfer pricing method is not recommended in most situations. However, if a company has only a small number of internal transfers, the volume of internal sales may be so small that the method will engender no incorrect cost-shifting activity. Given its ease of use, the method may be applicable in this one case, despite its other flaws.

TRANSFER PRICING BASED ON OPPORTUNITY COSTS

A completely unique approach to the formulation of transfer prices is based on opportunity costs. This method is not based precisely on either market prices or internal costs since it is founded on the concept of foregone profits. It is best described with an example. When a selling division can earn a profit of $10,000 by selling Widget A on the outside market but is instead told to sell Widget B to a buying division of the company, it loses the $10,000 it would have earned on the sale of Widget A. Its opportunity cost of producing Widget B instead of Widget A is therefore $10,000. If the selling division can add the foregone profit of $10,000 to its variable cost to produce Widget B, it will be indifferent as to which product it sells since it will earn the same profit on the sale of either product. Thus, transfer pricing based on opportunity cost is essentially the variable cost of the product being sold to another division, plus the opportunity cost of profits foregone in order to create the product being sold.

This concept is most applicable in situations where a division is using all of its available production capacity. Otherwise, it would be capable of producing all products at the same time and would have no opportunity cost associated with not selling any particular item. To use the same example, if there were no market for Widget A, on which there was initially a profit of $10,000, there would no longer be any possible profit, and consequently no reason to add an opportunity cost to the sale price of Widget B. The same principle applies if a company has specialized production equipment that can be used only for the production of a single product. In this case there are no grounds for adding an opportunity cost to the price of the product since there is no other use for the production equipment.

A problem with this approach is that there must be a substantial external market for sale of the products for which an opportunity cost is being calculated. If not, there is not really a viable alternative available under which a division can sell its products on the outside market. Thus, though a selling division may consider the current product pricing in a thin external market an opportunity cost, further investigation may reveal that there is no way for the market to absorb the division's full production (or can do so only at a much lower price), thereby rendering the opportunity cost invalid.

Another issue is that the opportunity cost is subject to considerable alteration. For example, the selling division wants to show the highest possible opportunity cost on the sale of a specific product, so that it can add this opportunity cost to its other transfer prices. Accordingly, it skews its costing system by allocating fixed costs elsewhere, showing variable costs based on high unit production levels and use of the highest possible prices, which results in a large profit for that product. This large profit is then used as the opportunity cost that is foregone when any other products are sold to other divisions, thereby increasing the prices other divisions must pay the selling division. Though this problem can be controlled with close oversight by the headquarters staff, the opportunity for a division manager to take advantage of this situation nonetheless exists.

This is a technique that is also difficult for the accounting staff to support. Their problem is that the opportunity cost appears nowhere in the accounting system. It is not an incurred cost (since it never happened) and therefore does not appear in the general ledger. Without "hard" numbers that are readily located in the existing

EXHIBIT 30.3. Impact of Opportunity Costs on Transfer Pricing

	10-Amp Motor	25-Amp Motor	50-Amp Motor
Variable cost ($)	24.00	27.00	31.00
Profit margin ($)	10.00	10.00	10.00
Price ($)	34.00	37.00	41.00

accounting system, accountants feel that they are working with "funny numbers." The lack of understandability does not stop with accountants, either. Division managers have a hard time understanding that a transfer price is based on a product's variable cost plus a margin on a different product that was never produced. Accordingly, gaining companywide support of this concept can be difficult.

Another problem occurs when buying divisions have no other source of supply because the products made by the selling division are unique. In this instance the managers of the buying divisions can appeal to the corporate headquarters staff to force the selling division to sell them products at a lower price, on the grounds that the selling division is in a monopoly situation, therefore can charge any price it wants, and consequently must have its pricing forcibly controlled.

Despite these problems, this is a particularly elegant solution to the transfer pricing problem. It helps division managers select from among a variety of alternative types of product by setting the prices of *all* their products at levels that will uniformly earn the same profit, as illustrated in Exhibit 30.3. In the example the profit margin on the 10-amp motor is $10, which is the highest profit earned by the division on any of its products. It now adds the same profit margin to its other two products, so that it is indifferent as to which products its sells—it will make the same profit in all cases. It is now up to the managers of the buying divisions to reject or accept the prices being charged by the selling division. If the price is too high, they can procure their motors elsewhere. If not, they can buy from the selling division, which not only allows this division to obtain a high profit on its operations but also proves that the resulting price is still equal to or lower than the price the buying division would have obtained if it had purchased elsewhere. Under ideal conditions this method should result in optimum companywide levels of profitability.

Unfortunately, the key words here are "under ideal conditions." In reality, many of the preceding objections come into play. For example, a selling division may find that its opportunity cost is a false one because the external market for its products is too small. As a result, it sets a high opportunity cost on its products, only to see all its interdivisional sales dry up because its prices are now too high. It then shifts all its production to external sales, only to find that it either cannot sell all its production, or that it can do so but only at a reduced price. Given the various problems with transfer prices based on opportunity costs, it is not used much in practice but can be a reasonable alternative in selected situations.

We have come to the end of several sections that covered different types of transfer pricing. Now we turn to a review of several ancillary issues pertaining to transfer pricing, including the uses of standard costs, fixed costs, and actual costs in the determination of transfer prices, as well as the impact of profit buildup on the selling activities of company divisions that sell to the external market.

TYPES OF COSTS USED IN TRANSFER PRICING DERIVATIONS

When creating a transfer price based on any type of cost, one should carefully consider the types of costs used to develop the price. An incorrectly considered cost can have a large, deleterious effect on the pricing structure that is developed. In this section we discuss the use of actual costs, standard costs, and fixed costs in the creation of transfer prices.

When *actual costs* are used as the foundation for transfer prices, a company knows that its prices reflect the most up-to-date costs, which allows it to avoid any uncertainty regarding sudden changes in costs that are not quickly reflected in prices. If such changes are significant, a company can find itself selling its products internally at price points that do not result in optimum levels of profitability. Nonetheless, these problems keep most organizations from using actual costs to derive transfer prices:

- **Volume-based cost changes.** Actual costs may vary to such an extent that transfer prices must be altered constantly, which throws the buying divisions into confusion—they never know what prices to expect. This is a particular problem when costs vary significantly with changes in volume. For example, if a buying division purchases in quantities of 10,000, the price it is charged will reflect that volume. However, if it places an order for a much smaller quantity, the fixed costs associated with the production of these units, such as machine setup costs which are spread over a much smaller quantity of shipped items, will drastically increase the cost and therefore the price charged.

- **Transfer of inefficiencies.** By using actual cost as the basis for its transfer pricing, a selling division no longer has any incentive to improve its operating efficiencies, for it can allow its costs to increase and then shift the costs to the buying division. This is less of a problem when the bulk of all sales are external, for the division finds that only a small proportion of its sales can be loaded with these extra costs. However, a situation where most sales are internal allows a division to shift nearly all its inefficiencies elsewhere.

- **Shifting of costs.** When actual costs are used, the selling division quickly realizes that it can load the costs it is charging to the buying division, thereby making its remaining costs look lower, which improves the division manager's performance rating. When these costs are shifted, the buying division's costs look worse than they really are. Though this problem can be resolved by constant monitoring of costs by the relatively impartial headquarters staff, the monitoring process is a labor-intensive one. Also, there are constant arguments between the divisions regarding what cost increases are justified.

In short, the use of actual costing as the basis for transfer prices is generally not a good idea, primarily because it allows selling divisions to shift additional costs to buying divisions, which reduces their incentive to improve internal efficiencies.

A better approach is to use *standard costing* as the basis for a transfer price. This is done by having all the parties agree at the beginning of the year to the standard costs to be used for transfer pricing, with changes allowed during the year only for significant, permanent cost changes, the justification of which must be closely audited to ensure that they are valid. By using this approach the buying divisions can easily plan the cost of incoming components from the selling divisions without having any concerns about unusual pricing variances arising. Meanwhile, the selling divisions no longer have an incentive to transfer costs to the buying divisions, as was the case with actual costing, and instead can now fully concentrate their attention on reducing their costs through improved efficiencies. If they can drop their costs below the standard cost levels at which transfer prices are set for the year, they can report improved financial results that reflect well not only on the division manager's performance but also on the performance of the company as a whole. Further, there is no need for constant monitoring of costs by the corporate headquarters staff since standard costs are fixed for the entire year. Instead, the headquarters staff can concentrate its attention on the annual setting of standard costs; this is the one time during the year when costs can be manipulated to favor the selling divisions, which requires in-depth cost reviews to avoid. As long as standard costs are set at reasonable levels, this approach is much superior to the use of transfer prices based on actual costs.

Yet another issue is the addition of fixed costs to variable costs when setting transfer prices. When these costs are combined, it is called full costing. When a selling division uses full costing, the buying division knows only that it cannot sell the purchased item for less than the price it paid. However, this may not be the correct selling strategy for the company as a whole. As noted in Exhibit 30.4, a series of divisions sell their products to a marketing division, which sells all products externally on behalf of the other divisions. The marketing division buys the products from the selling divisions at full cost. It does not know what proportions of the price it pays are based on fixed costs and which on variable costs. It can only assume that, from the marketing division's perspective, its variable cost is 100% of the amount it has paid for the products and that it cannot sell for less than the amount it paid. In reality, as shown in the exhibit, only 51% of the transfer price it has paid represents variable costs. If the marketing division were aware of this information, it would sell products at prices as low as the variable cost of $82.39. Though such a

EXHIBIT 30.4. Impact of Full Costing on Selling Decisions

	Division 1	Division 2	Division 3	Division 4	Cumulative Costs	Percent of Total
Transferred-in Cost	$ -	$ 41.58	$ 100.31	$ 171.98		
Division-Specific Variable Cost	$ 13.58	$ 41.02	$ 27.79	$ -	$ 82.39	51%
Division-Specific Fixed Cost	$ 22.58	$ 10.05	$ 34.53	$ 12.71	$ 79.87	49%
Total Division-Specific Cost	$ 36.16	$ 51.07	$ 62.32	$ 12.71	$ 162.26	100%
Margin on Division-Specific Cost (15%)	$ 5.42	$ 7.66	$ 9.35	$ 1.91		
Price Based on Division-Specific Costs	$ 41.58	$ 58.73	$ 71.67	$ 14.62		
Division Price + Transferred-In Price	$ 41.58	$ 100.31	$ 171.98	$ 186.60		

price would not cover fixed costs in the long run, it might be acceptable for selected pricing decisions where the marketing division has occasional opportunities to earn some extra margin on lower-priced sales.

The best way to ensure that the division making external sales is aware of both the fixed and variable costs included in a transfer price is to itemize them as such. When the selling division has full knowledge of the cumulated variable cost of any products it has bought internally, it can make better pricing decisions. This separation of a transfer price into its component parts is not difficult and can be done on a cumulative basis for all products that have been transferred through multiple divisions.

Another way to handle the pricing of fixed costs is to charge a budgeted amount of fixed cost to the buying division in each reporting period. Then there is no need to run a calculation in each period to determine the amount of fixed cost to charge at different volume levels. Also, the budgeted charge reflects the cost of the selling division's capacity used by the buying division and so is a reasonable way for the buying division to justify its priority in product sales by the selling division over other potential sales—it has paid for the capacity, so it has first rights to production.

Another school of thought is that no fixed costs should be charged to the buying division at all. One reason is that the final price charged to an external customer is based on market rates, not internal costs, so there is no reason to account for the cost if it has no impact on the final price. Another reason is that the fixed cost typically charged to the buying division rarely includes all fixed costs, such as general and administrative expenses—so if the fixed cost cannot be accurately determined, why charge it at all? Also, the fixed costs of a division are not closely tied to the volume of units produced (otherwise, they would be variable costs), and so it is not possible to accurately assign a fixed cost to each unit of production sold. In short, this viewpoint questions the reason for assigning any fixed cost to a product because of the difficulty of measurement and its lack of relevance to the ultimate price set for external sale.

Not including any fixed cost in the transfer price reduces the price the buying division pays and makes its profits look abnormally high since these costs are absorbed by the upstream divisions that supplied the product. However, the profits of the division that sells the product externally can be allocated back to upstream divisions in proportion to their costs included in the product, so there is a way to give these divisions a profit.

The arguments in favor of standard costing make it the clear choice over the use of actual costs in the derivation of transfer prices. However, the preceding arguments both in favor of and against the use of fixed costs are much less clear. A company can avoid the entire issue by simply basing intercompany transfers on market prices for each item transferred, but there is no outside market for many products, so managers cannot use this method to avoid the fixed cost issue. The author's preferred approach is to assign a standard lump-sum fixed cost to the buying division in each period; this avoids the issue of how to determine the fixed cost per unit and also gives the buying division the right to reserve the production capacity of the selling division related to the fixed cost being paid by the buying division.

IMPACT OF PROFIT BUILDUP

If an organization has many divisions that pass along products among themselves, it is possible that each successive division in the chain of product sales will tack on such a large profit margin that the last division in the chain will end up purchasing a product that is too expensive for it to make any profit on when it is finally time to sell it externally. This problem is known as profit buildup and is illustrated in Exhibit 30.5. In the exhibit the first three divisions add a preset profit margin to a product as each one adds value to it—the price accordingly increases as it advances through the chain of products. By the time the product reaches Division 4, the price is so high that it will lose $0.25 per unit on selling it. Because it will lose money, it has no incentive to sell the product, even though the company as a whole earns a profit of $6.35 (net of the loss on sale) over the course of its manufacture in the various divisions. We add up all the incremental margins added to the product in each division to arrive at the $6.35 figure, less the loss that occurs at the time of sale.

The profit buildup problem is most common when a company sets up profit margins for each successive division to add to products, based on a final market price that is no longer valid or is reduced in the case of a special sale price.

In this situation the final division in the chain has several alternatives. One is to purchase its component parts elsewhere. This option is the best when the supplying divisions can earn their standard profit markups by selling all their production elsewhere but is otherwise detrimental if the organization as a whole is not using excess production capacity to supply components to Division 4. Another option is to not sell the product at all, which may be acceptable if the division has other products it can sell that still earn a similar profit level; if not, however, the division does not optimize profitability by foregoing these sales. Yet another choice is to have the corporate headquarters staff review the margins added throughout the transfer process to see if they should be reduced to reflect actual market rates. This approach may interfere with the normal transfer price-setting structure within the company, however, and may also require considerable corporate intervention if the final product price constantly fluctuates. The best alternative for Division 4 is to negotiate with downstream divisions for special transfer price breaks as the final sale price moves up or down; this approach keeps the headquarters staff out of the picture and allows the selling division to react more quickly to sudden downturns in the final price that may still result in an overall profit for the organization.

A helpful method for determining the lowest price at which a company should sell its product is to divide the transfer price into two components—the cumulative variable cost and the cumulative margin added to the product at each transfer. In this way, the selling division can see the size of the cumulative variable cost, which

EXHIBIT 30.5. Profit Buildup Scenario

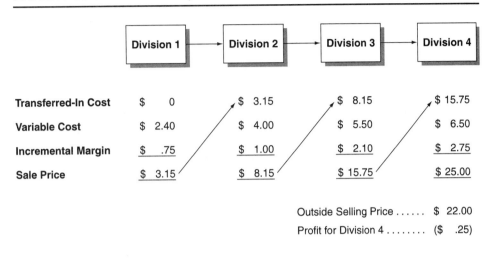

	Division 1	Division 2	Division 3	Division 4
Transferred-In Cost	$ 0	$ 3.15	$ 8.15	$ 15.75
Variable Cost	$ 2.40	$ 4.00	$ 5.50	$ 6.50
Incremental Margin	$ .75	$ 1.00	$ 2.10	$ 2.75
Sale Price	$ 3.15	$ 8.15	$ 15.75	$ 25.00

Outside Selling Price . . . . . . $ 22.00

Profit for Division 4 . . . . ($ .25)

represents the point below which it cannot drop the selling price without incurring an overall loss on the sale of the product. Without such a report the selling division does not realize that some portion of the cost that has been transferred to it is only a margin that has been added internally.

COMPARISON OF TRANSFER PRICING METHODS

In the preceding sections seven transfer pricing methods were described, as well as the advantages and disadvantages of each one. The wide array of methods may be confusing to someone attempting to select the method that best fits a company's particular circumstances. Accordingly, the summary table shown in Exhibit 30.6 may be of assistance. This table lists each transfer pricing method in the first column, in the order in which they were originally presented. The column heads are the three main criteria for selecting a transfer pricing method—profitability enhancement, performance review, and ease of use—as well as the problems that go along with each one.

When selecting from the list of transfer pricing methods, it is useful to follow a sequential list of yes/no rules that gradually eliminate a number of methods, leaving one with just a few to choose from. These decision rules are:

1. **Is there an outside market for a selling division's products?** If not, then throw out all market-based pricing methods and review cost-based methods instead.

   - *If so, the recommended methods are market pricing, adjusted market pricing, and negotiated pricing.*

EXHIBIT 30.6. Comparison of Transfer Pricing Methods

Type of Transfer Pricing Method	Profitability Enhancement	Performance Review	Ease of Use	Problems
Marketing pricing	Creates highest level of profits for entire company.	Creates profits centers for all divisions.	Simple applicability.	Market prices not always available; may not be large enough external market; does not reflect slightly reduced internal selling costs; selling divisions may deny sales to other divisions in favor of outside sales.
Adjusted market pricing	Creates highest level of profits for entire company.	Creates profits centers for all divisions.	Requires negotiation to determine reductions from market price.	Possible arguments over the size of reductions; may need headquarters intervention.
Negotiated prices	Less optimal result than market-based pricing, especially if negotiated prices vary substantially from the market.	May reflect more on manager's negotiating skills than on division performance.	Easy to understand but requires substantial preparation for negotiations.	May result in better deals for divisions if they buy or sell outside the company; negotiations are time-consuming; may require headquarters intervention.

Method				
Contribution margins	Allocates final profits among cost centers; divisions tend to work together to achieve large profit.	Allows for some basis of measurement based on profits, where cost center performance is only other alternative.	Can be difficult to calculate if many divisions involved.	A division can increase its share of the profit margin by increasing its costs; a cost reduction by one division must be shared among all divisions; requires headquarters involvement.
Marginal cost	Maximum profit levels for each division and in total.	Can measure divisions based on profitability.	Difficult to calculate the point at which marginal costs equal revenues.	Difficulty of cost and price measurement; reduced incentive to produce as marginal costs equal margin prices.
Cost plus	May result in profit buildup problem, so that division selling externally has no incentive to do so.	Poor for performance evaluation since will earn a profit no matter what cost is incurred.	Easy to calculate profit add-on.	Margins assigned do not equal market-driven profit margins; no incentive to reduce costs.
Opportunity cost	Good way to ensure profit maximization.	Drives managers to achieve companywide goals.	Difficult to calculate and to obtain acceptance within the organization.	Too arcane a calculation for ready acceptance; requires an outside market to determine the opportunity cost; the opportunity cost can be manipulated.

2. **Is the corporation highly centralized?** If not, avoid all cost allocation methods that require headquarters oversight.

- *If so, the recommended methods are contribution margin and opportunity cost.*

3. **Do the transferred items represent a large proportion of the selling division's sales?** If not, it may be best to simply transfer products at cost and have all profits accrue to the division that sells completed products externally. This means that all divisions selling at cost probably have no external market for their products. They should be treated as cost centers, with management performance appraisals tied to reductions in per-unit costs.

- *If so, the recommended methods are marginal cost and cost-plus.*

All the transfer pricing methods described in this chapter are based on the assumption that a company wants to treat all its divisions as profit centers. However, as noted in the last item in the preceding set of decision rules, under some circumstances it does not make sense to add any margin to a transferred product. In these cases, which usually involve the manufacture of products that cannot be sold outside the company and for which there is only one buyer—another company division—it is best to transfer at cost. Otherwise, the company creates a profit center that cannot be justified since there is no way to prove, through comparisons to external market prices, that profit levels are reasonable.

The number of cost centers a company allows should be kept to a minimum, for two reasons. First, the managers of a cost center are not concerned with the final price of a product and so may not make a sufficient effort to reduce their costs to a level necessary for the company as a whole to sell a product to the external market at a reasonable profit margin. For example, the manager of a cost center may think that a 5% reduction in costs is a sufficient target to pursue for 1 year, even though the marketing division that sells the final product is faced with falling market prices that call for a 20% reduction in prices in order to stay competitive. Accordingly, the behavior of a cost center manager may not be tied closely enough to an organization's overall needs. The second problem is that, since the cost center is driven to keep its per-unit costs at the lowest possible level, it resists any demands from buying divisions to increase its level of production to the point where its per-unit costs will increase. This typically happens when a production facility exceeds 60% to 70% of its theoretical production capacity level, requiring it to spend more on overtime and maintenance costs. Such behavior by the selling division does not maximize overall company profits as long as the marginal increase in costs does not exceed the profit to be gained by producing each additional unit.

In short, market-based transfer prices are to be preferred over all other methods because they result in the best level of conformance to a company's overall profitability, performance measurement, and ease-of-use goals. Other cost-based measures can also be used, but only as secondary measures in the event that market-based pricing is not possible.

In the next section we use the decision rules outlined in this section to complete a case study on transfer pricing.

CASE STUDY

The General Research and Instrumentation Company has developed a global positioning system device that requires the production of a highly specialized circuit board at its Cincinnati facility, for exclusive sale to its Boston plant where it will be included in final assembly and sold on the open market. Ms. Deirdre Corey, a member of the cost accounting staff, is asked to determine the best transfer pricing method for circuit boards sold by the Cincinnati plant to the Boston facility.

Ms. Corey finds that the circuit board is of such a specialized nature that there is no market for it outside the company; other GPS manufacturers have designed their own circuit boards, so this board is not compatible with the systems produced by competitors and therefore would not be purchased by them. She also notes that the accounting staff at the Cincinnati plant is of minimal size and is strictly concerned with the processing of daily production transactions. It has no capability to determine marginal costing levels for production in Cincinnati. In addition, the circuit board constitutes 75% of the total cost of the completed GPS unit. Another key point is that the GPS market is highly price-competitive, so there must be a strong emphasis on cost reductions. Finally, she finds that circuit board production makes up one-half of total production volume in the Cincinnati facility.

With this information she discards the possibility of using any market-based pricing since there are no market prices against which transfer prices can be set. This focuses her attention on cost-based pricing methods. She can reduce the list of options further by noting that the Cincinnati accounting staff is not equal to the task of determining marginal production costs, which eliminates the marginal costing methodology as a viable option. It is also inappropriate to use the opportunity cost method since it requires an external market for the circuit board in order to determine the opportunity cost that would be lost when sales are made to the Boston facility. By using decision rules to eliminate several transfer pricing options, Ms. Corey finds that she now has just two options to choose from—the contribution margin and the cost-plus method. The key difference between these two methods is that the cost-plus method does not place as strong a focus on cost reduction as the contribution margin method does. Because in this case there is such a strong emphasis on cost reduction in order to meet price competition, she recommends that the contribution margin method be used to develop transfer prices. The decision is particularly appropriate in this case, for the circuit board is 75% of the total product price, which means that the bulk of all cost reductions achieved by the

Cincinnati plant will be allocated back to that plant under the rules of the contribution margin approach, giving the manager of that division a strong incentive to cut costs as much as possible.

Ms. Corey followed a logical process of examining the particular circumstances calling for the use of a transfer price and discarding those methods that did not meet her criteria. This resulted in just two viable transfer pricing candidates, with sufficient differences between them for an easy decision to be made.

SUMMARY

Despite the wide array of transfer pricing methods noted here, some company managers claim that none of them work in their special situations. They are correct to a certain extent, for no method works perfectly in *all* situations. However, one must realize that it is sufficient to select the method that works the best in *most* situations, so that a reasonably efficient transfer pricing situation can arise. If management insists on continuing the search for the perfect transfer price, there will be endless bickering and debate over the shortcoming of any methods now in use, resulting in a general level of dissatisfaction. This sort of debate is most common in the area of transfer pricing because the profitability performance of divisional managers is directly affected by it.

CHAPTER 31

Pricing Decisions and Laws

Some companies operate in industries where their products—for example, commodities such as wheat and oil—command a market-driven price. However, a much more common occurrence is that a company has considerably more control over the prices it charges. If so, it should consult with its cost accountant to determine product costs, which should be the lowest possible prices that can be charged without incurring a loss. In this chapter we note how different product costs are used to develop prices under different pricing scenarios, as well as a number of special pricing issues such as target pricing, life cycle pricing, the pricing of bundled products, and price war scenarios. We also cover the various laws that control collusive and predatory pricing, as well as the dumping of products in the United States by foreign entities.

PRICING NOT BASED ON COSTS

Before delving into the various ways in which costs are used to derive prices, we briefly touch on the circumstances under which a company does not use its product costs to derive prices.

The main case where this occurs is when a company produces a commodity that cannot be distinguished from the same products sold by competitors. Examples of commodities are crops such as corn, soy, and barley. Other examples are wood products, oil, and minerals like gold, silver, and molybdenum. Commodities tend to be raw materials that are converted to other products that can then be differentiated, such as wood products that are turned into furniture.

When a company sells commodities, its prices are determined in the market-place. The only reason why it compares its prices to its costs is to ensure that it is making a profit at the current market price.

A similar pricing scenario occurs when there is a price leader in the marketplace who sets product prices. This leader tends to be a company with a dominant share of the market, and usually the lowest cost structure, who therefore can control the price of a large share of all products sold in a particular market niche. If another company tries to sell its products at a higher price, it will find that customers do not accept the increase, for they can still buy products from the price leader at a lower cost. If a company wants to sell its products for less than the prices set by the price leader, it can do so, but the leader's dominance will probably prevent it from gain-ing much market share through this strategy. Consequently, most companies in such industries tend to adopt whatever price points are set by the price leader. A good example of this is the Mars Company, which has a dominant share of the candy market. It sets the prices for the products one finds at the supermarket check-out lane, and all competitors are compelled to use the same pricing. In cases like this a company has no control over the price points at which it sells its products.

There are many cases where the underlying product is quite similar to others on the market, but a company bundles it with additional products or services or adds features to it in order to differentiate it. In these instances the cost accounting staff is frequently called on to determine the cost of the added services or features, which the marketing staff then uses to calculate a price that is added to the base price of the product. Thus, we have a mixed pricing situation where the base price is deter-mined by the marketplace, but the cost of additional features can be at least partly determined by the incremental cost of these features.

There are also a number of situations, all within the services industries, where companies use prices based on the value of the product received, which may have nothing to do with its cost. For example, a law firm's price for representing a client may be one-third of the award resulting from a lawsuit, rather than an hourly rate. Whether the law firm invests 1 hour or 1000 hours of its time on the lawsuit, the amount of the award is the same. This approach is being increasingly used by professional recruiting firms, which sometimes accept company stock as payment for their services rather than a fixed fee. Consultants also accept pay-ment in terms of a percentage of the savings resulting from their services. In all these cases there is no direct relationship between the cost of the services pro-vided and the price received.

A final case in which price determination departs from any cost basis is peak load pricing. This term refers to the practice of varying one's prices in direct re-sponse to changes in demand. For example, a street vendor can charge a high price for ice cream on a hot day but may have difficulty giving it away on a subzero day. Similarly, a bakery charges full price for its products in the morning but only half price for the same items at the end of the day, since most people buy their baked items first thing in the morning. This concept also applies to special locations rather than to peak periods of demand. For example, the same store in a franchise chain of restaurants may charge higher meal prices at a "hot" vacation location such as Aspen or Vail but charge much less for serving the same meal in a less desirable location. The classic example of this is the situation in a movie theatre, where food prices are astronomically high, because of the lack of competition for food sales within the theater.

These are all special cases where a cost accountant's services are usually not required, except to verify that the prices charged are not below variable costs. Prices are more closely related to the market forces of supply and demand than to the need to earn a specific margin on one's costs.

SHORT-RANGE PRICING

The preceding situations are ones where the cost accountant is not called on much to assist in setting pricing levels. The situation is entirely different when a company deals with short-range pricing arrangements. These are cases where a customer calls with a special request for an order that is priced very low. The customer may be playing off the company against another one of its suppliers, or perhaps has a large order, or maybe is just fishing for a good deal—the reason for a low pricing request does not matter. The company has to decide whether it will take the offer, and this is when the cost accountant becomes valuable.

The basic rule for short-range pricing is that the lowest price is the one that at least covers all variable costs of production, plus a small profit. Anything lower would cost a company money to produce and therefore would make no economic sense. The main issue becomes the determination of what variable costs to include in the variable cost calculation. They are:

- Direct labor
- Direct machine costs
- Inventory carrying costs
- Materials
- Ordering costs
- Quality costs (testing, inspection, and rework)
- Receiving costs
- Scrap costs

The costs on this list are those that vary directly with production volume. Not every item is considered a variable cost at some companies. For example, if the purchasing staff is unlikely to be laid off as a result of not taking the customer's order, the purchasing cost is probably not a variable one. The same reasoning can be used to assume that the receiving costs and even the direct labor costs are not really variable. Also, the direct machine costs, such as for utilities and any volume-related maintenance or machine labor, may still be incurred even if the order is not accepted and so are not considered variable. Given all these exceptions, it is apparent that the product's list of variable costs may be quite small, resulting in an equally small cost that must be covered by the customer's price.

A useful tool in determining a product's variable cost is activity-based costing, which is explained in detail in Chapter 16. This procedure accumulates costs for any corporate activity and allocates these activities to products or other cost objects. It is particularly useful because it traces costs to activities—which are, by definition, variable—if they do not happen, then the cost is not incurred. Because ABC is such a good tool for measuring variable costs, it is perfect for calculating these costs for short-range pricing purposes.

The variable cost used as the basis for a pricing decision should include one additional item. This is the lost margin on sales that will occur when the low-priced goods reach the market and replace sales of the company's products that are marked up at higher price levels. For example, if a company produces cereal that has a margin of $2.00 per box and a customer offers a special pricing deal that reduces the company's margin to $0.50 per box, the company should realize that the customer will simply sell the underpriced product on the open market at a lower price than the company's regular cereal, thereby eliminating the company's margin on its regular sales. This means that the company will experience a net loss of $1.50 per box on every box of cereal it sells at the lower price. However, this is not a valid argument if the company knows that the customer will sell the product in a new market where it does not compete with its existing products. This is a common situation where a company is asked to produce for a foreign market where it has no presence and where the company is confident that this is indeed the product's destination (perhaps because the product labeling is converted to a foreign language). Thus, this consideration arises only when a low-priced product will compete with a company's existing products.

The concept of short-range pricing is best illustrated with an example. A customer of the Low-Ride Bicycle Company wants to buy 1000 bicycles from it, which it will sell in a third-world country where it has recently opened a sales branch. The customer wants Low-Ride to offer its best possible price for this deal. The manager of Low-Ride knows that the same offer is being made to the company's chief competitor, Easy-Glide Bicycles. The company's cost to create a bicycle in a lot size of 1000 units is shown in Exhibit 31.1.

The owner of Low-Ride receives the pricing request at the slowest time of the production year, when he normally lays off several staff members. He sees this as a golden opportunity to retain employees, which is more important to him than earning a profit on the order. Consequently, he can charge a price of as little as $116.06 per bike, as derived in Exhibit 31.1, though this will leave him with no

EXHIBIT 31.1. Variable Costs Used for Short-Range Pricing

	Cost per Unit ($)
Direct labor	13.50
Direct machine cost	20.17
Inventory carrying cost	None
Materials	72.15
Ordering costs	Fixed
Quality costs	3.02
Receiving costs	Fixed
Scrap costs	7.22
Total cost	**116.06**

profit. He has recently hired the production manager away from Easy-Glide Bicycles and knows that Easy-Glide has a similar cost structure, except for 20% higher scrap costs. Accordingly, he knows that Easy-Glide's minimum variable cost will be higher by $1.44. This means that he can add $1.43 to his price and still be lower than the competing price. Therefore, he quotes $117.49 per unit to the customer.

Though short-range costing is used for many special pricing deals, a company cannot obtain a sufficient return on its investment if this is the only pricing method used. The more common method required for the bulk of all sales deals is based on long-range pricing, which is discussed in the next section.

LONG-RANGE PRICING

The pricing decisions just outlined for short-range situations can bring a company to the brink of bankruptcy if it uses them all the time, for they do not allow for a sufficient profit margin to pay for the company's overhead, not to mention the profit it needs to provide some return to investors on their capital. Proper long-range pricing requires the consideration of several additional costs. They are:

- **Product-specific overhead costs.** This is the overhead associated with the production of a single unit of production. It tends to be a small cost category, for if a cost can be accurately identified down to this level, it is considered a variable cost instead of a fixed one.

- **Batch-specific overhead costs.** A number of overhead costs are accumulated at this level, such as the cost of labor required to set up or break down a machine for a batch of production, the utility cost required to run machines for the duration of the batch, the cost of materials handlers needed to move components to the production area and to remove finished products from this area, and allocation of the depreciation on all machinery used in the process.

- **Product line–specific overhead costs.** A product line may have associated with it a product manager, a design team, a production supervisor, quality control personnel, customer service, distribution, advertising, and an ongoing investment in inventory. All these overhead costs can be allocated to the products that are the end result of the overhead costs incurred.

- **Facility-specific overhead costs.** Production must take place somewhere, and the cost of that "somewhere" must be allocated to the production lines housed within it, usually based on the square footage taken up by the machines used in each production process. The costs of overhead in this category can include building depreciation, taxes, insurance, maintenance, and maintenance staff.

The costs described here can exceed the total variable cost of a product, as described in the preceding section. When fully applied to all products manufactured, the marketing staff commonly finds that the resulting product costs are several times higher than is the case when only variable costs are considered. This is a particular concern for companies that require a large (and expensive) base of automated machinery to manufacture their products, for they have such a large investment in overhead that they must add on a large cost to their variable costs, as well as a reasonable profit, before arriving at a long-range price that adequately covers all costs.

The size of the markup added to the variable and fixed costs of a product should at least equal the target rate of return. This rate is founded on a firm's cost of capital, which is the blended cost of all debt and equity currently held. If the markup margin used is lower than this amount, a company will not be able to pay off debt or equity holders over the long term, thereby reducing the value of the company and driving it toward bankruptcy. It may also be necessary to increase the target rate of return by several additional percentage points, in case managers feel that the product in question may have a high risk of not selling at adequate levels over a prolonged period of time; by increasing the markup the price is driven higher, and the company earns back its investment sooner than would otherwise be the case (assuming that customers are still willing to buy the product at the higher price).

To continue with our example from Exhibit 31.1, if the Low-Ride Bicycle Company wants to determine its long-range bicycle price, it should include the additional factors noted in Exhibit 31.2, which lists all possible fixed costs, plus a markup to cover its cost of capital.

The primary difficulty with using a fully costed determination of a product's long-range price is that it can be difficult to calculate all the overhead costs that apply to each product. The best way to do this is to conduct an activity-based costing review (Chapter 16). However, such reviews can take a great deal of time, and so many companies conduct them only on a project basis, perhaps just once every few years. If a company measures these costs so infrequently, there may be a problem

EXHIBIT 31.2. Fixed Costs Also Considered for Long-Range Pricing

	Cost per Unit ($)
Total variable cost	116.06
Product-specific overhead costs	0.00
Batch-specific overhead costs	41.32
Product line–specific overhead costs	5.32
Facility-specific overhead costs	1.48
Markup of 12%	19.70
Total long-range price	**183.88**

EXHIBIT 31.3. Determination of Markup Percentage on Variable Costs

	Fully Costed Product	New Product with Only Variable Costs Available
Total variable costs ($)	152.00	129.00
Total overhead costs ($)	89.15	(assumed from markup percentage)
Grand total costs ($)	241.15	202.24
Markup over variable cost to equal grand total cost (%)	**58**	

with determining these costs for new products developed between activity-based costing reviews. A simple, moderately accurate way to avoid this problem is to determine the fully costed cost of a product that has undergone an ABC analysis and then determine the markup over the variable cost that equals the cost of all overhead added to it; this markup percentage is then used to determine the approximate amount of fixed costs that would probably be assigned to a new product with similar production characteristics. An example of this method is shown in Exhibit 31.3.

This method yields only an approximate full cost and should be verified with an activity-based costing study as soon as possible. Also, it is important to carry forward a markup percentage only for a product that is similar to the baseline product since this carries a better assurance that the new product will attract the same overhead costs used by the baseline product. If there is a significant difference between the two products in terms of the assets or activities used during the production process, this markup technique is much more likely to result in an incorrectly derived overhead cost.

LIFE CYCLE PRICING

It may not be sufficient to think of long-range pricing as just the addition of all fixed costs to a product's variable costs. Such an approach does not factor in all the changes in a product's costs and expected margins that can reasonably be expected over the course of its market life. For example, if one compiled the full cost of a product at the point when it has just been developed, the cost per unit would be high, for sales levels would be quite small; this means that production runs would also be short, so that overhead costs per unit would be high. Also, it is common for a company with the first new product in a market to add a high margin to this already high unit cost, resulting in a high initial price. Later in the product's life it gains greater market share, so that more products are manufactured, resulting in lower overhead costs per unit. However, competing products will also appear on the market, which will force the company to reduce its margins in order to offer competitive pricing. Thus, the full cost of a product varies, depending on the point at which it is currently positioned in its life cycle.

The best way to deal with long-range pricing over the course of a product's entire life cycle is to use a company's previous history with variations in cost, margin, and sales volume for similar products to estimate likely changes in a new product during its life cycle. An example of this is shown in Exhibit 31.4.

The exhibit shows that a company has a considerable amount of overhead costs to recoup during the startup phase of a new product life cycle, which requires a high price per unit, given the low expected sales volume at this point. However, setting a very high initial price for a product leaves considerable pricing room for competitors to enter the market; accordingly, many companies now choose to initially lose money on new product introductions by setting their prices at the long-range price rather than at the short-range price needed to recoup startup costs. By doing so they send a signal to potential market entrants that they are willing to compete at low initial price points that leave little room for outsized profits by new market entrants. This strategy foregoes large initial profits but may decrease the number of competitors, thereby reducing the level of competition in the long run.

The exhibit also shows that sales volumes gradually decline as a product enters the maturity phase of its life cycle. At this point price competition becomes fierce, as competitors strive to fill their production capacity by undercutting competitors. This is a good area for sensitivity analysis by the cost accountant, to determine the lowest possible price at which a company can compete and still earn a profit, as well as the minimum volume level that must be met before overhead costs cannot be covered. This analysis is good for determining the point at which a company should either terminate a product or replace it with an improved one just starting a new product life cycle.

Based on a table similar to that shown in Exhibit 31.4, a company can determine the most appropriate pricing strategy to adopt over a product's entire life cycle, so

EXHIBIT 31.4. Life Cycle Pricing

	Startup Phase	Growth Phase	Maturity Phase	Totals for all Phases
Unit volume	10,000	200,000	170,000	380,000
Variable cost/unit ($)	4.50	4.25	4.15	4.21
Fixed cost pool ($)	300,000	650,000	575,000	1,525,000
Fixed cost/unit ($)	30.00	3.25	3.38	4.01
Total cost/unit ($)	34.50	7.50	7.53	8.22
Expected margin (%)	30	20	15	19
Expected price/unit	**44.85**	**9.00**	**8.66**	**9.79**
Total revenue ($)	448,500	1,800,000	$1,472,200	4,720,700
Total variable cost ($)	45,000	850,000	705,500	1,600,500
Total fixed cost ($)	300,000	650,000	575,000	1,525,000
Total margin ($)	103,500	300,000	191,700	595,200

that the company is appropriately positioned in the marketplace and earns the greatest possible profit over the entire period during which the product is sold.

COST-PLUS PRICING

In some cases a company is asked by a customer to quote a price on a project or product that is so difficult to produce that the company is at great risk of incurring large cost overruns in attempting to complete it. An example of this is practically any new defense project involving leading-edge technology, such as weapons that have never even been designed before, much less produced. In these cases a company typically quotes an astronomically high price, which gives it a sufficient amount of margin cushion to obtain a healthy profit on the endeavor, no matter how expensive it is to complete. The customer usually cannot afford the high price and instead offers a cost-plus pricing contract.

With cost-plus pricing a customer reimburses a company for all the costs incurred in developing and producing a product it has ordered, plus a predetermined margin. There is a strong incentive for the company to agree to such a pricing deal, for there is no way to lose—all costs are guaranteed to be covered by the customer. For this reason, however, the customer is concerned that only the costs contractually agreed on in advance are charged to it. These allowable costs can be itemized in great detail in the contract with a customer. All variable costs are always reimbursable; the main issue instead is how much overhead can be charged to the contract. For example, there is a preset percentage of total plant or corporate overhead that can be charged, which cannot be exceeded. There may also be a pricing formula that allows only a certain amount of overhead incurred for a set of projects to be charged to a single project (such as the cost of an engineering supervisor who reviews the work for several projects at once). The amounts of these allocation percentages tend to be negotiated for each contract, so that they are never consistent. Given the level of uniqueness of each contract, it is useful to assign a separate cost accountant or contract administrator to each one to ensure that only the correct costs are billed under the contractual rules.

There may also be stipulations in a cost-plus agreement that some portion of the cost savings created by the company will be shared with the customer. This arrangement is required by many customers on the reasonable grounds that because they are footing the entire bill for any overruns in costs, they should be entitled to a share of any cost reductions. If this stipulation is present, then a cost accountant must create a tracking system that identifies and accumulates all cost savings, which can be a difficult chore.

Some contracts allow overhead to be allocated to a project (and then billed to the customer) based on a set dollar rate per unit of activity (e.g., $3.25 for every hour of direct labor). Customers realize that such overhead allocation clauses can be abused since charging an excessive number of units of activity to a project results in a large overhead cost being billed. Accordingly, a cost accountant must be particularly careful to charge these activities to the correct jobs and to maintain complete records to back up this information.

There are a large number of additional issues related to cost-plus pricing, but they are so specific to individual contracts that it is impossible to itemize them here. Suffice it to say that this type of pricing not only ensures a company of a profit but also guarantees all cost accountants full employment for the length of any such contracts, for there is a great deal of paperwork to be maintained, which customers can review repeatedly.

PRICING AND TARGET COSTING

The most common pricing practice is for a company's engineering staff to design a product and build a prototype, after which the cost accountants compile costs for it and the marketing staff develops a price based on this initial cost. The product is then released into the marketplace, where the company finds that its price is too high to attract any buyers or that it does not result in a sufficiently large profit. Company managers then order all department managers to look for ways to cut the cost of the product in order to bring its margin back in line with expectations. This proves hard to do since the product has already been designed, and most costs are irrevocably built into a product at the point when its design is approved. The best bet for cost reduction at this point is to authorize a series of engineering changes, which results in confusion on the production line since the manufacturing staff has already become accustomed to producing the original design; the purchasing staff must also find new component suppliers, while the warehouse staff finds that it must dispose of a pile of unused components that have been designed out of the product. All these items cost extra.

A better way to manage this process is to use target costing, which is described in detail in Chapter 17. In brief, this technique involves determining at the front end of the design process the best price that will sell a product, given customers' perceptions of product value and the price points at which competing products sell, and then forcing the engineering staff to design a product within the costing parameters that allows a company to earn an adequate margin at the target price. By using this approach a company finds that it cannot design a product at all, given the target price, or that it can do so and then does not have to go through a subsequent scramble to reduce costs—for the targeted costs have already been achieved.

This approach is a good one from the cost accountant's perspective, for her usual role in deriving prices is now reversed—instead of assisting in the search for ways to cut costs after a product is designed, she can assemble costing estimates in advance and as part of the initial design team and then focus on how to make the product design fit into a predetermined set of pricing parameters. This is a much more efficient use of a cost accountant's time. See Chapter 17 for more information about target costing.

PRICING OF BUNDLED PRODUCTS

When a company seeks to differentiate its products from competing products, or if it wants to achieve a higher level of perceived value in the marketplace, it may choose to bundle products together at a lower price than one would pay if purchasing all the component parts individually. For example, Microsoft Corporation bundles its Word, Excel, PowerPoint, and Access software together into Microsoft Office Suite. Similarly, many organizations now bundle service contracts with hardware sales, such as the many deals now available for low-priced personal computers that come with mandatory 3-year Internet service deals. Though bundling is a good value for the customer, it represents more work for the cost accountant, who must split the resulting revenue into sales for each of the component items sold so that profitability can be determined for each item.

One approach to splitting apart the component prices of a bundled product is to assign a proportion of the bundled price to each component product in exact proportion to the price at which each of the components sells on the open market. An example of this allocation method is shown in Exhibit 31.5, where we allocate a bundled price for a set of books and related services.

In the example the bundled set of products is sold for $150. In order to allocate the final price back to the individual component products, we determine the prices at which each item sells separately (e.g., a dinner with a golf professional is a real bargain at $78!) and calculate the total price for these items sold separately, which

EXHIBIT 31.5. Allocation of Bundled Product Prices Based on Separate Prices

	Separate Price ($)	Percentage of Total	Allocated Price ($)
Golf guide book	45	22	33
Golf vacations book	15	8	12
Golf club	42	20	30
Golf magazine subscription	25	12	18
Dinner with golf professional	78	38	57
Total	**205**	**100**	**150**

is $205 in the example. We then calculate the proportion of each item's price as a percentage of the total price and apply this percentage to the $150 at which the bundled set of products is actually sold.

One problem with this approach is that some of the component products may not be sold on their own—only as part of the bundle. Then it is not clear what price should be set for these items, which makes it impossible to apportion some percentage of the bundled price to them. One way to resolve this problem is to first allocate the bundled price to the component products at 100% of their stand-alone prices. Whatever price is left over (if any) can then be allocated to the products not sold separately, based on any reasonable allocation method such as the cost of these component products.

Another problem is that the price of a bundled set of products, or the prices of any of the component products, may change regularly, requiring the cost accountant to redo the calculation noted in Exhibit 31.5. This can be a time-consuming chore. An alternative approach to the problem is to agree on a standard set of prices at the beginning of the year and to apportion bundled prices to component products based on these standards. If the allocated amounts vary somewhat from the total revenues earned on sale of the bundled products, this variance can be charged to a variance account. The amount in the variance account can then be periodically allocated to the component products based on their relative percentages of sales revenues from the sale of bundled products. This is much easier than constantly rederiving the allocation calculation.

An alternative approach to allocations based on product prices is allocations based on product costs. With this approach the allocation previously noted in Exhibit 31.5 includes the cost of each bundled item in the second column, rather than each price. Then we can allocate bundled prices without any skewing based on relative differences in the margins attached to each product. For example, if the cost of the dinner with the golf professional were only $15, then the margin would be 81%, whereas the margin on the sale of either book in the bundle may be 15%.

Based on these relative differences, the dinner product is allocated far more revenue than the book products. This approach is not recommended in most cases, for the purpose behind allocating prices to an individual product is so that a company will know the profit level of each of its products—this is best discerned by allocating based on the actual prices that products can attract in the marketplace, rather than their internal costs. An extreme example of this issue is when an allocation of a bundled price to an inordinately expensive product *will* result in an allocation of the largest proportion of the bundled price to that product; this gives management the incorrect impression that the product is profitable and may even persuade managers to sell more of it at its current price, even though its high cost will result in minimal profits or even losses.

Thus, a proper price allocation system is necessary to ensure that managers are made aware of the profitability of individual products included in bundled product sales.

PRICE WARS

When there is too much production capacity in an industry and not enough available customer sales to use it up, a common occurrence is a price war, where one company lowers its prices in order to steal customers away from a competitor, who in turn matches or reduces these prices in order to retain its customers. During a price war the only winner is the customer, who experiences greatly reduced prices—however, it is ruinous for companies who are slashing prices. A cost accountant can be of great assistance in finding ways to avoid the debilitating effects of a price war.

One way to prevent a price war is to analyze the perceived value of each feature of a company's products in relation to similar products produced by competitors. If a company can clearly identify selected product features that competitor's offerings do not contain, these features can be heavily promoted in order to raise the perceived overall value of the products in the eyes of customers, allowing the company to avoid a price war. However, this analysis should be conducted well in advance of a price war, so that the proper mix of high-value features is present at all times. A discerning competitor is able to see this differentiation and may realize that a price war will not work.

Another option is for the cost accountant to conduct a competitive analysis of the company initiating a price war to see if its cost structure will allow it to cut prices to sustainable levels that are lower than what the company can support. If not, then a rational pricing move by the company is to briefly cut prices to levels below the variable costs of the competitor, thereby sending it a clear message that further price competition will put it out of business. This is a particularly effective approach if the cost accounting staff can discover if the competitor is outsourcing its production. If so, the entire cost of the outsourced product is variable, as opposed to a mix of fixed and variable costs when production is kept in-house. This gives an in-house manufacturer an advantage over an outsourced manufacturer because the in-house manufacturer has the option of not including fixed costs in its pricing calculations in the short run (see Short-Range Pricing earlier in this chapter), whereas the outsourced manufacturer has no fixed costs to exclude. This gives the in-house manufacturer an inherent advantage in the event of a price war. For example, Companies A and B produce exactly the same product. Company A manufactures it in-house and incurs a $10 cost that is half fixed and half variable. Company B, however, outsources its production and must pay $10 to its supplier for each unit it buys. This manufacturing scenario gives Company A a clear advantage over Company B in the event of a price war, for Company A can slash its price down to its variable cost of $5, whereas B can drop its price only to its variable cost of $10. Thus, the type of manufacturing system used has a direct bearing on the competitive positioning of companies locked in a price war.

Another option is for the cost accounting staff to develop a detailed rendering of the company's cost structure and release this information to the public, perhaps through a professional magazine or newspaper interview. Competitors who access this information will realize that the company's cost structure is lower than theirs and that waging a price war would result in a loss. This option, of course, is a viable one only for companies with a distinct cost advantage over their competitors.

Yet another way to deal with a price war is to contact key customers and offer them special long-term deals, which lock them into set pricing levels for what will presumably be the duration of the price war. This strategy was used by AT&T when it was in the midst of a major price war over long-distance phone rates with MCI and Sprint. Customers signed up for several years of phone service at slightly reduced prices, but they turned out to be higher prices than the going rate, as the price war drove long distance rates ever downward. This allowed AT&T to earn extra revenue that would otherwise have been lost.

Another strategy is to create a new product or product line with new features and a market positioning, while letting the old product gradually be eliminated by a price war. In this way a company allows competitors to reduce their margins to dangerous levels while it neatly sidesteps the entire problem by concentrating on a slightly different market. The approach can also be reversed by leaving the price point of the old product alone and instead designing a new, much lower-cost product that can compete more effectively in a price war. Yet another variation is to design a new product that is sufficiently different that customers are faced with an apples-to-oranges comparison of competing products; they cannot judge which product is the better value, and so the price war never gets started. Any of these approaches requires a considerable amount of time to implement and works best for companies with a significant ability to roll out new products on a regular basis.

If all these options fail, then the only alternative left is to participate in a price war. If this becomes necessary, the best thing to do is to cut prices at the first hint of the price war, to set deeply discounted prices, and to do so with great fanfare. This aggressive approach signals to competitors that a company is serious about its participation in a price war and that it intends to pursue the war until all other competitors back off. This "hard and fast" response can sometimes stop a price war before it has had time to build momentum. Some companies take this concept a step further by publicizing their intention to cut prices in the business press before anyone even attempts to initiate a price war; this tells everyone what kind of reception they can expect if they cut their prices and may keep them from starting a price war.

There are many alternatives to matching competitor price cuts—alternatives that can keep a company's margins at respectable levels while competitors slash their own margins. By using cost accounting to reposition products, add features, offer special customer deals, publicize costing levels, or analyze competitor cost structures, a company can withstand the negative effects of price wars.

COLLUSIVE PRICING

When several companies combine their pricing strategies in order to set prices in the marketplace that are higher than would normally be found in a competitive market, we experience collusive pricing results. This situation does not normally arise in fragmented industries with many competitors since it is difficult for so many companies to conspire in setting prices. The problem is more common in situations where there are only a few key manufacturers or service providers, because the collusion of only a few companies is required. The issue can arise when there is an excessive amount of industry capacity in relation to available sales; company executives are then faced with a drop in prices as competition for limited sales heats up (see the last section) or a private agreement to hold (or even increase) price levels. Allegations of collusive pricing have arisen in a number of industries over the years, including such areas as oil, drugs, and agricultural chemicals.

One of the oldest laws currently in force that impacts collusive pricing is the Sherman Act. Enacted in 1890, it states that anyone who attempts to or has succeeded in creating a monopoly is guilty of a felony and can be punished with a fine of up to $10 million and/or imprisonment of up to 3 years. This act has the broad, overriding purpose of attacking all forms of trade restriction that can lead to the establishment of a monopoly, rather than a specific, detailed description of what types of pricing policies are illegal. It can be, and has been, construed to apply to collusive pricing.

There is little a cost accountant can do to avoid collusive pricing, for it has little to do with a company's internal cost structure. Instead, collusive pricing issues typically arise in the marketing department, where prices are set, or within the management ranks of a company, which have the most contact with their counterparts at competing companies.

PREDATORY PRICING

A company can bring charges of predatory pricing against a competitor when it feels that the competitor is making deals with customers that prevent them from doing business with the company or that involve especially low pricing designed to drive the company out of business. Generally, one can consider predatory pricing to be pricing activities that aim to exclude competitors from the marketplace on some basis other than internal efficiency.

These issues are addressed by three acts of Congress. The first is the Clayton Act, which specifies that a company may not sell products or services to its customers on the express condition that they do not do business with a competitor. This exclusion of competitors can also be based on a special rebate or discount being offered to the customer. The second act is the Robinson-Patman Act, which is actually an amendment to the Clayton Act. It states that it is unlawful to discriminate in price between different purchasers of commodities of like grade and quality, where the effect is to substantially lessen competition or tend to create a monopoly in any line of commerce; however, one can change prices based on the cost of manufacture, sale, or delivery resulting from the differing methods or quantities in which such commodities are sold. The act does not prevent pricing changes related to the marketability of goods, such as the deterioration of perishable goods, obsolescence, distress sales under court process, or the discontinuance of a business. Finally, the previously noted Sherman Act can also be applied to cases of predatory pricing since they are a clear form of trade restriction.

The intent of these acts is to foster competition by outlawing any predatory pricing situations that will result in the elimination of competitors from the marketplace and which leads to a reduced number of competitors who thereby will have greater leeway to raise prices.

Proving a charge of predatory pricing is extremely difficult. One must show that a competitor has a specific intent to monopolize a market, that it has done so through predatory activities, and that it has a reasonably high chance of achieving its goal of creating a monopoly. The first two issues can be proven by showing that a competitor is indeed setting prices below its costs, while the probability of creating a monopoly is proven by presenting a case that the competitor is likely to recoup the costs incurred by its predatory pricing once other companies have been driven out of the market.

The two problems that arise in proving a case of predatory pricing involve the definition of a competitor's product cost and its likelihood of recouping its lost profits. The United States Supreme Court has left the first issue wide open by not defining the proper measure of cost, preferring to let lower courts decide the issue on a case-by-case basis. Should it be full cost, with all overhead allocated, or variable cost, with all overhead excluded, or some point in between? In order to have a clear chance of winning a predatory pricing case, one should be able to prove that the price charged by a competitor is below its variable cost, which is the lowest possible cost that can be applied to a product. If the price charged is higher than this level, then a competitor can probably successfully defend itself on the grounds that it is making short-range marginal pricing decisions (see Short-Range Pricing earlier in this chapter).

It is equally difficult to prove that a competitor is likely to recoup its lost profits from predatory pricing through the creation of a monopoly. One reason is that once the competitor drives other companies out of the marketplace, it raises prices again, which attracts new competitors to the market, thereby keeping it from raising prices to the high levels needed to recoup its lost profits. There must be significant barriers to entry that allow the competitor to "own" the market for a sufficiently lengthy period of time before new competitors arrive and drive down prices once again. Examples of such barriers are legal requirements, such as lengthy licensing procedures or patents, and capacity issues, such as long lead times to build production facilities.

Given the difficulty of proving predatory pricing, this is not a charge that is commonly won in court. However, such a lawsuit can soak up the resources of a competitor for a lengthy period, distracting it from daily business issues, and so such lawsuits appear with some regularity.

To guard against a predatory pricing lawsuit, a cost accountant should build a cost tracking system that details all variable costs associated with all products sold, so that this information can be easily compiled for presentation in court. Further, there should be excellent documentation of the costing information used to make short-range pricing decisions since these are the situations that are most likely to cause predatory pricing lawsuits to be filed. Also, this cost information should be retained for a number of years, so that it is available for all years contained within the statute of limitations for the states within which a company operates. Taking these precautionary measures makes a company much more capable of successfully defending itself against predatory pricing lawsuits.

DUMPING

A United States industry can experience a severe drop in sales if a competitor located in a foreign country imports competing goods into the United States at extremely low prices. This is known as dumping. When it occurs, an injured United States company can sue the competitor directly or can bring the issue to the attention of the Federal Trade Commission, which is empowered under the Federal Trade Commission Act to investigate the problem and increase import duties to a sufficient level to erase the pricing advantage. This is a difficult charge to prove if one bases the dumping charges on the cost of the product (see the last section), so the charge is instead based on the price at which the foreign company sells its products in its home market. If the price charged in the United States is lower than the price charged in the home country, then dumping is proven to have occurred. The exact text of Section 72 of the Federal Trade Commission Act, which deals with this issue, is:

> It shall be unlawful for any person importing or assisting in importing any articles from any foreign country into the United States, commonly and systematically to import, sell or cause to be imported or sold such articles within the United States at a price substantially less than the actual market value or wholesale price of such articles, at the time of exportation to the United States, in the principal markets of the country of their production, or of other foreign countries to which they are commonly exported after adding to such market value or wholesale price, freight, duty, and other charges and expenses necessarily incident to the importation and sale thereof in the United States: Provided, That such act or acts be done with the intent of destroying or injuring an industry in the United States, or of preventing the establishment of an industry in the United States, or of restraining or monopolizing any part of trade and commerce in such articles in the United States. Any person injured in his business or property by reason of any violation of, or combination or conspiracy to violate, this section, may sue therefore in the district court of the United States for the district in which the defendant resides or is found or has an agent, without respect to the amount in controversy, and shall recover threefold the damages sustained, and the cost of the suit, including a reasonable attorney's fee.

Dumping is of particular concern to cost accountants working for foreign-based corporations. They must be aware of the prices charged for their products in the entity's home countries, as well as all ancillary costs noted in the act, such as freight and duty costs, and be prepared to defend their companies in court with this information if the need arises.

CASE STUDY

The General Research and Instrumentation Company is notified that it is being sued by a competitor, AtoClock, over its low pricing of a new line of atomic clocks. The cause of the complaint is that the GRIN Company was offered a special deal to sell 500 of its atomic clocks to a distributor in Arizona. The price was $550 each, which was well below the usual company price of $1000. The price was based on the variable cost of the product, as produced in the company's New York facility, plus a 5% margin. The deal was accepted because the distributor also promised to buy a number of other related products from the GRIN Company as part of a package deal.

 The company counsel, Mr. Ervin Spectacle, called in Ms. Emily North, the corporate cost accountant, to discuss the matter. She brought with her the bill of materials for the atomic clock, which clearly stated that its variable cost was indeed $550. However, further investigation revealed that the freight cost associated with shipping the devices to Arizona was an additional 8%. Though this cost was mistakenly excluded from the initial pricing decision, in court it will appear as though the GRIN Company has been engaging in predatory pricing.

They then look at the second issue the court will review, which is the ability of the GRIN Company to recoup its losses by driving out all competitors. They find that AtoClock is the company's only competitor for atomic clock sales in the United States and that it will close its Arizona sales office as a result of the GRIN Company's sales into that state, which it cannot reopen without a significant expenditure. There are competitors located in other countries, but a 20% import duty on their atomic clocks prevents them from competing in this market. Thus, it appears that a court will find that the GRIN Company has achieved a monopoly situation in Arizona, even if it has done so inadvertently.

Mr. Spectacle calls the attorney for AtoClock to arrange for an out-of-court settlement, while Ms. North revises the cost accounting system to include freight costs on the bill of materials. She also has a discussion with the marketing manager and gives him a standardized checklist of all costs to include in his short-range pricing decisions. She then works with the marketing department's secretary to create a filing system for the documentation related to all short-range pricing decisions, so that this information can be properly stored. Finally, she submits a request to the internal auditing department to periodically review the costing information used by the marketing department, to ensure that her changes are properly implemented. These alterations will ensure that the GRIN Company is not involved in a similar debacle in the future.

SUMMARY

Pricing is an extremely complex area in which the cost accountant can be most helpful by assisting the marketing department in selecting the appropriate short-range and long-range pricing. It is also important for the cost accountant to become involved in the determination of full life cycle costs, as well as to review how well prospective price points over the course of a product's life allow a company to recoup its lifetime investment in the product. It is also important to know the various methods for allocating the prices of bundled products, so that the correct profitability of each subsidiary product in a bundled product can be determined for profitability purposes. There are also a number of federal laws that can reveal a company's pricing policies to be collusive or predatory, so the accounting staff should be aware of these laws and ensure that all pricing policies stay on the correct side of the law. Indeed, pricing is a most fertile ground for the cost accountant to plow.

PART VII

Other Topics

CHAPTER 32

Corporate Strategy
and Cost Accounting

The cost accountant is generally concerned with the daily analysis and transmission of information about product, product line, and customer costs and often has no idea of how his or her activities relate to the overall corporate direction, or strategy, that a company is pursuing. In this chapter we undertake a brief review of the components of strategy and how the cost accountant's work can be used to support it.

COMPETITIVE STRATEGY DEFINED

According to Michael Porter (1998, p. xxiv), competitive strategy is "a combination of the ends (goals) for which a company is striving and the means [tactics] by which it is seeking to get there." The first item he mentions is strategic: the overall plan of attack that a company follows in order to change or improve its position in the marketplace. Examples of strategies are:

- Attain cost leadership in the industry.

- Expand into the South American market.

- Develop innovative consumer electronics.

- Create a minerals location and development capability.

- Use acquisitions to obtain a 20% share of the shipping market.

- Integrate the supply chain in order to secure raw materials.

All these sample strategies have the same characteristics: they are high level and reveal the general direction the management team wants a company to follow. A soundly derived strategy is one that takes into account the current or prospective actions of competitors, potential market entrants, substitute products, and the relative power of both customers and suppliers to arrive at a company direction that is not only achievable but which will also carve out a solidly defendable niche in the marketplace that is also profitable. The five factors just noted are crucial to the development of a sound strategy. In more detail, they are:

- **Competitors.** There are other companies currently in the marketplace who sell products that compete with the company's offerings. One must understand the resources, intentions, and both current and future product offerings of these companies in order to determine the best way to counteract their activities. This may include obtaining patent protection for certain key product features that will yield a permanent advantage over competitors for the term of the patents, or perhaps the initiation of a price war to grab market share if the company knows that a certain competitor is weakened by a high debt load and cannot respond to lower pricing. Clearly, an intimate knowledge of competitors is crucial to the formulation of good strategy.

- **Potential market entrants.** There is always the risk that new competitors will arrive who will throw the market into disarray with new product offerings. These competitors can be kept away if there are high barriers to entry, such as large capital investments, government licensing, or long sales cycles to customers—these barriers are ones that a company can work to propagate.

- **Substitute products.** Products created in a different market may have a cross-market appeal, perhaps based on lower pricing or higher value, that suddenly poses a threat to continued sales of the company's products. This threat can be preempted by obtaining good market intelligence about these products, while also being willing to buy the companies that produce them.

- **Customer power.** The prices a company can charge are directly related to the ability of a customer to exact lower prices from it. This problem is most common where there are only a small number of large customers and there are many competitors, so that customers who place large orders can threaten to take their business elsewhere unless they receive lower prices. This problem can be avoided through the systematic collection of patents to cover key product attributes, as well as the erection of barriers to entry that will keep away new competitors and perhaps drive away existing ones.

- **Supplier power.** Similarly, large suppliers who have a singular level of control over a company's component parts can demand such high prices for them that the company cannot adequately pass these costs along to customers without seriously reducing sales. A company can avoid this problem by switching to alternate materials, which may require the redesign of products.

Once a company has considered the impact of these five competitive factors in deriving its strategy, it must drop down a level and formulate the tactics by which it will achieve the strategy. Tactics are the detailed operational steps taken in order to accomplish a strategy. Here are some examples of tactics:

- Develop target costing systems in order to improve product margins.
- Create customer service centers in order to enhance service levels.
- Build a new smelter in order to increase production capacity.
- Take the company public in order to secure additional funding.
- Replace production equipment in order to reduce scrap rates.

The tactics just noted are much more specific than the strategy examples and can be readily communicated to department managers for implementation. Traditionally, tactics are included in the annual budget, along with sufficient funding to ensure that they can be achieved. The human resources staff can create performance plans for managers that are tied to these tactics, to ensure that they are properly motivated to implement them. Accountants then measure budgeted against actual financial results and report on the success of the targeted tactics to the management team. By these means a company creates systems to implement the tactics that allow it to follow a designated strategic path.

PROBLEMS WITH MANAGING THE STRATEGIC DIRECTION

There are a number of ways in which a company can fail to follow through on the strategic direction the management team has determined is the correct one. Only by avoiding all the issues mentioned in this section can a company have a reasonable chance of attaining its goals. In reality, however, most organizations do not follow through on these items and consequently do not succeed.

First, there may be a weak linkage between a company's strategy and the tactics needed to attain it. This is a common problem for managers who are too "high level" in their thinking to work through the morass of seemingly innumerable tactical details that must be considered to ensure that all aspects of a company are oriented in the right direction. Instead, they set down the strategy in front of a group of lower-level managers, wave a hand, and issue a general order to get it done. Even if the management team does a reasonable job of creating a set of tactics to follow, it is likely that the tactical changes needed by some functions will not be thoroughly addressed or that the tactics adopted by different functions will conflict with each other. All these issues will guarantee the failure of a corporate strategy.

Another problem is that, even if all functional areas are carefully considered and excellent tactics are adopted, there may be no reward system in place that pushes employees to follow the tactics. For example, the traditional reward system for the purchasing staff may be to never have an inventory stockout that would keep the production line from running, whereas the newest tactic is to reduce working capital by paring down the raw materials inventory. Which approach will the purchasing staff follow? The one that rewards them the best, namely, the old approach, which is reinforced by an unchanged reward system. If new tactics are not reinforced with a closely linked reward system, it is still possible that the overall corporate strategy will fail because of inattention by employees.

In order for a reward system to function properly, there must be a measurement system in place that tracks a company's ability to complete its tactics. This is a serious issue, for most organizations have measurements that track only the performance of their currently followed tactics. There is probably no way to determine if a new tactic is succeeding or not, because there is no measurement available. For example, a traditional company may have financial measures in place, but the new tactics require close attention to customer satisfaction, which calls for information about customer surveys, complaints, and product returns. If a measurement system is not in place that can accurately and frequently collect and disseminate such information, then there is no way for employees to see if they are doing a good job or for managers to properly reward them for their activities. The result is adherence to the old reward system because the new system is inoperable.

A good strategy can fail because of a lack of comprehensive, nonconflicting tactics or a supporting reward or measurement system. In the next section we review a formal method for linking tactics to various strategies, as well as for deriving and reporting formal measurements to support these tactics.

LINKING STRATEGY, TACTICS, AND MEASUREMENTS

The linkage of strategy, tactics, and related measurements is usually an unplanned endeavor that is lacking some elements in even the best-run businesses. However, a tool has been developed to address this problem that is called the "balanced scorecard." It is described in detail by Kaplan and Norton (1996). These authors have determined that the proper mix of tactics and measurements a company must use to achieve its chosen strategy must encompass four key perspectives:

- **Financial perspective.** This is the area in which companies have traditionally focused all their attention, to the detriment of the next three items. The key tactical and measurement items included in this area should cover the rate of revenue growth and the mix of sales to be expected, as well as any cost reduction, productivity improvement, and asset utilization goals.

- **Customer perspective.** The focus of any company must be on its customers, or else there will be no company. The key tactical and measurement items included in this area should cover the company's overall and niche market shares, customer retention and acquisition rates, and the average levels of customer profitability and satisfaction.

- **Internal business processes.** Improvements in this area have been discussed in some detail in the business press of late, with a general focus on reengineering and process centering. A better way of looking at this area is to concentrate on the improvement of only those areas that have tactical relevance to a company's strategic direction, namely, innovation (i.e., product development), operations (i.e., production), and postsale service to customers.

- **Learning and growth.** A company cannot achieve specific goals unless its employees are both sufficiently trained and motivated. Further, they must be empowered and have their jobs aligned in such a fashion that they are fully supported and directed toward attaining these goals. There is also a need for company information systems to provide employees with the right kinds of information. All these items make up the final key perspective.

The tactics and measurements for these four perspectives can be grouped into a single-page "scorecard" showing the results from the learning and growth area leading to the internal business processes targets (since employees generally require training before they can bring about internal process improvements). This area in turn leads to the customer-related targets since better internal processes affect customer satisfaction and retention levels. Finally, the results from the customer-related targets impact the financial targets. Each cluster of tactics noted on the balanced scorecard should include the target measurement level and the actual measurement results as of the report date. It may also be possible to include the actual measurement results for the last quarter or year, in order to give some perspective to the company's level of progress in each area.

By formalizing the key tactical and measurement areas, companies can develop better planning that gives them a much greater chance of success. However, the types of tactics and measurements adopted vary for every company, given the particular strengths and weaknesses of each one. This calls for careful consideration of the correct tactics and measurements, possibly with the assistance of a consultant trained in the use of this methodology. The tactics certainly vary by the type of strategy followed. For example, Exhibits 32.1 through 32.3 note possible tactics to be followed for the three main growth strategies of product differentiation, cost

EXHIBIT 32.1. Balanced Scorecard for a Product Differentiation Strategy

Financial Perspective:

Tactics	Goal	Actual
Average Gross Margin	40%	34%
Proportion of Design Teams Using Target Costing	100%	29%
Proportion of Products Exceeding Budgeted Costs	0%	49%

Customer Perspective:

Tactics	Goal	Actual
Customer Satisfaction Level	95%	80%
Customer Returns	0.5%	1%
Proportion of Design Teams that Include Customers	100%	41%

Strategy: To grow by blanketing the market with a wide array of products.

Learning & Growth:

Tactics	Goal	Actual
Employee Turnover	10%	15%
Average Training	40hrs/yr	32hrs/yr
Employee Access to Management Information Systems	100%	42%

Internal Business Processes:

Tactics	Goal	Actual
Average Prototype Time to Complete	12 days	20 days
Proportion of Products Covered by Patents	100%	81%
Time to Market	150 days	210 days

reduction, and service. These are only examples, but they can serve as a guideline for a company's formulation of which tactics and measurements to use, given their particular strategic direction.

For the product differentiation strategy shown in Exhibit 32.1, the ultimate focus is on a wide array of diverse product offerings. For this to occur there must be exceptional concentration on the procurement and retention of a highly trained workforce, as well as on business processes tightly aligned in the direction of rapid product prototyping, patent procurement, and quick distribution. There must be a

EXHIBIT 32.2. Balanced Scorecard for a Cost Reduction Strategy

Financial Perspective:

Tactics	Goal	Actual
Average Gross Margin	40%	34%
Overhead Cost %	17%	29%
Inventory Turnover	12x/yr	7.5x/yr
Receivable Turnover	10x/yr	7x/yr

Customer Perspective:

Tactics	Goal	Actual
Customer Returns	0.1%	2.3%
Analysis of Customer Complaints within One Day	100%	27%
Customer Satisfaction	90%	75%

Strategy: To grow by selling products at the lowest possible prices.

Learning & Growth:

Tactics	Goal	Actual
Employee Turnover	20%	30%
Percent of Staff Trained in Process Analysis	50%	13%
Percent of Staff on Analysis Teams	50%	4%

Internal Business Processes:

Tactics	Goal	Actual
Average Shipment Cycle Time	40 hrs	82 hrs
Proportion of Scrap	0.1%	3.0%
Labor Efficiency	90%	73%

slavish devotion to customer preferences since their opinions drive the development of new products. Further, there must be high margins on product sales, which provide enough cash to support the infrastructure needed to pursue this strategy. Also, with so many products constantly under development, the accounting staff must have an intense interest in the use of target costing by each product development team, as well as in a continual comparison of projected to actual product costs. An additional measure not noted in the exhibit for lack of space is the constant replacement of old products with new ones; a good way to measure this factor is through the percentage of total sales derived from products developed within the past few years.

For the cost reduction strategy shown in Exhibit 32.2, the staff must be trained in the use of reengineering, process centering, and other analysis tools that allow the organization to concentrate its efforts on creating the most efficient set of company processes possible. Internal business processes must support this effort by collecting information about all types of waste in the system, such as cycle times needed to complete tasks, material scrap rates, labor efficiency, and costs by process. The customer focus in this case is on complaints by customers because these are evidence of quality problems in the system that can be tracked down and eliminated, thereby reducing the future cost of waste. Finally, the finance function has a large role—examining all processes and products to determine margins, recommending cost reductions, and conducting benchmarking studies to determine where there are opportunities for further cost reductions. This analysis should also focus on the use of capital, both in inventory and accounts receivable.

Many other measures can be used on the balanced scorecard for the cost reduction strategy because there are so many activities that can lead to lower costs. Here are a few to consider:

- **Cost of quality.** Some estimates have placed the cost of product quality at as high as 30% of total sales. If the actual figure is anywhere near this amount, managers will be intensely interested in breaking the cost down into its component parts and using this information to reduce quality costs. This topic is covered extensively in Chapter 28.

- **Equipment utilization.** If machines are not being used, they are a wasted asset. Consequently, a good measure is overall machine utilization, which can also be reported by individual machine, so that managers can eliminate unused equipment.

- **Field service expenses.** If a company sells products that must be serviced in the field, this activity should be structured as a profit center, so that managers can see if field service pricing is sufficient to cover related costs and if quality problems are resulting in an excessive amount of free field service repair work.

- **Machine age.** Older machines eventually require replacement, so managers must know the age of equipment so that they can budget for replacements.

- **Machine maintenance costs.** The cost of machine maintenance rises with age and also indicates which equipment is inherently poorly designed, is of low quality, or is being overworked. Managers can track down and correct these issues, resulting in lower maintenance costs.

- **Number of inventoried items.** In a cost-conscious environment the administrative cost of managing an excessive number of inventory items is not tolerated, for there is a direct relationship between administrative costs and the number of inventory items. This concept can be expanded to the number of parts per product, for (once again) the cost of managing all the parts required to create a finished product can be quite high.

- **Production backlog.** A low-cost strategy requires careful management of the flow of production so that materials, labor, and machinery can be scheduled in an efficient manner. To ensure that there is a sufficient amount of time available for this scheduling, there should be a reasonably lengthy backlog of orders. Thus, the size of the backlog or the ratio of backlog to sales is a good tactical measure for this strategy.

- **Setup time.** The time required to change over a machine for the production of a new product is wasted time that could otherwise be used to manufacture something. By closely tracking the setup time by individual machine, management can concentrate its efforts on bottleneck operations and any excessively long conversion times.

- **Space reduction.** The floor and cubic space taken up by a production facility can be expensive, and so the cost per square foot and the number of square feet used are useful measures, especially when there is a clear possibility of subleasing space to reduce costs.

For the service strategy shown in Exhibit 32.3, there must be an intense focus on locating, training, motivating, and retaining those rare employees who are naturally capable of providing the highest level of service to customers. (Note: This strategy is most commonly followed in the retail sector.) Business processes must be capable of tracking customer orders, not to mention complaints, and disseminating this information to all employees. These processes must also be oriented toward filling customer orders on time, avoiding inventory stockout conditions, and resolving customer complaints as rapidly as possible. Further, the closest possible monitoring of customer satisfaction, specific complaints, and suggested improvements is of the highest importance. Finally, financial goals must track the level of profitability by customer, not only in total but also for add-on sales, such as for product financing and servicing costs.

Despite the clear advantages of a balanced scorecard, it can be a difficult concept to create. The main problem is that it involves all parts and functions of a company, and so it is hard to establish a consensus on measurements. There are many fiefdoms in an organization, and there will be resistance to the concept from managers who will lose power (e.g., reduced staffing levels or authority over decisions) if changes are implemented. Even if they agree on a general tactical direction, they may take their resistance down to a lower level by arguing over the exact details of how performance measurements will be calculated, who will collect them, and how they will be used to evaluate manager performance. The cost accountant frequently becomes entangled in these debates, for she will possibly be in charge of these

EXHIBIT 32.3. Balanced Scorecard for a Service Strategy

Financial Perspective:		
Tactics	**Goal**	**Actual**
Average Profit Percent per Customer	50%	32%
Average Financing Profit per Customer	8%	4%
Average Servicing Profit per Customer	11%	9%

Customer Perspective:		
Tactics	**Goal**	**Actual**
Customer Satisfaction	98.0%	77.0%
Percent of Customers Contacted for Follow-Up	50%	10%
Customer Retention	95%	71%

Strategy: To grow by providing a superior level of service to customers.

Learning & Growth:		
Tactics	**Goal**	**Actual**
Employee Turnover	5%	15%
Percent of Staff Trained in Customer Service	100%	85%
Percent of Staff Undergoing Repeat Training	100%	40%

Internal Business Processes:		
Tactics	**Goal**	**Actual**
Proportion of Orders Filled on Time	100%	82%
Proportion of Inventory Stockouts	0%	8%
Percent of Customer Queries Resolved On First Contact	85%	41%

measurements and therefore under pressure to create measurement systems favorable to the managers whose performance will be evaluated under the new system. This may call for the intervention of senior managers to ensure that the proper systems are created to support the balanced scorecard.

When properly formulated, a balanced scorecard can be an excellent tool for ensuring that all key tactics a company follows are tightly integrated and will lead to the achievement of its chosen strategy. However, we have not yet considered who collects, measures, and disseminates the information noted on the balanced scorecard. This is the job of the cost accountant and is discussed in the next section.

ROLE OF THE COST ACCOUNTANT IN THE STRATEGIC FRAMEWORK

The cost accountant is not directly responsible for the formulation of strategy but can impact it in several ways. One is through advising management on the ability of existing systems to provide the tracking information needed for the balanced scorecard measurements to be used. If the requisite systems are not currently available, the cost accountant must be able to estimate the types of systems needed for this purpose, as well as the costs of obtaining, implementing, and operating them. This analysis should also include some discussion about the risks of inaccurate data being reported by the systems, so that the management team is aware in advance of the probability of working with inaccurate measurement information. These steps describe the cost accountant's involvement during the *strategy formulation* stage.

The primary task of the cost accountant in the strategy arena is in providing continuing information to management regarding the status of all the key tactical measures that support the strategy. These can be measures itemized on the balanced scorecard, or they can be a wide array of other measures that may be too detailed in nature to be included on the scorecard and are really at a level of supporting detail that underlies the scorecard.

The vast majority of the measures used to support a strategy are not financial in nature, as a perusal of any of the three balanced scorecard exhibits reveals. They are more concerned with levels of employee training or turnover, process efficiency, and customer satisfaction. Measuring these factors is a long step away from the traditional analysis of product and process costs in which cost accountants have been trained. This can be a difficult transition for an accountant to make, which must be bolstered by training the accountant in the reasoning behind the use of this more diverse set of measures and how they impact the overall direction and success of the organization as a whole.

The balanced scorecard is not yet used in many organizations. At companies where managers are not yet committed to the concept, the cost accountant can still provide assistance in following the company's strategic path, though in a more limited manner. A number of initiatives have been promulgated over the last few decades that can assist a company in accomplishing its goals. By reviewing the cost-effectiveness of each one and creating measurement systems for them, a cost accountant can have a significant impact on a company's tactics. Some of these activities are:

- **Activity-based costing.** As noted in detail in Chapter 16, this is a method for allocating costs to activities, and from there to products, which results in much more accurate cost allocations. Management frequently finds that the margins on its higher-volume products go up as a result of this analysis, while the margins on its low-volume products go down. When used properly, this analysis results in the resetting of product pricing, the abandonment of certain product lines, and an overall improvement in profitability. However, this methodology is not a strategy but rather a fine tuning of the costing system that is of most use to an organization that wishes to adopt a strategy of competition based on low prices.

- **Capacity management.** As described in Chapter 26, a fully implemented MRP II system allows a cost accountant to determine the usage levels of all machines in a facility. This information allows the management team to eliminate under-utilized equipment and purchase more equipment for bottleneck operations. The result of these actions is a much more efficient use of capital. This tactical improvement is most commonly used by companies competing on a strategy of low product pricing.

- **Discretionary cost containment.** This is the careful analysis of the benefits to be obtained from various overhead costs, such as advertising and research and development, so that only expenditures are made that result in the greatest return. This tactic is useful for any type of strategy, though it is of particular benefit to organizations competing on a low-price strategy.

- **Downsizing.** This tactic is designed to focus on the core activities of an organization and eliminate all tasks (and related personnel) that do not directly support these activities. It can be used by all companies in distressed financial conditions but (once again) is most useful as a cost reduction strategy for organizations that compete based on low prices.

- **Outsourcing.** This tactic is the practice of shifting activities to outside suppliers, leaving only a minimal internal presence to review or manage the activities of the suppliers [see Bragg (1998) for more details]. It can be used for a variety of reasons, such as anticipated cost reductions, skill improvement, or a reduced capital investment. It is useful for all strategies but must be used carefully to ensure that a company does not incur a significant run-up in costs or that it does not eliminate any core competencies.

- **Process centering.** This is a method for consolidating the number of steps performed in a process so that the smallest number of employees is involved. The ultimate result of this procedure is to have one person handle all the steps in a process, which completely eliminates the transfer, wait, and queue time that occurs when activities are shifted among a number of employees. This practice results in much shorter cycle times, which is a tactical advantage to companies using any of the three strategies outlined in this chapter.

- **Product complexity analysis.** A product has a high degree of additional overhead cost if it requires an inordinate number of parts or manufacturing processes. By focusing on a reduction in the number of parts, a simplification of the assembly process (which is assisted by designing the product so that parts can be assembled only in the correct way—called design for manufacture), and the standardization of parts across many product lines, a company can achieve significant reductions in its product cost structure. The cost accountant can be particularly useful in enacting this tactic by assisting in the analysis of potential cost reductions during the complexity analysis. This tactic is of particular value for a cost reduction strategy.

- **Quality improvement.** One of the most important tactical initiatives is the improvement of product quality. By attending to the myriad of issues that contribute to product quality, a company can not only effect a major reduction in product costs but also eliminate all warranty and field service costs caused by poor quality. The cost accountant can assist in this effort by identifying the most significant quality costs (see Chapter 28 for more information about the cost of quality). This tactic is particularly useful for the cost reduction and service strategies since it reduces product costs and improves the quality of products delivered to customers.

- **Reengineering/process flow analysis.** This concept is used to totally redesign a company's processes to arrive at much higher levels of efficiency and effectiveness. Though it has earned a reputation for failure at many companies, because of the numerous changes that must be enacted, the concept is a sound one and can result in outstanding benefits if implemented properly. This tactic is of use for all three main strategies since it impacts costs, cycle times, and customer service.

- **Target costing.** A useful activity for any organization that creates many of its own products is target costing. As described in Chapter 17, target costing requires the cost accounting staff to join all product development teams and assist them in developing price, cost, and profit targets during the design stage. If a design cannot meet its cost goals, then it is not produced. This concept is of great importance to companies that compete with a product differentiation strategy.

The just noted activities are all at the tactical level. By concentrating on them a management team essentially uses tactics to drive corporate strategy, rather than the reverse. For example, if managers decide to use reengineering as their "latest and greatest" way to improve company performance, they have not really defined the strategy for which it is being used. If the strategy is better customer service, then reengineering should be focused on reducing the cycle time of processes that have a noticeable impact on customer service. However, if the strategy is cost reduction, then the focus must be on the most expensive processes, whether they directly impact customers or not. Thus, the purposes for which these activities are used must still be driven by a strategy, or else the expected results may be worse than anticipated.

A final strategy-related issue that involves the cost accountant is the measurement of financial performance directly related to specific strategic initiatives. For

EXHIBIT 32.4. Calculation of Financial Benefits from Strategic Changes

Revenue/Expense	Baseline Revenues and Expenses	Actual Results	Variance
	15,000 units	20,000 units	
Price per unit ($)	14.00	12.00	
Total revenue ($)	210,000	240,000	+30,000
Cost per unit ($)	10,000	8.00	
Total cost ($)	150,000	160,000	−10,000
Gross margin	60,000	80,000	+20,000

example, if a company decides to adopt a cost reduction strategy, so that it can lower its prices and attract more customers, the cost accountant can determine the baseline price and cost information from the reporting period just prior to the start of this strategy and compare it to the new price and cost structure, obtaining a variance that is directly traceable to the strategy change. An example of this reporting format is shown in Exhibit 32.4, where we compare the new product sales volumes to the levels prior to adoption of a strategy to reduce costs so that prices can be lowered; the result is an increase in volume that leads to additional profits.

The trouble with the type of analysis shown in Exhibit 32.4 is that it can be difficult to precisely determine the effects of specific strategic changes, especially when a number of different tactics are being implemented at the same time, all of which may have an impact on the same financial measures. The problem is exacerbated when there are a multitude of product lines or divisions, which requires a separate analysis for each one. This does not mean that a cost accountant should abandon the effort—this would only eliminate a vital feedback loop to the management team regarding the effectiveness of its strategic direction. However, the cost accountant is likely to be required to make substantial in-depth analyses in order to report meaningful strategic variance information to the management team.

This concept can be expanded to include a number of different strategy scenarios. For example, if management wants to know the financial impact of cost centering, the cost accountant can determine the cost of all staff involved in the particular process being redesigned and then calculate the savings from a reduced head count after the process change is completed. However, these analyses can be difficult to complete when determining the costing impact of secondary activities. To continue the last example, process centering also has an impact on other staff who were responsible for expediting transactions through the earlier process model, as well as clerical staff who had to investigate and fix errors caused by the earlier transfers of transactions between a large number of employees, not to mention the lost sales to customers who canceled orders because they had to wait too long for transactions to be completed. Such secondary cost benefits occur for nearly all tactical changes but are difficult to quantify. The cost accountant must determine the time required to make such analyses, whether or not the resulting information will be accurate or usable, and decide at that point if the additional analysis is worthwhile or if a simple enumeration of the probable secondary benefits is sufficient.

In short, the cost accountant is not involved in the formulation of business strategy but has a predominant role in reporting back to management on the success of the tactics it is using to advance its strategy. This can involve a mix of operational and financial performance measures. The following section contains an analysis of such a measurement system.

CASE STUDY: A STRATEGY

Mr. Pryce B. Lowe, the appropriately named cost accounting manager of the General Research and Instrumentation Company, has just been told by the general manager that the company is switching to a product differentiation strategy, which will require particular attention to the time to complete prototypes, time to market, and target costing. The general manager asks Mr. Lowe to create measurement and reporting systems that will effectively support this new strategy.

The first measurement is the time to complete prototypes. Since this has nothing to do with the information collected by the current financial system (nor do the other two measures), Mr. Lowe must create a new data collection system. He does this by obtaining access to the project scheduling system maintained by the engineering staff. By accessing this database periodically, Mr. Lowe can easily determine when prototyping projects are started and completed. However, he notes that completion dates can be inaccurate, so he recommends an additional control point by reviewing his prototyping completion report (as shown in Exhibit 32.5) with the engineering manager to ensure that the dates are correct.

Mr. Lowe also puts the average prototyping measurement on a trend graph, so that management can see if there are changes over the course of the year.

The next measure is the total time to market for new products. This measure requires Mr. Lowe to use the engineering start dates located in the engineering database he has already accessed for the prototyping measurement. However, the engineers are not responsible for the dates of product release to the market—that information is available only through the marketing staff. Therefore, he considers combing through the price list information issued by the marketing staff each month to see when products are made available for sale. Alternatively, he can use the accounting database, which lists the dates shipped for all products. Since the accounting information is more organized, he chooses it as the best source of information for product release dates (though the accounting information reveals only when something ships, not when it is made available for sale—these can be different dates). He then constructs a report similar to the one shown earlier in

EXHIBIT 32.5. Prototyping Completion Report

Project Name	Project Manager	Start Date	End Date	Total Days
Speaker box 104	B. Haskins	01/04	01/25	21
Subwoofer 117	R. Tondorski	02/07	02/26	19
Amplifier 129	A. Altamonte	02/09	03/13	33
		Average completion days		24

Exhibit 32.5 and issues this report to the management team each month. He also creates a trend line analysis of the average days to market, so that management can work on reducing the measure.

The final measure is more difficult since there are several alternative measures available for describing target costing performance. They are:

- Measurement of the presence of target costing accountants on design teams

- Measurement of the number of design staff trained in target costing

- Measurement of the proportion of approved designs that meet target costing standards

- Measurement of the percentage by which the costs of produced designs exceed their original target costs

Mr. Lowe decides that the first two measures do not really show if target costing is successful, or the exact amount of its success, because they make the target costing concept available only to design teams. The third measure appears to be better since it tightly focuses on the ability of design teams to meet their costing goals. The fourth goal is also a good one, but since it focuses on product costs after release to production, he feels that this measure can wait until product designs are further along in the production process. Accordingly, he works with the cost accountants assigned to each design team to derive a weekly reporting system that yields the current estimated cost of each product, its targeted cost, and the percentage by which the two numbers vary. He then constructs a summary-level report itemizing all completed designs and their actual and targeted costs (as shown in Exhibit 32.6), while also making available to management an additional report that lists the same information for design projects still in progress. He feels that the latter report is equally necessary because it tells management well in advance if there are any prospective problems with attaining targeted costs, which focuses its attention on resolving the costing issues or dropping the designs before the design teams incur additional costs.

EXHIBIT 32.6. Target Costing Report for Completed Product Designs

Product Name	Actual Cost ($)	Target Cost ($)	Cost Variance ($)	Cost Percentage	Authorizing Manager[a]
GPS navigator	231.00	225.00	−6.00	−3	R. Donnelly
GPS antenna	15.25	15.25	0	0	A. Travis
GLS software	48.00	32.00	−16.00	−50	R. Donnelly
GPS holder	11.47	11.50	+0.03	0	A. Travis
		Average variance		−8	

[a]The name of the manager who authorized a design to proceed to production despite an actual cost that exceeds the targeted costs.

The actual costs for each of the products listed in Exhibit 32.6 are derived from product bills of materials, which Mr. Lowe can access through the engineering department's bill of materials database. The target costing information comes from the spreadsheets maintained by the cost accountants assigned to each design team.

At the completion of his project, Mr. Lowe notes that none of the three measurement systems he is recommending will result in a traditional cost accounting variance or numerical report of any kind. Also, only the release date information used in the time-to-market report comes from any accounting files—and this information is only to derive a date (the product release date), not a financially oriented number of any kind. He wryly (and correctly) assumes that much of his school training in cost accounting variances is no longer sufficient for the types of reporting systems now required to properly support a company's strategic orientation.

SUMMARY

Competitive strategy is more than the intention to follow a specific overall path. A company must also derive the supporting set of tactics and measurements to ensure that all resources are pointed in the direction of achieving the desired strategy. One approach to linking strategy and tactics in a coherent manner is a balanced scorecard, which a cost accountant can support not only by creating measurement systems but also by continually measuring, evaluating, and reporting on the results of these systems. If there is no balanced scorecard system in place, the cost accountant can still contribute to a company's strategic direction by analyzing the impact of various activities, such as outsourcing and reengineering, that have a strategic impact, though in a more focused and smaller set of areas than would be the case if a balanced scorecard approach were used.

REFERENCES

Bragg, S. (1998). *Outsourcing.* New York: John Wiley & Sons.

Kaplan, R. S., & Norton, D. P. (1996). *The balanced scorecard.* Cambridge, MA: Harvard University Press.

Porter, M. (1998). *Competitive strategy.* New York: Free Press.

CHAPTER 33

Benchmarking

An increasingly common way to improve many aspects of a company's operations is through the use of benchmarking. This is a process of obtaining information outside a company or an area of a company about how to do things better and then implementing these methods in-house. There are several types of benchmarking that target different types of company performance, though a standard benchmarking process is followed when researching improvements—both issues are covered in this chapter. Also, we discuss the role of the cost accountant in the benchmarking process, which is a considerable one.

DEFINITION OF BENCHMARKING

Benchmarking is the process of obtaining and productively using information about how to improve one's processes, products, and strategies. It is a systematic process, rather than one that is only occasionally engaged in; it requires the ongoing use of project teams that are continually renewed with well-trained employees from all parts of an organization and are adequately supported at the uppermost levels of the company.

Benchmarking ideas can be obtained from other departments or divisions of a company. This is most likely in cases where there is strong pressure from the top of the organization for company managers to regularly meet and exchange ideas related to best practices. It is least likely where all company departments are located so close together that they all already use the same procedures or think in the same way, or if the company is so centralized that there is no room for initiative and "free thinking" regarding how to do things better.

Benchmarking ideas can also be obtained from outside the organization. This requires regular contacts with members of other organizations, not only within the same industry but also outside it, so that unique ideas can be regularly identified and brought in-house for implementation. For the latter type of benchmarking data gathering to work, an organization must be willing to accept ideas from the outside, rather than to believe that the best ideas are generated only within the company. It also requires a new mind-set, that it is perfectly acceptable to steal good ideas from other organizations—this can be difficult for some long-term employees to accept.

Another approach to gaining acceptance for outside ideas is to carefully screen prospective employees for being open to new ideas and to constantly train the workforce in the concepts of idea generation and implementation. This level of training requires the commitment of a considerable amount of funding for the training budget, not only for training but also for ancillary activities, such as bringing in outsiders to give speeches or seminars to the staff, sending employees to the facilities of other companies, and reviewing current literature for new ideas. The management structure must also be changed, so that the staff gets used to investigating benchmarking ideas on their own, rather than waiting for a manager to tell them what ideas are going to be implemented next. This can be a difficult concept for some old-line managers to accept, which may result in some management turnover. To ensure that all employees are fully committed to the concept of benchmarking, it is also useful to include it as a line item in employee job descriptions and periodic performance reviews.

Clearly, there are many issues that a company must consider when it searches for benchmarking ideas. They are:

- Ongoing contact with other organizations and company divisions
- Mind-set change regarding where ideas come from
- New employee screening
- Increased budget for training
- Increased budget for idea generation
- Altered management structure
- Altered job descriptions and performance reviews

By following the benchmarking process a company can expect to lower its costs of doing business, reduce quality-related problems, and improve the speed of transaction processing. These enhancements should lead to higher customer satisfaction levels, and therefore lower customer turnover, as well as to increased profitability.

However, the disruption caused by the changes implemented as a result of benchmarking may lead to the loss of some employees who are uncomfortable with the types of changes being made. Since these employees are frequently long-term employees used to the old way of doing business, this may result in a significant loss of internal expertise. However, since these people are the ones most apt to resist any changes in the company, their absence may increase the pace at which changes can be implemented.

Benchmarking does not have to be focused on just one area of a company. Though much of the business literature emphasizes benchmarking for the production department, virtually any area can be subject to this type of review. This can include such disparate areas as the janitorial, engineering, food service, and accounting functions. The primary difficulty with using benchmarking to address some functional areas, however, is that a company has limited resources to use in its benchmarking efforts, so it is best to categorize potential projects based on the size of their payback, in terms of monetary or strategic results, and address the top-ranking ones first, wherever they are within the company.

For benchmarking to work properly, a company must be good at three things—collecting information internally about whatever needs to be improved, collecting the same information externally or in other divisions of the same company, and implementation. Though data collection efforts require great diligence to complete, it is the third factor that gives a company the greatest skill in this area. As noted in a later section of this chapter, a company must follow a series of well-planned steps to ensure that all recommended changes are implemented properly, that the results are measured and compared to initial measurements to verify that there has been an improvement, and that follow-up activities will ensure that all changes are permanently followed within the company.

It is not reasonable to ask a transient project team to efficiently perform all of the three functions just outlined since its members may have little experience in this area. Instead, there should be a permanent benchmarking department within a company that maintains a standard set of policies and procedures related to how benchmarking projects are to be conducted. These procedures can be used to start up and operate each benchmarking team in a consistent, reliable manner. Also, this department should supply ongoing services to all benchmarking teams, so that they have administrative, research, implementation, and legal help. This department will learn from each project team that works under its guidance, so its level of expertise can reasonably be expected to increase over time, allowing it to provide better advice to new project teams.

In summary, benchmarking is all about collecting information about better ways to conduct business and then implementing these changes. This results in better processes and products and leads to higher profits. However, this comes at the price of altering the organization to more readily accept change, which can be a difficult proposition. In the next section we review the different types of benchmarking a company can use.

TYPES OF BENCHMARKING

There are three types of benchmarking, each of which is targeted at a different part of a company's operations. The first is benchmarking for internal processes. Examples of processes subject to benchmarking reviews are the sales cycle and procurement cycles, which make up the primary ongoing operations needed to run a company. The sales cycle involves taking orders from customers, scheduling them for production, manufacturing them, shipping the products, issuing billings, and processing cash receipts. The procurement cycle involves placing purchase requisitions, searching for suppliers, negotiating with suppliers, placing purchase orders, accepting deliveries, processing rejected goods, processing billing paperwork, and issuing payments to suppliers. These two processes comprise the bulk of most company operations, though there are certainly many ancillary processes that can also be the subject of a benchmarking study.

Comparisons can be made with companies from markedly different industries since processes are readily adaptable across many industries. When one hears about how a company has conducted a benchmarking review with another company far outside of its normal field of competitors, it is most likely that process changes were involved.

When processes are the subject of benchmarking, the usual justification is that there will be immediate financial results, typically through the elimination of employee positions. Benchmarking can also achieve shorter processing intervals, which are readily measured. For these reasons process benchmarking is popular.

Another type of benchmarking is based on products or services. It uses comparisons between a company's own products or services and those of other organizations. The focus of such studies tends to be on the quality, reliability, and features of comparable products. This does not mean that benchmarking comparisons are confined to products created by companies in the same industry, since products can be broken down into their component parts which may individually be more readily compared with components of products from other industries. Product benchmarking can be performed without the approval of another company since one can simply buy its products and directly review them through reverse engineering or feature comparisons. Nonetheless, it is most useful to obtain the cooperation of the maker of each product since the review team can glean much additional information regarding the manner in which each product is manufactured, information not readily apparent from a direct review of the product itself.

The final form of benchmarking involves strategy; the review team wishes to discern if there are other ways to position the company within its industry that have not been considered but which other organizations are implementing with success. This usually requires a close look at other industries since the industry within which a company competes may be chock-full of organizations that all have the same strategic mind-set and therefore are not a good source of information. This type of review tends not to yield much in the way of short-term improvements since strategic changes typically require several years of effort to implement. Thus, only the most forward-looking management teams tend to engage in this type of benchmarking, however useful it may prove to be in the long run.

Though the preceding categories generally cover the bulk of benchmarking situations, there are also a few cases that are less easily categorized. One situation is when a company elects to use benchmarking to assist its business partners. This may involve its customers or its suppliers, but more commonly its suppliers. It usually does this in exchange for lower prices from its suppliers or larger or better-priced orders from its customers. Another category of benchmarking is centered on employees. This type of benchmarking addresses improvements in worker safety, training, morale, absenteeism, and retention. These are particularly important issues for any company whose primary asset is its employees, such as organizations in the service and software industries.

BENCHMARKING PROCESS

How does one conduct a benchmarking study? The process is relatively straightforward. First, because it may involve the detailed examination of a number of different departments, some of which may not be too thrilled to be receiving any attention, the support of the senior management team must be obtained. This means that the benchmarking team leader should present the objectives of the latest benchmarking project to a high-level senior manager, preferably at the vice president or CEO level, and request a written statement of support itemizing the objectives being authorized, as well as distribution to all departments that will be affected by the study.

Next, the benchmarking team requires financial support. This means that funds must be budgeted, which will probably require a shifting of budgeted funds from some other source to the benchmarking project. This frequently requires the intervention of the CFO or controller, who can authorize funding. Alternatively, one or more department managers who need the results of the benchmarking study may allocate funds to it from their internal budgets.

An additional preparatory step is to assign staff to the project. Though part-time staffing is possible, employees rarely have sufficient time to commit to an extra project, which results in missed deadlines for the benchmarking team. A better approach is to assign full-time personnel to the project. The mix of such staff will change by project, depending on what skills are needed for each one.

Next, the benchmarking team must be trained in the tasks they will be required to perform. Though they are already experts in their own fields of specialization, benchmarking requires additional skills in data collection, analysis, process flow modeling, and implementation, some of which they may not have had any experience with. This training may not take long, but it is important to complete nonetheless, to ensure that the same method is used by all members of the project team.

The next step is to decide exactly what to benchmark. Though there should already be some general idea of what is to be done (which was how senior management approval and funding were obtained), the topic initially presented may have been a broad one within which several more specific projects could be fitted. For example, the initial proposal may have been to shorten the cycle time of the disbursements business process. However, there are a number of steps within this process, such as ordering and receiving goods, forwarding the paperwork to accounting, matching accounts payable documentation, and issuing payment. The project team may select only one of these subprocesses for a more detailed review.

Once the specific subprocess has been selected, the project team can collect information about the performance level of whatever is targeted. This information is needed in order to compare it to the results of a review of outside entities or other departments or divisions of the same company. For example, a review of a process might require a work flow diagram detailing exactly how information flows through it, as well as the various control points and time requirements at each step in the process. Alternatively, a review of an existing product requires an analysis of its cost (which is where the cost accountant is extremely useful) and a complete description of its various features and level of quality. Finally, a review of strategy requires complete documentation of the existing in-house strategic direction, as well as supporting tactics. All this information should be compiled into a formal document, with a primary document being kept under the control of a librarian (or someone with a similar title) on the project team, so that it is not at risk of being lost or modified.

The next step is to determine what companies to benchmark. Some organizations put this step earlier in the benchmarking process, on the grounds that there is no point in completing other steps if there is no evidence of anyone against whom comparisons can be made. There are a variety of ways to make a list of benchmarking targets. One is to review professional publications to see which companies are improving themselves in specific areas; another is to review general or industry-specific publications for the same information. Another source is speeches at industry symposiums. Yet another source may be networking connections between companies. If there are many company divisions, still another source is one's counterparts in these divisions. In short, there are many possible approaches to developing a list of potential benchmarking candidates.

There may be some difficulty in setting up benchmarking meetings with competitors since these organizations obviously prefer to keep their most impressive results hidden as a competitive advantage. This issue should force one to look outside the industry. By doing so one can frequently spot organizations that have created outstanding processes, products, and strategies that exceed those of any company within one's own industry. Examples are L. L. Bean (distribution prowess), Ford Motor Company (accounts payable), and General Electric (Internet business processes).

Once a set of benchmarking targets have been selected, the project team must create a set of questions to ask the representatives of the companies with whom they will meet. This is an important step since the target companies are setting aside valuable time to meet with the team and should not have their time wasted. To this end the team should first create the largest possible list of questions and then winnow it down to the most critical ones that can definitely be handled during the assigned meeting time with the target company. There should also be a secondary list of follow-up questions that can be used if time is still available after the primary questions have been answered. The team may wish to role-play the meeting in advance, assigning roles to each person on the team, so that questions are posed with the greatest level of efficiency and notes are taken that are complete and comprehensive. If the team is particularly concerned about potentially missing any answers through the note-taking process, it can either assign several people to this role, on the grounds that their combined notes will contain all possible information, or by bringing a tape recorder to the meeting.

Once the initial interview has been completed, the project team should review it and compare it to the results it recorded when examining the company's internal process, product, or strategy, as the case may be. This review will almost certainly give rise to additional questions for the benchmarked companies. However, employees of these companies should not be continually bothered with requests for follow-up information since they are giving this time away free. Instead, the team should marshal all its remaining questions and run through them in a single phone call, thereby making the best use of everyone's time.

The completed review should give rise to a number of action items that can be used to modify or (more rarely) replace the internal process, product, or strategy. However, before implementing any changes, this is a good time to interact with the personnel who will be affected by them. The reason for doing so is because change can be difficult for anyone who has not previously reviewed the changes and agreed to them. Also, the person who will use the modification may be aware of internal problems the project team is not aware of that will make the change inoperable. In addition, even if the changes are good ones, there may be so much internal inertia (e.g., We've always done it this way, so why change?) that the project team should present its proposed changes to its senior management-level sponsor who can then assist in forcing the changes throughout the organization.

With these preparations completed, the team should create a thorough implementation plan that describes the precise changes, when they will take place, what they will impact, and who will be responsible for them, not to mention any required training, capital purchases, or personnel changes. This plan should be carefully reviewed to ensure that nothing is missing and that the time lines are reasonable.

Finally, the benchmarking changes can be made. During this key phase the entire project team should be available (no vacations!) to assist with any problems that might arise during the implementation. Despite the highest level of care used in planning for the changes, one can be assured that problems *will* arise. If the implementation requires the participation of multiple production shifts at a company, the team must schedule someone to be available all hours of the day.

Once the implementation has been completed, the team should meet to go over all the successes and problems encountered during the project. Not only is this a good time to cover issues that can be avoided in the future, but it also results in a document that can be passed to other benchmarking teams so that they too can avoid problems.

A final step is to schedule a review of all the changes after some time has passed and they have had a chance to "settle in" and either succeed or fail. If they have failed, the team must review the situation and recommend changes to the management team in regard to what further steps must be taken. If the changes have been a success, the benefits should be quantified and forwarded to the financial analyst reviewing the project, so that the management team can be informed of the return on investment of its benchmarking initiative.

Many steps have been described here; they are all necessary to the successful completion of any benchmarking project. By using these steps one can ensure that sufficient management backing, funding, and company buy-in are available to support a project and that the project is conducted in the most efficient manner possible.

ROLE OF THE COST ACCOUNTANT IN BENCHMARKING

So where does the cost accountant fit into the benchmarking process? She may not be a high-level decision maker, may not have the skills to manage the project team, and may not be involved in the implementation process. Nonetheless, she is positioned at the core of the benchmarking process.

A key part of benchmarking is understanding how a company's internal systems operate. This is a primary ongoing function of the cost accountant, who may already have compiled work flow diagrams itemizing all key processes—not because they will be needed for benchmarking but because the cost accountant is frequently involved in determining the cost to run transactions through key processes, particularly for use in an activity-based costing system (Chapter 16). In addition, any benchmarking project that investigates the improvement of a company's products and services needs to unearth information about their current cost. Once again, the cost accountant should have already compiled this information or at least have ready access to the databases that contain it. Thus, any internal costing information is most easily accessed by the cost accountant.

An additional task most easily handled by the cost accountant is obtaining benchmarking information from target companies. Though anyone properly prepared with a questionnaire could obtain this information, it is better to use the cost accountant, who is better trained to examine weak answers and discover key information whose absence may not be immediately apparent to anyone else. Further, the cost accountant can be used to compare the internal and external information about each project, not only to spot missing information but also to highlight key differences and verify that they are valid.

In short, the cost accountant acts as the chief financial analyst on a benchmarking team, both assembling and reviewing the key information used by the team to arrive at a list of suggested recommendations for improvement.

SUMMARY

The cost accountant is ideally positioned to assist a company in pursuing an aggressive benchmarking program, not only by assembling costing information about benchmarking targets but also by working with target companies to ensure that the most important information is extracted from them and verified against internal data. For more information about the extensive work plans that can be used as part of a benchmarking project, see Bogen and English (1994).

REFERENCE

Bogen, C., & English, M. (1994). *Benchmarking for best practices.* New York: McGraw Hill.

CHAPTER 34

Valuing Inventory

In many smaller organizations the cost accountant's key job function is considered to be the valuation of inventory—the rest of the company has less appreciation for the other issues discussed in this book, but for them, the valuation must be correct, so that financial statements have some degree of validity. This chapter addresses this most basic cost accounting function, describing how to conduct a month-end valuation for both periodic and perpetual cost systems, and goes on to discuss how to investigate inventory variances that interfere with an accurate valuation.

INVENTORY VALUATION STEPS FOR A PERIODIC INVENTORY SYSTEM

The most elementary system for determining the value of both inventory and the cost of goods sold is to accumulate all purchases made during the month, add this number to the value of the beginning inventory, subtract the cost of a physical inventory count at the end of the month, and—voila—you have both an inventory valuation and the cost of goods sold. Though this sounds like a simple approach, it is actually the valuation method most likely to be in error, for the mandatory month-end inventory count may be incorrectly performed or compiled, producing incorrect results. The perpetual inventory and standard costing systems, as described in the next two sections, are more accurate than the periodic inventory system.

Nonetheless, one should review this section in some detail, for it describes a number of inventory valuation steps that are referred to in later sections.

The steps to be followed in conducting an inventory valuation using the periodic inventory system are:

1. *Determine the ownership of inventory.* One should not count inventory if it does not belong to the company, so it is important to clearly identify and locate inventory prior to conducting a count. For example, consignment goods on the premises that are owned by someone else should be clearly marked and not counted. If the company owns consignment goods located elsewhere, arrangements must be made to have them counted.

2. *Determine matching of ownership paperwork with physical presence.* If inventory items are sitting on the receiving dock, be sure that supplier invoices are on hand that record their related cost, or that receiving documentation is available that can be converted to a cost. Otherwise, the items will be counted into inventory without any corresponding addition to purchasing costs, which will result in an excessively high inventory valuation and artificial profits. The same approach must be used for finished goods that are on the shipping dock. If invoicing documents have not yet been prepared, they should still be counted as part of inventory. Alternatively, if invoices have been issued, they must be excluded from the inventory count.

3. *Count the inventory.* Assign counting teams to the physical inventory count, use prenumbered sequential inventory count tags to record all counts, and closely monitor the results for accuracy.

4. *Identify material costs to use for inventory valuation.* Raw material costs always include the purchase price, to which can be added freight, handling, and related insurance costs (though these extra costs can more easily be charged to the current period). Also, any early payment discounts can be subtracted from the purchases account as a reduction in purchasing costs.

5. *Identify direct labor costs to use for inventory valuation.* Compile all direct labor costs incurred during the period. This involves separating supervisory labor costs from direct labor costs and including them in overhead costs (see the next item). The easiest way to compile direct labor costs is to add up the totals for all payroll expenses during the period and *subtract* any payments in payrolls that apply to the previous month, while estimating and *adding* the cost of any direct labor at the end of the month that has not yet been included in a payroll.

6. *Identify overhead costs to use for inventory valuation.* Generally accepted accounting principles mandate that certain costs be accumulated into overhead cost pools, which are then allocated to both inventory and the cost of

goods sold. These costs include machine and building repairs and maintenance, utilities, rent, indirect labor, the salaries of production supervisors, production supplies, all quality control costs, and the cost of small tools that are not otherwise capitalized. Not all of the enumerated costs should be included in the overhead cost pool if they also bear some relationship to general and administrative costs, which are charged to the current period. For example, the rent cost of a production facility is charged to overhead, but the cost of rent for the facility where the sales and accounting staff is located is charged to current costs.

7. *Cost the inventory with material costs.* Using a preset cost flow assumption (usually LIFO, FIFO, or average costing—see Chapter 13), create an inventory valuation that uses cost layers or a weighted average of all purchases. If LIFO is used, then there should be a database on hand that itemizes the oldest cost layers. If FIFO is used, then it can be constructed from scratch using the most recent inventory purchasing documents (since only the most recent costs are included in cost layers).

8. *Add direct labor costs to inventory.* The cost accountant already knows the total amount of direct labor incurred during the month (see step 5) but still needs to allocate this between the production that went into inventory and the production that was sold. To do this he must have a basis of allocation. This can be a standard amount of labor charged per hour of machine time used, square footage utilized, standard direct labor hours used, or some other allocation basis. The main point is to consistently apply the same allocation measure over multiple periods in order to show consistent financial reporting, as well as to use an allocation method that has some provable basis in fact. As an example of such an allocation, the cost accountant may determine that 1000 machine hours were used during the month to produce 500 units of production, of which 200 were stored in inventory and 300 were sold. This works out to 40% of the machine time used that can be applied to inventory. Therefore, if the total direct labor cost was $100,000, then $40,000 would be charged to inventory and $60,000 to the cost of goods sold.

9. *Cost the inventory with overhead costs.* The allocation of overhead costs follows the approach described for direct labor in step 8, except that the pool of overhead costs includes such a wide array of costs that several different forms of allocation may be needed to spread the costs between inventory and the cost of goods sold in a reasonable manner. For example, building insurance costs may be allocated based on a product's use of building square footage, while machine maintenance costs can be allocated based on the number of machine hours used.

10. *Determine the cost of goods sold.* Add the newly costed inventory valuation to the beginning inventory balance and subtract all purchases during the

month from this total to arrive at the total cost of goods sold. Since this may be a large lump-sum number that does not provide much information to management, it may be better to use several general ledger accounts to store different types of inventory and purchasing information, which can then be used to determine the cost of goods sold for a smaller number of items.

11. *Investigate inventory and costing variances.* It is a rare situation for the resulting cost of goods sold to be perfectly in line with expectations. Instead, use the variance analysis procedures described under Variance Investigation later in this chapter to determine where problems may have arisen, as well as to correct numerical problems and ensure that the underlying issues that caused them have been resolved.

INVENTORY VALUATION CHECKLIST FOR A PERPETUAL INVENTORY SYSTEM

The perpetual inventory system shares many valuation steps with the periodic inventory system but has a major advantage in that running balances are kept for all inventory items. As a result, if the management team has confidence in the accuracy of its inventory-related transactions, it can avoid month-end physical inventory counts entirely, which results in much shorter and less time-consuming inventory valuations.

Another change from the periodic inventory system is that there is no need for a purchases account. Instead, all incoming inventory is recorded as passing through the inventory account. When needed in production, a second transaction is created that shifts the raw materials inventory to work-in-process inventory. On completion, an additional transaction moves it to finished goods inventory, while a fourth transaction records a sale. The number of transactions involved highlights a key weakness of the perpetual method, for there is some risk that transactions will not be properly completed at all stages of the production and sales processes, resulting in an inaccurate inventory valuation. To avoid this problem, the physical inventory-taking step noted under Inventory Valuation Checklist for a Periodic Inventory System should be replaced by an ongoing step that requires daily cycle counting of inventory balances; this catches and corrects transactional errors.

Thus far, we have discussed keeping track of the cost of materials only within the perpetual inventory system. Though more useful than the periodic inventory system, which has no such feature, it does not provide a full cost for each item in stock. To do this we need to add direct labor and overhead costs. The cost of overhead will still be applied at the end of the accounting period (for a better approach, see the next section), but it is possible to add direct labor costs to inventory over the course of the month. To do so the direct labor staff must charge its time to specific products or jobs; this information is stored on time sheets and then entered into the accounting database, or entered automatically at a timekeeping terminal (Chapter 5). In either case the cost of labor is present in inventory at all times, which gives management a better view of its ongoing investment in inventory. Since the cost of overhead is added to the inventory only at the end of the month, however, this still does not yield an accurate ongoing full inventory cost. In order to achieve that goal, we must integrate standard costing into the perpetual inventory system, which is discussed in the next section.

INVENTORY VALUATION CHECKLIST FOR A STANDARD COSTING INVENTORY SYSTEM

Thus far, we have assumed that only actual costs are used during the inventory valuation process. The periodic costing system required us to wait until month-end, at which point we compiled actual costs; the perpetual system allowed for the constant use of actual costs throughout the month, but at the price of using many transactions and requiring direct labor personnel to code their time to specific products or jobs; and there still was no way to charge actual overhead costs to inventory on an ongoing basis. The integration of standard costing into a perpetual inventory system allows us to have reasonably current inventory costs at all times and in all three categories of costs—materials, direct labor, and overhead.

To use standard costs for inventory valuation, a company must first compile bills of materials for every completed product in stock. There must also be BOMs for all work-in-process items that have been partly completed, as well as a listing of the standard costs for all raw material items. These standard costs are then used to value the inventory. Though the creation and proper maintenance of BOMs is a major chore that may require the full-time use of several staff members, it carries with it the benefit of having immediate access to a fully costed inventory at any time—just multiply the perpetual inventory database by the current set of BOMs to arrive at a valuation. This feature is useful for organizations that like to issue financial statements more frequently than once a month and need reasonably accurate inventory information to do so.

Similarly, labor routings must be compiled for every work-in-process and finished goods item. A labor routing lists the exact amounts of labor time required to complete each step in the production process. As was the case with BOMs, labor routing records are then automatically multiplied by the inventory balance for each item in stock to determine the direct labor cost component of inventory.

Standard overhead costs must also be applied to inventory. This is done by compiling actual overhead costs from a previous period (or the average of such costs over several preceding periods, which smooths out unusual variations in the monthly level of costs), dividing them by some allocation basis, such as the number of direct labor hours used by each product, and arriving at a standard overhead cost per unit of allocation basis. This cost is then entered into the computer system, which automatically charges it to each inventory item.

Once all standard costs have been determined and charged to inventory, the cost accountant must still compare these costs to actual costs at month-end to ensure their accuracy. In one such step, the actual overhead cost must be determined at the end of each month, using the same compilation process described for the periodic valuation system. Once the actual overhead cost is available, the cost accountant must run a report that extracts the total amount of standard overhead cost already stored in the inventory and determine the difference between the total standard and actual overhead costs. The difference, either positive or negative, should be booked to the inventory account in the general ledger. Thus, the standard cost of overhead is supplemented at month-end so that it matches the actual amount of costs incurred.

The same approach must be used to ensure that direct labor costs are recorded at their actual values. The total amount of actual direct labor costs must be compiled for the month, and the appropriate amounts allocated between inventory and the cost of goods sold (precisely as was the case for the periodic inventory system). Again, a report must be run that notes the total amount of standard direct labor costs already stored in the inventory, which can then be adjusted in the general ledger to match the amount of actual direct labor costs incurred.

Also of considerable importance is the continuing use of some type of cost flow principle for the valuation of material costs, such as LIFO, FIFO, or average costing. The accounting system must still create layers of inventory costs or calculate an ongoing average cost, despite the use of a standard cost for inventory valuation. Then, at the end of the month, the total layered actual cost can be compared to the standard cost to determine the difference between the two valuations. Once again, the variance should be booked to the general ledger inventory account.

With so many variances being calculated and added to the general ledger, it is useful to divide the single general ledger account for inventory into at least three accounts, one each for materials, direct labor, and overhead. By doing so one can quickly compare account balances to total actual costs within each category to ensure that every item has been adjusted to actual cost at month-end. An alternative that requires even more accounts is to record raw materials in a separate account, with no further subdivision (since there should be nothing in it but materials), while separately dividing both work in process and finished goods into three accounts each (for materials, labor, and overhead). This approach not only makes it easier to reconcile accounts but also simplifies the compilation of totals for raw materials, work in process, and finished goods, which can be shown separately in the financial statements.

Consequently, the addition of standard costs to the perpetual inventory valuation system solves the problem of constantly charging actual costs directly to inventory (a particularly onerous chore for the direct labor personnel), while also providing for the use of a reasonably accurate overhead cost in the valuation that can be accessed at any time. The main problem with this approach is that the cost accountant must now conduct a reconciliation between the actual and standard costs of inventory to ensure that actual costs are still reflected in the total valuation from time to time. Most cost accountants conduct this comparison every month since they do not want to run the risk of reporting a valuation that is significantly different from actual costs. Others, with a greater degree of confidence in their BOMs and labor routings, conduct the comparison less frequently. Generally, it is best to err on the side of caution and run the comparison every month.

LOWER-OF-COST-OR-MARKET RULE

Though the preceding discussions provide the basic guidelines for valuing an inventory, they both require the addition of an accounting rule required by generally accepted accounting principles. It is called the lower-of-cost-or-market rule, and its explanation closely reflects its name. If the market value of an inventory item drops below the cost at which it is recorded in inventory, its cost must be written down to the market value. More specifically, the rule states that the recorded inventory cost should not be less than the net realizable value, as reduced by an allowance for a normal profit margin. This clarification keeps a company from reducing its inventory valuation too far, which it might otherwise be tempted to do in order to charge more costs through to the cost of goods sold, thereby reducing profits and (in particular) a firm's related income tax liability.

From a practical perspective this rule is usually enforced only when a company is about to be audited or to issue financial statements to the investing public. The reason for this delay is that it can be difficult to determine the market rate for many specialized items, so managers do not want to invest the time in an ongoing review of market rates. Even then, many corporations find that they simply have no means of determining market rates for many of their products or component parts and so cannot make a reasonable determination of the lower-of-cost-or-market rule. Still, there are some inventory items to which the rule can be applied. These items should be identified in the inventory database so that they can be located and reported on separately, thereby making adherence to the rule somewhat easier.

When applying the rule, one can review individual items or whole classes of inventory at the same time. Though the latter method may appear on the surface to require the least amount of work, in reality it is difficult to make broad-based comparisons and adjustments to large classes of stock. Consequently, the most common approach is to review specific inventory items that represent large proportions of the total inventory valuation and institute downward cost adjustments for these items if such changes are warranted. Reviews of smaller-dollar-value items are not worth the review effort in comparison to the size of any possible adjustments and so are generally ignored if there would otherwise be a minor impact on the level of reported profits.

VARIANCE INVESTIGATION

A large proportion of a company's costs are included in the inventory valuation process. Many transactions are involved in the storage and use of these costs, which means that there is a high likelihood of error in a large proportion of company costs. Consequently, the cost accountant is constantly employed in the analysis of inventory and cost-of-goods-sold amounts to see if there are errors. In this section we look at some of the variance investigation methods that can be used.

Before proceeding to specific variance investigations, one must understand that there are many ways in which the inventory and cost of goods sold can be made incorrect, involving such a wide array of problems as changes in units of measure, miscounted products, incorrect or missing data entry for inventory transactions, and scrap. The cost accountant cannot hope to accomplish a perfect variance analysis that finds and explains every last penny of variance. Instead, the best approach is to look back on the variance analyses from previous periods, find the variances that account for the largest proportion of incorrect costs, and complete them first; then work through variances that account for progressively smaller amounts until there is no time available to proceed any further. This results in some portion of the total variance being unaccounted for. Then, as the causes of the largest variances are dealt with, the overall variance size gradually shrinks, allowing one to address and correct smaller causes of variances. It is likely that a company will never achieve a perfectly accurate inventory valuation that contains no variances, but the size of the variances should decline over a period of several years.

The following is a list of suggested analyses covering the most likely causes of inventory-related variances. They are in no particular order of preferred implementation since the types of problems encountered by individual companies vary considerably; thus, one must sample each of the variance resolution methods to see how much of a variance is encountered and then use it only if the resulting variance is sufficiently large. The analyses are:

- **Unit of measure changes.** Costs are assigned to units of inventory based on a specific unit of measure. For example, a roll of tape may cost $1.50 for one roll. A roll is an ideal unit of measure for the warehouse staff since it must periodically count the rolls. However, the engineering staff may prefer to think of tape in inches since it uses this information to create bills of materials where listing a fraction of an entire roll may result in a small unit usage rate. If the engineering staff went into the computer system and altered the unit of measure to inches without telling anyone, the price per unit would stay the same although the unit of measure was changed. Thus, if the roll of tape contained 1000 inches, its cost in the inventory would jump from $1.50 to $1500. If there are many rolls of tape on hand, this will result in general consternation. This variance is best found by simply sorting the inventory in declining dollar order and looking for outrageously large dollar values. Another approach, if available, is to run a search of inventory transactions to see if any units of measure have been changed.

- **Incorrect inventory counts.** When the management group orders a physical inventory count to be taken, such as at year-end, it does not realize that the sudden mass counting of all items in stock may actually produce inventory records that are less accurate than before the count because the people doing the counting frequently are not warehouse employees and therefore do not know what they are counting. This problem can be detected by comparing before- and after-inventory valuations, item by item, to see which items have changed significantly as a result of the inventory count. Another approach is to backtrack through all the inventory receipts, pull transactions since the last inventory count to determine what the current inventory quantity should be, and compare this amount to what has been counted in the warehouse.

- **Unrecorded scrap.** A major problem in an undisciplined production process is not recording scrap use. When this happens, extra inventory must be requisitioned from the warehouse, perhaps to such an extent that it grossly exceeds the material quantities listed on the bills of materials for items being produced. This is a particular problem in a company that uses backflushing to relieve inventory as a result of production. In this instance quantities are backflushed based on bill of materials quantities *only;* if additional scrap is incurred during the production process and is not manually relieved from inventory, the inventory database will continue to show the scrapped quantities as part of the inventory balance. This problem can be detected through constant cycle counting but can be corrected only through intensive training of the production staff in how to handle the paperwork for scrap transactions.

- **Incorrect part numbers.** A surprisingly common issue is that parts are received into a warehouse using an incorrect part number, either because the part was initially misidentified, or because the part number was incorrectly entered in the database, perhaps on account of a transposition or a missing number. The result is excessively low quantities of parts under the correct part number and quantities that are too high under other part numbers. This is a particular problem if the costs of the parts are not roughly the same, since extended costs for different part numbers can be much higher or much lower than their actual values. This is a difficult problem to spot since the parts may be so thoroughly misidentified that their labels and storage boxes are also wrong. One approach is to conduct periodic audits that involve opening parts containers and manually verifying part numbers. Another alternative is to compile all receiving and issuing transactions for a part in order to arrive at a theoretical quantity that should be in stock and then investigate further to see if the actual quantity is significantly different. This is one of the most labor-intensive variance investigations.

- **Unauthorized obsolescence throwaways.** The warehouse staff may realize that inventory items are no longer of any use and throw them away without authorization. They may even enter a proper inventory transaction that records the reduction in inventory. Nonetheless, this practice blindsides the cost accountant, who finds that an additional charge to the cost of goods sold has occurred and does not know why. This is a difficult item to locate unless the computer system can automatically determine what inventory items should have been used, based on actual production figures, and then compare this theoretical use to actual transactions to highlight obvious differences.

- **Supplier pricing changes.** If there is a sudden change in the price a company pays for its components (usually upward), the expected inventory valuation and accompanying cost of goods sold will change. This can be a major problem if the component is a key one that makes up a large part of a finished product's cost, since the cost of goods sold is dramatically affected. This problem is more easily uncovered than some of the other variance issues because many computer systems have the capability to report on a history of pricing changes for each component, which allows the cost accountant to quickly spot the problem. It should be standard practice to run such a report every month for a selection of key components.

- **Changes in the bill of materials.** The inventory includes not just raw materials but also work in process and finished goods. These latter two categories are valued based on a list of components that are included in a bill of materials, which is usually maintained by the engineering department. If the engineers choose to alter some component of a BOM, a ripple effect will run through the cost of inventory for the item whose BOM they have changed. For example, if they decide to increase the amount of scrap cost assigned to a product, this will increase the inventory valuation by that amount. This problem is best detected through the use of a computerized change log that notes all changes in BOMs.

- **Changes in labor routings.** As in the case of BOMs, the industrial engineering staff maintains records of standard labor use for each product, called labor routings. If a labor routing is altered, it too will have an impact on inventory valuation. Again, this problem can be spotted with the use of an automated change log.

The variances noted here are by no means the only ones a cost accountant can find; they are just among the most common. The author once participated in a comprehensive review of inventory variances for a candy manufacturer, which found no less than 70 different potential inventory-related variances that could occur. Only a cost accountant with a great deal of experience with valuation systems can track down, account for, and correct all possible variances.

SUMMARY

From the length of the section dealing with variance investigation, it may be apparent that the cost accountant's job is rarely complete when the initial inventory valuation has been finished. There are so many transactions flowing through the inventory database that it is almost impossible not to have errors creep into the data used for the valuation. The result is an inventory or cost of goods sold that varies from expected levels and which must therefore be closely investigated and continuously monitored for problems. Knowing what the most likely transactional problems are, and what causes them, is a critical part of the inventory valuation task.

CHAPTER 35

Costing Best Practices

The bulk of this book has focused on the technical aspects of which cost accounting systems to use and how to use them. However, using the correct costing method does not mean that the resulting system will operate in an efficient or effective manner. Consequently, the material in this chapter is primarily concerned with those best practices that will result in the most efficient, effective costing system. In each of the following sections, we cover a best practice that reduces the time needed by the cost accounting staff to complete its work or improves the value of the information it creates.

ELIMINATE HIGH-OVERHEAD ALLOCATION BASES

One part of the cost accountant's job is to properly allocate overhead costs to various activities and products. If this is done incorrectly, management may decide to expand its sales efforts for a product that actually has substandard margins, or retire products that actually have excellent margins. Thus, the use of a proper cost allocation method is critical to the operational decisions made by management.

There are two criteria for a good allocation base. One is that it should have a tight causal linkage to the cost being allocated. For example, an increase in square footage is likely to result in an increase in utility costs. This concept is explained in detail in Chapter 16. The other criterion, which is of more concern to us here, is that a small change in the allocation base should not result in a disproportionately large cost allocation. The best and most common example of this problem is when a company allocates all its overhead costs based on the amount of its direct labor. If overhead costs are $100 and direct labor costs are $10 in a period, a $1 change in the amount of direct labor incurred will result in a $10 change in the amount of an allocated cost, which is a 10:1 ratio. This situation results in wide swings in the amount of allocated costs from period to period and plays havoc with the total cost figures supplied to management. To avoid this problem one should first determine which overhead allocation bases result in excessively high degrees of leverage in the amounts of costs allocated. Then one can find alternative allocation bases that have much lower leverage ratios and substitute them for the original allocation base. This may result in subdivision of the original pool of costs into a number of smaller pools, each of which uses a different allocation basis. This approach results in much more accurate cost allocations that have little variation from period to period. An additional benefit of substituting several smaller allocations for a single large one is that a number of allocations tend to result in further smoothing of the dollar amount of costs allocated since the allocation bases may not increase or decrease in concert with each other.

This best practice improves the *effectiveness* of cost accounting information since it provides management with allocated overhead costs that are applied more consistently from period to period. Unfortunately, it generally requires more work to calculate since there are usually several cost pools to accumulate and allocate, rather than a single large one.

FOCUS ON OVERHEAD COSTS

This may appear to be an excessively generic best practice, but it drives to the core of cost accounting effectiveness in many companies. Cost accountants spend the bulk of their time analyzing direct labor and material costs when the majority of total costs do not even lie in these areas—they are in the many cost categories that make up overhead. The solution to this dilemma is to categorize *all* company costs by the annual dollar volume expended and then direct the attention of the cost accounting department toward the largest categories—whether or not they are direct labor or materials costs.

By taking this approach cost accountants can focus the attention of management on far more than direct manufacturing costs, so that the cost effectiveness of all company functions is periodically reviewed. This results in a continual streamlining of all company functions, which may include downsizing, outsourcing, or automation.

This shift in focus is likely to result in additional analysis time on the part of the cost accounting department, but the added time requirements will be more than offset by an increase in the *effectiveness* of the information provided to management.

FOCUS ON THE CAUSES OF COSTING PROBLEMS

Too frequently the cost accounting department concentrates on churning out a standardized set of variance reports, month after month. Though this approach gives management a consistent set of information that it can track over many time periods to determine trends, it does not tell it what it really needs to know, which is *why* variances are occurring.

A truly *effective* cost accounting department should take the alternative approach of creating variance reports only as a basis for further investigation. It should spend only a few percent of its time creating these reports and the rest of its time roaming the facility, reviewing detailed cost reports, and interviewing employees to determine specifically why variances occur and how to avoid them in the future. If this allocation of time does not allow the cost accounting staff to continue to create and distribute its periodic variance reports, then so be it. It is acceptable to reduce the frequency of information distribution if the underlying causes of problems can be identified and resolved in the meantime. Accordingly, the cost accounting manager should consider the automation of standard cost reports or a switch to much less frequent reporting, such as once a quarter.

FOLLOW A SCHEDULE OF INVENTORY OBSOLESCENCE REVIEWS

At the end of each fiscal year, the typical cost accounting staff conducts a review of the inventory and usually discovers an inordinately large amount of obsolete items that have accumulated over the course of the year. This leads to recriminations among the management group in regard to who is responsible for the loss that must be recognized to write off the now useless inventory, and which may have a significant impact on the level of profitability. The cost accountants are then called back in to investigate and spend a disproportionate amount of their time tracking down the reasons why each item was purchased and why it was never used. Because of the politically charged nature of this problem, it is a high-priority one and so creates havoc with the work schedule of the cost accounting department. Furthermore, the issues that gave rise to the obsolete inventory problem have been occurring for the entire year, since no one has regularly discovered and reported their existence to the management group, which could have corrected the underlying problems months ago and kept the level of obsolete inventory much lower.

To fix both these problems, the cost accounting staff should build into its monthly calendar of activities a regular review of inventory, checking records to discover which items have not been used and which are in danger of becoming obsolete. The review should also include an examination of all problems previously reported to management in past months to see if any progress has been made in resolving them. Though it may appear that conducting so many reviews wastes more time than an annual review would, the overall impact of reducing inventory problems and the resulting writeoffs, which in turn increase profits, are well worth the extra effort.

Since the cost accounting staff is providing the rest of the company with higher-quality information, this is a best practice that improves the *effectiveness* of cost accounting information.

PLOT AND REVIEW COST TRENDS

When a cost accountant reviews the cost of a product, the review typically includes a summary of all component and labor costs, so that management can tell if these costs are excessive. However, this is just a snapshot of costs during one point in time, so managers have no idea if these costs have changed until a new product costing review is conducted, which could be a number of months in the future (if at all). Consequently, managers do not have enough information to take rapid action to correct product costing problems.

A good way to provide a higher level of information to managers in this area is to issue costing trend reports every month. These reports list the cost of each component or product at the end of each month and do so on a trend line for at least the last year. Such reports can take several forms. One is a simple listing of the cost trends for all components purchased. This is an easily automated report, but it may be so lengthy that managers do not have the time to peruse the costs of thousands of items. A better approach is to designate certain parts in the costing database as being high-cost parts (e.g., as "A" inventory items), so that the computer system can list only these items in the trend report, thereby greatly reducing the length of the report while still focusing on the most expensive items.

Another variation is to report only on the cost of completed products, rather than their component parts. This may reduce the report to a single page, depending on the number of products a company sells. Then, if managers want to see more detail, the cost accounting staff can print a more detailed report for each product that itemizes the costing trends for all component parts. This information can also be graphed.

If a company also has a target costing system in place (Chapter 18), it should have a specific set of target costs for each product or component, which can be incorporated into these reports so that managers see not only cost trends but also the previously planned costing levels. An example of such a report layout is shown in Exhibit 35.1.

This best practice has a significant impact on the *effectiveness* of the cost accounting information given to management. Since these reports can be automated, there should not be a significant degradation of the efficiency of the cost accounting staff as a result of their generating these reports.

EXHIBIT 35.1. Sample Cost Trend Report

Description	Actual Cost 3/31/02 ($)	Actual Cost 6/30/02 ($)	Actual Cost 9/30/02 ($)	Target Cost ($)	Target Date
Radio	31.02	31.47	32.02	30.49	5/31/03

REPORT ON RECURRING SYSTEM ERRORS

We have already noted that the cost accounting staff should concentrate its investigative resources on discovering the underlying problems that cause costing variances. There is another area of activity that causes costing problems, and that is recurring errors caused by the costing system itself. For example, failure to assign inventory receipts to the correct month at the receiving dock results in an incorrectly high cost of goods sold in one month and an amount that is too low in the next. Similarly, the lack of a procedure for recording goods that are returned to stock from the shop floor results in an excessively high cost of goods sold, while the inventory book balance is too low. The cost accounting staff can trace many of these issues quite easily and then determine their frequency of occurrence in order to establish the order of priority in which they will be fixed.

The best way to trace a recurring system error is to look in the company database for the correcting entry that was made to resolve the offending problem. In the inventory area this means that cycle counting adjustments are made to ensure that the book balance matches the actual amount of inventory on hand. By having cycle counters record the reasons for changes in the computer when they make adjusting entries, the cost accounting staff can summarize this data by type of problem and then sort the various systemic problems to determine which ones are most in need of repair.

A large part of the investigative work in this area can be automated by constructing standard computerized reports that itemize only correcting entries of various kinds. By focusing on creating these reports, the cost accounting staff does not become unduly burdened by extra work when it adopts this best practice.

Since this approach leads to a higher quality of information, it increases the *effectiveness* of the cost accounting department.

REVIEW BILL OF MATERIALS ACCURACY

The single most significant database the cost accounting staff uses is the one stored in the company's bills of materials. The BOM is an itemization of the parts and their quantities required to build a product. Cost accountants draw on this information to determine standard costs, as well as to create baseline information for variance calculations or to conduct backflushing transactions. If the information contained in a BOM is incorrect, many cost accounting analyses based on this information will be rendered useless.

Because of the critical nature of BOM information, the cost accounting or the internal auditing staff should regularly review the accuracy of the data in a large sample of bills. If there are any inaccuracies, the problem should be brought to the attention of the engineering staff immediately, so that it can be corrected. Also, accuracy information should be calculated and posted for all to see, and accuracy should be considered a major corporate performance measure. Only by focusing its attention on the accuracy of its bills of materials is a company able to correctly report on and analyze its product costs.

Given the extreme importance of bill of materials information, any reviews of and updates to its accuracy should be considered a significant improvement in the *effectiveness* of the cost accounting department.

REVIEW LABOR ROUTING ACCURACY

Another key source of information for the cost accounting department is the labor routing. This document identifies the amount of labor or machine time to be expended on a product as it passes through each manufacturing workstation on its way to conversion to a finished goods item. If the information in the labor routing is wrong, an incorrect amount of labor will be charged to a product. Also, if direct labor is being used as the basis for allocating overhead to a product, any inaccuracy in the amount of labor will be duplicated in the allocated overhead amount, resulting in a double inaccuracy.

To keep labor routing documentation as accurate as possible, either the cost accounting or the internal audit staff should regularly review routing records, much as was the case for the bill of materials reviews described in the last section. Given their highly technical nature, it may be more efficient for the cost accounting staff to conduct these reviews, since they call for a walk-through of all workstations itemized on a labor routing, as well as the timing of work in each process—tasks that are well within the group of chores to which the costing staff is accustomed.

Since the review of labor routings results in more accurate costing information, it enhances the *effectiveness* of the cost accounting function.

REVIEW ONLY MATERIAL VARIANCE LEVELS

As noted repeatedly throughout this chapter, the reports of cost accountants can be made much more *effective* by reducing them in size, concentrating instead on proper groupings of information and eliminating unnecessary information. The second item is the primary focus of this best practice.

The cost accounting staff should eliminate all nonmaterial variance information from both its reports and subsequent investigations. By doing so it provides far more focused information to management, while also eliminating its investigation of insignificant items. This reduction in scope is easily achieved by modifying the selection characteristics of standard computerized cost accounting reports so that only variances of a certain percentage or dollar size are printed.

The main issue is determination of the appropriate minimum variance levels below which variances will be ignored. For companies with a narrow costing focus, such as those in tight competitive markets, a variance of just 1% or a few pennies may be considered significant, whereas others with less profitability pressure may feel that higher cutoff levels are more appropriate. A valid reason for setting a high cutoff level may even be that there are too few cost accountants available to investigate all the items, so the cutoff is set at a level that yields just enough variances to fit the work schedule of the cost accounting department.

REVISE COSTING REPORTS

Cost accounting is a technical subject, and cost accountants lean in the direction of obfuscation when they prepare cost accounting reports, perhaps because they are so inured in the subject matter that they assume everyone who receives the reports must also have a similar grounding in this material. However, to think that (for example) a marketing manager will go out of her way to learn the intricacies of cost accounting would be a severe mistake. Consequently, we present in this section a number of suggestions for making costing reports more easily understood by their recipients.

The cost accounting department should not assume that its level of pay is based on the weight of the reports it issues. Managers are not inclined to read the tomes that cost accountants are prone to release since there is no time to wade through all the material. Instead, the cost reports should be limited to just exception situations. For example, a materials cost variance report does little good if it lists all the hundreds or thousands of parts that have no variance from the standard cost at all. Why not report on just those with a measurable variance? Even better, limit the list of items reported to those above a certain dollar or percentage amount. Best of all, try sorting the report so that the largest variances are at the top and the smallest at the bottom. This approach reduces the size of many cost reports and narrowly focuses everyone's attention on only the largest variances.

Another problem with cost reports is that they are issued too late for many problems to be resolved. Generally speaking, the cost accounting staff runs all its reports after the end of each month, so that managers may wait more than a month to receive information about events that occurred as early as the beginning of the previous month. By then, many employees have forgotten the circumstances that resulted in a variance or (if they caused the underlying problems) have had more than enough time to cover up their misdeeds. These issues are resolved by increasing the frequency of reporting. Since many cost reports are generated automatically by a computer system, it is easy to have the system automatically create variance reports every night during the standard batch processing period, which can then be reviewed by the cost accounting staff the next morning. In this way managers receive "fresh" information about cost problems, ones that they can more easily address. The only downside to this approach is the daily additional review chore that the costing staff must take on in reviewing cost reports. However, by setting reports to print only large variances (as noted in the preceding paragraph), the amount of paperwork to be reviewed can be significantly reduced.

The typical cost accounting report is a lengthy list showing actual costs and variances from standard costs for every component or product in a company's database. Sorting through this information is too much of a chore for managers, so the cost accounting staff should work on regrouping the data into relevant categories, perhaps by product line or customer, with subtotals, so that managers can obtain more relevant information.

Most cost reports are inward looking—that is, they focus on costs by component or product. However, this practice overlooks another large category, which is costs by customer. Though many costing systems are not designed to accumulate this information, the cost accounting staff will find it well worth its effort to periodically reshuffle its standard reports to arrive at a summarization showing the sales, cost of goods sold, and gross margin for every customer. If this is too much work, then the report can be reduced in size to address just the largest customers. This information is particularly valuable to managers, since it reveals which customers are so inordinately profitable that they should receive extra attention, and also indicates which customers are so unprofitable that a company may be able to increase its profits by dropping them.

A final variation on preparing the usual cost report is to replace or supplement existing information with direct costs. This adjustment shows managers the costs that can indisputably be assigned to specific products and represents the absolute minimum level to which prices can be dropped. Managers who are given only full costs (including allocated overhead) always find themselves in turf battles with other managers, arguing over which costs should be assigned to what products or customers. By eliminating overhead from the equation, management now has a base-level cost to use for selected decision making, though this must be supplemented by additional overhead costs in order to avoid encouraging managers to price products too low.

Since this best practice provides better and more frequent information to managers than was previously the case, it improves the *effectiveness* of cost accounting information.

SHIFT THE COST ANALYSIS FOCUS TO TARGET COSTING

When the cost accounting staff focuses on the production of traditional variance measures resulting from manufacturing activities, it overlooks the primary area of potential cost savings, which lies in the product design stage. Most of the costs of a product are permanently built into a product during the design stage because specific materials are used that cannot be substituted for less expensive materials during production, while the design itself may call for certain production and assembly techniques that cannot be further streamlined. Consequently, the cost accounting manager would be fully justified in shifting the bulk of her available staffing resources away from the production area and into the design stage.

The best cost accounting methodology now in use in the design stage is called target costing. As is more fully explained in Chapter 17, it focuses the attention of design teams on first determining the target price at which a product will be sold and then arriving at a target cost that cannot be exceeded, by subtracting a specific level of profitability from the target price. The design teams then use value engineering techniques (as also described in Chapter 17) to reduce costs to the targeted cost level. The role of cost accountants in this process is to provide constant feedback to the design teams regarding the current cost of ongoing designs and the amount of costs that must still be removed in order to meet cost goals. Cost accountants can also compare design costs to actual costs once a product reaches the production floor, thereby warning management about any areas in which actual costs are exceeding budgeted levels.

Target costing is the most proactive and beneficial of all costing activities and therefore results in a major improvement in the *effectiveness* of the cost accounting department.

STOP REPORTING LABOR VARIANCES

The traditional approach to reporting costing variances is to first create reporting systems for direct labor, which involves the tracking of labor costs per hour, total labor hours incurred, shift premiums, and overtime costs. While this method is thorough, there is no longer much of a need for such detailed reporting. This reporting system was developed many years ago when labor costs were a much larger proportion of total product costs than they are now. With the advent of automation, material and overhead costs now represent the lion's share of all product costs, while labor is frequently a mere 10% or so of the total cost. Consequently, collecting labor data and creating variance reports are incorrect uses of the cost accounting staff's time, which would be better spent in the review of other costs.

Though the existing direct labor reporting system may work quite well, the cost accounting manager should give serious thought to its complete elimination. Not only would this give the cost accounting staff much more time to devote to other types of costs, but it would also keep the direct labor staff from wasting its time filling out reporting forms that are subsequently loaded into the costing database for review. Thus, eliminating the direct labor cost reporting system may actually improve the efficiency of the direct labor personnel.

If the more tradition-bound members of the management team question the decision to eliminate the direct labor cost reporting system, a few additional arguments can be presented to them. One is that there is no point in tracking direct labor cost variances because this cost is really a fixed one in the short term—after all, how many companies hire and fire personnel based on each day's scheduled production? Not many, since they must keep qualified staff on hand even if it means paying them when there is no work to perform. And if the direct labor cost is fixed, the bulk of the variances being tracked are useless. Another point is that the real opportunity for cost reduction is in the design stage of a product, not in the production phase. By focusing the bulk of its attention on the design stage (for more information about this, read Chapter 17, which discusses target costing), the cost accounting staff can deliver much more value to a company; however, it can find time to do this only if it abandons other work, such as direct labor cost reviews. The best approach for convincing die-hard opponents is to conduct a detailed cost-benefit analysis that reveals the total cost of all steps in the direct labor cost reporting process and then offset this total with the projected benefit. Since there is little quantifiable benefit, this analysis always results in a net cost.

The main intent of this best practice is to improve the *efficiency* of the cost accounting staff by eliminating a task that produces little benefit, allowing it to focus on other activities that will result in a greater return on the effort invested.

USE AUTOMATED AND ACCESSIBLE COSTING REPORTS

A number of cost accounting reports are of the list variety. They present a broad swath of information about a large set of data, such as all the components or products in a database, one after the other. This information is usually run as a customized report by the cost accounting staff and then sent out to a standard distribution list of recipients. Because of the highly regimented nature of this information, it may be possible to convert the reports to a standard format that can be readily accessed and printed by the report recipients, thereby removing the cost accounting staff from the report printing and distribution business.

This approach is most likely when the reports can be accessed from or posted to a computer server linked to a local area network. This configuration allows employees to access the files if they have access to the network. When the costing information is considered confidential, password access can be built into the system so that it is available only to authorized users.

The main problem with this approach is that the cost accounting staff no longer has a chance to review the information for errors before it is released for general use. If there are many costing errors that must be repeatedly fixed, it may be better to avoid this best practice until the sources of the errors can be permanently corrected. Otherwise, it is generally sufficient for the cost accounting staff to periodically review the reports for errors and make corrections, perhaps at the rate of one review per month (with the exact frequency being largely dependent on the volume of recurring errors).

This best practice results in a reduced workload for the cost accounting department, so its primary focus is on improving *efficiency.* In addition, the resulting free time allows the cost accounting staff to focus on other issues, which may lead to further improvements in the quality of work completed.

USE AUTOMATED SYSTEMS FOR DATA COLLECTION

In many organizations the collection of costing data is a painful manual endeavor involving compilation of information from a variety of paper-based documents, data entry of daily status reports from the factory floor, and manual summation of this data into a set of cost reports that are necessarily brief and not thoroughly analyzed—all because the cost accounting staff has spent so much of its time on mundane data entry chores that it has no time left to interpret the results.

An excellent best practice that allows the costing staff to switch from data entry to data analysis is data collection automation. Two types of data can be entered by this means. One is bill of materials and labor routings, which should be loaded into a manufacturing database where they can be readily accessed and updated by all employees who need this information. By storing information in a computer, the cost accounting staff no longer has to recompile costs every time it conducts another cost analysis since it can create downloads and reports that yield all the necessary information. Also, a good database includes a transaction history tool that tells the costing staff who has made changes in these important records, as well what items were changed, in case these changes later result in variances that the costing staff must investigate.

The second type of data entry is of the daily transactional variety. This can include hours or minutes worked by job, as well as the quantities of various components used or products manufactured. The effort required to record direct labor can be automated by having employees "swipe" magnetized or bar-coded badges through readers that assign time worked to specific jobs and then automatically route the resulting data to a job costing database. Similarly, production can be tracked by attaching bar codes to products and automatically scanning the codes as they pass by a fixed scanner on a conveyor belt. This type of automation completely avoids any effort by the cost accounting staff to enter primary data, with the exception of a periodic review of data that appears to be out of the ordinary and which may require some adjusting entry to fix.

Both these solutions to data entry allow the cost accounting department to shift the bulk of its time to the analysis of costing data and the investigation of variances and away from the continual collection and entry of base-level data into a database.

Since the automation of data entry does not result in an increase in the quality of costing information but does reduce the effort of the costing staff, it is best categorized as an *efficiency* improvement.

SUMMARY

The majority of the best practices noted in this section were designed to improve the quality of information issued by the cost accounting department. They do this by focusing on the key periods during the production process when most costs are incurred (e.g., through target costing), or by concentrating the bulk of the costing staff's time on the areas responsible for most cost variances (e.g., overhead costs, bills of materials, labor routings, and obsolete inventory). A large minority of best practices are concerned with efficiency improvements, which can be achieved through automation (e.g., computerized data collection and reporting) or through the elimination of work tasks that do not result in meaningful costing information (e.g., minor variance investigation of all kinds, and labor variances). The sum total of all these best practices yields a cost accounting department that is highly focused on tasks that will result in the greatest value to the corporation.

CHAPTER 36

Cost Budgeting

The cost accountant is frequently called on to assist in the task of completing a company's budget. If there is no budgeting manager or financial analyst in an accounting department, then it is possible that the entire budgeting task will be assigned to the cost accountant. This chapter is intended to provide an overview of how the various budgets fit together, how the budgeting process is managed, the ancillary role of activity-based budgeting, and the role of the cost accountant in the process.

ROLE OF BUDGETING

Budgeting is a lengthy process that involves a large amount of employee time. Why invest so much effort in this document? One reason is that it establishes a standard against which performance can be measured. For example, the sales staff has a sales budget that itemizes the product quantities it is expected to sell in each reporting period. Similarly, the purchasing budget itemizes the costs of major raw materials that the purchasing staff should attain, while all department managers have cost budgets whose costs they should not exceed. This concept can be taken a step farther with the right features in a computerized accounting system, whereby purchase orders for costs that exceed the budgeted amounts are automatically rejected, ensuring that the budget is met. In short, the budget can be used to tightly link responsibility for both revenue and expense items to specific individuals and departments within the company.

Along similar lines, a budget can be used to review the performance of employees and determine the amounts of bonuses awarded. For this purpose the budget is linked to a separate employee evaluation system containing the exact reward amounts that will be achieved if certain preplanned target levels of performance are reached. Conversely, the evaluation system may flag poor performance for corrective action by management. In either case the budget is used to ensure that employee behavior is coincident with a company's financial goals.

Another role for budgeting is management by exception. There are hundreds, if not thousands, of different costs that a manager could potentially investigate each month to verify that they are within expected levels, but there is no time to do this. Instead, actual costs can be compared to budgeted levels, yielding variances from the budget that can in turn be reviewed more easily to see which ones are the largest. Then only the exceptionally large variances need to be investigated, which saves a great deal of management time.

Yet another role for the budget is in sensitivity analysis. One can change a few key variables in the budget model to see what the impact will be on cash flows and on the level of reported profits. For example, if there is some concern that the price of a key raw material will increase, this cost change can be easily added to the budget model, which recalculates itself to account for the change. Other common variables used in this regard are the price per unit of product, changes in the cost of direct labor due to unionization, changes in medical costs, and changes in the unit volume of sales.

In addition, the budget is used to quantify the current set of corporate strategies and tactics. Without the budget they would be merely words on paper, for there would be no way to determine their monetary impact. For example, through the use of a budget, a tactic to double the inventory turnover rate can be accomplished by specifying exact inventory levels to be attained, period by period, as well as the cost of capital investments and training programs required to ensure that this tactical goal is met.

From the perspective of employees the main attraction of the budget is that it stabilizes employment. It does so by allowing managers to determine attainable sales levels for given amounts of equipment and labor capacity, which in turn allows them to "level-load" production facilities to ensure that the highest possible levels of capacity utilization are maintained at all times. This approach avoids sudden declines in production levels that might lead to employee layoffs.

Similarly, the budget can be used both to obtain a high level of equipment utilization and to target equipment that can be sold off because of lack of use. For example, the budget can show the amount of machine time required to complete one unit of a product, which in turn can be multiplied by total production levels to determine total utilization rates. However, this requires a level of detailed information that many budgets do not include, so it is most commonly used when management is interested in the utilization of a specific (usually high-cost) piece of equipment; the budget is structured around the analysis of this specific item in order to obtain the required information.

A budget readily reveals the amount of cash needed to run each part of a business, as well as the profitability of each part. In doing so it reveals the investment required and the return that can be expected on that investment. By reviewing this information managers can determine where they should invest company funds to obtain the greatest possible return on investment.

Thus, there are many roles the budget can play, including the utilization of cash, employees, and equipment; the translation of the corporate strategy into a numerical model; and the linking of performance to responsible individuals within a company. For all these reasons the budget is one of the most valuable documents a company can create.

SYSTEM OF BUDGETS

Only the smallest company is able to contain its entire budget in a single page of numbers. A much more common practice is to divide it into a number of smaller, interlinked calculations that follow a specific sequential order.

The general system of budgets is shown in Exhibit 36.1. The flow of budgets goes from top to bottom in the exhibit. At the top we see that there are two primary sources for the budget. One is the sales budget, from which the production budget is derived. The other is the tactical plans used by a company to determine its budget for research and development, which is oriented toward the issuance of strategically positioned products into the marketplace at some point in the future. Also, tactical plans play a large role in the types of marketing used to sell products during the budget period, as well as to position brand awareness in the minds of consumers over the long term. The tactical plans also have an indirect impact on the sales budget since ongoing tactics may require a shift in a company's product offerings, which in turn impacts the unit sales volume.

The production budget is derived primarily from the sales budget but must also be netted against the inventory budget to determine the precise quantities of products to be built. For example, if there is an overage of products already stored in the warehouse, the production budget can be reduced by the amount of this overage when determining the amount of projected sales for which production must be completed. Also, if the management group wants to do a better job of fulfilling short-term deliveries to its customers, it may want to increase the size of the inventory, which calls for a production plan larger than what is strictly required by the sales budget.

The production budget also requires input from the purchasing budget, and vice versa. The purchasing staff may determine that some materials will not be available, necessitating the use of substitute components that will have an impact on the amounts, types, and timing of production. Also, the production schedule will require the purchasing staff to determine the available quantities of components in the inventory and to buy the remainder, with timing that is sufficiently in advance of production to ensure that all parts will be on hand at the time of production.

EXHIBIT 36.1. System of Budgets

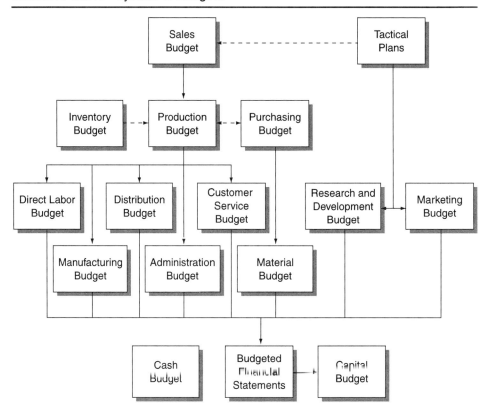

The production budget drives a series of other departmental and related budgets. For example, the amount of direct labor required for the production process is entirely determined by the timing and type of production contained within the production budget. The volume of production also drives the contents of the manufacturing budget, which contains the wide array of overhead costs needed to smoothly operate the manufacturing facility during the budgeted period. The distribution budget is based not only on the quantity of production that will be shipped to customers but also on any tactical changes in the number and positioning of warehouses used to store products, and the locations of customers. The administration budget is directly derived from the volume of overall activity in all other departments of the company, which in turn is largely driven by the production budget. The customer service budget is based on a combination of factors: the volume of sales, the number of new customers (since new customers generally call more frequently than old ones), and the number of new products (which are the most liable to require warranty or instructional assistance). The material budget is derived directly from the purchasing budget. Thus, the majority of departmental budgets are derived in some manner from the production budget, with lesser degrees of influence from other factors.

It is also useful to include in the budget model a section that itemizes a variety of budgeted operational and financial statistics, which should be presented alongside a set of comparative statistics culled from recent company results. By including this information, company managers can see if key statistical targets are being reached, or if some performance measures are below expectations and require improvement. For example, a creditor's loan covenant may specify that the current ratio always be no less than 2:1; if the projected ratio is worse than that minimum level, the budget must be adjusted to improve the ratio. Another example is revenue per person; if a possible sale of the business is partly based on the productivity of the business, as defined by revenue per person, the management team must pay special attention to it in the budget. Yet another situation is when the decision is made to improve inventory turnover on the grounds that it will reduce the company's investment in working capital. In all these cases the statistics page is frequently consulted at the end of each iteration of the budget, so that managers can see what the projected results are that will lead them into a round of adjustments to the model that will enhance these statistics.

Once all these budgets have been assembled, they are combined into a budgeted set of financial statements, as noted at the bottom of Exhibit 36.1. Linked to the financial statements are additional documents that detail the amount of financing needed to implement the budget, the amount and timing of capital expenditures, and (finally) the cash budget for each period listed in the budget. The last item is particularly important, for it is a cross-check on the validity of the entire budgeting process. If the cash budget yields an excessively large negative balance during any budget period, the management team must work its way back through the budget model, testing its assumptions and altering any issues that impact cash flows, until it arrives at a budget model that allows it to operate in a cash flow positive manner, thereby ensuring corporate survival.

The information that goes into the system of budgets is closely intertwined, which therefore requires that the budgeting model for each of the budgets also be closely linked. This is easily achieved with the use of a commercially available budgeting software package or with an electronic spreadsheet containing numerous, linked work sheets that automatically update each other when new information is entered. Using this approach the person updating the budget does not have to worry about making additional changes in the model that are downstream from any initial change.

BUDGET FORMAT

In general, the budget looks like a set of financial statements that typically cover every reporting period of a year. This section describes a few special considerations in regard to the format of the budget.

One issue is the time period to be covered by the budget. The most commonly accepted practice is for it to cover one year, simply because this matches the standard reporting cycle for annual financial statements. However, it may be useful to alter this period to match key operational issues within a company. For example, if the business is centered on the rate at which new products are developed, it might make sense to create a budget that matches the typical time period needed for new product development. Similarly, this period might be stretched to match the period needed for new facility construction, especially if the company is capital-intensive. Another option is to base it on the payout period for capital equipment (though this could result in a *very* long-term budget). However, there may be a number of projects, facilities, and other capital projects in operation, all with different time lines, making it difficult to settle on a reasonable budget period other than the traditional interval of one year.

One problem with setting any sort of limitation on the length of the budget is that at some point actual activities will butt up against the end of it, prior to the creation of an entirely new budget that addresses the next budgeting period. This may be a problem if management is accustomed to reviewing financial projections well into the future, since these projections will not yet exist. The best way to avoid this issue is to create a rolling budget in which old budget periods are dropped off one end and new periods are added at the other end, thereby always maintaining a number of budget periods into the future. The primary difficulty with this approach is that the company is always in budget creation mode, with some work to be done at all times to prepare the next section of the budget that is to be added. However, the company becomes accustomed to, and quite expert at, the budgeting steps, making each iteration of the process that much easier to complete.

One must also determine the number of periods within the budgeting cycle that will be included in the budget. It is most common to see a separate column for every month, but this leads to a great many numbers, not all of which are relevant and which require a great deal of updating effort. For example, a sales budget is probably not going to be accurate to within a month, despite the insistence of management on entering sales figures that are accurate to within one month. A better approach is to clump the months together into quarters, which allows estimates to be made that are more likely to be accurate within the broader time period. Also, switching to the quarterly format reduces the amount of numbers in the budget by two-thirds, so that the chore of data updating is correspondingly reduced.

Another issue is the level of detail to include in the budget, as well as the amount of stratification into different departments. Some budgets are painfully detailed, including accounts for which only $100 of expenses are charged during a year. This greatly contributes to the amount of work required to update the budget and is not recommended. Instead, small account balances should be grouped into an "other" account to restore some brevity to the budget. Also, a considerable degree of stratification is usually desirable. For example, a budget can contain a single "salaries" line item, but this might not include enough detail to see what parts of the company are incurring this large cost. A better approach is to divide expense line items into as many departments as there are managers in the company, so that the nature of each expense becomes more visible.

A final formatting issue involves the text that should accompany the numerical portion of the budget. This should contain a complete list of all assumptions used in deriving the budget, as well as an itemization of all risks. Risk analysis is particularly important, for it identifies the assumptions regarding such issues as potential sales fluctuations, changes in the competitive environment, scarcity of raw materials, and changes in technology that are fundamental to the quantifications noted in the budget. Without this information it is difficult to determine the risk of positive or negative changes in budgeted results.

SYSTEM OF BUDGETS: AN EXAMPLE

Most of the components of a budget are the same as those found in the financial statements and so need little explanation. These sections include the departmental expense budgets and pro forma income statements. However, other sections operate somewhat differently and so are explained with the help of two exhibits.

In Exhibit 36.2 we see the relationship between the tactical plans and two subsidiary-level budgets. In most cases departmental budgets are largely driven by the amount of forecasted sales volume. However, this is not necessarily the case for the research and development department or for the marketing department. In the exhibit we see that the company has set specific tactical goals for the repositioning of customer awareness of its products, as well as for firing up a new marketing campaign in a key sales region. The first goal is not tied to the rest of the budget—it involves a long-term customer awareness issue and may take several years to bear fruit in the form of increased sales. The second goal is tied to sales, since the lack of a marketing campaign on the West coast is likely to result in a drop in forecasted sales for the budget period. Consequently, marketing is an area that supports sales, but also has goals unrelated to short-term sales which are strongly driven by tactical plans.

The research and development budget is even more closely tied to tactical plans, for one cannot assume that any product currently in development will be released in time to contribute to the upcoming sales forecast (unless it is *very* close to completion). Instead, tactical plans may call for changes in the type of research and development being conducted, so that sales several years down the road will benefit from such direction.

In both the marketing and research and development areas, a great deal of judgment is required to construct a budget. This is because there is no clear change in profits in the short run as a result of expenditures in either area. Consequently, a considerable amount of time should be spent on obtaining the best possible "guesstimates" from both in-house and outside experts regarding the best possible expenditure levels in these areas.

The linkages between the sales, inventory, production, and purchasing budgets are close, and mirror the activities found in a material requirements planning system (Chapter 26). As shown in Exhibit 36.3, we begin with a sales forecast, which

EXHIBIT 36.2. Linkage between Tactical Plans and Subsidiary Budgets

Tactical Plans:

1. To extend research into automated lawn mower equipment.
2. To scale back further research on non-motorized lawn mowers.
3. To expand customer awareness of leading-edge mowing technology.
4. To extend seasonal marketing campaign to West coast in conjunction with opening of new warehouse in that region.

Research & Development Budget:

	Quarter 1	Quarter 2	Quarter 3	Quarter 4
Automation project team	$65,000	$100,000	$175,000	$225,000
Manual equipment project team	150,000	100,000	70,000	45,000
Cutting technology team	50,000	50,000	50,000	50,000
4-stroke engine project team	68,000	82,000	80,000	75,000
Total expense	$333,000	$332,000	$375,000	$395,000

Marketing Budget:

	Quarter 1	Quarter 2	Quarter 3	Quarter 4
Awareness advertising campaign	$258,000	$220,000	$210,000	$200,000
West coast advertising campaign	400,000	50,000	50,000	250,000
Staffing expenses	80,000	82,000	84,000	84,000
Travel and entertainment	35,000	8,000	8,000	35,000
Total expense	$773,000	$360,000	$352,000	$569,000

EXHIBIT 36.3. Linkages between the Sales, Inventory, Production, and Purchasing Budgets

Sales Budget:

	Quarter 1	Quarter 2	Quarter 3	Quarter 4
2-stroke lawn mower	$900,000	$1,200,000	$120,000	$40,000
4-stroke lawn mower	550,000	475,000	80,000	15,000
Self-propelled mower	1,450,000	1,575,000	275,000	150,000
Robotic mower	0	75,000	150,000	20,000
Manual mower	50,000	150,000	10,000	5,000
	$2,950,000	$3,475,000	$635,000	$230,000

Divided by price/unit of $100 = 500 mowers

Production Budget:

Manual mower	Quarter 1
Sales requirement	500
- Beginning inventory	150
= Production needed	350

Inventory Budget (units):

Beginning finished goods:	Quarter 1
2-stroke lawn mower	500
4-stroke lawn mower	125
Self-propelled mower	400
Robotic mower	75
Manual mower	150

Purchasing Budget:

Manual Mower Parts:	No. of Parts per Unit	Production Needed	Total Parts Needed	In Inventory	Net Purchases
Handles	2	350	700	200	500
Shafts	1	350	350	400	(50)
Wheels	2	350	700	50	650
Blades	1	350	350	15	335

Inventory Budget (units):

Beginning Raw Materials:	Quarter 1
Handles	200
Shafts	400
Wheels	50
Blades	15

then drives the expected results for the other three budgets. Within the sales budget we use just the sales forecast for the first quarter of the upcoming year for the manual push mower, which is $50,000. We must first convert the sales figure to units of production, which is calculated in the exhibit by dividing a sales price of $100 per unit into the total forecasted sales, giving us an estimated sales volume in units of 500 mowers. Next, we see how many of these mowers are already located in the finished goods inventory at the beginning of the production period; the more units in stock, the fewer units we will have to produce in order to meet the sales target. The left side of the exhibit contains the beginning inventory figures and shows that we already have 150 units in stock. Moving to the middle of the exhibit, we see that the production budget subtracts the beginning inventory from the sales forecast to arrive at a production requirement of 350 units.

We then move to the purchasing budget. This budget requires that we first determine all the components of the manual push mower and then multiply the total amount of required production by these components to determine the total number of components that must be purchased. This calculation appears on the right side of Exhibit 36.3. In addition, it subtracts the amount of components already in stock (as noted at the bottom of the exhibit), resulting in the purchasing budget shown on the far right. This is a complex derivation but is necessary to ensure that projected production and purchasing quantities are budgeted as close to reality as possible (after all, this is where most of a company's expenses are found, so accuracy here can save it a great deal of money). In order to reduce the burden of calculation, the forecasting function of an MRP system can be used to derive the information needed for these budgets.

These are the key areas in a budget that require either a high degree of judgment or in-depth calculations. The other areas, dealing with departmental budgets, generally involve using selective adjustments to current expense figures and then rolling them forward to create the new budget. There is less chance for error in these other areas, and they are more mechanical in construction.

FLEXIBLE BUDGETS

A key objection raised in regard to the use of budgets is that, if the sales budget is not attained, all other aspects of the budget, which are based on that preset volume of sales, will be rendered invalid. Thus, if sales are significantly off, the entire budget can be thrown out the window. For example, a startup company may plan on expanding its sales volume from 3500 units in the current year to 28,000 in the following year; to support this level of sales, the company includes in its budget the capital cost of buying and equipping a new building, as well as the hiring of 40 new employees. However, actual sales increase to only 5000 units, so the company stays in its existing building and only 5 people are hired. These expenditures are far be-

EXHIBIT 36.4. Comparison of Rigid and Flexible Budgets

	Actual Results	Rigid Budget	Variance	Flexible Budget	Variance
Unit volume	5,000	28,000	(23,000)	5,000	–
Price per unit	$ 10.00	$ 9.00	$1.00	$ 9.00	$ 1.00
Revenue	$ 50,000	$252,000	(202,000)	$ 45,000	5,000
Unit cost	4.25	4.15	(0.10)	4.15	(0.10)
Extended unit cost	21,250	116,200	94,950	20,750	(500)
Contribution margin	$ 28,750	$135,800	$(107,050)	$ 24,250	$ 4,500
Other cost					
Manufacturing	11,000	38,000	27,000	10,500	(500)
Sales and					
marketing	7,500	14,000	6,500	14,00	6.500
Engineering	4,000	9,000	5,000	9,000	5,000
Administration	5,250	11,000	5,750	11,000	5,750
Total other costs	$ 27,750	$ 72,000	$ 44,250	$ 44,500	$ 16,750
Profits before tax	1,000	63,800	(62,800)	(20,250)	21,250
Income taxes	400	25,520	25,120	(8,100)	(8,500)
Net profit	$ 600	$ 38,280	(37,680)	$ (12,150)	12,750

low expected levels, so it is impossible to make any valid comparison between the actual and budgeted results.

Flexible budgeting was developed to avoid this problem. Under this system a budget is created that uses a standard price per unit, a standard variable cost per unit, and a lump-sum set of fixed costs. When actual unit volumes of sales are known, these numbers are added to the model, which multiplies them by the variable price and cost information to create a budget that is sensitive to the volume of actual sales. Using the earlier example we can derive the flexible budget shown in Exhibit 36.4. This exhibit shows the traditional actual financial results in the first column and a "rigid" budget in the second column. The resulting variances are so far off that there is no point in even making a comparison. However, the fourth column presents a flexible budget, yielding a much higher degree of comparability, which results in much smaller variances in the fifth column. The fifth column shows a great deal of comparability between the actual results and the flexible budget for the revenue and cost of goods sold sections, since these are altered to match actual volumes; the fixed costs listed thereafter are less comparable, since no provision was made to budget different cost levels for them in the event of different sales volumes. The latter problem can be addressed by creating a series of budgeted fixed costs for each cost category associated with a given set of sales volumes. Though more complex to create, this approach results in a high degree of comparability between all actual and budgeted results.

Thus, flexible budgeting allows one to still derive some use from a budgeted-to-actual comparison, even if actual sales volumes are significantly different from expectations.

The key difficulty with using the flexible budget concept is that it presumes a relatively small number of products for which standard prices and costs can be easily modeled. If actual sales conditions result in a broad mix of product sales, as well as many different price points at which each product is sold, the results of a flexible budgeting system are less usable.

ACTIVITY-BASED BUDGETING

As may have been apparent in an earlier section, System of Budgets, the budgeting process is largely oriented toward departmental budgets. However, as described in Chapter 16, it is also possible to trace a company's costs in terms of activities rather than departments. This approach can be used within a budgeting system. To do so an activity-based costing system must be set up that stores overhead costs in cost pools and uses some reasonable basis of allocation to charge them to activities (also see Chapter 16). The system used is identical to the one used for a typical ABC system, except that budgeted costs are used in the cost pools and expected units of activity are used instead of actual ones.

The activity-based budgeting (ABB) approach is useful not only for determining the prospective cost of activities in the budget period but, more importantly, for determining what activity costs are most capable of being reduced. This allows a company to focus the bulk of its attention on activities that can be improved on, thereby effectively reducing activity-related costs throughout the budget period.

There are also several problems with an activity-based budget. One is that the level of detail required to construct such a budget is much higher than that required for a more typical budget, and this information is not accumulated through a typical accounting system. For example, a normal budget for the machining department accumulates the cost of operating a set of machines and depreciating them, whereas an ABB system requires the additional accumulation of information about the basis for allocation, as well as the level of activity use by all products passing through the department. Because of this extra level of detail, activity-based budgets tend to be constructed for only a few types of activities that will benefit the most from the resulting attention; this means that ABB becomes ancillary to the regular budgeting system since it is unlikely to cover all costs. Thus, an activity-based budget is presented along with a regular budget, and therefore extra work is required to maintain both.

The other problem with ABB is that it is not neatly contained within standard departmental boundaries, so that responsibility for its results is difficult to clearly identify. In our previous example an activity-based budget for a process within a machining department may also include the cost of maintaining the machines used within that department—this cost is the responsibility of the maintenance manager, so the costs identified by the activity-based budget are the responsibility of both the maintenance manager and the machining department manager. In such cases it is easy to shift responsibility among numerous candidates, making the implementation of budget-based improvements much more difficult.

The activity-based budget model is a good one for the targeted improvement of specific activities within a company but consists of a subset of total company costs. Thus, it is best used in conjunction with a departmental budget that more comprehensively addresses all the costs incurred during the budget period.

BUDGETING PROCEDURE

Compiling a budget requires the continual and prolonged interaction of nearly every manager in a company over a period of several months. Managing such a widespread process requires a detailed budgeting procedure that carefully itemizes the dates on which budgeting deliverables are due, who is responsible for delivering them, and what information is to be delivered. An example is shown in Exhibit 36.5, itemizing the sequential steps in the budgeting process. This is a bare-bones schedule of events and should be supplemented by a budgeting manual that lists examples of what each deliverable should look like (perhaps taken from the previous year's budget), as well as instructions on how to access the company's budget model to enter each deliverable.

A key factor in the budgeting process is how budgeting information is to be entered into the model, and there are varying degrees of sophistication. The most primitive (and most common) method is to assign complete responsibility for entering information into the budgeting model to a single individual, which means that this person has sole access to it and must complete all data entry efforts. Though this approach guards against unauthorized access to the budget, it can result in a considerable amount of data rekeying if a company has a large budget model with inputs from many departments.

An alternative approach is to issue a standard budgeting format on an electronic spreadsheet on which participating departments can enter their budget information. The spreadsheet can then be automatically merged into the budget model, eliminating any duplication of data entry. However, any change in the template may cause significant difficulty when it is merged back into the main budget model since cell cross-references may no longer function. This would render the budget model inoperable.

EXHIBIT 36.5. The Budgeting Timetable

Mavis Brick Company
20xx Budget Procedure

Date of Budget
Delivery to Board: First Monday of December   **Page Number:** 1 of 1
Send Deliverables to: Controller

Step	Date	Responsibility	Deliverable
1	10/05	Budget committee	Review strategic direction
2	10/15	Sales vice president	Present revenue plan
3	10/20	Marketing vice president	Present marketing plan
4	10/24	Production vice president	Present production plan
5	10/28	Engineering vice president, Management Information Systems vice president, CFO	Present engineering, administration, and MIS plans
6	11/02	Production vice president	Present facilities plan
7	11/08	CFO	Present capital expenditures plan
8	11/11	CFO	Present financing plan
9	11/20	Budget committee	Budget reiteration meeting
10	11/25	Budget committee	Budget reiteration meeting
11	11/30	Budget committee	Final management review meeting

Note: From *1998 Cumulative Supplement to Controllership* (p. 37), 1998, New York: John Wiley & Sons. Reprinted with permission. Steve Bragg and Janice Roehl-Anderson.

The best method is to create a central budgeting database which can be accessed through an intranet or the Internet and allows each department access to its own section of the budget. This variation does not allow for any changes in the format of the budget and so yields the best results. However, this is also the most expensive approach since the model may have to be custom-developed.

ROLE OF THE COST ACCOUNTANT IN BUDGETING

The cost accountant may be asked to develop the entire budget, but this task is usually left to a financial analyst or budgeting manager. More frequently, this person is assigned a partial role in the budgeting process, which may include these tasks:

• **Calculate overhead rates.** One job for the cost accountant is to develop budgeted overhead rates for the valuation of projected inventory levels. This involves the selection of an allocation base, the determination of what costs to associate with it, and the calculation of an overhead rate per unit of production.

- **Calculate unit costs.** A key part of developing the material and direct labor budgets involves determination of what it would cost to produce each item in the sales budget. The cost accountant is in an ideal position to work with the engineering staff to determine any prospective changes in costs in the upcoming year that will impact the cost of materials or direct labor.

- **Develop the capital purchases budget.** As noted in Chapter 25, the cost accountant has the analysis tools needed to determine the payback, net present value, and/or internal rate of return on all capital expenditure proposals and so is in an ideal position to compile this information and present it in the budget.

- **Determine target costs.** Part of the work required in creating the research and development budget involves projected costing for new products still in the development stage. The cost accountant plays a central role in the compilation of costs for as-yet uncompleted development projects, as described in Chapter 17, and so can supply much of the information for this budget.

- **Roll forward existing costs.** The cost accountant has extensive experience in reviewing the current level of costs and in determining the drivers that cause these costs to occur. Since the budgets for all departments are to some degree based on the level of costs incurred in the previous year, it is reasonable to assume that he or she will be called on by department managers to assist in constructing new budgets for the upcoming year.

SUMMARY

Budgeting plays a key role in the allocation of resources to the most profitable activities, as well as in controlling the rate of expenditure in every part of a company, both of which allows it to attain its stated operational and financial goals. The budget is a complex web of interrelated plans that describe every facet of a business and requires expert management to ensure that it yields valid results. The cost accountant is one of the people who assists in this management through his or her knowledge of unit costs, capital expenditures, target costs, and departmental expenses. Consequently, this person can expect to be involved in many aspects of the budgeting process.

CHAPTER 37

Cost Accounting for Services

The bulk of the cost accounting discussion in this book is based on the premise that all companies manufacture products for which costs can be calculated and inventories valued. In reality, many companies offer services instead, with no inventories or tangible products. Though many of the topics described in other chapters do not have direct applicability to these types of organizations, there are still a number of cost accounting issues that should be of concern to them. In this chapter we discuss the definition of a service business, how cost accounting has traditionally been conducted for it, what issues have been overlooked by these traditional systems, and what can be done to correct the problem.

WHAT IS A SERVICE BUSINESS?

A service business is one that produces an output that is not physical in nature. This definition covers a great many types of businesses. It includes all companies in the banking and insurance fields, as well as in the computer services, engineering, architecture, accounting, legal, consulting, and communications fields. These are industries in which the output is provided in the form of advice or information. The concept can be taken farther to include such industries as transportation, utilities, lodgings, recreation, and medical services. In the latter cases the service provided is still nonphysical in nature but includes a significant investment in fixed assets. For example, Walt Disney World provides a service—recreation or amusement—and has incurred multibillion-dollar fixed costs to do so. Alternatively, Ernst & Young provides in-depth accounting and consulting, which require a much smaller capital investment but a much larger investment in the recruitment, training, and retention of employees to provide these services.

Though the types of businesses in the service field and their levels of capital investment vary considerably, they all have one thing in common from a cost accounting perspective; there is no tangible unit of production to measure. Unlike the situation at a manufacturing facility, there is no physical entity that can be called work in process or finished goods, nor is there an inventory item sold to customers, nor is there a need to value any inventory left in stock. This singular difference calls for an entirely different approach to cost accounting. Before delving into this new approach, let us first review the historical foundations of cost accounting and why this difference has led to a gap in the use of cost accounting for services.

HISTORICAL USE OF COST ACCOUNTING FOR SERVICES

Cost accounting was founded in the industrial age, particularly during 1850–1950, when large corporations were being formed that produced tangible goods—steel, automobiles, and ships. At this time corporations worked hard to secure their sources of supply so that they were no longer forced to negotiate with suppliers over the prices and the supply of key materials. As more suppliers were bought by their customers, corporations became vertically integrated. Representative of this trend was the Ford Motor Company, which owned the iron ore mines and foundries that supplied it with steel for its cars, not to mention nearly all of its other sources of supply.

Once vertical integration took hold in industry, managers were no longer able to establish the profitability of each individual business unit, for each one was so commingled with its upstream suppliers that there was no way to determine unit sales and costs. This problem sent most cost accounting theoreticians in the direction of creating systems for cost centers and profit centers, followed closely by new systems that determined the profitability of specific product lines and individual products. Once this fine level of detail was achieved, there were few additions to the science of cost accounting until the advent of increased competition from overseas, which forced company managers to explore new ways to streamline organizations. This renewed interest led to the invention and increasingly widespread use of activity-based costing (Chapter 16), which allowed an organization to focus on and reduce the cost of specific activities. A further development was the use of target costing, which enabled managers to design products that closely matched targeted price and cost levels well before a product ever reached the production phase.

Though there was a steady advance of cost accounting theory and practical application throughout this series of events, little attention was paid to the key underlying issue arising as the 20th century drew to a close—the industrial age had ended, and the bulk of new business had now shifted to the provision of services. This became a considerable concern with the advent of government deregulation in a number of services industries, for it allowed companies to compete with each other much more aggressively, which called for the use of new costing tools to determine what services were more (or less) profitable than others. Cost accounting was ill-equipped to handle this shift, with nearly all of its tools positioned to assist solely in the management of manufacturing businesses. As a result, service businesses have essentially ignored the key role that cost accounting can play in their operations. Here are some examples:

- **No cost of goods sold.** There has been no attempt to determine the variable costs in a services business. Instead, all costs are considered to be fixed. This results in an income statement with no cost of goods sold. Instead, there is a revenue line against which are offset all costs, which are assumed to be fixed.

- **No profit centers.** There is no attempt to divide revenues and costs into profit centers. This is not an issue with dividing revenues into profit centers but rather with dividing the associated costs. Consequently, the income statement of a service business tends to carefully itemize all types of revenues but to then offset them with a lump-sum set of fixed costs.

- **No break-even analysis.** Since there is no cost of goods sold or any attempt to determine which costs are variable, the manager of a services company must assume that the break-even point at which zero profits are earned is identical to the point at which all costs equal revenues. This concept ignores the key issue that some additional costs must be incurred in order to generate additional sales, which increases the break-even point.

- **No pricing formulations.** When there is no attempt to determine what costs are variable, it is impossible to determine what price to charge for a service. By default, many service businesses charge whatever their competitors charge or what they are forced to charge by regulatory mandate.

- **Emphasis on responsibility accounting.** Because there has been no emphasis on tracing the costs of activities, cost accountants have been left with only one time-worn activity to implement—responsibility accounting. This is the careful tracing of all costs for a specific department, comparing its results to a budget, and reporting any variances back to the management team, which rewards managers based on their ability to match or beat budgeted results. This approach does not involve profitability concepts and so is much inferior to other profitability-based performance measures that determine a department's ability to contribute to bottom-line margin improvements.

All these shortcomings make it clear that services companies are not being served well by traditional cost accounting systems. They do not know the cost of providing services and so cannot determine a number of key factors that would allow them to better manage their businesses. In the next section we more clearly define the specific improvements that can be made to enhance cost accounting for services businesses.

IMPROVEMENTS TO COST ACCOUNTING IN A SERVICES ENVIRONMENT

In this section we clearly identify the most crucial cost accounting improvements that can be made to enhance the information provided to the managers of services organizations. They are:

- **Compile the cost of service activities.** The most crucial accounting effort must be directed toward the determination of all variable costs incurred whenever a service-related activity is completed. By doing so most of the remaining activities noted in this list can be readily completed. The use of activity-based costing to compile these variable costs is discussed in the next section.

- **Implement job costing where possible.** In addition to determining the cost of services, it may also be possible to calculate the cost of individual service jobs. Such jobs require some unique output, as can be found in the banking industry for an equity placement, or in public accounting, where a specific audit is completed. Time cards are kept to record all time spent working on these jobs, which is then costed out and summarized by job. If it is too much trouble to collect actual time and expenses charged to a job, it may be sufficient to use budgeted figures, though this approach may be inaccurate.

- **Use process costing for high-volume situations.** There are a few instances, always involving high service transaction volumes, when process costing can be used to determine the cost of specific activities. Examples of this are the processing of checks by a bank and the processing of insurance claim forms by an insurance company.

- **Assign fixed costs to specific activities.** Once the variable cost of each activity, or the cost of a job, has been assigned, the cost accounting staff should take the additional step of calculating the total amount of all fixed costs directly related to specific activities even though they do not change in amount as service levels vary. This information allows analysts to conduct cost-volume-profit analyses on each activity, as well as to create profit centers for each one, to which fixed costs can be assigned with some certainty.

- **Analyze activities with cost-volume-profit analysis.** With the variable and fixed cost of each activity now in hand, one can easily conduct a cost-volume-profit analysis (see Chapter 21 for more information) on each activity to determine the volume levels at which a company breaks even on various levels of pricing and unit volume.

- **Create profit centers.** The collection of variable costs and fixed costs by activity also allows a company to create profit centers for each one, with a cost-of-goods-sold section that refers to all variable costs incurred. Managers can use this information to adjust pricing levels, allocate capital, and measure profit center performance, as noted in the next three items.

- **Determine minimum prices based on unit costs.** Pricing for services is frequently driven more by the rates charged by competitors than by internal costs. Nonetheless, if the prices charged are less than their costs, a company will not survive long. Accordingly, managers can use variable costing by activity to determine the minimum price level at which a service will return a profit, as well as cost-volume-profit analysis to determine the unit volumes it wants to support at specified pricing levels. These actions keep an organization from providing "free" services to its customers that are really activities being subsidized by other activities. The classic case of such free services are banking services, especially automated teller machines, that have been offered free to banking customers for many years. Only recently have banks conducted costing reviews and found that these functions have costs, which they are now attempting to pass along to their customers—to the outrage of those who have grown accustomed to obtaining these services at no cost.

- **Recommend capital allocations based on profit center results.** Now that there is a profit center for each service provided, it is much easier to calculate the return on investment for each activity, which allows managers to determine which activities deserve more capital for expanded service levels and whether or not capital should be withdrawn from other service areas.

- **Measure manager performance based on profitability.** If managers are responsible for specific services, the profit center reporting format can be used to measure their performance. If some activities are in the responsibility areas of multiple managers, this may call for a realignment of their responsibilities before performance reviews can be used.

- **Assign costs to work in process.** In many cases costs are incurred during a reporting period for which billing will not occur until a later period. These costs are the service version of work in process and should be capitalized during the period. This topic is covered in a later section of this chapter.

- **Increase the speed of reporting feedback.** Once all data collection and reporting systems are in place, the accounting staff should review the systems with the managers who need the information and determine the timing of the reports they need. In many cases this results in an increase in the frequency of reporting or a reduction in the time period between the end of a reporting period and the issuing of all related reports.

- **Create measurement systems for quality cost tracking.** As in a manufacturing environment, quality problems of various kinds can cause a company to expend an inordinate amount of resources in corrective activities of various kinds. The cost accounting system should be designed so that the bulk of these costs are segregated and reported for management action. This topic is covered in a later section of this chapter.

Not every improvement noted here is applicable to every services industry, but the basic concept is clear—define the cost of activities and determine the variable nature of as many costs as possible, so that managers can determine proper pricing and break-even levels for every service they provide. In the next section we discuss the need for activity-based costing to analyze the most important of these issues— the costing of service-related activities.

APPLICATION OF ACTIVITY-BASED COSTING TO SERVICE BUSINESSES

A tool that was developed for tracing costs in a manufacturing environment is activity-based costing. As the name implies, this methodology involves determination of the cost of each activity in which a corporation is engaged; each of these costs is then charged to a product or customer, resulting in much more accurate costing than was previously possible (see Chapter 16 for a complete description of activity-based costing). This method is just as useful in a service environment for determination of the cost of activities.

Its use is best illustrated by an example. When an auditing firm wants to determine the actual cost of conducting an audit, there are considerably more activities to trace than just the labor of the auditors assigned to the audit itself. There are also a number of preliminary and support activities, such as:

- Annual sales meeting with client
- Audit preplanning meeting
- Creation of job number and work file for audit
- Audit of budget meeting
- Compiling of time sheets for audit staff
- Proofing of audit documentation

- Copying audit reports
- Periodic billing for audit
- Collection calls to client
- Processing of cash received from client

All these activities normally fall into the general cost category called overhead, where, unfortunately, most costs fall in the services business. However, by using ABC, we can make reasonable estimates regarding the costs of each of these activities and assign them to the audit, thereby presenting a more accurate picture of the true cost of the audit and at the same time reducing the total amount of costs included in the "overhead" category.

The first step in assigning costs to the categories just noted in our example is to create cost pools in which we can summarize selected costs. Each cost pool should correspond closely with an activity. To use the preceding example, a cost pool for the audit company can be a billing pool in which are stored the costs incurred when invoices are processed for clients. The pool can include costs for the labor and associated benefit costs of the accounting staff that are expended in this activity, as well as the cost of invoice forms purchased from a printer, a portion of the depreciation on any computer equipment used to process the invoices, and the costs of postage and envelopes. A cost pool such as this can be constructed for every activity noted earlier for the auditing firm.

The next step is to determine the most appropriate cost driver for each activity. A cost driver is any factor that causes a cost to occur (which in a services environment is generally the activity being measured). To use the ongoing example, the creation of an invoice is a cost driver. By dividing the number of invoices created into the total cost of the associated cost pool, we arrive at the cost per invoice.

The final step in the ABC process is to tally the number of times an activity has been used in the creation of the final product or job, which in the example is the audit of a client. If we say that the ABC project has determined that an invoice costs $13.72 to complete, and six invoices were issued to the client, then the total cost of this particular activity for a specific client is $82.32. When this cost is added to the costs of all the other activities included in the audit, company managers can arrive at a good idea of the total cost of the audit, which can then be compared to the total amount billed to determine the size of any profit or loss. To illustrate the results of an ABC analysis, Exhibit 37.1 shows all the activities associated with an audit, the cost of each one, the number of occurrences, and the resulting total cost of the audit. This information can be compiled in a similar manner for any service, providing a detailed cost analysis for management review.

The labor required to complete an ABC review of activities is considerable, for the measurement of cost pools and drivers falls outside the normal set of accounting activities, requiring the completion of an entirely new set of systems. Accord-

EXHIBIT 37.1. ABC Review of the Costs of an Audit

Activity	Unit Cost	Number of Occurrences	Total Cost ($)
Annual sales meeting with client	$50/hour	4	200.00
Audit preplanning meeting	$50/hour	3	150.00
Creation of job number and work file for audit	$40.50/setup	1	40.50
Audit of budget meeting	$50/hour	4	200.00
Cost of compiling time sheets for audit staff	$1.80/time sheet	14	25.20
Proofing of audit documentation	$220/review	2	440.00
Copying audit reports	$3.80/copy	10	38.00
Periodic billing for audit	$13.72/billing	6	82.32
Collection calls to client	$4.89/call	2	9.78
Processing of cash received from client	$9.03/check	6	54.18
Total			1239.98

ingly, many companies determine ABC information only on an occasional project basis, rather than doing so continually, and adjust their cost estimates from time to time with a new review. This approach is less accurate than an ongoing ABC system but results in fewer costs associated with the ABC system. Simply because it is so different from existing systems, an ABC analysis is difficult to shoehorn into existing work patterns, charts of accounts, and procedures.

An ABC system is well worth the effort of installation, for it gives a services company the ability to determine the cost of its key activities with some degree of precision, thereby allowing it to price its products correctly and determine which activities produce the greatest profits or losses.

WORK IN PROCESS IN A SERVICE ENVIRONMENT

A services firm typically charges off all costs to the current period. This is fine if all associated revenues are recognized at the same time or if any expenses with associated unrecognized revenues are so small as to be insignificant. However, there are many cases, especially in industries where services are provided on jobs that may last several months, where the costs incurred in a period are so significant that charging them off in the current period results in an excessively low level of reported profitability. Conversely, the associated revenues are likely to be recognized at the end of the job, when there are few costs left to charge against them, resulting in excessively high profits in these periods. Thus, such circumstances can result in inordinate and continuing swings in the reported levels of profitability that do not match what is actually happening. This problem is common in auditing, architectural design, consulting, and engineering firms, all of which engage in multiperiod projects for their clients but do not always issue billings at the end of each period that match their revenues to expenses incurred during the period.

The best way to avoid this problem of uneven reported profits is to capitalize all costs that have not yet been billed into an inventory account, such as "jobs work in process," and release expenses from this account as matching revenues are billed out. This results in a much more orderly flow of reported profits from period to period. Also, by reporting a summary, by job, of all costs in this work-in-process account, managers can see which jobs with an excessive store of costs need progress billing or job completion so that the matching costs can be expensed.

The main difficulty with this approach is that it requires employees to carefully compile and report the time they spend on jobs. This information must then be entered into the accounting system and a cost attached to each hour worked (based on a budgeted hourly amount or on an actual labor cost), so that the accounting staff can determine how many hours should be entered in the work-in-process account at the end of the period. Other types of period expenses can also be charged to the account, such as travel costs, though these tend to be a small proportion of total job-related costs. The main issue is that a time tracking system must be in place, so that the accounting staff can verify how many hours have been worked that have not been billed.

This approach is highly recommended for services companies that see their lov elo of profitability constantly change from period to period because large quantities of unbilled costs are charged to expenses.

QUALITY CONTROL AND COST ACCOUNTING IN A SERVICES ENVIRONMENT

A services company can suffer from quality-related problems as much as or more than a manufacturing firm. For example, an incorrectly processed insurance claim must be retrieved from a storage area, examined and corrected, the claimant contacted regarding the change, and (possibly) a new check issued that takes the place of a previous payment, which in turn must be canceled. All these activities are frequently much more costly than the single activity that caused them. Consequently, it is extremely important for a services company to have a good knowledge of what types of quality costs it incurs, as well as their size, so that it can take corrective action to reduce the most significant quality-related costs.

As described in some detail in Chapter 28, there are four types of quality costs. They are:

1. *Appraisal costs.* These are the costs of activities required to determine the size and extent of quality problems. In a services environment, they include

the cost of quality review audits by quality inspectors. These costs are easy to classify separately as quality costs and store in the general ledger, for they generally relate to specific activities or salaries.

2. *Prevention costs.* These are the costs of all activities needed to keep quality problems at a minimum. They include the costs of employee training, procedure writing, and remedial training for employees who continue to cause quality errors. These costs are also relatively simple to collect and report, for they involve activities that are easily traced.

3. *Internal failure costs.* These are the costs of all activities needed to correct quality problems that have already occurred within a company. They represent a difficult measurement task, for the tracing and correction of quality problems involves nearly all employees in a services environment at various times during the work week. Properly recording these costs requires detailed time tracking by all employees, which is not practical or tolerated in many businesses. Accordingly, these costs are frequently estimated.

4. *External failure costs.* These are the costs of correcting a quality problem once it has left the confines of a business and reached the customer and are even more difficult to measure. These costs involve dealing with customer complaints, correcting the service error, and lost profits on sales to customers who no longer do business with the company as a result of quality-related problems.

In a manufacturing environment the focus of most quality improvement activities is on the discovery of why quality issues arise in tangible products and what systemic changes are necessary to ensure that they do not occur again. The solution is somewhat different in a services environment, for there is no tangible product. Instead, the cause of nearly every quality problem can be traced to the chief resource of a services firm—its employees. To ensure that the staff is of the highest quality and does quality work, the cost accountant is most frequently employed in tracking down the causes of specific quality issues and recommending that specific staff areas undergo various types of training to ensure that they do not cause the same problems again. It is also of considerable importance in a services company to focus on recruiting the best possible employees and retention of those who produce the highest quality of work. These quality improvements are significantly different from those used in a manufacturing environment.

SUMMARY

As services have taken over the national economy from manufacturing, services companies have found that there are few tools in the cost accounting repertoire that can provide them with better control over or knowledge of their costs. These problems can be corrected by shifting the cost accounting system away from a focus on budgeting departmental costs and in the direction of deriving costs for specific services through the use of activity-based costing. This information can be used to create profit centers for each service provided, as well as to determine the proper minimum prices for all services. New systems can also result in a better matching of revenues and costs by using work-in-process tracking, as well as a greater knowledge of the cost of quality in a services environment.

CHAPTER 38

Cost Accounting with an Electronic Spreadsheet*

The cost accountant uses databases much more than electronic spreadsheets. Nonetheless, there are cases where the spreadsheet is an invaluable tool for completing selected analysis tasks. In this chapter we explore how to use Microsoft Excel to assist in regression analysis, as well as in determining net present value, internal rate of return, and project risk. These tasks are particularly applicable to determining cost variability, as previously noted in Chapter 29, and capital budgeting, as noted in Chapter 24.

REGRESSION ANALYSIS

A cost accountant is sometimes called on to create trend lines that forecast the variable cost to be expected at various levels of unit production. One of the better approaches for doing this is to mathematically fit a line to a set of data points that describe actual costs that have been experienced over a specific range of production levels. This line is then used to estimate costs at various production volume levels. The line can be created in Excel with a regression command.

*Portions of this chapter are adapted with permission from *Financial Analysis: A Controller's Guide* (Chapter 14), by S. Bragg, 2000, New York: John Wiley & Sons.

EXHIBIT 38.1. Regression Analysis in Microsoft Excel

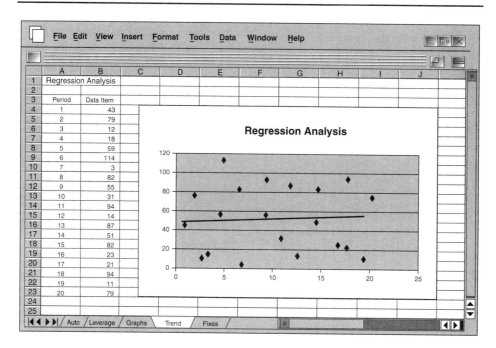

The regression command is a powerful tool for determining the trend line that best fits a disparate set of data and is most useful when dealing with a set of numbers that are widely scattered and show no apparent pattern. In essence, the method determines the trend line that minimizes the sum of all squared errors between all data points and the line. Rather than delve into the formula for this method, it is easier to plot the data elements and proceed immediately to the graph shown in Exhibit 38.1, where Excel superimposes a regression trend line on a set of data points. We have plotted down the left side of the exhibit 20 data items for 20 periods that differ widely from each other and have no apparent pattern. To create the chart shown in the exhibit, we complete these steps:

1. Highlight the range of numbers to be graphed on a trend line.

2. Click on the Chart Wizard icon.

3. The Chart Type = Scattergraph.

4. Enter the name of the graph in the Chart Title field.

5. Set the Legend option to Off.

6. Store the resulting graph on a separate work sheet.

7. Add the regression line to the graph by clicking on the completed graph, clicking on any data point within the graph, pressing the right mouse button, and picking "Select Trendline." Choose whichever of the six trend line options is most appropriate. The exhibit here uses a linear trend line.

The result appears in Exhibit 38.1, where we see a trend line with a slightly upward angle, indicating that there is some pattern in the data.

NET PRESENT VALUE ANALYSIS

When evaluating a capital asset proposal, there are many factors to review, such as expected market conditions, sales estimates, salvage values, and maintenance costs. After all these items have been reviewed and substantiated, they must all be input into a cash flow projection model to see if the project returns an adequate amount of cash. Excel supplies a formula that makes this an easy task, once the stream of all cash flows has been entered on a spreadsheet. A sample of such an analysis is shown in Exhibit 38.2, where we have simulated a typical cash-generating project involving a significant up-front expenditure to purchase and set up equipment, 5 years of progressively larger positive cash flows as more equipment capacity is used, and additional costs at the end of the project to dismantle the equipment, which is net of the salvage value.

Once this information is stored on a spreadsheet, we add the net present value formula, which is derived as:

NPV(interest rate, range of cash flow values)

The interest rate used in the formula should be the incremental cost of capital. For more information on this concept, refer to Chapter 24. The range of cash flow values listed in the second part of the formula represent the net cash flows for each period of the analysis. The formula then determines the current value of the expected future cash flows for each future period, using the cost of capital as the discounting factor, and summarizes all the separate discounted cash flows into a single dollar value of all cash flows for the project. In the example the formula uses a 13% cost of capital, which results in the formula:

NPV(.13,I6:I11)

The NPV formula is a powerful tool for determining the discounted cash flows of projects, but one must keep in mind that the cash flows used in these models are highly subjective in nature (depending on the extent of previous analysis work). As a result net present values appear to be accurate to the nearest penny but do not have solid quantitative underpinnings, yielding inaccurate results. For example, the cash flow analysis shown earlier in Exhibit 38.2 listed a large percentage of cash inflows in the later years of the project, which contributed to the small positive cash flow

EXHIBIT 38.2. Net Present Value Calculation

	A	B	C	D	E	F	G	H	I	J
1	Net Present Value Analysis									
2	[All figures in thousands]									
3						Personal		Net		
4		Equipment	Equipment	Testing	Maintenance	Property		Cash		
5	Period	Purchases	Installation	Codes	Costs	Taxes	Revenue	Flows		
6	1	(1,200)	(400)	(250)	(50)	(48)	300	(1,648)		
7	2				(55)	(48)	600	497		
8	3				(60)	(48)	650	542		
9	4				(65)	(48)	700	587		
10	5				(70)	(48)	750	632		
11	6	120	(75)			(48)		(3)		
12										
13										
14		Cost of Capital:	13%				Net Present Value:	8		
15										
16										
17	Notes:									
18	(1) Assumes a 10% salvage value at the end of the project.									
19	(2) Assumes that positive cash flows will commence half-way into the first year.									
20	(3) Assumes that personal property taxes will still be owed in the final year of operations,									
21	despite a projected disposal sometime during that year.									
22										
23										
24										
25										

anticipated for the project; unfortunately, cash flows several years into the future are more uncertain and unpredictable than those likely to occur in the near term, so these long-term estimates should be closely reviewed. In short, a cost accountant should spend lots of time questioning the expected cash flows used in a net present value analysis in order to be sure of the outcome.

Cash flow assumptions are not the only factor involved in the net present value calculation. The other factor is the cost of capital used to discount the stream of cash flows. If this factor is incorrect by even a small amount, the net present value will be incorrect, which can lead to an incorrect decision regarding the acceptance or rejection of a project. The simplest way to determine the potential severity of an error in the cost of capital is to recalculate the net present value using a cost of capital that is incrementally higher than the original interest rate. If the net present value drops below zero, it may be necessary to review the accuracy of the cost of capital to ensure that it is correct. A slightly more elaborate approach, as shown in Exhibit 38.3, is to plot a comparison of the net present value to the cost of capital to find the discount rate at which the net present value drops to zero. Using this graphical approach, we can see that, if the cost of capital increases by just 1% from the 13% used earlier in Exhibit 38.2, the net present value will turn negative. Consequently, though the original calculation shows a positive return, it is so small that

EXHIBIT 38.3. Comparison of NPV to Discount Rate

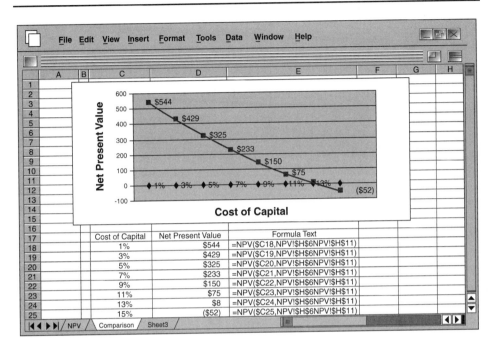

	Cost of Capital	Net Present Value	Formula Text
17			
18	1%	$544	=NPV($C18,NPV!$H$6NPV!$H$11)
19	3%	$429	=NPV($C19,NPV!$H$6NPV!$H$11)
20	5%	$325	=NPV($C20,NPV!$H$6NPV!$H$11)
21	7%	$233	=NPV($C21,NPV!$H$6NPV!$H$11)
22	9%	$150	=NPV($C22,NPV!$H$6NPV!$H$11)
23	11%	$75	=NPV($C23,NPV!$H$6NPV!$H$11)
24	13%	$8	=NPV($C24,NPV!$H$6NPV!$H$11)
25	15%	($52)	=NPV($C25,NPV!$H$6NPV!$H$11)

a reexamination of the cost of capital may be in order to verify that the discount rate used is the correct one.

The calculations used to create the graph in Exhibit 38.3 are shown at the bottom of the exhibit, with all the formulas noted in the lower right corner. Each net present value formula references the cost of capital immediately to its right, while also referencing the time-sequenced series of cash flows noted on the NPV work sheet shown in Exhibit 38.2.

INTERNAL RATE OF RETURN CALCULATION

As noted earlier in Chapter 24, one of the key determinants of the suitability of a capital project is its return on investment, which is described by the internal rate of return calculation. This can be a difficult manual calculation in which the cost accountant continually recalculates the discount rate at which a project's stream of cash flows will reach zero, requiring calculations at high and low estimated IRR discount rates and gradually closing in on the exact IRR value. A much faster approach is to let Excel do the work by automatically churning through the calculation iterations and returning the correct IRR value in moments.

EXHIBIT 38.4. Internal Rate of Return Calculation in Microsoft Excel

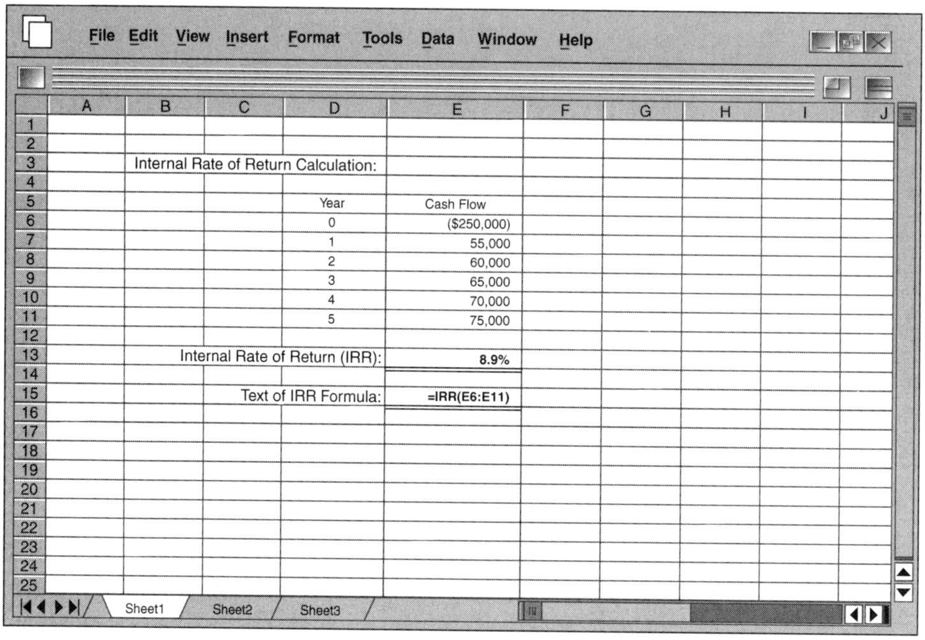

				Year	Cash Flow
				0	($250,000)
				1	55,000
				2	60,000
				3	65,000
				4	70,000
				5	75,000
		Internal Rate of Return (IRR):			8.9%
		Text of IRR Formula:			=IRR(E6:E11)

Internal Rate of Return Calculation:

The calculation of IRR is best illustrated with the example shown in Exhibit 38.4, where we itemize the cash flows for each year of a sample project and then enter the simple formula noted in cell E15, which references the range of cash flow values. The calculated IRR result appears in cell E13, where we see that the IRR of the presented set of cash flows is 8.9%. This formula represents a considerable improvement in speed over manual calculation of the same information.

RISK ANALYSIS

When constructing a financial analysis of the likely results of a set of projected cash flows, a cost accountant must always remember that these cash flows are projected—they are not facts and may vary considerably from reality. Given the level of uncertainty involved, it may be useful to determine the spread of possible outcomes. By doing so a cost accountant can see if all expected outcomes are grouped tightly about a single estimate, which relates to a low level of risk, or if there is a significant spread of possible outcomes, which greatly increases the risk of meeting the targeted outcome. Excel provides a wide array of statistical tools for determining the level of risk, and six that are easy to understand and use are described here.

The first step when using the following statistical tools is to generate a list of possible outcomes for whatever the analysis may be. For example, if a capital project is under discussion, try to obtain a number of possible outcomes, by polling several experts in the company or industry or from personal knowledge of previous actual outcomes for similar types of projects. Then, the first step in the risk analysis work is to determine the highest, lowest, and median values on the list of possible outcomes. These are shown in Exhibit 38.5, where we have itemized a dozen possible annual cash inflows from a project. All possible variations are noted at the top of the work sheet. Next to them are the Excel formulas that find the minimum, maximum, and median values on the list. However, these are not precise measures and do not give a sufficiently accurate view of the level of risk.

To provide us with a more detailed idea of the spread of possible outcomes, we can use the Excel quartile formula to generate the average outcome for the first, second, third, and fourth quartiles of all possible outcomes, which we have also converted to a graph with the Excel Chart Wizard icon. Yet another formula that tells us if there is a "lean" in the data toward the lower or higher end of the spectrum of possible results is the skew formula. This formula determines of the presence of skew toward the higher end of possible outcomes (which is positive skew) or skew toward the lower end of possible outcomes (which is a negative skew). A skew of zero indicates no skew in either direction. Finally, the standard deviation is an extremely useful tool for determining the dispersion of possible outcomes about the median of all outcomes. The larger the standard deviation of the sample, the larger the dispersion about the median and the greater the degree of risk that the average outcome will not be attained.

The details of the formulas shown in Exhibit 38.5 are simple. All the formulas reference the range of projected cash inflows, which are noted in cells C5 through C16. The only variation from this pattern is for the quartile formulas, which also require addition of the quartile number at the end of the formula.

The analysis shown in Exhibit 38.5 tells us that the project has a wide range of possible outcomes, with a maximum value that is more than four times higher than the minimum value. The range of possible outcomes has a positive skew of 0.24, which tells us that the people providing the estimates have generally guessed that the actual outcome will be higher than the projected average. Finally, the standard deviation from the mean is $1808, which is slightly more than a 40% variation from the median. With such a large dispersion of possible outcomes, the underlying data requires much more validation before the project can be approved. Also, given the higher degree of risk, the cost of capital used to discount the cash flows from the project can be set higher, thereby making it more difficult to obtain approval for the project.

EXHIBIT 38.5. Risk Analysis for a Capital Project

Projected Outcome	Projected Cash Inflow		Result	Text of Formula
1	$5,400	Minimum Value of all Outcomes	$1,700	=MIN($C$5:$C$16)
2	$3,200	Maximum Value of all Outcomes	$8,000	=MAX($C$5:$C$16)
3	$1,700	Median Value of all Outcomes	$4,475	=MEDIAN($C$5:$C$16)
4	$6,100			
5	$2,900	Minimum Value	$1,700	=QUARTILE($C$5:$C$16,0)
6	$4,700	Value of 25th Percentile	$3,125	=QUARTILE($C$5:$C$16,1)
7	$5,800	Value of 50th Percentile	$4,475	=QUARTILE($C$5:$C$16,2)
8	$8,000	Value of 75th Percentile	$5,838	=QUARTILE($C$5:$C$16,3)
9	$3,900	Maximum Value	$8,000	=QUARTILE($C$5:$C$16,4)
10	$4,250			
11	$5,950	Degree of Skew	0.24	=SKEW($C$5:$C$16)
12	$2,500	Standard Deviation	$1,808	=STDEV($C$5:$C$16)

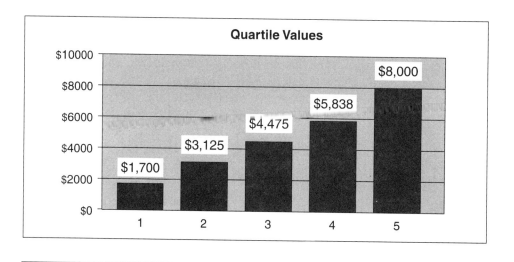

Quartile Values

SUMMARY

There are far more formulas on electronic spreadsheets related to financial analysis than there are for cost accounting. Nonetheless, the regression analysis, net present value, internal rate of return, and risk formulas presented here are of use to the cost accountant in selected situations, such as for capital budgeting evaluations and the determination of product costs at various volume levels. The use of an electronic spreadsheet greatly increases the speed with which one can complete what would otherwise be very labor-intensive calculations.

CHAPTER 39

Cost Accounting and Taxes

The cost accountant's typical duties are some distance from direct efforts to improve profitability. They normally involve generating reports that other employees can use as a basis for further efforts that can result in profitability improvements. However, there are two areas in which a cost accountant can have a direct immediate effect on profitability: the costing of inventory and the generation of transfer prices for product sales to other company entities. Both these activities can have a large impact on the income tax expenses paid by a company. In this chapter we explore how these activities can alter income tax payments, as well as some additional variables to consider when adopting new transfer price levels.

TAXATION AND INVENTORY VALUATION

The primary objective when preparing an income tax return is to keep the reported level of income as low as possible. However, there are few alternatives under generally accepted accounting principles that allow a company to meet this goal by reporting excessively low revenue or high expenses—except in the case of inventory. A company is permitted to use an alternative inventory valuation method for taxing purposes that yields a lower cost of goods sold than the method used for reporting the taxable amount of income.

This ability to employ two different sets of inventory valuations is especially attractive for companies using advanced accounting software that compiles inventory values by several different valuation techniques—and at the same time. Without this type of software a cost accountant might be faced with the formidable task of having to manually compile the secondary inventory valuation on paper, since low-end accounting systems do not have this dual valuation capability.

As an example of how this system works, a company may have had a long-standing valuation system that uses the first-in first-out methodology to value its inventory. In an effort to lower its taxes, it obtains a software package that allows it to value costs under the moving-average method at the same time. By reviewing the total inventory valuations under each method, the cost accountant determines that the moving-average method results in a lower inventory valuation than the FIFO method, which means that more costs are pushed out of inventory and into the cost of goods sold, which in turn reduces income for taxation purposes. Accordingly, the company adopts the moving-average method for tax reporting purposes.

The problem with using a dual valuation system is that this approach only delays the payment of income taxes to some future period—it does not result in the permanent reduction of taxes. To continue the previous example, if the company using the moving-average valuation system decides to reduce its inventory at some point in the future, perhaps in response to a just-in-time manufacturing initiative (Chapter 28), then there will be no inventory to shift costs into or out of. As a result, the reported levels of income for taxation and for financial reporting purposes will be equalized and there will no longer be a valid reason to use two separate inventory valuation methods.

The inventory method that companies prefer to use for tax reporting purposes is last in first-out because it results in the lowest inventory valuations and the highest cost of goods sold in an inflationary environment. For example, if the price of a unit of stock increases by 5% every year, the LIFO method will always charge off to expenses the most recently purchased (and most expensive) units, while leaving in stock the least expensive units that were purchased earlier. However, because this method can result in such a drastic reduction in reported income, the Internal Revenue Service (IRS) requires companies using it for tax purposes to also use it for financial reporting purposes. In doing this the IRS is essentially saying that you cannot have your cake (low taxes) and eat it too (high reported income). If a company wants to pay low taxes through the use of LIFO, it must also report a lower level of income in its external financial statements. This may not be a palatable alternative for publicly held companies whose investors have high earnings-per-share expectations.

Some companies tried to circumvent the IRS LIFO reporting rule by setting up parent companies that did not use the LIFO reporting method but compiled the financial reports of its subsidiaries (which did use the LIFO method) for taxation purposes. This allowed them to report LIFO costs for tax purposes while still reporting improved financial results to investors. The IRS put a stop to this practice by ruling that if LIFO is used in any one of a group of financially related companies, the entire group is assumed to be a single entity for tax reporting purposes, thereby forcing the consolidated external financial reports to be recorded under the LIFO costing method.

When reporting the impact of LIFO costing on a company's balance sheet, it is acceptable to separately itemize the original valuation that used a different costing methodology and the incremental change caused by the use of LIFO costing. An example of this format is:

$$\text{Inventory valuation (FIFO)} = \$2,350,000$$

$$\text{Incremental impact of LIFO} = -\$500,000$$

$$\text{Total inventory valuation} = \$1,850,000$$

It is also acceptable to the IRS if LIFO is reported for tax purposes, while actual market value is used for financial reporting purposes, as long as the market valuation method results in a lower inventory valuation than would be the case with LIFO costing. This is clearly not much of an incentive to use this approach since reported profits would be even lower than under the LIFO method, and so the IRS' magnanimous offer has not met with an enthusiastic response.

Just because the use of LIFO for tax reporting generally requires the use of the same method for external financial reports, there is no reason why a cost accountant should feel constrained to use LIFO for internal management reports. The IRS does not care what costing method is used here since such reports are not distributed outside a company and therefore cannot influence investors or creditors. Consequently, if the accounting system allows the use of multiple valuation methods and the cost accountant feels that the costs derived from a different costing method will be more useful than LIFO costs, he or she can populate management reports with inventory costs that use any other type of valuation methodology.

This section has itemized the reasons for using multiple inventory valuation methods for tax purposes, as well as the shortcomings of doing so. Conducting such reporting may be well worth the effort because a company can delay the reporting of taxable income until some future period, thereby obtaining the benefit of investing funds that would otherwise have to be paid out to cover its income tax obligations.

TAXATION AND TRANSFER PRICING

A highly fruitful area in which the cost accountant can reduce income taxes is transfer pricing between company locations in different countries. This is a particularly important topic, for income taxes can then be *permanently* reduced, not just pushed off into the future as is the case for inventory valuations.

The basic concept of transfer pricing is a simple one, as shown in Exhibit 39.1. In the example the income tax rate in country Alpha is 40% but is only 25% in country

EXHIBIT 39.1. Income Tax Savings from Transfer Pricing

	Country Alpha Location	Country Beta Location
Sales to subsidiary:		
Revenue	$1,000.000	
Cost of goods sold	850,000	
Profit	$150,000	
Profit percentage	15%	
Sale outside of company:		
Revenue		$1,500,000
Cost of goods sold		1,000,000
Profit		$500,000
Profit percentage		33%
Income tax percentage	40%	25%
Income tax	$60,000	$125,000
Consolidated income tax	$185,000	
Consolidated income tax percentage	28%	

Beta. If a company has a subsidiary in country Beta, it can sell its products to the subsidiary at a low price. By doing so it reduces its margins on the sale recorded on the corporate parent's books (located in country Alpha), which leaves it with a smaller profit that will be taxable at the higher income tax rate in country Alpha. Meanwhile, the subsidiary has an unusually low cost of goods sold, thanks to the low transfer price, and so records a higher than normal income at its location, which is country Beta. Since the income tax there is lower than in country Alpha, the company as a whole has recorded a permanent reduction in its overall income tax expense.

In the exhibit the company facility in country Alpha sells product to its subsidiary in country Beta at a low transfer price, resulting in the recognition of only 15% net income in country Alpha but 33% net income in country Beta. When the 15% net income in country Alpha is multiplied by that country's income tax rate of 40%, and the 33% net income in country Beta is multiplied by that country's income tax rate of 25%, the consolidated organization achieves an overall income tax rate of just 28%. Thus, alterations in product transfer prices can have a major positive impact on the income tax rates a company pays.

There are other types of transfer prices that a company can use to increase or decrease the expenses of its foreign subsidiaries. For example, when a subsidiary is located in a country with a high income tax rate, it behooves company management to increase the costs charged to that location. One way to do this is to charge the subsidiary a variety of royalty or licensing fees, perhaps for the use of patents or brand-name trademarks held by the corporate parent. Another alternative is to charge a subsidiary somewhat higher or lower than normal interest rates on funds loaned to it, depending on the need to increase or decrease reported income at that location.

All these changes make it appear that the cost accountant, or anyone else involved in setting prices to subsidiaries, is having a grand time altering accounting records to achieve a lower overall income tax rate. This is true to some extent, for the need to reduce income taxes can drive an organization to adopt pricing practices with its subsidiaries that do not even remotely follow generally accepted accounting principles. To keep these practices from getting out of hand, the United States government has adopted a set of rules (noted in Section 482 of the IRS code) that serve as guidelines for how transfer prices are to be constructed. Companies must follow these guidelines or expect the IRS to alter their prices for tax purposes, resulting in higher income tax percentages. The rules are:

1. *Market price.* The preferred transfer price is the market rate for a product. Since there is rarely a provable market rate for the bulk of products and components shipped between countries (because they are not precisely identical), there is some allowance for adjustments to the market price to account for the variability in the other products on the market against which the comparison is being made. The accounting staff can also adjust the market price for reasonable variations in administrative costs, such as an increase in the transfer price to reflect the extra effort associated with intercountry documentation requirements. These adjustments can be exploited to the fullest or ignored, depending on the level of transfer price desired by a company. If there is no reasonable basis for the construction of a market-based price, then a company can use the next method.

2. *Work back method.* This method starts with the sales price of the product that was used by the subsidiary to sell the product to a customer not related to the company (e.g., the first product sale in the sequence that is not intercompany). We then remove the subsidiary's markup from this price, as well as the cost of any additional work put into the product by the subsidiary, and the result should be a reasonable estimate of the transfer price that should have been used. The weakness in this method is that it can be difficult to compute the full cost of all the value added to a product by the subsidiary if the transferred item is only a component that goes into a much larger product. For example, this method would not work well if the transferred item were a computer chip included in a microwave oven, for the cost of the chip is only a small part of the total product price. When this is the case, a company can use the following cost-plus option.

3. *Cost plus.* This method involves the summation of all costs for the product to be transferred, followed by establishment of a satisfactory margin to be

added to the cost. The cost is easy to determine, but it can be difficult to establish the margin, and considerable negotiation with the IRS may be involved (which is why this is the least-favored pricing method from the viewpoint of the IRS).

In short, the IRS prefers to see transfer pricing that can be proven by a review of market prices since these cannot be altered by the cost accounting staff. Less-preferred pricing methods are those that are subject to some internal manipulation. Because of these rules, the cost accounting staff is constrained in its transfer pricing practices by general IRS guidelines. Nonetheless, many adjustments to transfer prices can be claimed as valid because of the special costs associated with transferring products between countries. These adjustments can be used or ignored in order to alter net income in locations where tax rates are at their lowest.

Section 482 of the IRS code also allows the government to assign different interest rates to intercompany loans if the existing booked rates used do not appear to match market rates. Similarly, the IRS can require a company to book expenses for services performed between subsidiaries, as well as for the prices of intangible items, such as royalties and commissions. In the case of intangible items, the IRS allows an expense to be charged to a subsidiary to the extent that the license or royalty will result in a level of income commensurate with the amount of expense charged, thereby keeping inordinately high expenses from being charged for such items.

The IRS does not have the same time or other resources available to it that an internal cost accounting staff has, and so cost accountants can still develop detailed and convincing proofs of why the IRS transfer prices should be altered in the company's favor. This results in considerable negotiation over the final transfer prices to be adopted, so the cost accounting staff can have a definite positive impact on transfer pricing even when the IRS steps in and alters prices.

Consequently, transfer pricing is an area that can save a company a considerable amount of money on reduced income tax expenses but can also raise warning flags to government tax authorities if excessively exploited. There are additional considerations to be aware of when determining the best transfer price, which are covered in the next section.

OTHER TRANSFER PRICING CONSIDERATIONS

The decision to alter transfer prices to a foreign subsidiary in order to reduce the overall level of income taxes is not as simple as it may at first appear. The calculation of net income, levels of custom duties, cash flow restrictions, and the level of reported subsidiary earnings are also factors to be considered.

When making a comparison of income tax rates charged in various countries, it is not sufficient to look at the percentage rate charged against the reported level of net income. It is also necessary to investigate the local accounting rules that determine the level of net income. For example, some countries may place severe restrictions on, or even eliminate the charging of, depreciation against net income, which raises the level of reported earnings. When this happens, the amount of income against which the income tax percentage is charged is higher, thereby negating some or all of any income tax advantage that the subsidiary's country at first appeared to offer. Consequently, it is best to have a tax expert with a knowledge of local tax laws prepare a sample tax return for a subsidiary that includes all local income recognition rules and see what impact this analysis has on the net income tax percentage charged.

Another issue to consider is that many corporate subsidiaries have lending arrangements with local banks, who require certain minimum profitability levels to be reported before they extend debt arrangements into future periods. In order to ensure that these minimum profitability levels are met, transfer prices may be set at lower than customary levels. Though this may result in additional income taxes being paid (if the local country charges a higher income tax rate than the country in which the corporate parent is located), the advantages of obtaining local financing may outweigh the extra income tax cost. This is a particular relevant issue in countries that tightly control cash outflows since a loan by a corporate parent to a subsidiary may not be allowed back out of the country at some future date. To avoid locking up cash flows in these cases, the procurement of local debt can be an overwhelmingly important issue, easily outweighing the increased income tax expense.

The restriction of cash flows out of a country may also force a company to charge high transfer prices to its subsidiaries located in these countries, which allows it to be paid back more cash through its accounts receivable than it is likely to be paid through dividend or income distributions (which are the most tightly controlled items in such situations). This practice may run counter to the objective of reducing income taxes since a country with tight cash flow restrictions may also have a low tax rate, which would make it advantageous to set much lower transfer prices in that country in order to recognize a high level of income there. Nonetheless, the ability to extract cash from such countries is generally considered more important than obtaining a favorable tax rate there, because it is not much use to a company to obtain low income tax rates if it cannot use the resulting additional cash flow.

Another consideration is the amount of customs duties charged at international boundaries. If a country charges a high customs duty but has a low income tax rate, the cost accountant must conduct an analysis to see if the savings on reduced income taxes is outweighed by the increased amount of customs duties charged. This is a more quantifiable issue than the previous items involving cash flows, as well as the ability to obtain local loans, and so can be readily analyzed at the cost accountant's level without requiring additional decision making by higher-level managers.

Another twist in the transfer pricing decision process is the impact of these prices on corporate activities. As noted in Chapter 30, a correctly set transfer price has a positive impact on a company's profit maximization decisions, as well as on the performance evaluations of the managers at each subsidiary receiving transferred products. When these transfer prices are altered to take advantage of local income tax rates, they are skewed away from the optimal levels at which profit maximization activities and performance evaluations are enhanced. To offset this problem a company can create two sets of accounting records—one for internal management purposes and one for external tax reporting. Unfortunately, though this is a legal approach, taxing authorities (rightly) look askance at the existence of two sets of accounting books and want to know why the internal transfer prices do not match those reported to them—and possibly require an adjustment in the prices to match those of the internally used accounting records.

The preceding issue brings up an important final topic—the impact of altered transfer pricing on local governments. When the local taxing authority sees that a company is continually shifting its transfer prices up or down in order to take maximum advantage of local tax rates, it may question the underlying basis for these changes, which can result in a tax audit that forces the company to alter its transfer prices. These activities may also lead to tax avoidance charges, which can include interest and penalties that exceed the tax savings that would otherwise have been recognized. Further, a government that sees a company persistently altering its pricing over time may adopt a permanently questioning and suspicious attitude toward that company, resulting in endless audits and other reviews that cost more in internal administrative time than the transfer pricing alterations are worth. In cases where there has been continual conflict with local tax authorities, it may be best to adopt a conservative transfer pricing strategy solely to improve relations with the local government.

All these issues must be considered, and reviewed repeatedly, as taxation and other changes occur in every country in which a company has operations. There is never a set-in-stone solution to the transfer pricing issue because of the fluid taxation environment of today's business world. Accordingly, the cost accounting and taxation staffs of modern international corporations are permanently employed in the daily search for the best overall pricing structure that will result in the lowest possible level of income tax expense.

CASE STUDY

Mr. Pryce B. Lowe, one of the cost accountants at the General Research and Instrumentation Company, has been asked to review the transfer prices used for a chip set manufactured in the United States and sent to Belgium for integration into an automotive testing product at that site. The United States has a 40% income tax rate, as opposed to the 33% rate charged by Belgium. Mr. Lowe knows that Belgium also charges a $4 customs duty on each chip set entering that country. Furthermore, the income tax calculation in Belgium excludes depreciation and any royalty

EXHIBIT 39.2. Calculation of Belgian Income Tax Rate

	Complete Income Statement	Adjustments for Belgian Tax Rules	Adjusted Belgian Income Statements
Revenue	$12,000,000		$12,000,000
Cost of goods sold:			
Materials	5,500,000		
Labor	1,200,000		5,500,000
Royalties	350,000	−$350,000	0
Depreciation	480,000	−480,000	0
Other overhead	2,250,000		2,250,000
Total cost of goods	9,780,000		4,250,000
Administrative costs	525,000		525,000
Net profit	$1,695,000		$3,725,000
Income tax paid	$1,229,250 ◄───────────────		$1,229,250
Income tax percent	**73%**		**33%**

charges made by the parent company to the subsidiary. The GRIN Company ships about 10,000 of these units to its Belgium facility each year. Mr. Lowe also knows that the IRS is scheduling an audit of the GRIN Company's transfer prices, so he must come up with a pricing structure that follows the IRS pricing guidelines. He decides that this is a two-step process. In the first step he will determine the actual income tax rate for Belgium and then decide on the correct IRS pricing guideline to derive a transfer price.

He begins with the income statement for the GRIN Company subsidiary for the previous year, which is shown in Exhibit 39.2. The exhibit lists the sale of other products to the subsidiary, as well as the chip set, and also includes the $4 customs duty. Based on this analysis it is apparent that the actual income tax rate is a high 73%, which is caused by the nondeductibility of intercompany royalty charges, as well as depreciation. Based on this information, Mr. Lowe decides that the transfer price of the chip must be as high as possible so that the subsidiary's cost of goods sold will be increased, thereby keeping the company from paying any extra income tax in Belgium.

He then reviews the IRS guidelines for determining the transfer price of the chip set. The preferred option is to obtain the market price for the chip set, but this is a completely unique item specially designed for the Belgian subsidiary—there is no way to obtain such information, so he moves to the next alternative. This is to take the price used by the subsidiary to sell the product containing the transferred parts and strip away all added costs and margins to arrive at the price of the transferred item. This approach also will not work, because the final product includes several hundred parts, of which the chip set is just one. It would be impossible to arrive at

EXHIBIT 39.3. Extra Costs Assigned to a Transferred Product

Description	Cost ($)
Bill of materials cost	129.17
Royalty for use of patents	10.00
Special packaging	8.03
Shipment insurance	1.92
Customs duties	4.00
Freight cost	0.99
Added administrative overhead	5.49
Subtotal	**159.60**
Margin (at 50%)	79.80
Total transfer price	**239.40**

a reasonable price figure for the chip set given the impact of so many other parts, several of which are also transferred to Belgium by the corporate parent. This leaves Mr. Lowe with the third option, which is to assemble the cost of the chip set from the records of the American parent company and add a reasonable margin to it to arrive at the appropriate transfer price.

With the objective of deriving the highest possible transfer price for the chip set, he starts with the bill of materials for the chip set and then adds overhead costs associated with the packaging, insurance, shipment, and customs duties for the product, as noted in Exhibit 39.3. Further, he assigns a high markup to the final product cost, on the grounds that he can always negotiate it back down if the IRS examiner disapproves of the resulting high cost. However, he knows that this high cost will result in a higher sale price being recognized in the United States, which will require a higher income tax to be paid in that country, so there should not be too much argument from the government over this issue.

The real problem with the transfer price Mr. Lowe has developed will be in Belgium. If that country's tax examiners choose to investigate the basis for the transfer price, there may be some negotiation over the high margin that was added to the price, as well as the royalty for use of the patents involved in manufacture of the product. If the government unilaterally reduces the Belgian transfer price, this will reduce the profit earned by the corporate parent. As a result, the American division of the GRIN Company will have to file with the IRS for a refund of excess income taxes paid in that country, while it pays a higher income tax to the Belgian government.

SUMMARY

Based on the information presented in this chapter, it is apparent that a cost accountant has considerable leeway in creating tax situations where taxes are either postponed or completely eliminated. The actions necessary to create these situations require an excellent knowledge of the government tax laws in every country in which a company operates, which calls for the assistance of in-house tax experts or outside consultants. Even with their aid, the cost accountant must be aware that aggressive alterations to inventory valuation methods or transfer prices may invoke the wrath of local tax authorities, resulting in negotiations over the income taxes charged. Just as important an issue is what impact these alterations will have on a company's internal management and performance measurement systems since they can skew the information used by these systems. To avoid problems in these areas, it may be necessary to create a secondary set of tax-specific accounting records with a reconciliation system that brings them into alignment with the primary accounting records. The effort required to do this is usually justified, given the large benefits to be gained from reducing income taxes.

CHAPTER 40

Fraud in Cost Accounting

An unfortunate fact of the business world is that some companies use cost accounting to commit fraud. This is not the deliberate theft of company assets—cost accounting is not a good foundation for that type of fraud. Rather, it is used to artificially inflate or deflate a company's reported profits. The underlying corporate assets are still there, but a misused cost accounting system can so thoroughly misstate a company's actual results that no one can tell how well the company is really performing. In this chapter we explore the reasons why cost accounting is used to commit fraud, consider how the cost accountant can either help or prevent this activity, and present descriptions and examples of the various types of fraud that can be committed with a cost accounting system.

REASONS FOR FRAUD IN COST ACCOUNTING

Cost accounting fraud is usually instigated at the management level, not by the cost accounting department. The reason for this is that when managers are compensated based on the profitability of the company as a whole or of their individual business units, they have an incentive to "stretch" reported results. The problem is exacerbated when a disproportionately large part of a manager's potential income is based on stretch profitability goals that can be achieved only through extreme efforts. The reverse situation may also be true for privately held companies that are more concerned with avoiding taxes—these organizations may reward their managers based on their ability to improve cash flow while holding down the amount of reported profitability. In either situation the level of fraud initially committed is relatively minor—perhaps a slight adjustment that results in a small change in income, but enough to reach a performance goal. However, this small step into the realm of fraudulent behavior makes it easier to make a larger adjustment in the next reporting period, and so on. Soon, a manager is incorporating fraudulent actions into his or her daily activities and develops a range of activities that will result in skewed financial results, most of which are described in this chapter.

FRAUD-ENABLING COST ACCOUNTANTS

A common ploy for a manager intent on using the cost accounting system to commit fraud is to reduce the cost accounting staff or to keep it so busy with other, completely unrelated tasks that there is little time to identify or investigate suspicious activities. Nonetheless, the majority of activities mentioned in this chapter are relatively easy to spot, especially for accountants who are trained in the nuances of costing systems.

The simplest approach for the cost accounting manager is to create a trend line of all major cost categories, inventory levels, and cost allocation pools and simply trace the levels of the items from as far back as possible, right up to the present day. Since these costs rarely change, in total or in proportion to each other, variations can reveal the presence of a tampering manager. The level of work required to keep track of this information is minimal, so even a reduced cost accounting staff or one whose activities are being deliberately forced in other directions should still be able to find time for such rudimentary analyses. If not, the cost accounting staff will enable the fraudulent manager to continue his or her activities by ignoring them.

Even after the costing staff discovers that a manager has altered the cost accounting system, a common response is that the cost manager chooses to ignore it, feeling that it is safer to go along than to buck the boss. This is especially common when the changes made by the fraudulent manager are widely spaced, so that the cost manager has time to get used to each incremental change before being hit with the next one. This sort of lax behavior by the cost manager only enables the fraudulent manager since a complete lack of resistance just emboldens him to make more future changes. A better approach is to prepare and actively promote a detailed study showing the effect of each change made by the fraudulent manager, the resulting changes in expense levels, and how these changes go against generally accepted accounting principles. If this resistance continues to arise every time the fraudulent manager attempts to make a change, there is much less chance that he or she will press for a full range of changes to the existing costing systems.

In addition to the initial analysis provided by the cost accounting manager in response to changes made by the fraudulent manager, there should also be a monthly summarization of the changes in expenses that result from each individual change that has been instigated, as well as notations regarding what the actual levels of inventory valuation and cost of goods sold should be. This constitutes an ongoing and highly detailed record of the fraudulent manager's activities. It is best to make this information as public as possible, which acts as a major deterrent. When there is a risk of retaliation, the cost accounting manager should continue to compile and store the information, releasing it to both the internal and external auditors when the opportunity arises.

These types of resistance to inappropriate changes in the cost accounting system, even if they involve only the tracking of cumulative costing changes, are an excellent tool for improvement once the information finds its way into the hands of someone who can counteract the fraudulent manager. If the cost accounting manager finds herself in a more high-level role where she can provide more active resistance, then so much the better. However, if these actions are not taken, the entire cost accounting staff will simply enable a fraudulent manager to make a number of harmful changes to existing systems that will result in severe skewing of reported financial results.

HOW TO STOP COST ACCOUNTING FRAUD

Cost accounting fraud is difficult to stop because it is generally initiated by members of the management team, those whose pay levels are driven by the need to report high levels of profitability. If the chief executive officer is one of the people behind the fraudulent activities, then there is no realistic way to stop them. Leaking information about the problems to the company's auditors will only result in their refusal to issue an opinion on reported results or their withdrawal from an auditing engagement. Under these circumstances a cost accountant is in a difficult situation that is best resolved by finding employment at a different company.

Situations where only lower-level managers are responsible for fraud are more preventable. In these cases the cost accountant should report any discovered problem to the cost accounting manager, who can then pass the information along to his or her supervisor—probably the corporate or divisional controller or the chief financial officer. This individual is then responsible for reporting the problem to the chief executive officer, who should deal with the offending manager(s). The main difficulty arises when the cost accounting manager reports directly to the person responsible for the fraudulent activity, for example, when the cost accounting manager works for a specific division and reports to its general manager, who is the one involved in the fraud. The problem is exacerbated when there is no division controller at all, just a corporate one, since this gives the cost accounting manager no local ally with whom to consult. In this situation the cost accounting manager is placed in the uncomfortable position of going around his or her manager; if this appears to be the correct action, then the issue should go to the manager of the internal auditing department, who generally reports straight to the board of directors and therefore is generally in a position to act on such tips without fear of retaliation from the offending manager.

Given the variety of circumstances that may arise, and the potentially severe backlash for employees who take on the "whistle blower" role in uncovering cost accounting fraud, it is best to take these steps prior to going public with fraud claims:

1. *Verify the information.* What may first appear to be fraudulent activity may actually be a misinterpretation of the data, or an innocent action by someone that can be quickly cleared up with some clarification of the issue. Be certain of your facts before proceeding with any publicity regarding the issue.

2. *Have another person verify the information.* Even after completing the first step, it is still possible that you will not have a complete picture of the situation in which the suspected case of fraud is occurring. Therefore, have an associate or your supervisor review the information to verify that there is indeed a problem.

3. *Consult a lawyer.* Though this step appears extreme, it is best to determine the extent of one's rights prior to pursuing a course of action that may result in retribution within an organization.

Then proceed with the most appropriate course of action, based on the available facts and a close analysis of the extent of fraudulent activity, as well as the available means for resolving the problem. The remaining sections of this chapter describe a variety of ways to commit fraud throughout the cost accounting system.

CHANGE THE BASIS FOR OVERHEAD ALLOCATION

When allocating overhead costs to products, the most common approach is to charge a predetermined amount of overhead to each dollar of direct labor used in each product. The direct labor component of the equation has been used for decades and is still the one most commonly employed, despite incursion of the much more sophisticated and accurate activity-based costing allocation system. When a manager wants to inflate the value of inventory, thereby driving down the cost of goods sold, one possible approach is to cast around for a different allocation system that results in more overhead dollars being allocated to the inventory. It does not really matter to the manager which system is more accurate; he just wants the one that allocates the most overhead dollars to inventory.

The way in which this type of fraud begins is that a manager piously proclaims that it is time to discard the outdated direct labor allocation system (which may be a valid claim) and commissions a study by the cost accounting staff to find several allocation systems that are "more accurate" (though that is not the point). The cost accountants go off in a corner, chuckling to themselves that they finally have a manager who cares about cost accounting, and come back with several possible allocation systems. The manager expresses deep interest in all the new systems and asks that the accountants revalue the inventory based on each system, just to see what happens. When the study is completed, the manager runs through the list of inventory valuations and picks the one that yields the highest possible valuation—he does not care about the theoretical underpinnings of the system selected but just wants a higher valuation.

Since this type of cost accounting change appears to be perfectly valid and cannot even be considered fraud (since the new system may actually allocate costs better than the old one), there is not much to be done about it. However, one should consider this a warning sign—if a manager is fiddling with the allocation system, he may have designs on other alterations to the costing system that will be revealed later.

CHANGE THE COMPONENTS OF THE OVERHEAD COST POOL

One of the areas that always seems to attract the attention of a fraudulent manager is the overhead cost pool. This pool of costs includes all overhead costs that will be allocated to inventory rather than directly expensed within the reporting period. If the number of expenses listed here can be increased, the proportion of costs charged to the current period will drop, resulting in an increase in profits for the period.

The types of costs charged to the overhead cost pool are relatively standard and are itemized in any number of publications by the Big Five accounting firms. Capitalizeable costs are:

- Depreciation of factory equipment and facilities
- Factory administration expenses
- Indirect labor associated with production activities
- Indirect materials expended in support of production activities
- Factory maintenance
- Officer's salaries related to production
- Benefits of production employees
- Quality control costs
- Rent of any production equipment or facilities
- Rework labor

- Taxes related to production assets

- Utilities related to production activities

Though the specific types of costs that can be allocated are clear-cut, there are still two ways to commit fraud in this area. The first approach is to dump unrelated costs into approved accounts that will be summarized into the overhead cost pool. For example, the manager may require the accounts payable staff to code all office supply billings into the "production supplies" account rather than a separate "office expenses" account. Another variation is to record all fixed asset purchases in the production equipment asset account, so that the resulting depreciation and personal property taxes are all loaded into the overhead cost pool. The second, and more common, approach is to increase the proportion of costs allocated between the production cost pool and period expenses. This is particularly likely when allocating the cost of officer salaries to production since this is a highly subjective measure that cannot be precisely proven without a time-consuming study of the activities of each company officer.

A combination of the activities noted here results in a larger overhead cost pool, which will increase profits as long as the amount of inventory (to which all these additional costs are being directed) does not fall, which would result in the expensing of some portion of these previously capitalized costs.

OVERALLOCATE OVERHEAD COSTS

The normal approach for allocating overhead to inventory is to compile all overhead costs for each reporting period and then allocate the actual amounts based on some allocation methodology, or to enter in the computer system a standard overhead cost for each item and then adjust the total standard amount at the end of the reporting period so that it matches the total cost actually accumulated during the period. The first method is difficult for a fraudulent manager to alter, but the second one is subject to some manipulation, with the assistance of the accounting staff.

If the standard overhead system is used (the second method just noted), the amounts automatically allocated to each item in inventory will stay the same in every period until someone goes into the computer records and manually alters them. A fraudulent manager can take advantage of this system by convincing the controller (which is easier if the manager supervises the controller!) that there is no need to adjust this standard amount to match actual overhead costs in each period; making an adjustment at the end of the reporting year is sufficient. The manager can then raise the standard overhead rates charged, which has a dramatic upward impact on the value of inventory, thereby showing excellent reported profits until the end of the year. Even then, knowing that auditors are sure to review the adequacy of the overhead allocation, a manager working in concert with the accounting staff can shift actual costs from other accounts into the overhead cost accounts to make it appear as though actual overhead costs have indeed risen, thereby validating the increased standard overhead costs charged to each product.

The greatest failing of this type of fraud is that it requires collusion between the fraudulent manager and the accounting staff—and the more people involved, the greater the chance that the secret will leak out. Also, a thorough auditing staff has a good chance of finding this type of fraud by carefully examining year-to-year changes in the various accounts used to compile overhead costs, and then closely investigating accounts in which large year-to-year cost increases have occurred.

SHIFT COST ALLOCATIONS AWAY FROM NONPRODUCTION DEPARTMENTS

When a company uses the traditional method of cost allocation, all overhead costs are assigned to production activities, which means that some of the costs will be charged to inventory and some will go into cost of goods sold. This is the ideal situation for the fraudulent manager since he can then concentrate on altering the system so that as much of the cost as possible is allocated to inventory, thereby driving down the cost of goods sold. However, if the cost allocation system is a more sophisticated one that also allocates costs to other departments, these costs will probably be charged directly to expense, which leaves fewer costs to be allocated to inventory. For example, if a company has one or more service departments that provide services to other departments within the company (such as the computer services department), a reasonable allocation approach is to determine the use of these services by all departments and allocate the costs accordingly; then, some costs will be charged to general and administrative departments, whose costs are always charged directly to expense in the current reporting period.

If a fraudulent manager is looking for costs to capitalize into overhead, such a sophisticated overhead allocation system will be a target for modification. The easiest approach is for this manager to order a reversion to the traditional allocation system that dumps all costs into production activities. If this direct conversion is not possible, the manager will attempt to alter the allocation system so that a higher proportion of service costs are allocated to production.

It will be clear to a cost accountant that the fraudulent manager is altering the system since such sophisticated allocation systems are directly under the control of most cost accounting staffs. The best response is to prepare a report clearly showing the impact on reported profits that result from the manager's changes, as well as how the new allocation system is clearly skewing costs. This information should be sent up the chain of command to the controller or the chief financial officer, who should use it to deal with the manager causing the changes.

ALLOCATE EXTRA COSTS TO SPECIFIC JOBS

Some companies enter into time-and-materials or cost-plus projects with their customers, especially governmental entities, that allow them to pass a number of costs through to their customers. However, there are rules under which these contracts operate that keep companies from entering a wide array of nonrelevant costs into job records that will eventually be charged to customers. These rules typically prevent various types of overhead costs from being charged to customers. In many cases such costs cannot be charged to *any* customer and so are written off to expenses and absorbed by the company.

This is a fertile situation for the fraudulent manager, for the results of a deliberate skewing of the cost accounting system are greater billings to customers and more cash when these bills are paid. The typical action taken is to deliberately change the rules regarding what expenses can be charged to specific jobs, leaving fewer expenses to be allocated to unbillable overhead accounts. This generally takes place in two steps, the first one being a few small changes in cost allocations to see if the customer notices any increases in its billings. If so, and the customer sends an audit team out to investigate, the manager can easily claim that there was a "screw-up" and adjust the billings as demanded by the customer. However, if there is no response from the customer, the next activity is a more blatant allocation of additional costs to customer-specific billings. This second step is more targeted than the first step since the manager may have learned to stay away from the billings of a few customers that reacted strongly to the first increase in billings, while dumping the bulk of extra costs into the billings of customers who did not react. This approach usually results in a significant increase in billings but runs the risk that customers will eventually discover what has happened and file a lawsuit against the company to recover their money, which will result not only in damage awards but also in public humiliation of the company.

Given the extent of damages that will arise if this type of fraud is discovered, it is greatly in the interests of the cost accounting manager to put a stop to it. Accordingly, the best prevention measure is to have the internal audit team schedule a recurring review that centers on the specific jobs to which various costs are charged, with the resulting report going straight back to the audit committee, which should include some members of the board of directors (who can take significant action if they discover problems).

CHANGE INVENTORY VALUATION METHODS

Every inventory is valued using some underlying valuation method, such as last-in first-out or first-in first-out. These methods are based on the assumed flow of inventory through a facility. For example, if you stock a shelf with inventory, the first inventory you load onto the shelf is positioned at the rear, where it stays until all the other inventory in front of it has been used. Under this assumption the last inventory in (i.e., at the front of the shelf) is the first inventory used (i.e., a shopper or picker always takes the items at the front of the shelf first). This is called the last-in first-out method. The reverse assumption applies to the FIFO method. Whichever valuation method is used (and there are several other valid ones), there is a different impact on the inventory's valuation. For example, when considerable inflation occurs over several years, the inventory stored at the back of the shelf is the oldest and so also has a lower cost than the more recent items near the front of the shelf. If a company currently uses the LIFO valuation methodology and a manager wants to increase the value of the inventory, he can switch to the FIFO method; in our example, this assigns the latest, inflated, costs to inventory, while using up the oldest, least expensive inventory items first. Therefore, by altering the valuation method, one can increase or decrease the value of the inventory, even though the inventory itself is never moved.

Altering the inventory valuation method is legitimate and may in fact better reflect the actual movement of costs through the inventory. However, such a change is discouraged under generally accepted accounting principles and requires a disclosure in the financial statements, which makes the impact of the change quite clear to readers of these statements. Nonetheless, if making such a change can improve the level of reported results, a manager may try it. If the cost accounting staff is unhappy about the switch, it can present its case to the outside auditors, who can determine if actual cost flows accurately reflect the proposed change and refuse to render an opinion on the statements if they feel the change will result in misleading financial statements.

CHANGE LABOR ROUTING ASSUMPTIONS

Though labor usually makes up a relatively small proportion of the total cost of a product, this cost can be artificially expanded to result in a much larger proportion, which then drives up the cost of inventory, reducing the cost of goods sold and resulting in a higher level of reported profitability.

The way to increase the labor costs charged to a product is to alter the labor routings so that they spread the cost of equipment setups over a smaller number of parts produced—this means that the assumed length of production runs is shortened. For example, if a metal stamping machine requires 10 hours of setup before it can stamp a particular part, then the cost of that setup can be charged to the resulting manufactured parts. If the setup cost is $1000 and the number of parts produced during the production run is 1000, then the cost of the operation per part will be $1. However, if the labor routing is altered so that the assumed length of the production run is much shorter, such as 100, then the cost allocated to each unit goes up to $10. Obviously, a small change in the assumption leads to a large change in cost, which makes this a worthwhile endeavor for a fraudulent manager to undertake.

The approach can be further disguised by making a series of small incremental reductions in the assumed production run lengths in the labor routings over several years, so that auditors do not see any sudden changes in costs at one time. The author observed one situation where a shaped metal part suddenly jumped in cost from $2 to $6000, which was so excessive that auditors spotted it at once, quickly uncovered the entire plot, and forced the company in question to restate its inventory based on prior-year labor routing information.

The best way to detect labor routing alterations is to review a selection of labor routings with the industrial engineering staff, to obtain its opinion regarding proper production run lengths. If there is some chance that the engineers are involved in the labor routing changes, bringing in an outside consultant who can review the data and observe actual production runs may be the best alternative.

CHANGE NORMAL SCRAP ASSUMPTIONS

Most bills of materials contain a list of each part or assembly used to manufacture a product, as well as the unit of measure for each part, the standard quantity used, and the standard scrap percentage assumed to arise in the course of production. This last item can be manipulated for short-term gains in reported levels of profitability.

If the scrap percentage is altered, a product's cost will increase in a standard costing environment since the cost of each inventory item is multiplied by the standard scrap percentage associated with it to arrive at the total cost. As a result, both the cost of goods sold *and* the value of all work in process and finished goods inventory increase, which does little to assist a fraudulent manager in the long run. However, if a company operates in a seasonal industry where there is a continuous inventory buildup for most of the year and then a short selling season, a fraudulent manager working toward a short-term profitability bonus can alter the scrap percentage upward, which can increase the inventory valuation by several percent, while the small proportion of sales during most months will have a minor impact on profitability. The result is a boost in the short-term reported level of profitability. However, the fraudulent manager will see these "paper profits" reversed as soon as the inventory is sold off, which should occur during the primary selling season. Consequently, this approach works only if the manager causing this activity is rewarded for a short-term run-up in profits. It also requires a standard costing system, which relies heavily on accurate bills of materials.

Though this is clearly one of the most short-term approaches to fraud, a clever manager can combine it with another method—a massive expansion in the level of inventory (see Increase Value-Added Inventory). By doing so the manager can apply the extra scrap percentage to more inventory irrespective of the level of sales. This is a particularly rewarding method if a manager is about to receive a performance bonus and then leave the company, since he or she does not care that the inventory levels and scrap percentages will have to be reduced at some point in the future, causing all paper profits to be reversed.

This type of fraud is most easily guarded against if the manufacturing software is designed so that a single change in a scrap percentage field on one screen results in an automatic cascading ripple effect that changes all a company's bills of materials. This is an easy field for a fraudulent manager to personally access and change, but it is equally easy to install password protection for it, thereby denying access to all but a few authorized employees. Given the critical nature of the information in a bill of materials, it is always a good idea to use password protection for this information irrespective of the likelihood of fraud.

CHANGE BILL OF MATERIALS COMPONENTS

The bill of materials is the most sacrosanct document used by the engineering and purchasing departments, and it is considered absolutely inviolable by both these departments. However, there is a way for a fraud-minded manager not only to alter bills of materials in order to skew financial results but also to make both departments go along with and even initiate the change.

A manager seeking to improve financial results wants to include every conceivable product component in a bill of materials since this creates a higher per-unit cost for each item in inventory (including those already in inventory), yielding a higher inventory valuation. An easy way to do this is to put into the bills all fittings, fasteners, and shop supplies that are even remotely connected to a specific product. Members of the engineering staff, whose job it is to do this, thinking they have a micromanager on their hands, make the changes just to humor him. Consequently, a fraudulent manager can quickly engineer a reduction in the cost of goods sold in the 1% to 2% range without raising the suspicion of anyone.

The adjustments are small enough that most cost accountants and auditors will probably not notice them. The best way to detect such changes is to keep tabs on the amount of monthly expense in the manufacturing supplies area; this expense should drop precipitously since the expense is being capitalized into the inventory. This is a difficult practice to stop because of its limited nature and theoretical justification. The best approach is to adopt a companywide policy regarding the treatment of supplies, fittings, and fasteners, so that a fraudulent manager cannot alter bills of materials without breaking company policy.

DELAY BACKFLUSHING ADJUSTMENTS

Most companies use the picking system for withdrawing goods from or entering them into the warehouse area, resulting in a specific inventory pick or receipt transaction that is easily traceable. However, backflushing does not work this way. Under this methodology the production staff reports the total number of products produced, which is then entered into the manufacturing computer, which in turn multiplies the total amount produced by the related bills of materials for each item, providing a total amount of each component that should have been used, which the computer then deducts from the inventory records. This procedure, though a technically elegant one, is also less easy to trace back through the system because an auditor must first determine the quantity produced, then locate the bills of materials for each item produced, then manually calculate the quantities of components that should have been withdrawn from inventory, and then inspect the backflushing transactions to see if these quantities were actually withdrawn. This is a tedious, highly error-prone process that only an experienced auditor can properly complete. Knowing how difficult it is to trace this information, a fraudulent manager can simply delay the backflush processing at the end of a reporting period so that the inventory is not reduced until the first day of the next reporting period. The result is an overinflated inventory for the reporting period, which may be useful to a manager who needs to attain a monthly or quarterly profit figure in order to earn a bonus. Once the bonus is paid, the manager lets subsequent backflushing transactions occur at their normal times, which results in reduced profits in the next month since the backflushing that should have occurred in the previous month leads to a charge to inventory in the next month.

This is a surprisingly easy type of fraud to commit, for the fraudulent manager only has to know how to access the nightly batch processing file that schedules the backflushing transaction to run. When he accesses this file and stops that single transaction, no one suspects that there is a problem. As long as the transaction is turned on again within the next few days, it is also unlikely that anyone will notice that the resulting inventory records indicate quantities that are somewhat higher than what is actually in stock.

The best way to spot a delayed backflush is to conduct an inventory count at the end of the reporting period, during which any excessive book balances can be spotted and corrected, with the adjustments being charged to the correct reporting period. However, most companies do not count their inventories every month. Also, a clever manager can sometimes convince auditors to conduct inventory counts slightly in advance of or after the period end, using roll-back or roll-forward calculations to verify balances; these calculations can be off by small amounts, giving the manager sufficient room to delay a backflush and create a small change in the reported levels of profitability.

ALTER THE PERIOD-END CUTOFF DATE

By far the most common type of cost accounting fraud is a simple alteration in the date when a product is shipped. Many corporate managers are under intense pressure to ship as much product as possible during the last few days of a month, so that sales will be at the highest possible levels, and feel it necessary to record shipments that actually went out in the first day or two of the next month as shipments from the previous month. This is an easily detected fraud if a company uses a third-party carrier, since all shipping documentation will clearly point toward a shipment that occurred in the next month no matter what the internal documentation says. This problem is so common that auditors make the cutoff review a key part of every audit.

However, the trail is somewhat more difficult to follow if a company has its own fleet of trucks, for it can alter bills of lading and shipping records to make shipments appear as though they were actually sent out in the previous month. In this case there are still ways to detect the fraud. They are:

- **Issue financial statements rapidly.** If there is a tightly enforced policy to complete financial statements as soon as possible, the controller must complete all invoicing within the first few hours of the first day of the next month, which means that any later shipments must, by default, be recorded in the next month. This practice limits the time period when the cutoff can be extended to only a few hours past the end of the reporting period.

- **Compare driver logs to shipping documentation.** All commercial drivers must keep a detailed daily driving log. If they are caught without an up-to-date log book, their licenses can be suspended or revoked, and so logs tend to be well kept. By comparing the driving activities noted in the logs to the shipping documentation accompanying the items being shipped, one can also detect timing differences.

- **Send an auditor to the shipping dock.** If there is an independent witness in the shipping area, there is not much chance of a cutoff problem occurring. However, this person must also examine the dates listed on all shipping documentation that then goes to the accounting department to ensure that dates are not altered.

- **Confirm shipments with recipients.** One can also contact customers and ask them when they received shipments from the company, which is quite telling evidence if the customers experience a long delay in receiving shipments from the date when a company claims they were sent out. However, the confirmation process is a time-consuming one and is not normally used unless there are strong suspicions that intentional cutoff fraud exists.

The biggest problem with fraud related to the cutoff issue is that the entire management group of a company is frequently well aware of the problem and chooses to ignore it because they all stand to gain financially from the enhanced financial results that will be reported.

RECORD SALES THROUGH BILL-AND-HOLD TRANSACTIONS

When a manager is having difficulty selling products, a clever alternative approach is to enter into arrangements with customers whereby they can purchase additional quantities of product, frequently at a significant discount, but do not have to take delivery or pay for the items until they are shipped, which may be some months in the future. Since the products do not meet the basic accounting test of having been shipped, auditors examine these transactions in great detail and request written confirmation from customers that they are legal, nonreversible sales.

Though bill-and-hold transactions are not technically illegal, the end result is that a company stuffs an excessive quantity of product into its distribution pipeline—to such an extent that some of it "backs up" into the company's facilities. At some point in the near future, so many sales will have been recorded through bill-and-hold transactions that customers will no longer need to purchase additional products until they have flushed out the bulk of their bill-and-hold inventories. When that time arrives, sales plunge, resulting in major losses. The fraudulent manager tries to build up bill-and-hold transactions to the greatest possible extent, collect his or her performance-based bonus, and leave the company just before sales suddenly dive.

This is not a difficult transaction to detect since there must be a reasonable amount of accompanying documentation to satisfy the outside auditors. Also, it is visually apparent, since the warehouse is overloaded with finished products being held for customers. The best way to stop this practice is to point out to senior management that working capital requirements have greatly expanded, since the company has now invested in inventory that is technically owned by customers who do not have to pay for it until after they accept delivery.

IGNORE OBSOLETE INVENTORY

In even the best-run companies, there is always some obsolete inventory that is written off each year. The largest number of write-offs occur in situations where there are poor inventory tracking systems, since employees tend to ignore or re-purchase components that are already in stock if these parts cannot be found. Obsolescence also occurs when the purchasing staff buys excessive quantities of parts under the misguided notion that it is reducing per-unit costs by buying in bulk. Finally, obsolete inventories arise when the engineering staff switches over to new parts for an existing design without first drawing down existing stocks of old parts. When all three of these issues are present in a company, the annual write-off due to obsolescence can be remarkably high—well in excess of 10% of the total inventory balance.

Given the potential size of the write-off each year, it is no surprise that many managers vigorously deny the existence of such large quantities of unusable inventory. Their method for eliminating this expense can involve several actions. One is to sharply reduce the obsolete inventory allowance, which is a reserve that the accounting staff accrues in each reporting period in anticipation of a future write-off of inventory. They can also pressure the warehouse and cost accounting staffs to stop or sharply reduce the number of actual write-offs taken against this reserve, thereby leaving so much of it in place that they can successfully argue in favor of no further expense accruals to add to the reserve. They can also clean up or reshuffle the inventory, so that a casual or inexperienced observer does not notice any items covered with dust or that have clearly not been used for a long period of time. The author is aware of one company that even hired a maid to dust off the inventory! Finally, a manager can disable reports that itemize components or products that have not been used recently and are the principal and most accurate tools for identifying obsolete inventory. The combination of all these activities can severely reduce or eliminate obsolescence write-offs.

The truly clever manager does not implement all these changes at once but rather gradually increases the use of each technique or implements each one in staggered fashion. If this is done, the external auditors will not see a sudden, highly suspicious drop in obsolescence write-offs but rather a gradual decline, which the manager will have a much easier time explaining away as being caused by a gradual improvement in the company's ability to control its inventory.

This is a difficult activity to stop, especially if a manager is reducing the obsolescence write-offs in only small increments. One action is to respond promptly and in detail to any special request by the outside auditors for reports that show the age of selected inventory items, while another possibility is to ensure that the auditors have discussions with members of the warehouse staff who can identify old inventory items; however, in this case the possibility of severe retribution from the responsible manager may keep anyone from talking. A final possibility is to suggest that the auditors run a trend line of inventory write-offs in relation to inventory turnover, since this ratio should be relatively steady from year to year. The auditors can then calculate a probable obsolescence expense based on this calculation and force the manager to accept the extra expense as part of the audit.

INCREASE VALUE-ADDED INVENTORY

One of the most common forms of cost accounting fraud discussed in business schools occurs when a manager deliberately increases the amount of value-added inventory on hand, which results in a much larger allocation of overhead costs to inventory, thereby keeping the overhead from being charged to expense.

To do this the fraudulent manager first obtains a copy of the inventory that breaks down the amount of direct labor charged to each product at either the work-in-process or finished goods stage of production (or something besides direct labor, if some other method is used to allocate overhead costs to the inventory). He then sorts the list to determine which inventory items have the highest labor content and then issues orders for exceptionally large quantities of these inventory items to be produced, usually far beyond what will actually be needed in the normal course of business. The cost accounting staff then allocates overhead to the inventory in its usual manner, which is probably by summarizing the direct labor content of the inventory and charging the monthly pool of overhead costs to the inventory by multiplying a standard cost of overhead by each direct labor dollar. For example, if the preset overhead allocation rate is $2.50 to be applied to each $1.00 of direct labor, then the overhead cost applied to inventory for $20,000 of direct labor will be $50,000. When so much additional overhead cost is shifted to the inventory, there is less left over to charge to the cost of goods sold, which results in a higher profit. The fraudulent manager then collects his performance bonus, before anyone realizes just how much larger the inventories have become, and leaves the company.

This is a dangerous practice to pursue from the perspective of overall company health, since there must be a considerable additional investment in inventory before there is a noticeable increase in profits. The cash invested in this inventory may not be recovered for some time, since the inventory may have been expanded to one or more years worth of inventory; and the larger the inventory, the greater the chance that some of it will be written off because of obsolescence or sold at a discount.

The best way to avoid this type of fraud is to reward managers based not only on bottom-line profitability but also on the amount of working capital invested in the business. Under this approach an increase in inventory results in an increase in working capital, so the manager receives no bonus and therefore does not have an incentive to perpetrate this type of fraud.

ACCRUE COSTS TO SPECIFIC JOBS FOR PERIODIC PAYMENTS

When a company bills its customers on a cost-plus basis, it compiles costs under a job number and bills the customer based on the total amount of costs accumulated for the job. To increase the amount of cost in each billable job, a fraudulent manager can charge accrued costs to them that have not yet been incurred (and may never be incurred). If customers do not closely review the contents of their job accounts to see what they are paying for, it is quite likely that these cost increases will be successfully billed to them. The trouble is that there may be no basis for the accrued expense—it was all a fabrication.

Once the customer has been billed, the job is closed down in the accounting system, so that no transactions can be made to or from the account. The fraudulent manager waits until the job is closed and then reverses the accrual to some other account, allegedly because the computer system no longer allows any transactions to be made to it (which freezes the accrued expense into that account). This approach permanently leaves an unreversed accrual in the job account, so it is not at all difficult to detect the transaction. However, if the accrued amounts are kept relatively small, their presence may escape detection by anyone reviewing only larger transactions on an audit basis. This approach is particularly effective for large job accounts, where a single moderate-sized accrual may be lost in a sea of other transactions.

This is a difficult situation to detect. The best method is to look for unreversed accruals in all job accounts. Also, customers who *do* review the costs in their job accounts may file a complaint about it, which is a clue to look for more widespread use of this practice.

ALTER UNIT COSTS

A good accounting computer system records the exact unit cost of any item purchased, so that the per-unit cost passes into a LIFO, FIFO, or some similar database that carefully tracks the costs of all parts kept in stock. When operated properly, the system represents an extremely accurate picture of all inventory costs, which can then be traced back through the accounting system to the exact supplier invoice that provides evidence of each cost. However, this system can be skewed in two ways.

One approach is to gain access to the costing data and directly alter the per-unit costs of all or selected inventory items. If the changes made are extremely small, such as tenths of a cent, the differences may appear so insignificant that an auditor does not bother to find out why there is such a tiny difference in the computer's recorded cost and the cost on the supplier's invoice. However, when there are many units of a particular item in stock, the small incremental change in the cost can result in a significant alteration in the value of the inventory and so is worth the effort of a fraudulent manager.

The best way to spot this problem is to use an accounting system that records and reports all transactions in the system. Then a periodic trace of transactions relating to costing records can provide abundant evidence that someone has altered records. Another approach is to lock down all access to the costing records to all but high-level personnel. Under normal circumstances there is no valid reason for anyone to access these records, so limiting access should not be an issue.

The other way to alter costing records is to change the assumptions under which costs are recorded from noting just the actual per-unit cost of each item to adding on the freight cost of each delivery from a supplier. This is perfectly acceptable under generally accepted accounting principles, but it results in a higher unit cost for each item in inventory, which leads to a lower cost of goods sold and a higher level of profitability. If a company is using LIFO or FIFO costing, the change will be gradual since the new, higher costs take over only gradually as older layers of inventory costs are used up. However, under a standard costing system where all inventory costs are replaced at once with the new cost, there will be a marked one-time jump in the inventory value that is sufficiently large to attract the attention of a fraudulent manager.

SUMMARY

There are a number of categories into which fraudulent cost accounting activities fall. As noted in this chapter, they include alteration of cost allocation methods, changing cost assumptions, altering the recording of transactions at the end of a reporting period, altering unit costs, changing inventory levels in order to alter the associated overhead costs, and recording sales that have not yet occurred. These activities are usually driven by the need of company managers to falsely improve reported earnings because their compensation is tied to these earnings by various means. The cost accountant is frequently aware of these issues and is in a unique position to put a stop to them.

Glossary

ABC method A method for separating inventory items by cost of use, volume of use, or valuation. In its most common form, the 20% of inventory items that typically make up 80% of total costs are given an "A" designation, the next 30% of items are given a "B" designation, and all the remaining items are given a "C" designation. This approach results in a useful categorization of the inventory, which can then be used to determine which items should be most carefully costed or counted.

absorption costing A methodology under which all manufacturing costs are assigned to products, while all nonmanufacturing costs are expensed in the current period.

accelerated depreciation Any of several methods that recognize an increased amount of depreciation in the earliest years of asset use. This results in increased tax benefits in the first few years of asset use.

activity-based budgeting A budgeting methodology that traces the use of activities to provide services and create products, rather than using the more traditional approach to budgeting costs for specific departments.

activity-based costing (ABC) A cost allocation system that compiles costs and assigns them to activities based on relevant activity drivers. The cost of these activities can then be charged to products or customers to arrive at a much more relevant allocation of costs than was previously the case.

activity-based management (ABM) A methodology that uses the information uncovered by activity-based costing to manage activities. Its primary objective is to determine whether activities add value and how these activities can be conducted to further maximize value to the customer.

actual cost The actual expenditure made to acquire an asset, including the supplier-invoiced expense, plus the costs to deliver and set up the asset.

allocation The process of storing costs in one account and shifting them to other accounts, based on some relevant measure of activity.

allowable cost The difference between the target price and the target profit in a target costing environment. It is the maximum cost that a company can tolerate if it is to meet its profit objectives at specific price points.

applied cost A cost that has already been assigned to an expense category.

average inventory The beginning inventory for a period, plus the amount at the end of the period, divided by 20. It is most commonly used in situations where just using the period-end inventory yields highly variable results because of constant large changes in the inventory level.

avoidable cost A cost that will not be incurred if an activity is halted. For example, closing a factory results in the elimination of all costs directly associated with it; these costs are therefore avoidable.

backflushing A method for recognizing incurred costs from the production process that records transactions at the point when production is completed, rather than when materials are released from the warehouse area.

batch cost A cost incurred in the production of a group of products or services that cannot be identified with specific items in the group.

benchmarking The process of comparing a company's processes and outputs to those of other organizations to determine the "best of class," which a company can then emulate internally to improve its profitability, efficiency, or competitive position.

bill of materials A listing of the quantities of all parts and subassemblies that make up a product. It frequently includes additional information, such as the standard scrap rate to be expected when using each component. It is of considerable value for a number of applications, such as backflushing and product costing.

book inventory The amount of money invested in inventory, as per a company's accounting records. It consists of the beginning inventory balance, plus the cost of any receipts, less the cost of sold or scrapped inventory. It may be significantly different from the actual on-hand inventory if the two are not periodically reconciled.

book value An asset's original cost, less any depreciation that has been subsequently incurred.

bottleneck An operation in the midst of a manufacturing or service process in which the required production level matches or exceeds the actual capacity.

break-even point The sales level at which a company, division, or product line makes a profit of exactly zero. It is computed by dividing all fixed costs by the average gross margin percentage.

break-even point, composite The break-even point for an entire division or company, utilizing the summary-level information for all its products and costs.

budgetary slack Insufficiently high levels of expense in a budget used to make the performance of managers appear better than it really is when their operating results are then compared to the budget.

bundled product A group of two or more products, services, or a mix of the two sold under a single price and for which separate prices are available for each component part of the group.

by-product A product that is an ancillary part of the primary production process, having a minor resale value in comparison to the value of the primary product being manufactured. Any proceeds from the sale of a by-product are typically offset against the cost of the primary product or recorded as miscellaneous revenue.

capacity The ability of a production process to create a product or service, given the constraints of equipment, space, and available time.

capacity, ideal The theoretical maximum capacity at which a production facility can manufacture products, assuming that all machines are operating properly, there are no breakdowns, and that logistical support is available to the facility. This level is rarely reached under normal operating conditions.

capacity, practical The maximum level at which a production facility can realistically be expected to produce, given the variables of staffing problems, material shortages, and machine downtime. This is the maximum level at which one should plan for ongoing production levels without investing in additional production equipment, facilities, and personnel.

capital budgeting The series of steps followed when justifying the decision to purchase an asset, usually including an analysis of costs and related benefits, which should include a discounted cash flow analysis of the stream of all future cash flows resulting from the purchase of the asset.

carrying cost The variety of costs associated with keeping inventory on hand, including the costs of storage, damage to inventory, insurance, interest costs for invested funds, and taxes.

collusive pricing The "fixing" of prices by a group of companies in the same industry deliberately working together to adjust prices or to control levels of production to ensure that prices stay within a narrow range.

committed cost A cost that a company has made a prior decision to incur, perhaps signified by a contract or purchase order. This term frequently refers to costs incurred for the purchase of capital equipment.

common cost   A cost shared by two or more products or entities. For example, building rent is a common cost for two departments housed in the same building.

complete reciprocated cost   The costs of a support department, plus any costs that have been allocated to it from elsewhere in an organization. The complete reciprocated cost can then be allocated in its entirety to other departments or cost pools within the company.

concurrent engineering   The technique of bringing together representatives from most major departments to design new products. These design teams typically include members of the engineering, production, accounting, and marketing functions. This approach avoids the more traditional sequential process whereby designs are passed from department to department, with lengthy iterations required to fix design problems.

conference method   A group approach to determining costs and related drivers by collecting opinions about them from members of the departments involved in the accumulation or use of costs.

constant dollar accounting   A method for restating financial statements by reducing or increasing reported revenues and expenses by changes in the consumer price index, thereby achieving greater comparability between accounting periods.

contribution margin   The margin that results when variable production costs are subtracted from revenue. It is most useful for making incremental pricing decisions when a company must cover its variable costs, though perhaps not all its fixed costs.

controllability   The degree of influence a manager has over specific revenue or expense items purportedly under his or her area of responsibility.

controllable cost   Any cost that a specific manager has the authority to increase or decrease. The concept is most frequently applied to department-specific income statements because only costs directly controllable by each department manager should be included in the report.

conversion cost   Any cost required to change materials into a finished product.

cost   The expense incurred to create and sell a product or service. If a product is not sold, it is recorded as an asset, whereas the sale of a product or service results in the recording of all related costs as an expense.

cost accumulation   The process of categorizing and recording all costs as incurred in the accounting books of record. Costs are most commonly accumulated by job or department.

cost allocation   The process of assigning a specific or pool of indirect costs to a cost object, using some predefined and logically derived method of allocation.

cost center   An entity within a corporation against which costs are recorded, but no revenues. This results in a financial statement for the entity that totals to a cost figure rather than a net profit. Examples of departments that are cost centers are accounting and human resources.

cost depletion   A method of expensing the cost of a resource consumed by first determining the total investment in the resource (such as the procurement of a coal mine), determining the total amount of extractable resource (such as tons of available coal), and assigning costs to each consumed unit of the resource based on the proportion of the total available amount that has been used.

cost driver   A factor that directly impacts the incidence of a cost and is generally based on varying levels of activity.

cost estimation   A process used to determine the approximate cost of an item or service by compiling the costs of its component parts, labor, and applied overhead.

cost leadership   The ability of a company to attain the lowest possible costs in its industry by focusing closely on cost reduction in such areas as product design, process efficiency, and the elimination of waste.

cost object   An item for which a cost is compiled. For example, it can be a product, a service, a project, a customer, or an activity.

cost of capital   The blended cost of a company's currently outstanding debt instruments and equity, weighted by the comparative proportions of each one. During a capital budgeting review, the expected return from a capital purchase must exceed this cost of capital or else a company will experience a net loss on the transaction.

cost of goods sold   The accumulated total of all costs used to create a product or service which is then sold. These costs fall into the general subcategories of direct labor, materials, and overhead.

cost of quality   The sum total of all costs a company incurs when it produces inferior products, such as costs for inspection, warranty returns, lost customers, and rework.

cost-plus pricing   A pricing method that first accumulates the total cost of a product and then adds a planned margin to arrive at a selling price.

cost pool   A cluster of cost items.

cost-benefit analysis   The process of assembling information about the timing and amounts of both incoming and outgoing cash flows related to the purchase of an asset.

current cost   Under target costing concepts, the cost that would be applied to a new product design if no additional steps were taken to reduce costs, such as through value engineering or kaizen costing. Under traditional costing concepts, this is the cost of manufacturing a product with work methods, materials, and specifications currently in use.

depletion   The reduction in a natural resource, which equates to the cost of goods sold in a manufacturing organization.

development cost   The one-time cost for designing and developing a product.

differential cost   The difference between the costs of two alternatives.

direct allocation   A method for assigning the costs of service departments to production activities. It does not allocate the cost of services between service departments before assigning all service costs to production activities.

direct allocation methodology   A system for allocating support costs directly to operating departments without first pooling them and reallocating them in an intermediate step.

direct cost   A cost that can be clearly associated with specific activities or products.

direct costing   A costing methodology that assigns only direct labor and material costs to a product and does not include any allocated indirect costs (which are all charged off to the current period).

direct labor   Labor specifically incurred to create a product.

direct materials cost   The cost of all materials used in a cost object, such as finished goods.

direct materials mix variance   The variance between the budgeted and actual mixes of direct materials costs, both using the actual total quantity used. This variance isolates the unit cost of each item, excluding all other variables.

discounted cash flow   A technique that determines the present value of future cash flows by applying a rate to each periodic cash flow that is derived from the cost of capital. Multiplying this discount by each future cash flow results in an amount that is the present value of all future cash flows.

discretionary cost   A cost that can be incurred or not without a direct or immediate impact on outputs.

driver   A factor that has a direct impact on the incurring of a cost. For example, adding an employee results in new costs to purchase office equipment for that person; therefore, an addition to the head count is a cost driver for office expenses.

dual-rate cost allocation   An approach to allocating costs that separates costs into variable and fixed costs and places each one in different cost pools for further allocation.

dumping   The sale of products in the United States by a foreign-based company at a price lower than that at which they are sold in the company's home country. It is economically detrimental to U.S. industries.

economic order quantity   The purchasing quantity at which a company minimizes the sum of its ordering and carrying costs.

external failure costs   The costs a company incurs from the sale of a product that fails after shipment to a customer. These costs can include freight for the product's return, repairs, freight for shipment back to the customer, and the cost of prospective lost sales to that customer in the future.

factory overhead   All the costs incurred during the manufacturing process, minus the costs of direct labor and materials.

failure cost The series of costs associated with a product or service that does not meet a company's minimum quality standards, including the cost of receiving, investigating, and returning customer complaint calls, warranty expenses, and the loss of customers.

finished goods inventory Goods that have been completed by the manufacturing process, or purchased in a complete form, but have not yet been sold to customers.

first-in, first-out (FIFO) A process costing methodology that assigns the earliest cost of production and materials to units being sold, while the latest costs of production and materials are assigned to units still retained in inventory.

fixed asset An item with a longevity greater than 1 year that exceeds a company's minimum capitalization limit. It is not purchased for immediate resale but rather for productive use within a company.

fixed cost A cost that does not vary in the short run irrespective of changes in any cost drivers. For example, the rent on a building does not change until the lease runs out or is renegotiated, irrespective of the level of business activity within the building.

fixed overhead The portion of total overhead costs that remains constant in size irrespective of changes in activity within a certain range.

full cost method A methodology used by companies involved in the exploitation of natural resources whereby they capitalize the cost of all exploration and expense these costs as discovered resources are used.

gross margin Revenues less the cost of goods sold.

historical cost The original cost required to perform a service or purchase an asset.

homogeneous cost pool An accumulated pool of costs in which all represented costs have a similar causal relationship to the common base of cost allocation.

hybrid costing system A costing system that blends various characteristics of the process costing and job costing methodologies.

idle time The cost of direct labor for employees who are unable to conduct productive activities because of system breakdowns. This cost is included in factory overhead.

incremental cost The difference in costs between alternative actions.

indirect cost A cost not directly associated with a single activity or event. Such costs are frequently lumped into an overhead pool and allocated to various activities, based on an allocation method that has a perceived or actual linkage between the indirect cost and the activity.

indirect labor The cost of any labor that supports the production process but is not directly involved in the active conversion of materials to finished products.

indirect material Any material that cannot be directly traced to the production of a finished goods item. The term generally refers to manufacturing supplies.

insourcing The use of internal production methods to produce items that would otherwise be purchased from outside suppliers.

internal failure costs The set of costs incurred by a company when a nonconforming product is created but has not yet been shipped to a customer. These costs can include inspection, repair, and scrap costs.

internal rate of return The rate of return at which the present value of a series of future cash flows equals the present value of all associated costs. This measure is most commonly used in capital budgeting.

job A distinctly identifiable batch of a product.

job costing A system for developing a product cost by accumulating costs by lots or batches.

joint cost The cost of a production process that creates more than one product at the same time.

joint product The product with the highest sales value of any product in a group of products resulting from a joint production process.

just-in-time (JIT) Refers to several manufacturing innovations that result in a "pull" method of production in which each manufacturing workstation creates just enough product for the immediate needs of the next workstation in the production process.

kaizen costing The process of continual cost reduction that occurs after a product design has been completed and is in production. Cost reduction techniques can include working with suppliers to reduce the costs in *their* processes, implementing less costly redesigns of the product, or reducing waste costs.

kanban A Japanese term for a production system that pulls materials through a production facility by using cards to indicate a workstation's need for additional materials from the workstation(s) that supplies them.

labor efficiency variance The difference between the amount of time budgeted to be used by the direct labor staff and the amount actually used, multiplied by the standard labor rate per hour.

labor rate variance The difference between the actual and standard direct labor rates actually paid to the direct labor staff, multiplied by the number of actual hours worked.

last-in, first-out (LIFO) An inventory costing methodology that bases the recognized cost of sales on the most recent costs incurred, while the cost of ending inventory is based on the earliest costs incurred. The underlying reasoning for this costing system is the assumption that goods are sold in the reverse order of their manufacture.

life cycle costing The compilation of all costs associated with a product from the time of initial development, through production, to its abandonment or destruction.

locked-in cost A cost that has already been or will be incurred, based on past decisions. The term most commonly refers to product designs since a design specification calls for certain component parts whenever a product is manufactured in the future.

lower of cost or market An accounting valuation rule used to reduce the reported cost of inventory to its current resale value if that cost is lower than its original cost of acquisition or manufacture.

manufacturing resource planning (MRP II) An expansion of the material requirements planning concept, with additional computer-based capabilities in the areas of direct labor and machine capacity planning.

marginal cost The incremental change in the unit cost of a product as a result of a change in the volume of its production.

material requirements planning (MRP) A computer-driven production methodology that manufactures products based on an initial demand forecast. It tends to result in more inventory of all types than a just-in-time production system.

materials price variance The difference between the actual and budgeted cost to acquire materials, multiplied by the total number of units purchased.

materials quantity variance The difference between the actual and budgeted quantities of materials used in the production process, multiplied by the standard cost per unit.

mixed cost A cost that contains both variable and fixed elements.

moving-average inventory method An inventory costing methodology that calls for recalculation of the average cost of all parts in stock after every purchase. Therefore, the moving average is the cost of all units subsequent to the latest purchase, divided by their total cost.

negotiated price A price that two divisions of a company have mutually agreed to use as a transfer price between them.

net present value A discounted cash flow methodology that uses a required rate of return (usually a firm's cost of capital) to determine the present value of a stream of future cash flows, resulting in a net positive or negative value.

non-value-added cost A cost that does not impact the value a customer obtains from receipt of a product or service if that cost is eliminated.

opportunity cost Refers to the incremental increase in revenue that is foregone when a resource is not used in its most productive manner.

original cost The expense initially incurred to acquire or build an asset. It excludes any subsequently incurred costs, such as costs for asset additions.

outsourcing The practice of obtaining services from outside a company rather than performing them with company staff.

overallocated cost An indirect cost for which more has been allocated than was actually incurred during an accounting period.

Pareto analysis The 80:20 ratio stating that 20% of the variables included in an analysis are responsible for 80% of the results. For example, 20% of all customers are responsible for 80% of all customer service activity, or 20% of all inventory items make up 80% of the inventory value.

payback method A capital budgeting analysis method that calculates the amount of time it will take to recoup the investment in a capital asset with no regard for the time cost of money.

peak load pricing The practice of charging a higher amount for a product or service during peak demand periods.

penetration pricing A low level of initial pricing that a company adopts for its products in order to quickly build market share, though at the cost of profitability.

period cost A cost that must be charged to expense during the current period, rather than capitalized into inventory.

perpetual inventory A system that continually tracks all additions to and deletions from inventory, resulting in more accurate inventory records and a running total for the cost of goods sold in each period.

predatory pricing The dual practice of first reducing prices below one's costs in order to drive competitors from a market and then raising prices with impunity in order to maximize revenue.

price discounting The practice of reducing prices below published levels in order to encourage customer purchases, usually in greater volumes than was previously the case.

price discrimination The practice of charging different prices to different customers for the same products or services.

price variance The difference between the actual and budgeted prices of a product, multiplied by the actual quantity of product sold.

process A series of linked activities that result in a specific objective. For example, the payroll process requires the calculation of hours worked, multiplication by hourly rates, and subtraction of taxes before the final objective is reached, which is the printing of the paycheck.

process costing A costing methodology that arrives at an individual product cost through the calculation of average costs for large quantities of identical products.

product cost The total of all costs assigned to a product, typically including direct labor, materials (with normal spoilage included), and overhead.

product life cycle The time period beginning with initial research on a new product; passing through its design, production, and sale; and ending when either customer support or spare parts for it are no longer offered to customers.

production yield variance The difference between the actual and budgeted proportions of product resulting from a production process, multiplied by the standard unit cost.

profit center An entity within a corporation against which both revenues and costs are recorded. This results in a separate financial statement for each such entity, which reveals a net profit or loss, as well as a return on any assets used by the entity.

proration The allocation of either under- or overallocated overhead costs among the work-in-process, finished goods, and cost-of-goods-sold accounts at the end of an accounting period.

raw materials inventory The total cost of all component parts currently in stock that have not yet been used in work-in-process or finished goods production.

recurring cost Any cost that occurs on a regular basis. It can be associated with a product, a service, or an activity. Commonly recurring costs are rent and utilities.

redistributed cost A cost that has first been recorded in one cost pool and then allocated elsewhere.

reengineering The complete revamping of an existing process, with the objectives of greatly reducing the time and cost required to achieve specified outputs from that process.

reorder point The inventory level at which a purchasing system automatically notifies the purchasing staff of the need to buy more inventory.

replacement cost The cost that would be incurred to replace an existing asset with one having the same utility.

responsibility center A portion of a company, usually a department, whose manager is directly responsible for a specific set of outcomes.

revenue An inflow of cash, accounts receivable, or barter from a customer in exchange for the provision of a service or product to that customer by a company.

revenue center A responsibility center for which the manager is solely responsible for the level of revenue generated; this excludes responsibility for all costs.

rework Refers to a product that does not meet a company's minimum quality standards but which is then repaired in order to meet these standards.

safety stock An additional inventory level that is kept on hand at all times to guard against sudden reductions in inventory that would lead to stockout conditions.

sales value at split-off A cost allocation methodology that allocates joint costs to joint products in proportion to their relative sales values at the split-off point.

scrap The excess unusable material left over after a product has been manufactured.

selling price variance The difference between the actual and budgeted selling prices for a product, multiplied by the actual number of units sold.

sensitivity analysis A technique for arriving at a range of possible outcomes to an analysis when a number of key inputs to the analysis, such as assumptions or activity levels, are changed.

service department A responsibility center within a company, not directly involved with operations, that provides services to other entities within the company.

setup cost The cluster of one-time costs incurred whenever a production batch is run, which includes the cost to configure a machine for new production and all batch-related paperwork.

shrinkage The excess of inventory listed in the accounting books of record but which no longer exists in the actual inventory. Its disappearance may be due to theft, damage, miscounting, or evaporation.

skimming pricing A staggered pricing strategy that initially sets a high product price in order to gain the largest possible profits before competing products reach the market. Prices

are then lowered in stages, with the intent of reaping the greatest possible profits before being forced by competing prices to reduce to lower price points.

split-off point The point in a production process when clearly identifiable joint costs can be identified within the process.

spoilage, abnormal Spoilage arising from the production process that exceeds the normal or expected rate of spoilage. Since it is not a recurring or expected cost of ongoing production, it is expensed to the current period.

spoilage, normal The amount of spoilage that naturally arises as part of a production process, no matter how efficient the process may be.

standard A predetermined price or cost arrived at through a careful analysis by the sales and marketing staff (in the case of a price) or by the engineering staff (in the case of a cost), either of which is used for comparison to actual results on a per-unit basis.

standard cost A predetermined cost based on original engineering designs and production methodologies. It is frequently used to determine the degree of additional actual costs incurred above the standard rates.

static budget A budget that is frozen at a predetermined level of production output and is not subsequently changed to more closely parallel actual activity.

step cost A cost that does not change steadily but rather at discrete points. For example, a facility cost remains steady until additional floor space is constructed, at which point the cost increases to a new, higher level.

stockout A condition occurring when a company runs out of a final product that is needed by a customer or out of a sublevel or component part required by an internal production process.

sunk cost A cost that was incurred in the past and cannot be reversed.

support department A department that provides services to other departments rather than to customers.

target cost The amount of cost that must be eliminated from a product design so that a company can achieve its target profit. In some organizations it is the highest cost that can be reached while still achieving the target profit.

target price The price that a company has determined to be the one that customers will pay for a product, based on competitive pressures, customer perceptions of how much they will pay for certain features, and the willingness of the company to price low if it wants to obtain additional market share.

target profit The standard profit a company assigns to a new product design. It is typically based on a firm's cost of capital and can be adjusted for the perceived risk or amount of required capital associated with a specific product design.

total cost The sum of all costs incurred, which generally includes direct labor, material, and overhead costs.

traceable cost A cost that can be clearly assigned to a specific activity or item.

transfer price The price at which one part of a company sells a product or service to another part of the same company.

transferred-in cost The cost a product accumulates during its tenure in another department earlier in the production process.

unexpired cost A cost that is not recognized as an expense until related revenue is recognized in some future period.

unit cost The cost assigned to a single unit of production. It is calculated by dividing a cluster of costs by the number of units of production created as a result of these costs.

value engineering Improving the value of a product by systematically examining its design, related production processes, and component parts, especially in relation to the perceived value of its various features by customers, which results in a lower-cost, higher-value product from the perspective of the customer.

value-added cost A cost incurred in order to specifically increase the value to the customer of the product or service being provided.

variable cost A cost that changes in amount in relation to changes in a related activity.

variable costing A methodology that assigns only variable costs to a product, excluding all indirect costs. Also known as direct costing.

variance The difference between an actual measured result and a basis, such as a budgeted amount.

work-in-process inventory Inventory that has been partially converted through the production process but for which additional work must be completed before it can be recorded as finished goods inventory.

Bibliography

Ansari, S., & Bell, J. E. (1997). *Target costing: The next frontier in strategic cost management.* Chicago: Irvin Professional Publishing.

Applications of direct costing. (1961). Montvale, NJ: National Association of Accountants.

Atkinson, J. H., Jr., et al. (1991). *Current trends in cost of quality.* Montvale, NJ: National Association of Accountants.

Benke, R. L., Jr., & Edwards, J. D. (1980). *Transfer pricing.* New York: National Association of Accountants.

Brackner, J. W., & Skousen, C. R. (1996). *Manufacturing accounting and support of manufacturing excellence.* Montvale, NJ: IMA Foundation for Applied Research.

Bragg, S. M. (1997). *Advanced accounting systems.* Altamonte Springs, FL: Institute of Internal Auditors.

Bragg, S. M. (1999). *Accounting best practices.* New York: John Wiley & Sons.

Compton, T. (1994). *Strategy for success: Implementing an activity-based costing system.* Denton, TX: Professional Development Institute.

Cooper, R., & Slagmulder, R. (1999, August). Designing ABC systems for strategic costing and operational improvement. *Strategic Finance,* 18–20.

Cooper, R. & Slagmulder, R. (1999, October). Activity-based cost management system architecture—Part I. *Strategic Finance,* 12–14.

Corbett, T. (1998). *Throughput accounting.* Great Barrington, MA: North River Press.

Corr, A. (1983). *The capital expenditure decision.* New York: National Association of Accountants.

Dhavale, D. G. (1996). *Management accounting issues in cellular manufacturing and focused-factory systems.* Montvale, NJ: IMA Foundation for Applied Research.

Frigo, M. L., & Kos, H. A. (1999, August). Navistar's dream team. *Strategic Finance,* 38–45.

Goldratt, E. (1990). *What is this thing called the theory of constraints and how should it be implemented?* Croton-on-Hudson, NY: North River Press.

Hertenstein, J. H., & Platt, M. B. (1998, April). Why product development teams need management accountants. *Management Accounting,* 50–55.

Implementing target costing (1994). Montvale, NJ: Institute of Management Accountants.

Martinson, O. B. (1994). *Cost accounting in the service industry.* Montvale, NJ: Institute of Management Accountants.

Morse, W. J., Roth, H. P., & Poston, K. M. (1987). *Measuring, planning, and controlling quality costs.* Montvale, NJ: Institute of Management Accountants.

Mowen, M. (1986). *Accounting for costs as fixed and variable.* Montvale, NJ: National Association of Accountants.

Noreen, E., Smith, D., & Mackey, J. T. (1995). *The theory of constraints and its implications for management accounting.* Great Barrington, MA: North River Press.

Practices and techniques: Implementing activity-based costing. (1993). Montvale, NJ: Institute of Management Accountants.

Siegel, J. G., & Shim, J. (1995). *Dictionary of accounting terms.* Hauppage, NJ. Barron's Educational Series.

Standard costs and variance analysis. (1974). Montvale, NJ: Institute of Management Accountants.

Steedle, L. F. (1990). *World-class accounting for world-class manufacturing.* Montvale, NJ: Institute of Management Accountants.

Index